T0368026

Facility
Management

Facility Management

Second Edition

Edmond P. Rondeau, AIA, CFM, IFMA Fellow
Robert Kevin Brown, PhD, GRE, AICP
Paul D. Lapides, CPA, MBA

WILEY

John Wiley & Sons, Inc.

Library of Congress Cataloging-in-Publication Data:

Rondeau, Edmond P.
   Facility management / Edmond P. Rondeau, Robert Kevin Brown, Paul D. Lapides. 2nd ed.
     p. cm.
   Includes bibliographical references and index.
   ISBN-13 978-0471-70059-3 (cloth)
   ISBN-10 0-471-70059-2 (cloth)
   1. Real estate management.   2. Facility management.   I. Brown, Robert Kevin.
  II. Lapides, Paul D.   III. Title.
   HD1394.R66 2006
   658.2—dc22
                                             2005010713

10 9 8 7

Foreword

Not until the 1980s did facilities management (FM) come into its own. Even though FM had always been around in one form or another, it lacked a focus, even a name. It did not command a presence either within the organization or without. In fact, practitioners didn't know that "someone else does what I do," as the FM vice president of a Midwest bank told me in 1980.

Indeed, the 1980s can be considered the decade of facilities management. Associations of professional FM practitioners were formed, colleges and universities developed FM degree programs, publications exclusively for FMs appeared for the first time, and manufacturers and consultants hopped on the FM bandwagon with marketing plans to serve this newly identified buyer with clout.

In short, the sleeping discipline emerged from its cocoon and matured to benefit the corporation and its employees. Facilities managers turned their attention to critical issues, from human factors to new technologies, energy conservation to indoor air quality, and the means to integrate them all in the total workspace.

But by the end of the decade, the flourishing economy took a nosedive with a recession unlike those of the past. The recession of the 1990s was deeper and steeper, and business is seemingly unable to make a fast rebound to anything we might consider normal. Reflecting business in transition, the early 1990s saw new words enter corporate America's lexicon: reengineering, restructuring, reinventing, and downsizing, rightsizing, smartsizing. No matter what the euphemism, employees were pink-slipped by the tens of thousands.

Nor were facilities managers immune to wholesale layoffs. In some cases, the entire FM department was disbanded, giving meteoric rise to outsourcing as a word and a business concept. American business was indeed in the throes of transition, and FMs struggling for survival diligently searched for new means to meet belt-tightening mandates with bottom-line measures. In response came such concepts as hoteling, telecommuting, virtual offices.

The first five years of the twenty-first century have seen economic recession after 9/11 and the growth of business mergers have continued to force reconsideration of many long-accepted practices. As economists forecasted a slow recovery after 9/11 American business continue to pull out of this long slump.

In the 2000s, facilities management executives are facing even greater pressures to sharpen their strategic skills to match those of every other top executive in the corporate structure. As a result, educational tools will be in demand by those eager to move ahead. This book by three highly regarded professionals serves as a solid foundation for the principles and practice of facilities management. The challenges ahead may be great, yet meeting those challenges can be professionally and personally rewarding.

ANNE FALLUCCHI

IFMA Fellow
Editor Emerita and Founding Editor,
FACILITIES DESIGN & MANAGEMENT

Preface

The facility management profession has been and continues to evolve as an in-house service to corporate employers. Many experienced corporate facility management professionals and product and service providers have been working to improve the profession, information, products, and services they provide their in-house customers and clients. A 1991 market study by a national real estate services group stated, "More than seven billion square feet of building space and four quadrillion square feet of land are owned by corporate America. It is often the most valuable asset on U.S. company balance sheets. As the nation's businesses continue to undergo a fundamental restructuring—through mergers and acquisitions, decentralization, new technologies, changing markets and tightening profits—the pressure is on to better manage corporate facilities and make those assets work harder."[1]

As local, national, and global economies and services change, providing information and services that lead to informed and financially sound decisions about these assets becomes even more important in protecting them and improving the value of your corporation. Ideally, this book will help you and your company protect and more effectively and efficiently use its assets to improve shareholder value.

This book contains up-to-date information about the evolving facility management profession that will help facility professionals and their service providers meet the current and long-range challenges and opportunities they face.

Among the book's outstanding features are its hands-on approach and many relevant exhibits, including samples, policies, procedures, forms, and examples. This book takes a practical approach to the activities facility and outsource professionals must address to successfully manage their responsibilities and career.

This book provides the facility professional with a detailed review of facility management issues. *It* does not *provide a detailed review of or instructions regarding legal details, issues, or requirements; the facility management professional should review and address these topics with corporate or outside legal counsel.*

The book is divided into ten chapters designed to help you look at the services and issues facility professionals and consultants face in the ongoing cycle of successfully meeting their customers' requirements and completing facility management assignments.

Chapter 1 provides an overview to facility management, including a brief discussion of the evolution of the profession, definitions, organizational and personnel

---

[1]Arthur Andersen & Co., Real Estate Services Group, Marketing Publication, 1991, p. 2.

issues, ethics, the facility management mission, you and your customer, negotiation strategies, service level agreement (SLA), total quality management (TQM), balanced scorecard, the Sarbanes-Oxley Act of 2002, LEED, and the Americans with Disabilities Act (ADA).

Chapter 2 presents information on long-range and annual facility planning with reference to complementing the business plan and synchronizing corporate planning. It also looks at corporate facility planning, strategic planning, the annual operating plan, the long-range plan, strategic real estate and facility planning, strategic corporate facility management information, and the disposition of assets.

Chapter 3 reviews facility financial forecasting and management. Areas covered include the annual operating plan, the long-range plan, appropriations request, trend and ratio approach, capital budgeting evaluation, financial and facility alternatives, the development and use of capital project tracking, disposing of assets, and outsourcing.

Chapter 4 examines real estate considerations, analysis, and planning. With the vast amount of corporate resources and funds invested in corporate real estate and their associated legal commitments, it is important that facility professionals understand the responsibilities and objectives of the real estate function, best practices in corporate real estate management, issues to review and analyze, real estate and facility inventory, site criteria considerations, determination of customers' requirements, selection of a real estate broker, principal analytical and transactional activities, acquisition, site evaluation criteria, customers' site evaluation criteria, environmental and due diligence issues, and the legal document review process.

Chapter 5 reviews architectural and engineering planning and design: development of design requirements and layout, design firm selection process, programming and design, LEED (Leadership in Energy and Environmental Design), budgeting, contract document review, bidding the project, closing and costs, building programming and design illustrated, and campus and high-rise office concepts.

Chapter 6 provides interior programming and space-planning information. It considers space and furnishing standards, national purchasing contracts, space programming, alternate project delivery systems, ergonomic and life safety issues, additional planning and design requirements, the need and requirements for a facility management system (FMIS), and work environment trends that influence space and how people work.

Chapter 7 discusses construction and renovation work such as capital and churn projects; permitting, reviewing, and awarding the construction contract; the preconstruction meeting; construction and renovation; project costs; the certification of occupancy and the punchlist; owner-furnished items; relocation; build-to-suit concerns; new paradigms; and private funding initiatives the FM must face and manage.

Chapter 8 considers the many details of facility maintenance and operations requirements. It reviews the importance of maintenance and operations, its goals and alternatives, time facility maintenance management function, management planning process, managing the physical asset, intracompany and customer relations, financial reporting and controls, administrative responsibilities, and marketing and leasing owned and leased facilities.

Chapter 9 provides an overview of general administrative and technology services: telecommunications and computer integration, security and safety in light of 9/11, disaster avoidance and recovery, records management, furnishings and equipment inventory, mail and copy center services, audiovisual equipment services, conference room scheduling, food and beverage service, and recycling and confidential destruction services.

Chapter 10 examines integrated asset management, technological changes, communication and leadership, successful facility management, and the anticipated evolution of the FM profession. Topics reviewed include hands-on experience, education, and traditions.

We hope that after you read this book you will share with us your thoughts and comments about additional material and exhibits that should be included in the next edition. Also, we are interested in learning about your facility management experiences, trends, rules of thumb, and other relevant information. To communicate errors, suggestions, and experiences to us, please contact our publisher: John Wiley & Sons, Inc., Professional & Trade Division, 111 River Street, Hoboken, NJ 07030.

Thank you for your support; we look forward to hearing from you.

EDMOND P. RONDEAU
ROBERT KEVIN BROWN
Atlanta, Georgia   PAUL D. LAPIDES

Acknowledgments

The authors acknowledge and thank the following professionals, in-house customers, and corporate clients whose experience, writing, speaking, and sharing contributed to many of the concepts, ideas, and experiences utilized in the development, realization, and evolution of the facility management profession and practice.

Bill Adams, Project Management; Parkash Ahuja; Keith Alexander, IFMA Fellow, Centre for Facilities Management, UK; David Armstrong, IFMA Fellow, Armstrong Associates; Alvin Arnold, BDO Seidman; Bill Back, CFM, IFMA Fellow; David Baer, UPS Supply Chain Solutions; Pat Bailey, GSA Real Estate Sales; Diane Barnes, Wilkhahn, Inc.; Dr. Franklin D. Becker, Cornell University; Katleen Beeckmann, CoreNet Global (Belgium); Charles Bennett, CPA; Susan Biggs; Stephen Binder, Cushman & Wakefield; Michael Bourque, Earl R. Flanshtirgh & Associates; Rebecca Bray, UPS Supply Chain Solutions; Robert Brosseau (Canada); Richard Burroughs, Applied Software; Derek K. Butcher, Centre for Facilities Consultancy (UK); Malcolm Campbell (Australia); Deborah G. Carlston, Synnax Corporation; Alan Clayton, UPS Supply Chain Solutions; Roy Cloudsdale, Johnson Controls World Services; Peter A. Conlin, CFM; McKinley Conway, Conway Data; Dick Cooper, CFM, IFMA Fellow; David Cotts, CFM, IFMA Fellow (retired); Kreon L. Cyros; Marvin Dainoff, M. Dainoff Associates; John Diefenbach, AIA, JIA, PAE International (Japan); Ben DeVries; Jeff Dimond; R. Landon Doggett (retired); John Dues; Dr. Francis Duffy, DEGW Architects (UK); Marty Dugan; Raymond G. DuPont; Lawrence L. Edge, Medallion Group LLP; Behrooz (Ben) Emam, AIA, CFM; Eleanor Estacio, CoreNet Global; Anne Fallucchi, IFMA Fellow (retired); Carol Farren, CFM, IFMA Fellow, Facility Management Worldwide; Rudy Flores; Bruce Kenneth Forbes; John Fox (Australia; retired); Geoff Gidley, Facility Management Solutions Ltd. (UK); George Graves, IFMA Fellow (retired); Robert Gross, IFMA Fellow, Vanguard; Jeffrey Hamer, Asset Direction, Inc.; Philip E. Hammel, Honeywell; Dorothy Harris; Ernesto Hernandez; C. Frederick Hess, CFM, IFMA Fellow; James Hickey, CFM, IFMA Fellow (retired); Gerry E. Higgs, CFM, PE; Melanie Hill, CoreNet Global (UK); Ken Hitchcock, Marcus & Millichap; Gerald Hubbard, CFM, IFMA Fellow; John Igoe; David Jarman, Price Waterhouse; Lois Johnson; Samuel Johnson, CFM, IFMA Fellow; Diana Jones, The Home Depot; William Joseph; Maury Keiser, CFM, IFMA Fellow (retired); Peter S. Kimmel, AIA, IFMA Fellow; Prentice Knight, CoreNet Global; Sigeru Kuwabara, NTT Power and Buildings (Japan); Alex Lam, CoreNet Global (Canada); Earnie C. Leake, CFM, IFMA Fellow; TaeGoo (Ty) Lee, System-O Consultants (Japan); Scott Levitan, Georgia Institute of Technology; Chad Lewis; Dennis Longworth, CFM, ASAE Fellow;

Harry Ludwig, King & Spalding; Erik Lund, IFMA Fellow (retired); Jean Lusso, Kerry Lydon (Belgium); Barry Lynch, AIA; Dr. Josef Mack, Facility Management Institute (Germany); Diane MacKnight, CFM, IFMA Fellow; Professor Stephen Margulis, Grand Valley University; Jon Martin, Carter; Mike McGahagin; Mary McGrath, CFM (Canada); Sandra Moss Mallory, Smith, Gambrell & Russell; Jim Moss, Applied Software; Sharon Mount, AIA; Motosugu Nakatsu (Japan); Christine H. Neldon, CFM, IFMA Fellow, St. Paul Travelers; Makato Ogawa, Nomura Research Institute (Japan); Richard Palmer, CFM; Hazel Pankey, Conway Data, Inc.; Jack Parker, Corporate Space Services; Joel Parker, Conway Data, Inc.; Sterling Pettefer; Norman Polsky (retired); Joy Pooler; Helen Rauch, Helen Rauch & Associates; Alex Robertson, Siemens Real Estate, Inc.; J. Peter Ruys, AIA, ASID, Ruys & Company; Mel Schlitt, The Merchandise Mart; Michael Schley, FM Systems; Dr. William R. Sims, CFM, IFMA; Henry Howard Smith, AIA (retired); Stan Stanton, Huntress Executive Real Estate Search; Richard Stonis, Associated Space Design; David Taylor (Australia); Tom Tillman; Dr. Andres F. van Wagenberg, Eindhoven University of Technology (Netherlands); Larry Vanderburgh, BOMI; Duncan Waddell, Corporate Facility Management Resources (Australia); Ken Walker, UPS Supply Chain Solutions; Ray Wallace; Lei Wu (China); Syd Welch; Martha Whitaker; Barry J. Yach; Don Young, IFMA.

The authors further acknowledge and thank the following professional associations and education organizations whose leadership, vision, sharing, research, educational programs, and service to members and students help shape and provide guidance for the evolution of the facility management profession and practice:

- American Institute of Architects (AIA)
- American Society of Interior Designers (ASID)
- American Society of Real Estate Counselors (ASREC)
- Association National des Responsables de Services Generaux (France)
- British Institute of Facilities Management (BIFM)
- Building Owners and Managers Association (BOMA)
- Building Owners and Managers Institute (BOMI)
- Business and Institutional Furniture Manufacturers Association (BIFMA)
- CoreNet Global
- Danish Facilities Management Association (DFMA)
- EUROFM
- Facility Management Association of Australia Limited (FMA)
- German Facility Management Association (GFMA)
- Industrial Asset Management Council (IAMC)
- Institute of Business Designers (IBD)
- Institute of Real Estate Management (IREM)
- International Facility Management Association (IFMA)
- International Society of Facility Executives (ISFE)

- Japan Facility Management Association (JFMA)
- National Office Products Association (NOPA)
- Netherlands Facility Management Association (NEFMA)
- Norwegian Network of Facility Management (NNFM)
- Urban Land Institute (ULI)

Thanks also to John Czarnecki of John Wiley & Sons, Inc., for his patience and support with this second edition.

Finally, we wish to thank those professionals and organizational leaders who care and who persevere in providing a humane, environmentally friendly, safe, and secure work environment for their colleagues, clients, and employees.

E.P.R.
R.K.B.
P.D.L.

About the Authors

EDMOND P. RONDEAU, AIA, CFM, IFMA Fellow, is the general manager, real estate, in the Real Estate Development Office, where he manages owned and leased property for the Georgia Institute of Technology in Atlanta, Georgia. Previously, Ed was the director of global operations for Conway Data, Inc., an Association Management Company based in the Atlanta, Georgia, area, where he was responsible for association management–related assignments primarily outside of North America. Ed has been responsible for the International Development Research Council's member and chapter development programs, world congresses, and staff for Asia, Australia, Europe, and Latin America regions. His work experience includes serving as the director of consulting services for the Integrated Facility Management business unit of Johnson Controls, Inc.; as the manager of corporate real estate for Contel Corporation; as the vice president of property management for the National Bank of Georgia; as the vice president of real estate and construction for Arby's, Inc.; as a construction manager for the Coca-Cola Company; and as a staff architect for Auburn University.

Ed holds a master's in business administration in real estate from Georgia State University and a bachelor of architecture from Georgia Tech, is a registered architect in Georgia, holds a NCARB certificate, and is a Certified Facility Manager. He was the 1988 president of the International Facility Management Association (IFMA), served as the 1990 chair of the IFMA Foundation, was elected an IFMA Fellow in 1992, and was the 1994/1995 president of the IFMA Real Estate Council. He served on the board of directors for the Board Certified in Corporate Real Estate (BCCR), was a member of the IDRC Financial Review Board, was a trustee of the IFMA Foundation, has served as the chair of the Advisory Committee for the Georgia Tech Integrated Facility and Property Management masters degree program and is a member of the Core Global Finance Committee.

He has worked for spoken on corporate real estate and facility management issues throughout the United States and internationally, including in Argentina, Australia, Austria, Belgium, Brazil, Canada, China, Cuba, Denmark, Japan, Germany, Hong Kong, India, Italy, Mexico, the Netherlands, New Zealand, Philippines, Singapore, South Korea, Spain, Sweden, Trinidad and Tobago, the United Kingdom, and Venezuela. Ed has authored numerous articles and is a coauthor of two books on corporate real estate and three books on facility management. He is the author of numerous facility management and corporate real estate articles, the author of *Principles of Corporate Real Estate,* a coauthor of *Managing Corporate Real Estate* and *Managing Corporate Real Estate: Forms and Procedures,* the coauthor of the real estate management information system LeaseKiT, and the coauthor of the capital project budget tracking system CaProKIT. He is the lead author of the book *Facility Management,* which received the 1997 IFMA Author of the Year Award; is coauthor, with Dr. Walther Moselener, of *Facility Management 2,* published in Germany; and is the coauthor of *The Facility Manager's Guide to Finance and Budgeting,* for which he received the 2004 IFMA Distinguished Author Award.

ROBERT KEVIN BROWN, PhD, CRE, AICP, is president, Robert K. Brown & Associate. He is the chair emeritus of real estate and the originator and former chairman of the Department of Real Estate, College of Business Administration, Georgia State University. He served previously as corporate director of real estate, Rockwell International Corporation; vice president, Rockwell Graphics Systems Group; and president, Narland Corporation and Standard Property Land Company, wholly owned Rockwell subsidiaries.

Dr. Brown holds a bachelor's degree from the Johns Hopkins University and master's and doctoral degrees from the University of Pittsburgh. A nationally known lecturer and consultant on asset management strategies to many Fortune 500 companies, he is the codeveloper of the first commercially available PC-based corporate real estate asset management system. He is the author of numerous articles and 11 books on real estate, including *Managing Corporate Real Estate, The Real Estate Primer, Essentials of Real Estate, Real Estate Economics,* and *Corporate Real Estate: Executive Strategies for Profit Making,* and is the coauthor of *Managing Corporate Real Estate, Managing Corporate Real Estate: Forms and Procedures,* and *Real Estate Asset Management: Executive Strategies for Profit Making.* Dr. Brown was the contributing editor of the corporate real estate column in *National Real Estate Investor Magazine.* He also serves as a member of the Asset Management Editorial Board of *National Real Estate Investor Magazine* and the board of advisors of *The Arnold Encyclopedia of Real Estate.*

Dr. Brown is a member of the American Society of Real Estate Counselors (GRE) and served as a member of its board of governors. He holds memberships in the American Real Estate Society (ARES); American Institute of Certified Planners (AICP); International Facility Management Association (IFMA); and International Association of Corporate Real Estate Executives (NACORE), where he served on the board of directors. He served as a member of the board of directors of Underground Festival, Inc., the governing board of Underground Atlanta. More recently, Dr. Brown served an appointment as visiting professor in the Graduate School of City Planning, College of Architecture, Georgia Institute of Technology.

PAUL D. LAPIDES, CPA, MBA, is a professor of management and entrepreneurship at the Michael J. Coles College of Business at Kennesaw State University (Georgia), where he founded and serves as director of the nationally recognized Corporate Governance Center.

Mr. Lapides is a member of the board of directors of Sun Communities, Inc. (NYSE: SUIT), and the Board of Directors Network, Inc. (BDN), and serves on the advisory boards of the National Association of Corporate Directors (NACD) and the Newman Real Estate Institute at Baruch College. His business and consulting experience includes advising hundreds of start-up, growth, and midmarket companies, as well as many of America's Fortune 500 companies.

Mr. Lapides is the author of more than one hundred articles and twelve books, including *Managing and Leasing Residential Properties*; coauthor of *Managing Corporate Real Estate, Managing Corporate Real Estate: Forms and Procedures, Real Estate Investment: Strategy Analysis Decisions*; and contributing author of *The Public REIT Legal Source, Real Estate Investment Trusts, Problem Real Estate, Real Estate Syndication Manual, Real Estate Transactions,* and *The Arnold Encyclopedia of Real Estate.* A frequent speaker at business, professional, and academic organizations, his opinions have appeared in more than 500 publications and on national and local television and radio.

Mr. Lapides received a bachelor's degree with honors in economics from the Wharton School of the University of Pennsylvania and a master's of business administration from New York University. Prior to joining the faculty at Kennesaw State University, he was an adjunct professor of real estate at New York University and Columbia University.

Contents

Chapter One

An Overview of Facility Management

How did facility management evolve into the current profession? In this chapter, we describe facility management of the past and the changes that have brought the profession and practice to its current state. The directions we believe facility management will take in the United States and Canada are discussed in chapter 10.

Only in the past thirty years has facility management become a recognized and required process of organizations throughout the world that expend resources on people, their work environment, and the ways they work. Why has this come about? Is it new? Not really. For many years, universities, colleges, and major corporations, as well as government agencies with numerous large facilities, extensive maintenance and operating budgets, and scarce capital budgets, have been developing and using management practices and procedures that are now widely accepted by professionals.

Such organizations, with minimal financial and human resources, have had to closely manage their day-to-day requirements and the details of their expenditures. They have had to think, plan, and develop their facility programs based on long-term goals, political reality, and economic necessity.

Organizations with less restrictive economic or physical requirements traditionally spent little time on long-range or day-to-day facility issues or details. Such expenditures did not comprise a large percentage of the budget, nor was the planning, implementation, and operation of a small number of facilities complex.

Design a building, build it, put up office partition walls, doors, and so on; hook-up the AT&T-provided phone; install a desk, chair, credenza, side chairs—and move in, with few complications.

What changed this process, and what impact have the changes had on the way we develop and manage work environments? Thirty-five years ago, many companies were smaller than they are today; they were often state or regionally focused; had relatively cheap energy, construction, and work space costs; and focused on short-term goals, objectives, and requirements.

In the early 1970s, inflation became a threatening issue. The oil embargo brought fuel shortages that spurred a dramatic increase in the cost of materials and the financing of all endeavors. Capital funds and materials became scarce, and the deregulation of monopolies and previously regulated services (phone, fuel, airline, etc.) required many large companies to compete more effectively and efficiently in the marketplace.

Increased competition from foreign companies filled some of the material and services void, while many U.S. companies that reacted positively with innovation and alternate solutions prospered. Inefficient manufacturing processes, nonproductive work environments, and higher worker expectations required senior management to seek alternatives, to plan for the long term, to "work smarter," to be more productive and become more competitive.

One result of this business crisis and upheaval in U.S. companies was the evolutionary management of scarce resources—the transition to managing facilities as an asset. Facility management as a practice and profession is continuing to evolve to provide management services that meet strategic long-range and short-term corporate requirements. These business practices combine proven and innovative methods and techniques with the most current technical knowledge to achieve humane, productive, and cost-effective work environments. Strong central threads of quality of life, cost-effectiveness, flexibility, and environmental considerations run through the technical components of the practice. In most cases, facility professionals are corporate generalists or boundary spanners who recruit and manage a variety of specialists such as in-house staff, consultants, or outsourcing firms.

Facility professionals must look ahead with minimal knowledge and be able to both perform and improve routine tasks. The desire and ability to work well with people in a service capacity, to be practical, economical, available, tactful, flexible, persuasive, responsive, and timely, are additional facility management traits and requirements.

Corporate or organizational owners/tenants and their staffs have always had facility management responsibilities, handling them with varying degrees of success depending on the manager's training, capabilities, and interest. Whether corporations or organizations own or lease their office, factories, retail space, warehouses, or specialty business locations, they have found it necessary to assign one or more employees the tasks of planning, budgeting, securing a location, designing, constructing, furnishing, occupying, managing, maintaining, redesigning, reconstructing, relocating, and disposing of corporate facilities.

Corporations with approximately 100,000 rentable square feet of office space or 100 to 200 employees often find that they need a structured way to deal with project budgets, planning, project delivery and internal coordination, authority, and responsibility for major capital projects, day-to-day customer building change requests, and building/site management issues. Thus, many corporate leaders have created or chosen one internal department, Facility Management (FM), to manage and coordinate these issues.

The facility management profession continues to change and evolve. Corporate mergers and buyouts have required facility professionals to compete for limited career opportunities and to become more proactive within their organizations. The recession of the 1990s and early 2000s taught facility professionals some hard lessons. To remain in business and excel, we must have informed and knowledgeable service partners in the facility management process who are trained, educated, and prepared to address the challenges and opportunities that await them.

The trend of outsourcing facility management and other corporate services continues as organizations seek to focus long-term personnel and resources on core business requirements. Outsourcing has changed the way management and service providers look at the in-house staff because these same support employees—with little advance notice—may become outsourced employees as service providers or contract consultants.

The pressure to reduce staff costs through downsizing, which continued into the early 2000s, has been replaced by programs to actively reduce all real estate and facility management expenses. We find that senior executives in many corporations are requiring reductions in annual operational costs in the range of 10 to 30 percent from the previous year's operational costs—and all without loss in the quality of real estate and facility services provided. To achieve these savings, many corporate real estate and facility professionals have had to become agents and leaders of change.

Facility professionals have had to look at all service levels, service specifications, and the personnel costs associated with their staffs and service providers. Facility organizations have had to grow and mature toward leading-edge ways of doing business while providing equal or better services to their customers. Some who have not grown or developed new ways of producing more with less have failed and are no longer in corporate real estate or the facility management profession. New ways of doing business include:

- Globalization of real estate portfolios and associated facility management strategies
- Total energy management—addressing supply, demand, and operational energy management issues as an integrated solution
- Performance-based contracts—partnerships designed to create incentive and reward innovation
- Focus on workplace management rather than asset management only
- Bundling and integration of services that affect the workplace environment—proximity (workplace configuration and move management), connectivity (IT/LAN), and comfort (HVAC)
- Service levels rather than performance specifications
- Setting up and maintaining a balanced scorecard process to measure performance against goals and regularly reporting this information to customers
- Implementing a Six Sigma program as a measure of quality that strives for near perfection
- The Sarbanes-Oxley Act of 2002—a federal law that created a new era in financial reporting for public companies. The facility professional must consider practical means of assisting companies to comply with this important federal legislation.
- The importance of energy and environmental design and Leadership in Energy and Environmental Design (LEED) as developed by the U.S. Green Building Council (see chapter 5)

DEFINITIONS

In the late 1970s, the profession began to receive recognition and to define itself more formally within U.S. and Canadian corporations, becoming known as *facility management*. During this period, the Facility Management Institute, a nonprofit educational and research organization, described the profession as managing and coordinating interrelated "people, process, and place" issues and functions within the corporation or organization. The U.S. Library of Congress, in 1982, defined *facility management* as "the practice of coordinating the physical workplace with the people and work of the organization; it integrates the principles of business administration, architecture, and the behavioral and engineering sciences." [Library of Congress Professional Definitions, Library of Congress News #82–115.]

The International Facility Management Association (IFMA) now defines *facility management* as "a profession that encompasses multiple disciplines to ensure functionality of the built environment by integrating people, place, process and technology" (see Exhibit 1.1) and has grouped the numerous job responsibilities of facility professionals under nine major functional areas, as shown in Exhibit 1.2.

Other management terms represent related issues. For example, *property management* is frequently described as the profitable operation and management of owned, leased, or subleased real property including land, buildings, assets, equipment and legal commitments for an owner, developer, or landlord. The facility professional does not usually manage corporate facilities for a profit; the mission of this person and staff is to provide high-quality, cost-effective service to in-house customers in support of the corporate business plan—that is, people and process issues rather than just place issues.

Another example is *asset management*, which is often described as the administration, operation, and management of a real property portfolio including land, facilities, and legal commitments controlled by an owner, tenant, developer, or landlord. Asset management can be a function within property management or a service outside of property management. It can be included within facility management as a function that usually focuses on the physical land, building, and/or

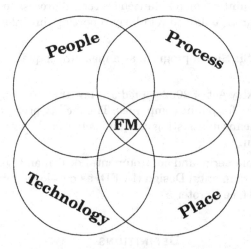

Exhibit 1.1   People, Process, Place, Technology *(Developed by the International Facility Management Association in response to the evolution and the importance of Technology in FM and with FM customers)*

1. Long-range facility planning

2. Annual facility planning (tactical planning)

3. Facility financial forecasting and management

4. Real estate acquisition and/or disposal

5. Interior space planning, work specifications, and installation and space management

6. Architectural and engineering planning and design

7. New construction and/or renovation work

8. Maintenance and operations of the physical plant

9. Telecommunications integration, security, and general administrative services (food services, records management, reprographics, transportation, mail services, etc.)

Exhibit 1.2   Nine Facility Management–Related Job Responsibilities

space, and the operation and management of the asset. Asset management usually does not address people issues.

At the end of the text is a glossary of facility management definitions and buzzwords.

As the owner's representative, the facility professional is an expert in almost all aspects of the corporation's internal culture and should have unique insight to personnel, personalities, other support departments, and business history and real estate/facility requirements. This position title may be facility manager, director of facilities, vice president of facilities, or even others, depending on the size and history of the organization, related activities, and internal politics. This person, who may or may not be trained in another profession (e.g., architecture, engineering, interior design, business administration, accounting, finance, human resources), uses his or her corporate business experience and people skills to manage some or all of the nine job responsibilities listed in Exhibit 1.2 and at times takes on additional corporate business responsibilities.

Facility professionals are generalists who understand the corporate business philosophy; respect its financial, legal, and quality requirements; know who the company's decision makers are; and recognize those with the authority to sign legal documents. They facilitate and manage budgeting; interview and hire consultants; set design, construction, furnishings, scheduling, space and office furnishing standards; institute capital purchasing programs; and translate corporate customer facility requirements into a cost-effective, environmentally safe, and aesthetically pleasing workplace. Their role is to ensure that the customer and the corporation have an on-time and on-budget project with the best possible site, space, facilities, furnishings, and support systems to serve their needs today and tomorrow. Further, facility professionals have the responsibility to identify, secure, and work with qualified and high-quality service and product providers (see Exhibit 1.3).

The information in Exhibit 1.2 and Exhibit 1.3 is graphically combined in Exhibit 1.4, which shows the central management role of the facility professional.

- Municipal code and regulatory officials
- Utility suppliers
- Real estate developers, brokers, and tenant representatives
- Soil and material testing engineers
- Architects
- Engineers
- Interior designers
- Estimators and schedulers
- Systems furniture installers
- Movers
- General contractors and their subcontractors
- Consultants for art, computer, energy, food service, landscaping, lighting, records management, relocation, risk, management, telecommunications, security, signage, and other services
- Landlords, property managers, and asset managers
- Maintenance, janitorial, and other vendors and specialty suppliers

Exhibit 1.3   Quality Service and Product Providers

Facility managers must handle increasingly complex processes with an expanding number of team members. For example, consider the differences in designing and building a Model T Ford in the 1920s and today's complex technological cars. Today's practice must address diverse technological and economic changes:

- Increasing use and reliance on technology, including more and more computers, telecommunications devices, and their support requirements
- Continuing significant cost of leased or owned facilities, materials, human resources, benefits, costs of capital, taxes, and fixed operating costs
- Evolution of the closed-office concept to the needs, flexibility, and cost-effectiveness of the open-plan/open-office concept
- Increasingly complex telecommunications, computer cabling, power, backup power, heating, ventilating, and air conditioning, lighting, life safety, security systems, environmental and ergonomic requirements
- Higher worker expectations for pleasant, ergonomic, secure, and cost-effective environments coupled with limited time, space, staff, and funds
- Competitive and economic pressures to reduce or hold the line on expenditures; increase profits; reduce staff, and buy out, merge with, or take over competitors
- Pressure to mesh personnel and facility requirements with long-range regional, national, and international business issues, as well as to develop an integrated strategic corporate business and facility plan

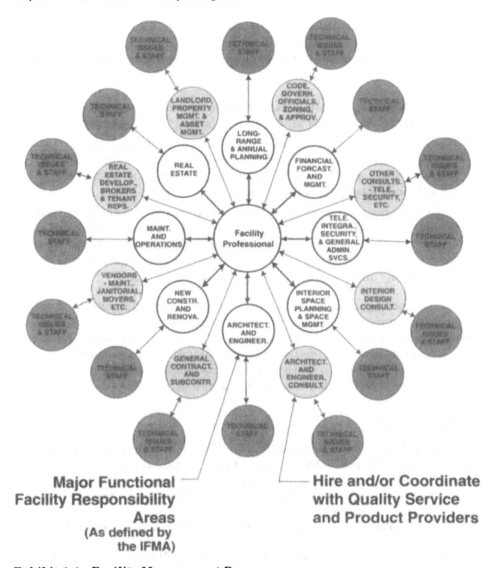

Major Functional Facility Responsibility Areas
(As defined by the IFMA)

Hire and/or Coordinate with Quality Service and Product Providers

Exhibit 1.4   Facility Management Process

- Requirement to provide high-quality, integrated in-house services in a timely, coordinated, cost-effective manner based on an intimate knowledge of the corporate culture and politics, including customer and senior management service expectations

Facility management is known primarily by its effects, principally acquisition, design, construction, maintenance, and operation and support services for in-house customers and the physical facilities.

ORGANIZATIONAL AND HUMAN RESOURCES ISSUES

Senior corporate management deals with facility management issues and services in one of three ways:

1. Senior management continues to maintain the status quo, which may appear to meet current requirements and is the politically safe thing to do.

2. If senior management perceives or believes facility management change is necessary, it may give an available in-house person the responsibility for resolving the problems while delegating little or no authority, regardless of the individual's training or experience.

3. Knowledgeable and experienced senior managers provide strong leadership by making substantial commitments to dealing with facility issues and services by identifying and placing a qualified, knowledgeable, and experienced in-house or outside person in the role of facility professional with the responsibility and *authority* to carry out his or her mission.

There is a growing understanding among corporate senior leaders of the need to delegate authority as well as responsibility to facility professionals charged with the strategic planning and management of the corporations' fixed assets, facilities, and services. Their mission is to enable substantial savings of funds, worker hours, and resources. These achievements reduce overhead, raise productivity, and increase profits, thus improving the bottom line.

Organizational Issues

The facility management department functions within a formal organizational structure. It must, therefore, be responsive to the organization's internal philosophy as well as to external market influences that affect the organization's ability to perform. We discuss methods for performance measurement later in this chapter; here we concentrate on organizational issues.

How do formal structures vary? We can perceive variations in terms of:

1. The number of interdependent units established within the total organization
2. The levels of formal authority designated in the hierarchy
3. The size of each formally designated unit within the organization
4. The kind of authority formally delegated to the various units
5. The work done by the formally designated units
6. The location of the work
7. The degree of autonomy granted to each unit

Throughout this book, we describe the specifics of facility management department organization with these seven points in mind. Exhibit 1.5 is a schematic of a hypothetical corporate office organizational chart. We use a large, multinational service conglomerate as our reference base, for three reasons. First, this type of company is complex operationally, with a full complement of line and staff depart-

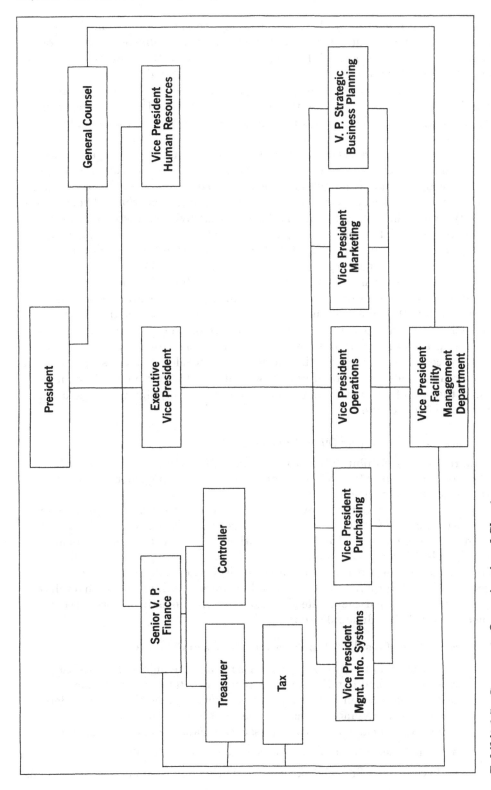

Exhibit 1.5 Corporate Organizational Chart

ments; thus, it provides excellent organizational perspectives. Second, because the facility management department is assumed to be established as an operational entity from day one, it inherits little in the way of nonproductive attitudes or personnel. Third, we assume senior management created the type of facility management atmosphere that will make the facility management program work. Exhibit 1.6 shows a design for organizing our hypothetical facility management department to implement the example corporation's facility management and services program in a manner that is both cost and operationally effective.

Designated interface personnel, carried on division and group budgets, assist the facility management department. The liaison group is a key ingredient in the program because it not only provides knowledgeable personnel, maintained at noncorporate expense, but also creates a responsive communications channel between the facility management department and the operating division. A second interface group consists of other corporate departments and corresponding division and staff groups that provide advice, counsel, and expert support in a wide variety of technical areas, without appearing on our example's departmental budget.

Extending the organization chart upward (see Exhibit 1.5), the vice president, Facility Management Department, reports through the operations side of the corporate staff to the senior vice president, Finance. In some cases, the direct-line reporting relationship is different; the senior vice president, Human Resources; the vice president, Operations; and the general counsel are among other prevalent choices. The corporate facility executive also develops relations with division and group presidents and their respective line and staff personnel. Without these links, the lack of two-way communication would probably signal serious faults in program effectiveness.

Interface Relationships with Other Corporate Staffs

Now, referencing Exhibits 1.5 and 1.6, we examine the functions of each of the other primary corporate staffs to see how the facility management department relates to and complements them.

Exhibit 1.6 portrays the many continuing interface relationships with other corporate office staffs. The level at which these relationships occurs depends a good deal on company size and on the relative position of the staffs on the hierarchical scale. We make two assumptions here: first, that the influence of the facility management department permeates all levels of corporate management; second, that our corporation is large and has numerous divisions, with a full complement of staff departments. Readers can scale their existing or preferred alignment to suit their individual situation.

1. Senior Vice President, Finance/Chief Financial Officer (CFO)

   The voice and influence of the CFO permeates the highest levels of corporate decision making. Financial decisions are interwoven with operating and related decisions into composite decisions that set the tone and determine the posture and character of the corporate business mission.

   Every financial officer has five essential management requirements:

   a. To make sure corporate goals are financially attainable

   b. To contribute financial expertise and viewpoint to management decisions

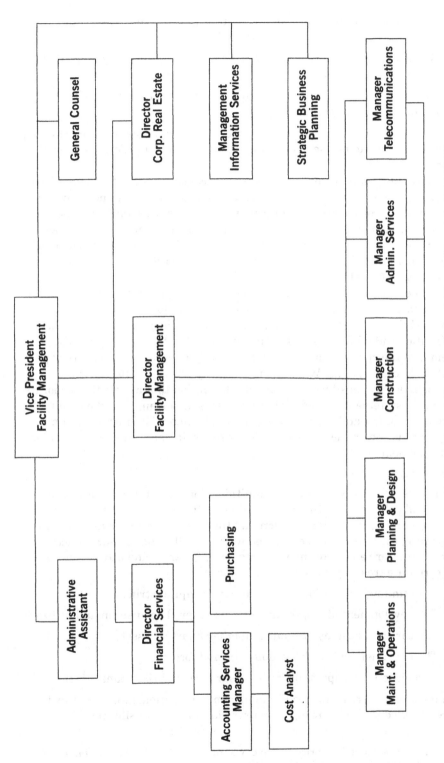

Exhibit 1.6　Corporate Facility Management Department Organizational Chart (Copyright 1994 IFMA)

    c. To serve as communicator on financial aspects of the business to investors, employees, and the public

    d. To insist on corporate conduct that adheres scrupulously to ethical practices in financial matters[1]

    e. To ensure compliance with the requirements of the Sarbanes-Oxley (SOX) Act of 2003 in the United States.

These requirements are achieved by means of a philosophical impact on top-level strategy and by the establishment and implementation of financial goals and controls.

    The facility management department becomes an arm of financial policy through its understanding of corporate financial objectives and its implementation of corporate financial policy. We suggest that top management creates broad policies, that the facility management department is cognizant of those policies, and that the actual implementation and the resultant corporate staff interfacing occur at levels subordinate to the top management level.

    In the context of the financial scandals and bankruptcies of a number of major corporations in the late 1990s and early 2000s, the U.S. Congress enacted the Sarbanes-Oxley (SOX) Act of 2002, which amended the U.S. securities and other laws in significant ways. Most compellingly, SOX demands the criminal prosecution of willfully noncompliant officers of publicly held corporations. With this potentiality, SOX has affected every department responsible for financial information that affects the corporate financial statement, including facilities. It is important that the facility professional understand how SOX affects the financial information and reports that he or she is responsible for reviewing and providing to senior management.

2. Treasurer

In a substantial, diversified, and multidivision company, the CFO is the financial policy maker. Subordinate finance functions may be split between the accounting controller function and the finance treasurer function. In this case, the treasurer is entrusted with the following primary functions: The treasurer reports to the vice president, Finance, and directs the conduct of corporate treasury activities, including:

    a. A continuing evaluation of the company's capital structure

    b. The development of long-range plans for capital acquisition and utilization

    c. The care and custody of funds and other financial assets

    d. The supervision of banking, domestic and foreign

    e. Corporate-level aspects of credit, insurance, and risk management

In terms of the treasury–facility management relationship, these functions are reflected in the following treasurer planning responsibilities:

[1]Source: J. Fred Weston and Maurice B. Goudzwaard (eds.), *The Treasurer's Handbook* (Homewood, IL: Dow Jones—Irwin, 1976), 114.

    a. Preparing long- and short-range plans and strategies for short- and long-term debt

    b. Reviewing the foreign and domestic cash positions of the company daily through cash and other financial forecasts

    c. Planning for the maintenance of adequate funds to meet outstanding and planned commitments

    d. Reviewing the implications of general economic, business, and financial developments and forecasting their impact on the corporation's treasury operations, policies, and cash requirements.

Thus, the cash or credit conditions of surplus real estate sales and the lease-versus-buy considerations of facility acquisitions fall within the treasurer's province in exercising custodial responsibilities over cash and debt and their interplay in the corporate capital structure.

3. Controller

If we view the treasurer as the corporate money financier, the other side of the finance function—the budget, accounting, financial controls and systems; financial reporting; and internal auditing—is administered by the corporate controller, who reports to the vice president, Finance. The controller directs the corporation's accounting, financial reporting, contracts and pricing, financial planning, operations analysis, and government fiscal relations activities on a global basis. The main functions of this position include:

    a. Exercising direction over the entire company's accounting, contracts and pricing, government fiscal relations, and financial planning and procedures

    b. Executing arrangements with outside auditors

    c. Directing the preparation of the company's official financial statements

    d. Reviewing all major contracts and proposals and amendments and changes thereto, including proposed pricing strategy

    e. Establishing corporate financial goals and preparing long-range and annual operating plans, forecasts, and associated operating and capital budgets

    f. Analyzing the corporation's operating results and the operating results of its various elements, identifying and analyzing potential problem areas, and presenting the results and recommended corrective action plans to operations corporate senior management

    g. Evaluating major investment opportunities

The facility management department works routinely with the controller's office when transmitting cash deposits on surplus sales, total remainder cash payments on prior sales upon the closing of the sale, and on final payments for large construction or furnishing projects.

Beyond this obvious relationship, though, the facility management department is (or should be) deeply involved in financial planning and controls activity. This involvement is heightened in companies that have a

formal procedure for capital dollar requests (both for acquisitions and dispositions). This procedure, requiring the submission of a formal document
commonly known as an *appropriation request* (AR), is examined in detail in
chapter 2. Our major point here is that all such requests require input from
each participating corporate staff department as well as the originating
division and group documentation.

Because the facility management department is called upon to comment
on and analyze the facility management aspects of the AR, the department is
part of the corporate financial control mechanism. In the most complex case,
the department is intimately involved in the planning behind the proposed
acquisition/construction/remodeling/disposition so it can act on the program
ensuing from approval smoothly, knowledgeably, and enthusiastically.

4. The Tax Affairs Department

The tax consequences of acquisitions, construction, remodeling, and
dispositions permeate every facility management transaction. Accordingly,
there should be heavy activity between the tax and facility management
departments. Let us illustrate the general responsibilities of the tax affairs
department by citing part of a fairly typical job description for a senior
corporate tax person: "To handle all tax affairs of the corporation and its
related entities with a view to ensuring compliance within the limits of all
applicable laws in a multinational environment at the least cost to the
overall organization. In addition, to handle all matters relating to the
renegotiation of contracts with the U.S. government."

The principal responsibilities of the tax affairs department are:

a. Negotiating and/or reviewing and approving major transactions in their
   formative stages and proposing changes to achieve the best tax results

b. Studying existing corporate structures, policies, operations, procedures,
   and business practices and recommending changes that would reduce
   tax costs

c. Requesting rulings from and conducting negotiations with taxing
   authorities

d. Formulating policies for and administering compliance with tax laws.
   This includes preparing and filing returns, approving and scheduling tax
   payments, and negotiating with tax examiners.

e. Advising senior management on the impact on its strategic plans of new
   tax laws, decisions, regulations, rulings, and proposed tax legislation

f. Recommending, authorizing, and conducting or controlling tax litigation

g. Filing corporate renegotiation reports and handling the audits and
   administrative proceedings relating thereto

The principal contacts between the tax affairs department and the facility
management department occur in the following areas:

a. The administration and evaluation of sales and property taxes

b. The analysis of the tax implications of sales (capital gains or losses)

c. The analysis of the tax implications of acquisitions (industrial revenue bond financing, for example)

d. The analysis of extended term sales (evaluation of the credit risk and gain or loss implications)

A lot of action should occur between tax and facility management, and the dollar aspects are significant.

5. The Corporate General Counsel

The most obvious of the interface staff relationships is that between the facility management department and the office of the corporate general counsel, as all real estate, construction, and major facility purchases transactions require the use of legal contracts and should be negotiated with professional guidance from the office of the corporate general counsel, which performs these functions:

a. Protecting the company's interests through the drafting or review of effective legal documents

b. Offering opinions and recommendations, based on sound legal interpretations, concerning problems posed by corporate staffs and divisions

c. Participating in the preparation of cases in litigation

d. Collaborating with outside legal counsel in various legal matters

e. In addition to reviewing or drafting legal documents and all required forms for real estate, construction, and major facility purchases, participating in contract negotiations and supervising the preparation of closing documents for real estate acquisitions and dispositions

If a company has a large legal staff with a corresponding volume of facility management activity, one or more staff members may be assigned to the facility management department on a full-time or first-call basis. Frequently, a legal staff member participates in contract negotiation, particularly for complex, big-ticket deals, so the development of good working relationships between the two staffs is obviously beneficial.

6. Other Corporate Staff Relationships

In addition to the preceding staff relationships, the facility management department interacts with the following departments: insurance, business development, management information services, marketing, purchasing, human resources, and public relations. The primary elements of these interdepartmental contacts are as follows:

a. *Insurance Department.* The insurance department is notified of any changes in the real estate inventory—owned or leased, acquisitions or dispositions—so excesses or inadequacies in insurance coverage can be avoided. Where the acquisition of an existing facility is contemplated, the insurance department can arrange for the independent inspection of the facility by an underwriter—for example, Industrial Risk Insurers (IRI)—to evaluate potential loss exposures and the costs of eliminating them.

b. *Purchasing Department.* In much the same manner, the facility management department works with the purchasing department primarily when
seeking a site, seeking design and associated services, seeking furnishings, construction, bid document review, bid announcement, bid opening
and review, and bid award. Because purchasing is involved in architectural, engineering, construction, furnishing, and service contracts (such
contracts represent purchased services), lead time notification from the
facility management department increases corporate operating efficiency.

c. *Human Resources.* The relationship between the facility management
department and human resources is extremely important both internally,
to ensure the proper hiring, training, and management of staff, and
externally, to provide studies on union matters in potential locations.
These items weigh heavily in financial decisions on new facility locations.

Working relationships also exist between the corporate facility management
department and other group/division staff personnel, particularly finance and
operations. The facility professional maintains many one-on-one relationships
with senior group/division presidents, vice presidents, and so forth. The peer
group pressures of corporate management require strong support from the corporate front office if real estate profit opportunities are to be maximized.

Corporate Directives and Procedures

As a first step toward dollar effectiveness, written corporate directives and procedures that provide a realistic framework for achieving defined goals should be
developed, approved by senior management, and implemented. (We cannot
emphasize too strongly the importance of senior management commitment to the
success of the facility management program.)

The key corporate directive, signed by a corporate officer, provides the muscle
for the facility management program. Its key operating words should state,
"Authority for the negotiation and document preparation and/or execution for all
acquisitions, design, construction, furnishings, disposals, and similar transactions which affect the rights of the corporation in real property and facilities are
retained in the Corporate Offices."

The series of supporting procedures should be designed to instruct divisions on
the proper ways of complying with the corporate directive.

While the organizational structure just described is patterned to achieve both
perceived and defined goals, it is only one possible solution to the intricate problems of effective facility management. Your solution may be different. We urge
you to make the effort to fully comprehend the wondrous ways in which an effective facility management program can help your company and then to design a
plan that works for you.

Human Resources Issues

Facility professionals often find that whereas organizational issues may be well
defined, human resources involves ongoing problems that must be addressed and
managed. Hiring, training, counseling, managing, cutting back on staff, and even
firing nonperforming employees are tasks that the facility professional must

accomplish to ensure the developing departmental team includes mature, efficient, and knowledgeable members.

Many corporations set up facility management departments based on past work requirements, and the job titles may or may not adequately reflect the work or responsibilities performed. The following titles are often used:

Administrative Coordinator	Building Manager
Administrative Director	Construction Coordinator
Administrative Manager	Construction Manager
Architectural Manager	Construction Director
Area Manager	Customer Service Manager
Assistant Director	Development Manager
Director	Interior Designer
Director, Physical Assets	Interior Design Manager
Division Manager	Maintenance Manager
Engineering Director	Maintenance Supervisor
Engineering Manager	Manager, Building Services
Facilities Engineer	Manager, Custodial Services
Facilities Design Coordinator	Manager, Facilities Operations
Facilities Planner	Real Estate Coordinator
Facility Coordinator	Real Estate Director
Facility Director	Real Estate Manager
Facility Manager	Real Estate Representative
Facility Supervisor	Vice President, Facility Management

Many facility management departments have a number of supervisory levels denoting experience, expertise, supervisory responsibilities, and leadership standards. Through a number of research projects, the IFMA has developed the following five supervisory levels that encompass most job descriptions:[2]

1. Professional/Specialist (no subordinates)

2. Unit Supervisor (subordinates but no supervisors)

3. Section Heads (supervisors who supervise others)

4. Managers (supervisors who supervise others)

5. Directors (supervisors who supervise other supervisors)

Exhibit 1.7 provides brief descriptions for the positions noted in the preceding list. Each description summarizes the position, its major responsibilities, the reporting hierarchy, and basic qualifications.

All position descriptions should meet the following criteria: realistic responsibilities; clear expectations and defined work requirements; clear reporting line to a specific stated position; clear reporting lines from other positions; qualifications commensurate with the responsibilities and authority granted by senior management through policies, procedures, and executive authority.

[2]*Source*: International Facility Management Association (IFMA) "Research Report #24," *Profiles 2003, Salary Report*, p. 23. Copyright 2004 IFMA.

Level 5 Management	**Senior Vice President, Corporate Services**
Summary	Provide overall strategic facility management and service-related planning to support the development of facilities and services to meet strategic operational business requirements.
Major Responsibilities	Establish, maintain, and promote an ongoing work-responsive relationship with senior line organization management.
	Direct and ensure the coordination, scheduling, budgeting and completion of facility and service requirements such as long-range planning, real estate acquisition, management and disposal, purchasing, capital and churn construction and renovation projects, maintenance, security, telecommunications, word processing, travel, food service, mail, receiving and shipping, records management, and reprographics.
	May also direct other support services such as human resources, computer services, and public relations.
Reports to:	Executive Vice President; Chief Financial Officer; Chief Executive Officer
Reporting to This Position:	Senior facility/service-related officers and directors
Qualifications	Undergraduate degree in management or technical area. Graduate degree in business administration, law, or finance. Minimum of 15 years of progressively responsible facility and service-related experience.

Exhibit 1.7   Position Descriptions (*Developed by Edmond P. Rondeau, BDO Seidman, for the International Facility Management Association (IFMA)). "Research Report #12," Profiles '94, Salary Report, 1994, p. 48.*)

Level 3 Management	**Supervisor, Construction Management**
	Other Titles: Building Construction and Renovation Chief, Construction
Summary	Supervise departmental staff, oversee the delivery of quality construction on time and within budget. Set standards for quality of construction and set and interpret departmental policy for departmental staff.
Major Responsibilities	Provide leadership, supervision, and direction to departmental staff.
	Complete the construction plan each year in cooperation with other departments within the company.
	Develop and monitor construction documentation to ensure corporate financial protection, particularly in the area of progress payments, retainage, and general bonding procedures.
	Monitor and review new materials, advanced technology, construction techniques, schedules, and cost.
	Establish, maintain, and promote an ongoing work-responsive relationship with the line organization.
Reports to:	Manager, Facilities Construction; Director of Facilities; Vice President, Real Estate and Construction
Reporting to This Position:	Construction Manager; Construction Coordinator; Department Assistant; Cost Analyst; Project Manager
Qualifications	Six to eight years of construction and planning experience and an undergraduate degree in a technical area (engineering, construction, or architecture). State registration as a licensed engineer or architect.

Exhibit 1.7 Position Descriptions (Continued)

Level 3 Management	**Supervisor, Corporate Real Estate**
Other Titles:	Real Estate Manager
Summary	Supervise departmental staff, and oversee the timely acquisition, management, and disposal of real estate. Coordinate with other departments for input before formalizing decisions and provide real estate personnel as authorized to implement approved real estate plans.
Major Responsibilities	Provide leadership, supervision, and direction to Real Estate Managers and Real Estate Coordinators. Negotiate and acquire real estate locations consistent with needed criteria as set forth by senior management. Organize, staff, train, and motivate departmental staff and other outside professionals as required. Supervise the market analysis, business decisions, and site selection of the Real Estate Managers. Establish, maintain, and promote an ongoing work-responsive relationship with the line organization.
Reports to:	Director of Finance; Comptroller; Manager, Facilities Management
Reporting to This Position:	Real Estate Manager; Real Estate Coordinator; Real Estate Assistants; Property Coordinator; Site Manager
Qualifications	Undergraduate degree in business administration, real estate, or law. Advanced study or graduate degree in business administration with emphasis in real estate, finance, and strategic planning.

Exhibit 1.7 Position Descriptions (Continued)

Level 2 Management	**Project Manager**
Other Titles:	Construction Manager, Project Engineer
Summary	Manage and coordinate the budgeting, scheduling, design, bidding, construction, furnishings and relocation requirements for renovation and new construction projects.
Major Responsibilities	Determine the scope of the work, prepare cost estimates, schedules, correspondence, contracts, and purchase requisitions for assigned projects.
	Review and manage project budgets, consultants, contractors, and other associated product and service providers.
	Inspect and coordinate construction, telecommunications, security, data processing, furniture, furnishings, signage, landscaping, and move-in requirements.
	Prepare and issue a final punch list and review all requests for payment. Ensure all punch list items are complete, lien waivers have been received, and a Certificate of Occupancy has been obtained before the final request for payment is approved.
Reports to:	Supervisor, Construction Management; Director of Construction
Reporting to This Position:	Project Coordinator; Facility Planner; Site Engineer; Cost Analyst
Qualifications	Degree in building construction, engineering, or architecture plus four to six years' experience. Professional registration often desired, sometimes required.

Exhibit 1.7   Position Descriptions (Continued)

Level 2 Management	**Real Estate Manager**
Other Titles:	Real Estate Representative, Property Manager
Summary	Provide corporate-wide expertise in real estate and coordinate assigned real estate activities. Provide consistent dissemination of knowledge and application of real estate policies, procedures, and practices.
Major Responsibilities	Assist in the development, implementation, and maintenance of corporate real estate policies, procedures, and practices.
	Represent the corporation in specified real estate assignments, including real estate analysis, broker selection, site selection, coordination with legal counsel, lease negotiation, and property acquisition.
	Provide ongoing management of existing corporate leased properties and other properties as required.
	Evaluate and analyze corporate real estate opportunities, including site selection and negotiation, strategic real estate planning, and disposition requirements.
Reports to:	Director of Real Estate; Director, Facilities Management
Reporting to This Position:	Real Estate Coordinator; Real Estate Assistant
Qualifications	Undergraduate degree in business, real estate, or construction. Graduate studies or continuing professional education in real estate, law, finance, or marketing. Five or more years of management experience in corporate real estate or property management.

Exhibit 1.7   Position Descriptions (Continued)

Level 1 Management	**Project Coordinator**
Other Titles:	Facility Coordinator, Project Planner
Summary	Coordinate corporate construction and renovation projects and interface with in-house customers and service providers.
Major Responsibilities	Coordinate and follow up on construction documentation and construction progress daily.
	Assist in the selection of design, construction, furnishings, and other project-related service providers.
	Manage correspondence, project documents, contracts, change orders, project budgets and schedules as they relate to architectural, construction, furniture, furnishings, signage, relocation, and landscape contracts.
	Coordinate project requirements with in-house service providers.
Reports to:	Director of Construction; Construction Manager; Project Manager
Reporting to This Position:	Rarely has direct supervision of subordinates but often acts in an advisory capacity to all organizational units.
Qualifications	Bachelor's degree in business administration, construction, architecture, or interior design. Entry level to three years' experience or no degree and four to eight years' experience.

Exhibit 1.7 Position Descriptions (Continued)

Level 1 Management	Real Estate Coordinator
Other Titles:	Real Estate Analyst, Site Coordinator, Property Coordinator
Summary	Coordinate the processing of real estate contracts, land purchase requisitions, rent and subtenant invoices and the monthly lease payment schedule with legal counsel, landlords, and sellers.
Major Responsibilities	Assist in the acquisition, management, and disposal of corporate real estate.
	Maintain, review, and track lease, tax, common area maintenance, and operating expense pass-through payments and increases from and to landlords.
	Maintain the real estate management information system database and the monthly status reports.
	Review owned and leased real property documents and provide timely notice for lease expiration and option renewal to the appropriate in-house parties.
Reports to:	Director, Manager, or Supervisor of Corporate Real Estate
Reporting to This Position:	Rarely has direct supervision, but often coordinates the day-to-day activities of consultants, attorneys, paralegals, landlords, and/or contractors for Real Estate Managers.
Qualifications	Bachelor's degree in business administration, paralegal, or real estate. Entry level to three years' experience or no degree and four to eight years' experience.

Exhibit 1.7   Position Descriptions *(Continued)*

   The management and human resources department must be involved in the development of position descriptions including work requirements and responsibilities, reporting lines, qualifications, training, compensation, and personnel performance evaluation. The facility management position and salary responsibility factors matrix shown in Exhibit 1.8 may prove useful when evaluating departmental compensation plans with your management and human resources department.
   Exhibit 1.9 provides a number of executive observations to consider in the development and organization of a facility management department.

		CORP. HQ. POSITION	DIVISION POSITION			SUPER-VISORY LEVEL
			DIVISION HQ.	Operating Unit		(See Levels Below)
				Op. Unit Hq.	Sect. in Unit	
HISTORY OF INDUSTRY, ORGANIZATION & CHURN	De-clining					
	No Growth					
	Small Growth					
	Medium Growth					
	Large Growth					
MGMT. STYLE	Decen-tralized					
	Cen-tralized					
LOCA-TION	Living & Labor Costs					
BUSINESS FOCUS	Service — New					
	Service — Exist.					
	Product — Static					
	Product — Dy-namic					
FIRM SIZE (No. of Employees)	Small (Less Than 1,000)					
	Medium (1,000 To 10,000)					
	Large (Over 10,000)					
FM REPORTS TO	Line Mgmt.					
	Staff Mgmt.					

5 Supervisory Levels:
1. Professional/Specialist (no subordinates)
2. Unit Supervisor (subordinates but no supervisors)
3. One level of supervisor (who supervise others)
4. Two levels of supervisors (who supervise others)
5. Three or more levels of supervisors report to you

Exhibit 1.8   FM Position and Salary Responsibility Factors Matrix

Discussion Items:
- Teamwork Issues
  - Image externally and internally
  - Consistency and oversight opportunities
  - Management plans
  - Implementation plans and follow-up
- Management Issues
  - Accountability and responsibility
  - Financial control
  - Project management
- Organizational Issues
  - Ongoing organization
  - Training: technical and management
  - Job rotation
  - Job description, objectives and performance appraisal
  - Administrative and technical support
- Communication Issues
  - Senior management expectations
  - Customer expectations
  - Employee expectations and requirements
  - Supplier expectations and requirements
- Marketing Issues
  - Customer master plan requirements
  - Master planning strategies
  - Benchmarking, excellence and quality programs
- Mission and mission statements
- Customer expectations, services, benchmarking, excellence, quality, and service level agreements
- Policies and procedures including responsibility and authority
- Position descriptions and job performance
- Cost versus customer service
- Training, job switching, and career paths
- Large customer perceptions
- Staffing, job perceptions, hiring and firing
- Marketing to future service growth areas
- Executive communication, organization, and reorganization
- Implementation and executive follow-up
- What does your boss expect? What does his boss expect?
- Imprinting
- Project management
- Handbook for Architects and Engineers
- Real estate service, negotiating strategy, budgeting, accountability, recurring rent payments, and audit trail
- Design and construction management budgets and control
- Team concepts versus individual units
- Automation: Real Estate and Project Management

Exhibit 1.9   Executive Observations

ETHICS

Because your reputation for honesty, professionalism, integrity, and standing with your customers and within your corporation is one of your most valuable assets, you must protect it at all times. The ethics you live and work by provide a base of trust that enables your boss, customers, staff, service and product providers, and acquaintances to believe you will be fair and honorable in your dealings with them.

Facility professionals often make decisions or recommendations about purchasing costly services or products that may indebt the organization through major legal commitments. Most organizations have written codes of ethics that govern many aspects of doing business for and with the firm. Many organizations prohibit accepting or giving gifts, no matter how small (even a cup of coffee); others permit small gifts appropriate to the event or occasion, such as a business lunch. Still other organizations permit the presentation of gifts personally paid for by the giver. Whatever your organization's code of ethics requires, your actions set the example for staff and others who observe your conduct of business activities.

The code of ethics usually states, as a minimum, that "employees shall not discriminate because of race, sex, creed, age, handicap, or national origin." In many organizations, employees must sign a statement acknowledging that they have read and understand the organization's code of ethics.

The International Facility Management Association (IFMA; see Exhibit 1.10), the Industrial Asset Management Council (IAMC; see Exhibit 1.11), and CoreNet Global (see Exhibit 1.12) have each developed a code of ethics for their members.

All IFMA members are expected to comply with the IFMA Code of Ethics. When in doubt, members have the responsibility to seek clarification from IFMA.

IFMA members shall treat each other with respect when dealing with matters that could affect their professional reputations. All members shall recognize that the profession will be judged by the conduct of individual members.

IFMA members shall maintain the highest professional standards and ethical behavior in their Association relationships. This includes, but is not limited to, the use of mail lists, membership information and membership resources, or any calls, contacts or working relationships outside of IFMA.

IFMA members shall use IFMA membership as a means of professional development for themselves and not personal aggrandizement.

IFMA members shall be responsible for providing educational and professional development information to the membership.

IFMA members shall not buy or sell products or services at IFMA functions, except at trade shows or displays established for that purpose.

IFMA members shall not discriminate because of race, sex, creed, age, disability or national origin as it relates to their Association relationships.

Exhibit 1.10   IFMA Code of Ethics (Source: International Facility Management Association; the Revised IFMA Code of Ethics was adopted by the International Facility Management Association in September 1995.)

IFMA members shall abide by the Constitution and Bylaws of the Association and shall support the objectives of its strategic plan and the interests of the Association stakeholders (members' business entity and leadership, government regulatory agencies and IFMA staff).

IFMA members are responsible to report the actions of individuals or companies considered contrary to the Code of Ethics to IFMA. These actions may include, but are not limited to, cases of professional malfeasance, discrimination or incompetence.

The IFMA Ethics Committee shall investigate complaints received and may issue sanctions for code violations.

This document is a guideline and does not represent the entire breadth of what constitutes good conduct and ethical behavior.

CODE OF ETHICS ISSUE RESOLUTION PROCEDURE

Individuals applying for and being accepted for membership in IFMA implicitly agree to abide by the rules and regulations that govern the Association. This includes adherence to the Association's Code of Ethics as last amended September 1995.

By extension all chapters, councils and other constituent groups that operate under a charter granted by IFMA, or which otherwise function at the behest of the Association, shall abide by the same rules and regulations and shall enforce them vigorously and fairly in all matters.

In the event of an ethical conflict between two or more members of the same chapter, council or constituent group, the elected or appointed leadership of that group shall serve as the primary mediator of such issues. It is assumed that most ethical questions will be resolved at this level.

Should the chapter, council or other constituent group fail to resolve the issue at hand to the satisfaction of all concerned, or if the issue directly involves an officer or officers of that group, it shall be brought before the member of the IFMA Board of Directors having oversight over that group for mediation.

Should any issue not be resolved to the satisfaction of all stakeholders at the Director level, it shall be brought before the Association's Ethics Committee which will serve as a "court of last resort." Written statements of the facts and opinions surrounding the issue shall be solicited from all those directly involved. The committee may also seek input from leadership, administrative and legal resources of the Association as it deems necessary and appropriate.

Ethical issues brought by individual members and/or constituent groups which directly involve the Association and/or a member of its Board of Directors or staff shall be referred directly to the Association's Ethics Committee.

The Immediate Past Chairperson of the Association shall chair the Ethics Committee, which also shall include the three previous chairs of the Association and its Vice President of Administration and Membership Services.

After due consultation with all stakeholders in an issue, and not later than six months after the issue has been formally brought before it, the Ethics Committee shall render a judgment which shall be accepted by all as final.

Exhibit 1.10   IFMA Code of Ethics (Continued)

Act with integrity.

Maintain standards of conduct above the legal limitations.

Honor commitments to others.

Avoid and disclose potential conflicts of interest.

Accept no gift which might appear to imply obligation.

Tell the truth.

Give accurate, complete information.

Deal with facts, not presumption and supposition.

Keep commitments.

Meet obligations.

Respect requests for confidentiality.

Support programs of the organization.

Represent fairly the interest of the organization.

Treat people with dignity and respect.

Assume the best about others.

Maintain a courteous and considerate manner.

Promote positive relationships.

Talk to, not about, people.

Contribute to the advancement of colleagues.

Protect the environment.

Conserve natural resources.

Maintain aesthetic values.

Excel.

Do your best.

Draw out the best in others.

Exhibit 1.11   Code of Ethics and Conduct (Source: *Industrial Asset Management Council, 2003. The IAMC was founded in May 2002 in the United States for real estate and facility professionals who primarily focus on the acquisition, management, and disposal of corporate industrial and manufacturing facilities.*)

The purpose and objectives of CoreNet Global are outlined in Article II of the Bylaws of the Association. It is expected that all members of the Association will adhere to and support the Bylaws.

The Association's "Code of Ethics and Standards of Professional Conduct" establish professional guidelines that fellow members and others can expect CoreNet Global members to practice in their business and Association activities. Each member is responsible to practice his/her profession according to these standards:

Each member shall endeavor to:

1. Practice one's profession in a manner which will uphold and maintain the integrity, reputation and expertise of CoreNet Global, one's company and the individual member.

2. Positively promote the perception of the real estate profession in order to improve the member's personal impact on the company's decision-making process.

3. Willingly and actively communicate with fellow members to enhance their understanding and education in the areas of real estate without compromising confidential or proprietary information.

4. Respect the business practices of one's company and those in the real estate community.

5. Accept no form of remuneration in regard to any company-related transaction other than compensation from one's company.

6. Use sound professional judgment for the benefit of one's company.

7. Pursue the interests of one's company judiciously and diligently within the bounds of conscience and law.

8. Not engage in unlawful discrimination on account of race, color, religion, sex, age or national origin in business or hiring practices or transactions.

9. Claim only those credentials, degrees, qualifications, experience or relationships which each member does, in fact, possess.

10. Refrain from using membership in CoreNet Global for personal or company gain or gratification at the exclusion or expense of others.

CoreNet Global was founded for the purpose of enhancing the corporate real estate profession. Relationships and business transactions by members with other persons in the real estate profession, governmental bodies and other CoreNet Global members should always be conducted with fairness, professionalism and courtesy. Infractions of these standards will be reviewed and may result in a forfeiture of membership.

Exhibit 1.12   ARTICLE 15 CoreNet Global Code of Ethics (Source: CoreNet Global Bylaws. CoreNet Global, a global corporate real estate association, was founded in April 2002 with the merger of the International Development Research Council (IDRC) and the National Association of Corporate Real Estate Executives (NACORE).)

The Facility Management Mission

As a facility professional, you have a unique opportunity to improve your corporation's bottom line each time a leased or owned property is acquired, leased, subleased, remodeled, sold, or donated. Your knowledge of your mission (see Exhibit 1.13), services provided (see Exhibit 1.14), corporate culture, policies and procedures, and the inventory of facilities and property (see chapter 4) help set the tone, schedule, and successful completion of a facility requirement.

Corporations that provide a rapidly expanding product or service, or that are shrinking in sales and staff, usually do not make a substantial investment in fixed equipment. If they can live with a variable lease cost, they will most likely choose to lease rather than to own property and facilities. These corporations, often small manufacturers, retailers, or service providers, tend to seek three- to five-year lease commitments and use cash for operations. They do not invest heavily in equipment and are mobile in their geographic service area. They must be flexible in their business operations and able to reduce lease occupancy expenses when required.

To help your in-house customers, your staff and management must understand and agree to the corporate facility management services offered by your department. You may wish to develop a written service level agreement with your customer(s) to define and quantify the quality, level, and types of real estate service your department will provide, performance objectives and measurements of service against objectives, and the information and help your customer(s) will provide to you. The service level agreement is usually for a term of one year and includes a page for the signatures of the service provider (you) and the senior level manager (your customer) of the department, company, or operations group. It should not be a lengthy document, but it should contain the detail necessary to provide a clear understanding between the parties.

FACILITY MANAGEMENT

The mission of the Corporate Facility Management Department is to serve ABC Company and our Customers by providing and delivering timely, quality, professional facility management analysis, and consulting support services. Doing so enhances ABC's long-term competitive position through the acquisition and management of efficient, cost-effective facilities.

We provide high-quality facility management services essential to productive work and support environments.

**STRATEGIC FACILITY MANAGEMENT
SERVICES DELIVERED FOR ABC CO.**

Exhibit 1.13   Mission Statement

Department: **Facility Management and Planning**
Resp. Area: **1460**

A. Service/Function: <u>Real Estate Services</u> Annual Cost: $_____

   1. DESCRIPTION OF SERVICE/FUNCTION:

Serve ABC Company and our customers by providing and delivering timely,
quality, professional real estate analysis, and consulting support services. This
also includes traveling to the business units upon request or when required,
implementation of Corporate Real Estate Policies and Procedures, and staying
informed on real estate markets and field operations.

   2. VALUE CREATED BY SERVICE/FUNCTION:

Providing this service enhances ABC Company's long-term competitive position
through the acquisition and management of efficient, cost-effective real estate.
This includes assisting Division customers to obtain cost-effective brokerage
services, determining real estate requirements, recommending alternative
strategies and lease or purchase concessions to obtain, providing lease or purchase document review, provide financial analysis, and reduce business unit
exposure and financial obligations to help ABC Company/business unit bottom-
line performance.

   3. IMPACT FROM LOSS OF SERVICE/FUNCTION:

Business unit customers are aware of their immediate needs and resources.
Real Estate Consulting Services provides an additional level of real estate
expertise and corporate strategic direction to assist the customers and ABC
Company to make a more informed, consistent decision to increase shareholder
value and protect ABC Company's resources. Without the current service, which
focuses on the management of ABC Company real property assets, there would
be no overall corporate strategic asset management planning, policies or focus
on the over _____, _____ owned and lease properties and the over $ _____,
_____ in yearly expenditures.

B.   Service/Function: <u>Facility Management</u>   Annual Cost: $_____
                                    <u>ABC Bldg., Chicago, IL</u>

   1. DESCRIPTION OF SERVICE/FUNCTION:

Provide professional facility management services to in-house customers and
manage the funds and services necessary to support the business, operational
and legal requirements for ABC Company. This includes maintaining, and operating the building and managing all facility expenditures including taxes and
utilities.

Exhibit 1.14 Service Function Justification

2. VALUE CREATED BY SERVICE/FUNCTION:

In 2001, the ABC Company had spent over $ _____, _____ more than bud-
geted on facilities and services. In 2002, this budget overrun was reduced by
$ _____, _____ to $ _____, _____. In 2003, it was reduced by $ _____,
_____ to a $ _____, _____ budget overrun; in 2004 it was reduced by
$ _____, _____ to a $ _____, _____ budget overrun; and in 2005, ABC
Company will not sustain a budget overrun but will receive a cost savings of
over $ _____, _____. Facility budget overruns have been reduced through a
successful management program that has controlled the facilities' variable
costs and stabilized fixed costs.

3. IMPACT FROM LOSS OF SERVICE/FUNCTION:

ABC Company has a legal obligation to manage and operate its facilities and to
pay all building expenses totaling over $ _____, _____ in 2005. ABC Com-
pany's Facility Management Department is responsible for the management and
costs to maintain and operate the building.

C. Service/Function: **Facility Management Information System (FMIS)**
                       Implementation and Support   Annual Cost: $_____

1. DESCRIPTION OF SERVICE/FUNCTION:

The ABC Company Facility Management Information System (FMIS) is an asset
management and a graphic database system designed to address ABC Company and business unit real estate, facility management, and facility maintenance requirements, while maintaining a decentralized management of assets
and resources, and providing for local control over facility decisions.

2. VALUE CREATED BY SERVICE/FUNCTION:

The ABC Company Facility Management Information System has been designed
to provide the following objectives, benefits, and value to the ABC Company
and to each business unit user:

• Know what we own, lease, and manage, including real estate, buildings,
  plans and space, budgets and expenditures, construction, furniture, equipment, maintenance, plans and operating manuals, life safety, records,
  telecommunications, computer, and fixtures.

• Save time and manpower for users.

• Identify opportunities to reduce real estate, facility, and operating expense.

• Increase accuracy and eliminate duplication of records.

• Provide reports and analytical tools not feasible with manual systems.

Exhibit 1.14 Service Function Justification (Continued)

- Help formulate short- and long-term real estate, facility, and operational strategies.

- Efficiently transfer data between users at the unit level and master files at the Company and business unit levels.

3. IMPACT FROM LOSS OF SERVICE/FUNCTION:

The ABC Company Facility Management Information System provides the ability to strategically manage the over _____, _____ properties owned and leased by the ABC Company totaling over $_____, _____ a year in expenditures. Without the Facility Management Information System, the graphics and database of information would not be readily or easily available, and the real estate, buildings, plans and space, budgets and expenditures, construction, furniture, equipment, maintenance, life safety, records, telecommunications, computer, and fixtures would not be readily accessible for planning and daily use by the FMIS business unit customers in a timely and consistent format.

Exhibit 1.14   Service Function Justification (*Continued*)

YOU AND YOUR CUSTOMER

It is important that you and your customer take the time necessary to understand your customer's business requirements and your mutual roles as team members to meet those needs. You should discuss how you propose to organize the facility management assignment and support the project after completion. Include a review of the following aspects of your department:

- Department mission
- Previous real estate assignments
- Measuring performance and service against specific standards
- Staff
- Quality, excellence, and customer satisfaction programs

You may find the Lease Property: Site Criteria Considerations (Exhibit 4.14) and the Purchase Property: Site Criteria Considerations (Exhibit 4.15) in chapter 4 valuable in helping you and your customer (including management) focus on specific requirements by asking your customer to weigh each criterion. The completed checklist identifies your customer's initial expectations and requirements.

The Facility Management Team

Your facility management team includes the customer and your staff. The team may also include the assistance of your corporate or outside legal real estate counsel, in-house support services (e.g., telecommunications, management information system, finance, records management), a real estate broker, a design or engineering consultant, and a general contractor; others, such as a facility management relocation consultant, also may be required (see Exhibit 1.15).

THIS AGREEMENT (the "Agreement") is made and entered into this _____ day of_____ 20_____, by and between _____, a _____ (the "Company") and_____, a _____ (the "Contractor").

WITNESSETH:

WHEREAS, Company is currently planning the construction and furnishing of and the move into new office space approximating _____ usable square feet located on the _____, _____, _____ floors of _____ (the Project), an office building located at _____ (city), _____ County, _____ (state) (the Premises); and

WHEREAS, Contractor represents that he is knowledgeable and experienced in the areas of interior construction and furnishing and planning and executing moves into office space; and

WHEREAS, Company desires to engage Contractor as an independent contractor to assist Company in constructing, furnishing and moving into the Premises; and

WHEREAS, Contractor desires to be engaged as an independent contractor by Company on the terms and conditions as hereinafter set forth;

NOW, THEREFORE, for and in consideration of the premises and the mutual promises and covenants contained herein, and for other good and valuable consideration, the receipt, adequacy and sufficiency of which is hereby acknowledged, the parties hereto agree as follows:

1. Services. The Company hereby retains Contractor for the purposes of and the Contractor hereby agrees to perform facilities construction management services, furnishing management services, moving coordination services and such other services on behalf of Company in connection with the Project and the move into the Premises as Company may from time to time request during the term of the Agreement. Contractor's work shall include, but is not limited to, coordination of design plans and furnishing plans with Company and Company's interior designers and architects, attendance at all planning and construction meetings, participating in bidding out of all construction and furnishing contracts, monitoring construction progress and coordinating construction and installation of all furnishings and equipment with all contractors, subcontractors and vendors and such other coordination and management services as requested by Company from time to time during the term hereof. Contractor agrees that he will be available on a full-time basis for the period beginning three (3) weeks prior to Company's announced move-in date and terminating one (1) week after said date. Contractor's services and duties shall at all times be performed in a competent and professional way.

Exhibit 1.15   Independent Contractor Agreement

2. Term. The term of this Agreement shall commence on the date hereof, and unless sooner terminated pursuant to Section 4 hereof, shall expire on _____, 20____ (the Expiration Date). Notwithstanding anything in this Agreement to the contrary, the covenants contained in Section 4(d) shall survive the expiration or termination of this Agreement.

3. Compensation, Reimbursements, Deductions.

(a) Contractor shall be compensated for his services to the Company pursuant to this Agreement _____, payable in semimonthly installments on the 15th day of each month for the period from the 16th through the last day of each previous month and on the last day of the month for the 1st through the 15th day of each month. Contractor shall account for his time spent working for Company in a manner satisfactory to Company. Should this Agreement terminate for any reason prior to the Expiration Date, Contractor shall only receive that portion of his compensation as he may have earned for the period prior to such termination.

(b) As an independent contractor and not an employee, Contractor acknowledges, understands and agrees that the Company is not required to withhold federal, state or local income taxes from any compensation paid Contractor hereunder, or to otherwise comply with any local, state or federal law concerning the collection of income taxes at the source of payment of compensation; that the Company is not required under the Federal Unemployment Tax Act and the Federal Insurance Contribution Act to withhold taxes for unemployment compensation and for Social Security on behalf of contractor or his dependents; and that the Company is not required under the laws of any state to obtain workers' compensation insurance or to make state unemployment compensation contributions on behalf of Contractor. Contractor expressly releases the Company from any liability arising from its failure to withhold such taxes, to provide such unemployment compensation, Social Security benefits and workers' compensation insurance, and Contractor hereby agrees to indemnify and hold the Company harmless from all liability it may incur as a result of such failure. Contractor assumes full responsibility for the payment of all federal, state, and local taxes for contributions imposed or required under unemployment insurance, Social Security, and income tax laws with respect to Contractor's performance pursuant to the terms of this Agreement.

(c) In accordance with and subject to Company's normal policies, Contractor shall be reimbursed for all actual, reasonable, and direct expenses which, after the Company's prior written approval, were incurred by him in the performance of his duties hereunder. Contractor shall provide the Company with written documentation of such expenses in a form complying with the records required by the Internal Revenue Service and appropriate state authorities for tax deductibility purposes, and reimbursement for each item of expense shall be made within reasonable time after receipt by company of the written documentation therefore.

Exhibit 1.15 Independent Contractor Agreement (Continued)

4. Termination.

(a) The Company or Contractor may immediately terminate this Agreement for cause at any time, the determination of which shall be made by Company or Contractor, without notice of any kind. Cause as used herein shall include but shall not be limited to the following: conduct by Company or Contractor amounting to fraud, dishonesty, intentional misrepresentation, embezzlement, gross negligence, wilful acts of moral turpitude, or wilful misconduct or other acts reflecting discredit upon the Company or Contractor's failure to adequately fulfill his obligations hereunder, or the breach by Company or Contractor of any written agreement with the Company or Contractor.

(b) This Agreement may be terminated without cause thirty (30) days following Company's or Contractor's written notice of termination to the other party.

(c) This Agreement shall terminate upon the death or total disability of Contractor (total disability meaning the failure or inability of Contractor to perform his obligations hereunder for a period of sixty (60) consecutive days by reason of Contractor's mental or physical disability as so determined by a licensed physician selected by the Company).

(d) This Agreement shall terminate upon the total inability of Company to pay Contractor (total inability meaning the failure or inability of Company to perform its obligations hereunder for a period of sixty (60) consecutive days by reason of Company's financial inability or refusal to pay Contractor as so determined by the Contractor).

(e) Upon the termination or expiration of this Agreement whether for cause or otherwise, Contractor, within seventy-two (72) hours thereof, shall deliver, or cause to be delivered, to the Company originals and all copies of any documents or other items containing Confidential Information held or in possession or control of Contractor and a list of contractors, subcontractors, and vendors involved with or connected to the Project whose names are known to Contractor. The failure of the Contractor to deliver such Confidential Information and list shall result in the forfeiture of any additional compensation due but not yet paid to the Contractor under the terms hereof. Further, the Contractor hereby covenants and agrees to direct to the Company any and all subsequent inquiries from contractors, subcontractors, and vendors respecting the Company or the Project.

For purposes of this Section 4, the term Confidential Information means any and all data and information relating to the Premises or the Project (whether constituting a trade secret or not) which is or has been disclosed to Contractor or of which Contractor became aware as a consequence of or through his relationship with the Company and which has value to them Company and is not generally known by unrelated third parties. Confidential Information shall not include any data or information that has been voluntarily disclosed to the public by the Company (except where such public disclosure has been made without authorization), or that has been independently developed and disclosed by others, or that otherwise enters the public domain through lawful means.

Exhibit 1.15 Independent Contractor Agreement (Continued)

5. Assignment. Contractor acknowledges that the services he is to perform pursuant to the provisions of this Agreement are personal in nature and may not be delegated or assigned by him without the prior written consent of the Company, and that his right to any monies due or to become due as a consequence of the terms hereof is not assignable without the prior written consent of the Company.

6. Relationship. It is distinctly understood and agreed between the parties hereto that the Contractor is retained and engaged by the Company only for the purposes and to the extent set forth in this Agreement, and during the period he renders services hereunder, his relation to the Company shall be that of an independent contractor in the performance of each and every part of this Agreement. The Contractor shall not be considered by reason of any of the provisions of this Agreement or otherwise as having an employee status or as being entitled to participate in any plan, arrangements, or distributions by the Company pertaining to or in connection with any employment benefits enjoyed by the Company's regular employees.

7. Indemnification by Contractor. In consideration of his being retained and engaged by the Company, and as a further inducement to the Company to enter into this Agreement, Contractor agrees to the following:
   (a) Contractor shall have no authority to bind the Company by any promise or representations, whether written or oral, express or implied, made by him. Contractor shall not have the right to make or enter into any contracts or agreements of any nature whatsoever for or on behalf of the Company.
   (b) Contractor agrees to indemnify and hold the Company harmless from and against any and all loss and cost or damage to the Company arising out of or as a direct or indirect result of: (i) any representation or promise made by Contractor, or anyone in his employ or control, in violation of the provisions of subparagraph (a) of this Section 7; and (ii) any contract or agreement entered into on behalf of the Company without the written approval of the Company as provided in Section 7(a).
   (c) Contractor further agrees to release, indemnify, and hold forever harmless the Company from any and all claims for damage to person or property and for any and all liability of any other nature arising out of any act or omission on the part of the Contractor in connection with the performance of this Agreement.

8. Company Indemnification. The Company hereby agrees to defend, indemnify, and forever hold harmless the Contractor against any and all liability, loss, claims, cost, and expense (including reasonable attorney's fees and costs of litigation) that may be incurred by the Contractor arising out of, in connection with, or that might be incurred as a result of the Company's being negligent or derelict in performance of obligations under this Agreement or being in breach of any of the covenants or warranties given herein.

9. Facilities. The Company will provide Contractor, at no cost to the Contractor, with facilities, supplies and support necessary to comply with all obligations in accordance with this Agreement.

Exhibit 1.15 Independent Contractor Agreement (Continued)

10. <u>Reports</u>. The Contractor shall make reports of periodic progress and results to the Director of Administration in written activity reports in a form and frequency to be prescribed by the Director of Administration and shall give prior notice of any scheduled meetings, presentations, or demonstrations.

11. <u>Warranty</u>.

(a) The Contractor hereby warrants and represents to the Company that he is entitled to use and offer for sale the materials, analyses, data, programs and services to be delivered or rendered hereunder; that all such materials, analyses, data, programs and services will be of the kind, nature, quantity and quality designed herein; and that the performance of Contractor's obligations under this Agreement will not cause Contractor to be in breach of any obligation to any third party.

(b) Contractor warrants and represents that the execution of this Agreement and the performance of the obligations hereunder does not and will not constitute a breach of, or default under, any other written or oral agreement or contract entered into by him.

12. <u>Notice</u>. Any notice, schedule, or other document or communication permitted or required to be given to Contractor pursuant to the terms hereof shall be deemed given if personally delivered to Contractor or sent to him, postage prepaid by registered or certified mail, to:

_____ (contractor name)

_____ (contractor address)

_____ (contractor address)

_____ (contractor city, state, zip)

Attention: _____ (contact name)

Any notice required or permitted to Company shall be deemed given if sent to it by registered or certified mail to:

_____ (company name)

_____ (company address)

_____ (company address)

_____ (company city, state, zip)

Attention: _____ (contact name)

Either party may change its address by notifying the other party in the above-stated manner.

Exhibit 1.15 Independent Contractor Agreement *(Continued)*

13. <u>Benefit</u>. This Agreement, and the rights and obligations hereunder, shall inure to the benefit of and be binding upon the Company, its successors and assigns, and upon Contractor, his heirs and personal representatives.

14. <u>Governing Law</u>. This Agreement is entered into and in all respects shall be interpreted, construed, and governed by and in accordance with the laws of the State of _____.

15. <u>Headings</u>. Section headings are inserted for convenience only, are not part of this Agreement, and are not to be considered in the construction or interpretation of this Agreement.

16. <u>Severability</u>. The invalidity or unenforceability of any section or subsection of this Agreement shall not affect the validity or enforceability of any other section or subsection of this Agreement.

17. <u>Entire Agreement</u>. This Agreement embodies the entire agreement of the parties hereto relating to the subject matter hereof. This Agreement supersedes all prior agreements and understandings, and all rights and obligations thereunder are hereby canceled and terminated. No amendment or modification of this Agreement shall be valid or binding unless it is in writing and signed by the parties hereto.

18. <u>Waiver</u>. The waiver by either party of a breach of any provision of this Agreement by the other shall not operate or be construed as a waiver of any subsequent breach of the same or any other provision by the breaching party.

19. <u>No Setoff by Contractor</u>. The existence of any claim, demand, action, or cause of action by the Contractor against the Company, whether predicated upon this Agreement or otherwise, shall not constitute a defense to the enforcement by the Company of any of its rights hereunder.

IN WITNESS WHEREOF, Contractor has set his hand, and the Company has caused this Agreement to be duly executed, and the parties have caused this Agreement to be delivered, all on the day and year first above written.

COMPANY NAME   *CONTRACTOR NAME*

_____   _____

_____   By: _____

_____   By: _____

(Title)   (Title)

Exhibit 1.15   Independent Contractor Agreement *(Continued)*

You should be prepared to help your customer obtain management approval for preliminary costs and budgets—both expense and capital—the schedules, and the total funds your corporation must be willing to finance or commit to for a given term. The team members should also provide input and advice on the time requirements and the proposed schedule.

The positive relationships you develop through your understanding of your company and customer's requirements and culture can help ensure that you and your staff are valuable contributors to your company's success.

NEGOTIATION STRATEGIES

An increasing number of corporations are developing detailed real estate, design, furnishing, building, and service requests for proposal (RFPs) that require service and product providers to meet stringent financial and facility obligations.

As the corporate facility professional, you should put together a negotiating team of in-house specialists including the corporate customer (purchaser or tenant), legal counsel, finance, and other departments with intimate awareness of the corporate culture and the details the project must address. This team may also include outside specialists, including a real estate broker or tenant representative, a design or engineering consultant, and legal counsel as required to ensure that your customer and the corporation are protected in all business and legal issues.

The team reviews negotiation strategy, real estate, facility, and business issues before producing an RFP and agrees on a model of expected purchase price, building costs, rental rates, warranties, and other tangible values for your customer. A short list of prospective service and product suppliers is developed based on an initial analysis of the responses to the RFP. Using the agreed-on negotiation strategy, the corporate facility professional with staff members or a consultant refers to this list to try to obtain the targeted model or better.

Negotiation involves give and take by both sides, and the team members must understand the strengths and weaknesses of their position and the service or product supplier's bargaining position. Reasonable expectations of the corporate customer can be met if the team members are aware of their options, if they test their assumptions, if they take shrewdly calculated risks based on solid information, and if they believe they have power in the market. On occasion, however, the facility professional's customer may have to pass on an opportunity because it would be necessary to rush into a particular solution without addressing legal or business items that could later adversely affect its bottom line and business plans as well as those of the service and product suppliers and the corporation.

Gone are the days where senior corporate professionals could commit to major capital decisions without input from others within the corporation. In today's economy, it is becoming more common for corporations to reduce the length of lease commitments to a five-year (or less) initial commitment with one or more three- to five-year options to extend the lease. Corporations are beginning to spend the time necessary to understand the power their company has in the marketplace. With this and other negotiating information, corporations are obtaining favorable service or product solutions that maximize the value of their facilities and increase shareholder value in the corporation.

Many service or product transactions are complex because each acquisition or lease is unique, and negotiation priorities vary from one transaction to the next. As a successful negotiator, the facility professional is able to identify and define the customer's requirements and business objectives, evaluate the service or product supplier's position to determine strengths and weaknesses, engage in mutual accommodations, and justify the team's position in reasonable terms. The facility professional must also be thoroughly prepared to offer and handle the compromises and concessions necessary to reach an agreement and close the purchase or secure the service or product for the customer.

The negotiating checklist given in Exhibit 1.16 lists items and issues you may wish to use in developing and conducting your real estate and facility negotiations. Dr. Chester Karrass, a noted negotiator, author, and speaker, states, "In business, you don't get what you deserve, you get what you negotiate." [From Marketing Material for Karrass Negotiating Seminar.] In developing your strategy, you and your customer may choose to use this key business philosophy along with the negotiating principles of time, power, and information.

Time

Time is a valuable component that is often overlooked in real estate and facility requirements. Allot sufficient time to review the market realistically and negotiate terms at or below market for the facility professional's customer's required services or products. Otherwise, the customer may be in the undesirable position of having only a few options to choose from and need to take what is offered because the facility professional has not had enough time to negotiate a good deal.

During the first meeting with the customer, the facility professional should review the customer's perception of the available services and the market and determine what quality the customer requires, expects to obtain, and can afford as well as how this requirement fits in with that customer's business plan. These expectations may or may not be easily satisfied and may have to be revised in keeping with current or future space and furnishings standards and with policies and procedures. The assessment of need must be supported by management to provide all with a clear definition of the requirement before beginning the service or product search.

If the customer's current operation is providing support for computer or clerical activities, the facility professional will be looking for space and furnishings with certain characteristics, and these will be unlike those needed for, say, an office for the chairman of the board. The timing, costs, and terms of the lease or purchase, the location, quality, and the costs for constructing and furnishing the space will therefore vary according to the customer's needs and resources.

For example, a customer may not have capital funds and therefore will be willing to pay a higher rental rate or lease the space for a longer term to receive a larger upfit allowance. Or the customer may be willing to fund a part of the capital improvements and would like to have these costs applied to lower the rental rate. These and other strategies are all part of putting together a financial model that provides the facility professional's customer with the best solution for the smallest financial and legal exposure and commitment. In developing a financial model and strategy, the facility professional may wish to confer with the corporate legal counsel, finance department, and broker.

Achieving Acceptable Terms for Both Parties

- Determine product or service provider market activity.
  - Is it a seller's or buyer's market?
  - Is it a normal or balanced market?
- Understand local product and service provider business terminology, cap rates, prices, etc.
- Determine your customer's unique dilemmas and those of product and service providers.
- Use financial concepts such as market value, most probable purchase price, leasing costs, ROI, ROE, investment value, etc.
- Evaluate in advance the range of product and service provider offers and your and their counteroffers.
- Consider and understand in advance the subjective factors that may affect your customer's selection process.

Negotiating Psychology

- Know your customer and the product and service providers.
- Who are you trying to satisfy?
- Who is the product or service provider trying to satisfy?
- Who are you, your customer, the product, or service provider accountable to during this process?
- Understand pertinent corporate, cultural, and business traits and practices.
- Know the roles being performed by the negotiating parties.
- Know your and your customer's negotiation style.
- Manage the desire to control others.
- Avoid being overly confident, trusting, or overly suspicious.
- Avoid being overly manipulative or exploitive.
- Recognize the need to win, succeed, and close by both parties.
- Know your opponent's negotiation style.
- Be alert to flashy, steamroller, or rigid negotiators who may convey:
  - "Trust me—I'm honest."
  - "Trust me—I only want what's right."
  - "Don't trust me. I'm out to get you."
- Consider and carefully plan the physical factors that can affect negotiations.
  - The location—yours, your customer's, the product or service provider's, or a neutral place.
  - The facility—table and chair types, where to sit, colors, breaks and refreshments, meals, HVAC, and other comfort or distress factors.
  - Are there time limits to each session and to complete the process?
- Where appropriate, use professionals ("who care, but not that much") to represent you in negotiations.

Exhibit 1.16 Negotiating Checklist (Copyright 1994 IFMA.)

- Ensure that during negotiations all parties know:
  - Who is the spokesperson for each side?
  - What are the limits of the spokesperson's authority and flexibility?

The Process Should Meet Corporate Objectives

- Use cooperative bargaining rather than confrontation.
  - Try to achieve a satisfactory and sound solution.
  - The goal is a basic meeting of the minds.
- Control the process based on your negotiating strategy and model.
  - Use your negotiating model.
  - Determining essential facts is essential to defining business and negotiating issues.
  - Prudent preparation should result in understanding the assumptions.
  - Discover the strengths and weaknesses of both sides.
- Be prepared for reciprocal provisions.

Ensuring You Get What You Thought You Were Getting

- What are the necessary requirements for your customer? Are they satisfied?
- What conditions does the product or service provider require to close?
- Where possible, require specific remedies and liquidated damages.

Concluding the Negotiating Process: The Final Agreement and Closing the Deal

- Be ready to concede appropriate items or issues within your negotiating model.
- Use an attorney whose experience includes closing the deal where the purchase is being made.
  - Require the right to assign the purchase or lease without unreasonable restraint.
  - Do not waive essential contingencies, warranties, and representations that must survive the purchase of the product or service.
  - Require an inspection as appropriate.
  - When rights and duties are indisputably clear in the product or service contract, take a firm position.
  - Support your leasing or closing attorney while achieving your business objectives.
  - Do not forget that you can stop the process or reschedule a closing or contract signing if required business terms and issues have not been achieved.
- Be gracious, civil, and professional.
- If you decide to try to squeeze the last buck out of the deal, understand what this will mean to both parties to the deal. If it is a good deal, close the transaction.

Exhibit 1.16 Negotiating Checklist (Continued)

Power

Negotiating involves give and take by both sides, and the facility professional must understand the strengths and weaknesses of his or her bargaining position. Herb Cohen, another noted negotiator, in his book *You Can Negotiate Anything*, states:

> ... in order to influence an outcome ... you must realistically analyze the other side's position, as well as your own, in light of three ever-present tightly interrelated variables:
>
> 1. Power
> 2. Time
> 3. Information
>
> ... Within reason, you can get whatever you want if you are aware of your options, if you test your assumptions, if you take shrewdly calculated risks based on solid information, and if you believe you have the power.[3]

The negotiator's role requires that the facility professional remain focused on the requirement and keep in mind the words of Herb Cohen: "I care, but not that much." The facility professional's customer is often vitally concerned with locating a service or product, negotiating quickly, and getting the issue settled. The facility professional must keep the program moving at a quick pace but should also take a more detached view to ensure that the customer and the corporation get the best deal possible.

Information

It is the corporate facility professional's responsibility to identify the customer's current and future needs during the negotiation process. A broker or consultant may provide advice and assistance, but it remains the facility professional's responsibility to obtain the best deal possible. To do this, he or she needs information about the market, the economy, the area, and the available workforce. It is important to know where the facility professional's customer lives, where his or her staff live, and what immediate and long-range plans have been made for transportation. Will there be relocation costs. Does the potential community offer single and multifamily housing, shopping, recreation, medical services, including hospitals and doctors, legal and banking services, religious activities, holidays, garbage disposal, and day-care centers? Myriad other matters may call for consideration: utilities, taxes, political and community events, natural resources (e.g., clean air, water, and soil), lease or purchase costs, operating expenses, common area maintenance costs, special assessments, hazardous waste or pollutants, schools, colleges, airports, parking, construction activity, leasing, subleasing, purchasing activity,

[3]From *You Can Negotiate Anything* by Herb Cohen. Copyright © 1980 by Herb Cohen. Published by arrangement with Carol Publishing Group. A Lyle Stuart Book.

free rent, work letter or up-fit allowances, moving expenses, construction costs, furnishing costs. These are just some of the facts the facility professional may need to weigh in helping the customer generate the best real estate decision.

Be sure to judge accurately the power of your organization and your customer in the marketplace. With this and other information, you can begin the process of obtaining a favorable solution for your customer's requirements.

TOTAL QUALITY MANAGEMENT[4]

Total quality management (TQM) is also called by many other names, including quality control, quality circles, and quality-centered culture. The name is not really important. What *is* vital is the understanding that a true quality-centered culture is a way of thinking about and doing business that breaks with traditional methods and offers new directions for managers and employees alike.

The greatest impediment to quality in facility management is not ignorance; it is the illusion of knowledge. What senior management and industry eventually learn is that continual arbitrary cost-cutting is not an effective strategy.

A quality-centered culture is an organizationwide, standardized system of service delivery that is:

- Customer-driven
- Statistically aided
- Management led
- Constantly changing toward continuous improvement

Unlike traditional management, which focuses on finding errors and often on allocating blame, TQM focuses on analyzing work systems and on preventive and continuous training for ongoing improvement.

A quality-centered culture is a real process of management with provable results; it is not this year's slogan or promotion. Nor is TQM an exotic discipline, applicable only in the classroom. If you cannot show tangible, realistic results using total quality management, you should not be talking about TQM.

Defining Quality

Before quality can be managed, it must be defined. You cannot manage in general; management must be specific. You must identify the item and condition that meet the customer's expectations and perception of quality. At that level, you can manage quality.

Quality has two aspects: the absence of defects and the perception of excellence. Each work process has innumerable points at which defects may occur. For example, in cleaning a desk, defects may occur in the dusting, streaks in the pol-

[4]Reprinted with permission from the September/October 1993 issue of the *Journal of Property Management,* published by the Institute of Real Estate Management, Chicago, Illinois. (312) 329-6000. All rights reserved.

ishing, failure to replace items on the surface correctly, and so forth. Every major area in which defects could occur should be identified.

Another way to review quality is to benchmark your facility management performance against another organization's facility management department that has been identified as best in its class. The benchmarking survey addresses the following questions: What is the norm? What services should be provided? What should our customers expect, and by when? What are the relative costs and benefits for providing these services? What does senior management expect?

Benchmarking is described by one corporate executive as "the continuous process of measuring products, services and practices against the toughest competitors of those companies recognized as industry leaders."[5] The International Facility Management Association (IFMA) has developed a process for benchmarking which the facility professional may find useful in developing a benchmark for current facility management services (see Exhibit 1.17).

Why should you consider benchmarking your organization's facility services? Consider the following authoritative reasons:

- "More than seven billion square feet of building space and four quadrillion square feet of land are owned by corporate America."[6]

- "Corporations account for almost 75% of the nation's real estate capital . . . with $2.6 trillion of equity in plants, warehouses, land and office buildings."[7]

- "The goal is to achieve superiority and leadership in the marketplace."[8]

The next step is to survey clients to determine which defects are most unacceptable and to rank defects based on the customer's determination of its impact on quality. While ideally all defects should be eliminated, in most cases the majority of complaints center on a relatively small number of problems. Once you have surveyed customers to determine which criteria drive customer satisfaction (see Exhibit 1.18), you can concentrate on eliminating defects and on preventing future ones in new areas.

The customer satisfaction survey is a useful performance measurement format that should help you and your staff understand your customer's view of your performance on a completed project. It will also help you review performance in comparison to the quality and levels of service you established when benchmarking your department.

This survey is just one of many methods for obtaining customer feedback to assess performance. In today's service-versus-dollar environment, the continued high quality of your services in conjunction with an intimate knowledge of your

[5]Mr. David T. Kerns, CEO, Xerox. Xerox Corporation, "Competitive Benchmarking, What It Is and What It Can Do for You," Quality Office, Internal Publication, Stamford, CT, 1987.

[6]Arthur Andersen & Company's Real Estate Services Group 1991 Marketing Publication.

[7]Roulac Real Estate Consulting Group of Deloitte & Touche, "The Flow of Money into Real Estate," *Wall Street Journal*, July 24, 1989.

[8]Xerox Corporation, "Competitive Benchmarking: What It Is and What It Can Do for You," Quality Office, Internal Publication, Stamford, CT, 1987.

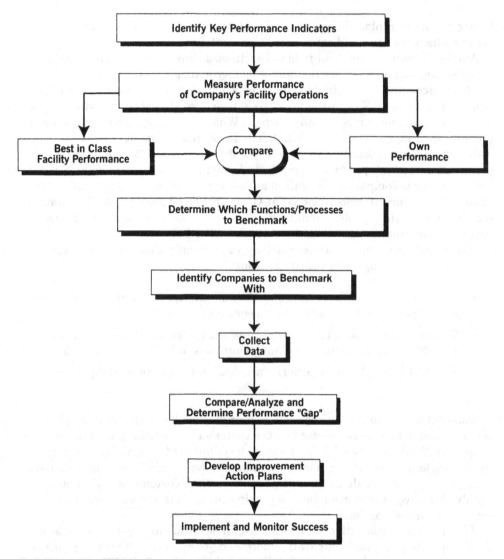

Exhibit 1.17   IFMA's Benchmarking Methodology (Source: International Facility Management Association, Research Report #7—Benchmarks, 1991. IFMA has also published Benchmarks III, Report #18 (1998) and Benchmarks IV, Report #25 (2004).)

customer's expectations—and your customer's awareness of the services you can provide—may very well decide your department's continued existence. The results of your customer satisfaction survey should provide a performance measurement tool that resembles Exhibit 1.19.

The perception of quality is a different matter, and the process that drives it is very different from the identification of defects. You can have a relatively defect-free environment and still have an unhappy customer.

The gap may result because the customer's expectations are higher than the service being delivered. Whether a customer is happy or unhappy is the result of

---

MEMO

FROM: Bill Roberts   **DATE:** November 14, 2005

TO: Carol Rogers   **SUBJECT:** Customer Satisfaction Survey

The Corporate Facility Management Department has an ongoing Quest for Quality program that includes a formal review of services to our customers. This process requires us to look at everything we do on a service and product basis with an eye toward improvement.

Only the people we work with can give us a true sense of whether we are meeting their needs in a timely and efficient manner.

Please take a few minutes to complete the attached customer satisfaction survey, which will help us to continually improve our activities and, consequently, make progress toward our quality goals.

Exhibit 1.18   Customer Satisfaction Survey

Customer Name: Carol Rogers   **Date:** November 14, 2005
                   Vice President

Address: ABC Company
                    Retail Operations
                    2538 North Michigan Avenue
                    Suite 710
                    Chicago, IL 60632

Telephone: (302) 555-1700

QUEST FOR QUALITY

CUSTOMER SATISFACTION SURVEY

Corporate Facility Management Department

A. The mission of the Corporate Facility Management Department is to serve ABC Company and our customers by providing and delivering timely, quality, professional facility management analysis and consulting support services. Doing so enhances ABC Company's long-term competitive position through the acquisition and management of efficient, cost-effective real estate. We provide high-quality real estate services essential to productive work and support environments.

The major services we provide are categorized in the general areas listed below. Please check those services that you requested or used in the past 12 months.

CHECK ALL THAT APPLY.

[ ] Strategic Facility Planning

[ ] Product and/or Supplier Selection

[ ] Product and/or Service Negotiation

[ ] Lease and Construction Document Review and Execution

[ ] Ongoing Management of Facility Relocation Requirements

[ ] Facility Management Consulting on Request

[ ] Facility Management Information System (FMIS)

[ ] Other—Write In: _____

_____

_____

Exhibit 1.18   Customer Satisfaction Survey (Continued)

B. Please circle the performance **NUMBER** rating (Poor = P, Fair = F, Good = G, Excellent = E, or N/A for Not Applicable) and add comments and note problems as desired for the most recent service provided:

1. Do you feel the leasing process for office space at 1265 East Wacker Drive, Suite 345, Chicago, IL, addressed all areas of your real estate needs?

	P	F	G		E
N/A 0	2	4	6	8	10

Comments and/or Issue: _____

_____

_____

2. Do you feel the information prepared to quantify your preliminary space requirements adequately met your quality, price, and space needs?

	P	F	G		E
N/A 0	2	4	6	8	10

Comments and/or Issue: _____

_____

_____

3. Do you feel you were provided with a sufficient number of sites, floor plan layouts, review opportunities and information to make an informed location decision?

	P	F	G		E
N/A 0	2	4	6	8	10

Comments and/or Issue: _____

_____

_____

4. Regarding your lease with the XYZ Group, do you feel the lease negotiations were accomplished with:

	P		F	G		E
A. Professionalism by the Broker Representing ABC Company?	N/A	0	2	4	6	8	10
B. Professionalism by the Corp. Facility Dept.?	N/A	0	2	4	6	8	10
C. Minimum Problems?	N/A	0	2	4	6	8	10
D. Maximum Administrative Services Assistance?	N/A	0	2	4	6	8	10
E. Maximum Legal Assistance?	N/A	0	2	4	6	8	10

Exhibit 1.18 Customer Satisfaction Survey (Continued)

Comments and/or Issue: _____

_____

_____

5. Are you satisfied with your new leased facility and the quality of the space?

	P		F	G		E
N/A	0	2	4	6	8	10

Comments and/or Issue: _____

_____

_____

6. Are there any problems with your relocation that are still unresolved?

	P		F	G		E
N/A	0	2	4	6	8	10

Comments and/or Issue: _____

_____

_____

7. Do you feel the handling of your facility management requirements
   has been:

		P		F	G		E
A. Professionally managed and presented?	N/A	0	2	4	6	8	10
B. Handled in a timely manner?	N/A	0	2	4	6	8	10
C. The services you expected?	N/A	0	2	4	6	8	10
D. Sensitive and attentive to your needs?	N/A	0	2	4	6	8	10

Comments and/or Issue: _____

_____

_____

8. How do you rate our overall performance?

		P		F	G		E
A. Orientation of Facility Management Services	N/A	0	2	4	6	8	10
B. Site and Space Specifications	N/A	0	2	4	6	8	10
C. Sites and Space Located	N/A	0	2	4	6	8	10
D. Sites and Design Reviewed	N/A	0	2	4	6	8	10
E. Site and Design Recommendations	N/A	0	2	4	6	8	10
F. Product and Supplier Negotiations	N/A	0	2	4	6	8	10
G. Service Quality	N/A	0	2	4	6	8	10
H. Response Time	N/A	0	2	4	6	8	10
I. Professionalism	N/A	0	2	4	6	8	10
J. Project Management Expertise	N/A	0	2	4	6	8	10
K. Budget and Schedule Performance	N/A	0	2	4	6	8	10

Exhibit 1.18   Customer Satisfaction Survey *(Continued)*

Comments and/or Issue: _____

_____

_____

9. From the listing of major services shown on page 1, in what area(s) do you feel we need to improve? Please be specific.

_____

_____

_____

10. What other facility management services do you feel are needed that you would use if available?

_____

_____

_____

C. Other comments and/or issues you wish to share:

_____

_____

_____

Thank you for your help. Please return a completed copy of this Customer Satisfaction Survey to the Corporate Facility Management Department, ATTN: Bill Roberts.

WR:bw   Initials: _____

                                                Date: _____

Exhibit 1.18   Customer Satisfaction Survey *(Continued)*

% DELIGHTED

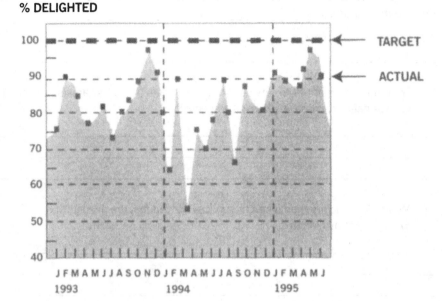

Exhibit 1.19   Performance Measurement: Delighted Customers

the difference between perception and expectation. Focus groups and spot interviews with customers are effective in assessing customer perceptions because the interviewer can note perceptions during questioning.

Ask focus group members to rate quality on a scale of 1 to 5. Segment and examine the extremes, either the excessively demanding or the completely satisfied, and look for patterns in the problems the majority of people perceive. By identifying these prevalent problems and by then improving the associated process, you achieve success.

Of course, not just service delivery but also the process of this delivery is important to the customer. Therefore, you must expand the criteria beyond the actual service to include such factors as the behavior of the service providers, their appearance, and so forth. However, each criterion should still be addressed quantitatively.

The focus in TQM is not on the technical aspect of service delivery, although technical skills are important. Customers usually do not know or care about the technique; they are only interested in the end results.

Measuring Quality

Once you have defined quality, you must develop a system to measure quality on a continuous basis. You must achieve a measurable way to:

- Say that you have greater customer satisfaction.
- Show that management is prevention directed.
- Show that the cost of quality is going down.

The measurement of quality requires two prongs: a measurement of defects and a measurement of the perception of excellence. You must measure and monitor both.

Measuring quality begins by establishing customer-defined targets of acceptable quality through focus groups with customers. In focus groups, customers first talk in general about their perceptions of quality and then move to an item-specific definition of what they consider quality.

Target levels may differ depending on the customer's needs; for example, a customer may want an executive boardroom clean with only 5 percent acceptable defects, while the mail room will be acceptable with 10 percent defects. Remember, it is the customer's perception of quality that is measured, not the supervisor's or yours.

After a target level is established, specific points are designated for each item type (e.g., work order item, items to be cleaned). A score is given for each customer-designated item in the process. Quality is measured by making random inspections within each stratum. Thus, cleaning is measured by examining a certain number of randomly selected offices, a certain number of randomly selected corridors, and so forth. Random spot interviews of customers are conducted on a regular basis.

In measuring quality, the principal goal is not to determine if a particular desk is dirty. A certain number of defects, realistically, are inevitable. The key is to identify management patterns in which all or most of the desks have the same problem. If you find a pattern of one error recurring, then the management system for eliminating that error is at fault and must be changed to prevent future errors (see Exhibit 1.19).

Managing Quality

Too often, facility professionals spend management time managing complaints. In effect, they are managing failure, trying to solve problems after the process has failed.

Instead, quality-oriented facility professionals manage the process itself, looking for and preventing flaws that permit errors and result in customer complaints. You can train people to eliminate the defects if you perceive a pattern, either in an individual employee or in a group of employees. The measurements of performance should be tracked monthly by employee and by task. In this way, the improvement of each employee can be plotted, and areas that hinder quality can be pinpointed and improved.

By testing alternatives, management may determine which change or combination of changes prevents problems and improves actual quality ratings. In addition to improving processes, managers must work to develop a system that encourages and rewards the achievement of quality. You cannot tell people you want quality if you reward for lower cost or greater productivity only.

Because all employee performance is numerically measured, performance tracking is objective instead of subjective. Bonuses and other incentives can be tied to reaching or exceeding established quality goals. For example, in working with a contractor, you can define three levels of quality: not acceptable, acceptable, and above acceptable. Set ranges for each level of performance.

If the contracting firm performs in the acceptable range, it could receive cost plus profit; if it performs below acceptable, it could receive cost minus profit; if it performs above acceptable, it could receive cost plus profit plus a sizable incentive. Contractors should be encouraged to divide the incentive money among their employees.

Implementation of Total Quality Management

A fully implemented system of defining goals, measuring performance, and training for continuous improvement will not appear overnight. It will probably take at least 90 days to reorient management and employees to the new demands. However, within six months, real change is possible, and within a year, a company should be able to establish a stable, quality-oriented culture.

While the commitment is significant, the payoffs are even more so. Costs to achieve a TQM culture could equal 2 to 4 percent of gross revenues. However, most companies achieve a 20 to 30 percent reduction in errors that more than offsets these costs. Productivity increases, and costs drop significantly.

Management time also drops significantly if TQM is in place. Because managers spend much less time putting out fires, they have time for training and planning to improve quality even further. Genuine quality success guarantees higher productivity, lower costs, and more satisfied customers.

Business Process Improvement

During your TQM and benchmarking review, you may need to look at the business processes currently in use. These may require radical redesign to provide more efficient, cost-effective, and timely services, especially if you are automating a process or service.

Reengineering is one of the buzzwords that identify this process. We prefer the term *business process improvement*, as it connotes reviewing the current business process and recommending a new approach to provide a service or product. Business process improvement is defined as "the radical redesign of business processes to achieve major improvements in your organization's profit margins and market share."[9] The objective of business process improvement is to improve the effectiveness, efficiency, and adaptability of a business process.

The benefits of business process improvement can be significant—even remarkable—gains in productivity and customer satisfaction. They are achieved through:

- Bureaucracy elimination
- Duplication elimination
- Value-added assessment
- Process simplification
- Process cycle-time reduction

[9]BDO Seidman, Accounts and Consultants, "Business Process Improvement" brochure, 1994.

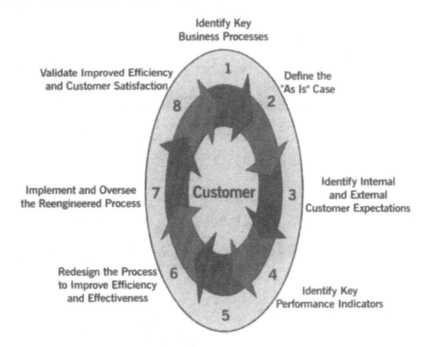

Identify Key
Business Processes

Validate Improved Efficiency
and Customer Satisfaction

Define the
"As Is" Case

Implement and Oversee
the Reengineered Process

Customer

Identify Internal
and External
Customer Expectations

Redesign the Process
to Improve Efficiency
and Effectiveness

Identify Key
Performance Indicators

Observe Process Performance
Objectively Using Statistical Methods

Exhibit 1.20   Business Process Improvement Methodology

- Error proofing
- Standardization
- Supplier partnerships
- Big-picture improvement
- Automation and/or mechanization

The need for and scope of modifications to your facility management organization's current and proposed business processes can be identified by means of the methodology shown in Exhibit 1.20. Exhibit 1.21 compares a traditional view and a process view of business operations. While a task may not cross a particular organization's lines in this exact sequence, you can get an appreciation for the nature of many major business process.[10] The flow of work is often across the boundaries of departments, functions, and even divisions within the overall organization. Things fall through the cracks. Things get lost, delays occur—often for good reasons, as viewed by the person who appears to cause the delays.

What one person or organization provides may be unusable for what another person or organization must do with it as part of the process. The item may be

[10]Business Process Improvement Workshop, *Participant Guide,* Council for Continuous Improvement, San Jose, CA, 1993, Module 2, pp. 6–7.

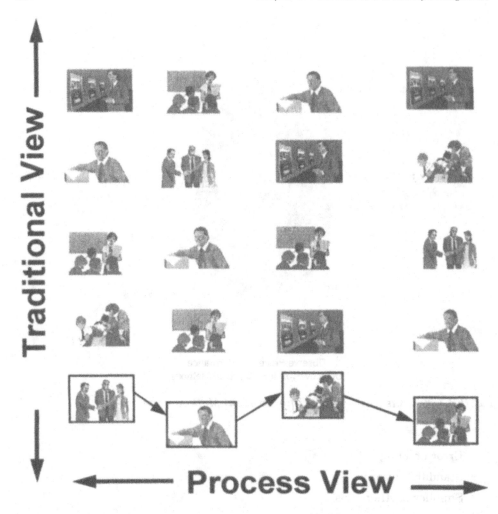

Exhibit 1.21   Traditional versus Process View of Business Operations

defective, incomplete, in the wrong format, or simply too late. For the overall process to work effectively, every step in the process must be executed effectively.

Balanced Scorecard[11]

What Is the Balanced Scorecard?

A new approach to strategic management was developed in the early 1990s by Robert Kaplan and David Norton. They named this system *the balanced score-card*. Recognizing the weaknesses and vagueness of previous management approaches, the balanced scorecard approach provides a clear prescription of what companies should measure in order to balance the financial perspective.

[11]You might want to consult the Balanced Scorecard Institute for additional information at their website: Balanced Scorecard Institute, 1025 Connecticut Ave. NW, Suite 1000, Washington, DC 20036, (202) 857-9719, *www.balancedscorecard.org*.

The balanced scorecard helps managers at all levels monitor results in their key areas. An article by Kaplan and Norton entitled "The Balanced Scorecard: Measures That Drive Performance," which appeared in the *Harvard Business Review* in 1992, sparked interest in the method and led to their business bestseller, *The Balanced Scorecard: Translating Strategy into Action* (1996).

You can't improve what you can't measure. So metrics must be developed based on the priorities of the strategic plan, which provides the key business drivers and criteria for metrics managers most desire to watch. Processes are then designed to collect information relevant to these metrics and reduce it to numerical form for storage, display, and analysis. Decision makers examine the outcomes of various measured processes and strategies and track the results to guide the company and provide feedback.

The facility professional should understand that the balanced scorecard is a *management* system (not only a *measurement* system) that enables organizations to clarify their vision and strategy and translate them into action. It provides feedback around both the internal business processes and external outcomes in order to continuously improve strategic performance and results. When fully deployed, the balanced scorecard transforms strategic planning from an academic exercise into the nerve center of an enterprise.

Kaplan and Norton describe the innovation of the balanced scorecard as follows:

The balanced scorecard retains traditional financial measures. But financial measures tell the story of past events, an adequate story for industrial age companies for which investments in long-term capabilities and customer relationships were not critical for success. These financial measures are inadequate, however, for guiding and evaluating the journey that information age companies must make to create future value through investment in customers, suppliers, employees, processes, technology, and innovation.

The balanced scorecard suggests that we view the organization from four perspectives (see Exhibit 1.22) and develop metrics, collect data, and analyze it relative to each of these perspectives:

The Learning and Growth Perspective

The Business Process Perspective

The Customer Perspective

The Financial Perspective

The balanced scorecard methodology builds on key concepts of previous management ideas such as TQM (discussed above), including customer-defined quality, continuous improvement, employee empowerment, and—primarily—measurement-based management and feedback.

Double-loop Feedback

In traditional industrial activity, *quality control* and *zero defects* were the watchwords. In order to shield the customer from receiving poor quality products, aggressive efforts focused on inspection and testing at the end of the production line. The

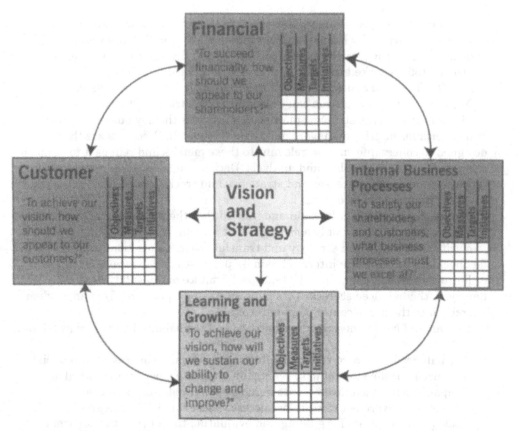

Exhibit 1.22   Four Perspectives.

problem with this approach, as Deming pointed out, is that the true causes of defects are never identified, and there are always inefficiencies due to the rejection of defects. What Deming saw was that variation is created at every step in a production process, and the causes of variation must be identified and fixed. If this can be done, then there is a way to reduce the defects and improve product quality indefinitely. To establish such a process, Deming emphasized that all business processes should be part of a system with feedback loops. The feedback data should be examined by managers to determine the causes of variation and the processes with significant problems; then they can focus attention on fixing that subset of processes.

The balanced scorecard incorporates feedback around internal business process outputs, as in TQM, but adds another feedback loop around the outcomes of business strategies. This creates a double-loop feedback process.

Outcome Metrics

The value of metrics is their ability to provide a factual basis for defining:

Strategic feedback to show the present status of the organization from many perspectives for decision makers

Diagnostic feedback into various processes to guide improvements on a continuous basis

Trends in performance over time as the metrics are tracked

Feedback around the measurement methods themselves, and which metrics should be tracked

Quantitative inputs to forecasting methods and models for decision support systems

Management by Fact

The goal of measurement is to permit managers to see their company more clearly —from many perspectives—and hence to make wiser long-term decisions. The Baldrige Criteria (1997) booklet explains this concept of fact-based management:

Modern businesses depend upon measurement and analysis of performance. Measurements must derive from the company's strategy and provide critical data and information about key processes, outputs and results. Data and information needed for performance measurement and improvement are of many types, including: customer, product and service performance, operations, market, competitive comparisons, supplier, employee-related, and cost and financial. Analysis entails using data to determine trends, projections, and cause and effect—that might not be evident without analysis. Data and analysis support a variety of company purposes, such as planning, reviewing company performance, improving operations, and comparing company performance with competitors' or with "best practices" benchmarks.

A major consideration in performance improvement involves the creation and use of performance measures or indicators. Performance measures or indicators are measurable characteristics of products, services, processes, and operations the company uses to track and improve performance. The measures or indicators should be selected to best represent the factors that lead to improved customer, operational, and financial performance. A comprehensive set of measures or indicators tied to customer and/or company performance requirements represents a clear basis for aligning all activities with the company's goals. Through the analysis of data from the tracking processes, the measures or indicators themselves may be evaluated and changed to better support such goals.

Six Sigma: What Is Six Sigma?

Six Sigma, in many organizations, simply means a measure of quality that strives for near perfection. Six Sigma is a disciplined, data-driven approach and methodology for eliminating defects (driving toward six standard deviations between the mean and the nearest specification limit) in any process—from manufacturing to transaction and from product to service.

The statistical representation of Six Sigma describes quantitatively how a process is performing. To achieve Six Sigma, a process must not produce more than 3.4 defects per million opportunities. A Six Sigma defect is defined as anything outside of customer specifications. A Six Sigma opportunity, then, is the total quantity of chances for a defect. Process Six Sigma can easily be calculated using a Six Sigma calculator.

The fundamental objective of the Six Sigma methodology is the implementation of a measurement-based strategy that focuses on process improvement and varia- tion reduction through the application of Six Sigma improvement projects. This is accomplished through the use of two Six Sigma sub-methodologies: DMAIC and DMADV. The Six Sigma DMAIC process (define, measure, analyze, improve, con- trol) is an improvement system for existing processes falling below specification and looking for incremental improvement. The Six Sigma DMADV process (define, measure, analyze, design, verify) is an improvement system used to develop new processes or products at Six Sigma—quality levels. It can also be employed if a current process requires more than incremental improvement. Both Six Sigma processes are executed by specially trained, in-house Six Sigma Green Belt and Six Sigma Black Belt personnel, and are overseen by in-house Six Sigma Master Black Belt personnel. According to the Six Sigma Academy,[12] Black Belts save companies approximately $230,000 per project and can complete four to six proj- ects per year. General Electric, one of the most successful companies implementing Six Sigma, has estimated benefits on the order of $10 billion during the first five years of implementation. GE first began Six Sigma in 1995 after Motorola and Allied Signal blazed the Six Sigma trail. Since then, thousands of companies around the world have discovered the far-reaching benefits of Six Sigma.

> Six Sigma is a customer-centered, systematic, data-driven method for doing things better.

> *Customer-centered* means that projects start with, and are measured by, meet- ing customer wants and needs.

> *Systematic* means that the Six Sigma tools are applied in concert, which makes them vastly more powerful than they are alone.

> *Data-driven* means that facts and data are used for making decisions.

> *Doing things better* means, in some measurable, meaningful way, improving the situation of customers, workers, or shareholders of the organization.

Public Relations

In today's business environment, facility management departments must keep in close touch with their customers through internal relations programs. This includes developing and implementing a public relations plan with the following features:

- A market services strategy
- A defined market
- An ongoing customer contact program
- A public relations plan; an insurance policy

---

[12]For the Six Sigma Academy, see *www.six-sigma.com*, 8876 East Pinnacle Peak Road, Suite 100, Scottsdale AZ 85255, Phone: (480) 515-9501, Fax: (480) 515-9507.

Before completing your public relations plan, be sure you understand top management's business and facility agenda.

Your marketing services strategy should include:

- Understanding company objectives
- Marketing objectives
    Increase awareness of services.
    Improve the image of your organization.
    Enhance customer knowledge of services.
    Disclose specific qualifications.

While developing your marketing services strategy, you should also be defining your market and your competition:

- Market analysis
    Who are your customers?
    Where are they headed?
- Competitive analysis
    Avoid surprises.
    Understand perception versus reality.
    Understand the competition.

You may find that your marketing services strategy indicates that you must entirely change the way you and your staff do business, and with customers. Many facility management departments are now charging their customers for their services and have become a profit center in lieu of being a cost center. Other departments are not only changing the way they do business but are even in the marketplace actively selling their facility management services to other organizations on a fee/consulting or contract basis.

The public relations and marketing services strategy should include major customer contact and management by walking around (MBWA). You must ensure that you and your staff plan for time outside of your office to involve and meet your customers through:

- Questionnaires
- Telemarketing
- Response/service cards
- Focus groups

Your public relations plan should anticipate market needs including:

- Perception of service
- Expectation of service
- Anticipation of service
- Previous personal experience
- Cost of service

- Value-added service
- Preparation for outcomes
- Management of service perceptions/expectations
- Development of marketing packages
  Visit customers.
  Tell your story.
- Follow-up and service recovery
- Development of performance criteria
  Measure performance.
  Report performance to customers.
  Improve performance.

The preceding public relations and marketing services strategy provides the basis for changing the facility management department to meet your customers' and senior management's expectations and requirements.

AMERICANS WITH DISABILITIES ACT

Along with the many existing federal, state, and local regulations, your corporation should have a policy and procedures to address and implement associated facility management requirements contained in the 1990 Americans with Disabilities Act (ADA). This federal antidiscrimination statute is designed to remove barriers that prevent qualified individuals with disabilities from enjoying the same employment opportunities that are available to persons without disabilities.

The ADA seeks to ensure access to equal employment opportunities based on merit. It does not guarantee equal results, establish quotas, or require preferences favoring individuals with disabilities over those without disabilities. When an individual's disability creates a barrier to employment opportunities, however, the ADA requires employers to consider whether reasonable accommodation could remove the barrier.

The ADA thus establishes a process whereby the employer must assess a disabled individual's ability to perform the essential functions of the specific job held or desired. While the ADA focuses on eradicating barriers, it does not relieve a disabled employee or applicant of the obligation to perform the essential functions of the job. To the contrary, the ADA is intended to enable disabled persons to compete in the workplace based on the same performance standards and requirements that employers expect of persons who are not disabled.

However, where that individual's functional limitation impedes such job performance, an employer must take steps to *reasonably accommodate*, and thus help overcome the particular impediment, unless to do so would impose an undue hardship.

Such accommodations usually take the form of adjustments to the way a job customarily is performed or to the work environment itself.

This process of identifying whether, and to what extent, a reasonable accommodation is required should be flexible and involve both the employer and the

individual with a disability. The determination of whether an individual is qualified for a particular position must necessarily be made on a case-by-case basis,
and no specific form of accommodation is guaranteed for all individuals with a
particular disability. Rather, an accommodation must be tailored to match the
needs of the disabled individual with the demands of the job's essential functions.

The Equal Employment Opportunity Commission (EEOC) is responsible for
the enforcement of Title I of the ADA, which prohibits employment discrimination
on the basis of a disability. Discrimination on the basis of disability is dealt with
under the same guidelines as cases of discrimination on the basis of race, sex,
national origin, and religion.

The ADA includes implementing and following objective and nondiscriminatory
practices involving all employment issues of qualified disabled persons and ensuring access to company products and services by persons who are disabled. This
statement applies to all situations involving personnel and business outlets providing products or services to customers.

The Americans with Disabilities Act, Public Law 101–336, was enacted on July
26, 1990, with varying implementation and effective dates for different sections.

Title III of the Americans with Disabilities Act (ADA), which became effective
January 26, 1992, prohibits discrimination of the basis of a disability in places of
public accommodation controlled by a private entity. In such facilities, building
owners are required to eliminate barriers that exclude disabled individuals from
equal access to public buildings, and all new public buildings and commercial
facilities must "be designed and constructed so as to be readily accessible to and
usable by persons with disabilities."

Definition of Disability

The ADA defines a disability as "a physical or mental impairment that substantially limits one or more of the major life activities," such as seeing, hearing,
walking, speaking, breathing, learning, and working.

Physical or mental impairment refers to "any physiological disorder, or condition, cosmetic disfigurement, or anatomical loss affecting one or more of the following body systems: neurological, musculoskeletal, special sense organs,
respiratory (including speech organs), cardiovascular, reproductive, digestive,
genito-urinary, hemic and lymphatic, skin, and endocrine; or any mental or psychological disorder, such as mental retardation, organic brain syndrome, emo-
tional or mental illness, and specific learning disabilities." Disabilities include
such conditions as visual and hearing impairments, physical impairments (cere-
bral palsy, arthritis, epilepsy), physical disfigurements, psychological or emo-
tional impairments, mental handicaps or learning disabilities (retardation, brain
injuries, dyslexia), contagious and noncontagious diseases (heart disease, cancer,
AIDS, infection with HIV), and others such as sleep disorders, alcoholism, and
recovery from a drug addiction, including nicotine withdrawal, which limit an
individual's ability to perform major activities. The duration of the condition also
affects whether or not it would be considered a disability. Temporary impairments
with little or no permanent impact, such as broken limbs, concussions, appendici-
tis, and, except in rare cases, obesity, are not included as disabilities.

Removal of Architectural Barriers

The ADA requires that public accommodations "remove architectural barriers in existing facilities, including communication barriers that are structural in nature, where such removal is readily achievable, i.e., easily accomplishable and able to be carried out without much difficulty or expense." Examples include:

- Installing ramps.
- Making curb cuts in sidewalks and entrances.
- Repositioning shelves.
- Rearranging tables, chairs, vending machines, display racks, and other furniture.
- Repositioning telephones.
- Adding raised markings on elevator control buttons.
- Installing flashing alarm lights.
- Widening doors.
- Installing offset hinges to widen doorways.
- Eliminating a turnstile or providing an alternative accessible path.
- Installing accessible door hardware.
- Installing grab bars in toilet seats.
- Rearranging toilet partitions to increase maneuvering space.
- Insulating lavatory pipes under sinks to prevent burns.
- Installing a raised toilet seat.
- Installing a full-length bathroom mirror.
- Repositioning the paper towel dispenser in a bathroom.
- Creating designated accessible parking spaces.
- Installing an accessible paper cup dispenser at an existing inaccessible water fountain.
- Removing high-pile, low-density carpeting or installing vehicle hand controls.

The ADA Accessibility Guidelines list specific alterations that should be made. Construction standards for new buildings are outlined in Title III.

Priority of Barrier Removal

After surveying the property, a list of all potential barriers should be identified and a plan devised to remove them. The ADA suggests a formula to prioritize phases of barrier removal. Top priority should be given to barriers that restrict access to the building from public sidewalks, parking lots, and public transportation. Barriers to entrance of the facility typically could be removed by the addition of handicapped parking, ramp construction, and wider doorways.

After barriers to entrances are removed, the ADA recommends taking measures to allow access to "those areas of a place of public accommodation where goods and services are made available to the public." For example, after a shopping mall is renovated to allow access from the parking lot, barriers to store access should be removed. This process may include widening doorways, rearranging display racks, providing raised character and Braille signs, and installing access ramps. The third priority should be to enable access to public restroom facilities.

For questions pertaining to: Consult these governmental agencies:

Employment   Equal Employment Opportunity Commission (R, TA, E)
                          President's Committee on Employment of People with
                             Disabilities (TA)
                          Small Business Administration (TA)
                          National Institute on Disability and Rehabilitation
                             Research (TA)

Public accommodations   Department of Justice (R, TA, E)

Public services   Department of Justice (R, TA, E)

Rehabilitation and   Department of Education (P)
   independent living
   services

Tax law provisions   Department of Treasury (TA)

Accessibility   Architectural and Transportation Barriers Compliance
                          Board (G, TA)

Work incentive   Social Security Administration (P)

Key   R: Issued regulations.
        TA: Provides technical assistance on how to comply.
        E: Has enforcement authority.
        P: Administers programs relevant to successful implementation of the Act.
        G: Issues guidelines.

Additional information about compliance with Title III can be obtained by contacting the U.S. Department of Justice at the following address:

Civil Rights Division

Office on the Americans with Disabilities Act

U.S. Department of Justice

P.O. Box 66118

Washington, DC 20035-6118

202-514-0301 (voice)

202-514-0383 (TDD)

The ADA Reference Guide[13] provides information regarding governmental agencies to contact for answers to ADA questions.

---

[13]Reprinted from the *Americans with Disabilities Handbook,* published by the Equal Employment Opportunity Commission and the U.S. Department of Justice, October 1991.

Conclusion

This overview provided a brief commentary of the history of facility management, associated definition, organization and personnel issues, ethics, departmental management, total quality management, the balanced scorecard, Six Sigma, public relations, and information on the Americans with Disabilities Act. Entire books have been written on some of these topics; we encourage you to seek additional information in areas that pique your interest and that you will need to review with your management. Our intent in this chapter is to provide a foundation for the material in the following pages.

The next chapter begins an in-depth look at why and how the facility department should be tied into the organization's long-range business plans.

Chapter Two

Long-range and Annual Facility Planning

LONG-RANGE FACILITY PLANNING PROCESS

Managing change is the single largest issue facing senior management today. Predicting change is so problematic that the only effective response is a stance that poises a company to act on opportunities as they arise and to proceed with full awareness of relative risks. The corporate facility management department's objective is to help the customer's organization make real estate and facility decisions that accommodate potential future changes—for example, expanding staff, restructuring, or contracting with minimum penalties. Strategic facility management planning should be designed to give the customer's organization the same thorough, rational, and methodical approach to facility management that the customer's management brings to the corporation's overall business strategy.

Corporate planning is a formal, systematic, managerial process organized by responsibility, time, and information to ensure that operational planning, project planning, and strategic planning are carried out regularly, to enable top management to control the future of the enterprise. This generally accepted definition of the planning process within the corporate structure suggests that a substructure of three distinct types of planning occurs within the general concept of corporate planning. These types are:

1. Strategic planning
2. Operational planning
3. Project planning

We are going to spend a moment or two on each type so you will understand exactly what we mean when we refer to it in this text. In Exhibit 2.1, note that despite critical differences among the three levels of planning, each level relates to the primary thrust of the planning mission, which is to reduce uncertainty and control the risk inherent in a business decision.

We define *strategic planning* as providing the overall corporate direction subject to the external environment, resources available, and resources obtainable. Strategic planning typically involves complex and abstract issues because the ripple effects of their implementation through the organization are difficult to anticipate.

Operational planning primarily involves the more detailed, specific aspects of implementing strategic plans or changing current operating activity. Strategic

	Degree of Uncertainty	Degree of Complexity	Penalties for Errors
Strategic planning	Very high	Very high	Possible loss or bankruptcy
Operational planning	Low in the short-term, but increasing with time	Low	Short-term loss
Project planning	Ranges from high to low, depending on project	High-medium	Loss of capital or opportunity

Exhibit 2.1   Types of Corporate Planning

planning, in contrast, normally considers the broad approaches or general plans needed to achieve certain long-term objectives.

Project planning is the generation and appraisal of, the commitment to, and the working out of the detailed execution of an action outside the scope of present operations that is capable of separate analysis and control. Normally, the corporate facility management executive is involved only in the project planning phase of the total corporate planning process, if serving as a member of the planning team. If the executive is not a member, he or she is simply consulted before implementation of a plan that has already been finalized. In our view, such organizational exclusion is an error both for the facility management department and for the corporation. The facility professional can be an exceptionally valuable ear in the marketplace as well as a contributing ally when new or alternative facilities are required.

It is important to stress at the outset that the word *strategic* does not always mean that the planning activity underway is more important than any other. Frequently, operational planning decisions affecting the day-to-day existence of the business enterprise are more important than the ultimate fulfillment of long-run objectives. Refer to the pyramid in Exhibit 2.2 and note that the broad strategic planning approach is at the base, operational planning activities are in the middle, and project planning, where the greatest concentration of effort is required, is at the apex.

Exhibit 2.3 shows that in strategic, long-range planning, the business decisions consist of a number of relatively commonsense factors and involve actions normally performed every day. The dotted lines indicate that feedback is essential to the strategic planning process: Input from the corporate facility management professional should be an important part of that feedback. How does the corporate facility management department relate to business planning? At what level of decision making is the department's input valuable?

Within your own internal strategic planning function, you may find a high degree of indifference and even resistance to the inclusion of lower-level executives in efforts to chart the overall business mission of the corporation. This, again, is an error. Although the input of your facility management department is

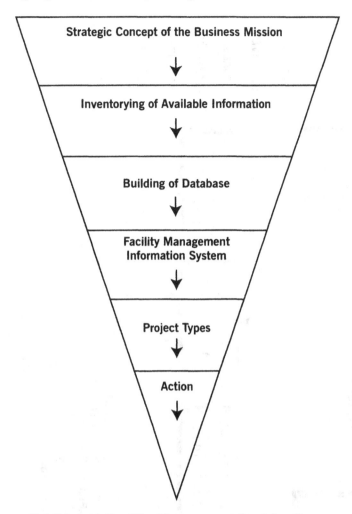

Exhibit 2.2   Facility Management Decision System

normally solicited only at the project planning stage, you can find opportunities to plug in its opinions and points of view at other points in the planning process, to the profit advantage of your company.

The traditional concept of strategic planning is becoming outmoded as the time horizon for investment planning shrinks and, thus, moves closer to the plateaus of operational and project planning—your facility management department's acknowledged sphere of experience. Also, your corporate facility management staff routinely handles both new facility acquisition programs (including design, estimating, and construction) and surplus furnishings and property marketing efforts.

Decisions related to new facility acquisitions and surplus property dispositions are based on the same kind of logic—that is, both types of decisions imply that an operating division (and this relates to the entire corporate mission) requires facilities in certain market areas and not in others. If properties are no longer

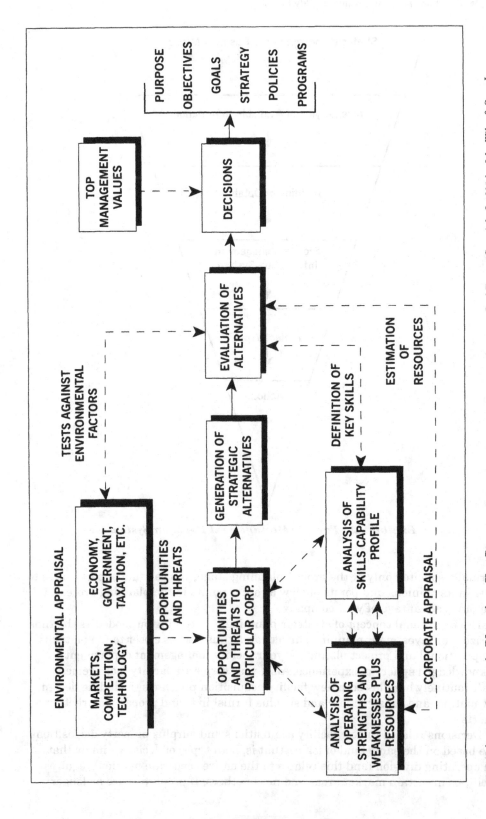

Exhibit 2.3 Strategic Planning: Key Steps *(From Robert Kevin Brown, Managing Corporate Real Estate, Copyright © 1993 by John Wiley & Sons, Inc.*

Reprinted by permission.)

required in certain locations, they are normally replaced with facilities in other locations. Knowledge of long-term economic and social factors that make certain regions attractive is a significant asset in the creation of a viable real estate/facilities inventory.

Let us sharpen our focus by relating strategic planning to a facilities acquisition problem. We believe facilities searches and similar activities are better accomplished in-house, simply because no one is more familiar with your internal operating posture than your own operating and staff personnel.

If you refer to Exhibit 2.3, you can readily perceive how new facilities information should be required input for both the environmental appraisal and the corporate appraisal that enter into strategic planning.

STRATEGIC FACILITY MANAGEMENT FUNCTIONS

Facility management is the process of managing all aspects of real estate and facility assets from acquisition to disposition. More specifically, the functions of real estate and facility asset management are:

1. Protection of the market values of the real estate inventory
2. Assisting in capital accumulation
3. Origination of strategic moves
4. Information networking among divisions and operations, which provides the basis for:
   - Annual Operating Plan (AOP)
   - Long-Range Business Plan (LRBP)
   - Strategic Business Plan (SBP)
   - Long-Range Facilities Plan (LRFP) as part of the manufacturing strategic plan
5. Risk assessment and control
6. Deal structuring:
   - Lease versus buy
   - Specific project assignments, including making hold-versus-sell decisions
   - Acquisitions and divestitures
   - Buy/sell
   - Lease arbitrage
   - Market studies
   - Highest and best-use analyses
   - Strategic management reports on the inventory status and forecast
   - Miscellaneous studies
7. Facility design
8. Construction

9. Maintenance and operations

10. Administrative services

All the preceding functions represent profit opportunities for both the client/user and the facility management expert, with success depending on the skill with which the opportunities are exploited.

For all these reasons, corporate facility management executives must believe strongly that the genius of the future lies not in technological achievements alone but also in the executive's ability to manage them—and, more specifically, the ability to manage effectively in a practiced, everyday way the real estate, facilities, and related fixed assets so necessary to technological and business success.

SYNCHRONIZING CORPORATE PLANNING AND CORPORATE FACILITY MANAGEMENT

The strategic implications of fixed-asset facility support plans will receive increasing capital planning attention in this decade as businesses strive to maximize bottom-line performance. Realistic facilities delivery and construction schedules are required to develop accurate capital expenditure forecasts for calculating many important financial ratios used in planning. Therefore, the preparation of the interdependent strategic business plan and the facilities support plan must be concurrent. Neither can be prepared in a vacuum.

The moment of truth comes when strategic business plans are received at the corporate offices and the requirements for capital facilities investments are reviewed. Answers must be found for a host of questions: How much capital should the company invest each year? How does the firm compare with its competition? Should the company spend more to improve productivity? Is it investing in facilities for products that have a declining market? Will the new facilities improve competitive posture? Are the new facilities properly located? Are these capital programs affordable? The list can seem almost endless, and most questions are strategic rather than operational. This is why we place the corporate facility executive at the strategic level of corporate planning. He or she has much to contribute to these decisions.

The fixed-asset facilities support plan must be based on the operational plans of the operating divisions. Similarly, business plans must reflect the realities of existing capacities and operating costs as well as requirements for additional capital investment, real estate leases, and other facilities expenses. Acquisition or construction of new facilities also takes time. Consequently, facilities must be planned on a long-term basis, but with contingency plans that can accommodate short-term deviations in business projections.

Early on, the corporate facility management department should perform a facilities utilization audit. The purpose of the audit is to answer the following three groups of questions:

1. How much space is needed to generate a project at a given location for a given segment of a business? What types of useful standards can be devel-

oped to measure facility utilization, such as square feet of space per employee dollar of profit?

2. How does productive capacity of a business relate to its near-term and longer-term marketing objectives? Simply put, how many offices, manufacturing plants, and distribution facilities does a business have? Do their locations relate efficiently to the business plan, to one another, to availability of raw materials, to cost-effective labor, and to designated markets and customers?

3. How much physical office and production capacity is needed—and when—to meet growth objectives? Should the facility even be located on its present site, or are substantial incremental investments needed at existing locations just because they are there?

Corporate decisions to acquire or dispose of real estate and facilities are investment decisions. Operating divisions compete for corporate dollars according to traditional methods that allocate resources with capital budgeting techniques, particularly where those resources are being committed to long-term fixed capital assets. Generally, fixed-asset values relate to manufacturing, distributing, and marketing corporate goods. On the other hand, the dominant measure of the profitability of an individual real estate investment decision is the discounted cash flow, where the timed sequential return of investment dollars receives priority.

Evaluation motives clash, then, as the traditional corporate financial executive thinks about ways to publicize the shareholder ownership value through earnings per share (EPS) growth, dividend policy, and stock and bond prices (normally on a short-term basis), whereas the real estate investment analyst is looking at available depreciation that can be added to net income. It appears that much more effort will be expended over the balance of the 2000s to resolve the bookkeeping and reporting paradox that now exists, and that fixed-asset investments must be looked at in ways that now differ from accepted practice. We believe the corporate facility management executive will be called on increasingly to provide reasoned, factual advice on this important point.

How has the evolving investment climate affected the corporation's need for specialized real estate and facility services? The dramatic expansion of required services means the real estate and facility analyst or marketing specialist must have the expertise and insight necessary to take advantage of the following new opportunities:

- Real estate portfolio review and analysis through the establishment of corporate real estate program/profit objectives, along with corporate real estate policy and procedures.

- Raising corporate funds through the planning, packaging, and marketing of surplus corporate assets; the disposition and marketing of surplus corporate buildings and leaseholds; corporate real estate financing.

- Analyses and implementation of corporate plans for growth and contraction through merger, acquisition, divestiture, and liquidation of assets.

- Marketing and management of fixed-asset projects.

STRATEGIC PLANNING

Strategic planning with respect to the corporation's facilities is at the heart of an effective facility management function. The information and strategy exchange (see Exhibit 2.3) is essential to producing a useful document and game plan. While a purely top-down approach should be avoided, it is critical that corporate policy be carefully observed and integrated into the strategic facilities plan. This can include policies such as make-or-buy preferences (revolving around the corporation's strategic competencies), investment focus (e.g., research and development, inventory, facilities), and customer service. Information should be gathered from whatever sources are appropriate (see Exhibit 2.4). Some of the best sources are the operating plans for the corporation's strategic business units, the corporation's general policies and business plan, and historical data for the corporation as well as its various interfaces. No two strategic facilities plans are alike, nor should they be. Therefore, the following material provides a menu of important items from which the corporate facility executive can select to structure a plan best suited for his or her corporation.

Issues to Address in a Strategic Facilities Plan

- Capacity requirements forecast
- Facility location, relocation, expansion, and consolidation
- Facility acquisition, utilization, and divestiture

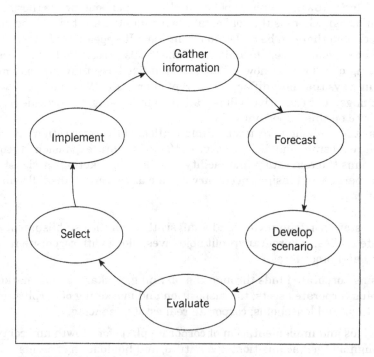

Exhibit 2.4   Strategic Planning Process

- Life-cycle costing and productivity incorporating perspectives on trade-offs
- Facilities financing, including the capital budgeting plan
- Financial statement effects of real estate organizational structure, management policies, and action
- Implementation policies and procedures
- Facilities standards

Information Required to Develop the Strategic Facilities Plan

- Marketing distribution plans, inventory management, and sales forecasts by product/service type
- Financial objectives, including funding, profitability, and profile
- Organizational structure for operating, regulatory, and liability management
- Human resources as related to site-specific operating costs and relocations
- Real estate and facility inventory and utilization data, historical and forecasted
- Strategic and operating requirements for each strategic business unit
- Ancillary services related to facility operations (utilities, amenities, etc.)
- Market information respecting the commodity (space and location)
- Corporate policies related to or involving facilities including:

  Real property interest preferences (owned or leased)

  By facility type and location (foreign or domestic)

  Risks (environmental, financial, market)

  Financing methods—internal, seller financing, third-party (e.g., banks), or leases

  Financial statement objectives—asset, liability, or expense recognition and timing

  Cash flow impact

  Management of financial, market, and legal risks and contingencies

  Strategic aspects of real estate (e.g., image, worker morale, environmental protection)

The Planning Process

- Parties involved in the development of the strategic facilities plan:

  CEO and CFO, and an executive committee representing senior management

  Representatives of departmental functions (e.g., human resources, finance)

  Representatives of the strategic business units operating within the corporation

  Corporate facility management department executive

- Corporate strategy input:
  Product and packaging impact—changing consumer acceptance
  Marketing strategy impact—changing customer location
  Manufacturing technology selection
  Materials sourcing program
  Production planning and control—changes in volume
  Logistical strategy—purchasing, packaging, shipment
  Inventory planning—demand and factors variation
  Capital funding
  Organizational design
  Human resources program (labor pool, benefits, etc.)
- Operations management: the dynamics of the environment and potential for:
  Changes in demand
  Changes in supply (competition)
  Changes in technology
  Changes in management methods (e.g., just-in-time)
  Changes in management objectives (e.g., total quality)
  Changes in organizational objectives/structure
  Changes in labor pool size or quality
- Physical plant inventory management:
  Impact on corporate profitability and risk profile
  Schedule and delivery date coordination

Identification of Space Requirements
- Present—this operating period
- Future—short term and long term
- Space requirements affected by:
  Employee efficiency
  Technology used in operations (e.g., telecommunications)
  Land and building costs
  Development or land banking potential for proposed or adjacent sites
  Timing considerations
  Legal and/or environmental considerations
  Locus of decision-making ability and acquisition authority
  Evaluation of alternatives, especially short- versus long-term solutions

Single-purpose versus multiple-purpose solutions

Image and prestige considerations

Assembly of a Strategic Facilities Plan

- Statement of corporate objectives for the upcoming period, players, timetable, resources, constraints

- Identification of specific facilities requirements per strategic business unit (type, amount, where, when, budget, linkages):

  Define the objective(s) of the function requiring a facility.

  Define relationships and contributions of other corporate functions.

  Establish space requirements.

  Identify and evaluate alternative facility plans.

  Select and implement the plan.

  Reprogram the facility in step with operational objectives.

  Identify existing inventory and capacity of facilities in relation to policies addressing utilization and performance standards.

- Identification of alternative solutions to accommodate the objectives, with specific notation as to the related costs, benefits, trade-offs, risks, impact, and externalities. This requires the input of the staff and operating personnel noted.

- Identification of a comprehensive and integrated set of recommendations and rationale for the actions proposed, constituting a basic strategic facilities plan

- Senior management review and adoption (with modifications)

- Development of implementation plans and procedures for both corporate facility management personnel and the strategic business units and staff departments involved in executing the action plans

- Implementation monitoring, notation of feedback, and realignment of plan details as necessary

Implementation Program

- Capital allocation requests and acquisitions
- Land and space banking
- Divestitures
- Inventory redeployment
- Cost management measures
- Refinancing of real property interests
- Pursuit of cost-offsetting opportunities
- Relocation

ANNUAL OPERATING PLAN

The annual operating plan (AOP), or annual budget, represents the short-term part of the budgeting cycle, normally restricting the operating unit to plus and minus forecasts of one year. Preparation of the AOP begins at the office, plant, or department or division level, with each operating unit submitting its short-term "hopes and fears" forecasts to company levels, where the individual reports are combined into one plan. This consolidated company plan is then submitted to corporate headquarters for further analysis and synthesis into an AOP for the corporation.

A division-level AOP includes a letter of transmittal from the division president to the company CEO summarizing the financial results to date, measured against the previous year's AOP and the division long-range plan (LRP), and discussing critical issues and key assumptions of the plan under review. It also contains comments on the following:

- *Net Cash Flow* (after taxes). The department prepares a detailed explanation for business areas planning a full-year negative net cash flow and explains the management actions (receivable collections, inventory control, reduced capital expenditures, etc.) required to support cash flow improvements.

- *Risks and Opportunities.* The department identifies and describes potential risks and opportunities not included in the plan, quantifies the potential in terms of sales and profit impact, and details the management action required.

- *Forecast Variance.* The department identifies major differences, if any, between current forecast and the most recent previous forecast. In addition, a forecast variance schedule is included as an attachment to the letter of transmittal.

Specific AOP contents describe and analyze the proposed plan of operation under a number of topical headings, all illustrated by narrative and quantitative material. These operational items normally include:

- Executive summary
- Sales and profit summary
- Annual operating plan
- Operating results by quarter (sales, PBT, inventories, and receivables)
- Objectives and major management actions
- Risks and opportunities—short-range, but related to forecasts
- Staff operating expenses—for purposes of division allocations
- Staff engineering expenses—for purposes of division allocations
- Staff marketing expenses—for purposes of division allocations
- Staff administrative expenses—for purposes of division allocations

- Net assets employed
- Cash flow schedule
- Current year plan compared with last year's actual
- Preceding year's plan compared with that year's forecast
- Current year plan compared with long-range plan
- The projected base and method for allocations
- Capital authorization and expenditures

Several of these items are of particular importance to the facility management department, which should provide input on the numbers and strategies outlined in the AOP. Some of these items are discussed in greater detail in chapter 3.

THE LONG-RANGE PLAN

Just as the Annual Operating Plan (AOP) signifies by its title the short-term nature of the projection cycle, the long-range plan (LRP) denotes an attempt to forecast corporate business prospects over a longer period—usually five years or more (see Exhibit 2.5). Therefore, the span of interest widens significantly when corporate, group, and division leaders create a framework within which long-term growth opportunities can be extrapolated from sequential AOPs. To be effective, however, the LRP must be more than the AOP repeated five times.

The basic objectives of an LRP are as follows:

1. To assess and define the economic and competitive environment that is likely to be faced within the LRP period.
2. To establish goals for the LRP that are consistent with the company's approved strategic objectives.
3. To identify and define the major actions required to achieve the LRP goals.
4. To determine the timing, scope, resource requirements, and major milestones of each planned action.
5. To prepare reasonable estimates of the probable financial effect of implementing the LRP.
6. To assess the major risks of accomplishing the LRP objectives, to identify key early warning indicators, and to prepare contingency plans for responding to significant changes in the external environment.
7. To evaluate the aggregate resource requirements and the availability of the necessary resources and to reach resource allocation decisions.
8. To arrive at an agreed-on plan for the managing of the business during the LRP period and to establish preliminary estimates of the probable operating results for each of the fiscal years included in the plan.

The LRP presentation format closely duplicates that of the AOP—from plant to division to company or operation to a concise document submitted for corporate

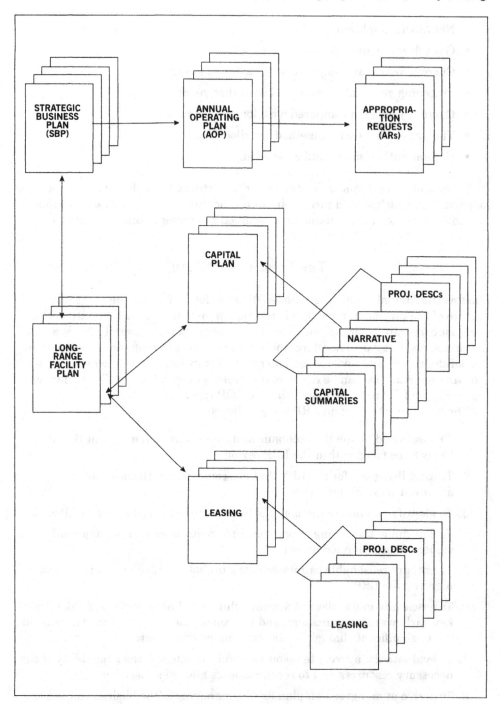

Exhibit 2.5   Basic Planning Document Relationships

office review and evaluation. The basic purpose of the LRP presentation is to describe business strategy of each division over a five-year period (or whatever other term is chosen) and to identify the major management actions included in the LRP to implement the strategy.

The major actions may be specific planned events or milestones. These may include major new product developments or introductions, capacity expansions, market penetration objectives, critical decision points, and management organization changes.

The presentation format for an LRP, as shown in the following sample, normally addresses key long-term planning objectives in the following topical sequence:

1. Statement of charter
2. Summary of economic and competitive assumptions
3. Strategic plan summary
4. Division goals and major management actions
5. Risks and opportunities
6. Early warning indicators and contingency plans
7. Summary of product line business strategies
8. Product line analysis—history and future trends
9. Research and engineering plan summary
10. New product contributions
11. New product contribution trends
12. Major new programs/products—investment/expense and timing
13. Capacity utilization by major process/facility
14. Capital plan summary
15. LRP summary
16. Four-box chart—sales, profit, assets, and cash flow
17. Four-box chart—inventories, receivables, working capital, and noncurrent assets
18. Division profit and loss statement
19. Summary of changes in sales and profit
20. LRP assumptions—pricing, economics, and performance improvements
21. Operating results by product line—long-range plan
22. Division net assets employed
23. Division cash flow
24. Foreign location after-tax cash flow (in local currency)
25. Projected base for allocations

The items are relatively self-explanatory. The emphasis leans toward existing and emerging market analyses than toward past events. For example, the eighth item, "Product line analysis—history and future trends," normally addresses the following issues:

1. Market developments and forecasts—industry—general
   - The basis for industry forecasts and growth trends
   - Technology developments and trends
   - Governmental influences
   - Competitive actions
   - Import/export considerations
   - Country market considerations versus world market considerations
   - The industry capacity/market demand relationships
   - Market behavior versus general conditions (and major economic indicators)

2. Marketing plans—company-specific:
   - Market share targets, changes versus competition
   - New product development and introduction plans
   - Product obsolescence and deletion
   - Pricing strategy
   - Distribution strategy
   - Marketing and sales organization
   - Advertising and promotional strategy

The LRP's emphasis on the future is important because the facility management department is involved in the development of LRP forecasts that relate to changing real estate and facilities requirements that support forecasted market programs and company marketing plans.

SAMPLE: Corporate Facilities Procedures

INTERNAL LETTER   XYZ Corporation International

Date: May 2, 2005   No:

TO: (Name, Organization, Internal Address)   FROM: (Name, Organization, Internal Address, Phone)

- Distribution   - William K. Smith
- •   - Corporate Offices—Chicago
- •   - 0870,001, PROS

Subject: Revision of Corporate Facilities Procedure
           Facilities Planning, FAC 04. 04

The attached April 30, 2005, revision of the subject procedure replaces the original procedure
dated November 9, 2000. The following changes are highlighted:

- Coordination with Purchasing is required only if quotations are needed.
- Investment categories are defined.
- Project description forms are no longer mandatory for projects less than $100,000.
- Total dollars for fourth and fifth years of the SBP long range capital plan are to be veri-
  fied using overall relationship basis (ratios).
- Specific projects for the fourth and fifth years are to be listed only to the extent
  possible.
- Longer-range facilities planning is recommended for major changes beyond five years.
- A subsection on forecasting has been added to the Long-Range Facilities Planning
  Section.
- Requirements for area planning statistics have been reduced.
- Project description forms are being revised to:
  Orient expenditure items by fiscal year.
  Eliminate certain appropriation request type data requirements.
- Requirements for the schedule of capital projects have been reduced.

In addition to the foregoing, other minor changes have been made.

William K. Smith
Staff Vice President
Facilities and Services

                                        FAC04.04
                                        April 30, 2005
                                        Replaces: November 9, 2000

                                        _____
                                        William K. Smith

FACILITIES PLANNING

I. PURPOSE

To establish guidelines and requirements for development of Long-Range Facilities Plans, including Capital and Leasing Plans used for Strategic Business Plans and Annual Operating Plans.

II. APPLICABILITY

All organizational components of the Corporation, as defined in Corporate Directive A-01.

III. PROCEDURE

Long-range facilities planning and capital planning will be performed in accordance with attachment #1 of this procedure, entitled *Facilities Planning Manual*.

REFERENCES

Finance Policy 12–10-01, Capital Expenditures and Extraordinary Expense Policy and Procedure
Finance Policy 65–10-01, Capitalization of Company Owned Property
Corporate Facilities Procedure FAC 04.02, Life Year Assignment Guide Corporate Facilities Procedure FAC 04.03, Proposal Requirements and Funding Analysis

FAC04.04
Attachment #1

XYZ CORPORATION INTERNATIONAL

FACILITIES PLANNING MANUAL

CORPORATE OPERATIONS STAFF
CORPORATE OFFICES
APRIL 30, 2005

FOREWORD

Orderly and well-planned capital spending is a fundamental process essential to the long-term profitability and growth of XYZ Corporation International. A good facilities plan is an integral part of successful long-range and annual business plans. This Facilities Planning Manual is designed to enhance the ability of each of our Divisions to create successful and meaningful capital plans that are well coordinated with our other business planning and forecasting procedures. The process outlined in this manual is also intended to facilitate the timely approval and implementation of these capital plans with a minimum of delay and repetitive review. Your observance of the guidelines and procedures contained in this manual is vital so that we can improve our performance in acquiring and maintaining the facilities necessary to the profitable operation of our business.

CONTENTS

I. OVERVIEW

INTRODUCTION

The Capital Appropriations Committee has requested the development of procedures to establish an effective, well-coordinated, and efficient system for planning, forecasting, and controlling capital expenditures throughout the Corporation.

The intent of the manual is to provide instructions and guidelines covering the development and implementation of facilities plans over a five-year period for the acquisition of fixed assets. The procedures in this manual are applicable to all domestic and international locations of the company, including all Operations, Groups, Divisions, and Subsidiaries.

Basic concepts in the capital planning and appropriation process are briefly described in this section as an overview and are described in detail in subsequent sections of the manual.

REFERENCES

This manual is based on the following references:

1. Corporate Directive—Facilities Planning (11-09-01)
2. Finance Policy—Capital Expenditures and Extraordinary Expense Policy and Procedure (12-10-01)
3. Finance Policy—Capitalization of Company-Owned Property (65-10-01)
4. Corporate Facilities Procedure—Life Year Assignment Guide (FAC 04.02)
5. Corporate Facilities Procedure—Proposal Requirements and Funding Analysis (FAC 04.03)

DEFINITIONS

For purposes of this manual, the following definitions are applicable:

Average Growth Rate. The percent average annual compound growth rate determined from compound interest tables by the percent increase over the planning period and by the number of years of the planning period.

Capital Project. The largest practical grouping of related effort to accomplish a specific facilities objective for which capital expenditures or leasing of property is proposed.

Capital Planning. The advance identification of capital projects, including description, justification, timing, and estimated cost.

Capital Expenditures. Expenditures for Company-owned property, certain property-related expenditures, and special tools that, except for land, are written off to expense over a period of two or more years. Included are expenditures that substantially increase the value of previously obtained property (improvements and betterments including major rearrangements and renewals) and expenditures that significantly extend the previous depreciable life (rebuilding, rehabilitation, restoration).

Facilities. Personal property utilized for production, maintenance, research, development, test, performance of services, administrative purpose or general plant purpose, and real property. This term applies as well to such personal property and real property provided by a customer under a facilities contract agreement. Excluded are customer-funded special tooling and special test equipment.

Facilities Planning. Periodic or continuous activity intended to lead to documentation of timely and economical acquisition, utilization and disposition of facilities required in the pursuit of business objectives.

Investment Categories. New programs or products, expansion, cost improvement, replacement or overhaul, energy, environment, and other.

Net Property. Property at original cost at time of acquisition less accumulated depreciation and amortization—also known as *book value*.

Personal Property. Machinery, equipment, general purpose laboratory instruments and test equipment, furniture and fixtures, vehicles, and machine tool accessories and auxiliary items, whether owned or leased.

Real Property. Land, buildings, and improvements to owned or leased land and buildings.

Strategic Business Plan (SBP). The primary five-year plan used by each business unit of XYZ Corporation to specify and carry out strategies to achieve its objectives. The early stages of development provide the basis for developing the Long-Range Facilities Plan, including the Capital and Leasing plans, which become part of the SBP. *Long-Range Plan* or *LRP* as used throughout this manual is intended to mean *Strategic Business Plan*.

Strategic Business Plan

The primary planning document within the Corporation is the Strategic Business Plan. This plan, for each business segment, sets out the directions, strategies, and overall implementation plans to be pursued by the respective units. Strategic business planning and facilities planning require full coordination early and throughout the strategic planning process in order to develop a long-range facilities plan that includes the information required for the preparation of the SBP. Both the Long-Range Facilities Plan and Capital Plan document the specific implementation actions.

Concepts developed and evaluated in the process of preparing strategic plans often involve major capital requirements and therefore significant capital investment programs in the future. Capital planning provides the necessary information regarding the capital resources required to carry out the approved strategic plan or for strategic alternatives that are being evaluated. Exhibit 2.5 indicates basic planning document relationships.

Long-Range Facilities Plan

Facilities planning is intimately associated with the capture of new business programs and penetration into new product lines. Facilities planning that calls for aggressive expansion or new business penetration is generally initiated by top management. Facilities proposals relating to methods improvements, replacement economics, and other investments of a technological nature more often are initiated by operating personnel and manufacturing/industrial engineers.

In support of the Strategic Business Plan and based on related long-range facilities strategies and objectives, a documented Long-Range Facilities Plan is prepared for each Division at least once each year that indicates how the major facilities in the possession of each division are expected to change and be utilized over the five-year planning period.

Long-range planning of facilities is essential because of the long lead time for construction or purchase and installation of facilities, their high cost and long life, their impact on the business unit, and the low cost of planning relative to the benefits achieved.

It is essential to good capital planning that adequate time be provided for implementing major facilities projects involving selection of new plant sites, acquisition and rezoning of additional real estate, design and construction of new facilities or plant expansions, phase-out and disposition of current operating facilities, and acquisition of new facilities to meet forecasted production, engineering, research, laboratory, warehousing, and distribution needs. In order to avoid the disadvantages of last-minute decision making in this important area, the Long-Range Facilities Plan provides a master plan that establishes the timing, size, location, funding method, and expected cost of facilities actions, including dispositions, needed to implement strategies and to meet profit objectives and long-term business growth.

Capital Project Concept

A Project Description (PD), Form 130-R-12, is initiated for each project to serve as the source of information about it, including description, cost, timing, and justification. The PD is considered a basic building block and fundamental working document for constructing the capital plan. PDs describe the purpose of the project, methods and facilities to be used to implement it, alternatives considered, costs, and preliminary financial justification. This description is usually less complete for projects scheduled to be initiated during the fourth and fifth years of the planning period. PDs are updated, modified, or canceled over the term of the planning period due to improved or revised definition of needs, requirements, specifications, and costs, or as business conditions dictate.

The PD is used as the basis for capital and leasing planning and as the basis for the Appropriation Request (AR). The PD is developed through the addition of detailed marketing, engineering, production, and financial data for preparing the AR.

All related capital and project expense requirements necessary to accomplish a specific objective are grouped as a single project so the planning, evaluation, and approval of capital transactions can proceed on an integrated basis without the need for incremental or piecemeal planning and approval decisions.

No commitments can be made unless an AR is authorized in accordance with the procedures and approval authority specified in Finance Policy 12-10-01. However, an expenditure of the lesser of 5 percent of the AR or $50,000 is permitted for preliminary planning work to adequately define major construction projects prior to submittal of the AR.

SBP and AOP Integration

The capital plan for the SBP is a five-year plan for capital expenditures and leasing of property based on the Long-Range Facility Plan. The capital plan for the AOP is for the first year only and is expected to be the same or nearly the same as the first year of the long-range capital plan resulting from Corporate reviews and recommendations.

Division-level sections of the SBP and AOP contain a narrative summary of the Long-Range Facilities Plan defining facility-related objectives, master area plan changes, new brick-and-mortar project rationales, and any other important data such as expected production capacity shortages, facility divestments and consolidations, and major facilities replacements.

Individual projects of $100,000 and higher are listed in the SBP-AOP capital schedules by investment category showing authorization amounts and timing and expenditure amounts calendarized by appropriate fiscal year. PDs are submitted with the AOP or SBP for all projects of $250,000 or more scheduled for approval during the planning period. The dollar amounts specified include all anticipated follow-on costs.

Detailed engineering, marketing, and financial analyses are not mandatory during the SBP-AOP planning cycle but must be completed prior to submission of an Appropriation Request for authorization to make commitments or expenditures for the project.

Appropriation Requests

Appropriation Requests are prepared in accordance with Finance Policy 12-10-01: Capital Expenditures and Extraordinary Expense Policy and Procedure.

Reports and Audits

In order to improve the management of capital expenditures and project implementation, a Schedule of Capital Projects, Form 130-Y-7, is originated and maintained to monitor progress. This report is date-oriented relative to the long-range and annual capital plans. The report is originated and maintained by the Division with the Schedule of Capital Projects to be submitted with the SBP and AOP. The report is revised at least quarterly thereafter.

Audits of the capital planning process and related implementation, reporting, and monitoring are conducted periodically by Corporate Operations.

II. GENERAL PLANNING GUIDELINES

Long-Range Facilities Plan

The Long-Range Facilities Plan (LRFP) is prepared at the Division level and describes proposed facility expansions, relocations, plant closings, and new site acquisitions. The facilities plan should summarize Division-wide facilities requirements and must be based on approved strategic business objectives as well as current marketing and sales forecasts by major program or product. The probable impact of new product introductions, changing research and engineering requirements, competitive cost and pricing pressures, environmental regulations, and energy availability must all be considered.

The first pages of each Division's Long-Range Facilities Plan contain a statement of facilities-related objectives established by division management as necessary or desirable to accomplish division goals and strategies. Typical facilities objectives are "Increase utilization of engineering office space," "Reduce cost of injection-molded plastic parts," or "Automate assembly and testing of products."

Each Division's Long-Range Facilities Plan consists of a five-year forecast of required plant or site area at year-end, displayed by individual plant location or site and substantiated by sales volume forecasts and related head count projections that correlate with the planned area forecast. Utilization of current facilities versus total capacity by shift should be shown to evaluate alternate methods of satisfying planned area requirements. For each year of the five-year forecast, all planned Division area changes, major equipment replacements, capacity additions, or other new facilities projects of significant size should be briefly described. Examples are "Construction of finished goods warehouse in 2005 and close regional distribution centers," "Purchase land and construct 300,000 sq. ft. engineering and manufacturing facility for Missile x production," or "Expand numerical control machining capability and capacity." The Facilities Plan serves as the basis for planning and evaluating capital funds specifically required for land acquisition, new building construction, plant expansions, new leased facilities, plant divestitures, facility consolidations, and other major capital projects.

The same Capital Plans and Leasing Plans are included in the Strategic Space Plan (SSP) as in the LRFP. The LRFP and the SSP, as submitted, must be in consonance by update or revision. The LRFP must be updated to include changes required for the AOP.

Longer-range facilities planning is advisable for major changes beyond five years such as site saturation, new sites, new plants, or major changes in products, technology, make/buy structure, or capacity. For this planning, longer-range forecasts of sales volume should be obtained from the sales/marketing function. Related head count and area requirements based on application of planning ratios or relationships and how needs are to be met should be determined and documented for at least every fifth year after the first five years.

Initiation of Capital Plans

A five-year capital authorization and expenditure plan is prepared by Operations personnel (usually manufacturing/industrial engineers) at each Division or manufacturing location based on specific capital projects. This expenditure plan, known as the long-range capital plan (LRCP), serves as a guide in forecasting the timing and amounts of capital funds required to accomplish the business objectives of the division. The LRCP is based on SSP considerations and the Long-Range Facilities plan. The annual capital plan (ACP) is the first year of the LRCP and is expected to be based on the best possible definition and estimates.

Coordination with Purchasing

Engineering estimates for major facilities expenditures for budgetary and planning purposes are usually satisfactory. When quotations are needed from contractors or suppliers, they are obtained in coordination with the purchasing function.

Impact of Inflation

The impact of inflation on all authorizations and expenditures must be recognized and provided for in the capital planning. Dollars current to the year under consideration must be used for each year of the planning period.

Replacement of Productive Capacity

Replacement of productive capacity should be considered on the basis of cost-effective application of available technology, not on the basis of one-for-one replacement with assets of like kind.

Leasing Policy and Considerations

The XYZ Corporation philosophy on leasing versus owning as stated in Finance Policy 12-10-01 is excerpted here.

It is company policy that manufacturing facilities be owned and not leased.

Short-term leasing is to be considered only when the requirement is temporary, where high risk of technological obsolescence exists, or under other conditions of great uncertainty.

Long-term leases of facilities must be justified by a leasing versus owning financial analysis with due consideration given to risk of the venture.

All highway vehicles except transportation trailers will be leased and not owned.

A leasing versus owning financial analysis must be performed for all other capital projects where leasing appears to be a viable alternative.

In the evaluation of capital projects where leasing is an alternative, two separate decisions must be considered.

1. The justification for the project and its related economic benefits to the Corporation must be established. In the case of a project justified on the basis of economic benefits, the analysis should be based on purchase of the capital items. If the facilities being considered are not available for purchase (e.g., additions to existing facilities financed by a regional development authority), the capitalized value of the lease should be used as the purchase price. The capitalized value of the lease is the present value at the current after-tax long-term borrowing rate, specified by the Corporate Treasurer, of all future lease payments.

2. The desirability of leasing all or a portion of the capital items as an effective method of utilizing the debt capacity of XYZ Corporation must be determined on the basis of leasing-versus-owning analyses and instructions from the Treasurer's Office regarding the preferred method of financing.

Plans to lease rather than own must be reviewed by the appropriate senior financial executive.

Leased property that is to be capitalized in accordance with Finance Policy 65-10-01 is treated as purchased property for capital planning purposes. All other property planned to be leased is included in the long-range and annual leasing plans. PDs include terms of applicable leases.

New Business Proposals

Capital requirements associated with new business proposals to NASA, the Department of Defense, Department of Energy, and other government agencies must be defined and analyzed prior to submitting signed proposals to the customer. (Reference: Corporate Facilities Procedure, FAC 04.03, "Proposal Requirements and Funding Analysis.")

Content of Capital Plans

The capital plan consists of a brief narrative summary, capital plan summaries, and PDs for projects equal to or greater than $250,000. The narrative summary highlights key issues, facilities strategies, key investment risks and benefits, and major facilities actions for the planning period.

The capital plans are based on the results of long-range facilities planning. The capital plan contains brick-and-mortar type requirements, machinery and equipment type requirements, and a definition of all other facilities requirements foreseeable over the five-year planning period for meeting division objectives. Facilities for performance of new military or other government-funded programs are included if the sales and profit forecasts for these programs are included in the SSP and AOP.

Capital plans do not include expenditures for acquisitions or equity investments in other companies. Capital requirements associated with divestiture or sale of a product line, business unit, or complete facility are included (e.g., severance and separation of common utility and fire protection systems, relocation and reinstallation of production equipment, and make-ready costs prior to sale).

III. Long-range Facilities Planning

Forecasting

The forecasting process consists of four steps:

1. Gather and record past data (sales, personnel, area).
2. Develop trends (sales, personnel, and area) and relationships (sales/employee, sales/sq. ft.) based on past data.
3. Project trends and relationships into the future to determine basis for facilities requirements.
4. Adjust projections for changes in product, technology, make/buy structure, etc. to establish a forecast.

The forecast should be based on the best sales information available and make reasonable sense relative to past data, projections, and future changes.

Past and future data in dollars for determining activity or volume should be in constant dollars to remove distortions due to inflation. Dollar figures should be converted to constant dollars of a base year in the past, preferably the same or an earlier year than the first historical year considered. The average annual producer price index (formerly wholesale price index, or WPI) for industrial commodities or for the specific commodities being manufactured should be used for U.S. offices and plants. Most governments publish an index of the change in monetary values. For locations outside the United States, use indexes published for that country.

The net effect of growth curves and their timing for each product or business segment, including the phasing in of new and phasing out of old products/business segments, should be considered in determining future volumes. Volume should be expressed in units relating to manufacturing activity, such as number of units produced or total manufacturing costs in constant dollars by year. Sales dollars can be used when they represent manufacturing activity. Manufacturing and sales dollars can be adjusted when necessary to eliminate effects not related to manufacturing activity such as material and/or component costs when manufacturing consists of assembly only.

It is generally desirable to use more than one type of unit (dollars, units, area) as a basis for historical growth and for projection to determine which results make the most sense.

Sources of data and bases for projections should be documented.

Division Long-Range Facilities Plan

Each Division or equivalent organizational unit that prepares an AOP prepares its own LRFP covering a five-year period. This plan addresses Division issues and strategies, additions and deletions of facilities, area utilization, facilities action plans, and capital investment. In some instances, an integrated LRFP is prepared by a Group or lead Division, especially where several Divisions of one or more Groups occupy the same major location or site. In such instances, LRFPs of the Divisions affected must reflect the results of the integrated plan. The documented plan comprises the following elements:

- Introduction and Objectives
- Division Facilities
- Sales Growth
- Personnel Forecast
- Facilities Issues
- Facilities Strategies
- Area Plan and Statistics
- Significant Facilities Projects
- Capital Investment Plan
- Leasing Plan
- Summary Charts and Data
- Conclusion or Summary Statements

Introduction and Objectives

A brief introduction is prepared together with a tabulation of facilities-oriented objectives for the five-year period.

Division Facilities

This section consists of brief statements, tabulations, and charts indicating the makeup of the Division in terms of organizations, major locations, number of personnel, number of buildings, and number of square feet of building area. Included is a plot plan for each major location showing present occupancy by organizational function of the Division for each building. Areas not occupied by the Division or areas occupied by other Divisions or organizations should not be shaded. A tabulation should also be prepared showing number of square feet occupied, number of Division personnel for each building, and number of square feet assigned to the Division but not in use for each building.

Sales Growth

This section shows the sales growth in dollars over the five-year planning period and compares this growth in percent to the growth in percent of personnel and building area. In addition, risks and opportunities relative to sales should be discussed briefly. Included is a tabulation of sales for the preceding year, this year, and the next five fiscal years using Format FP-l, as shown below.

Personnel Forecast

Schedules are prepared summarizing Division personnel by type (factory, office, lab, etc.), shift, and location, with subtotals by shift for each location and a grand total for the Division by year using Format FP-l (shown below). The schedules may be supplemented by charts.

Facilities Issues

This is a brief discussion of key considerations, problems, shortcomings, and needs affecting facilities requirements and utilization. This presentation may be made by major location or by organization. Unresolved issues that affect facilities should be highlighted.

			(TITLE)	
			Five-Year Plan	
Description	Last FY	F'CST This Year	___ ___ ___ ___ ___	Average Growth Rate
Totals			___ ___ ___ ___	

Format FP-1

Facilities Strategies

This section is a concise presentation of major planned short- and long-term facilities actions to achieve key objectives, solve serious or key problems, and/or satisfy basic needs. Included are planned expansions, phase-outs, consolidations, major relocations, centralization, offloading, establishment of offsite locations, improved utilization of existing facilities, modernization, major technological improvements, and major replacements.

A site saturation plan for building and land areas should be prepared. If a site will be saturated or replaced in less than 20 years, preliminary plans for additional or replacement sites should be developed.

Area Plan and Statistics

The area plan is a presentation of occupancy, area requirements, availability, and area utilization.

A schedule should be prepared showing occupancy for the Division by end of the present year by building and by location. Occupancy should show leased area, owned area, occupants (functions), total personnel, and first-shift personnel.

A schedule of area requirements by type and in total for each location and in total for the Division by year must be prepared using Format FP-1. A similar schedule must be prepared showing area availability by building and in total for each location by year using Format FP-1. Planned new sites and expansions must be identified and included. Total area available by year is determined and compared with area requirements by year to enter area excess or shortfall by year.

A summary must be prepared by location by year of total area owned, leased, and government-owned; area additions and deletions for each type of ownership; and changes in lease-outs of Company property and subleases to non–XYZ Corporation.

A summary is presented showing area utilization in square feet per person by type (e.g., factory, office, laboratory) and in total by major location by year using Format FP-1. A summary of major site statistics may be included.

Significant Facilities Projects

This section comprises a brief description of each facilities project of significant size.

Capital Investment Plan

This section comprises the Capital Plan as defined in this manual. The Capital Plan may be supplemented by additional narrative summaries, schedules, and charts as deemed desirable or necessary.

In addition, major expenditures in percent of total by investment category are presented. The capital programs are discussed briefly for those investment categories that constitute the major percentages of total capital expenditures.

Leasing Plan

This section comprises the Long-Range Leasing Plan. This plan may be supplemented by narrative, schedules, and charts as deemed desirable or necessary.

Summary Charts and Data

A summary chart of data and indexes for the Division should be prepared. The data should include sales, capital expenditures, personnel, gross area, and net book value by year using Format FP-1 (without average growth rate). The indexes should include net sales per person, capital expenditures as a percent of sales, capital expenditures per person, net sales per square foot, square feet per person, net book value per person, net property to gross property, and other meaningful indexes by year using the same format.

Sales-related indexes and human resources related indexes should be plotted on separate charts.

Summaries by Group or Operation

If desired or meaningful, human resources, area, capital plans, and leasing plans may be summarized by business segment, Group, or Operation, at the option of each Group or Operation, in addition to the individual Division summaries specified here.

Reviews of Long-Range Facilities Plans

LRFPs are mainly for review and use by the Division, Group, and Operation. LRFPs may be requested on an exception basis by Corporate Operations for review.

IV. CAPITAL PLANNING PROCEDURE

Capital Project System

Capital planning is performed by/for each Division or equivalent organizational unit that prepares an AOP. Capital planning is performed on the basis of a Project System whereby all related capital requirements necessary to accomplish a specific objective are grouped for approval as a single transaction. Tooling costs and related project expense items are included.

Determination of Capital Projects

Each department or function at the plant or Division level should be contacted at least once a year by responsible operations personnel, who will assist the user in determining the requirements for and the specifications of individual candidate items for projects for inclusion in the five-year capital plan.

Capital projects are developed with the active participation of shop supervision and by supervision of other functions affected. Operations personnel, usually Manufacturing Engineers or Industrial Engineers, at the plant or Division are responsible for coordinating and processing PDs and for making certain that the LRFP, the Capital Plan, and Capital projects take into account provisions of the strategic plan for the business unit. Capital projects are based on the following considerations:

- New or changing needs, requirements and conditions
- Operational changes
- Principal action programs
- Long-range facility plans
- Increased/decreased capacity requirements
- Cost/performance improvements
- New or improved technology or products
- Layout, methods, or process changes/improvement
- Replacement and modernization requirements
- Legal, governmental, health, and/or safety regulations, requirements, or standards
- Other considerations directly related to profitable operation of the business

Facilities requirements for identification of capital projects must be related to production processes and functions performed at the plant or Division, including:

Research	Receiving
Engineering	Warehousing
Design Quality	Control
Testing	Sales
Planning	Spare Parts
Scheduling	Service
Purchasing	Shipping
In-plant Material Handling	Distribution

Also included are requirements for offsite locations such as field offices, sales offices, service centers, and regional warehouses or distribution centers.

Adequate provisions should be made for long-term considerations such as properly maintaining the condition of facilities and cost-effective replacement and modernization of facilities.

Individual equipment items are grouped into projects based on a specific facility objective, such as "Replace mechanical calculators in the Accounting Department with electronic machines" or "Upgrade test equipment in Inspection and Quality Control Laboratories." Considerable latitude is permitted in the definition and dollar value of the project, but the scope must be broad enough to cover the overall objective so as to avoid the hazards of incremental approvals without full knowledge of the total program.

Each project is classified by one of the following investment categories that most accurately describes its primary purpose based on capital investments in facilities.

- *New Programs or Products.* Authorizations and expenditures made to enter a new business, develop, and launch a new product, facilitate new programs, or perform research and development (R&D) that may lead to new products.

- *Expansion.* Authorizations and expenditures to expand or increase capacity for current products or programs or to support growth related to present product lines.

- *Cost Improvement.* Authorizations and expenditures made to improve performance, reduce labor, or otherwise improve efficiency and reduce costs.

- *Replacement/Overhaul.* Authorizations and expenditures required to replace or rebuild worn out or damaged equipment and facilities.

- *Energy.* Authorizations and expenditures made to conserve energy through reduced consumption of electricity, oil, natural gas, coal, gasoline, and miscellaneous petroleum products. Also included are expenditures to implement alternative fuel supplies and other facilities directed toward mitigating production interruptions due to energy shortages.

- *Environment.* Authorizations and expenditures made to comply with federal, state, or local regulations concerning air and water quality and disposal of solid wastes.

- *Other.* Authorizations and expenditures that cannot be classified in any of the preceding categories, such as health and safety.

Addition of Capacity

When a capital project includes provisions for addition of productive capacity, assessments should be made of industry capacity to determine whether industry capacity already is adequate. Available capacity at other company locations must also be determined and evaluated. If expansion is still required, sales forecasts for the planning period must be obtained and translated to capacity requirements. In the case of machine tools, existing capacity in machine hours by machine type is determined based on the number of shifts and working days to be utilized. Utilization factors are calculated and applied to determine practical existing capacity. Deficits of capacity are translated to the number of additional machines required by type. An earnest search should be made within and outside XYZ Corporation to determine the availability of the needed capacity. When all or part of the needed capacity is located, the practicality of using this capacity is analyzed, assessed, and documented. The foregoing is performed during the planning stage prior to submission of an AR, becomes part of the project documentation, and is available for review.

Expansion of Building Areas

When a capital project includes provisions for building expansion, new construction, or leasing of space exceeding 5,000 square feet, block layouts should be prepared showing planned use of additional space and existing space that will be rearranged. Block layouts are an important aid in properly planning functional relationships, work flow, and material-handling concepts and in recognizing building, utility, and other constraints. These layouts should incorporate building architectural floor plans, utility installations, crane coverage, ceiling height identification, and any other important considerations. The block layouts become part of the project documentation and should be available for review.

Identification of Alternatives

For each capital expenditure project or project involving leasing:

1. Alternatives must be identified, including other methods, make versus buy, leasing versus owning, use of capacity at other divisions, and employment of additional shifts and overtime.

2. Alternatives must be assessed.

3. The best alternative is selected for proposal.

Timing of Expenditures

The timing and amount of capital expenditure and associated expense by fiscal year is determined for each capital project. Capital and expense are recorded separately for each fiscal year. The timing of construction projects affected by inclement weather requires special consideration. Planned dates should take into account realistic lead times and capacity for processing and approving project requests, writing specifications, obtaining and evaluating bids, etc.

Project Description Documentation

Project Documentation

Each capital project of $100,000 or greater is documented by Operations personnel at the Division or operating location through the use of a Project Description (PD), Form 130-R-12. A project number is assigned to each PD, and the PD is maintained and used as the basic form for capital planning. PDs are submitted with the SBP and the AOP for each project of $250,000 or more.

Expenditures less than $100,000 are grouped as "Miscellaneous" by investment category for planning and control purposes on the Capital Plan Summary. For such expenditures to be initiated during the first three years of the planning period, each grouping must be backed by a single PD to which is attached a listing of the individual projects with their estimated authorization and expenditure amounts and timing.

When capital projects include provisions for addition of capacity or expansion of area, the PD must be supplemented by additional documentation.

A PD is initiated whenever the need for a capital project is recognized, even if expenditures are not expected until some future year. New business proposals to government customers as defined in Facility Procedure FAC 04.03 generally result in preparation of a PD. PDs used for facilities planning purposes do not require detailed engineering, marketing, financial, or vendor quotation data in order to qualify for inclusion in the Long Range Capital Plan (LRCP) or the Annual Capital Plan (ACP) submittals. Cost estimates in PDs may contain provisions for contingencies due to lack of substantive data. PDs are updated, modified, or canceled throughout the planning period as business conditions warrant.

The impact of inflation must be reflected in the dollar amounts used in the PD. Dollars current to the year under consideration must be used for each year of the planning period.

Instructions for Preparing the PO

Part 1

Refer to Form 130-R-12 (shown on the following page) for reference numbers for the following instructions:

Form 130-R-12

1. *Project Name.* Enter the full descriptive title of the proposed project. This normally starts with an applicable verb (e.g., "Expand," "Modernize," "Rebuild").

2. *Division / Location.* Designate the office, plant, and/or location to which the project applies.

3. *Project No.* Assign a project number based on the following:

    First three digits—Division number.

    Fourth digit—Fourth digit of fiscal year in which initial expenditure will occur (for FY2000, use "0"). This digit is not to be revised after submittal of the first LRP.

    Last three digits—Sequence number of project for the division and year indicated.

4. *AR Quarter and Year.* Expected quarter and fiscal year for submitting the AR for approval.

5. *Origin Date.* Date of origin of the PD.

6. *Action.* Enter the following based on the stage of processing the PD.

    F/C—The project as defined for the LRCP or ACP.

    MOD—Modified to conform to the annual capital allocation or modified for other changes.

7. *Investment Category.* Check the one block that most accurately describes the investment category.

8. *Page Numbers.* Assigned at the time of submission and at each subsequent revision. Each revision starts with page 1, followed by consecutive page numbers.

9. *Responsible Person and Telephone.* Enter name of Operations person or equivalent person responsible for planning and implementing the project and his/her telephone number for contact.

10. *Revision Date.* Enter date of revision number indicated.

11. *Revision Number.* Enter sequence number of revision since origination.

12. *Description and Purpose of the Project.* Enter an explanation of what is to be done with the investment of company resources and enter the explanation of why the investment is required, its justification including economic analysis when appropriate, or other anticipated results. In the case of leases, also enter the planned initiation date, period of the lease, location of use, reason for use, reason for leasing rather than owning, lease terms,

XYZ CORPORATION INTERNATIONAL   **Project Description**
                                                                      Part 1

Project Name	Division/Location	Project No. (3)
(1)	(2)	⌐⌐⌐⌐⌐⌐⌐⌐⌐

	AR Qtr. & Yr.	Orig. Date	Action
	(4)	(5)	(6)

Investment Category (7)		(8)
[ ] New Program/Product [ ] Cost Improvement [ ] Energy		
[ ] Expansion [ ] Replacement/Overhaul [ ] Environment [ ] Other		Page of

Responsible Person	Telephone	Rev. Date	Rev. No.
(9)		(10)	(11)

Description and Purpose of the Project

(12)

Alternate Solutions Considered

(13)

Preliminary Financial Justification

(14)

Form 130-R-12

and whether the lease is new or a renewal. In the case of leased equipment, state whether the equipment is available for purchase, and for lease renewals, state whether credits toward purchase have been accumulated.

13. *Alternative Solutions Considered.* Summarize the principal alternative solutions considered and why they were rejected.

14. *Preliminary Financial Justification.* Enter preliminary financial results of the project on the basis of rough calculations until definitive return on asset and payback information is available.

Part 2

Refer to Form 130-R-13 (shown on the following page) for reference numbers for the following instructions:

Form 130-R-13

1. *Planned Completion.* Enter month or quarter and fiscal year that project is planned to be completed.

2. *Action.* Same as reference number 6 for Part 1. To be entered when continuation pages are used.

3. *Revision Number.* Same as reference number 11 for Part 1. To be entered when continuation pages are used.

4. *Page Numbers.* Continuation from page 1 outlined in reference number 8 for Part 1.

5. *Project Number.* Enter same number as indicated in Part 1.

6. *Item.* Enter consecutive sequence number for each line item listed.

7. *Fiscal Year.* Enter the fiscal year of expenditures.

8. *Description.* Enter the major elements of the project by line item with estimated cost of $25,000 or more by fiscal year of expenditure. List expense items separately if not associated directly with listed capital expenditures. Create one or more line items for lease expenditures.

9. *Cost Basis.* Enter basis for each cost entry according to the following codes:

   1—Firm bid (when obtained for AR)

   2—Contractor's or supplier's estimate

   3—Engineering estimate

   4—Other

10. *Capital Dollars.* Enter the total capital dollars, including freight, installation, and sales tax, for each line item. Do not include cost of items that will be funded by or paid for by the government.

11. *Expense Dollars.* Enter total expense dollars associated with each line item when applicable.

12. *Total Cost.* Enter the total of capital and expense dollars for each line item.

13. *Totals.* Enter cumulative totals of each of the columns indicated.

14. *Fiscal Year.* Enter each fiscal year of the project beginning with the year in which initial expenditure will occur.

15. *Capital.* Enter total capital dollars planned to be spent on the project for each fiscal year indicated.

16. *Expense.* Enter total expense dollars planned to be spent on the project for each fiscal year indicated.

17. *Totals.* Enter the total project expenditure by type (capital, expense) for all the applicable fiscal years.

XYZ CORPORATION INTERNATIONAL   **Project Description**
Part 2

I t e m	FY	Description	C B	Capital $	C B	Expense $	Total Cost $
Planned Completion (1)			Action (2)		Rev. No. (3)	Page of (4)	Project No. (5) ⅼⅼⅼⅼⅼⅼⅼⅼ
(6)	(7)	(8)	(9)	(10)	(9)	(11)	(12)
			Totals	(13)		(13)	(13)

		FY (14)	FY (14)	FY (14)	FY (14)	FY (14)	FY (14)	Totals
Capital		(15)	(15)	(15)	(15)	(15)	(15)	(17)
Related Expenses		(16)	(16)	(16)	(16)	(16)	(16)	(17)

Form 130-R-13

SBP Capital and Leasing Plan Preparation

Long-Range Capital Plan

Each year, an LRCP is developed by Division for the next five years by Operations personnel at the plant or division level. The LRCP is based on the Project Description (PO), Form 130-R-12, for capital projects $100,000 and above.

In the fourth and fifth years, the LRCP total dollars should be verified using some overall relationship basis such as indexes to make certain that reasonable capital is planned. Specific projects for these years should be listed to the extent possible.

The LRCP is summarized on a Capital Plan Summary, Form 130-Y-5, and submitted with the LRP to Corporate Financial via Division, Group, and Operations management.

Preparing the Long-Range Capital Plan Summary

Refer to Form 130-Y-5 (shown on the following page) for reference numbers for the following instructions.

Form 130-Y-5 (New 12/03)

1. *Division.* Self-explanatory.
2. *Year.* Enter fiscal year of the SBP or AOP as appropriate.
3. *Year.* Enter the first fiscal year of the five years planned.
4. *Year.* Enter the last (previous) fiscal year.
5. *Year.* Enter the current fiscal year (the year in which the LRCP is originated).
6. *Year.* Enter the second fiscal year of the planned period.
7. *Year.* Enter the third fiscal year of the planned period.
8. *Year.* Enter the fourth fiscal year of the planned period.
9. *Year.* Enter the fifth fiscal year of the planned period.
10. *Project Name.* For each investment category, enter the name of each large project in reverse sequence of capital dollar amount, starting with the largest amount. Large project is defined as (1) $100,000 and above for Corporate review; (2) lesser amounts if desired by Division, Group, or Operation reviews.
11. *Miscellaneous.* For each investment category, enter the dollar amount summation of the balance of the capital projects.
12. *Totals.* For each investment category, enter the total dollar amounts, the summation of items (10) and (11) for each applicable column.
13. *Project Number.* Enter project number as entered on the PO for the project.
14. *Fiscal Year.* Enter fiscal year of capital authorization.
15. *Capital Dollar Amount.* Enter capital dollars of authorization for each investment category line item for which a capital expenditure is forecast for one or more years of the planning period. Include authorizations made in the current or prior years.
16. *Actual Expenditures.* Enter capital dollar expenditures for last fiscal year by investment category line item for all projects that had expenditures last year and will have expenditures in one or more years of the planning period.
17. *Forecast Expenditures.* Enter forecast of capital dollar expenditures for the current fiscal year (the year in which the LRCP is originated) for each applicable investment category line item for projects that will have expenditures in one or more years of the planning period.
18. *Carryover Expenditures.* Enter the capital dollar expenditures for the first fiscal year of the five-year planning period as a result of authorizations or contractual obligations prior to the first fiscal year. Make these entries for each investment category line item.

Capital Plan Summary

XYZ CORPORATION INTERNATIONAL

Division _____ (1)

(2) _____ Strategic Business Plan
(2) _____ Annual Operating Plan

(In Thousands of Dollars)

Projects By Investment Category (1)	Project Number (13)	Authorizations FY (14)	Authorizations $ Amount (15)	Expenditures Actual (4) (16)	Expenditures Forecast (5) (17)	Expenditures C'Over (18)	Expenditures New (3) (19)	Expenditures Total (20)	(6) (21)	(7) (21)	(8) (21)	(9) (21)	Totals (22)
New Program/Products (10)													
■ Misc (11)													
■ Totals (12)													
Expansion													
■ Misc													
■ Totals													
Cost Reduction													
■ Misc													
■ Totals													
Replacement/Overhaul													
■ Misc													
■ Totals													
Energy													
■ Misc													
■ Totals													
Environment													
■ Misc													
■ Totals													
Other													
■ Misc													
■ Totals													
Totals (23)													
Memo: Project Rel. Exp. (24)													

Form 130-Y-5 (New 12/03)

19. *New Expenditures.* Enter new capital expenditures planned for the first fiscal year of the five-year planning period for each investment category line item.

20. *Total Expenditures.* Enter total of carryover and new capital expenditures for the first fiscal year of the five-year planning period for each investment category line item.

21. *Capital Expenditures.* Enter total planned capital expenditures by applicable fiscal year for each investment category.

22. *Total Capital Expenditures.* Enter total planned capital expenditures by investment category line item for the five-year planning period.

23. *Totals.* Enter total for each applicable column.

24. *Project-related Expense.* Enter project-related expenses other than for leasing for each applicable column.

Projects with expenditures occurring in the fourth quarter of the first two fiscal years are identified and determinations made for each relative to expenditure amount, month, and probability of actual expenditure by end of fourth quarter. This information is entered for the project on the Capital Plan Summary using footnotes.

Other Capital Summaries

Authorization and expenditure summaries can be prepared by business segment for Divisions or by investment category by organizational unit above the Division level if desired or required.

Recent and Current Capital Expenditures

A summary is compiled and submitted with the LRP Capital Summary showing total capital expenditures by investment category for the last fiscal year and for the current fiscal year (a forecast).

Long-Range Leasing Plan

Each year, a long-range leasing plan is developed for all new leases and lease renewals for authorizations during the five-year planning period. The leasing plan is developed for each Division by Operations personnel based on the PD for capital projects as previously described.

The long-range leasing plan is summarized on a Leasing Plan Summary, Form 130-Y-6, and submitted with the LRP to Corporate Financial via Division, Group, and Operations management.

Preparing the SBP Leasing Plan Summary

Refer to Form 130-Y-6 (shown on the following page) for reference numbers for the following instructions.

Form 130-Y-6 (New 1)

1. *Division.* Self-explanatory.

2. *Year.* Enter the first fiscal year of the planning period of the leasing plan opposite Long-Range Plan or Annual Operating Plan, as appropriate.

XYZ CORPORATION INTERNATIONAL

Leasing Plan Summary

Division _____ (1)

(2) _____ Strategic Business Plan

(2) _____ Annual Operating Plan

(In Thousands of Dollars)

Projects By Leasing Category	Project Number	Type Property	Location	Lease Mo. And Year	Lease Period	Footnotes	Authorization	
							FY	$ Amount
New								
■ ( ) (3)								
■ ( )								
■ ( )								
■ Misc (4)	(5)	(6)	(7)	(8)	(9)	(10)	(11)	(12)
Renewals								
■								
■								
■ Misc								

Form 130-Y-6 (New 1)

3. *Project Name.* For each leasing category, enter the name of each large leasing project in reverse sequence of dollar amount by fiscal year, starting
   with the largest amount. A large project is defined as (1) for Corporate
   review: $100,000 and above over the lease period, and (2) for Division,
   Group, or Operation reviews only; lesser amounts if desired.

4. *Miscellaneous.* For each leasing category, enter the dollar amount summation of the balance of the leasing projects by fiscal year.

5. *Project Number.* Enter project number as entered on the PD for the project.

6. *Type Property.* Enter the appropriate type of property from the following:
   Real property, data-processing equipment, machinery and equipment,
   transportation equipment, and other.

7. *Location.* Enter the location for use of the leased property.

8. *Lease Month and Year.* Enter the effective month and year for the new
   lease or lease renewal.

9. *Lease Period.* Enter the initial period of lease (excluding options or
   renewals) in months.

10. *Footnotes.* Enter footnote number and explain footnote below when
    appropriate.

11. *Fiscal Year.* Enter fiscal year for authorization (one of the years of the plan-
    ning period) of leasing expenditure.

12. *Leasing Dollar Amount.* Enter amount of authorization in dollars for the
    fiscal year indicated for each leasing category line item.

Major Expenditure Projects

For each project whose capital expenditure or leasing expenditures will equal or
exceed $250,000, the PD must be submitted to Corporate Financial with the SBP
Capital and Leasing Plan summaries and SBP for review by Corporate Operations. PDs for lesser amounts may be requested and reviewed as necessary.

AOP Capital and Leasing Plan Preparation

Annual Capital Plan

Each year, an Annual Capital Plan (ACP) is developed by Division for the next fiscal year by Operations personnel at the plant or division level. The ACP is based
on the PO for capital projects as previously described and the first year of the
LRCP. This plan is expected to be the same or nearly the same as the first year of
the approved LRCP.

The ACP is summarized on the Capital Plan Summary, Form 130-Y-5, and submitted with the AOP to Corporate Financial via Division, Group, and Operations
management.

Preparing the Annual Capital Plan Summary

Use the Capital Plan Summary, Form 130-Y-5, which is the same as that used for
the LRP Capital Plan Summary.

Refer to the instructions for filling out the Long-Range Capital Plan Summary. The last four years are not required for the AOP.

Annual Leasing Plan

An annual leasing plan is developed for all new leases and lease renewals for authorization during the next fiscal year. The leasing plan is developed for each Operation and Group by Division by Operations Personnel based on the PO for capital projects as previously described and the first year of the long-range leasing plan. This plan is expected to be the same or nearly the same as the first year of the long-range leasing plan as submitted with the SBP.

The annual leasing plan is summarized on Leasing Plan Summary, Form 130-Y-6, and submitted with the AOP to Corporate Financial via Division, Group, and Operations management.

Preparing the AOP Leasing Plan Summary

Refer to instructions for originating the SBP Leasing Plan Summary, Form 130-Y-6. The instructions are the same for both SBP and AOP leasing summaries.

Major Expenditure Projects

For each project having capital expenditures or leasing expenditures that will equal or exceed $250,000, the PO must be submitted to Corporate Financial with the AOP Capital and Leasing Plans and AOP for review by Corporate Operations. PDs for lesser amounts may be requested and reviewed as necessary.

Review and Assessment of Capital and Leasing Plans

Capital Plans and Leasing Plans are reviewed by the appropriate senior financial executive.

Finalized Capital Plan and Leasing Plan Summaries are submitted to the senior Operations executive at the Division level for review and approval. The senior Operations executive considers strategic plans and ensures that issues identified by Corporate Operations staff are addressed in reviewing and approving capital and leasing plan summaries.

Typical strategic planning considerations include:

1. Acquisitions
2. Expansions
3. Curtailments
4. New products or programs
5. Product phase-outs
6. Divestitures
7. Plant phase-outs
8. Plant relocations
9. Consolidation

The senior Operations executive, in conjunction with the senior financial executive, reviews Capital Plan Summaries relative to established or specified capital expenditures and performance targets and makes necessary adjustments for inclusion in the SBP.

Appropriate management and staffs at the Group and Operations levels review and modify or direct modification of capital plans originating at the Divisions based on strategic plans, greater visibility, performance improvements, etc. Where overall Operations, Group, or Division adjustments are made to planned capital or leasing expenditures, these adjustments are reflected in the Capital Plans and Leasing Plans by individual project and not as a general adjustment. Multiple iterations among Operations, Group, and Division levels for improving and approving capital plans are expected.

Operations management and staff at the Division, Group, Operations, and Corporate levels review the results of capital planning and make recommendations for modification/disapproval/approval.

Backup information leading to Capital Plan or Leasing Plan Summaries may be requested by higher organizational levels from lower organizational levels in order to make assessments and recommendations.

Capital plans are sent to the Corporate Capital Appropriations Committee with recommendations by Corporate Operations and Financial Analysis for approval/disapproval/approval with modifications. The Capital Appropriations Committee presents recommendations to the Management Committee.

Revision of Capital and Leasing Plans

As a result of Corporate reviews and recommendations, Capital and Leasing Plans are revised by appropriate management/staffs at the Division, Group, and Operations levels to comply with project recommendations and capital expenditure guidelines by the Corporate Offices.

V. REPORTS AND AUDITS

Scheduling, Reporting, and Monitoring Progress

The capital and leasing plans are reviewed by Operations personnel at the Division, and the initiation of projects are scheduled for management approval and implementation, taking into account efforts and time required for preparation, approval, design/specifications, bidding, procurement, construction, and installation. In many cases, the lead time is in excess of one year. Preparatory efforts include improved definition of requirements, determining and assessing viable alternatives, developing specifications, and obtaining more accurate cost data.

The following events are scheduled and entered on Schedule of Capital Projects, Form 130-Y-7, for each project equal to or greater than $100,000.

1. Appropriation Request submission and approval
2. Initiation of:
   a. Design/specification development
   b. Bidding

c. Procurement (building materials and components, machinery and equipment, etc.)

d. Construction

e. Installation (machinery and equipment, furniture and fixtures, etc.)

3. Project completion

For the LRCP, events for items 2 and 3 need not be scheduled for the fourth and fifth years. For the ACP, events for items 1, 2, and 3 must be scheduled for the first three years only.

Actual dates of occurrence for the preceding items are also entered and maintained on the Schedule of Capital Projects by the Division.

The Schedule of Capital Projects is submitted annually with the SBP and AOP. It should also be updated at least quarterly and monitored for timely action.

Operations management at the Division, Group, and Operations levels is responsible for monitoring progress of project implementation and funds commitment and taking corrective action whenever projects appear to fall behind schedule.

Preparing the Schedule of Capital Projects

Refer to Form 130-Y-7 (shown on the following page) for reference numbers for the following instructions for preparing the Schedule of Capital Projects.

Form 130-Y-7 (1/89)

1. *Division.* Self-explanatory.
2. *Report.* Enter the quarter of the fiscal year represented by the report.
3. *Date.* Enter date of report (should be within 15 days from end of quarter).
4. *Project Name.* Enter the name of each project.
5. *Project Number.* Enter the project number from the PD.
6. *AR Submission.* Initiation dates.
7. *AR Approval.* Initiation dates.
8. *Design/Specification Development.* Initiation dates.
9. *Bidding.* Initiation dates.
10. *Procurement.* Initiation dates.
11. *Construction.* Initiation dates.
12. *Occupancy/Installation.* Initiation dates.
13. *Project Completion.* Dates of completion.
14. *Plan.* Enter planned date for applicable event indicated at the top of the column.
15. *Actual.* Enter actual date for applicable event indicated at the top of the column.

XYZ CORPORATION INTERNATIONAL

Schedule of Capital Projects

Division (1)   Group (1)   Operation (1)   Report (2)   Date (3)

Project Name	Project Number	AR Submittal (6)		AR Approval (7)		Design/ Specifications (8)		Bid (9)		Procurement (10)		Construction (11)		Occupancy/ Installation (12)		Project Completion (13)	
		Plan	Actual	Plan	Actual	Plan	Actual	Plan	Actual	Plan	Actual	Plan	Actual	Plan	Actual	Plan	Actual
(4)	(5)	(14)	(15)	(14)	(15)	(14)	(15)	(14)	(15)	(14)	(15)	(14)	(15)	(14)	(15)	(14)	(15)

Form 130-Y-7 (1/89)

Audits

Audits of the capital planning process and related implementation, reporting, and monitoring as practiced by Operations, Groups, and Divisions are conducted periodically by Corporate Operations for conformance to Corporate Directives, Policies, Procedures, and this capital planning and appropriations manual.

STRATEGIC REAL ESTATE AND FACILITY PLANNING

Strategic corporate real estate and facility planning is the application of the best management techniques for the operation of existing facilities and for the acquisition and disposition of facilities. With the cost to acquire and operate facilities often being second only to personnel costs, applying the same forward-thinking management principles of the core business to this major overhead component can improve the function and reduce its overall cost.

Strategic corporate facility management planning necessitates a proactive rather than reactive approach to facility management decision making. It requires vision to anticipate the problems that may materialize over time and to develop contingency solution plans today that will address those problems. The overall objectives of this approach are to:

- Minimize long-term occupancy costs.
- Avoid facility obsolescence.
- Plan interior space for longest functional and aesthetic life.
- Provide for most cost-effective and functional future expansion.
- Provide for contraction rights with greatest flexibility and least cost.
- Minimize need and cost for future remodeling.

SAMPLE—STRATEGIC REAL ESTATE/FACILITY AND MARKET POLICY

Policy:

1. The organization shall adopt a policy and a procedure to identify and designate which real estate, facilities, and markets shall be declared strategic and non-strategic.

2. Every facility in the organization's real estate portfolio shall be designated as non-strategic unless designated as strategic.

3. A strategic facility will be designated as such by the Business Operations Committee and approved by the Finance Committee. The criterion of the Business Operations Committee shall use the designation as set out below.

4. It shall be the duty of the Real Estate and Facilities Department to track such designation in the organization's Real Estate database.

Purpose:

1. Provide a consistent and rational process for the identification of strategic market locations and whether a facility should be recommended as a strategic (own/lease) or a non-strategic facility (lease) in a specific market.

2. Provide the Business Operations Committee with a process with a detailed and analytical procedure to recommend if a facility should be considered strategic or non-strategic to the Finance Committee.

3. For the Business Operations Committee to provide a formal recommendation to the organization's Finance Committee that may or may not support the strategic ownership or long-term lease, or non-strategic lease of a facility in a specific market.

4. Provide a related investment strategy for strategic facility development versus an investment strategy for non-strategic facility development.

Designation:

The procedure and schedule for such designation shall be as follows:

1. For all real estate/facilities acquired in the future:

   At such time as a new facility is acquired, the appropriation form shall indicate the recommended designation of the Business Operations Committee. Unless the Finance Committee disagrees, the recommendation of the Business Operations Committee shall apply.

2. For such real estate/facilities currently in the real estate portfolio, the schedule shall be as follows:

   Until such time as all existing real estate are designated (as set out below), when a lease is extended or renewed a designation shall be recommended by the Business Operations Committee (with a statement that the District or Region agrees or disagrees with such designation), unless rejected by the Finance Committee such designation shall apply.

3. Designation of strategic or non-strategic shall be designated by the Business Operations Committee and presented to the Finance Committee for approval under a schedule to be determined and approved.

4. The implications of such designation are as follows:

   A strategic facility is one the organization would choose to keep whether or not it lost the customer(s) for which that facility was acquired (owned or leased).

   Example: A facility in a strategic market location or a facility whose unique characteristics could help to draw new customer(s).

   A non-strategic facility is one the organization would not want to keep if the organization lost the customer(s) for which it was acquired (leased).

   Example: A facility in a non-strategic market location or a facility that does not meet long-term use, access, labor market, etc., requirements and may or may not be in a strategic market location.

5. Strategic real estate/facilities are more likely to:

   Be owned if in a strategic market and if owned is not available, obtain site/building in a long-term lease (10+ years).

   Be obtained to meet the needs of a number of customer(s)—consider a multi-facility site.

   Where leased, obtain multiple lease renewal options and expansion options.

   Where leased, obtain a purchase option where possible.

   Be located on purchased property and build a new facility where purchasing an existing facility or leasing is not the best organization business option.

   Include the planning for facility expansion as the organization business grows in a strategic market.

   Have excess leasehold improvements (above standard).

6. Strategic real estate/facility considerations/recommendations:

   Purchase real estate and/or a facility in a strategic market and, if not available, obtain a long-term lease (10+ years)

   Lease the real estate/facilities to meet the needs of a number of customer(s)—consider a multi-facility site.

   Obtain multiple lease renewal options and expansion options where leased.

   Obtain a purchase option if leased where possible.

   Purchase real estate and build facility requirements where purchasing real estate and/or a facility or leasing is not the best organization business option.

   Plan for facility expansion as organization business grows at strategic market location.

7. Non-strategic real estate/facility considerations/recommendations:

   Where possible, do not develop a one-off facility for one customer in a non-strategic market location.

   Lease as small a facility as possible to meet the customer(s) needs.

   Obtain a short-term lease (3 to 5 years).

   Obtain buy-out clause in the lease where possible.

   Spend minimal capital on the leasehold improvement and site improvements.

   Spend minimal capital on equipment—consider installing used equipment.

8. A facility may be in a strategic or a non-strategic geographic market:

   Geographically, a significant market location and a location where the organization can secure a number of major customers.

   Customer(s) want/need/will agree to be housed in this market location.

The long-term business/political/environmental climate in this market location supports the organization business model.

The organization can profitably secure business, operate logistically, and grow the business from this market location.

The organization can obtain (purchase/lease) existing real estate/facilities or purchase/build new real estate/facilities for a reasonable price in this market location.

9. Within a geographic market, the eventual real estate/facility recommendation may be to own or to lease for a long term based on financial recommendations in conjunction with the above.

    Example: The organization would most likely choose to own a facility in a strategic market. If owning is not possible, then a long-term lease is sought.

10. Within a geographic market, a site/facility may be recommended by the Business Operations Committee to be a strategic or a non-strategic site/facility based on specific market and facility criteria shown on next page.

Designation Guidelines

While the criteria utilized by the Business Operations Committee to determine a recommended status are somewhat subjective, the decision procedure and criteria guidelines are followed as shown below. Over time, more information may be added to the process and procedures for the Business Operations Committee to implement this policy and to become the process owners.

Strategic/Non-strategic Decision Process—Market and Facility Criteria

Facility Criteria: Strategic and Non-strategic Considerations (see Exhibit 2.6)

Strategic Considerations:

- Term—Many years/10 or more years = higher strategic value
- # of Customer(s)—3 or more in one facility = higher strategic value
- Service(s)—Higher number of services = higher strategic value
- Facility Attributes—Higher fit = higher strategic value
- Facility Improvements—Higher dollar value = higher strategic value

Non-strategic Considerations:

- Term—One or a few years = less strategic value
- # of Customer(s)—1 customer in one facility = less strategic value
- Service(s)—Fewer services = less strategic value
- Facility Attributes—Less of a fit = less strategic value
- Facility Improvements—Less dollar value = less strategic value
- Market Criteria: Strategic and Non-strategic Considerations

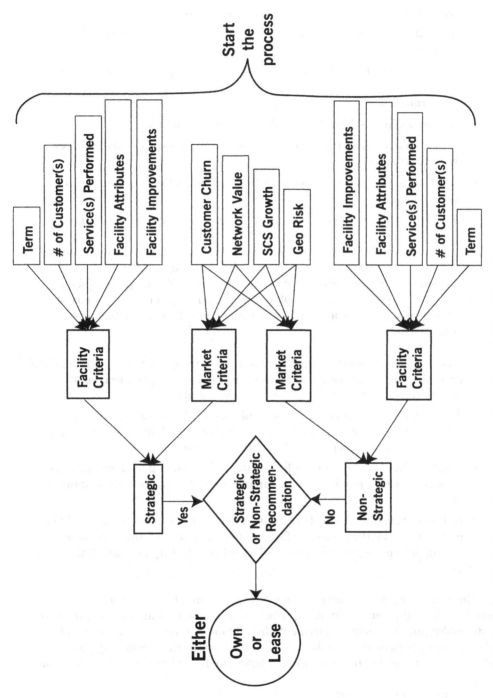

Exhibit 2.6 Facility Criteria: Strategic and Non-Strategic Considerations

121

Strategic Considerations:

- Customer Churn—Lower churn/turn = higher strategic value
- Network Value—Integral part of network = higher strategic value
- Organization Growth—Higher growth projected in that market = higher strategic value
- Geo Risk—Lower risk for facility to sit vacant = higher strategic value

Non-strategic Considerations:

- Customer Churn—Higher churn/turn = lower strategic value
- Network Value—Not integral part of network/a one-off location = lower strategic value
- Organization Growth—Lower growth projected in that market = lower strategic value
- Geo Risk—High risk for facility to sit vacant = lower strategic value

Corporations should consider the potential impact of mergers and acquisitions, reorganization, consolidation, technological change, financial flexibility, and growth when making real estate and facility decisions. The corporate facility management approach to strategic planning should help the in-house customer apply important corporate operational considerations to all dimensions of real estate decision making:

- *Customer Needs Assessment.* Current and future space needs and locational priorities should be comprehensively assessed to integrate real estate and facility considerations with other corporate needs.
- *Analysis.* Every alternative market solution to the customer's specific real estate and facility requirements should be identified and objectively analyzed based on the corporation's specific objectives.
- *Strategy Development.* A detailed strategic plan should be developed to optimize transaction results by maximizing market competition and minimizing risk.
- *Implementation.* The efforts of all members of the project team should be orchestrated by the corporate facility management executive to negotiate, document, and deliver the best real estate and facility product at the least cost.

The customer needs assessment phase is the foundation for strategic real estate and facility decision making. Working with senior management, the corporate facility management department should help determine locational and financial criteria, operational considerations, and overall corporate facility goals and objectives. During this important first phase, the following should be determined:

- Locational preferences
- Timing constraints

- Space required at occupancy
- Growth/contraction projections
- Image and character desired
- Occupancy cost objectives
- Performance criteria for building systems
- Space utilization/efficiency/adjacencies
- Optimum floor configuration and size
- Amenities required/desired

The customer needs assessment phase serves to identify practical real estate alternatives and analyze their suitability in consideration of the customer's actual business objectives.

Data Collection Process

The customer needs assessment phase can be achieved through a review of corporate information and a data collection process that includes structured interviews with selected senior management and the facility management department. The results of the interviews are tabulated in the rankings in the example matrix shown in Exhibit 2.7. The following is an interpretation of these findings from example interviews and the matrix for ABC Company:

Absolutely Important

- *ABC Company's Strategic Direction.* The interview process reinforced the strategic direction with a location and facility that fosters openness and communications, supports ABC Company's being the preferred service provider, and helps develop an image of stability.

- *Interrelationship Development.* Those interviewed felt it was important to foster group cohesiveness and to build a culture of teamwork between the groups that do not normally talk together. The facility should stimulate interrelationships, not suppress interrelationships.

- *Developing an ABC Company Image.* All those interviewed supported developing a company image of a solid organization that will ensure respect from customers and employees.

- *Floor Plan Flexibility.* Many of those interviewed who had experienced rapid growth in their departments or had a need to reorganize rated this as a key issue. The current facility is 98 percent occupied, and many of the floors are subleased with numerous fixed-wall offices. It does not provide the design flexibility that could be available with a new facility, especially if the occupied area could be in the 90 percent range.

- *Public Relations.* The general impression from those interviewed was that few in Chicago had heard of ABC Company, let alone knew what it did or was. Public relations was viewed as an effective means to support community activities and develop more public information in the media about the company.

ABC Company REAL ESTATE/FACILITY STRATEGY ISSUES	WEIGHTED ISSUES RANKINGS										
	ABSOLUTELY IMPORTANT				ESPECIALLY IMPORTANT			NOT VERY IMPORTANT			
	10	9	8	7	6	5	4	3	2	1	0
ABC Company's *Strategic Direction* - 21 Responses		X									
Interrelationship Development - 21 Responses			X								
Developing an ABC Company Image - 20 Responses			X								
Floor Plan Flexibility - 21 Responses				X							
Public Relations - 21 Responses				X							
Location - 21 Responses				X							
Informal Meetings and Conversations - 21 Responses				X							
Business/Adjacency Interrelationships - 19 Responses					X						
Building Visibility - 21 Responses					X						
Community Relations - 21 Responses					X						
Food Service Facility: On Site - 18 Responses					X						
Building Signage - 21 Responses					X						
Building Quality - 15 Responses					X						
Campus vs. High-Rise: Campus - 8 Responses					X						
High Rise - 9 Responses					X						
Building Security - 15 Responses						X					
Parking Security - 14 Responses						X					
Parking: Covered - 10 Responses							X				
Customer Training Facility: Remote - 13 Responses							X				
Travel Time - 7 Responses									X		
Elevator Service - 7 Responses									X		
Growth: None - 1 Response											X
Small - 7 Responses										X	
Modest - 11 Responses									X		
Large - 0 Responses											X
Unknown - 2 Responses											X
Health Facility - 4 Responses										X	
Access to Airport - 1 Response										X	
Access to Hotels, Restaurants, etc. - 2 Responses										X	
Customer Training Facility: On Site - 3 Responses										X	
No Opinion - 4 Responses											X
Parking: Surface - 3 Responses										X	
Food Service Facility: Remote - 1 Response										X	
No Opinion - 2 Responses											X
Campus vs. High-Rise: No Opinion - 4 Responses											X

Exhibit 2.7   Real Estate/Facility Strategy Issues Matrix

- *Location.* Almost all interviewed stated that the current location was satis-factory and that they would not want to move far from the downtown loca-tion. The area of site consideration discussed during the interviews by Susan Richards was an area bounded by South Shore/downtown area to the south, Redding to the west, Harding to the north, and IL 605 to the east. This appeared acceptable, especially as most employees who have moved into Chicago chose homes or apartments based on the current downtown location. No one interviewed felt the new facility should be near the airport.

- *Informal Meetings and Conversations.* There is a feeling that the facility must support and encourage informal meetings and conversations. One of the best ways to successfully develop an ABC Company culture is to provide the opportunity for members from different departments and backgrounds to share ideas and information informally.

Especially Important

- *Business/Adjacency Interrelationships.* The facility should promote free thinking, creativity, and work group communications, and should foster ad hoc interrelationships between various teams.

- *Building Visibility.* Some thought this was not an important issue, while others felt that having a recognizable building would help in public and community relations areas and stimulate a sense of pride for ABC Company employees. Also, this would help support customer perceptions that ABC Company is a "real" company with a presence in the marketplace and the community.

- *Community Relations.* A number of those interviewed felt that ABC Com-pany would gain more exposure from an active community relations pro-gram in lieu of building signage.

- *Food Service Facility.* An overwhelming number (18) felt that regardless of the type of facility, an onsite high-quality, affordable food service operation was especially important for employee use and for catering in-house meet-ings.

- *Building Signage.* Some interviewed felt that building signage was extremely important, while others saw no advantage to signage.

- *Building Quality.* No one interviewed felt the general quality of the build-ing, furnishings, or associated services should be reduced. The quality of the current location was acceptable, but some expressed concern that the twenty-first floor was too expensively finished. Others felt that the level was acceptable, especially to visiting overseas customers.

- *Campus versus High-Rise.* Responses on the interrelationship benefits of a campus versus a high-rise were split with 8 responses for a campus, 9 for a high-rise, and, surprisingly, 4 who had no opinion. Some who responded do not like elevators and feel they are bottlenecks. Several felt the high-rise is not conducive to a one-company environment and teamwork, whereas others felt a well-designed high-rise would be better because informal meetings would not readily be available in a campus setting. The findings are based on the definition of an urban campus.

- *Building Security.* Most felt the current building security was adequate and the current card access system was working. Escorting service after office hours to and through the parking deck was a major requirement for any location.

- *Parking Security.* The large majority of those responding felt the current covered/deck parking was preferable to on-grade parking where employees would have farther to walk to the building. The downtown area, with its large volume of shoppers, provides an opportunity for criminal activity that the current parking security appears to be handling satisfactorily.

- *Parking.* Covered parking was the clear choice. Many appreciated the location of the Building 1510 parking deck, especially its closeness to the ground-floor entrance lobby.

- *Customer Training Facility.* Many felt the customer training facility should be offsite. If it were to remain at the Corporate location, there was a desire that the new facility provide public and nonpublic space. The public space, on the first two floors, could accommodate trainees and reduce their need for elevator service.

Not Very Important

- *Travel Time.* While this item is not rated high, it was a real concern to some who felt that the time waiting for the elevator or the time traveling from Building 1510 to Building 1500 should be addressed in a new facility.

- *Elevator Service.* This was another concern for some, as the number of elevators serving the floors was not adequate for the number of ABC Company employees, tenants, and visitors to the 1510 Building. Other corporate planners have provided their high-rise facilities with more elevators than are usually found in typical tenant office buildings.

- *Growth.* Most felt that growth in their departments had peaked. Should ABC Company make another acquisition or successfully win major contracts, growth space takes on a unique requirement that may not be easily solved.

- *Health Facility.* As seen in Exhibit 2.7, a small number of those interviewed felt strongly that a health facility should be included for the benefit of employees. One nearby company is providing a facility within the four-story atrium, and another is contracting with the office park developer for use of the future office park health facility.

- *Access to Airport.* This issue is not highly rated or discussed. Customer training and the cost of bringing customer trainees to the downtown area were issues, but not critical to changing the current procedure.

- *Access to Hotels, Restaurants, etc.* Customer trainees appear to be satisfied with the shopping and restaurants downtown. There was a consensus that location should be adjacent to or near to hotels, shopping, and restaurants for customer trainees and for use by ABC Company employees.

The interviews and research show a consistent and overwhelming support for the current ABC Company strategic direction and for the development of an ABC

Company culture. Also, there is a significant conviction that the facility should support, encourage, and foster departmental interrelationship development and business/adjacency interrelationships.

The resulting Real Estate/Facility Strategy Issues Matrix (Exhibit 2.7) indicates that regardless of the type of location and facility(s) ABC Company chooses, campus or high-rise, certain items are *absolutely important* and critical to support and foster ABC Company's mission and strategic direction. Other items shown in the matrix are *especially important* and are significant in their support of the absolutely important requirements.

There is no clear choice for an urban campus or high-rise office setting. The choice may be made by default depending on economic cost constraints, the choice to own or lease via a build-to-suit, and/or location zoning and development costs. Also, community and neighborhood groups could affect development and associated scheduling and cost.

In the analysis phase, the corporate facility management department should evaluate the data gathered in the customer needs assessment phase and identify all viable market alternatives. Each option should be analyzed according to:

- Locational considerations and access
- Proximity to labor/clients/competitors
- Operational considerations
- Time required for implementation
- Total net present value occupancy costs
- Detailed construction specifications and costs
- Architectural efficiency of alternative buildings
- Comprehensive evaluation of building systems
- Site/parking/amenity evaluation

The analysis should be summarized to provide a concise and objective presentation of relevant considerations for each option. The customer can then proceed more rapidly through the decision-making process and objectively weigh the economic and functional strengths and weaknesses of each alternative. The discipline of the corporate facility management department's methodology promotes rational, methodical evaluation of alternatives to arrive at the optimum real estate and facility solution.

The importance of strategy development cannot be underestimated in the process of negotiating a real estate and facility requirements transaction. Negotiating, discussed in chapter 1, is in a number of ways exactly like playing poker. Perceptions can be as important as reality. To achieve the best terms that dynamic market conditions allow requires:

- Developing maximum negotiating leverage.
- Understanding each landlord's unique agenda.
- Recognizing changing market conditions.

- Defining risks.
- Controlling privileged information.

Project implementation requires a team of professionals skilled in negotiation tactics, real estate space programming, interior design, construction management, contract law, and facility management. When the corporate facility management team has achieved maximum landlord concessions and tenant contractual rights, the department can then utilize its project management organization to protect those gains during the important phases of design, construction, and relocation.

- Finalize lease negotiations.
- Prepare final space plans.
- Bid construction work.
- Supervise construction document preparation.
- Negotiate construction pricing and contracts.
- Administer construction to control costs.
- Negotiate contracts for furnishings and the physical move.
- Schedule the relocation.
- Punchlist construction.

Completing all the tasks that must be performed during a corporate office relocation or renegotiation is a complex and time-consuming process. The efforts of corporate and consultant professionals in real estate consulting, architecture, finance, construction, contract law, telecommunications, MIS, and facility management must be coordinated. In practice, however, the corporate facility department supports the customer in the crucial areas of lease contract negotiation, real estate acquisition, space planning and design, construction management, data and telecommunication planning and installation, and the physical relocation.

The section "Sample Corporate Facilities Procedures" in this chapter provides a detailed sample of a corporate policy and procedure process for acquiring leased or owned property and for constructing, managing, and disposing of these assets.

STRATEGIC CORPORATE FACILITY MANAGEMENT INFORMATION

After you have developed and implemented your real estate management information system, as discussed in chapter 4, and have abstracted and loaded all information on owned and leased property, you will have also developed a strategic corporate real estate information system. Using this information, you can now provide all levels of corporate management with up-to-date property, space, and cost data that may influence consolidation, location, real property, and facility strategies. Your system will be able to produce strategic planning information and reports such as those shown in chapter 4 (see Exhibits 4.2, 4.3, and 4.4).

On a micro level, the corporate facility management department should also have an integrated facility management information system (FMIS), discussed in chapter 6. This database or computer-aided design (CAD) system can easily and consistently deliver information such as the location of every department (floor and building), square feet occupied by each department, total space occupied and/or vacant on each floor and in each building, the current adjacencies on each floor, the age of each facility, and the advantages/disadvantages of each facility.

Your facility management information system should not only support day-to-day real estate and facility activities but also, and often more importantly, provide senior management with timely and effective strategic information. You and your staff are now the keepers and managers of accurate data that you can place at management's fingertips.

DISPOSITION OF ASSETS

Property, facilities, and furnishings deemed unnecessary to the pursuit of the corporation's strategic objectives should be identified as surplus and the corporation's interest therein divested. This rule should have no exceptions. For example, if a new property will better serve the corporation, the old property should not be ignored but rather considered surplus and sold. On the other hand, if the corporation does not need a property for current operations yet determines that it should be held for future use, the property is not surplus. If, to enhance corporate profitability, a corporation determines that it should lease or sublease idle space for which it has identified no current or future use, that space is *not* surplus; it is a key asset in the corporation's (presumably) new business mission, effectively or in fact. In this situation, however, the corporation should clearly state its intention to be active in the business of real estate investment (at least with respect to this property), as it is now competing in a new marketplace for profitability rather than for income that might offset the cost of carrying idle property held for a separate purpose.

The determination that a property is surplus should be made as quickly as possible because the cost of carrying idle assets can be substantial (see Exhibits 4.5 and 4.6). Moreover, in the case of owned surplus property, furnishings, and equipment, the proceeds from the disposition of these assets can be substantial and of considerable aid to the corporation's cash position. Therefore, in addition to absorbing the out-of-pocket carrying costs of surplus assets, the actual carrying cost also includes the cost of the capital not realized by virtue of the continued holding and investment in unproductive property. Finally, once the surplus determination is made, the corporation should also act quickly to dispose of the asset in the most profitable manner.

There are several ways of disposing of surplus real estate. If the asset is owned, the corporation can consider:

- Selling it as is.
- Selling it after enhancing its value by:
  Rezoning
  Development analysis and planning
  Premarketing
  Securing key adjacent parcels, etc.

- Partially divest through leasing (as a landlord).
- Donate the land and/or buildings to obtain the tax benefit.
- Abandon otherwise unmarketable property, letting ownership revert to the state by escheat (or to a local jurisdiction via a foreclosed tax lien).
- Contribute the property for an interest in another business.
- Exchange the property for other property the corporation can either use currently or bank for future use, preferably in a tax-deferred exchange.

If the asset is leased, the corporation can consider:

- Subleasing all or a part of the space (in which the corporation conveys less than its full leasehold interest).
- Assigning the lease, conveying all of its right and interest in the property to another.
- Donating the leasehold interest, if permitted, to obtain a tax benefit.
- Abandoning the premises, which would typically revert to the landlord by operation of law (though legal complications could arise here).
- Contributing the property for an interest in another business.
- Exchanging the property, perhaps in a tax-deferred exchange, for another lease the corporation can either use currently or justify banking.
- Buying out the remaining lease obligation at an effective price lower than the present value of the remaining lease payments.

There is often merit to exploring each of these alternatives. Disposing of assets always involves cost (e.g., commissions, carrying costs, deferred maintenance). Therefore, to ascertain the net benefit, some form of cost-benefit analysis should be implemented (using present value methods, if necessary). Attempting to convey an interest in real estate for a reasonable amount of consideration (money or other items of value) may also require marketing savvy. Disposing of property is much more than putting up a "For Sale" sign. Even the most straightforward disposal can be complicated. Considerations such as broker selection and fee-splitting with cooperating brokers currently receive much examination in the literature.

Although the prompt (though not hasty) disposition of surplus property, furnishings, and equipment is always in order, the facility professional should be aware that, from time to time, certain constraints may hinder the disposal of assets. The most obvious is the simple lack of a strong enough market, one in which buyers are few or marketing time is long. Sometimes, due to the nature of the property, its location, or the improvements thereon, there are no ready buyers, even in an otherwise strong general commercial market.

The specter of environmental liability under federal or state legislation enacted over the past three decades poses serious realty divestment problems for certain corporations. In years past, it was not uncommon practice, even for the federal government, to dispose of toxic waste by putting it in the ground at or near the site where it was produced. In most instances, the waste can no longer be recovered or treated, except at extraordinary expense. Nobody wants to buy trouble. Therefore, even if the property may no longer be of use to its owner, it is unlikely that it will ever be sold. Asbestos in buildings poses a similar problem. Many investors will not acquire properties that contain asbestos. Even willing buyers typically approach the matter prudently by requiring that the seller remove the asbestos at its own cost as part of a buy/sell agreement. If the cost to cure the asbestos problem exceeds the property's value, which can happen, selling the property may not be cost-effective.

Finally, even though an asset may be both marketable and in demand, there may be legal hurdles or prohibitions to disposition. Perhaps the most common prohibition for property is the right to sublet or assign leased space. Reasonably constructed lease clauses that restrict the corporate lessee from subleasing or assigning a lease to a third party by requiring the lessor's consent are often upheld if challenged in court or ignored. The court's rationale respects the lessor's interest in protecting the value and income stream from the property, which might be put in jeopardy by an unwelcome tenant. While corporate property owned in fee simple may generally be sold in spite of alienation restrictions included in the deed, other hurdles may still complicate the disposal.

CONCLUSION

The material in this chapter provides the cornerstone on which you, as a facility professional, should base the development of your Long-Range and Annual Facility Planning. This process requires that you look beyond your daily concerns and activities to the business concerns your customers are facing. Your challenge is to determine how can you support their growth, no-growth, or reduction requirements. This begins the process of providing value and helping your customers to succeed. If you and your facility staff can be at the right place at the right time with your FM services and products, then you are part of the strategic development and process for your organization. What more can you and your staff do to plan for and be ready for the immediate and long-range future?

Chapter Three

Facility Financial
Forecasting and Management

To accomplish corporate goals and objectives, management must first carefully plan and organize the activities that must be performed during future days, weeks, months, quarters, and years. These operating plans enable management to direct and control operations by providing targets to evaluate company performance on an ongoing basis. The formal process of planning these future business activities is called *budgeting*. Included in this planning, organizing, directing, and controlling should be the reasonable sorting out of capital requests from operating divisions and product groups into "go" and "no-go" decisions.

This chapter describes key elements of financial reporting and control procedures that provide companies with a framework for directing and controlling operations and for presenting real estate and facilities performance and analysis. This analysis, with the accompanying evaluation of real estate and facilities, has been receiving greater attention as businesses striving to maximize bottom-line performance recognize that the efficient allocation of company resources to capital projects is essential to the health of the company.

ANNUAL OPERATING PLAN

Chapter 2 discussed the annual operating plan (AOP), or annual budget, which represents the short-term part of the budgeting cycle, normally restricting the operating unit to plus and minus forecasts of one year (see the section "Sample Corporate Facilities Procedures" in chapter 2). The following sections discuss in detail the operational items normally addressed in the AOP.

Net Assets Employed

One of the basic measures of executive performance at the plant, operations, division, or corporate level is the effectiveness with which assets are employed to produce profit. Accordingly, the return-on-assets ratio (ROA) is one of the most significant yardsticks of performance measurement. ROA can be calculated by dividing the net assets employed, expressed by the following formula:

$$\text{Return on assets} = \text{Net income/Net assets employed}$$

The numerator, net income, comes from the income statement, or statement of operations. (After-tax cash flow comes from the statement of cash flows.) To determine the denominator, net assets employed, prepare a schedule of net assets employed. Exhibit 3.1 shows a sample schedule of net assets employed. Note that net assets employed equals the sum of (1) working capital (current assets minus current liabilities); (2) property, plant, and equipment; and (3) other assets.

The real estate department affects the schedule by additions to (acquisitions) and deductions from (surplus property dispositions) the asset base (property and plant). The more effective the real estate asset management program, the higher the ROA *ceteris paribus* (all else remaining equal), and the more accolades and rewards for the operating executive.

The net assets employed schedule demonstrates several attributes of AOP preparation and the manner in which the information is collected and presented for short-term evaluation purposes. The schedule emphasizes relative performance. The proposed AOP, divided into three-month intervals, is evaluated on this and other schedules against the two previous years' actual performance, the last quarter of the current year's forecast, the total current year's forecast, and the current long-range plan (LRP), or five-year forecast. Also note that real estate is included as property, facilities, plant, and equipment, not as current assets. This is indicative of the short-term illiquid nature of real estate and facilities. It is difficult to convert real estate and facilities into liquid assets (such as cash or other assets easily exchanged for cash) that can be used to pay current liabilities.

Real estate and facilities are often given minor attention in the AOP preparation, as many corporate executives still have the attitude that real estate and facility assets are a sort of necessary and cumbersome burden on the company's real moneymakers—production, marketing, and sales.

Cash Flow Schedule

Although the evaluative rationale remains consistent, the emphasis of the cash flow schedule is on assessing the operation's pure cash position, both actual and forecast (see Exhibit 3.2).

Note that although property, facilities, and accumulated depreciation items are excluded from formal presentations (as testimony to their noncontribution to operations-level liquidity), they are nevertheless important when companywide cash forecasts are made. As mentioned earlier, adding such items increases the asset base and dispositions reduce it. Other things remaining equal, additions reduce ROA, and dispositions have the opposite effect.

Finally, capital leases are now included under capital expenditures and consequently are receiving renewed accounting attention. Wall Street financial analysts gauge the performance of a company by analyzing the available public documents, such as the annual report and the end-of-quarter reports. There is little question that disclosures more accurately reflecting a company's financial posture will be required as the impact of the Federal Accounting Standards Board is increasingly felt. The facility management department may well play a pivotal role in the published financial posture of the company by conducting knowledgeable negotiations.

	9/30/02 Actual	9/30/03 Actual	9/30/04 Forecast	12/31/04	3/31/05	6/30/05	9/30/05	2004 B/(W) Than 2002 Forecast	2004 B/(W) Than 2005 LRP
Current assets:									
Formula cash (2.2)	$	$	$	$	$	$	$	$	$
Receivables									
Trade accounts									
Notes									
Allowance for doubtful account									
Net receivables									
Inventories:									
Finished goods									
Work in progress									
Raw materials and other									
Gross inventories									
Valuation reserves									
Obsolescence reserves									
LIFO reserves									
Other (specify)									
Net inventories	$	$	$	$	$	$	$	$	$
Other current assets	$	$	$	$	$	$	$	$	$
Total current assets	$	$	$	$	$	$	$	$	$

Exhibit 3.1 Net Assets Employed (in $ Millions)

Current liabilities:						
Trade payables						
Cash advances						
Other accrued liabilities						
Total accounts payable	$___	$___	$___	$___	$___	$___
Other current liabilities						
Total current liabilities						
Working liabilities						
Property, plant, and equipment						
At cost	$___	$___	$___	$___	$___	$___
Less accumulated depreciation						
Net property						
Other noncurrent assets						
Investments						
Other						
Total other assets	$___	$___	$___	$___	$___	$___
Net assets employed	$___	$___	$___	$___	$___	$___
Average net assets	$___	$___	$___	$___	$___	$___

Exhibit 3.1 Net Assets Employed (in $ Millions) (Continued)

135

| | 9/30/02 Actual | 9/30/03 Known | 9/30/04 Forecast | 2005 Plan | | | | | 2004 Forecast | 2004 Plan B/(W) Than | |
				1st Qrt.	2nd Qrt.	3rd Qrt.	4th Qtr.	Full Year		2004 Forecast	2005 LRP
Cash Receipts	$ ___	$ ___	$ ___	$ ___	$ ___	$ ___	$ ___	$ ___	$ ___	$ ___	$ ___
Capital gain/(loss)	___	___	___	___	___	___	___	___	___	___	___
Book value of property, plant, and equipment sold	___	___	___	___	___	___	___	___	___	___	___
Total cash from operations	$ ___	$ ___	$ ___	$ ___	$ ___	$ ___	$ ___	$ ___	$ ___	$ ___	$ ___
Cash used for:	$ ___	$ ___	$ ___	$ ___	$ ___	$ ___	$ ___	$ ___	$ ___	$ ___	$ ___
Working capital requirements:	$ ___	$ ___	$ ___	$ ___	$ ___	$ ___	$ ___	$ ___	$ ___	$ ___	$ ___
Accounts receivable	$ ___	$ ___	$ ___	$ ___	$ ___	$ ___	$ ___	$ ___	$ ___	$ ___	$ ___
Inventories:											
Other current assets[1]	___	___	___	___	___	___	___	___	___	___	___
Accounts payable	___	___	___	___	___	___	___	___	___	___	___

1 Includes changes in formula cash.

Exhibit 3.2 Cash Flow Schedule

Total working capital	$ ___	$ ___	$ ___	$ ___	$ ___	$ ___	$ ___
Cash receipts:	$ ___	$ ___	$ ___	$ ___	$ ___	$ ___	$ ___
Capital gain/(loss)	___	___	___	___	___	___	___
Other assets and liabilities requirements:	___	___	___	___	___	___	___
Capital Expenditures[2]	$ ___	$ ___	$ ___	$ ___	$ ___	$ ___	$ ___
Other assets	___	___	___	___	___	___	___
Other liabilities	$ ___	$ ___	$ ___	$ ___	$ ___	$ ___	$ ___
Total other	$ ___	$ ___	$ ___	$ ___	$ ___	$ ___	$ ___
Total cash used	$ ___	$ ___	$ ___	$ ___	$ ___	$ ___	$ ___
Net cash flow (pretax)	$ ___	$ ___	$ ___	$ ___	$ ___	$ ___	$ ___
Less: taxes of PBI dividend Allocation							
Net cash flow	$ ___	$ ___	$ ___	$ ___	$ ___	$ ___	$ ___
Exclude from presentation:							
Gross property:							
Capital Expenditures[2]	$ ___	$ ___	$ ___	$ ___	$ ___	$ ___	$ ___

2 Includes all capitalized leases; excludes project expense.

Exhibit 3.2 Cash Flow Schedule (Continued)

Cash receipts:	$ ___	$ ___	$ ___	$ ___	$ ___	$ ___	$ ___	$ ___
Capital gain/(loss)	___	___	___	___	___	___	___	___
Transfers in	___	___	___	___	___	___	___	___
Disposition of existing property at cost								
Gross property	$ ___	$ ___	$ ___	$ ___	$ ___	$ ___	$ ___	$ ___
Accumulated depreciation:								
Depreciation expense	$ ___	$ ___	$ ___	$ ___	$ ___	$ ___	$ ___	$ ___
Transfers (net)								
less:								
Accumulated depreciation on disposition of existing assets	___							___
Accumulated depreciation	$ ___	$ ___	$ ___	$ ___	$ ___	$ ___	$ ___	$ ___

Exhibit 3.2 Cash Flow Schedule (*Continued*)

Capital Budgeting Plan

After due process, the aggregate of capital dollars projected as available for corporate investment is allocated among various groups and divisions. Exhibit 3.3 illustrates a hypothetical capital plan summary schedule showing the status of new authorizations and previously approved expenditures.

Note, again, the relative nature of the schedule; AOP authorizations and expenditures are evaluated against the current LRP as well as previously established corporate AOP guidelines.

The inclusion of specific expenditures for new real estate and facilities in the AOP capital plan serves as an advance indicator to the facility management

		Expenditures		
	Authorizations	Carryover	New	Total
Group A:				
Division A	$____	$____	$____	$____
Division B	____	____	____	____
•	____	____	____	____
•	____	____	____	____
Total Group A	____	____	____	____
Group B:				
Division A	____	____	____	____
Division B	____	____	____	____
•	____	____	____	____
•	____	____	____	____
Total Group B	____	____	____	____
•	____	____	____	____
•	____	____	____	____
•	____	____	____	____
Total operations	$____	$____	$____	$____
Operations LRP	____	____	____	____
AOP over/(under) LRP	$____	$____	$____	$____
AOP guidelines	$____	$____	$____	$____
AOP over/(under) AOP guidelines	$____	$____	$____	$____

Exhibit 3.3   Capital Plan Summary

department of potential, near-term acquisition, construction, and major renovation projects. If the department has had an advisory role in AOP preparations and review, several additional benefits may result.

1. The facility management department may be aware that a proposed disposition by one division of property not yet officially declared surplus fits a proposed acquisition program of another division.

2. The facility management department can provide input on the anticipated timing and yield from projected surplus property sales.

3. The efforts of the facility management and other support departments normally responsible for equipment redeployment can be coordinated.

4. The proposed cost of facilities that are scheduled "as required" can be more accurately stated, providing the base for a better understood appropriation request.

Long-range Plan

Just as the title of the annual operating plan signifies its short-term projection cycle, the long-range plan denotes an attempt to forecast corporate business prospects over a longer period—usually five years or more. The span of interest widens significantly when corporate, company, and division leaderships create a framework within which long-term growth opportunities can be extrapolated from sequential AOPs (see chapter 2 for a detailed discussion of the LRP).

Appropriation Request

The appropriation request (AR) is the principal vehicle by which the operating division seeks operations, company, and corporate approval for virtually all proposals affecting operating division financial commitments. The AR has several objectives:

- It advises management of the full extent of the financial commitment involved in a proposed action.

- It demonstrates that the action is consistent with the fundamental business objectives of the company as stated in the AOP and the LRP.

- It proposes that the expected financial results or other considerations justify the commitment.

- It shows that the proposed appropriation is the most attractive way to accomplish the desired objectives.

No capital transaction should be started prior to the approval of an appropriation request by the authorized level(s) of management as spelled out in the financial policy. No operations, group, or division person, regardless of position, should be empowered to negotiate the acquisition or disposition of any real estate or major facilities transaction—or to sign any documents pertaining thereto—without specific authority regarding each property or facility. The right to perform these actions should be retained by the corporate office, with signature authority subject to delegated limitations.

The AR and its financial justification should be prefaced by a summary narrative addressed to succeeding approval levels, with approval signatures required at each designated level of authority (e.g., the signature approval of the chief financial executive at each level should be required on every AR). The summary letter generally includes the following:

1. A description of current operations and of how the project relates to the achievement of the divisional objectives and funding plan contained in the LRP and the AOP.

2. The purpose of the proposed project, including what the facilities, tooling, and so on, are intended to accomplish and how they relate to the operations of the location.

3. The aggregate amount to the request, the amounts previously approved, the future requirements, and the total commitment expected at the completion of the project; further, the relationship of the requested fund to previous and future requirements.

4. The amount of the request (capital plus related expense) compared to the amount included in the AOP and the LRP.

If the project was not included in the AOP or the LRP, a comprehensive statement of the project's forecasted impact on planned results should be included.

Financial justification should be presented in a series of exhibits supporting the summary letter, the required detail being determined by project complexities. Note that this chapter is primarily concerned with the philosophy of the AR and LRP process and, more specifically, with real estate department involvement in their preparation, review, and implementation, not with the procedural detail of the AR or LRP.

TREND AND RATIO ANALYSES

Management should use trend and ratio analyses to compare operating data that covers a number of periods (e.g., months, quarters, years). This analysis should be an integral part of the AOP and LRP. In addition, this analysis should be used to evaluate operating efficiency and profitability, liquidity, and risk and capital structure.

Trends can be stated in terms of percentage increases or decreases, and charted and graphed as a visual presentation of performance and changes during the period covered. Ratios are calculated by dividing one number into another and, based on company or industry standards, comparing the result with stated or anticipated goals (see Exhibit 3.4).

Ratio	Use
Short-term Liquidity	
Current ratio = $\dfrac{\text{Current assets}}{\text{Current liabilities}}$	Measure of ability to pay current obligations
Acid test ratio = $\dfrac{\text{Cash + Short-term investments + Current receivables}}{\text{Current liabilities}}$	Measure of short-term liquidity
Accounts receivable turnover = $\dfrac{\text{Credit sales}}{\text{Average accounts receivable}}$	Measures relative size of receivable balance and effectiveness of credit policies
Days' sales uncollected = $\dfrac{\text{Days in year}}{\text{Accounts receivable turnover}}$	Measures time it takes to collect receivables
Inventory turnover = $\dfrac{\text{Cost of goods sold}}{\text{Average inventory}}$	Measures relative size of inventory
Days' sales inventory = $\dfrac{\text{Inventory}}{\text{Average days' sales}}$	Measures effectiveness of inventory policies
Long-term Solvency and Capital Structure	
Debt to equity ratio = $\dfrac{\text{Total liabilities}}{\text{Total stockholders' equity}}$	Measure of relationship of debt to equity financing
Times interest charges earned = $\dfrac{\text{Net income before interest and taxes}}{\text{Interest expense}}$	Measure of protection of the return to creditors
Profitability and Operating Efficiency	
Profit margin = $\dfrac{\text{Net income}}{\text{Net sales}}$	Measures net income produced from sales
Contribution rate = $\dfrac{\text{Sales price per unit – Variable costs per unit}}{\text{Sales price per unit}}$	Measures percentage by which sales price exceeds variable costs per unit
Breakeven point in dollars = $\dfrac{\text{Fixed costs}}{\text{Contribution rate}}$	Amount of sales at which earnings are zero

Exhibit 3.4   Commonly Used Ratios

Ratio	Use
Total asset turnover $= \dfrac{\text{Net sales}}{\text{Average total assets}}$	Measures how efficiently assets are used to produce sales
Return on assets (ROA) $= \dfrac{\text{Net income}}{\text{Net assets employed}}$	Measure of operating efficiency and management performance
Return on total assets employed $= \dfrac{\text{Net income}}{\text{Average total assets}}$	Measure of operating efficiency and management performance
Return on common stockholders' equity $= \dfrac{\text{Net income} - \text{Preferred dividends}}{\text{Average common stockholders' equity}}$	Measure of profitability of common stockholders' investment
Earnings per share (EPS) $= \dfrac{\text{Net income}}{\text{Weighted average outstanding shares}}$	Measure of past, present, and future performance, and basis for comparing investment opportunities
Price earnings (P/E) ratio $= \dfrac{\text{Market price per common share}}{\text{Earnings per share}}$	Measure of market value of earnings and profitability of alternative investments
Dividend yield $= \dfrac{\text{Annual dividends declared}}{\text{Market price per share}}$	Measure of current return to investor
Real Estate	
Loan to value $= \dfrac{\text{Mortgage loan funds}}{\text{Property cost}}$	Measure of relationship of debt and equity financing
Debt service coverage $= \dfrac{\text{Net operating income}}{\text{Debt service}}$	Measure of the protection of the return to investors
Margin of safety $=$ Net operating income $-$ Debt service	Measure of protection of the return to lenders
Gross rent multiplier $= \dfrac{\text{Purchase price of property}}{\text{Annual gross rental income}}$	Measure of the purchase price of a multiple of rental income, basis for comparing investment alternatives

Exhibit 3.4 Commonly Used Ratios (Continued)

A company's AOP, LRP, balance sheet, and income statements supply information needed to perform ratio analyses. Identifying trends and calculation ratios serves a number of analytic needs, principally the following:

1. Comparing financial performance with prior and expected performance.

2. Providing financial performance data to support the planning, organizing, directing, and controlling functions of the company.

3. Performing credit analysis by commercial loan officers and suppliers' credit managers looking to extend short-term credit or working capital or long-term capital loans to a company.

4. Evaluating specific public (and private) entities by securities analysts or individual investors, comparing performance with other companies in the same industry.

Exhibit 3.4 shows some of the common financial statement ratios and other performance measures used to evaluate (1) short-term liquidity, (2) long-term solvency and capital structure, (3) profitability and operating efficiency, and (4) real estate.

Capital Budgeting Evaluation

The implementation of strategic, financial, and operational plans often requires managers to choose between two or more alternative courses of action, each requiring the commitment of significant capital resources. A typical objective of these situations is to achieve the highest return on capital invested or the greatest cost savings. While such decisions are generally made without complete information and require a great deal of business judgment, some information can be reduced to a quantitative basis. This quantitative information can and should be systematically measured, evaluated, and compared.

Capital budgeting evaluation, also called *project evaluation, project selection, capital budgeting, capital expenditure decisions,* and *investment analysis,* is used in a variety of decision-making situations. These include planning the acquisition or development of property, facilities, plant and equipment; analyzing leases; and evaluating business expansion alternatives and acquisition and disposition opportunities.

This section introduces some of the approaches used to measure financial dimensions and provide quantitative data for making real estate decisions—payback period, rate of return, and present-value models.[1] All these approaches have strengths and weaknesses; accordingly, most executives use several of them to track corporate capital expenditures and evaluate proposed projects.

[1]Portions of the information in this section are adapted from chapters 6, 7, and 8 of *Real Estate Investment: Strategy, Analysis, Decisions,* 2d ed., by Stephen A. Pyhrr, James B. Cooper, Larry E. Wofford, Steven O. Kapplin, and Paul D. Lapides (New York: John Wiley & Sons, 1989).

All the approaches require estimates of (1) cash inflows and outflows of each proposed project, (2) timing of the cash inflows and outflows, and (3) the tax impact of the alternatives on these cash flows.

A cash flow schedule for each proposed project should be prepared for this purpose (see "Estimating the Required Rate of Return" later in this section). The proposed project generates cash inflows from (1) the cash received from additional sales, (2) the financing of the project, and (3) the sale of the project in the future. Cash outflows are caused by (1) the cost of the project and the timing of the payments, and (2) the additional cash disbursements required to generate the additional sales. The net cash inflow/(outflow) is the result of subtracting the cash outflows from the cash inflows.

To determine the net cash inflow, the effects of depreciation and taxes must be calculated. Depreciation accounting allocates the cost of plant and equipment over the periods during which the assets are used. Although depreciation does not involve a cash outflow, it is a deductible in arriving at (taxable) net income and thereby reduces the amount of cash outflow for income taxes. For example, if depreciation (a noncash expense) is $100,000 during a period, net income before taxes is $100,000 less than actual cash flow. If the company's incremental federal income tax rate is 34 percent, income taxes are reduced by $34,000 for that period using the following formula:

$$\text{Tax savings} = \text{Tax rate} \times \text{Depreciation expense}$$

This $34,000 reduction in income taxes increases the project's net cash flow (after tax) by the same amount.

Payback Period

The payback period method is the most popular of the capital evaluation techniques and the simplest to use and understand. It determines the time required for the cumulative net cash inflow from a specific project to equal the related capital outlay. Based on the payback period approach, a project is deemed acceptable when cash flows are adequate to pay back the initial capital outlays in less than a specified number of years or faster than alternative projects. The payback period model is:

$$\text{Payback period} = \text{Cost of project/Annual net cash flow}$$

For example, if a proposed retail outlet requires an initial cash outlay of $100,000 for build-out and fixtures and is expected to generate $25,000 in annual net cash flow (after tax), the payback period is four years ($100,000/$25,000).

For projects with cash flows that vary from year to year, the payback period should be determined by preparing a schedule of annual net cash flows to determine when the cumulative annual net cash flows will equal the cost of project.

The primary reason that payback is so popular is its simplicity to calculate and understand. A short payback period is preferred because (1) the invested funds are at risk for a shorter period, and (2) the sooner cash is received, the sooner those funds are available for other uses.

The payback period also has weaknesses. It does not consider (1) the actual timing of the net cash flows during the payback period, or (2) the amounts and timing of cash that will continue to be received after the payback period. For an example of the latter case, consider the preceding retail example with two locations—one in a trendy area that is undergoing major changes (e.g., zoning, access) with little certainty about cash flow after the fourth year, and the second with strong prospects for this cash flow to continue for seven years. While both locations have a four-year payback period, the second location is clearly preferable.

These weaknesses are significant. Accordingly, other capital evaluation techniques should be used in addition to payback period.

Rate-of-Return Approach

The rate-of-return approach calculates returns by dividing average annual income or cash flow by the total estimated cost of the project. The result is the estimated percentage return on invested capital. This number can be compared with the estimated returns on alternative proposed projects.

The rate-of-return decision approach calculates returns by dividing average annual net income or cash flow by the total estimated cost of the project. The result is the estimated percentage return on invested capital. This number can be compared with the estimated returns on alternative proposed projects.

The rate-of-return decision approach requires management to perform the following three steps to arrive at a go/no-go decision for a project:

1. Estimate the expected rate of return.

2. Estimate the rate of return necessary to justify the investment and to compensate for the risks.

3. Compare the expected and required rates of return to make a go/no-go decision.

If the expected rate of return (ROI) is greater than or equal to the required rate of return (RROI), the project meets the company's financial criteria for a go decision.

Estimating the Expected Rate of Return

The expected rate of return can be measured in a variety of ways, not one of which is universally accepted. Four of the more popular accounting or rule-of-thumb measures that can be computed on a before- or after-tax basis follow:

1. Rate of return = $\dfrac{\text{Net income before depreciation and debt service}}{\text{Total capital invested (purchase price)}}$

2. Rate of return = $\dfrac{\text{Annual cash flow after debt service}}{\text{Cash equity investment}}$

3. Rate of return = $\dfrac{\text{Annual cash flow } plus \text{ Debt principal amortized}}{\text{Cash equity investment}}$

4. Rate of return = $\dfrac{\text{Annual cash flow plus Debt principal amortized } \textit{plus} \text{ Property appreciation}}{\text{Cash equity investment}}$

Although most managers use these measures to calculate the rate of return for a one-year period only, it is beneficial to compute them for each year of a projected holding period on a before- and after-tax basis.

Estimating the Required Rate of Return

Estimation of the required rate of return, the *hurdle rate,* against which management measures expected return is a subjective judgment that management makes on the basis of experience, the available rates of return on alternative investments, inflation expectations, and the riskiness of the property. The required rate of return should include (1) a real return—that is, a return for deferred consumption, (2) an inflation premium, and (3) a risk premium. Together, the real return and the inflation premium make up a so-called risk-free rate of return, representing the return management could expect from investments that are free of risk (e.g., Treasury bills) and of equal duration.

Management should, therefore, require that the expected cash flows from a project compensate for deferred consumption, for the expected rate of inflation over the holding period, and for the chance that actual cash flow may not equal expected cash flow.

PRESENT-VALUE MODEL

Real estate, facility, and other capital investments should be made when management expects the investment to generate sufficient cash flows to provide a return of the capital invested (the initial cash outlay) and a satisfactory return on the investment. Fundamental to understanding return on the investment is the concept of present value. The concept of present value is based on the idea that the right to receive some amount (often stated as $1) in the future (one year) is worth less than that same amount received today. The amount of the difference depends on how much can be earned on the funds if they are invested (e.g., in Treasury bills or corporate bonds). For example, if a 10 percent annual rate of return can be earned, the right to receive $1 in one year has a present value of $0.909091. This can be calculated using financial tables or a financial calculator. To confirm this present value calculation, $0.909091 invested today at 10 percent will earn $0.0909091 in one year ($0.909091 × 10%), and when the amount earned is added to the amount invested, the total equals $1.00 ($0.0909091 + $0.909091 = $1.0000001).

Present-value models are comparatively sophisticated evaluation techniques because they incorporate many of the variables not included in the payback period and rate-of-return methods. Many of these models have been adapted for computer software programs and desktop calculators to make their application easier for corporate real estate executives and students.

Discounted Cash Flow Model

The present-value model, also called the *discounted cash flow (DCF) valuation model*, emphasizes (1) defining income flows as after-tax cash flows, (2) placing cash flow in specific time periods, (3) accounting for each type of cash flow to reflect exposure to income taxes, and (4) relying on compound interest discounts. The discount rate is the required rate of return.

With the aid of financial tables or calculators, each year's net after-tax cash flow is discounted by applying a present-value factor derived from formulas based on the time value of money. The present value of each cash flow is computed, and all present values are added to get the total present value of the income stream generated by the investment during the specified holding period.

The present-value decision rule is the same as that for the traditional models: If the investment value is equal to or greater than the cost, the investment is acceptable; otherwise, the investment is rejected or modified.

Here is the basic after-tax present-value model:

$$PV_E = \frac{CF_1}{(1+R)^1} + \frac{CF_2}{(1+R)^2} + \ldots + \frac{CF_n}{(1+R)^n} + \frac{SP}{(1+R)^n}$$

$$PV_P = PV_E + PV_M$$

where:

$$PV_P = \text{present (investment) value of project}$$

$$PV_E = \text{present value of equity returns}$$

$$CF_1, CF_2, \ldots, CF_n = \text{equity cash flow; annual after-tax cash flow over the holding period } (n)$$

$$SP = \text{after-tax cash flow from sale of project (reversion cash flow)}$$

$$PV_M = \text{amount of debt borrowed to finance project}$$

$$R = \text{required rate of return on investment}$$

$$n = \text{holding period of investment}$$

The after-tax cash flow received in each period $(CF_1, CF_2, \ldots, CF_n)$ is discounted back to the point of initial investment at the required (internal) rate of return on equity (cash). The series of discounted cash flows is then totaled to measure the present value of the equity returns (PV_E). The present value of the property (PV_P) is then computed as the present value of the equity returns (PV_E) plus the amount of debt borrowed to finance the property (PV_M). If the present value of the project (PV_P) is equal to or greater than the total investment costs $(C, C = PV_E + PV_M)$, the project is acceptable using the decision rule. If PV_P is less, the project should be rejected or modified either to raise the present value of the property or to lower the total project investment costs.

Net-Present-Value Model

The net present value (NPV) of a project is determined by estimating the cash flows from the project, discounting them at a rate that represents an acceptable return, and then subtracting the initial cost of the project from the sum of the present values.

The preceding basic present-value model can be used to find the net present value of any series of cash flows by subtracting the total project cost from the present value of the property $(NPV = PV_p - C)$. The decision rule when using the net-present-value calculation is that as long as the net present value is zero or greater, the project is considered acceptable.

Internal-Rate-of-Return Model

Internal-rate-of-return (IRR) models, or discounted cash flow rate-of-return models, as they are sometimes called, are also popular tools for evaluating and comparing real estate investments. Many financial managers and analysts consider this rate-of-return measure, or some modified version of it, the proper yardstick for comparing returns between real estate and other investment opportunities, such as bonds, stocks, and annuities.

The internal rate of return is the rate, expressed as an annual percentage, at which the present value of the net cash flows equals the present value of the equity investment. IRR can be calculated on a before- or after-tax cash flow basis on either total capital or equity capital invested. Most managers prefer an after-tax model in which IRR is computed on the amount of equity investment.

The after-tax return on equity is generally recognized as the most significant measure of real estate returns because it explicitly considers the time value of money and management's ability to use financial leverage to increase the return and then shelter a portion of the return from income taxes.

The decision rule for investing is the same as the basic rule stated earlier: Accept projects that have IRRs equal to or greater than management's minimum required IRR (IRR = R, where R is the investor's minimum required IRR on equity). Projects should be rejected or modified if IRR is less than R.

RISK ANALYSIS MODELS

Internal-rate-of-return and present-value models are said to be *deterministic* in nature—that is, a specific value for each input variable is entered into the model to calculate the desired output. In contrast, a risk analysis model is said to be *probabilistic*—that is, the values of many of the input variables are uncertain and must be defined as ranges with associated probability distributions rather than as single-point estimates. A risk analysis model thus generates a range of possible returns rather than a single value; ideally, it also computes the probability of receiving different rates of return, depending on how the uncertain future unfolds.

Without the knowledge of how to deal explicitly with risk in decision making, managers typically concentrate on a few key assumptions about the future, examine a few rules of thumb, mull over the situation, and then make a decision. Although some of the risk consideration may be explicit, the mathematics of risk is often left largely to the four horsemen of the implicit decision-making apparatus: judgment, hunch, instinct, and intuition.

In contrast, financial theory attempts to make risk analysis more explicit and to suggest improved procedures. Three common methods of analyzing risk are as follows:

1. The payback decision rule, which focuses on how long it takes management to recover the initial cash investment (see "Payback Period").

2. The risk-adjusted discount rate, which attempts to account for risk by adding a premium to the required rate of return demanded (see "Net-Present-Value Model").

3. Conservative forecasts, which deal with risk by reducing forecasted returns to a more conservative level.

These three methods, however, have been subjected to increasing criticism. Although they are simple and familiar, they contain assumptions that are not only unclear but may be erroneous and could lead to decisions at odds with the company's objectives and goals. In addition, they ignore much information that could be valuable in sharpening the decision process.

Sensitivity Analysis

Additional property or project risk information can be calculated using the techniques of ratio and sensitivity analysis. Ratios can be used to measure the level and trends of risk by comparing various output data from a cash flow analysis. Popular ratio measures of risk are the debt coverage ratio and the breakeven point. In contrast, sensitivity analysis measures risk in the cash flow model by assigning different values to the input variables considered to be uncertain and then measuring their relative impact on the rate of return or other important output variables. With either ratio or sensitivity analysis technique, the project is rejected or modified if the data indicate a level of risk that is not commensurate with the expected level of return.

Portfolio Analysis

Risk analysis in real estate and facilities can be divided into two categories: individual project risk and portfolio risk. Analysis of individual project risk examines a single project and implicitly assumes the risk associated with it can be considered independently of the risk in other investments. Analysis of portfolio risk, in contrast, notes the relationships of various investments. For example, the overall risk profile of a portfolio of diversified real estate projects with different cyclical characteristics may be significantly less than the mean of the individual project risks because the contracyclical return patterns of some of the projects in the portfolio have a stabilizing effect.

INVESTMENT VALUE APPROACH

The most common technique for measuring returns for traditional real estate investment analysis is the investment value approach. Investment value is the present value of expected future net returns capitalized at the rate of return required to induce the investment in the first place. Using the investment value approach requires estimates of the investment value and investment cost for each project being considered. According to the decision rule, projects are accepted only if the investment value is equal to or greater than the investment cost.

The basic model for computing the investment value of a real estate project is the general appraisal capitalization model, as follows:

$$v = I/R$$

where

   v = investment value (present worth of future rights to income)

   I = net operating income before depreciation and debt service (rental income less operating expenses)

   R = capitalization rate (required rate of return on total capital to induce investment)

The capitalization rate (R) is determined in the same manner used to estimate the required rate of return used in the rate-of-return approaches (see "Estimating the Required Rate of Return").

Assumptions underlying this model are limiting; they are: (1) all cash outflows occur at one time, (2) income is a stabilized amount, and (3) capital is recaptured from income. Accordingly, while the generalized model of investment is a quick and easy way to calculate estimation of value, it is really appropriate for the preliminary evaluation of a project only.

FINANCIAL AND FACILITY ALTERNATIVES

At times, corporate management desires to develop a facility but lacks the expertise and, sometimes, the initial capital. A build-to-suit turnkey process may be an advantageous solution for corporations that can provide performance specifications and, in time, obtain a completed facility without having to manage the details of real estate acquisition, design, construction, and inspection. Your knowledge of these policies, available alternatives, and changes in corporate objectives can help ensure that your proposed real estate and facility solutions are responsive to current management, financial, and business requirements.

The following list identifies key financial and business items to consider in the analysis portion of buy/build decisions. You may wish to include other items that are unique to your corporation's financial, business, and legal requirements:

• Remaining first and/or second mortgage balance outstanding

• If the seller has a financial partner, the requirements to satisfy that partner

- Date for closing of the sale
- Occupancy date or certificate of occupancy date
- Options to purchase additional property; if yes, number of options, years for each option period, and dates options begin and end
- Amount of option period cost: fixed, consumer price index (CPI), percentage per year, or other
- Amount of earnest money deposit required, refundable under what circumstances, and applied to purchase price, etc.
- Seller or purchaser to pay for all, a share, or part of the closing costs, attorney fees, prorated property taxes, prorated insurance, prorated municipal special assessments, boundary surveys, legal descriptions, easements, environmental audits, soil testing, soil borings, soil engineering, zoning fees, filing and recording fees
- The contingency of sale and purchase on certain conditions that must be completed to the satisfaction of the purchaser and that may include:

  Closing takes place only after work permit is obtained from local governmental authorities

  Initial and final approval of the parent company

  Existing required zoning permitting the proposed use

  Letter from local utility providers and local governmental authorities verifying that the quantity and quality of utility and site services (water, sewer, natural gas, electricity, fire protection, etc.) are available for the specific purchaser's project at the time required

  The seller and purchaser to meet certain key dates to complete preliminary plans, to obtain design development and construction permits, to obtain construction or permanent financing or mortgage, etc.

  A bonus/penalty (monetary, etc.) if certain key dates or events are bettered or not met by either party

  Obtaining a general warranty deed

  The removal of liens, back taxes, easements, or items that prohibit or cloud clear title to the property

  Clear title and title insurance for the property

  Written confirmation from an independent testing firm that the site and adjacent sites (subsurface, surface, and airborne) do not contain soil pollutants, hazardous waste, buried obstructions, etc.

  Soil investigation report stating that the soil beneath the proposed improvements can support proposed traffic and building loads and/or site use

  Ability of the purchaser to obtain insurance

  Limit on purchaser's initial property taxes for a specified period of time

  Purchaser's ability to obtain a specified mortgage at a specified percentage rate

Purchaser's ability to obtain favorable financing or waiver of taxes from the local governmental authority

Acceptance of restrictive covenants and site developments including utilities, roads, and services by the local governmental authorities before closing

Obtaining an inspection and a bond from a local pest control company that the facility is free of specific pests (termites, mice, rats, ants, etc.)

Obtaining continued warranties for major building mechanical and electrical systems

- Onsite parking for staff and visitors; reserved parking
- Cost for parking if there is no onsite parking (if not free, try to lock in a long-term rate)
- Total purchase commitment
- Cost per square foot of property and/or building
- Mortgage payment per month, mortgage percentage for a specified period, and total mortgage cost per year
- Availability of local municipal development bonds or industrial development revenue bonds
- Operating expenses per month
- Size of property area in square feet and acres to three decimal places
- Common-area maintenance costs, especially for site utilities, landscaping, insurance, etc.
- Total building square footage (SF) being purchased and how it is calculated by the seller [as defined by Building Owners & Managers Association (BOMA) or the commonly accepted/recognized local method]
- Rentable square feet (RSF) and usable square feet (USF) per floor in the facility
- Total USF in the facility and how it was calculated by the seller (as defined by BOMA or the commonly accepted/recognized local method)
- Common-area factors in the facility (as defined by BOMA or the commonly accepted/recognized local method)
- Preceding year's taxes, this year's taxes, and next year's estimated taxes
- Tax advantages:

  No local or business taxes

  No local or state income taxes

  State revenue bonds for historical restoration, etc.
- Occupancy or use tax (established by local government)
- Insurance costs
- Porter service and costs, if any

- Written statement from seller that the site and/or building contains no sub-surface, surface, or airborne friable asbestos, contains no hazardous waste or soil pollutants, and meets ADA requirements, etc.

- Environmental site audit acceptable to the purchaser

With few exceptions, a corporation purchases property for a specific requirement. Each property must be evaluated in light of this requirement and how the corporation will use and improve the property. As discussed in detail later in this chapter, the corporation may:

- Acquire improved property and modify the property and existing facilities.

- Acquire land and make all improvements through new construction.

- Acquire a developed property and facility through a build-to-suit turnkey acquisition.

CAPITAL PROJECT TRACKING[2]

Facility management professionals, their staff, and management often find that standard corporate accounting systems cannot provide the capital budget management control, information, and timely reports they need for assistance in the consistent management of their capital project budgets and expenditures.

A *corporate capital tracking system* is defined in this chapter as a process that provides an integrated, consistent methodology to create and manage a computerized capital project budget database in conjunction with the capital budget approval process, preliminary budgets, and approved funding, purchase and change orders, invoices, payments, and project closeout in accordance with corporate capital project budget policies and procedural requirements.

The corporate capital tracking system provides a straightforward, organized system to help the department-level facility management professional manage project financial responsibilities and track such functions as:

- Capital project approval process
- Preliminary and approved budgets
- Purchase orders
- Change orders
- Invoices
- Payments
- Project close-out

[2]This information is based on the PC database software product CaProKIT(R), which was developed jointly by Edmond P. Rondeau and Applied Software Technology, Inc., Atlanta, Georgia, specifically for the corporate professional who manages and is responsible for tracking corporate capital project funds and expenditures.

The system's user-friendly database design permits the user to generate reports at any time throughout the life of a proposed or approved project. It also provides a method to ensure that *only* approved expenditures are charged against a specific project, and it produces specific reports for the project manager and corporate management to use in tracking and documenting departmental performance. Additionally, the system provides an audit trail for specific projects or departmental expenditures as well as a method of asset management after the project is complete.

The system's main menu allows access to submenus similar to the following:

- New Projects allows you to:

  Develop and revise a budget using your own or any of the system's UCIC (Universal Construction Index Code) numbers for each project budget category.

  Create a new and unique alphanumeric Project ID number. The Project ID is the basis of tracking *all* project information.

  Edit and print project budgets for review before being sent for approval.

  Print and post approved budgets to the database (see Exhibit 3.5).

- Current Projects allows you to select a current approved project and enter a submenu where the following functions can be performed using the approved Project UCIC Budget.

  Write, edit, print, and post project purchase requisitions or purchase orders.

  Write, edit, print, and post project change requisitions or change orders.

  Update project estimates.

  Enter invoice and print a disbursement approval form (see Exhibit 3.6) and enter check numbers and check dates.

- Reports allows you to selectively generate standard reports for each project by:

  Project financial status (see Exhibit 3.7)

  Cost history report (see Exhibit 3.8)

  Cost distribution by vendor (see Exhibit 3.9)

  Purchase order cost distribution (see Exhibit 3.10)

  Project financial status summary (see Exhibit 3.11)

  Asset code

  Project budget

  Outstanding purchase orders

```
                          ABC COMPANY CAPITAL TRACKING SYSTEM
      CP95-0001    RENOVATIONS TO SUITE 404, XYZ BUILDING, 234 RANDOLPH STREET, CHICAGO, IL 60339
                                      August 25, 1995
   Company Code: ABC
   Category:     RENOVATION

                                            INITIAL                      APPROVED
     UCIC       DESCRIPTION                  BUDGET                        BUDGET

     00300   CONSULTING FEES                  3,500.00                     3,500.00
     00301   CONSULTING REIMBURSABLE EXPENSES   350.00                       350.00
     DIVISION TOTAL:                          3,850.00                     3,850.00

     0200    GENERAL CONTRACTOR             105,000.00                   105,000.00
     0209    ASBESTOS REMOVAL                70,000.00                    70,000.00
     DIVISION TOTAL:                        175,000.00                   175,000.00

     06400   ARCHITECTURAL WOODWORK           1,500.00                     1,500.00
     DIVISION TOTAL:                          1,500.00                     1,500.00

     09682   CARPET                          50,000.00                    50,000.00
     DIVISION TOTAL:                         50,000.00                    50,000.00

     12220   MOVING EXPENSES                  4,500.00                     4,500.00
     12600   FURNITURE AND ACCESSORIES       32,000.00                    32,000.00
     DIVISION TOTAL:                         36,500.00                    36,500.00

     PROJECT SUBTOTAL:                      266,850.00                   266,850.00
     TAX:                                        0.00                         0.00
     FREIGHT:                                 3,000.00                     3,000.00

     PROJECT TOTAL:                         269,850.00                   269,850.00



     THIS RENOVATION WORK WILL UPGRADE THE EXISTING OFFICE SPACE
     FINISHES, PROVIDE FOR THE RE-LOCATION OF EXISTING WORK
     STATIONS AND PROVIDE POWER, TELEPHONE AND CABLING FOR EIGHT
     NEW WORK STATIONS.

     THE PROJECT IS SCHEDULED TO BEGIN ON OCTOBER 1 AND BE
     COMPLETED BY DECEMBER 17, 1995



     Prepared by:

     _____  08/25/95
     SAM JONES



     Approved by:

     _____ _/_/_  _____ _/_/_  _____ _/_/_
     WILLIAM J. SMITH      FRED A. FLEMING       TOM MOSS
```

Exhibit 3.5   Project Budget Approval Form

CAPITAL PROJECT TRACKING SYSTEM PROCESS AND SEQUENCE

The system should be based on a capital project tracking process that reflects good business practice and is familiar to the corporate project manager, staff, finance, and accounting departments and management. The system should follow the capital project budgeting and project management sequence and might appear as the following:

- *Project and Project Number.* The project manager completes a project data entry file form for the project. The department system manager then assigns the project a unique number (e.g., CP05–0001: CP for Capital Proj-

```
ID: CP95-0001      PO: 0003    INVOICE: ARGA-93-23456 DATE: 11/02/95
VENDOR: ASBESTOS REMOVAL OF IL

Purchase Order TOTAL:                  $   70000.00
Previous payments:                     $   63000.00
Previous balance:                      $    7000.00

TOTAL Invoice (less tax and freight): $    7000.00
Less Deposits:                         $       0.00
TOTAL Tax:                             $       0.00
TOTAL Freight:                         $       0.00

TOTAL AMOUNT:                          $    7000.00

AMOUNT PAID THIS INVOICE:              $    7000.00
Check Number:                              9876567898
Check Date:                                11/17/95

BALANCE REMAINING:                     $       0.00

INVOICE APPROVED AS SUBMITTED
There is retainage held on this P.O.

THIS P.O. HAS BEEN CLOSED

    UCIC: 0209  Asset code:     Title: ASBESTOS REMOVAL
    Ordered:  $   70000.00
    Received: $   70000.00
    Reference:  P.O.s 0003/000
            Invs.  ARGA-93-01-12  ARGA-93-12324  ARGA-93-23456


Comments:

THE REMOVAL OF ASBESTOS WAS COMPLETED ON 10/01/95 AND ALL
APPROVALS AND FINAL INSPECTIONS WERE OBTAINED ON 10/23/95.
FINAL PAYMENT IS BEING MADE AS THE CITY AND OTHER INSPECTION
AUTHORITIES HAVE APPROVED THE WORK AND HAVE INSURED A
CERTIFICATE OF OCCUPANCY TO ABC COMPANY IN CONJUNCTION WITH
THE GENERAL CONTRACTORS WORK.



Approved for payment: _____  _____
                          SAM JONES                        Date
```

Exhibit 3.6   Disbursement Approval Form

ect, 05 (the year 2005) for the project approved in 2004, -0001 for the first project in the year).

- *Budget.* The project manager develops a budget for the project based on the known scope of the work.

- *UCIC Number(s).* The project manager completes the Uniform Construction Index Code (UCIC) budget worksheet form for the project and attaches it to the project data entry file form. The system manager makes sure the project data and budget data are entered into the project data file using the assigned unique project number (see Exhibit 3.5).

- *Vendor(s).* The project manager provides the vendor(s) name(s) and information about the consultant(s) and vendor(s) to be used on the project.

- *Purchase Order(s).* The project manager completes the purchase order data entry form, which is based on the UCIC number(s) budget for the project, and the vendor for each purchase order. The system manager reviews the completed form and sees that the information is entered into the project

```
                              ABC COMPANY CAPITAL TRACKING SYSTEM                          PAGE 1
                                    REAL ESTATE DEPARTMENT
                                      FEBRUARY 11, 1996

                                    Project ID:CP95-0001
                                    RENOVATIONS TO SUITE 404,
                                      Manager: SAM JONES
                                          Region: N
```

UCIC	DESCRIPTION	BUDGET: CURRENT/ ORIGINAL	FUNDS COMMITTED	EST COSTS: CURRENT ORIGINAL	AMOUNT SPENT: THIS YEAR/ PRIOR YEARS	TOTAL SPENT/ OVER-UNDER BUDGET
00300	CONSULTING FEES	3,500.00	3,500.00	3,500.00	0.00	3,500.00
		3,500.00		3,500.00	3,500.00	0.00
00301	CONSULTING REIMBURSABLE EXP ENSES	350.00	338.45	350.00	0.00	338.45
		350.00		350.00	338.45	-11.55
0200	GENERAL CONTRACTOR	105,000.00	105,000.00	105,000.00	10,500.00	105,000.00
		105,000.00		105,000.00	94,500.00	0.00
0209	ASBESTOS REMOVAL	70,000.00	70,000.00	70,000.00	0.00	63,000.00
		70,000.00		70,000.00	63,000.00	0.00
06400	ARCHITECTURAL WOODWORK	1,500.00	1,500.00	1,500.00	0.00	0.00
		1,500.00		1,500.00	0.00	0.00
09682	CARPET	50,000.00	50,000.00	50,000.00	0.00	0.00
		50,000.00		50,000.00	0.00	0.00
12220	MOVING EXPENSES	4,500.00	4,500.00	4,500.00	0.00	0.00
		4,500.00		4,500.00	0.00	0.00
12600	FURNITURE AND ACCESSORIES	32,000.00	32,000.00	32,000.00	0.00	0.00
		32,000.00		32,000.00	0.00	0.00
	ADVANCE PAYMENTS/DEPOSITS:				0.00	25,000.00
					25,000.00	
	TAX:	0.00	0.00	0.00	0.00	0.00
					0.00	0.00
	FREIGHT:	3,000.00	3,000.00	3,000.00	0.00	0.00
					0.00	-3,000.00
	PROJECT TOTAL:	269,850.00	269,838.45	269,850.00	10,500.00	196,838.45
		269,850.00		269,850.00	186,338.45	-3,011.55

Exhibit 3.7   Project Financial Status Report

data file using the unique project number assigned to the project. Each purchase order number (or purchase requisition) has a unique number tied to the project number (e.g., CP9S-0001–001, where 001 is the next sequential purchase order number).

- *Change Order(s).* The project manager completes the purchase order data entry form for each change order based on a previously issued purchase order. The system manager reviews the completed change order form and sees that the information is entered into the project data file using the unique purchase order number assigned to that project (e.g., CP05–0001001-01, where 01 is the next sequential change order number).

- *Invoice(s).* The project manager reviews, approves, and codes all invoice(s) for payment with the unique project number. The system manager reviews each invoice to ensure it has been signed off, approved, and coded by the project manager; copies each invoice; sees that the information is entered into the database; and is responsible for sending the invoice(s) to Accounting for payment (see Exhibit 3.6).

ABC COMPANY CAPITAL TRACKING SYSTEM
CP95-0001   RENOVATIONS TO SUITE 404,
Project Manager: SAM JONES
REAL ESTATE DEPARTMENT
FEBRUARY 11, 1996

P.O.	VENDOR	P.O./ INVOICE DATE	INVOICE	CHECK	DATE PAID	FUNDS COMMITTED	CHARGES APPROVED AND PAID	COMMITTI BUT NO' PAID
0001/000	ASSOCIATED OFFICE DESIGN, INC.	08/19/95				3,850.00	0.00	
0001/001		09/25/95				-11.55	0.00	
0001		11/12/95	B12393-11.01	9287029827	11/15/95		3,520.24	
0001		11/25/95	B12395-11.15	9876543221	11/30/95		318.21	
PO TOTAL						3,838.45	3,838.45	0.
0002/000	METRO CONSTRUCTION	09/25/95				105,000.00	0.00	
0002/001								
0002		12/30/95	1234-D87638	9345678930	01/03/94		18,600.00	
0002		01/29/94	1234-D98273	9876544567	01/29/94		10,500.00	
0002		11/30/95	3456-0234120	94234567788	12/01/95		75,900.00	
PO TOTAL						105,000.00	105,000.00	0.
0003/000	ASBESTOS REMOVAL OF IL	09/25/95				70,000.00	0.00	
0003		12/04/95	ARGA-12-01-12	9832134567	12/05/95		17,450.00	
0003		11/01/95	ARGA-93-12324	987654678	11/02/95		45,550.00	
PO TOTAL						70,000.00	63,000.00	7,000.
0004/000	CARPETS OF IL	09/25/95				50,000.00	0.00	
PO TOTAL						50,000.00	0.00	50,000.
0006/000	OFFICE MOVERS, INC.	09/25/95				4,500.00	0.00	
PO TOTAL						4,500.00	0.00	4,500.
0007/000	NORTHSIDE OFFICE INSTALLATIONS	09/25/95	1234569025 INITIAL DOWNPAYMENT	2394879	10/10/95	35,000.00	25,000.00	10,000.
PO TOTAL						35,000.00	25,000.00	10,000.
0640/000	WOODWORK OF NORTH IL	09/25/95				1,500.00	0.00	
PO TOTAL						1,500.00	0.00	1,500.
PROJECT TOTAL						269,838.45	196,838.45	73,000.

Last approved budget: 269,850.00   08/25/95

Exhibit 3.8   Cost History Report

```
                        ABC COMPANY CAPITAL PROJECT SYSTEM                          PAGE:   1
                        CP95-0001    RENOVATIONS TO SUITE 404,
                                REAL ESTATE DEPARTMENT
                                  FEBRUARY 11, 1994
```

VENDOR NAME	VEND ID P.O. UCIC DESCRIPTION	FUNDS COMMITTED	CHARGES APPROVED AND PAID	COMMITTED BUT NOT PAID
ASSOCIATED OFFICE DESIGN, INC.	0002 0001 00300 CONSULTING FEES	3,500.00	3,500.00	0.00
	0002 0001 00301 CONSULTING REIMBURSABLE EXPENSES	338.45	338.45	0.00
	PO TOTAL	3,838.45	3,838.45	0.00
	VENDOR TOTAL	3,838.45	3,838.45	0.00
METRO CONSTRUCTION	0003 0002 0200 GENERAL CONTRACTOR	105,000.00	105,000.00	0.00
	PO TOTAL	105,000.00	105,000.00	0.00
	VENDOR TOTAL	105,000.00	105,000.00	0.00
ASBESTOS REMOVAL OF IL	0004 0003 0209 ASBESTOS REMOVAL	70,000.00	63,000.00	7,000.00
	PO TOTAL	70,000.00	63,000.00	7,000.00
	VENDOR TOTAL	70,000.00	63,000.00	7,000.00
WOODWORK OF NORTH IL	0005 0640 06400 ARCHITECTURAL WOODWORK	1,500.00	0.00	1,500.00
	PO TOTAL	1,500.00	0.00	1,500.00
	VENDOR TOTAL	1,500.00	0.00	1,500.00
CARPETS OF N. IL	0006 0004 09682 CARPET	50,000.00	0.00	50,000.00
	PO TOTAL	50,000.00	0.00	50,000.00
	VENDOR TOTAL	50,000.00	0.00	50,000.00
OFFICE MOVERS, INC.	0007 0006 12220 MOVING EXPENSES	4,500.00	0.00	4,500.00
	PO TOTAL	4,500.00	0.00	4,500.00
	VENDOR TOTAL	4,500.00	0.00	4,500.00
NORTHSIDE OFFICE INSTALLATIONS	0008 0007 12600 FURNITURE AND ACCESSORIES	32,000.00	0.00	32,000.00
	FREIGHT TOTAL	3,000.00	0.00	3,000.00
	ADVANCE PAYMENTS	(	25,000.00)	
	PO TOTAL	35,000.00	25,000.00	10,000.00
	VENDOR TOTAL	35,000.00	25,000.00	10,000.00
PROJECT TOTAL		269,838.45	196,838.45	73,000.00

```
  Last approved budget:    269,850.00  08/25/95
```

Exhibit 3.9   Cost Distribution by Vendor Report

- *Report(s)*. The system manager reviews and manages the printing and distribution of reports as required to the project manager and monthly as required by management (see Exhibits 3.7–3.11).

DISPOSING OF ASSETS

Corporations change management or direction, grow or decline. As your corporation goes through these cycles, you may find that leased space has been vacated or owned property is now surplus and the space, property, or furnishings, or equipment is not required to meet the corporation's immediate business plans. Your corporation or customer may wish to keep the vacant leased space or surplus

ABC COMPANY CAPITAL TRACKING SYSTEM
CP95-0001   RENOVATIONS TO SUITE 404,
REAL ESTATE DEPARTMENT
FEBRUARY 11, 1994

P.O.	VEND ID	UCIC	DESCRIPTION	VENDOR NAME	FUNDS COMMITTED	CHARGES APPROVED AND PAID	COMMITTED BUT NOT PAID
0001/000	0002	00300	CONSULTING FEES	Associated OFFICE DESIGN INC.	3,500.00	3,500.00	0.00
0001/000	0002	00301	CONSULTING REIMBURSABLE EXPENSES		338.45	338.45	0.00
P.O. TOTAL					3,838.45	3,838.45	0.00
0002/000	0003	0200	GENERAL CONTRACTOR	METRO CONSTRUCTION	105,000.00	105,000.00	0.00
P.O. TOTAL					105,000.00	105,000.00	0.00
0003/000	0004	0209	ASBESTOS REMOVAL	ASBESTOS REMOVAL OF IL	70,000.00	63,000.00	7,000.00
P.O. TOTAL					70,000.00	63,000.00	7,000.00
0004/000	0006	09682	CARPET	CARPETS OF IL	50,000.00	0.00	50,000.00
P.O. TOTAL					50,000.00	0.00	50,000.00
0006/000	0007	12220	MOVING EXPENSES	OFFICE MOVERS, INC.	4,500.00	0.00	4,500.00
P.O. TOTAL					4,500.00	0.00	4,500.00
0007/000	0008	12600	FURNITURE AND ACCESSORIES	NORTHSIDE OFFICE INSTALLATIONS	32,000.00	0.00	32,000.00
(ADVANCE PAYMENTS:						25,000.00)	
FREIGHT:					3,000.00	0.00	3,000.00
P.O. TOTAL					35,000.00	25,000.00	10,000.00
0640/000	0005	06400	ARCHITECTURAL WOODWORK	WOODWORK OF NORTH IL	1,500.00	0.00	1,500.00
P.O. TOTAL					1,500.00	0.00	1,500.00
PROJECT TOTAL					269,838.45	196,838.45	73,000.00

Last approved budget: 269,850.00 08/25/95

Exhibit 3.10   Purchase Order Cost Distribution Report

REAL ESTATE DEPARTMENT
FEBRUARY 11, 1994

Project Manager: SAM JONES

PROJECT	BUDGET: CURRENT/ ORIGINAL	FUNDS COMMITTED	EST COSTS: CURRENT ORIGINAL	AMOUNT SPENT: THIS YEAR/ PRIOR YEARS	TOTAL SPENT/ OVER-UNDER BUDGET
BRANCH RELATED REGION: CATEGORY:					
CP95-0001	269,850.00	269,838.45	269,850.00	10,500.00	196,838.45
RENOVATIONS TO SUITE 404,	269,850.00		269,850.00	186,338.45	-3,011.55

Exhibit 3.11   Project Financial Status Report

owned property and be willing to carry the ongoing costs if there is or may be a business need for it in the near future.

If there are no business plans to use the vacant leased space or surplus owned property, the large monthly carrying expenses and the accompanying legal issues will usually dictate timely disposal of the space or property. You and your customer should review the financial, legal, and market issues with your legal counsel and real estate broker and then adopt a disposal marketing strategy that could include one of the following:

- Locate another in-house division or department that could use the space and/or property and is willing to take over all or part of the remaining obligation.

- Sublease all or part of the space or property, if leased.

- Negotiate a buyout of the remaining lease obligation.

- Sell, if owned.

- Lease all or part of the space or property, if owned.

- Donate, if owned, to a governmental agency, a nonprofit organization, or a university or college where a tax credit could benefit your corporation and customer.

If another in-house user cannot be located, listing the space and/or property with a real estate broker may be chosen as a disposal strategy. Choose the listing real estate broker with the same care as the leasing or purchase real estate broker, as your corporation or customer is now a landlord or seller, with the space or property competing with offerings of landlords and/or sellers in the local market. A subleasing model of before-tax income or loss or an acceptable sales price should be developed according to corporate policies and procedures and what you, your customer, and the listing broker agree is realistic based on market conditions (see Exhibits 3.12 and 3.13).

The timing and associated economic/real estate activity will indicate whether the market is a seller's or a buyer's market. When you are subleasing, leasing, or selling space or property, market conditions and how anxious your customer is to divest the space or property are often a function of the time it will take to dispose of the asset.

The expense items for subleasing space or leasing property include the lease or mortgage payments for the remaining term of the obligation, insurance, a percentage commission for the listing real estate broker; space planning fees, permits, construction and depreciation costs, and income taxes. The expense items for selling a property include the mortgage payments, the cost of capital or interest, taxes and insurance, maintenance and operating costs, service contracts, a percentage commission to the listing real estate broker; and, often, a part of the closing costs. Once you have found a tenant to sublease your surplus leased property, a sublease agreement should be prepared based on your prime lease and the lessor's approval.

The Sublease Analysis shown in Exhibit 3.13 is designed for a spreadsheet file named "XYZBLDG1.WK1." The sublease analysis spreadsheet is specifically designed to be used as a tool with PC spreadsheet software to help develop a model income/(loss) for a sublease property based on the local real estate market, competition, the size, and the time remaining on the current lease. You (the sublandlord) can run numerous iterations against the model to develop a subleasing strategy and run a pro forma against each proposal for each proposed subtenant; these moves will help you make an informed management and real estate decision.

To use this spreadsheet, you must have a basic knowledge of a spreadsheet software package (Lotus, Excel, etc.) and of the modification and/or development of the spreadsheet formulas. Also, you should be familiar with real estate terminology and with lease and sublease analysis techniques.

The spreadsheet is set up based on subleasing office space. You must be able to supply all the variables in the items in the upper part of the spreadsheet.

- If an item does not apply to a particular analysis, enter zero (0) in the variable cell in lieu of leaving a blank.
- If an item or items do not appear on this spreadsheet and you want to include them as a separate line item (e.g., electricity or real estate taxes), new items can be added. You must be aware of how these items will affect the existing formulas and the analysis results. Items in the spreadsheet below the line of asterisks should also be modified to suit each analysis.
- If the sublease term is less than six years, which most are, it is necessary to modify the initial year (cell) formula to reflect the specific starting month and date of the sublease. The sixth-year (cell) formula assumes a partial year, which must be modified to meet the particular sublease termination date.
- Each year of the analysis starting with Cell _____ may need to be modified manually to reflect the particular lease term.

Based on the variable items and the modifications to the cell formulas, the spreadsheet analysis is executed automatically as the input variables are entered. It is recommended that you check initial results manually to ensure that modifications to the formulas reflect the correct sublease terms and expected results of income/(loss).

The sublease analysis spreadsheet provides an organized methodology for establishing an individualized subleasing program. It will help you understand how the cash flow and income (or loss) of each sublease will affect your company's bottom line. Because the spreadsheet is not fully automated, you must spend time reviewing how it works, learning the formulas, and tailoring modifications to take advantage of the power and speed of this computer-aided real estate tool.

Exhibit 3.12   Sublease Analysis

```
****************************************************************************************************
XYZBLDG1.WK1              SUBTENANT:  C.O.D. CORPORATION - SUBLEASING P & L          (NAME OF PREPARER)
PAGE 1                    SUBLANDLORD: ABC COMPANY - FINANCIAL ANALYSIS #1           (DATE ANALYSIS MADE)
****************************************************************************************************
```

Building & Address: XYZ BUILDING, 1234 MAIN STREET	ABC COMPANY Lease Information:
City, St. & Zip: CHICAGO, IL. 50515-1234	Lease Ends: OCTOBER 31, 1998
Sublease Fl.(s): 7TH FLOOR (SUITE 703)	Total Leased Area: 25,250 Rentable Square Feet (R.S.F.)
Subleased Area: 17,022 Rentable Square Feet (R.S.F.)	Rentable To 22,250 Usable Square Feet (U.S.F.)
15,000 Usable Square Feet (U.S.F.)	Usable Factor: 88.119%
Subl. Start Date: NOVEMBER 1, 1992	Current Lease Rate: $19.00 /R.S.F.
Subl.Term/End Date: 72 MONTHS - OCTOBER 31, 1998	Lease Rent Increase: 104.50% Per Lease Year
Sublease Rate: $20.00 /R.S.F.	Income Tax Rate: 0.34 % Of Before Tax Income Or (Loss)
Subl. Allowances: $15.00 /R.S.F. For Upfit	Net Present Value: 0.08 %
Subl. Rent Increase: 103.50% PER SUBLEASE YEAR	Sublandlord Upfit: $0.00 /RSF For Multi-Tenant Construction
Subl.Rent Abatement: 12 MOS. - RENT STARTS NOV. 1, 1993.	Brokerage Commission 6.00%
2 MOS. IN 1992	Space Planning, Etc. $0.75 /RSF
10 MOS. IN 1993	Park. Sp. Cost Incr. 103.50% Per Lease Year
# of Parking Spaces: 45 Cost/Sp./Mo $30 THRU 10/93	# of Parking Spaces: 67 Cost/Sp./Mo. $30 Thru 10/93

	Year 0 Costs	1992 (2 MO.)	1993 (12 MO.)	1994 (12 MO.)	1995 (12 MO.)	1996 (12 MO.)	1997 (12 MO.)	1998 (10 MO.)	TOTAL (6 YRS 0 MO)
Sublease Revenues:									
Rent Income		$56,742	$342,435	$354,421	$366,825	$379,664	$392,952	$336,956	$2,229,996
Parking Income		$2,700	$16,295	$16,865	$17,455	$18,066	$18,698	$16,034	$106,112
Less Rent Abatement		($56,742)	($283,708)	$0	$0	$0	$0	$0	($340,449)
NET REVENUES		$2,700	$75,022	$371,285	$384,280	$397,730	$411,651	$352,990	$1,995,659
EFFECTIVE RENT $19.54 /R.S.F.									
Tenant Part Of Upfit Cost:	$0								
ABC COMPANY EXPENSES:									
Space Planning, Etc.	$12,767								$12,767
Brokerage Fee	$113,373								$113,373
Upfit/Depreciation	$255,337	$7,093	$42,556	$42,556	$42,556	$42,556	$42,556	$35,463	$255,337
Rent & Oper Expense	N/A	$53,904	$325,853	$340,516	$355,839	$371,852	$388,585	$335,874	$2,172,424
Parking Expense	N/A	$2,700	$16,295	$16,865	$17,455	$18,066	$18,698	$16,034	$106,112
TOTAL EXPENSES	$381,477	$63,697	$384,703	$399,937	$415,851	$432,474	$449,840	$387,371	$2,660,013
NET EFF. RENT $16.91 /R.S.F.									

```
CUM. BEFORE TAX INC.(LOSS): ($126,140) ($187,137) ($496,818) ($525,470) ($557,040) ($591,784) ($629,973) ($664,354)
CUM. YEARLY INCOME (LOSS):       $0     ($187,137) ($309,681)  ($28,652)  ($31,570)  ($34,744)  ($38,189)  ($34,382)
```

BEFORE TAX INCOME OR (LOSS):									($664,354)
									============
INCOME TAXES:									$225,880
NET INCOME OR (LOSS):									($438,474)
Tenant Improvements:	($255,337)								
Add Back Depreciation:		$7,093	$42,556	$42,556	$42,556	$42,556	$42,556	$35,463	$255,337
NET CASH FLOW:	($255,337)	$7,093	$42,556	$42,556	$42,556	$42,556	$42,556	$35,463	($183,137)
NPV (THRU 10/31/98) =	($157,010)								

```
****************************************************************************************************
                                             PROJECTED INCOME OR (LOSS) =        ($664,354)
                            INITIAL MODEL FOR 7TH FLOOR PROJECTED INCOME OR (LOSS) =  ($670,354)
                                                                                 -----------
                                             ADDITIONAL INCOME OR (LOSS) =           $6,000
****************************************************************************************************
```

Exhibit 3.13   Sublease Analysis Spreadsheet

AGREEMENT OF SUBLEASE

This Sublease Agreement is made and entered into this 5th day of December, 2004, by and between ABC Company, a Delaware corporation, ("Landlord"), and Ross, Jones and Smith, Inc., a Delaware corporation ("Tenant").

WITNESSETH:

WHEREAS, Landlord is itself a tenant under that certain Lease dated August 10, 1991, entered into between ABC Company and West Wacker Towers, L.P. (Prime Landlord);

WHEREAS, Article 7 of the Prime Lease permits Landlord to sublease all or a portion of the demised premises on the prior express written consent of the Prime Landlord; and

WHEREAS, Tenant and Landlord desire to obtain the Prime Landlord's consent hereto:

NOW THEREFORE, in consideration of the agreements hereinafter set forth, the parties hereto mutually agree as follows:

1. DEMISED PREMISES. Landlord hereby leases to Tenant, and Tenant hereby leases from Landlord, certain space (the "demised premises") on the second floor of the Building (the "Building") situated at 4425 West Wacker Drive, Chicago, Cook County, Illinois 60630, assigned Suite 201 (outlined on Exhibit A, attached hereto). The demised premises constitute approximately 2,000 square feet of net rentable area, which constitutes approximately 1,800 square feet of net usable area.

2. TERM. This Sublease agreement shall be for a term of two (2) years and three CD months beginning on the Sublease Commencement Date, which shall be January 1, 2006, and ending on March 31, 2008 (the "Expiration Date"), provided, however, that in the event the demised premises are not substantially completed in accordance with the provisions of Article 6 by said date, for any reason or cause, then the Sublease Commencement Date shall be earlier of (i) the date the demised premises are occupied by Tenant, or (ii) the day which is fifteen (15) days after Landlord has certified in writing to Tenant that all work to be performed by Landlord pursuant to Article 6 has been substantially completed, in which event Landlord shall not be liable or responsible for any claims, damages, or liabilities by reason of such delay, nor shall the obligations of Tenant hereunder be affected. In the event the demised premises are occupied by Tenant prior to the Sublease Commencement Date, such tenancy shall be deemed to be by the day, and Tenant shall be responsible for payment of monthly rental, for each day of such occupancy prior to the Sublease Commencement Date. Within thirty (30) days after the Sublease Commencement Date, Landlord and Tenant shall execute Exhibit D, attached

Exhibit 3.14 Sublease Agreement Sample for ABC Company

hereto and made a part hereof by reference confirming the dates of commencement and expiration of the term of this Sublease Agreement in accordance with the provisions of this Article 2.

3. <u>USE</u>. Tenant will use and occupy the demised premises solely in accordance with the terms of the Prime Lease. Tenant will not use or occupy the demised premises for any unlawful, disorderly, or hazardous purpose, and will not manufacture any commodity or prepare or dispense any food or beverage therein without Landlord's and Prime Landlord's written consent. Tenant shall comply with all present and future laws, ordinances, regulations and orders of all governmental authorities having jurisdiction over the demised premises.

4. <u>RENTAL</u>. Tenant shall pay to Landlord an annual rental of <u>Forty Thousand</u> Dollars (<u>$40,000.</u>), payable in monthly installments, in advance, on the first day of each calendar month during the term of this Sublease, equal to <u>Three Thousand Three Hundred Thirty-Three and 33/100</u> Dollars (<u>3,333.33</u>) per month for the period beginning with the Sublease Commencement Date through <u>December 31, 2006</u>. Beginning on the first anniversary date of the Sublease Commencement Date and at each anniversary date thereafter, the annual rental due each year shall be increased by *4.5%*. If the Sublease Commencement Date occurs on a day other than the first day of a month, rent from the Sublease Commencement Date until the first day of the following month shall be prorated at the rate of one-thirtieth (1/30th) of the monthly rental for each such day, payable in advance on the Sublease Commencement Date. Tenant will pay said rent without demand, deduction, setoff, or counterclaim by check to Landlord at <u>4425 West Wacker Drive, Suite 200, Chicago, IL 60630</u> or to such other party or address as Landlord may designate by written notice to Tenant. If Landlord shall at any time or times accept said rent after it shall become due and payable, such acceptance shall not excuse delay upon subsequent occasions, or constitute a waiver of any or all of Landlord's rights hereunder.

5. <u>DEPOSITS</u>. Upon execution of this Sublease, Tenant shall deposit with Landlord the sum of <u>Three Thousand Three Hundred Thirty-Three and 33/100</u> Dollars (<u>$3,333.33</u>) as a deposit to be applied against the first month's rent. In addition, Tenant shall pay to Landlord as a security deposit the sum of <u>Three Thousand Three Hundred Thirty-Three and 33/100</u> Dollars (<u>$3,333.33</u>). Such security deposit (which shall bear interest at the then market rate) shall be considered as security for the performance by Tenant of all of Tenant's obligations under this Sublease. Upon expiration of the term hereof, Landlord shall (provided that Tenant is not in default under the terms hereof) return and pay back such security deposit including interest to Tenant, less such portion thereof as Landlord shall have appropriated to cure any default by Tenant. In the event of any default by Tenant hereunder, Landlord shall have the right, but shall not be obligated, to apply all or any portion of the security deposit to cure such default, in which event Tenant shall be obligated to deposit with Landlord upon demand therefore the

Exhibit 3.14   Sublease Agreement Sample for ABC Company (Continued)

amount necessary to restore the security deposit to its original amount and such amount shall constitute additional rent hereunder.

6. <u>WORK LETTER AGREEMENT</u>. Landlord will finish the demised premises in accordance with the provisions set forth in Exhibit B, attached hereto and made a part hereof. Landlord shall have no obligation to make any alterations or improvements to the demised premises except as set forth in Exhibit B.

7. <u>MAINTENANCE BY TENANT</u>. Tenant shall keep the demised premises and the other fixtures and equipment therein in clean, safe, and sanitary condition, will take good care thereof, will suffer no waste or injury thereto, and will, at the expiration or other termination of the term of this Sublease, surrender the same, broom clean, in the same order and condition in which they are on the commencement of the term of this Sublease, except for ordinary wear and tear and damage by the elements, fire, and other casualty not due to the negligence of the Tenant, its employees, invitees, agents, contractors, and licensees: and upon such termination of this Sublease, Landlord shall have the right to reenter and resume possession of the demised premises. Tenant shall make all repairs to the demised premises caused by any negligent act or omission of Tenant, or its employees, invitees, agents, contractors, and licensees.

8. <u>ALTERATIONS</u>. Tenant will not make or permit anyone to make any alterations, additions, or improvements, structural or otherwise (hereinafter referred to as "Alterations"), in or to the demised premises or the Building without the prior written consent of Landlord and Prime Landlord, which consent shall not be unreasonably withheld. If any mechanic's lien is filed against the demised premises, or the Building for work or materials done for, or furnished to, Tenant (other than for work or materials supplied by Landlord), such mechanic's lien shall be discharged by Tenant within ten (10 days) thereafter, at Tenant's sole cost and expense, by the payment thereof or by the filing of any bond required by law. If Tenant shall fail to discharge any such mechanic's lien, Landlord may, at its option, discharge the same and treat the cost thereof as additional rent hereunder, payable with the monthly installment of rent next becoming due and such discharge by Landlord shall not be deemed to waive the default of Tenant in not discharging the same.

Tenant will indemnify and hold Landlord and Prime Landlord harmless from and against any and all expenses, liens, claims, or damages to person or property which may or might arise by reason of the making by Tenant of any Alterations. If any Alteration is made without the prior written consent of Landlord and Prime Landlord, Landlord may correct or remove the same, and Tenant shall be liable for all expenses so incurred by Landlord. All Alterations in or to the demised premises or the building made by either party shall immediately become the property of the Landlord and shall remain upon and be surrendered with the demised premises as a part thereof at the end of the term hereof; provided, however, that if Tenant is not in default in the performance if any of its obligations under this Sublease, Tenant shall have the right to remove, prior to the expi-

Exhibit 3.14   Sublease Agreement Sample for ABC Company (*Continued*) ration of the term of this Sublease, all movable furniture, furnishings, or equipment installed in the demised premises at the expense of Tenant, and if such property of Tenant is not removed by Tenant prior to the expiration or termination of this Sublease, the same shall at Landlord's option, become the property of the Landlord and shall be surrendered with the demised premises as a part thereof. Should Landlord elect that Alterations installed by Tenant be removed upon the expiration or termination of this Lease, Tenant shall remove the same as Tenant's sole cost and expense, and if Tenant fails to remove the same, Landlord may remove the same at Tenant's expense and Tenant shall reimburse Landlord for the cost of such removal together with any and all damages which Landlord may sustain by reason of such default by Tenant, including cost of restoration of the premises to their original state, ordinary wear and tear excepted.

9. <u>INDEMNITY AND PUBLIC LIABILITY INSURANCE</u>. Tenant will indemnify and hold harmless Landlord from and against any loss, damage, or liability occasioned by or resulting from any default hereunder or any willful or negligent act on the part of Tenant, its agents, employees, contractors, licensees, or invitees. Tenant shall obtain and maintain in effect at all times during the term of this Sublease a policy of comprehensive public liability insurance naming Landlord, Prime Landlord, and any mortgagee of the Building as additional insureds, protecting Prime Landlord, Landlord, Tenant, and any such mortgagee against any liability for bodily injury, death, or property damage occurring upon, in or about any part of the Building or the demised premises arising from any of the items and coverage as set forth in the Prime Lease against which Tenant is required to indemnify Landlord with such policies to afford protection to the limits and coverage as set forth in the Prime Lease.

10. <u>RIGHT OF LANDLORD TO CURE TENANT'S DEFAULT: LATE PAYMENTS</u>. If Tenant defaults in the making of any payment or in the doing of any act herein required to be made or done by Tenant, then after ten (10) days' notice from Landlord, Landlord may, but shall not be required to, make such payment or do such act, and the amount of the expense thereof, if made or done by Landlord, with interest thereon at the rate of the prime interest rate charged by the <u>Chicago National Bank</u> during the period of such default plus <u>two</u> percent (<u>2.%</u>) per annum (hereinafter referred to as the "Default Interest Rate"), from the date paid by Landlord, shall be paid by Tenant to Landlord and shall constitute additional rent hereunder due and payable with the next monthly installment of rent; but the making of such payment or the doing of such act by Landlord shall not operate to cure such default or to estop Landlord from the pursuit of any remedy to which Landlord would otherwise be entitled. If Tenant fails to pay any installment of rent on or before the first day of the calendar month when such installment is due and payable, such unpaid installment shall bear interest at the rate of the Default Interest Rate, from the date such installment became due and payable to the date of payment thereof by Tenant. Such interest shall constitute additional rent hereunder due and

Exhibit 3.14   Sublease Agreement Sample for ABC Company (Continued)

payable with the next monthly installment of rent. In addition, Tenant shall pay to Landlord, as a late charge, five percent (5%) of any payment herein required to be made by Tenant which is more than ten (10) days late or cover the costs of collecting amounts past due.

11. <u>NO REPRESENTATION BY LANDLORD</u>. Neither Landlord, Prime Landlord, nor any agent or employee of Landlord or Prime Landlord has made any representations or promises with respect to the demised premises or the building except as herein expressly set forth, and no rights, privileges, easements, or licenses are granted to Tenant except as herein set forth. Tenant, by taking possession of the demised premises, shall accept the same as is, and such taking of possession shall be conclusive evidence that the demised premises are in good and satisfactory condition at the time of such taking of possession.

12. <u>BROKERS</u>. Tenant represents and warrants that it has not employed any broker other than <u>Professional Brokerage Company and Mid-Town Realty, Inc.</u>, in carrying on the negotiations relating to this Sublease. Tenant shall indemnify and hold Landlord harmless from and against any claim for brokerage or other commission arising against any claim for brokerage or other commission arising from or out of any breach of the foregoing representation and warranty. Any representation or statement by a leasing company or other third party (or employee thereof) engaged by Landlord as an independent contractor which is made with regard to the demised premises or the Building shall not be binding upon Landlord or serve as a modification of this Lease and Landlord shall have no liability therefore, except to the extent such representation is also contained herein or is approved in writing by Landlord.

13. <u>NOTICE</u>. All notices or other communications hereunder shall be in writing and shall be deemed duly given if delivered in person or sent by certified or registered mail, return receipt requested, first class, postage prepaid, (i) if to Landlord:

<u>ABC Company</u>
<u>4425 West Wacker Drive</u>
<u>Suite 200</u>
<u>Chicago, IL 60630</u>
<u>Attention: Facility Management Department</u>

and (ii) if to Tenant:

<u>Ross, Jones and Smith, Inc.</u>
<u>4425 West Wacker Drive</u>
<u>Suite 201</u>
<u>Chicago, IL 60630</u>
<u>Attention: President</u>

unless notice of change of address is given pursuant to the provisions of this Article 13.

Exhibit 3.14 **Sublease Agreement Sample for ABC Company** *(Continued)*

14. <u>COVENANTS OF LANDLORD</u>. Landlord covenants that it has the right to make this Sublease and that if Tenant shall pay the rental and perform all of Tenant's obligations under this Sublease, Tenant shall, during the term hereof, freely, peaceably, and quietly occupy and enjoy the full possession of the demised premises without molestation or hindrance by Landlord or any party claiming through or under Landlord. In the event of any sale or transfer of Landlord's interest in the demised premises, the covenants and obligations of Landlord hereunder accruing after the date of such sale or transfer shall be imposed upon such successor-in-interest (subject to the provisions of Article 22 of the Prime Lease) and any prior Landlord shall be freed and relieved of all covenants and obligations of Landlord hereunder accruing after the date of such sale or transfer.

15. <u>LIEN FOR RENT</u>. Tenant hereby grants to Landlord a lien on property of Tenant now or hereafter placed in or on the demised premises (except such part of any property as may be exchanged, replaced, or sold from time to time in the ordinary course of business), and such property shall be and remain subject to such lien of Landlord for payment of all rent and all other sums agreed to be paid by Tenant herein or for services or costs relating to the demised premises that Tenant may hereafter agree to pay to Landlord. Said lien shall be in addition to and cumulative of the Landlord's lien rights provided by law.

16. <u>PARKING</u>. Landlord grants to Tenant the right to park <u>six (6)</u> automobiles for no additional monthly rental for the first year of the Prime Lease term, and Landlord grants to Tenant the right to park <u>one (1)</u> automobile for no additional rental for the balance of the Sublease term on parking levels 1, or 2 as set forth in Exhibit E. Starting <u>January 1, 2007,</u> through the balance of the term of the Sublease, Landlord grants to Tenant the right to park five (5) automobiles for additional rent, which shall be the then market rate for comparable parking in a Class A office building in the Chicago, Illinois, metropolitan area. Nothing herein shall be construed to grant to tenant the exclusive right to a particular parking space, and as appropriate, Landlord may rearrange parking spaces or may provide assigned spaces, and may provide attendant parking or such other system of management of parking as it deems necessary. Landlord shall not be liable to Tenant, its invitees, employees, or guests because of failure to promptly remove snow, ice, or water from the parking area and/or structure or because of any injury or damage that may be sustained due to holes or defects that may develop or arise in the parking areas or due to any inconvenience that may arise due to temporary closure of parking areas for repair, maintenance, or snow, ice, or water removal.

17. <u>ENTIRE AGREEMENT</u>. This Sublease, together with the Exhibits and any Addenda attached hereto, contain and embody the entire agreement of the parties hereto, and no representations, inducements, or agreements, real or otherwise, between the parties not contained in this Sublease, Addenda (if any), and Exhibits shall be of any

Exhibit 3.14   Sublease Agreement Sample for ABC Company *(Continued)*

force or effect. This Sublease may not be modified, changed, or terminated in whole or in part in any manner other than by an agreement in writing duly signed by both parties hereto.

18. <u>DEFINED TERMS</u>. All terms used herein which are defined in the Prime Lease shall have the same meaning as in the Prime Lease.

19. <u>ASSUMPTION OF OBLIGATIONS BY TENANT</u>. Tenant hereby expressly assumes each and every obligation of Landlord set forth in the Prime Lease (Exhibit G) with respect to the demised premises to the same extent as if Tenant had directly entered into a lease with the Prime Landlord for said demised premises. Notwithstanding the foregoing, Landlord acknowledges its continuing obligation to the Prime Landlord under the Prime Lease with respect to the demised premises.

20. <u>LANDLORD'S CONSENT REQUIRED</u>. Notwithstanding anything to the contrary contained herein, this Sublease shall be null and void, and of no force and effect whatever, unless executed by the Prime Landlord in the space provided. Prime Landlord's execution of the Sublease signifies its consent to every provision contained herein and permits Landlord to sublease the demised premises in accordance with its rights to do so under the Prime Lease.

21. <u>SPECIAL STIPULATIONS</u>. Landlord and Tenant agree to the following special stipulations to this Sublease which shall take precedence over other Articles in this Sublease:

(1) With Prime Landlord's consent, Landlord shall provide to the Tenant, at no additional rental for the term of the Sublease, use of the Building's 250 square-foot Conference Room, which Landlord shall construct at no additional cost to the Tenant. The Conference Room shall be located on the first floor of the Building adjacent to the public rest rooms, as shown and specified on Exhibit F, and shall be available for Tenant use on a first-come basis from 7:30 AM to 6:00 PM (CST) Monday through Friday and from 7:30 AM to 12:30 PM (CST) on Saturday.

(2) Landlord shall provide the Tenant with <u>one (1)</u> Option to renew the Sublease for an additional <u>two (2)</u> year and <u>nine (9)</u> month term which shall commence on <u>April 1, 2008</u>, and terminate on <u>December 31, 2010</u>. Tenant shall notify the Landlord a minimum of 180 calendar days in advance of the beginning of the Option date should Tenant choose to exercise this Option to extend the Sublease.

(3) Landlord shall provide the Tenant with <u>one (1)</u> month of Rental Abatement commencing on <u>January 1, 2006</u>, and ending on <u>January 31, 2006</u>. Tenant shall pay as monthly rental during this Rent Abatement period Tenant's share of 2006 Operating Expenses which are $6.45 per rentable square feet which shall be <u>One Thousand Seventy-Five and 00/100</u> Dollars (<u>$1,075.00</u>) per month.

Exhibit 3.14   Sublease Agreement Sample for ABC Company (Continued)

In WITNESS WHEREOF, Tenant and Landlord have each executed this Lease as of the day and year first above written.

TENANT:
Ross, Jones, and Smith, Inc.

Attest: By: _____

_____   Title: President_____
(Corporate Seal)

LANDLORD:
ABC Company

Attest: By: _____

_____   Title: Vice President_____
(Corporate Seal)

ACCEPTED AND AGREED TO THIS _____ DAY OF _____, 2004.

PRIME LANDLORD:

West Wacker Towers, L.P.

By: _____

Name: _____

Title: General Partner_____

Exhibit 3.14   Sublease Agreement Sample for ABC Company (Continued)

EXHIBIT A
FLOOR PLAN—SUITE 201

EXHIBIT B
WORK LETTER AGREEMENT
(Not Included)

EXHIBIT C
RULES AND REGULATIONS
(Not Included)

EXHIBIT D
ADDENDUM TO LEASE COMMENCEMENT DATE
(Not Included)

EXHIBIT E
LEVELS 1 AND 2 PARKING PLAN
(Not Included)

EXHIBIT F
CONFERENCE ROOM PLAN
(Not Included)

EXHIBIT G
PRIME LEASE
(Not Included)

Exhibit 3.14   Sublease Agreement Sample for ABC Company (Continued)

A buyout of the lease is another viable option should your landlord need your space for an existing tenant or for a new tenant. If the landlord has too much vacant space, similar space is overabundant, or you are currently paying market or above rent, a lease buyout is seldom possible. However, a landlord who needs cash, wants to provide a more marketable space or contiguous floor area to sign a new tenant, or has a qualified tenant to take over your space at a higher rate *may* consider buying out your lease. The transaction must provide an economic benefit to the landlord, and it is usually up to the tenant (you or your customer) to make the initial offer on the buyout amount. This cash sum should take into account the:

- Remaining value of the space at the current rate multiplied by the time remaining on the lease.

- Plus or minus the remaining value of the space at today's market rate multiplied by the time remaining on the lease.

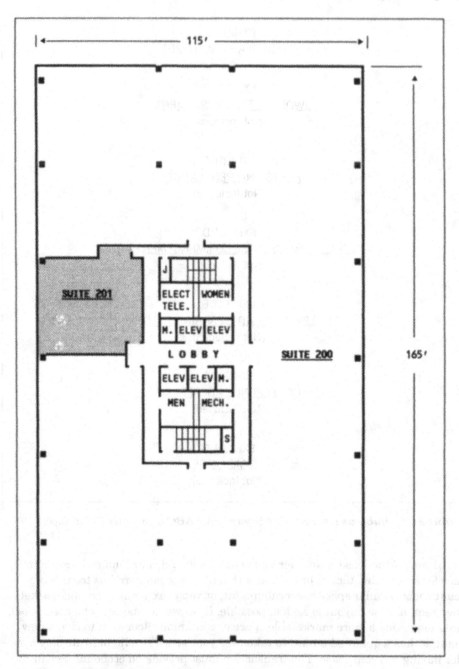

Exhibit A   Floor Plan—Suite 201

- Plus a recapture of the value of the remaining undepreciated improvements made by the lessor.

- Plus a recapture of a value for a pro rata amount of any other costs or cash inducements (moving costs, etc.).

- Plus a recapture of the value on the pro rata number of months of free rent (if any).

- Plus a recapture of a pro rata value of design and project management fees.

- Plus a recapture of a pro rata value of the real estate commissions paid by the lessor.

- Plus an estimated marketing cost to acquire a new tenant, which is added to the preceding amounts and totaled.

The net present value (NPV) of the total tells you or the landlord its value today (the time value of money); it is the *breakeven point* in the proposed buyout. To obtain the net present value, you must determine the financial value of money today. This value is the percentage of interest that your company or the landlord would usually have to pay to borrow money from a financial institution.

The breakeven point amount can provide the basis for establishing your initial buyout offer, which may be higher or lower than that figure. Whether your first offer is acceptable depends on the market, the landlord's immediate need for cash, and how much that party feels your company is willing to pay to get out of the lease. Again, your negotiation skills, strategy, and help from your real estate broker can help establish your initial offer, subsequent offers, and final offer.

A lease buyout can be beneficial to your customer and corporation in removing a legal and financial obligation from today's balance sheet. It is important that you and your legal counsel review this document carefully to ensure that the buyout amount is the *final* payment and your customer will have *no* further obligations to the landlord for this space. This document should remove all liability from your customer for all past or future rents, costs, expenses, liens, fees, taxes, and assessments. After the buyout is completed, it is not unusual to receive a bill(s) for additional operating expenses, fees, or taxes for the space; your buyout document should protect your customer from any further legal or financial requirements to the space or to the landlord.

Example. ABC Company currently is a tenant in the XYZ Building—a downtown mid-rise building. The company is planning to relocate the operation in the XYZ Building to another city and believes the relocation will provide considerable marketing and income opportunities. But at the time the company will relocate the operation, 36 months will be remaining on the current five-year lease. The company does not want to sublease the space but rather wishes to buy out the remaining lease commitment. The local real estate market surrounding the XYZ Building is soft, and the XYZ Building is 30 percent vacant. The landlord of the XYZ Building needs cash, however, and may consider a buyout of the lease, but will not make you an offer. What offer could (should) you make to the landlord?

Before determining your offer, you must take into account the issues the landlord will consider, as described earlier. Based on the lease agreement, here is one approach to looking at the remaining investment in the lease space:

Total Leased Area   25,550 Rentable Square Feet (RSF)
Current Lease Rate $18.00/RSF
Lease Rent Increase   3% Per Year
NPV Rate   8%

ABC Company Expenses	2003	2004	2005	2006	TOTAL
	(9 mo)	(12 mo)	(12 mo)	(3 mo)	(3 yr 0 mo)
Upfit /depreciation	$24,388	$32,518	$32,518	$8,130	$97,554
Rent and operating expense	$374,165	$513,852	$529,268	$133,288	$1,550,573
TOTAL EXPENSES	$398,553	$546,371	$561,786	$141,417	$1,648,127

Recapture Expenses	(9 mo)	(12 mo)	(12 mo)	(3 mo)	(3 yr 0 mo)
Recapture of undepreciated improvements =	$8,130	$32,518	$32,518	$8,130	$81,295
Recapture of 6 months free rent and 4 months marketing expo	$337,357				$337,357
Recapture of fees and commissions =	$6,676	$27,252	$27,997	$8,858	$70,783
36 MONTHS RECAPTURE COSTS					$489,435

TOTAL POSSIBLE BUYOUT
OBLIGATION $2,137,562

As shown here, the remaining rent and depreciation on premises improvement due to the landlord over the 36-month period is $1,648,127. The recapture of prior expenses and project expenses totals $489,435. So we know the total possible obligation may be approximately $2,137,562 in future dollars to buy out the lease obligation. If we take a net-present-value rate of 8 percent of the cash requirements for each year, we can determine the current total dollar value the future $2,137,562 represents today.

Once we have the possible buyout breakeven number, this becomes the basis for the initial offer. It is not uncommon to offer one-half or less of the breakeven sum as an initial buyout amount and then, based on the landlord's response, continue with negotiations or call off the buyout process. Some landlords will negotiate and some will not depending on what you are paying, their vacancy rate, cash flow situation, current debt service requirements, relationships with their mortgage lender or financial partners, and marketing prospects for leasing the space you propose to vacate at a higher rate than you are currently paying.

OUTSOURCING

Today, few facility organizations perform the same tasks they did ten years ago. More private and public organizations are outsourcing some or all of their real estate and facility management services to third-party integrated service providers. In the mid-1990s, outsourcing was focused on cost reduction, head-count reduction, and the out-tasking of certain functional non-strategic facility areas. Today, many organizations in the private and public sectors are looking for one or a few high-quality service providers to provide and manage a wide variety of integrated corporate real estate and facility management services, including strategic facility services. These private and public FM organizations may have a small core of corporate real estate and facility staff professionals who manage strategic real estate and facility issues for the organization and manage the outsourcing service provider(s). Where the real estate/facility management organization may have numbered 500, there may now be only five to ten employees who manage the outsourcing contract and provide strategic asset management and capital planning services for corporate senior executives.

Rather than managing a few to hundreds of contract service providers, many corporate real estate and facility professionals now have only one or a few invoices and contract(s) to manage. Their outsourcing provider now provides and manages services such as asset management, real estate lease administration, lease acquisition, management and disposal, design and construction, furnishings, food services, mail and copy services maintenance and operations, energy, safety, environmental issues, cleaning, move management, furniture and inventory management, landscaping, transportation, and so on. Many private and public sector real estate and facility employees are hired by outsource providers, and some find new career paths that sometimes prove very rewarding, as they have more opportunities for advancement than they would have had within their previous organizations.

CONCLUSION

This chapter reviewed a number of financial forecasting and planning concepts, issues, and procedures. To fully integrate your facility department into the financial world of your organization, it is essential that you and your staff become fully aware of your organization's process, requirements, and presentation requirements. Many a great facility management department has floundered because department management and staff did not understand the process or know the financial language to explain and promote their ideas and requirements. The challenge for facility professionals is to be proactive in their organization's financial world. Operating and capital funds are given to those FMs who can best promote their and their customers' real estate and facility requirements.

Chapter Four

Real Estate Considerations, Analysis, and Planning

RESPONSIBILITIES AND OBJECTIVES OF THE REAL ESTATE FUNCTION

The real estate function within a corporation exists mainly to support the company's strategic and operational objectives. It provides support to both senior and line management in the form of strategic facilities planning as well as specific analytical and transactional activities. These services, orchestrated by the professionals of the corporate real estate and facility function, enable the corporation to acquire, manage, and dispose of its real estate interest within acceptable time and cost parameters. While the objectives of the real estate function tend to focus on cost, space, and risk minimization, they do not end there but extend also to broader strategic matters involving senior management.

Senior management, in most organizations, acknowledges real estate's substantial role in corporate affairs. With real property interests representing such a substantial portion of corporate book and, particularly, market value, facility and real estate personnel in light of the requirements of the Sarbanes-Oxley Act of 2002 (mentioned in chapter 1) must continue to inform senior management about the ways in which corporate real estate can substantially affect corporate profitability, strategy, and organization. The inflationary period of the 1970s, followed by the generous tax environment of the 1980s, substantially increased the market values of the real estate owned by corporations. Suddenly, corporations began to recognize the vast reservoir of untapped wealth, salable or mortgageable, in their real estate. If they did not, others did, transforming unobservant corporations into acquisition targets. Some corporations, hoping to cash in on the unrealized equity, even went into real estate development temporarily. By the end of the 1980s, through the 1990s, and into the 2000s, times changed for real estate, and, consequently, the attitude of senior management toward it.

The lesson that senior management has learned in the past 30 years is that real estate and facilities can have substantial effects—both positive and negative—on corporate value and strategy. As noted, changes in the real estate market of the order experienced during this period required a management response. Because the risks and rewards for the corporation can be so great, information regarding real estate market changes, their impact on the corporation, and strategy recommendations relating thereto must be available to the decision makers. It is incumbent on the real estate and facility function to provide this support.

Generally, corporations emphasize that "they are not in the real estate business." While this may be true, virtually every corporation is *invested* in real estate—in some cases, to the extent of billions of dollars. Therefore, the present or forecasted impact of real estate on the corporation, as developed by the real estate function, should be presented in an annual *strategic facilities plan,* described later in this chapter. For example, this plan might recommend, based on observed real estate market activity, acquiring or leasing, on a long-term basis, property in specific submarkets due to historically low values being available at the time. In so doing, the corporation, while modifying its balance sheet, may be able to secure long-term cost advantages over its competitors, or at least remain competitive with respect to occupancy costs. In the alternative, it may be advantageous to dispose of property due to the specter of litigation, consequent major financial losses, and contingent liabilities stemming from, for example, persons occupying buildings that contain asbestos.

Finally, the facility management department might recommend forming or spinning off a real estate subsidiary to deal with either risk avoidance or profit opportunities. In all these instances, the real estate and facility function can affect organizational structure, financial profile, and profitability through its interface with senior management.

Corporate real estate and facility personnel typically spend most of their time and resources on servicing line management at operational levels. It is in connection with these responsibilities that the real estate function acts to acquire, manage, and dispose of the real estate the corporation requires to pursue the objectives of the strategic business units. Real estate and facility personnel may also contribute to divisional operating plans and the capital budgeting process with respect to real estate acquisition/disposition and operating costs. Such planning and analytical activities are becoming increasingly important to the real estate and facility function's interactive, rather than reactive, role in corporate operations. Generally, the skills of real estate and facility personnel should be applied to such tasks in a manner that adds value to the activities of the strategic business units.

Value may be added by minimizing costs and offsetting costs, the latter by creating or augmenting cash inflows—for example, by enhancing property value prior to disposition. Generally, however, cost minimization is of principal importance to the corporation's strategic business units, and this concern is present in all property acquisition and management activities. The disposal of real estate no longer required by the corporation is often underappreciated by line management, who may be inclined to just get rid of it. Again, real estate personnel act to minimize costs, realizing that it would be better for the corporation as a whole if property no longer needed by one division were transferred to another division that needs such facilities, perhaps avoiding higher new acquisition costs.

Sometimes, corporate real estate and facility personnel fail to realize that minimizing occupancy costs or enhancing property values does not always translate into increased corporate profitability. A less expensive site, in terms of acquisition costs, could require the corporation to incur additional transportation costs if it were poorly located. The configuration of a less expensive building might limit the type of equipment that could be used therein, thus increasing equipment costs or inhibiting productivity. Although a property considered disposable by one corporate division might generate a substantial profit if sold, it could be a cost-effective acquisition for another division. Selling the property at a substantial profit might bring special recognition to both the selling division and the real estate function. Nevertheless, overall corporate cash requirements might be minimized by transferring the property to the other division, especially as capital gains taxes could be avoided. The distinction between realizing real estate values and corporate profitability must be acknowledged by real estate and facility personnel in executing their responsibilities within the corporation.

An additional distinction between traditional profit-oriented real estate activity and the corporate perspective on managing interests in real estate is the form in which economic benefits are derived and reported with respect to these holdings. This is an important concept: In all their activities, corporations are concerned with both when economic benefits are obtained and when and how they are reported in financial statements. Whether the corporation is publicly or privately held, even closely held, reports concerning the corporation's financial performance and status are frequently examined by others, including banks, equity investors, regulatory agencies, credit rating agencies, and securities firms. All these outside entities are agents in determining the corporation's future. The financial statements they examine and on which they rely are almost always prepared according to generally accepted accounting principles (GAAP). The principle of conservatism—which, in part, directs the recognition of profit (and, to some extent, losses) in financial statements prepared under GAAP—sometimes heavily influences or even dictates corporate behavior, particularly at the level of the individual who has bottom-line responsibility.

This effect can be seen most vividly with respect to the prospect of recognizing gains and losses on the disposition of realty, and the effect of such recognition on the measured performance of management.

Corporate management is typically rewarded for performance measured at quarterly or annual intervals. As noted earlier, corporations, by virtue of requiring a location in which to conduct business, are necessarily invested in real estate. The value of those real estate interests can be managed to the benefit of the corporation by applying the principles discussed in this chapter. Changes in the value of real estate typically occur rather slowly. Current rental income from realty investments is often nominal and can take years to substantially change a property's market value. Furthermore, the increased value is not recognized under GAAP until the property is sold. Therefore, appreciation of real estate values tends to be of less concern to line management than how properties can contribute to current earnings. Over the long run, returns from real estate investments have generally not exceeded corporate earnings. Also, those returns tend to be based, in part, on the ability of real estate investments to shelter a certain amount of cash flow from taxation as ordinary income, converting some ordinary income to capital gains. While the 1986 Tax Act eliminated much of the tax sheltering available through real estate investments, the nature of economic gains in real estate has not changed.

There are additional reasons why managers with bottom-line responsibility might not want to sell properties even though doing so might be beneficial to the corporation. For example, rather than being unconcerned about realizing value appreciation, line management might be concerned about reporting a loss on a sale of realty. Land held by a corporation for expansion purposes may no longer be needed. Furthermore, its market value over time may have decreased below its acquisition costs. In fact, if the value of the property were continuing to decrease, it may be that a greater loss could be avoided by selling as soon as practicable. However, if sold, a loss would be reported, and, if sizable, might seriously affect a division's short-term financial performance. Consequently, the general manager of the division might be reluctant to act to minimize real economic losses. Still, the reduced economic value of such a property asset might be reported in spite of management's reluctance to act. Under GAAP and according to the Statement of Finance and Accounting Standards (SFAS) 33 the corporation's auditors might be required to report the loss of value, recognizing an unrealized loss based on the present value of the property's future cash flows (fair rental value).

Furthermore, the timing and amount of proceeds from prospective sales of real property are sometimes difficult to forecast, and such sales are therefore unlikely to be included as a source of funds in the operating subsidiary's formal capital expenditures plan submitted to its parent. As a result, property may not be formally declared surplus, and not made available for sale. Alternative strategies respecting surplus land might be to (1) execute a land lease to another party, (2) contribute the property to a development joint venture, or (3) exchange the property (perhaps in a tax-deferred exchange) for another parcel that better meets the subsidiary's operating requirements.

Alternatives 1 and 2 would not prohibit a later sale or exchange for other realty (as in 3), as long as the joint venture was structured as a tenancy in common, as opposed to a partnership. Consequently, an exchange of real estate (two-way or three-way) can be a useful way to address the matter of surplus property.

As can be seen in the foregoing, a corporation's real estate function must recognize the needs not only of different levels of management but also of individual managers who may have somewhat differing interests. Therefore, it is likely that the real estate function's objectives and responsibilities will depend on its own reporting responsibilities and location within the organization as a centralized or distributed function. This also applies to outside consultants who must consider how to balance objectivity with the objectives of the individuals who retain advisory services.

BEST PRACTICES IN CORPORATE REAL ESTATE MANAGEMENT

Best practices are used by corporate real estate and facility personnel to accomplish their objectives. The most important concern, as noted throughout much of the following material, is strategic planning. With respect to real estate and facility management, strategic planning has to do with the exchange of information and proposed strategies between comprehensive corporate planners and facility management planners. The next section focuses on the issue of strategic planning for corporate real estate by examining it in three ways. First, several areas are identified in which real estate can significantly affect the strategic or financial posture of the entire corporation. The two items that follow—managing values and managing risk—are like yin and yang; each complements and is necessary for the other, and each is in some way contained in the other, even though they are polar opposites. The importance of the information and strategy exchange is stressed.

Learning Research from CoreNet Global: *Corporate Real Estate 2010*

In the early 1990s, the International Development Research Council (IDRC) published a research report, *Corporate Real Estate 2000,* that created a powerful new vision for the corporate real estate industry. Almost a decade later, in 2003, a new corporate real estate vision emerged from the successor to IDRC, CoreNet Global, and this vision was published as *Corporate Real Estate 2010.* This report states that in 2010, corporate real estate will be a network, an enterprise within the corporate enterprise. It will be flat and fast and have the capability to explore new markets, tap new resources, develop new products, and deliver services faster and more efficiently than ever before.

The networked enterprise will expand, contract, and leverage its resources in ways that have not been practical in the past, all while providing decision makers with better visibility over their extended operations. At the core of the enterprise will be new ways to think about how and where people work, as traditional boundaries become irrelevant. The subtle but steady advance toward the networked world is becoming one of the most significant long-term trends in business. This trend has the potential to fundamentally transform society and almost every aspect of the way in which firms operate. The companies that grasp this vision will have a unique opportunity to benefit from the profound changes about to occur.

The Corporate Real Estate 2010 Research and Leadership Development Program and Vision, published by CoreNet Global, are designed to guide your organization and mentor your new leaders through this transformation. A full set of reports, listed below, is available from the CoreNet Global Report:

Enabling Work in a Networked World: A Research and Leadership Development Program for Corporate Real Estate Professionals:

- The Changing Nature of Work and the Workplace
- The Strategic Role of Place
- Solutions Delivery
- Asset Management and Portfolio Optimization
- Integrated Resource and Infrastructure Solutions (IRIS)
- The Role of Technology and the Web
- Enterprise Leadership
- Corporate Social Responsibility and Sustainability
- Summary: CoreNet Global Gallup CORE 2010 Research Reports
- Synthesis Report on Corporate Real Estate 2010 Research Reports[1]

[1]From the CoreNet Global website, *www.corenetglobal.org*, February 20, 2004.

STRATEGIC PLANNING

The responsibilities and objectives of the real estate and facility function should be established through strategic planning, from which all other real estate and facility plans and action should emerge. The strategic planning process should not operate in a top-down fashion only. This approach ignores the real estate and facility function's valuable knowledge of the market, inventory status, and the risks and opportunities surrounding its real estate asset base. The real estate and facility function and other corporate functions (especially senior management) involved in the strategic planning process should have an interactive and, in many instances, a proactive relationship. There is much value in the information and recommendations the real estate and facility function can generate for comprehensive corporate strategic planning. Moreover, this contribution can extend into fundamental corporate concerns, such as capital accumulation.

The ability to raise capital is fundamental to operating a business. This is true for an entirely new venture, an initial public offering (IPO), as well as the recapitalization of an existing corporation. Businesses must secure funds, and a corporation's real estate and facility assets can contribute significantly to that objective. Corporations typically obtain additional funds from retained earnings and issuance of debt or stock securities. If managed properly, real estate and facility assets can significantly enhance retained earnings through gains realized on sale. Rather than sell real estate assets, a corporation might elect to leverage its net worth as augmented by the unrealized equity it holds in real estate assets. Again, if properly managed, real estate and facility assets may allow a corporation to issue additional debt or stock in amounts that can significantly enhance its strategic posture. In fact, at times, if management does not act on the unrealized equity in its real estate, others may force it to, as witnessed by the takeover activity of the 1980s, late 1990s, and early 2000s.

The real estate function can be a key player in recognizing such opportunities, or necessities, and be the initiator of efforts to recapitalize or assume various defensive postures to ward off a takeover attempt. On the other hand, the real estate function can also identify and evaluate acquisition opportunities for its own corporation based on its understanding of market values and capacity utilization.

In addition, real estate and facility personnel might recommend acquiring realty that may be beneficial to the corporation (e.g., by identifying long-term economic or social factors in specific locations that increase a property's value or the corporation as a whole). Finally, real estate and facility personnel might identify opportunities to maintain or enhance a corporation's product or service market share by securing key sites (especially with retail or service companies and facilities) that would preclude or counterbalance competitor activity.

Apart from opportunities, risks are always present. A close watch on the factors affecting real estate can help the corporation avoid general or local hazards that present potential adverse effects such as hazardous waste regulation, plant-closing legislation, historic preservation laws, escalating energy costs, trends toward nuisance challenges relating to major installations in communities or states, and evolving worker safety regulations affecting facility designs (expensively reconfigured). These kinds of concerns should be addressed in assembling the corporation's strategic facility plan, as shown in the menu of items in Exhibit 4.1 (see also chapter 2).

Corporate real estate and facility management are becoming a readily recognized function as chief executive officers, heads of organizations, and chief government administrators increasingly perceive their value. Facility management "already is a useful tool for strategic planning because planning today involves the expenditure of billions and billions of dollars," said Lee A. Iacocca, chairman, Chrysler Corporation. "You don't spend that kind of money unless you're confident that the facilities you're building with it can be managed efficiently, provide a return on your investment over time, and do the competitive job you intend them to do. Our overall goal is to design, develop, and build the world's best automotive products. We will do that only if we have the best facilities."[2]

Annual and long-range planning requires basing site analysis and real estate selection on a realistic schedule that supports the business plan. While this may appear obvious, failures in the scheduling of plans often lead to disadvantageous site selections. Scheduling must be included in the strategic planning process for each business unit with a corresponding review at the corporate level.

With the information gained through your facility inventory, you can provide a Real Estate Property Inventory (Exhibit 4.2), an Office Facilities Summary (Exhibit 4.3), and a strategic listing of square footage and total value of the leases in the Leased Office Facilities (Exhibits 4.4–4.7).

Workplace Management

Businesses are pursing more aggressive workplace strategies to attract and retain employees, drive effectiveness and productivity, and measure workplace contribution to shareholder value. The value that can be achieved by increasing the employee productivity by creating a productive working environment is far greater than the value realized by reducing the cost of facility operations by several percentage points.

For example, a significant trend in corporate workplaces is the configuring and reconfiguring of work teams to foster communication and interaction. These teams perform better together, facilitate collaboration, nurture employee satisfaction, and improve productivity. It is essential to successfully manage the entire process relating to physical reconfiguration in the workplace and to control cycle time, cost, and coincidental disruption of the activity. Many companies find that their churn projects are moving more than 50 percent of their workforce every year. They must achieve the reconfigurations without disruption to their business. Project management is tied closely to the overall business asset management plan to ensure uninterrupted operations in the workplace.

Future real estate and facility management strategies recognize the link between employee satisfaction and productivity—and will be designed to focus on the linkages and factors that affect the building occupants.

---

[2]Quoted in Anne Fallucchi, Editorial, *Facility Design and Management* (October 1989), p. 6.

Issues to Address in a Strategic Facilities Plan

- Capacity requirements forecast
- Facility location, relocation, expansion, and consolidation
- Facility acquisition, utilization, and divestiture
- Life-cycle costing and productivity incorporating perspectives on trade-offs
- Facilities financing, including the capital budgeting plan
- Financial statement effects of real estate organizational structure, management policies, and action
- Implementation policies and procedures
- Facilities standards

Information Required to Develop the Strategic Facilities Plan

- Marketing distribution plans, inventory management, and sales forecasts by product/service type
- Financial objectives including funding, profitability, and profile
- Organizational structure for operating, regulatory, and liability management
- Human resources as related to site-specific operating costs and relocations
- Real estate inventory and utilization data, historical and forecasted
- Strategic and operating requirements for each strategic business unit
- Ancillary services related to facility operations (utilities, amenities, etc.)
- Market information respecting the commodity (space and location)
- Corporate policies related to or involving facilities, including:
  Real property interest preferences (fee or leaseholds)
  By facility type: location (foreign?), risks (environmental, financial, market)
  Financing methods: internal, seller financing, third-party (e.g., banks), or leases
  Financial statement objectives: asset, liability, or expense recognition and timing
  Cash flow impact
  Management of risk: financial, market, and legal risks and contingencies
  Strategic aspects of real estate (image, worker morale, environmental protection, etc.)

The Planning Process

- Parties involved in the development of the strategic facilities plan:
  CEO and CFO, and an executive committee representing senior management
  Representatives of departmental functions (e.g., human resources, finance)

Exhibit 4.1   Strategic Facilities Plan Checklist

Representatives of the strategic business units operating within the corporation

Corporate real estate department professionals and facilities professionals

- Corporate strategy input:

  Product and packaging impact—changing consumer acceptance

  Marketing strategy impact—changing customer location

  Manufacturing technology selection

  Materials sourcing program

  Production planning and control—changes in volume

  Logistical strategy—purchasing, packaging, shipment

  Inventory planning—demand and factors variation

  Capital funding

  Organizational design

  Human resources program (labor pool, benefits, etc.)

- Operations management: The dynamics of the environment and potential for changes:

  In demand

  In supply (competition)

  In technology

  In management methods (e.g., just-in-time)

  In management objectives (e.g., total quality)

  In organizational objectives/structure

  In labor pool size or quality

- Physical plant inventory management:

  Impact on corporate profitability and risk profile

  Schedule and delivery date coordination

  Identification of space requirements

- Present—this operating period
- Future—short term and long term
- Space requirements affected by:

  Employee efficiency

  Technology used in operations—telecommunications, etc.

Exhibit 4.1 Strategic Facilities Plan Checklist (Continued)

Land and building costs

Development or land banking potential for proposed or adjacent sites

Timing considerations

Legal and/or environmental considerations

Locus of decision-making ability and acquisition authority

Evaluation of alternatives, especially short- versus long-term solutions

Single-purpose versus multiple-purpose solutions

Image and prestige considerations

Strategic Facilities Plan Assembly

- Statement of corporate objectives for the upcoming period players, timetable, resources, constraints
- Identification of specific facilities requirements per strategic business unit (type, amount, where, when, budget, linkages):

   Defining the objective(s) of the function requiring a facility

   Identifying relationships and contribution of other corporate functions

   Establishing space requirements

   Identifying and evaluating alternative facility plans

   Selecting and implementing the plan

   Reprogramming the facility in step with operational objectives

   Identifying existing inventory and capacity of facilities in relation to policies addressing utilization and performance standards

- Identification of alternative solutions to accommodate the objectives, with specific notation as to the related costs, benefits, trade-offs, risks, impact, and externalities. This requires the input of the various staff and operating personnel noted.
- Identification of a comprehensive and integrated set of recommendations and rationale for the actions proposed, constituting a basic strategic facilities plan
- Senior management review and adoption (with modifications)
- Development of implementation plans and procedures for both corporate real estate personnel, but also the strategic business units and staff departments involved in executing the action plans
- Implementation monitoring, notation of feedback, and realignment of plan details as necessary

Exhibit 4.1   Strategic Facilities Plan Checklist (Continued)

Implementation Program for the Strategic Facilities Plan

- Capital allocation requests and acquisitions
- Land and space banking
- Divestitures
- Inventory redeployment
- Cost management measures
- Refinancing of real property interests
- Pursuit of cost-offsetting opportunities
- Relocation

Exhibit 4.1   Strategic Facilities Plan Checklist (Continued)

ISSUES FOR REVIEW AND ANALYSIS

Your company's annual and long-range business, real estate, and facility plans should address the general geographic locations where a site or space is required. These requirements should be part of an overall understanding of the current and future inventory of real estate available for current use and possible future uses. The inventory review should support the corporate plan by acknowledging that the geographic location can support the proposed use and is available within specific and acceptable cost ranges. The inventory should address what your company currently has in the geographic location, whether owned or leased, size, type, and age of existing property and facilities, possible use of vacant space, expiration date, and option date for leased properties, including monthly lease and operating expenses.

The inventory can also include an inventory of the trained labor force available, whether the local government will support the expected use, and the strengths and weaknesses of existing and future utilities, roads, housing, retail, education facilities, fire and police services, and environmental conditions.

A number of communities and even some states encourage or discourage the development of certain types of businesses. Many such communities use zoning to achieve these goals, and the facility professional must verify that the property under consideration is currently available with proper zoning or can be zoned for the proposed use. The time frame to change the zoning for a site varies by community. The process can be simple and quick or take years depending on the process, the number of hearings, and the number of approvals required to obtain the desired zoning. You must also address the cost for this change as well as the intangible cost to your company's business image within the community.

Ideally, you will be able to identify a sufficient inventory of zoned property in each area to meet your company's requirements without having to go through a zoning process. If you must request a zoning change, be prepared with alternate site locations should the effort not succeed.

Loaded in the Real Property Information System as of June 18, 2004

A. Divisions	Archived* Filter	ABC Company	Battery	Tire			Retail	Total
Total leased	96	35	101	156			879	1,267
Total subleased	0	15	1	4			21	41
Total owned	0	2	0	9			2,296	2,307
Total	**96**	**52**	**102**	**169**			**3,196**	**3,615**

B. Retail Division Western Region	CA	WA	TX			Western Region Hq.	Total
Total leased	118	8	118			1	245
Total subleased	0	0	0			0	0
Total owned	153	182	165			0	500
Total	**271**	**190**	**283**			**1**	**745**

C. Retail Division Central Region	MO	MN	KY	IL	Central Region Hq.	Total
Total leased	44	41	10	5	1	101
Total subleased	1	2	0	0	0	3
Total owned	372	298	84	115	0	869
Total	**427**	**341**	**94**	**120**	**1**	**973**

D. Retail Division Eastern Region	PA	VA	NY	GA	MA	Eastern Region Hq.	Total
Total leased	60	108	76	90	35	0	369
Total subleased	3	8	3	0	0	0	14
Total owned	132	188	150	171	84	1	726
Total	**195**	**304**	**229**	**261**	**119**	**1**	**1,109**

E. Retail Division Corporate	Hq.	L.S.	Office Svcs.	Ware. Dist.	Credit	Total
Total leased	1	9	67	9	57	143
Total subleased	0	13	1	0	1	15
Total owned	1	2	0	1	87	91
Total	**1**	**24**	**68**	**10**	**145**	**249**

Exhibit 4.2   ABC Company Real Estate Property Inventory

Your corporation should have a policy (written or unwritten) regarding the owning or leasing of real estate. Some corporations have a policy to own certain types of property for certain divisions and lease property only for certain other divisions. This policy is a function of several factors: the business product; the need for fixed real estate costs; the location; the age of the company or its business division; its status as a regulated or unregulated business; the availability of capital; the costs

	Divisions:	# Of Leased Offices	Total Leased Office Sq. Ft	# Of Owned Offices	Total Owned Office Sq. Ft.
	As of June 18, 2005				
1)	ABC Company	27	349,103	2	122,346
2)	Battery	33	720,567	0	74,238
3)	Tire	83	541,672	4	59,534
4)	Retail	101	1,141,169	88	78,415
	GRAND TOTAL	244	2,752,511	94	334,533

Exhibit 4.3   ABC Company Office Facilities Summary

of leasing, taxes, and insurance; local development surcharges; and the stability (perceived or historically) of the business and the local or national economy.

For example, a company whose major business income comes from federal, state, or local government consulting contracts is not able to charge the cost of capital or mortgage interest but can charge lease payments. Therefore, this type of company's policy must be to lease rather than own property. A manufacturing company that makes a substantial long-term investment in equipment usually owns property and associated facilities, but the same manufacturing company usually leases regional sales offices. The value of your company's owned or leased facilities can also be important if the company is a takeover target. Owned property is often viewed as an asset to a takeover company, whereas leased property, depending on total dollar amount and years of commitment remaining, is often viewed as a liability. Your company may choose to use owned versus leased property as a strategy

	Divisions:	Total Leased Offices	Total Leased Office Square Footage	Monthly Operating Expenses	Yearly Operating Expense	Annual Lease Commitment
	As of June 18, 2005					
1)	ABC Company	27	349,103	$373,425	$4,481,100	$6,713,486
2)	Battery	33	720,567	$99,911	$1,198,932	$11,216,448
3)	Tire	83	541,672	$57,527	$690,324	$17,624,493
4)	Retail	101	1,141,169	$52,817	$633,804	$12,127,127
5)	Filter*	96	1,069,709	$ —	$ —	$407,739
	GRAND TOTAL	340	3,822,220	$583,680	$7,004,160	$48,089,293

Exhibit 4.4   ABC Company Leased Office Facilities Square Footage and Total Value Summary (these properties will be deleted from the Database on June 22, 2005)

```
                                                      RECORD      STAT    X   COMP
                        AS OF: 06/18/95               SELECTION   BISU        ACCT
        PAGE    1                                                 BLDG        PRCL


                         LOCATION                                     MONTHLY/
                         TYPE FACILITY            LEASE      NET RENTABLE  YEARLY
        REAL ESTATE FILE NO.  CANCELLATION PENALTIES  EXPIRATION  SQUARE FEET  COMMITMENT
        --------------------  ----------------------  ----------  ------------  ----------------
        IL-A-624-1000-1000-00  CHICAGO, IL            01/01/95       35,000  $      68,211.49
                               DIVISION HEADQUARTERS                         $     818,537.88
                               NO CANCELLATION CLAUSE

        CA-A-103-1102-1010-00  LOS ANGELES            05/01/97      165,000  $      19,166.67
                               WESTERN DISTRIBUTION CENTER                   $     230,000.00
                               6 MONTHS RENT & SEE LEASE
```

Exhibit 4.5   ABC Company Leased Vacant Property

```
                                                      RECORD      STAT    X   COMP
                        AS OF: 06/18/95               SELECTION   BISU        ACCT
        PAGE    1                                                 BLDG        PRCL


                         LOCATION                  PURCHASE          BOOK VALUE    BUILDING(S)
        REAL ESTATE FILE NO.  TYPE FACILITY        DATE    ACREAGE   LAND & BLDG.  GROSS SQ. FT.
        --------------------  -------------------------  --------  --------  ---------------  -------------
        NJ-O-534-1034-1023-00  NEWARK, NJ          07/12/85  23.823  $  9,682,931.83     125,000
                               EASTERN REG. DISTRIB. CENTER

        GA-O-214-1021-1237-00  ATLANTA, GA         11/08/88   5.243  $ 18,919,349.27     189,500
                               S.E. REGION HEADQUARTERS
```

Exhibit 4.6   ABC Company Owned Surplus Property

```
                                                      RECORD      STAT    IL   COMP
                        AS OF: 06/18/95               SELECTION   BISU        ACCT
        PAGE    1                                                 BLDG        PRCL


                                                                              MONTHLY/
                                       LEASE      NET RENTABLE  NET USABLE     YEARLY
        REAL ESTATE FILE NO.  LOCATION NAME       EXPIRATION  SQUARE FEET  SQUARE FEET  COMMITMENT
        --------------------  -------------------------  ----------  ------------  ------------  ----------------
        IL-A-601-1000-1000-00  CHICAGO DIVISION HEADQUARTERS  01/31/95   35,000       31,500  $      68,211.49
                                                                                              $     818,537.88

        IL-A-702-1000-1210-00  CHICAGO DISTRIBUTION CENTER    09/30/94  175,000       ------  $      25,500.00
                                                                                              $     306,000.00

        IL-A-329-1000-1000-00  CHICAGO-O'HARE SERVICE OFFICE  06/15/93   23,000       21,754  $      57,500.00
                                                                                              $     690,000.00

        IL-A-493-1000-1210-00  CHICAGO-DOWNTOWN COMPUTER CTR  11/30/99   43,285       39,752  $      72,141.77
                                                                                              $     865,700.00
```

Exhibit 4.7   ABC Company All Leased Property in Chicago, IL to discourage takeover suitors. Your annual and long-range real estate planning must take into account your company's own-or-lease philosophy.

If you will be looking at leased property/space during the site evaluation process, you must review your current inventory of leased property/space for use, size, rental costs, expiration dates, escalation costs, and operating expenses. This can be compared with new, second-generation, or sublease property/space for each requirement. For example, should your company seek to consolidate facilities in a certain city or geographic area, the expiration or option date for each lease is a critical factor in planning the change. In fact, the consolidation may be driven by a long-term lease commitment at a site that proves a more economical location for the company than a new facility. To maintain your options during the negotiation phase, it is important that this strategy remain confidential (see chapter 1).

You could also use the preceding strategy to help provide an upgraded working environment for employees by obtaining the landlord's concession to refurbish the property/space. Negotiating refurbishment at a future date or option date in the lease agreement encourages the landlord to maintain the current space and thus reduce the refurbishment that must be completed by the specified date. The lease agreement can state refurbishment as an allowance per usable square foot, state exactly what will be refurbished (e.g., new carpet, new wall covering, walls repainted), or state a total amount the landlord must agree to spend. Because refurbishment can be an influential factor when renters decide whether to stay in a location or to move, landlords are using this feature to renegotiate leases, or renegotiate them early.

Another consideration is whether the real estate investment will appreciate or depreciate in value. A reliable and knowledgeable real estate broker in the area can assist you in evaluating possible sites that have historically appreciated in value. A property may be purchased and improved with a specific time frame in mind; because the facility is flexible and can be easily adapted for other uses without major rework or rezoning, it can be sold quickly for a profit when the company needs cash. Appreciation is seldom acknowledged by company accounting procedures but should be one of your considerations in deciding whether a location should be retained, sold, leased, or subleased. The appreciation of an accurately appraised property may be important if your company has a donation program through which it can realize good local public relations while using the donated gain to offset corporate taxes. You should know whether properties are appreciating or depreciating in each real estate market and for any specific property, whether it is better to sell or buy, lease, or sublease, or avoid a specific location because of the historical lack of appreciation or sales activity.

Taxes and Assessments

Taxation has become a major factor in many corporate annual and long-range planning programs. Many municipalities and states have enacted new or substantially increased property, business, and income taxes that increase the cost of doing business and may reduce the company's competitiveness, ability to grow, or likelihood of making a profit. Numerous corporations have relocated large operations and corporate headquarters to gain tax advantages in areas with lower or fewer taxes; these companies often obtain substantial tax concessions or a reduction in taxes for many years. Also, a number of states have established development authorities to market their state's ability to provide corporations with a profitable work environment. If your corporation is planning to relocate, state and local governments may agree to pay considerable relocation and site costs. These states or communities often make presentations to sell a company on relocation to their area. Benefits may include free or reduced land cost; free site development, including roads, rail, water, sewer, and power; free utilities for a time; plant or office facility construction costs provided or financed at a low cost (revenue bonds); rezoning; and other options unique to your company's requirements.

REAL ESTATE AND FACILITY INVENTORY

Real estate and facility professionals have a unique opportunity to affect and improve the corporation's bottom line each time a leased or owned property is acquired, leased, subleased, sold, or donated. Their knowledge of their real estate market; corporate culture, policies, and procedures; and the inventory of facilities and property (see Exhibits 4.8–4.10) helps set the tone, schedule, and successful completion of a real estate requirement.

Peter R. Veal, a research affiliate with the Laboratory of Architecture and Planning at the Massachusetts Institute of Technology, conducted a study in 1987 for the National Association of Corporate Real Estate Executives (NACORE) International entitled *Managing Corporate Real Estate Assets: A Survey of U. S. Real Estate Executives.* One of his most significant conclusions was that large numbers of corporate real estate professionals in the United States did not maintain adequate information on their real estate assets. Two out of three who responded in the 1987 study did not maintain a real estate management information system.

Since the study was made, many corporations have been addressing this issue. A number of them had gone through years of rapid growth due to acquisition, mergers, or internal development, and over time their investments in leased and owned facilities of varied types and at various locations became a critical business issue. The basic real estate and facility management questions that many corporate managers felt should be reviewed and addressed were:

- Where and what do we as a corporation own, lease, and sublease?
- Are we acquiring and disposing of these real estate and facility assets based on a policy that maximizes shareholder value?
- What is the book and market value of these real estate and facility assets (e.g., what do we have in our corporate asset checkbook)?
- What long-term liabilities that affect the bottom line are we committed to paying out in the form of rent, operating expenses, common area maintenance, utilities, property taxes, insurance, and so forth?
- How many properties or facilities are surplus or vacant?
- Do we have or can we develop a consistent computerized database system that will help each business unit more easily use, maintain, manage, and track its real estate portfolio and provide information and reports for itself and the corporation?

The facility manager's real estate management system should be able to provide standard reports for the facility manager to produce and use in the facility manager's long-range and day-to-day management of the real property requirements. Examples:

1. FACILITY LISTING REPORT

This report is a shorthand address/telephone book listing of the Real Estate (RE) File Number, location name, address, city, state, ZIP, location manager, area code, telephone and extension, and is sorted by property that is leased or owned. The report should list properties either by the RE File Number or location name. The facility manager should also be able to list just the state at the RE File Number and issue a report with all the locations in that state.

2. OPTION EXPIRATION REPORT

This report lists the RE File Number, location name, current beginning and ending option date, property owner, total area, monthly rate, and yearly rate. The report should be sortable by the RE File Number, the location name, or the option date. The facility manager should be able to further select to print the data for a range of dates. For example, the facility manager may want the report to list properties whose option occurs within the next 60 days, 90 days, or even a particular year (see Exhibit 4.9).

3. LEASE EXPIRATION REPORT

This report lists the RE File Number, location name, termination date, property owner, total area, monthly rate, and yearly rate. The report should list properties by the RE File Number, the location name, or the termination date. The facility manager should be able to further select to print the data for a range of dates. For example, the facility manager may want the report to list properties whose expiration date occurs within the next 60 days, 90 days, or even a particular year.

4. VACANCY/SURPLUS REPORT

This report covers all company-owned, leased, and subleased properties that are vacant or surplus. It should include the business unit, location, county, owned or leased, cancellation penalties, rent(s), remaining term options (if any), rentable square feet size, and purchase price of the property for owned locations. The report should also include vacant land, parking areas, buildings, and areas in buildings, floors, or parts of floors that are not being used and are available to another business unit within the business unit, other business units, or a subtenant. The report could be generated by business unit, company, state, and for all corporate business units, including corporate property (see Exhibits 4.5 and 4.6).

Exhibit 4.8   Corporate Real Estate Management System Reports

5. SQUARE FOOTAGE LISTING REPORT

This report covers all owned and leased property for a default area or over a given number of rentable square feet. The default amount can be changed to any area amount the facility manager desires. The report should be developed by RE File Number or location.

6. RECURRING EVENT REPORT

This report lists either the individual/company that rent is payable to, the RE File Number, the location, the business unit, the state, or a specific location. This report is generated only for leased or subleased property. It should be capable of being generated for a specific month, with totals given for that month. Up to four signature block names to be printed with comment lines can be included on the report.

7. RENT HISTORY REPORT

The real estate management system should be able to post and save monthly rent payments and sublease income by month and year. At the end of each month and when a change is made the base monthly rent, operating expenses and common area mainte-nance costs should be saved and posted to the facility manager's real estate manage-ment system database. The facility manager should also be able to save some, all, or a particular rent history for properties in the facility manager's business unit and company number.

8. RENT PAYMENT SCHEDULE

This report summarizes in a single page the monthly and annual lease payments and sub-lease income on each leased and subleased property. These data can be compared with Accounts Payable and Accounts Receivable to ensure that the amount paid or amount received, to whom, and the check address of the landlord or income address of the sub-tenant are correct (see Exhibit 4.10).

9. MASTER LISTING REPORT

This report lists all the information entered into the database catalogue by RE File Number or location alphabetically by location name. The report can also be selected for just one property, a small set of properties, by business unit, company, state, or account number (see Exhibits 4.11 and 4.12).

Exhibit 4.8   Corporate Real Estate Management System Reports (Continued)

---

10. USER-DEFINED REPORTS—REPORT WRITER

Report Writer allows the facility manager to create reports from the database of information within the facility manager's real estate management system (see Exhibit 4.7). The Report Writer should be able to:

a. Create the format of the report, including the report heading, which fields to print, the column sequence, column heading(s), and which columns will have totals.

b. Select the database from any subdirectory.

c. Sort the file in the sequence desired.

d. Select the desired records.

e. Create user-defined calculations.

f. Search for specific fields and report only on those fields.

g. Preview the report format on the screen.

h. Specify that the output be sent to the screen, a specific printer, an ASCII text file or a comma-delimited data file.

i. Preserve index, report generation, and printer configuration files for future use.

j. Provide Report Writer configuration options.

k. Interface with other user database and software configurations (software and hardware).

l. Import or export data from any other user mainframe, PC, or software system such as unique company software programs, spreadsheets, word processors, facility management database systems, graphics, or any system capable of producing an ASCII file.

Exhibit 4.8   Corporate Real Estate Management System Reports *(Continued)*

```
                                                      RECORD    BISU    X   COMP
                      AS OF: 06/18/95                 SELECTION STAT        ACCT
   PAGE    1                                                    BLDG        PRCL

                      LOCATION                                  TOTAL SQ FT/    MONTHLY
                      OWNER'S REPRESENTATIVE/  NOTICE  ---OPTION DATES---  RATE  NET RENTABLE/   YEARLY
   REAL ESTATE FILE NO.  LEASE   TERMINATION    DATE    BEGINS     ENDS   /SQFT NET USABLE   COMMITMENT
   --------------------  ------------------------------  ---------  -------------------  -----  ------------  ----------------

   X-100-01-1000-1000-01 CHICAGO, IL          01/01/95 07/01/95 06/30/00 20.00   35,000  $   68,211.49
                         RAYSON DEVELOPMENT CO.                                  31,500  $  818,537.88
                         06/30/95
```

Exhibit 4.9   Option Tracking Data by Option Expiration Date—2004

```
                                                      RECORD    BISU    X   COMP
                      As of 06/18/95                  SELECTION STAT        ACCT
      Page 1                                                    BLDG        PRCL

      REAL ESTATE FILE NO.:      X-100-01-1000-1000-01

      Location Name:             TEST FOR ABC CO. REAL ESTATE
      Business Unit:             ABC DIVISION
      Property Address:          235 EAST WACKER DRIVE
                                 SUITE 1700
      City/State/Zip:            CHICAGO              IL   60634-6578
      Country:                   USA

      Landlord:                  RAYSON DEVELOPMENT COMPANY
                                 c/o UNIVERSAL FINANCIAL LIFE
      Address:                   550 SOUTH MADISON AVENUE
                                 SUITE 900
                                 MAIL CODE 907
      City/State/Zip:            NEW YORK            NY   20246-1234
      Phone:                     (201) 555-0222   Ext. 1234

      Rent Payment Payable To:   PROFESSIONAL BROKERAGE COMPANY
                                 AS AGENT FOR
                                 RAYSON DEVELOPMENT COMPANY
      Address:                   PROFESSIONAL BROKERAGE COMPANY
                                 P.O. BOX 329856

      City/State/Zip:            CHICAGO             IL   60634-9856

      Lease Effective Date:      06/18/90
      Lease Termination Date:    06/30/95

      Base Rent Payment/Month:   $    58,333.33
      Operating Expense/Month:   $     8,956.82
      Common Area Maint/Month:   $       921.34
      Total Monthly Payment:     $    68,211.49

      Total Rentable Area:        35,000 Square Feet

      Escalation Terms:          1. RENT WILL ESCALATE AT A RATE OF 3% PER
                                    SQUARE FEET PER YEAR.
                                 2. OPERATING EXPENSE STOP IS $6.30 PER USABLE SQUARE FEET.

      Business Unit Approval:    Jane M. Simpson, Vice President     Date Lease Signed: 05/01/90
```

Exhibit 4.10   Rent Payment Schedule Report

```
            MASTER LISTING BY LOCATION              PROPERTY   BISU   X    COMP   100
                  AS OF: 06/18/95                   SELECTION  STAT   01   ACCT   1000
PAGE   1                                                       BLDG   1000 PRCL   01
REAL ESTATE FILE NUMBER: X-100-01-1000-1000-01

Lease/Ground lease/Easement:  L          Dates:
New lease/Extension/Renewal:  L          Submitted  04/07/90
Vacancy Approval ..........:  Y          Changed    06/17/90
Sublease ..................:  Y

Location Name ..:  TEST PROP. FOR ABC CO. REAL ESTATE    Landlord ......:  RAYSON DEVELOPMENT COMPANY
Business Unit...:  ABC DIVISION                                            C/O UNIVERSAL FINANCIAL LIFE
Property Address:  235 EAST WACKER DRIVE                 Address .......:  550 SOUTH MADISON AVENUE
                   SUITE 1700                                              SUITE 900
City/State/Zip .:  CHICAGO         IL    60634-6578                        MAIL CODE 907
County .........:  COOK                                  City/State/Zip.:  NEW YORK        NY  20246-1234
Country.........:  USA

Location Manager:  SANDRA STEPHENS                       Phone..........:  (201) 555-0222  ext.  1234
          Phone:  (312) 555-5432 ext.  2345

Legal Review By.......:  ROBERT ADAMS          03/15/90      Floors.......:   02
Financial Review By...:  KATHERYN SMITH        04/13/90      Type Facility:   CORP. HEADQUARTERS
Auth. Request required:  N
Auth. Request approved:  N
Internal Letter Only..:  Y                     10/02/89

                                                            Leasing Agent........:  PROFESSIONAL BROKERAGE
Owner's Representative:  WILLIAMS INVESTMENTS, INC.         Agent's Representative:  SANDRA K. BROKER
          Phone......:  (312) 555-3209 ext.  4309                    Phone.......:  (312) 555-8067

Rent Payment      PROFESSIONAL BROKERAGE COMPANY         Correspondence:  PROFESSIONAL BROKERAGE COMPANY
   Payable To:    AS AGENT FOR                            Notification:   304 EAST WACKER DRIVE
                  RAYSON DEVELOPMENT COMPANY                  Address:    SUITE 400
Rent Payment      PROFESSIONAL BROKERAGE COMPANY         City/State/Zip:  CHICAGO,        IL    60631
   Address:       P. O. BOX 329856

City/State/ Zip:  CHICAGO         IL    60634-9856

Lease   Effective..:  06/18/90        Total   Years :  5
Dates:  Occupancy..:  06/15/90        Term:   Months:  0
        Termination:  06/30/95                Days..:  12      Holdover:  1.25 TIMES BASE RENT

Options...............:  Y            No. of Option Periods:  2      For Years Per Option:  5
                                      Days Notice Required.:  180

Option For Other Space:  Y (If Yes, See Lease)
Option For Purchase...:  Y (If Yes, See Lease)
                                                                            Exercise Notification
Option          1. ABC COMPANY HAS THE RIGHT OF FIRST REFUSAL    Option              To Landlord:
Information:       ON 20,000 R.S.F. ON THE 3RD FLOOR, 8,000       Begins     Ends     Deadline Sent
                  R.S.F. ON THE 4TH FLOOR AND 3,000 R.S.F.
                  IN THE BASEMENT.                            1. 07/01/95  06/30/00   01/01/95
                2. ABC CO. HAS THE OPTION TO PURCHASE THE     2. 07/01/00  06/30/05   01/01/00
                   BUILDING ON 07/01/95. LANDLORD MUST BE     3.
                   NOTIFIED 180 DAYS IN ADVANCE - BY 01/01/95 4.
                   IF ABC CO. WILL PURCHASE THE BUILDING.

Rent/Penalty........:  5% OF MO. AMOUNT DUE.
Cancellation/Penalty:  NPV OF BALANCE OF RENT @ 10% + 12%.
```

Exhibit 4.11   Leased Property Master Listing Report

To answer these and many other questions, a number of corporations have developed and implemented an integrated, consistent methodology of inventorying owned and leased property through a user-friendly computerized program and database in accordance with their corporation's real estate and facilities policies and procedures. These computerized systems (mainframe and/or PC-based) are designed to address corporate and business unit real estate assets and requirements while maintaining the decentralized or centralized management of real estate assets and providing for business unit control or corporate control over real estate decisions.

```
              MASTER LISTING BY LOCATION              PROPERTY    BISU   X   COMP  100
                    AS OF: 06/18/95                   SELECTION   STAT   01  ACCT  1000
      PAGE    2                                                   BLDG  1000  PRCL  01

REAL ESTATE FILE NUMBER: X-100-01-1000-1000-01

Deposit.............:  Y  Amount   $     10,000.00
Parking/1000 Sq. Ft.:  3.21                           Floors Leased....:   17th and 18th.
Upfit Allowance.....:  Y  Amount   $    345,245.00    Date of Agreement:   05/01/90

Total Lease Commitment    $    3,500,000.00           Areas:  Total.......:    35,000
Rate/Rentable Sq.Ft./YR   $           20.00                   (Sq.Ft.) Office......:    35,000
Base Rent Payment/Month   $        58,333.33                   Warehouse...:
Operating Expense/Month   $         8,956.82                   Production..:
Common Area Maint/Month   $           921.34                   Net Rentable:    35,000
Total Monthly Commitment  $        68,211.49                   Net Usable..:    31,500
Total Annual Commitment   $       818,537.88          Annual Commitment Due Date..: $
Option Period Cost        $         5,000.00
Option Period Cost Info:  AMOUNT IS CHARGED AGAINST RENT

Common Area:            Property Area....:      95,348  Sq. Ft. OR    2.189 Acres
Factor.....:  10.021%   Additional Area Affected By Option....:    31,000  Sq. Ft. -  Land:    0.712 Acres

Escalation Clause: Y                              Periods   Begins      Ends        Rent/Month
Escalation   1. RENT WILL ESCALATE AT A RATE OF 3%    1.    07/01/91  06/30/92   $   60,083.33
Terms:          PER YEAR.                             2.    07/01/92  06/30/93   $   61,885.83
             2. THE EXPENSE STOP IS $6.30.            3.    07/01/93  06/30/94   $   63,742.40
             3. FOR THE OPTION PERIODS, THE RENT FOR  4.
                THE 1ST AND 2ND OPTIONS WILL BE       5.
                MARKET.                               6.
             4. AT THE END OF THE INITIAL 5 YEAR TERM 7.
                THE RENT WILL INC. A MIN. OF $1.50/YR.8.
                                                      9.
                                                     10.

Property Tax I.D. Number:   373-2949-12-04
Property Taxes By Lessee:   Y
   Last Year:    /  /      $                     Insurance By Lessee:   Y     Coverage:  $1,000,000/OCCURRENCE
   This Year:  12/31/90    $     13,238.92
   Next Year:  12/31/91    $     15,000.00       Utilities By Lessee:   Y     HVAC FOR COMPUTER AND SWITCH RM.

Services Included            0 - No Svcs Incl   2 - HVAC       4 - Plumbing   6 - Roofing   8 - Lighting
1  2  3  4  5  6  7  8  9    1 - Janitorial     3 - Electrical 5 - Grounds    7 - Signage   9 - Exterior

General     1. ORIGINAL SPACE DESIGN BY: INTERIOR
Comments:      DESIGN OF CHICAGO.                                  Approval            Date
            2. BLDG. PLANS LOCATED IN FACILITY DEPT.
            3. ENTIRE BUILDING IS BEING UPGRADED       Division..: Jane M. Simpson, V.P.    05/03/90
               FROM THE LOBBY TO THE PENTHOUSE         Unit......: Richard P. Frye, Sr. V.P. 05/04/90
               ELEVATOR.                               Corporate.: Samuel R. Wilson, Ex. V.P. 05/05/90
            4. THE BUILDING FITNESS CENTER IS AVAIL.
               AT NO COST TO ABC CO. EMPLOYEES.
```

Exhibit 4.11   Leased Property Master Listing Report (Continued)

This section focuses on the real estate management requirements of multi-location corporate business units with a highly decentralized approach. If a corporation's business environment is centralized or has a small number of locations, the basic approach is similar but usually less complicated to implement.

System Objectives

The corporate real estate and facility inventory system should allow users to fulfill the following objectives:

- To know what they own and lease.
- To know and track all financial and legal real estate obligations.
- To save time and human resources.

```
                    MASTER LISTING BY REAL ESTATE FILE NUMBER          PROPERTY   BISU   X   COMP   100
                              AS OF: 06/18/95                          SELECTION  STAT  05   ACCT  1005
PAGE    1                                                                         BLDG 0823  PRCL    02

REAL ESTATE FILE NUMBER: X-100-05-1005-0823-02

Location Name ..:  TEST PROP. FOR ABC CO. OWNED PROPERTY              Surplus Approval:    Y
Business U./Div.:  ABC DIVISION                                       Dates:
Property Address:  334 EAST WACKER DRIVE                              Submitted.......:    05/04/90
                   SUITE 200                                          Changed.........:    06/18/90
City/State/Zip .:  CHICAGO              IL    60634-6578
County/Country .:  COOK                       USA                     Floors: 2

Location Manager:  SANDRA STEPHENS, FACILITY MANAGER
Phone ..........:  (312) 555-5432 ext. 2345

Legal Review By ......:  ROBERT ADAMS                    01/06/90     Land ...:        6.12   Acres
Financial Review By ..:  KATHERYN SMITH                  03/21/90     Building:      42,789   Sq.Ft.
Auth. Request Required:  Y                                            Other ..:     266,587   Sq. Ft.
Auth. Request Approved:  Y
Internal Letter Only .:  N     If Yes,                   10/15/90
                                                                     Property Tax I.D. No.   373-2949-11-43
Topo Available ..........:  Y                            05/07/90     Property Taxes:
Survey/Plot Plan Available: Y                            05/10/90     Last Year:  12/31/89 $ 112,345.11
Appraised Value ......... $    12,345,678.90             08/08/87     This Year:  12/31/90 $ 127,853.94
Pictures Available ......:  Y                                         Next Year:  12/31/91 $ 130,000.00
Zoning Jurisdiction ......:  CHICAGO      Zoned:  O-1

Mortgage Dated:  06/02/90    In The Amount Of:   $  6,000,000.00  @ 9.70%   For 10 Yrs. 06 Months
Payoff Date:     12/31/00    Monthly Payment:    $     55,555.56  For   126 Months

Mortgage Payable To.....:  FIRST UNITED SAVINGS AND LOAN ASSOCIATION
                           OF GREATER CHICAGO
Mortgage Payment Address:  FIRST UNITED SAVINGS AND LOAN ASSOCIATION
                           4390 NORTH MICHIGAN AVENUE
                           SUITE 120
City/State/Zip..........:  CHICAGO          IL    60634-6578   Country:    USA

Deed Dated:   06/02/90    Deed Recorded: 06/06/90    Book Volume: 65-2375   Page: 4321

Purchase Price:      $   8,065,432.01      06/02/90          Insurance Coverage:  $10,000,000.00
Book Value:  Land:   $   2,665,872.09
       Improvements: $   5,348,625.90      06/12/90

General Warranty:  Y                                     Purchaser:  ABC COMPANY
Special Warranty:  N
Quitclaim ......:  N
Grant ..........:  N                                     Seller ..:  RAYSON DEVELOPMENT
Title Insurance :  Y     Amount $   8,065,432.01                     COMPANY

General     1. THIS BUILDING HAS BEEN PURCHASED TO        Easement(s) At Purchase ..:  Y  If Yes, See Deed
Comments:      PROVIDE A HEADQUARTERS FOR ABC CO.         Easement(s) After Purchase:  N  If Yes, See File
            2. THE ENTIRE BUILDING WAS RENOVATED IN
               1987 BY RAYSON DEVELOPMENT.                              Approval                      Date
            3. PARKING FOR ABC MANAGEMENT AND STAFF
               WAS INCLUDED IN THE PURCHASE FOR       Division   JANE M. SIMPSON, V.P.             10/18/89
               190 SPACES AT 330 EAST WACKER DRIVE.  Bus. Unit   RICHARD P. FRYE, SR. V.P.         10/18/89
            4. ASBESTOS WAS REMOVED IN 1985.         Corporate   PHILLIP S. MILLER, EXEC. V.P.     10/18/89
```

Exhibit 4.12   Owned Property Master Listing Report

- To identify opportunities to reduce real estate expense.

- To increase accuracy and eliminate duplication of records.

- To provide reports and analytical tools not feasible with manual systems.

- To help formulate short- and long-term real estate strategies.

- To efficiently transfer data between users at the business unit level and master files at the corporate level.

The development, implementation, and maintenance of the system is an ongoing and evolving program.

The real estate inventory system[3] must support the corporation's objectives and the particular objectives of the business units, which may include:

Corporate Objectives	Business Unit Objectives
Plan ahead.	Support the corporate business plan.
Maximize the use of resources.	Minimize or reduce the increase in additional resources.
Increase productivity.	Meet competitive pressures and lead the competition.
Manage real property resources.	Identify employee and space requirements to meet business and competitive situations.
Identify, consolidate, sublease, or dispose of real property.	Reduce expenditure, sell or sublease property that is productive, take advantage of market/synergy situation, and reduce unprofitable commitments.

Economic Impact

The development and implementation of this system provides a necessary tool in the annual and long-range planning process discussed in chapters 2 and 3. With the information in the database, the business unit user and the corporation can easily determine the responsible business unit; total number of properties owned and leased by the corporation by type; and the individual and total amount of monthly and yearly rent, operating expenses, taxes, and insurance paid by the business unit or the corporation for each property location.

Many corporations cannot tell their stockholders the value of their real estate and facility holdings or the yearly rent payments. The system can, given accurate input, easily and quickly provide management and control information to answer management's questions.

Historically, accounts payable departments pay by landlord or vendor name, not by location name, which is the file name used by the business unit user. By using reports such as the Rent Payment Schedule Report shown in Exhibit 4.10, the business unit user can now review monthly and cross-check payments made to landlords and other vendors against the amounts paid by the business unit's accounts payable department.

The facility inventory system is a management tool that can help corporations and facility professionals use sound business principles to realistically and strategically manage their corporation's real estate equity, assets, and capital expenditures. The purpose, use, and maintenance of the system does not stop with

---

[3]An example of such a system is LeaseKIT(TM), a PC database software product developed jointly by Edmond P. Rondeau and Applied Software Technology, Inc., Atlanta, Georgia. This system was designed specifically for the corporate facility and real estate professional who manages leased and owned corporate properties. Exhibits 4.8 through 4.12 are reports from this software. Robert Kevin Brown also pioneered the development of PC-leased corporate real property information systems.

implementation but must be continuously assessed and this assessment must become an ongoing, regular process for all business unit users. The development and implementation of such a system is more than just a project. It involves spending many hours to learn about the people, the corporation, the business units and their cultures, and the current avenues of information. More importantly, these questions must be answered: Who performs the real estate and facilities tasks? How could this system help them? Who at the business unit will be maintaining the database after implementation?

DETERMINING YOUR CUSTOMER'S REQUIREMENTS

Your real estate broker can help, advise, and assist you in property negotiations, but it remains your responsibility to obtain the best deal possible. To do this, you need information about many factors such as the market, the economy, the area, and the available workforce. You need to know where your customer lives, where his or her employees live, and what the immediate and long-range plans are for transportation, utilities, and taxes. You must be aware of political and community events; natural resources such as clean air, water, and soil; the presence of hazardous waste or pollutants; lease or purchase costs, operating expenses, common area maintenance costs, and special assessments; schools, colleges, airports, and parking; construction activity; leasing, subleasing, and purchasing activity; free rent, work letter, or up-fit allowances; moving expenses and housing (single and multifamily); community amenities—shopping, recreation, medical services, legal services, banks, religious activities, garbage disposal, and day-care centers. These are just some of the topics you may need to research to help your customer make the best real estate decision (see Exhibits 4.1, 4.19, 4.20, 4.21).

Take enough time to understand your customer's annual and long-range business plans and requirements. In discussing your role and theirs as team members to meet their needs, explain how you propose to organize their real estate assignments and how your department will support their project before, during, and after the real estate acquisition. This includes a review of your department mission, staff, previous real estate assignments, quality, excellence, and customer satisfaction programs, and how you measure performance and service against specific standards for this requirement, as discussed in chapter 1.

The Real Estate Team

In support of the corporation's annual and long-range planning process, your real estate team may also include your corporate or outside legal real estate counsel, in-house support services, a real estate broker, a design or engineering consultant, a general contractor, and others. You may use one or a combination of real estate options to solve the real estate requirement:

- Lease a new or existing facility.
- Lease the land or facility with an option to purchase.
- Lease the land; build and own the new facility.

- Build to suit if capital expenditure and ownership are not desired.
- Form a joint venture between the corporation and a developer.
- Purchase the land; build and own the new facility.
- Sell/lease back an existing facility, which usually includes the land.
- Dispose of existing vacant space or surplus property by:

  Locating another in-house division or department that could use the space and/or property and is willing to take over part or all of the remaining obligation

  Subleasing, if leased

  Negotiating a buyout of the remaining lease obligation

  Selling, if owned

  Leasing, if owned

  Donating, if owned, to a governmental agency or a nonprofit organization such as a university or college where a tax credit could benefit the facility professional's corporation and customer

Be prepared to help your customer obtain management approval for preliminary costs and budgets—both expense and capital—the schedules, and the total funds the facility professional's corporation must be willing to finance or commit to for a given term. The team members should also provide input and advice on the time requirements and the proposed schedule (shown in Exhibit 4.13) needed to:

- Define the negotiating and selection strategies.
- Identify and visit a number of possible sites.
- Develop and send out the request for proposal (RFP).
- Receive responses to the RFP (see samples in the next section).
- Make a comparative analysis of each response to the RFP.
- Begin negotiations; make real financial and space design comparative analyses based on the results of ongoing negotiations.
- Make a site recommendation to your customer.
- Review your customer's site selection.
- Make a presentation to management and obtain management's approval.
- Proceed with detail negotiations for the selected site.
- Review the legal documents, including exhibits, for legal and business issues to ensure that your corporation's interests are protected.
- Review and request revisions to the legal documents and exhibits.
- Review revisions to the legal documents and exhibits.
- Obtain the appropriate management signatures on the legal lease or sale and purchase agreement documents.

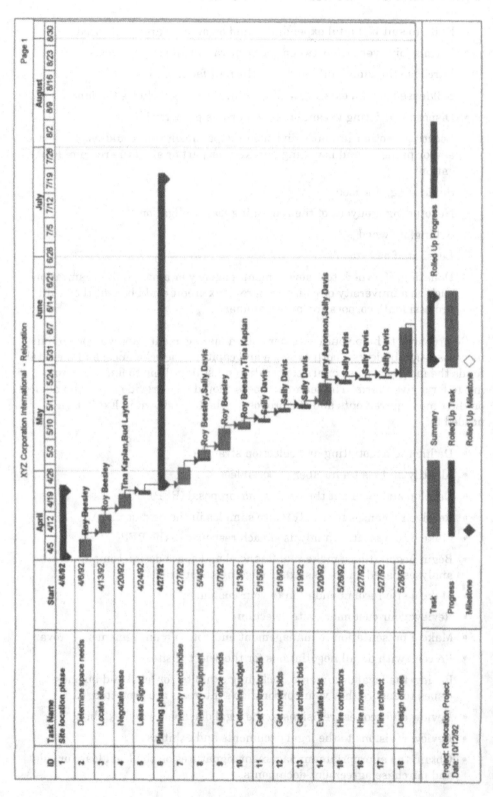

Exhibit 4.13   GANTT Chart—Relocation of XYZ Corporation International

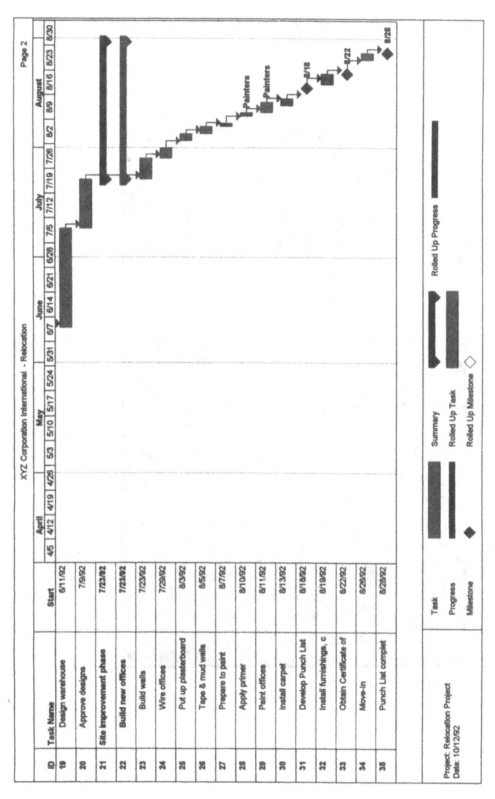

Exhibit 4.13   GANTT Chart—Relocation of XYZ Corporation International (Continued)

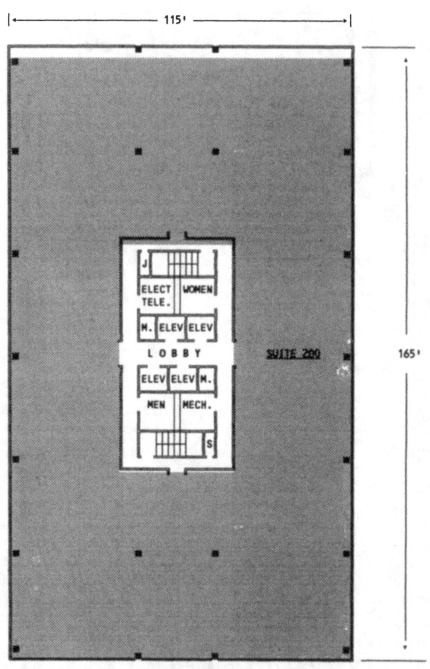

Exhibit 4.13A   Floor Plan

- Implement the construction or renovation phase.
- Obtain the occupancy permit before move-in.

The positive relationships you develop through your understanding of your company and customer's requirements and culture can help ensure that you and your staff are valuable contributors to your company.

LEASE PROPERTY NEGOTIATING CHECKLIST

You should consider the following items while negotiating a lease. You may want to include others that are unique to your customer's requirements and corporate legal requirements.

Property Information
- Property street address, county, city, ZIP code.
- Landlord (Lessor) name, address, city, ZIP code, telephone number
- Property leasing agent, representative, telephone number
- Rent payments payable to, rent payment address
- Landlord correspondence notification address
- Does the landlord have a financial partner? If yes, who?

Terms of the Lease
- Effective or commencement date
- Occupancy date
- Termination date
- Total initial term of lease in years/months
- Holdover capability (Can you stay on after the end of the lease on a month-to-month basis, and, if yes, for what additional percentage of rent?)
- Options—yes or no; if yes, number of options, years for each option period and dates options begin and end
- Number of days required to notify landlord to take option
- Option for other space within the property with amount of space being optioned
- Amount of rent for option period—fixed, consumer price index (CPI), percentage per year, etc.
- Specific option information unique to your location, landlord, right of first refusal of specific floors or space, etc.
- Rent or cancellation penalties
- Deposit required (your company's basic policy may be *not* to pay a deposit, as the deposit represents risk your company may not pose to a landlord). If

a deposit cannot be negotiated out of the deal, ideally, it should be no more than one month's rent and should earn interest for your company.

- Free rent (with today's soft markets, free rent is an appropriate method to gain financial benefit and reduce the effective rate)
- Parking per 1,000 rentable square feet
- Parking for visitors
- Reserved parking (ideally at no cost)
- Cost of parking (if not free for the term of the lease, try to lock in the rate for the term and option periods)
- Up-fit allowance or work letter, and the quality this will provide
- Purchase option; if yes, cost and date to notify landlord or date of purchase
- Floors to be leased and total number of floors to be leased
- Floor plans exhibits
- Date the agreement is signed
- Density of employee restriction
- Ability to sublease or assign the lease and restrictions, if any
- A contingency or special stipulation clause to provide a requirement for:

  Permitting the work

  Obtaining a certificate of occupancy

  Approval of the parent company

  Existing required zoning permitting the proposed use

  Letter from local utility providers stating that the amount and quality of services are available for the specific project

  The landlord and tenant to meet certain key dates to complete preliminary plans, design development and construction and interior design documents, permits, order special materials, begin construction, percentage of construction progress, move-in, substantial completion, certificate of occupancy, etc.

  A bonus/penalty that may be monetary, additional days of free rent, delay of the start of the lease effective date, etc.

  Cost of the work within the specified work letter or landlord's allowance

Rental Information

- Total lease commitment over the initial term of the lease
- Rental rate per rentable square foot
- Base rent payment per month and total rent per year
- Operating expenses per month (this complicated and expensive item should be thoroughly detailed in the lease, especially with regard to the percentage of expense pass-through, the base amount and base year, etc.)
- Common area maintenance (especially for properties where the site maintenance is managed by the landlord and you pay utilities, landscaping, etc.)

- Option period cost(s)
- Total rentable square footage (RSF) being leased and how it is calculated by the landlord (as defined by BOMA or the commonly accepted /recognized local method)
- RSF per floor
- Total usable square footage (USF) and how it is calculated by the landlord (as defined by BOMA or the commonly accepted /recognized local method)
- USF per floor
- Common area factors (as defined by BOMA or the commonly accepted/recognized local method)
- Property area in square feet and acres, if this is a ground lease
- Escalation clause (this is an important aspect where the details establish future rents with specific information on what is being escalated)

Tenant / Landlord Responsibilities

- Property taxes (these may or may not be included, depending on your market)
- Property Tax ID Number, if you must pay the taxes directly to the taxing agency
- Last year's taxes, this year's taxes, and next year's estimated taxes
- Occupancy or use tax (established by local government)
- Insurance—coverage(s) requested by the landlord or financial partner
- Services included in the lease; may be "none" or:
  Janitorial
  Signage
  Grounds/Common Area Maintenance (CAM)
  Electricity
  Exterior/Window repair
  Plumbing repair
  HVAC (heating, air conditioning, and ventilating)
  Lighting
  Roofing
- Window washing schedule
- After-hours HVAC and cost
- Hours of normal HVAC service (Is Saturday morning included? Building holidays at property?)
- Service elevator and hours of operation
- Porter service and costs, if any
- Loading dock(s), hours of operation, and trash disposal

- Security: Guards, access card (cost), cameras, parking, after-hour access, fire stair access, keys, police, etc.
- Fire and life safety, fire stations, hospitals, etc.
- Basement or tenant storage
- Signage: Suite, lobby directory, building, building pylon, etc.
- Noncompetitive tenants
- Building rules and regulations
- Smoking/no smoking policy in building
- Written statement from landlord that the building contains no friable asbestos

Amenities

- Food service, type, location, hours of operation, etc.
- Vending, location, serviced _____ times per week
- No smoking or smoking areas
- Tenant conference facility at no cost to tenant
- Health/fitness center, location, cost(s), if any
- Executive dining, type, location, hours of operation, etc.
- Retail services: bank, copy center, laundry, etc.
- Mail or postal facility
- Handicapped parking, access, rest rooms, etc.
- Public transportation:
  Roads
  Bus
  Airlines
  Pedestrian sidewalks
  Interstates
  Rapid transit/subway
  Ferry
- Tax advantages:
  No local or business taxes
  No local or state income taxes
  State revenue bonds for historical restoration, etc.
- Access to the building: pedestrian, vehicular, and services
- Shared telephone switch, telephone services, etc.
- Normal building hours
- Adequate and clean rest room facilities

PURCHASE PROPERTY NEGOTIATING CHECKLIST

Consider the following items while negotiating the sale and purchase of property. You should also include other items unique to your customer's requirements and corporate legal requirements.

Property Information

- Property street address, county, city, ZIP code
- Seller name, address, city, ZIP code, telephone number
- Property leasing agent, representative, telephone number
- First and/or second mortgage payments payable to, payment address
- Does the seller have a financial partner? If yes, who?

Terms of the Sale and Purchase

- Letter of intent
- Date of the sale and purchase agreement
- Date for closing of the sale
- Occupancy date or certificate of occupancy date
- Options to purchase additional property—yes or no; if yes, number of options, years for each option period and dates options begin and end
- Number of days required to notify seller to take option
- Option for other space within the property with amount of space being optioned
- Amount of option period cost—fixed, consumer price index (CPI), percentage per year, etc.
- Specific option information unique to your location, landlord, right of first refusal of specific floors or space, etc.
- Earnest money deposit required and refundable, nonrefundable, applied to purchase price, etc.
- Seller or purchaser to pay for all, share, or part of the closing costs, attorney fees, prorated property taxes, prorated insurance, prorated municipal special assessments, boundary surveys, legal descriptions, easements, soil testing, soil borings, soil engineering, zoning fees, filing and recording fees
- Purchase contingencies may include:

  Closing to take place only after work permit is obtained from local governmental authorities

  Initial and final approval is obtained from the parent company

  Existing required zoning permits the proposed use

  Letter is obtained from local utility providers and local governmental authorities stating that the quantity and quality of utility and site services (water, sewer, natural gas, electricity, fire protection, etc.) are available for the specific purchaser's project at the time required

The seller and purchaser agree to meet certain key dates to complete preliminary plans, design development and construction permits, obtain construction or permanent financing or mortgage, etc.

A bonus/penalty, which may be monetary, etc., agreed on if certain key dates or events are not met by either party

Obtaining a general warranty deed

Liens, back taxes, easements, or items that prohibit or cloud clear title to the property are removed

Clear title and title insurance for the property is obtained

Written confirmation is obtained from an independent testing laboratory that the site on and below grade does not contain soil pollutants, hazardous waste, buried obstructions, etc.

Soil investigation report is obtained stating that the site can support the proposed building and/or site use

The purchaser is able to obtain insurance.

Purchaser's initial property taxes are limited for a specified period

Purchaser is able to obtain a specified mortgage at a specified percentage rate

Purchaser is able to obtain favorable financing or waiver of taxes from the local governmental authority

Restrictive covenants and site developments, including utilities, roads, and services, are accepted by the local governmental authorities before closing

An inspection and bond is obtained from a local pest control company that the facility is free from specific pests (termites, mice, rats, ants, etc.)

Continued warranties are obtained for major building mechanical and electrical systems

- Number of parking spaces available
- Parking for visitors
- Reserved parking
- Cost for parking if there is no on-site parking (if not free, try to lock in a long-term rate)
- Site, boundary, and floor plans exhibits
- Site covenants or restrictions, if any

Mortgage Information
- Total purchase commitment
- Cost per square foot of property and/or building
- Mortgage payment per month, mortgage percentage for a specified period, and total mortgage per year
- Availability of local municipal development bonds or industrial development revenue bonds

Operating Information

- Operating expenses per month
- Common area maintenance (especially utilities, landscaping, etc.)
- Option period cost(s)
- Total square footage (SF) being purchased and how it is calculated by the seller (as defined by BOMA or the commonly accepted/recognized local method)
- RSF per floor
- Total usable square footage (USF) and how it is calculated by the landlord (as defined by BOMA or the commonly accepted/recognized local method)
- USF per floor
- Common area factors (as defined by BOMA or the commonly accepted/recognized local method)
- Property area in square feet and access to three decimal places
- Property taxes (these may or may not be included, depending on your market)
- Property Tax ID Number
- Last year's taxes, this year's taxes, and next year's estimated taxes
- Occupancy or use tax (established by local government)
- Insurance
- Porter service and costs, if any
- Loading dock(s), hours of operation, and trash disposal
- Security: Guards, access card (cost), cameras, parking, after-hour access, fire stair access, keys, police, etc.
- Fire and life safety, fire stations, hospitals, etc.
- Basement or tenant storage
- Signage: Suite, lobby directory, building, building pylon, etc.
- Nearest competitive company
- Building rules and regulations
- Building and/or municipal smoking/no smoking regulations
- Written statement from seller that the site or building contains no friable asbestos, hazardous waste, soil pollutants, etc.

Amenities

- Food service, type, location, hours of operation, etc.
- Vending, location, serviced _____ times per week
- No smoking or smoking areas
- Conference facility

- Health/fitness center, location, cost(s), if any
- Executive dining, type, location, hours of operation, etc.
- Retail services: bank, copy center, laundry, etc.
- Public transportation:

  Roads

  Bus

  Airlines

  Pedestrian sidewalks

  Interstates

  Rapid transit/subway

  Ferry
- Tax advantages:

  No local or business taxes

  No local or state income taxes

  State revenue bonds for historical restoration, etc.
- Mail or postal facility
- Access to the building: Pedestrian, vehicular, and services
- Handicapped parking, access, rest rooms, etc.
- Shared telephone switch, telephone services, etc.
- Normal building hours
- Adequate and clean rest room facilities

SAMPLE LEASE: PROPOSAL LETTER

WEST WACKER TOWERS, L.P.

4425 West Wacker Drive
Suite 2100
Chicago, IL 60630
(312) 555–3400

Ms. Sandra K. Broker   June 30, 2005
Vice President—Brokerage
Professional Brokerage Company
304 East Wacker Drive
Suite 2210
Chicago, IL 60630

    Re: West Wacker Towers
           Second Floor Lease Proposal
           4425 W. Wacker Drive
           Chicago, IL 60630

Dear Ms. Broker:

In response to your Request for Proposal dated June 18, 2005, I have been authorized by Westland Development Company, Inc. (Landlord) to submit the following proposal to your client, ABC Company (Tenant), for the leasing of new office space at the referenced location:

PREMISES: Approximately 16,535 rentable square feet (15,683 usable square feet) on the second (2nd) floor known as Suite 200 and as shown in the enclosed Exhibit A.

COMMENCEMENT: October 1, 2005.

LEASE TERM: Five (5) years—October 1, 2005, to September 30, 2010.

RENEWAL OPTIONS: Two (2) options for five (5) years for each option. Landlord must be notified in writing one hundred eighty (180) days in advance of the end of the current lease term if Tenant elects to remain in the lease space.

RENTAL RATE: $21.00 per rentable square foot, which includes a Base Rental component of $13.41 per rentable square foot and an Operating Expense component (expense stop) of $7.59 per rentable square foot.

ESCALATION: On the first day of each lease year, commencing October 1, 2005, the Base Rental component shall be increased by four and one half percent (4.5%). Option period Base Rent and Operating Expense component shall be market.

IMPROVEMENTS: Landlord shall provide to the Tenant an allowance of $17.00 per rentable square foot toward the Tenant's improvement of the space. Should Tenant elect to take the option to extend the lease term, Landlord shall provide Tenant an allowance of $8.00 per rentable square foot at the beginning of each option period for painting, carpeting, and minor alterations.

RENT ABATEMENT: Tenant shall receive twelve (12) free months of Base Rent abatement starting on October 1, 2005, and will begin Base Rental payments effective October 1, 2006. Operating Expenses shall be paid for the term of the lease.

PARKING: Landlord shall provide to the Tenant three (3) parking spaces per thousand rentable square feet at $10 per month per space through September 30, 2006. Landlord shall provide Tenant five (5) reserved and free spaces for the initial term of the lease on the 1st parking level.

CONF. FACILITIES: Landlord's 600 square feet conference facilities on the first floor shall be available for reservation by the Tenant at no additional cost.

HEALTH FAC.:   Landlord shall provide five (5) Executive memberships in the West Wacker Towers Health Club at no cost to the Tenant through the end of the initial term of the lease. Landlord shall provide up to seventy-five (75) Standard memberships for Tenant employees in the Health Club at $40 per month per member through September 30, 2006, when these memberships are paid by the Tenant.

SECURITY DEPOSIT: One (1) month's rent to be held for the term of the lease.

ASBESTOS: Landlord warrants to the Tenant that the space, building systems, and the building contain no friable asbestos.

If the terms and conditions set forth in this proposal are acceptable, please have the proposal executed by your client where indicated below and return one executed copy to my attention not later than 5:00 P.M. (CT), July 6, 2005. Should you have any questions please do not hesitate to contact me.

Sincerely,

Robert A. Thompson
Vice President
Property Management

enclosures

cc: Linda B. Stone (w/enclosures)
      W. Wacker/ABC Co. file (w/enclosures)

AGREED AND ACCEPTED:
ABC Company

By: _____   Date: _____

Title: _____

SAMPLE PURCHASE: LETTER OF INTENT

This Letter of Intent is made and entered into this <u>15th</u> day of <u>September, 2005</u>, by and between <u>ABC Company</u> ("Purchaser") and <u>Warehouse Developers, Inc.</u> ("Seller").

In consideration of the agreements hereinafter set forth, the parties hereto mutually agree as follows:

1. Seller agrees to sell and Purchaser agrees to purchase the property located at <u>2548 West Wacker Drive, Chicago, IL 60638,</u> in the County of <u>Cook,</u> State of <u>Illinois,</u> as more specifically described in Exhibit A, which is attached hereto and incorporated herein by this reference, together with all rights and appurtenances thereto and all rights, title, and interest of Seller in and to any and all roads and streets bounding such property. A more definitive description shall be provided by the Seller to the Purchaser from an accurate boundary and topographic survey acceptable to the Seller and Purchaser, at Seller's cost, to be reimbursed by Purchaser at closing.

2. The purchase price shall be as agreed to by the Seller and Purchaser based upon an appraisal of the property not later than 90 days from the date of this Letter of Intent by a minimum of three (3) appraisers retained by the Purchaser and approved by the Seller. Seller and Purchaser agree that the purchase price shall not exceed <u>$6.60</u> nor be less than <u>$5.15</u> per square foot of the appraised and surveyed property. Failure to agree on a reasonable purchase price shall render this Letter of Intent null and void.

3. Conveyance of the property shall be by general warranty deed and shall be covered by a fully paid title insurance policy.

4. Purchaser proposes to use the property for the construction and operation of a free-standing warehouse distribution center with outside storage. In the event that the property is restricted in any way which prohibits, limits or restricts the use of the property for such purpose, Seller shall obtain appropriate authorization so that the property may be used for the purposes described above. In the event Seller is unable to secure the authorization necessary for utilizing the property within 180 days from the date of this Letter of Intent, Purchaser may so notify Seller in writing, whereupon this Letter of Intent shall become null and void.

5. Further, Purchaser's obligation to purchase is also subject to the following within 180 days from the above date:

   a. Purchaser's obtaining approval and funding of the purchase of the property and construction of the warehouse distribution center from their parent company, <u>XYZ Corporation</u>;

   b. Seller's acquisition of clear title to an entrance way to the property from the adjacent property owner (whereby the adjacent property owner will exchange a portion of the adjacent property to create an entrance way to the subject property in exchange for a portion of the subject property which borders <u>West Wacker Drive</u> and <u>4th Avenue</u> and the adjacent property);

   c. Seller's obtaining results of soil borings and tests of the entrance way and the property stating that the property can be used by the Purchaser as intended without requiring major additional soil, subsoil, drainage, or structural improvements to the site or to the construction;

d. Purchaser's obtaining the necessary licenses, permits, and other authorizations, including curb cuts for reasonable traffic access;

e. Seller's obtaining letters of service and supply from the appropriate agencies for water, gas, electricity, sanitary sewer, storm sewers, and any other necessary public utilities stating that the services and supply are immediately on or contiguous to the subject property and are available to the Purchaser for a connection fee for all such utilities; and

f. Seller's obtaining title insurance binder.

6. Real estate taxes for the current year shall be prorated as of the date of closing.

7. The closing of the herein described purchase and sale shall be subject to the conditions set forth in this Letter of Intent and shall be scheduled at a mutually agreeable time and date on or after 180 days following the date of this Letter of Intent.

In WITNESS WHEREOF, the Seller has caused this Letter of Intent to be executed on the date noted above.

Witness: SELLER:
                                                     WAREHOUSE DEVELOPERS, INC.

_____   By: _____
                                           Walter H. Simpson

                                       Its: <u>President</u>

In WITNESS WHEREOF, the Purchaser has caused this Letter of Intent to be executed on the date noted above.

Witness: PURCHASER:
                                                     ABC COMPANY

_____   By: _____
                                           Robert C. Wilson

                                       Its: <u>President</u>

SITE CRITERIA CONSIDERATIONS

During the first meeting with your customer's representatives, review their perception of the market, their requirements and expectations, and their proposed budget for the project by using a Lease Property: Site Criteria Considerations questionnaire (see Exhibit 4.14) or a Purchase Property: Site Criteria Considerations questionnaire (see Exhibit 4.15). Their expectations may or may not be easily satisfied and may need to be revised in keeping with current space and furnishings standards and corporate policies and procedures. Their management

Location: _____ Date: _____ Evaluator Name: _____	CRITERIA WEIGHTS									
	NOT VERY IMPORTANT			IMPORTANT			ESPECIALLY IMPORTANT			
CRITERIA CONSIDERATIONS	1	2	3	4	5	6	7	8	9	10
Sq. Ft. Required: _____; ☐ Rentable or ☐ Usable										
Lease Term: ☐ 1 Yr. ☐ 3 Yrs. ☐ 5 Yrs. ☐ ___ Yrs.										
Occupancy Date: _____, 2___										
Access To: ☐ Interstate ☐ Public Transportation										
Bldg. Quality Type: ☐ A+ ☐ A ☐ B ☐ C ☐ ___										
Interior Upfit (Type): ☐ Low ☐ Med. ☐ High ☐ ___										
Building Lobby Image										
Window Views, Executives										
Window Views, Staff										
Floor Plan Flexibility										
Rental Rate Per RSF: ☐ $12 ☐ $15 ☐ $18 ☐ $___ /Yr.										
Interior Budget/U.S.F.: ☐ $10 ☐ $15 ☐ $20 ☐ $___										
Upfit Cost/U.S.F. By: Landlord ☐ $___; Tenant ☐ $___										
Rent Abatement - Free Rent: ☐ ___ Months										
Rent Escalation: ☐ Fixed % ☐ CPI ☐ % of CIP ☐ ___										
Options: ☐ 1 ☐ 2 For ☐ 3 Yrs. ☐ 5 Yrs. ☐ ___ Yrs.										
Expansion Options: ☐ ___ ☐ R.S.F. or ☐ U.S.F.										
Parking: ☐ Covered ☐ Reserved										
Building Security										
Loading Dock										
Freight Elevator										
After Hours HVAC										
Stand by Generator/Emergency Power										
On Site Food Service Facility										
Conference Facility										
Health Facility										
Building Management and Maintenance										
Other										

Exhibit 4.14   Leased Property Site Criteria Considerations

Location: _____	CRITERIA WEIGHTS									
Date: _____ Evaluator Name: _____	NOT VERY IMPORTANT			IMPORTANT			ESPECIALLY IMPORTANT		ABSOLUTELY NECESSARY	
CRITERIA CONSIDERATIONS	1	2	3	4	5	6	7	8	9	10
Acreage Required: _____										
Building Size/Gross Square Feet: _____										
Number of Floors: _____										
Occupancy Date: _____ ____, 2____										
Site Use/Zoning: _____										
Access to: ☐ Interstate ☐ Public Transportation										
Site Image/Landscaping										
Bldg. Quality Type: ☐ A+ ☐ A ☐ B ☐ C ☐ __										
Interior Upfit (Type): ☐ Low ☐ Med. ☐ High ☐ __										
Building Lobby Image										
Floor Plan Flexibility										
Purchase Price Per Acre: $_____										
Purchase Price: Building/Improvements $_____										
Deed/Clear Title										
Title Insurance										
Taxes										
Existing Easements										
Option For Additional Property: _____ Acres										
Signage										
Number of Spaces of Parking Spaces: _____										
Building Security										
Loading Dock										
Freight Elevator										
Utilities										
Stand By Generator/Emergency Power										
Food Service Area										
Trained Local Work Force										
Other										

Exhibit 4.15   Purchase Property Site Criteria Considerations

must support the assessment of need to provide all with a clear definition of the requirement before the real estate search begins.

The terms of the lease or purchase, as well as the location, quality, and costs for constructing and furnishing the space, will vary according to your customer's needs and resources. The real estate broker will expect you to be the spokesperson for the corporation and your customer during the search and negotiating phase. You, your customer, the broker, and other appropriate team members should agree on a negotiating strategy before writing the Request for Proposal (RFP), as discussed later in this chapter.

You may ask your broker to do a ZIP code search of home addresses for all your customer's employees whose jobs will be relocated to determine a feasible geographic area in which to locate a site and to perform a preliminary assessment of the market and the available sites. If the resulting data indicate that what is needed is not readily available or affordable, you may need to expand the geographic area of your search.

The requirements of the RFP usually include a number of nonnegotiable items such as usable square feet, geographic area, term, expansion options, parking, and security. Other items in the RFP may be negotiable: free rent, rate, escalations, base-year operating expenses, option rate, up-fit allowances or tenant work letter, space planning, general contractor, construction and property management fees, after-hours HVAC costs, and cash inducements. Failure to obtain nonnegotiable items may kill the deal, whereas other items are potential throwaways that could be modified or omitted from the requirement.

For example, your customer may not have capital funds and so be willing to pay a higher rental rate or sign a longer-term lease to receive a larger up-fit allowance. A customer needing low rental payments may be willing to fund a part of the capital improvements in return for a discounted rental rate. These and other strategies are all part of putting together a financial model that provides your customer with the best solution for the smallest financial and legal exposure and commitment. You may wish to involve the resources of your corporate legal counsel, finance department, and broker to develop the financial model and strategy.

SELECTING A REAL ESTATE BROKER

Unless you have a very small requirement or will be acquiring or disposing of property from or to another division within your corporation, you may choose to call on one or more licensed commercial real estate brokers to assist you. Some managers in your corporation may believe it is better to work directly with the landlord or the property owner than with a broker because the deal will not include a broker's commission. This sounds easy in theory, but in practice, savings may be unrealistic.

Dealing directly with the landlord or owner may be the way to go if you are adding a small space to your current leased space. But if you are getting started in corporate real estate, your time, real estate expertise, and knowledge of the local and out-of-town markets will be limited. A well-qualified real estate broker can provide you with years of hard-won experience and counsel that are probably not available to you from your legal counsel, customer, or anyone within your corporation.

The real estate broker serves as your expert and resource on the health and availability of real estate in the local or other geographic markets. His or her knowledge and contacts for the type of real estate you are seeking to acquire or dispose of can help you identify potential sites and acquire real estate in a timely manner that meets your customer's requirements.

With few exceptions, a corporation purchases property for a specific requirement. Exhibits 4.16 and 4.17 list information that a real estate broker can fur-

MARKET SURVEY ITEMS	BLDG. 1	BLDG. 2	BLDG. 3	BLDG. 4	BLDG. 5
Building Name	Park Plaza	191 Union Tower	Westfield Place	Sutton Building	1 Crown Square
Building Quality (A, B, or C)	A	A	B	C	A
Landlord	Main St. Ltd.	Wright & Partners	Associated Developers	Metro Properties	Brown & Thomas
Financial Partner	Major Life Insurance	Western Casualty	Chicago Nat'l Bank	Metro Properties	Teacher's Pension Fund
Total Building Rentable Sq. Ft.	258,000	487,400	281,500	110,700	879,550
Building Occupancy %	78.3%	85.2%	67.8%	59.6%	62.4%
Available Rentable Sq. Ft.	55,986	72,137	90,562	44,723	330,711
Available Contiguous R.S.F.	43,000	23,210	31,760	27,610	201,040
Floor Plate Size (R.S.F.)	21,500	23,210	18,750	18,450	25,150
Number of Floors	12	21	15	6	35
Efficiency Factor (rsf/usf)	1.143	1.112	1.136	1.162	1.122
Rate Per Rentable Square Foot	$18.00	$20.50	$15.00	$12.00	$23.00
Rent Escalation	5% /yr.	C.P.I.	3% / yr.	$.15/rsf/yr	7% / yr.
Operating Expense Cost Per RSF	$8.10	$7.05	$6.50	$7.73	$9.12
Blocks from ABC Building	Adjacent	2 North	1 South	3 East	2 West
Building Age	6 yrs.	7 yrs.	10 yrs.	14 yrs.	6 mos.
Floor to Ceiling Height	9' - 0"	8' - 6"	8' - 6"	8' - 3"	9' - 0"
Improvement Allowance/U.S.F.	$22.00	Turnkey	$15.00	Work Ltr.	$27.50
Free Rent On Five Year Term	12 months	9 months	10 months	5 months	12 mos.
Expansion Options	Yes	No	Yes	Yes	Yes
Cancellation Option Available	No	Unknown	Yes	Yes	No
Building Security	Card Access	Sign In/Out	Key and After Hrs.	After Hrs. Only	24 Hrs./On Site
Sprinklered	Yes	Yes	Yes	No	Yes
Conference Room/Facility	No	Yes	No	No	Yes
On Site Parking Available	Yes	No	Yes	Yes	No
Available Parking Cost/Space	$3.15/day	$2.25/day	$2.75/day	No cost	$3.50
Food Service	Yes	Yes	No	Yes	Yes
Computer Room Available	Yes/5th Fl.	No	Yes/Bsmt.	Yes	No
Freight Elevator	Yes	Yes	No	No	Yes
Loading Dock	Yes/3 bays	Yes/2 bays	Yes/2 bays	No	Yes/4 bays

Additional Market Survey Information:

Building 1 - Landlord has been aggressively marketing the building as a number of the 1st five year tenants have left the building. Building includes a quality sit down sandwich shop and is frequented by building tenants and tenants from adjacent buildings. No asbestos.

Building 2 - Landlord's Financial partner has previously taken 3 to 6 months to review each proposal and 2 to 4 months to sign off on the lease for this quality building. A new property management company has been hired and building janitorial services have improved. No Asbestos.

Building 3 - A major corporation which occupies 4 floors will be moving out of the building in 60 days. This space includes a 3,000 square foot computer room with 12" raised floor and a 2 hour UPS system in the building basement. Landlord has been marketing the space and may be close to leasing 2 floors. No asbestos.

Building 4 - Landlord has a good reputation and has numerous office properties throughout Chicago. Building is in good repair and lobby/elevator has recently been renovated. One of the tenants is a small competitor of ABC, Inc. and has three years remaining on their lease. Asbestos has been partially abated.

Building 5 - This is a landmark design and is the newest office building in town. A major corporation has leased 50% of the building for 15 years. There is a lunch/dinner club on the top floor, the ground floor contains a number of food and retail shops, and the conference facility will accommodate 50 in a classroom setting.

Exhibit 4.16   Lease Property Market Survey

MARKET SURVEY ITEMS	BLDG. 1	BLDG. 2	BLDG. 3	BLDG. 4	BLDG. 5
Building Name	132 Union Center	Summitview Terrace	832 Ridgecrest	4420 Main Street	1st Nat'l. Bank Bldg.
Prop./Bldg. Quality (A, B, or C)	B	A	C	B	A
Property Owner	Associated Developers	Brown & Thomas	Smith Properties	Teacher's Pension Fund	Sumitzu Bank & Trust
Acreage Available	6.112	4.231	5.568	3.827	2.969
Site Terrain	Sloping	Level	Sloping	Level	Sloping
Bldg. Size (Gross Sq. Ft.)	77,848	253,000	127,680	375,138	372,806
Number of Floors	4	10	7	18	14
Gross Square Feet Per Floor	19,462	25,300	18,240	20,841	26,629
Efficiency Factor (gsf/usf)	1.123	1.142	1.109	1.136	1.157
Blocks From Stealth Building	1 West	2 South	4 North	Adjacent	3 East
Sale Price For Property/Sq. Ft.	$7.00	$12.00	$10.00	$15.00	$17.00
Total Property Sale Price	$1,597,400	$2,211,600	$2,425,450	$2,500,000	$2,198,600
Sale Price For Building/GSF	$78.00	$93.00	$69.00	$82.00	$104.00
Total Building Sale Price	$6,072,144	$23,529,000	$8,809,920	$30,761,316	$38,771,824
Total Property/Building Sale Price	$7,669,544	$25,740,600	$11,235,370	$33,261,316	$40,970,424
Building Age	8 yrs.	5 yrs.	12 yrs.	10 yrs.	16 yrs.
Building Occupancy %	72.8%	0%	87.2%	77.6%	62.4%
Operating Cost Per GSF	$6.96	$8.21	$7.24	$8.47	$9.91
On Site Parking Spaces/1,000 GSF	3.11	1.13	2.2	2.5	None
Number of Mos. On The Market	3	6	10	7	9
Previous Office Use	Spec.	Corp. HQ	Spec.	Spec.	Bank/Spec
Floor To Ceiling Height	8' - 8"	9' - 0"	8' - 2"	8' - 6"	9' - 0"
Building Security	Sign In/Out	Card Access	Key and After Hours	After Hours Only	24 Hrs./On Site
Asbestos/Structure	No/Steel	No/Steel	Yes/Steel	No/Concrete	No/Concrete
Computer Room	Yes/1st Fl.	Yes/Bsmt.	No	No	Yes/Bsmt.
Sprinklered	Yes	Yes	Partial	Yes	Yes
Food Service	Yes	Yes	No	No	Yes
Loading Dock	Yes/1 Bay	Yes/2 Bays	Yes/1 Bay	Yes/2 Bays	Yes/3 Bays
Freight Elevator	Yes	Yes	No	No	Yes

Additional Market Survey Information:

Property 1 - Seller is slowly leasing the building after a major tenant moved out to Building 5. Majority of leases have 3 or less years until termination. Seller is very interested in selling for cash.

Property 2 - A major corporation headquarters has left town and the building is vacant. This building includes a 5,000 square foot computer room with 18" raised floor, a 4 hour UPS system and an emergency generator in the building basement.

Property 3 - Seller has a good reputation and has numerous office properties throughout Chicago. Building is in good repair and lobby/elevator has recently been renovated.

Property 4 - A new brokerage company has just listed the building and is known for getting "top dollar" for sellers.

Property 5 - This is an older landmark design and a major bank is in the process of relocating to a new building. There is a full service restaurant on the ground floor which also contains a number of retail shops, and a health facility which can accommodate 100 members at a time.

Exhibit 4.17   Purchase Property Market Survey

nish before you begin analyzing available sites. Each property must be evaluated in terms of how the corporation will use and improve it.

The Lease Property Market Survey (Exhibit 4.16) may be prepared on a number of office buildings for lease in a particular section of a metropolitan area. The survey provides competitive information on five office buildings by comparing items that are important for you and your customer's evaluation. In addition, there is some subjective information at the bottom of the survey about each site and landlord. Exhibit 4.17 is a Purchase Property Market Survey that provides similar information on several properties and sites for sale in a particular section of a metropolitan area.

A knowledgeable real estate broker can provide geographic cost information for a specific application at different locations (see Exhibit 4.18). The key variables are land cost, site development cost, fees and building cost, taxes, and utility/operating cost for each location. Remember that these costs are only for *development* of the facility. The cost of living, availability of a trained workforce, transportation, housing, income taxes, and many other business and operational issues must also be obtained and included before making a final selection.

A growing number of tenant representation brokers do not market properties for landlords and will represent you for a fee for services or a commission paid by the landlord or seller. A number of companies also market their services as real estate counselors or corporate real estate advisory consulting services for projects involving large, complex requirements to lease, sublease, acquire, or dispose of property.

JUNE 18, 2005

FAC #	ZIP	CITY	ST	LAND COST PSF	SITE DEV COST PSF	FEES & BLDG COST PSF	TOTAL DEV COST PSF	REAL PROP TAXES PSF	ELECT PSF	GAS PSF
1	82	351 PHOENIX CITY	AL	$0.22	$6.00	$26.70	$32.92	$0.25000	$0.400	$0.200
2	95	302 THOMASTON	GA	$0.12	$6.00	$26.70	$32.82	$0.20000	$0.400	$0.200
3	81	300 ATLANTA	GA	$2.00	$7.50	$30.00	$39.50	$0.35000	$0.400	$0.200
4	83	088 NEWARK	NJ	$6.88	$6.90	$31.30	$45.08	$0.55000	$0.420	$0.550
5	80	122 ALBANY	NY	$1.15	$6.90	$31.30	$39.35	$1.53000	$0.370	$0.300
6	101	120 JOHNSTOWN	NY	$0.05	$6.90	$31.30	$38.25	$1.48000	$0.370	$0.300
7	87	641 KANSAS CITY	MO	$1.75	$6.00	$28.00	$35.75	$0.83000	$0.410	$0.150
8	98	633 ST. CHARLES	MO	$0.80	$5.10	$24.70	$30.60	$0.55000	$0.380	$0.150
9	94	982 BELLEVUE	WA	$1.75	$6.90	$31.30	$39.95	$0.65000	$0.320	$0.240
10	99	982 BURLINGTON	WA	$1.50	$6.90	$31.30	$39.70	$0.62000	$0.320	$0.240
11	84	907 ANAHEIM	CA	$10.00	$6.90	$31.30	$48.20	$0.54000	$0.340	$0.400
12	86	917 ONTARIO	CA	$6.00	$6.90	$31.30	$44.20	$0.54000	$0.340	$0.400
13	85	924 SAN BERNADINO	CA	$3.00	$6.90	$31.30	$41.20	$0.54000	$0.340	$0.400
14	100	923 VICTORVILLE	CA	$1.50	$6.90	$31.30	$39.70	$0.54000	$0.440	$0.400

NOTES:
1. INCLUDES GRADING, UTILITIES, YARD FENCE, YARD CRUSHER RUN, BLDG. SHELL, PAVING &
2. LAND COST PSF IS THE ESTIMATED COST OF AN IMPROVED INDUSTRIAL SITE READY FOR
3. $6.00 PSF OF BLDG COST ARE FEES FOR: LEGAL COSTS, ETC. ($.50 PSF).
                                          PROGRAMMING, ARCH., ENG, SURVEYING, &
                                          GENERAL CONTINGENCY ($2.00 PSF).
                                          LANDSCAPING AND IRRIGATION ($1.00 PSF).

Exhibit 4.18   Geographical Analysis for ABC Company

```
                              JUNE 18, 2005
****************************************************************************
                        S Q U A R E   F O O T   V A L U E S
              TOTAL   10 ACRES    10 ACRES    7 ACRES     4 ACRES     4 ACRES
   WATER &    OPER    BUILDING    BUILDING    BUILDING    BUILDING    BUILDING
   SEWER      COST    200,000 SF  150,000 SF  100,000 SF  60,000 SF   30,000 SF
   PSF        PSF     56,000 SF   40,000 SF   35,000 SF   20,000 SF   10,000 SF   NOTES
****************************************************************************
   $0.050    $0.900  $2,791,032  $2,063,832  $1,601,582   $932,333    $485,333  1, 2 & 3
   $0.050    $0.850  $2,747,472  $2,020,272  $1,571,090   $914,909    $467,909  1, 2 & 3
   $0.050    $1.000  $4,051,200  $3,196,200  $2,409,840  $1,398,480   $873,480  1, 2 & 3

   $0.052    $1.572  $6,129,728  $5,283,928  $3,883,350  $2,238,771  $1,718,771  1, 2 & 3

   $0.050    $2.250  $3,633,740  $2,787,940  $2,136,158  $1,240,376   $720,376  1, 2 & 3
   $0.050    $2.200  $3,152,402  $2,306,602  $1,799,221  $1,047,841   $527,841  1, 2 & 3

   $0.050    $1.440  $3,530,300  $2,782,300  $2,113,610  $1,224,920   $764,920  1, 2 & 3
   $0.050    $1.130  $2,751,680  $2,101,480  $1,618,436   $939,392    $539,392  1, 2 & 3

   $0.050    $1.260  $3,895,100  $3,049,300  $2,319,110  $1,344,920   $824,920  1, 2 & 3
   $0.050    $1.230  $3,786,200  $2,940,400  $2,242,880  $1,301,360   $781,360  1, 2 & 3

   $0.050    $1.330  $7,488,800  $6,643,000  $4,834,700  $2,782,400  $2,262,400  1, 2 & 3
   $0.050    $1.330  $5,746,400  $4,900,600  $3,615,020  $2,085,440  $1,565,440  1, 2 & 3
   $0.050    $1.330  $4,439,600  $3,593,800  $2,700,260  $1,562,720  $1,042,720  1, 2 & 3
   $0.050    $1.430  $3,786,200  $2,940,400  $2,242,880  $1,301,360   $781,360  1, 2 & 3
****************************************************************************

   INTERIOR FINISH.
   BLDG. AND BLDG. COST PSF ASSUMES A BASE BUILDING COST FOR TILT-UP CONSTRUCTION.

   INSPECTION ($2.50 PSF).
```

Exhibit 4.18　Geographical Analysis for ABC Company (Continued)

Real Estate Broker Selection Process

Ideally, you should select, cultivate, and develop a relationship with a qualified real estate broker before a customer asks for your help on a real estate assignment. The process is in many ways similar to selecting a design firm or general contractor for ongoing facility management requirements.

Each metropolitan area has a number of qualified, professional, commercial real estate firms who understand the local market and have contacts in other metropolitan areas if you have an out-of-town requirement. Ask your management, other facility managers, other corporate real estate managers, bankers, and landlords to identify real estate brokerage firms with a superior real estate and customer service reputation. If you are currently using a brokerage firm that you inherited or one your customer wishes to use, determine whether it can provide the services you need and is included among the recommended firms in your poll.

The object of this research is to identify a firm that will create value for your company by increasing your capabilities, effectiveness, and efficiency. Invite the high-caliber firms you identify to make presentations using a format that describes these attributes:

- Customer service orientation
- Available in-house services:

    Research capability

    Real estate financial analysis capability

    Marketing skills

    Sales

    Leasing

    Subleasing

    Property management
- History and ownership of the brokerage company
- Experience as brokers
- Experienced brokers
- Financial capability
- Follow-up procedures
- Request for Proposal (RFP) capability
- Methods of compensation for services:

    Percentage fee from the landlord

    Construction management

    Specializations (office, industrial, warehouse, etc.)
- Contacts with brokers in other cities

    Consulting fee from the corporate customer
- Means of measuring their performance and service
- Reputation and references

After this review, select the best two or three firms and determine how well you feel they:

- Will be sensitive and flexible in quickly adapting to you and your customers' special needs.
- Will listen and act to provide creative alternatives if the real estate requirement runs into major problems.
- Will work with you and your customers. Is this a good match?
- Are able to use the in-house real estate and financial analysis expertise they profess to have.

The broker's commission for services usually is paid by the landlord (leased property) or by the seller (purchased property). For leased property, the commission is usually a percentage of the total rent to be paid over the term of the lease; for purchased property, it is often a percentage of the total price.

Many corporate real estate managers are now using the brokerage selection process to leverage their company's singular or multiple real estate requirements to obtain service or financial concessions from the brokerage company they select. Depending on your agreement with your broker, including the reduction of risk, the commission fee paid by the landlord can be used by your broker to assist your corporation in securing an improved concession package for your customer and corporation. This may include but may not be limited to:

- Lower initial rent
- Additional free rent
- Additional design, construction, or moving allowance(s)
- Relocation and/or telecommunication services

When you feel comfortable that one or possibly two firms can provide the real estate services or financial concessions you desire, make a selection and begin the commitment and investment process. In making a commitment between you and the brokerage firm, agree to invest the time necessary to learn about each other. For the real estate broker, this can include the history of your corporation, the corporation's business and how it is organized, the decision-making process, its position in the marketplace, and the competition.

Your broker should clearly understand your mission and your department's standards of quality, excellence, and service. Thoroughly discuss the services you expect from the broker, including your and their post-occupancy performance review of how well the requirement was satisfied and any adjustments that should be made before the next assignment.

As with a design or construction project, the real estate requirement must be managed through strong lines of communication among all team members so everyone understands what is to be accomplished and who is responsible for specific actions based on an established schedule. We recommend that you select *one* senior person from the brokerage firm to be your primary contact and responsible for coordinating all activities with you. For the sale of property, you might want to consider developing and executing a sales agency agreement similar to the sample shown below to formalize the work to be accomplished by your selected brokerage firm.

SAMPLE SALES AGENCY AGREEMENT

ABC COMPANY, INC.
324 East Wacker Drive
Chicago, IL 60631

Professional Brokerage Company   December 31, 2004
304 East Wacker Drive
Chicago, IL 60631

Re: Approximately 12.9-acre site, together with approximately 95,500 square feet of existing improvements, located at 315 East Wacker Drive, Chicago, IL 60631 (the "Premises")

Gentlemen:

ABC Company, Inc. ("Seller"), hereby appoints Professional Brokerage Company ("Broker"), as its sole agent and grants to Broker the exclusive right to sell the Premises.

AGENCY AGREEMENT

Broker's appointment as Seller's exclusive agent with the exclusive right to sell shall be upon the following terms and conditions:

The term of this Agreement shall commence as of December 30, 2004, and shall continue in effect until December 30, 2005. Seller shall, however, at any time, have the right to remove the Premises from the market by giving written notice to Broker. Should Seller return the Premises to the market before the expiration date of this Agreement, Broker shall be the broker under the terms hereof. At any time after June 30, 2005, Seller shall have the right to terminate this Agreement for any reason upon thirty (30) days prior notice. In the event that Broker fails to diligently pursue this assignment, in Seller's reasonable opinion, or otherwise is in default under the Agreement, Seller shall have the right to terminate the Agreement, at any time, on fifteen (15) days prior notice.

Broker agrees that it will use its best efforts to secure a satisfactory purchaser for the Premises and, if Broker deems it necessary, Broker will also solicit the cooperation of other licensed real estate brokers. Broker represents that it possesses all of the consents, approvals and licenses required to perform the services contemplated by this Agreement.

Ms. Sandra D. Broker, Vice President, with Professional Brokerage Company, Chicago, IL, will be Broker's account representatives throughout the term of this Agreement and will be available for regular status meetings with Seller's representatives.

Broker, at its own expense, shall develop a marketing program to properly advertise the availability of the Premises, which program may include special plans, signs, brochures, circular matter and/or other forms of advertising, subject to Seller's prior approval. Broker shall prepare a color marketing brochure consistent with local market practice.

All materials and information relating to the Premises, Seller, or its affiliates given to the Broker must be kept confidential and no such information or materials may be released to third parties without the prior approval of Seller, except to the extent required by law.

During the term of this Agreement, Seller will refer to Broker all inquiries and offerings received by Seller with respect to the Premises, regardless of the source of such inquiries or offerings, except as to those potential purchasers identified in Exhibit A hereto.

Subject to Paragraph 10 hereof, in the event that, at any time during the term of this Agreement, the Premises are sold upon terms acceptable to Seller, in its sole and absolute discretion, then Seller shall pay to Broker one (1) full commission computed and payable in accordance with the applicable commission rate hereunder. Notwithstanding anything contained herein to the contrary, no commission shall be due Broker in connection with any sale or transfer of title to any affiliate or subsidiary, direct or indirect, of ABC Company or any party identified on Exhibit A. If, upon the expiration or earlier termination of the term of this Agreement, Seller shall have neither accepted an offer for the sale of the Premises nor have entered into a contract of sale for the Premises, Broker shall submit to Seller a list of the parties with whom Broker has had active negotiations for the sale of the Premises and who have made a written offer to purchase the Premises. Seller agrees that if, within three (3) months after the expiration or earlier termination of the term of this Agreement, Seller shall execute a contract of sale for the sale of the Premises with any of the parties disclosed in the list referred to in the preceding sentence, subject to Paragraph 10 hereof, Seller shall pay Broker one (1) full commission with respect thereto at the time and in the manner set forth in this Agreement.

If a licensed real estate broker other than Broker is the effective procuring cause of any sale covered by this Agreement, Broker shall have such other broker (i) agree to accept, as its sole compensation, an equitable portion of the commission payable to Broker pursuant to this Agreement, and (ii) unconditionally release Seller from all liability and obligations to such other broker in a written agreement acceptable to Seller. Broker shall indemnify, defend, and hold Seller harmless from and against any loss, cost, liability, and expense (including, without limitation, reasonable attorneys' fees and disbursements) incurred in connection with any claim for any commission, fee, or other compensation made by any broker, person, or entity claiming to have dealt with Broker in connection with the Premises, provided that Broker's liability pursuant to the indemnity set forth in this sentence shall not exceed the aggregate commission paid or payable to Broker with respect to the transaction in question.

On any sale of the Premises for which Broker is entitled to receive a commission hereunder, Broker shall, subject to the terms and conditions of this Agreement, receive a commission equal to _____ percent (___%) of the gross purchase price paid for the Premises.

The commission shall not be deemed earned until the unconditional transfer of legal and beneficial title to the Premises in accordance with the contract of sale and payment in full of the purchase price provided in the contract of sale, at which time the commission shall be due and payable.

The commission computed in accordance with the rates set forth in Paragraph 9 above shall be based upon the total sales price, which shall include the principal amount of any mortgages, loans, or other obligations of Seller which may be assumed by the purchaser or which the purchaser takes title "subject to" and the principal amount of any purchase money loans or mortgages taken back by Seller.

In the event a contract of sale is signed, but title is not transferred for any reason whatsoever, Broker shall receive no commission or other compensation, regardless of whether or not Seller is entitled to retain any down payment made by the purchaser. Seller has no responsibility to pay any fee or compensation to Broker (including reimbursement of any costs incurred by Broker in connection with the Agreement), except as specifically provided in this Agreement.

This Agreement shall be binding upon the parties hereto, their respective successors, and assigns.

This Agreement contains the entire understanding of the parties. Broker may not assign this Agreement nor may Broker assign its rights, duties, or obligations under this Agreement. This Agreement may not be changed or modified orally but only by written instrument signed by the party to be charged.

All notices sent pursuant to the terms of this Agreement, in order for same to be effective, must be sent by certified or registered mail, return receipt requested, to the respective parties at the addresses set forth below:

To Client: ABC Company, Inc.
              324 East Wacker Drive
              Chicago, IL 60631
              Attention: Bill Smith

With a copy to: ABC Company, Inc.
                   Legal Department
                   324 East Wacker Drive
                   Chicago, IL 60631
                   Attention: Real Estate Counsel

To Broker: Professional Brokerage Company
              304 East Wacker Drive
              Chicago, IL 60631
              Attention: Sandra D. Broker

With a copy to: Outside Professional Counsel, LLP
                   632 East Wacker Drive
                   Chicago, IL 60634
                   Attention: John Boxley

Any notice so posted shall be deemed effective upon receipt thereof by the party for which the same is intended. Either party hereto, upon notice to the other, may designate a different address for the sending of notices.

In the event that the Premises are transferred to an unaffiliated third party pursuant to a leasehold structure, Seller and Broker shall negotiate in good faith to reach any agreement with respect to the amount of commission which shall be paid to Broker for its services in connection with such a transaction.

If the foregoing accurately sets forth our Agreement, please sign and return the enclosed duplicate original of this letter.

Very truly yours,

ABC COMPANY, INC.

By:

Name:

Title:

By:

Name:

Title:

ACCEPTED AND AGREED:

PROFESSIONAL BROKERAGE COMPANY

By:

Name:

Title:

EXHIBIT A
List of Prospective Purchasers Excepted from Agreement: None

PRINCIPAL ANALYTICAL AND TRANSACTIONAL ACTIVITIES

Corporations, through their real estate function, buy or lease, hold, and sell or sublet property. Specific actions in these areas should be directed by the strategic business and facilities plan. Real estate and facility personnel, however, can employ a range of methods to accomplish their objectives. Of course, an endless variety of methods is available to the real estate function; we mention only the most important here. The following discussion is divided into the three principal postures of the corporation with respect to its real estate: acquisition, management of its portfolio, and disposition.

Acquisitions

In considering what real estate service to acquire and where to locate it, the focus is on how it should be acquired: whether by purchase or lease, and whether by building new facilities or occupying existing facilities. The alternative you choose should rest on its ability to provide the desired utility at the lowest possible cost to the corporation. Some trade-offs are likely in the decision-making process unless there are no alternatives, due either to specification requirements or the lack of market sites. Note further that decisions about financing, such as whether to fund an acquisition through the capital budgeting process, the use of mortgages, or the use of an operating lease, are usually made separately, by the finance function. Still, real estate acquisitions can often be considered investment decisions rather than decisions only about how to fund the cost of consuming an acquired resource, as is the case with most equipment financing decisions. Therefore, the real estate function, with its unique access to information about the real estate market, must examine the typical financing decision in light of the relevant market conditions. This is true of the basic lease-versus-buy decision.

The decision to lease rather than buy space should be based on a lower net cost to the corporation, all other things being equal. However, all other things usually are *not* equal. For reasons of flexibility, timeliness, economies of scale, and the availability of funds, leasing property may make better sense or simply be necessary. Otherwise, this decision is based on the present value of the cash flows related to the two alternatives. The selection of a discount rate is often a critical factor. For most true financing decisions, the after-tax cost of debt is used. However, for investment decisions, such as certain real estate acquisitions, the preferred discount rate is the after-tax cost of capital. In instances of pure cost (funds are being consumed), where the only cash flows being considered are negative, the lowest net present value of the cash flows related to each alternative indicates the more advantageous alternative; otherwise, the highest net present value indicates the better choice.

The decision to acquire and occupy existing facilities versus constructing new facilities is based on an analysis similar to the lease-versus-buy analysis, with an important additional component: whether the same real estate service, or utility for the user, is available with facilities not originally designed for the prospective user. The lack of utility is roughly equivalent to the functional obsolescence concern. The cost to cure the obsolescence must be identified and added to the acquisition cost of the existing facility to compare apples with apples. Unfortunately, not all obsolescence can be cured, which might adversely impact productivity. Therefore, in considering existing facilities for acquisition, an additional analysis must be performed to determine that impact as well as the implicit additional costs of the existing facility. Because many markets are oversupplied from time to time (as was the case in the early 1990s and early 2000s), it is likely that the costs to acquire and cure the obsolescence of existing facilities will comprise the less costly alternative. This may not be true, however, for specialized facilities, such as research and development (R&D) headquarters and specialized manufacturing property (high-tech or heavy industry). Bargains, if available, are likely to be in markets for rather homogeneous space—for example, administrative office and warehouse facilities.

THE PROCESS OF ACQUISITION

Who, What, When, How Much, How Long, Where

Your customers' needs for space and furnishings are often translated into a design program. The real estate requirement can also be translated into a document called a Request for Proposal (RFP), which answers the following questions:

- Who will occupy the space or property?
- What kind of space or property is needed—leased or owned?
- What type or types of space or property is needed?
- What growth space will be required now and in the future?
- When is the requirement needed?
- How much space or property is needed?
- How long will the facility professional's customer need to use the space or property?
- Where should the space or property be located?
- Will any other pertinent data enhance, clarify, or describe the specific requirements of the facility professional's customer and the facility professional's corporation?

The RFP is often written by your real estate broker based on specifications supplied by you and your customers. It is tailored to particular real estate and facility requirements and should include key requirements you will use in the evaluation and analysis of each response.

Items to Consider in the Lease or Sublease RFP

Your lease or sublease RFP should state exactly what landlords must know and include in their response to the following issues (and/or additional items unique to your business and/or location and required by your corporation's legal counsel). A lease or sublease RFP shows many of the following items:

Premises requirements (number of rentable or usable square feet)

Term of the lease

Term commencement date

Rent abatement (free rent)

Rental commencement date

Rental rate

Escalation and any other rental adjustment clause(s)

Improvement allowance

Space planning and design services

Expansion option(s)

Renewal option(s)

Property management and tenants

Operating hours

ADA compliance and access

Extended or after-hours HVAC

Telecommunication and shared-tenant services

Security

Parking (on-grade, structured, number per 1,000 RSF, etc.)

Asbestos (test results and a written statement from the landlord that the building and site contains no friable asbestos)

Amenities (conference rooms, food service, health club/fitness center, postal services, child care, branch bank, stationery, etc.)

Non-disturbance

Other landlord services

Surcharges

Landlord's broker

Agency disclosure

Response to RFP due date

Exhibits (as applicable)

Items to Consider in the Sale and Purchase RFP

Your purchase RFP should state exactly what sellers must know and include in their response to the following issues (and/or additional items unique to your business and/or location and required by your corporation's legal counsel). A sale and purchase RFP shows many of the following items:

Proposed property street and city initial address

Seller name, address, phone number

Property developer and/or developer's financial partner

Total acreage, land, building, improvements, square feet, etc.

Topographical data, survey/plot plan

Subsoil and hazardous material investigation

Purchase price and earnest money

Deed type available (general warranty, special warranty, grant, or quitclaim)

Existing easement(s)

Clear title and existing title insurance

Photographs required

Zoning jurisdiction and zoned

ADA compliance

Applicable building code(s) and floor area ratio (FAR)

Site plan agreement or subdivision of property agreement

Signage restrictions

Covenants and restrictions

Roads dedicated to the municipality

Landscaping and site lighting requirements

Site drainage and site stormwater retention requirements

Municipal water, service, and municipal sewer or well water and/or septic system, including fire hydrant service

Electrical service

Property taxes (last year, this year, estimated next year)

Tax advantages (local or business taxes, local or state income taxes, local occupancy or use taxes, state or local development bonds, etc.)

Air rights

Mineral rights

Environmental issues (asbestos, soil or air pollution, radon, etc.)

Noise pollution

Security (guards, access card cost, cameras, parking, after-hour access, fire stair access, keys, police, etc.)

Trained labor force availability

Fire and life safety, fire stations, hospitals, etc.

Adjacent or nearby competition

Asbestos (test results and a written statement from seller that the building and site contains no friable asbestos)

Local government smoking policy

Contingencies

Amenities (food service, conference/health/fitness facilities, bank, copy center, postal service, public transportation)

Parent company approval

Seller's broker

Agency disclosure by your broker

Response to RFP due date

Exhibits (when applicable)

Negotiating Psychology

It is often said that the party with a negotiating advantage (e.g., a corporate user seeking to lease space in a buyer's market) has leverage, strength, or power over the other party. Historically, though, corporations did not recognize this leverage even when they had it, whereas entrepreneurial developers, with better information about the marketplace and more skilled real estate negotiators, felt they had power even when they did not (e.g., in a buyer's market). Often, this feeling of negotiating strength had a tremendous impact on the final terms of the transaction.

Negotiations are conducted in a potentially antagonistic, emotionally loaded environment. However, tension need not lead to insurmountable conflict. If the negotiators keep in mind their knowledge of human nature, consider carefully when choosing which individuals to bring to the bargaining session, and are aware of physical factors affecting the negotiations, they can carry out bargaining in an atmosphere conducive to successful negotiation. Chapter 1 (Exhibit 1.16) provides a Negotiating Checklist to help you set and carry out your negotiating requirements.

YOUR SITE EVALUATION CRITERIA

After you, your customer, and the real estate team have developed the specific requirements for a real estate need, a Request for Proposal (RFP) can be written and sent to prequalified building owners and/or landlords. You or your real estate broker should receive and deliver a copy of the responses to the RFP to your customer. Some of the responses may not follow the requested response format or provide the requested information. Your customer will expect to receive an apples-to-apples comparative financial analysis of the responses to help in reviewing and identifying the responses that meet the stated requirements. Depending on the extent of the requirements and the complexity of the RFP, the apples-to-apples analysis may be simple and straightforward or complex. Unless you have the time and resources to perform the more complex financial evaluations, your broker should have and provide this capability and service to you and your customer.

The financial analysis should be provided in a format you and your customer can understand. All responses should be listed with each item quantified and responses addressed in the same comparative format. As in the following example, the facility professional may find that each response quotes different rentable square feet (RSF) while the usable square feet (USF) number, which is a function of the efficiency (EFF) of the floor and building design, is quoted as requested:

				Rent	Rent
Location	USF	EFF	RSF	RSF	Per Yr	5 YR
Building A	13,500	10.0%	15,000 × $15.00 = $225,000 = $1,125,000
Building B	13,500	12.5%	15,429 × $15.00 = $231,435 = $1,157,175
Building C	13,500	15.0%	15,822 × $15.00 = $238,230 = $1,191,150

These calculations easily show that based on RSF alone and assuming that all landlords quoted a $15.00/RSF rental rate, your customer would be paying over $6,000 more per year at Building B than at Building A and over $13,000 more per year at Building C than at Building A. The total rent for the five-year term, assuming a constant $15.00 per RSF, would amount to more than $30,000 in savings at Building A over Building B and more than $66,000 at Building A over Building C.

But your analysis must also look at many additional items:

- The up-fit allowance
- What it includes in real dollars based on new or existing space
- Comparing and equating floor-to-ceiling or floor-to-bottom of structure costs versus landlord's improvement allowance or work letter
- In-place or to-be-installed mechanical, electrical, ceiling, and sprinkler systems, etc.
- The rental rate
- Escalations
- Building core and design layout efficiency
- Free rent
- Parking costs
- ADA compliance, operating expenses, etc.

It may be necessary to compare a number of variables to achieve an apples-to-apples analysis that will determine the net present value (NPV) and effective level rent for each property. When you know these figures, the reputation of the landlord, and the response to the RFP, you will be in a position to make a site recommendation.

Exhibit 4.19 shows a site evaluation matrix for three sites. This spreadsheet format provides an objective ranking of weighted site evaluation criteria. Each criterion is scored by the customer and other members of the site identification team, and the average ratings and scores for each criterion are shown. The analysis provides a total score for each site, and notes are provided at the bottom of the page for weighting, site upfit, and general site selection notes and information to assist in the decision-making process. In any event, your line operating executives

Evaluation Date: JUNE 18, 2005
Evaluation By: BILL ROBERTS, SUSAN ADAMS, AND WALTER LITTLE.

OFFICE LOCATION/LANDLORD			SUMMERFIELD/GLENV¹. MAYFIELD INVEST.		RICHLAND/NILES FAIRFIELD DEVELOP.		WESTLAKE/SKOKIE WESTLAKE & ASSOC	
EVALUATION CRITERIA	WEIGHT		Rating	Score	Rating	Score	Rating	Score
Total Cost/Value	9.0		9.5	85.5	9.0	81.0	9.0	81.0
Land Cost/Value	7.0		9.0	63.0	8.5	59.5	5.0	35.0
Upfit Cost/Value	8.0		9.5	76.0	8.5	68.0	9.5	76.0
Location	8.0		10.0	80.0	9.0	72.0	8.5	68.0
Building Configuration	6.0		10.0	60.0	8.5	51.0	8.5	51.0
Amenities (Food Service,)	10.0		9.5	95.0	8.5	85.0	8.5	85.0
Free Parking	9.0		9.5	85.5	9.5	85.5	7.0	63.0
Building Services & Security	8.0		9.5	76.0	9.0	72.0	6.0	48.0
Collocation With XYZ Corp.	6.0		6.0	36.0	9.5	57.0	6.0	36.0
Bus Route To & From Site	8.0		9.0	72.0	8.0	64.0	8.0	64.0
Courier Service Available	10.0		9.0	90.0	8.5	85.0	8.5	85.0
Real Property, etc. Taxes	6.0		8.0	48.0	8.0	48.0	8.5	51.0
Housing/Local Labor Market	6.0		8.5	51.0	8.0	48.0	8.0	48.0
Operational Cost Savings	7.0		9.0	63.0	8.0	56.0	8.0	56.0
Human Resources Issues	7.0		8.0	56.0	8.0	56.0	8.0	56.0
Ability To Meet Schedule	10.0		9.5	95.0	9.0	90.0	10.0	100.0
Landlord Resources Avail.	9.0		9.5	85.5	9.5	85.5	10.0	90.0
Overall Landlord Exper.	9.0		9.5	85.5	9.0	81.0	9.0	81.0
Overall Evaluation	8.0		9.5	76.0	9.0	72.0	8.5	68.0
TOTAL SCORE:				1379.0		1316.5		1242.0

Evaluation Notes: Upfit Notes:
1. Weights are between 0 and 10 (10 being best) 1. Full Turnkey $38.00 Per Sq. Ft.   Full Turnkey
2. Rates are between 0 and 10 (10 being best)   Construction.   For Office & $95.00   Construction.
3. Ratings x weights = score   For Computer Room.

Information Notes:
1. TAXES: NILES (City & County)   GLENVIEW (City) and SKOKIE (City)
     Real Estate $1.38/$100 + Fire & Rescue Levy $0.88/$100
     Personal Property $3.75/$100 $4.20/$100
                             No Merchants Capital Tax   No Merchants Capital Tax
                             Gross Receipts Tax In Effect   Gross Receipts Tax In Effect
2. HOUSING COSTS
     2 Bedroom (Median-1991) $99,500 $136,000
     3 Bedroom (Median-1991) $107,000 $193,000
     2 Bedroom - Rental $570 per month $690 per month

Exhibit 4.19   Site Evaluation Matrix

should concentrate on making their plan by manufacturing and marketing product lines, not by real estate sales.

Exhibit 4.20 shows a relocation analysis for three buildings, including building rent, parking, and operating expense, for a five-year term. The analysis provides a year-to-year comparison of expenses and what the purchase option would be, if any.

Exhibit 4.21 shows a comparative analysis of five buildings and the lease and capital costs for each location. The subjective information in the notes at the bottom of the page is drawn from the landlords' proposals and from research on each location. This analysis provides objective bottom-line comparisons to use in making a selection.

```
BCCOIN1.WK1                                                          Prepared By: BILL ROBERTS
AGE 1                                                                Date:      JUNE 18, 2005

Development Name:  SUMMERFIELD        Development Name:  RICHLAND OFFICE PARK    Development Name:  WESTLAKE TERRACES
Address:           3298 Summers Ct.  Address:           9100 Bakers Avenue      Address:          West Terrace Drive
                   Suite 100                            Suite 120                                 Building 200, Suite 105
City, St. & Zip:   GLENVIEW, IL.     City, St. & Zip:   NILES, IL.              City, St. & Zip:  SKOKIE, IL.
Lease Starts:      DECEMBER 1, 1995  Lease Starts:      DECEMBER 1, 1995        Lease Starts:     DECEMBER 1, 1995
Lease Ends:        NOVEMBER 30, 2000 Lease Ends:        NOVEMBER 30, 2000       Lease Ends:       NOVEMBER 30, 2000

Total Leased Area: 32,000 Square Feet Total Leased Area:  32,000 Square Feet   Total Leased Area:    32,500 Square Feet
  Yr 1 Lease Rate: $7.00 /S.F.;         Yr 1 Lease Rate: $7.20 /S.F.;            Yr 1 Lease Rate:    $6.10 /S.F.;
  Yr 2 Lease Rate: $8.28 /S.F.;         Yr 2 Lease Rate: $7.42 /S.F.;            Yr 2 Lease Rate:    $6.10 /S.F.;
  Yr 3 Lease Rate: $8.75 /S.F.;         Yr 3 Lease Rate: $7.64 /S.F.;            Yr 3 Lease Rate:    $6.10 /S.F.;
  Yr 4 Lease Rate: $8.88 /S.F.;         Yr 4 Lease Rate: $7.87 /S.F.;            Yr 4 Lease Rate:    $6.10 /S.F.;
  Yr 5 Lease Rate: $9.34 /S.F.          Yr 5 Lease Rate: $8.10 /S.F.             Yr 5 Lease Rate:    $6.10 /S.F.
Bldg. Rent Inc.:   100.00% Per Year   Bldg. Rent Inc.:   100.00% Per Year      Bldg. Rent Inc.:     100.00% Per Year
Tot. Parking Area: 50,000 Square Feet Tot. Parking Area: 48,875 Square Feet    Tot. Parking Area:   0 Square Feet
  Yr 1 Park. Rate: $0.00 /S.F.;         Yr 1 Park. Rate: $1.21 /S.F.;            Yr 1 Park. Rate:    $0.00 /S.F.;
  Yr 2 Park. Rate: $0.00 /S.F.;         Yr 2 Park. Rate: $1.25 /S.F.;            Yr 2 Park. Rate:    $0.00 /S.F.;
  Yr 3 Park. Rate: $0.00 /S.F.;         Yr 3 Park. Rate: $1.28 /S.F.;            Yr 3 Park. Rate:    $0.00 /S.F.;
  Yr 4 Park. Rate: $0.00 /S.F.;         Yr 4 Park. Rate: $1.32 /S.F.;            Yr 4 Park. Rate:    $0.00 /S.F.;
  Yr 5 Park. Rate: $0.00 /S.F.;         Yr 5 Park. Rate: $1.36 /S.F.;            Yr 5 Park. Rate:    $0.00 /S.F.;
Park. Rent Inc.:   100.00% Per Year   Park. Rent Inc.:   100.00% Per Year      Park. Rent Inc.:     100.00% Per Year
  Yr 1 Total Rate: $7.00 /S.F.;         Yr 1 Total Rate: $8.41 /S.F.;            Yr 1 Total Rate:    $6.10 /S.F.;
  Yr 2 Total Rate: $8.28 /S.F.;         Yr 2 Total Rate: $8.67 /S.F.;            Yr 2 Total Rate:    $6.10 /S.F.;
  Yr 3 Total Rate: $8.75 /S.F.;         Yr 3 Total Rate: $8.92 /S.F.;            Yr 3 Total Rate:    $6.10 /S.F.;
  Yr 4 Total Rate: $8.88 /S.F.;         Yr 4 Total Rate: $9.19 /S.F.;            Yr 4 Total Rate:    $6.10 /S.F.;
  Yr 5 Total Rate: $9.34 /S.F.;         Yr 5 Total Rate: $9.46 /S.F.;            Yr 5 Total Rate:    $6.10 /S.F.;
Total Rent Inc.:   106.69% Per Year   Total Rent Inc.:   102.89% Per Year      Total Rent Inc.:     100.00% Per Year
Purchase Option:   $3,395,000 @ YEAR 5 Purchase Option:  First Right of Refusal Purchase Option:    NONE
Lot Size:          5.21 Acres         Lot Size:          3.75 Acres            Lot Size:            NONE
Operating Expense  $6.50 /RSF         Operating Expense  $6.55 /RSF            Operating Expense    $6.35 /RSF
Oper. Ex. Inc.:    104.50% Per Year   Oper. Ex. Inc.:    105.50% Per Year      Oper. Ex. Inc.:      104.75% Per Year
```

	YEAR 0	1995 (1 Mo.)	1995 (12 Mos.)	1997 (12 Mos.)	1998 (12 Mos.)	1999 (12 Mos.)	2000 (11 Mos.)	Total (60 Mos.)	LESS 1 YR. FREE RENT
SUMMERFILED EXPENSES:									
Building Rent Expense	N/A	$18,667	$227,413	$266,213	$280,347	$285,387	$273,973	$1,352,000	($ 224,004)
Parking Expense	N/A	$0	$0	$0	$0	$0	$0	$0	
Operating Expense	N/A	$4,000	$48,180	$50,348	$52,614	$54,981	$52,471	$262,594	
TOTAL EXPENSES	N/A	$22,667	$275,593	$316,561	$332,960	$340,368	$326,444	$1,614,594	$1,390,590

	YEAR 0	1995 (1 Mo.)	1996 (12 Mos.)	1997 (12 Mos.)	1998 (12 Mos.)	1999 (12 Mos.)	2000 (11 Mos.)	Total (60 Mos.)	LESS 1 YR. FREE RENT
RICHLAND EXPENSES:									
Building Rent Expense	N/A	$19,200	$230,987	$238,027	$245,093	$252,453	$237,600	$1,223,360	($ 230,400)
Parking Expense	N/A	$4,928	$59,302	$61,216	$62,723	$64,678	$60,931	$313,778	
Operating Expense	N/A	$4,000	$48,180	$50,348	$52,614	$54,981	$52,471	$262,594	
TOTAL EXPENSES	N/A	$28,128	$338,468	$349,591	$360,430	$372,113	$351,002	$1,799,732	$1,569,332

	YEAR 0	1995 (1 Mo.)	1996 (12 Mos.)	1997 (12 Mos.)	1998 (12 Mos.)	1999 (12 Mos.)	2000 (11 Mos.)	Total (60 Mos.)	LESS 1 YR. FREE RENT
WESTLAKE TERRACES EXPENSES:									
Building Rent Expense	N/A	$16,521	$198,250	$198,250	$198,250	$198,250	$181,729	$991,250	($ 198,252)
Parking Expense	N/A	$0	$0	$0	$0	$0	$0	$0	
Operating Expense	N/A	$3,656	$44,040	$46,021	$48,092	$50,256	$47,962	$240,027	
TOTAL EXPENSES	N/A	$20,177	$242,290	$244,271	$246,342	$248,506	$229,691	$1,231,277	$1,033,025

Exhibit 4.20   Relocation Analysis for ABC Company Headquarters in Northern Chicago, IL

June 18, 2005

Proposed Location/Term	Rate/ R.S.F.	Esc./ Year	Total R.S.F.	Total U.S.F.	First Years Rent	Upfit Allow./ U.S.F.	Total Allow.	Estimated Total Improve. Cost	Total Rent	Total Commitment = Total Rent + Total Improve. Cost	Estimated Balance Of Improve. Cost Paid By XYZ CO.	Remarks
1. 1265 Wacker Avenue, 3rd & 4th Floor												
24 Months	$17.75	4%	50,000	44,000	$875,500	$5.00	$250,000	$480,000	$1,798,500	$2,278,000	$230,000	Note 1
2. 769 Michigan Drive, 4th Floor & partial 2nd, 5th & 8th Fls.												
24 Months	$19.50	3%*	45,000	40,284	$877,500	$8.00	$322,272	$445,000	$1,782,000	$2,227,000	$122,800	Note 2
30 Months	$19.50	3%*	45,000	40,284	$877,500	$10.00	$402,840					Note 2
36 Months	$19.50	3%*	45,000	40,384	$877,500	$12.00	$484,608					Note 2
3. 849 Wacker Avenue, 5th & 6th Floors												
18 Months	$12.00	Fixed	47,743	45,481	$572,916	$1.00+	$ 45,481	$446,600	$1,160,200	$1,606,800	$204,700	Note 3
24 Months	$12.15	Fixed	47,743	45,481	$580,078	$1.00+	$ 45,481					Note 3
4. 982 Michigan Drive, 14th & 15 Floors, with Basement/Computer Rm.												
18 Months	$15.00	Fixed	49,439	44,754	$741,585	$4.47	$200,000	$380,400	$1,483,200	$1,863,600	$ 80,400	Note 4
24 Months	$15.00	Fixed	49,439	44,754	$741,585	$6.70	$300,000					Note 4
5. 1200 Richards Street, 8th & 9th Floors												
18 Months	$14.66 Net	Market	47,000	43,519	$806,500	$8.00	$348,152	$522,300	$1,397,100	$1,919,400	$174,200	Note 5
24 Months	$12.00 Net	Market	47,000	43,519	$681,500	$8.00	$348,152					Note 5

Notes:

1. 1265 Wacker Avenue did not make an 18 month proposal, but they stated that this would not be a deal-breaker. Proposal provided an option for an additional 18 months and included the Landlord providing preliminary and working drawings.

2. 769 Michigan Drive did not make an 18 month proposal, and again, they expressed a serious interest in ABC Co. If 18 months is required, the upfit allowance would be $0.00 (i.e. that cost would be totally ABC Co.'s). Rent would be $20.10 for year 2 and $20.70 for year 3.

3. 849 Wacker Avenue proposal provides for re-carpeting and repainting and an additional upfit allowance of $1.00 per usf. The lease term may be extended to a total of 60 months at a rental rate of $13.00/rsf at the end of the initial lease term.

4. 982 Michigan Drive proposal recognized the possible need to alter 60% of the space and has provided for a renewal term of 36 or 42 months at $16.00/rsf. This is the only proposal to include a computer room which meets ABC Co.'s needs without having to build one from scratch. This proposal includes our subleasing and using the current major tenant's facilities including food service, catering, vending, parking, security, and card access, and includes space planning, construction drawings, building permits, and certificate of occupancy. The above yearly rental includes an existing Computer Room of 3,878 rsf and not all of this space has to be leased.

5. 1200 Richards Street proposal is a net of janitorial and utilities which are estimated to be $2.00 to $2.50/rsf. Existing space will be vacated by Jan. 15, 2005 by the current tenant and because of the age of the building and wear on the space, the entire inside of the existing office/warehouse will require gutting and is included in the $8.00/rsf. Proposal includes one preliminary drawing and on completed set of construction documents.

Exhibit 4.21 Analysis of 24-Month Proposals for the Relocation of ABC Company

Cost Issues and Items to Review and Analyze

There are times when management could choose either to own or to lease a facility. Within the corporation, the decision is often a function of corporate policy, politics, operational need, and financial resources. Outside the corporation, the financial, real estate, and construction marketplace may provide a financial opportunity to choose ownership rather than leasing. Interest rates may be low, rental rates may be low, and construction costs may be lower than recent historical costs. Changing conditions may dictate a financial opportunity or confirm previous policies.

Should you be faced with a slumping real estate market, low interest rates, low inflation, and lower construction costs, your own-versus-lease feasibility analysis may project a net cost/breakeven point over ten years out. In this case, it may not make financial sense to own when it is less expensive to lease a facility for ten years. But it may make better business sense to own because the ongoing capital investments in the facility over the next ten years would be lost at the end of the lease term. But if interest and inflation rates are high and rental rates are moderate, the breakeven point for leasing may be at five years, and the advantages of a long-term lease would be readily apparent.

A breakeven point with a short time frame may make owning rather than leasing financially attractive, especially if interest rates are low and there is a substantial cash difference after the breakeven point when this cash could be used for other business or operational purposes. The longer the time frame to the breakeven point, the closer either decision could prove to be acceptable, assuming the corporation has the financial resources and time to select either alternative. But some corporations that expect to make substantial capital investments at the site will not consider a lease scenario unless they can obtain a 15-year or longer lease term with options.

A number of variables must be considered in the own-versus-lease comparison. An analysis completed today can be quite different from an analysis made five years ago or five years in the future depending on variables such as the cost of financing, rent payments, operating expenses, escalations, and construction costs. The numbers will not be exactly the same for two similar corporations and should be based on your corporation's financial condition and particular financial leverage in the financial, real estate, and construction marketplace.

Remember to include in your analysis the value of the facility at the end of its asset life compared with the value of the property or lease. In some marketplaces, the value of the building at the end of its asset life may appreciate substantially if the building has been well maintained and kept clean, current with codes and enhanced building systems, and aesthetically competitive. The market value of the asset above its book value in an appreciating real estate market at the end of its asset life or sooner could provide an opportunity for substantial capital gain and nonoperational income to improve your corporation's bottom line. Your corporate finance and operations management will undoubtedly be careful with how such a capital gain and income are treated and reported internally and externally.

The financial analysis should be provided in a format you and your customer can understand. All responses should be listed with each item quantified and responses addressed in the same comparative format (see Exhibits 4.19, 4.20, and 4.21).

Present Value Analysis—Annual Weighted Cost Factors

Effective level rent translates a net present value (NPV) of periodic lease payments into an annualized dollar amount per square foot. A net-present-value calculation is one of the few ways in which all the dollar values of the concession package are taken into account while allowing for the alternative cost of money leasehold. The advantage of using a constant payment as the net effective rent is that it is easier to compare in different transactions and is close to the actual rent that would be paid on an annualized basis.

Example. The mechanics of this calculation explain the concept of effective level rent:

- Alternative 1

    1,000 square feet

    One year free rent

    $10.00 per square foot for years 2–5

    9% discount rate

Solution. The net present value at 9% equals $29,722.20. The level annual payment for five years at 9% using this net present value equals $7,641.35. Thus, the effective level rent per square foot equals $7.64.

- Alternative 2

    1,000 square feet

    No free rent

    $8.00 per square foot for 5 years

    9% discount rate

Solution. The net present value at 9% equals $31,117.21. The level annual payment for five years at 9% using this net present value equals $8,000.00. Thus, the effective level rent per square foot equals $8.00.

Both alternatives yield the same amount of gross dollars, $40,000, and, as quoted by the landlords, the same effective rent at $8.00. However, because of the present value impact of the timing of the lease payments, Alternative 1 has a lower *effective* level rent. Please note that this lease analysis computes the present value using monthly lease payments with the payment made at the beginning of the month.

YOUR CUSTOMER'S SITE EVALUATION CRITERIA

When the initial analysis of the responses to the RFP is complete, you may find that your customer is interested in two or three locations. A preliminary space plan for each location should be completed to demonstrate which building shape and floor layout most efficiently meets the RFP and design program requirements for the least cost and the most value to the customer.

At this point, the facility professional's broker often goes back to each selected landlord and describes the lease/upfit/concession package you are looking for or asks the landlord to improve on the initial response. Some may drop out at this time, and others may come back with alternatives that may or may not be acceptable.

Knowing the revised NPV and effective level rent analysis, the reputation of the landlord, and the landlord's response to the RFP, you should be in a position to formally present a site recommendation to your customer. The customer may or may not agree with your recommendation, as its management may have other objective or subjective valid concerns. For example, the RFP may have specifically requested that the landlord provide a conference room to accommodate 30 people at the location at no initial cost or ongoing user fee. If your customer has repeatedly stressed this concern, then you should expect that the location providing this requirement may strongly influence your customer's choice above other locations that cannot meet the conference room requirement even though they have a lower rental rate and other amenities.

ENVIRONMENTAL AND DUE DILIGENCE ISSUES

An increasingly important contingency issue that the real estate and facility professional and senior management must take into account in site acquisition planning is the physical condition of the site and surrounding environment. Failure to understand and heed environmental laws could result in fines, penalties, or enforced cleanups costing the facility professional's company millions of dollars.

Environmental issues have become legislative issues in many areas, and to protect the facility professional's company, the real estate and facility professional must be aware of the requirements of state, county, and local regulatory agencies as well as the ramifications of the federal government's 1969 National Environmental Policy Act and the regulations developed by the Environmental Protection Agency (EPA), which was established in 1970. The focus of this Act and these regulations is to preserve the environment by addressing:

- Asbestos
- Polychlorinated biphenyls (PCBs)
- Hazardous materials
- Water pollution
- Radon
- Underground Storage Tanks (USTs)
- Solid waste
- Air pollution
- Lead
- Hazardous waste
- Indoor air

Federal environmental/legislative regulations since 1969 include:

- National Environmental Policy Act of 1969 (NEPA)
- Comprehensive Environmental Response Compensation and Liabilities Act (CERCLA), and it's Superfund for environmental cleanup
- Resource Conservation and Recovery Act of 1984 (RCRA)
- Superfund Amendments and Re-authorization Act of 1986 (SARA) plus Title III
- Safe Drinking Water Act of 1986 (SDWA)
- Federal Insecticide, Fungicide, and Rodenticide Act (FIFRA)
- Toxics Substance Control Act (TSCA)
- Clean Water Act (CWA)
- Water Quality Act of 1987
- Pollution Prevention and Recycling Act of 1990
- Clean Air Act of 1990 (CAA)

These environmental issues have become more important since the passage of CERCLA, Superfund, and SARA. These acts provide a federal framework to require owners of real property, operators, and others designated as responsible parties to clean up contaminated soil, polluted water, and other discharges to the environment. These acts also require responsible parties to participate actively in the cleaning up of hazardous waste sites. Potential environmental problems come in a multitude of forms, and the identification of these problems through the due diligence environmental site audit is a fundamental and extremely important requirement before property purchase and closing takes place.

It is imperative to make a due diligence environmental audit (see Exhibit 4.22) for any site the facility professional is proposing for the customer's purchase, long-term tenancy, or tenancy in a build-to-suit lease. This audit is designed to assure the health and safety of the organization purchasing the property and employees occupying it. It provides protection from having to conduct expensive environmental cleanups, protection from liability claims of individuals, employees, tenants, or customers for health hazards associated with the environmental situation, and, finally, the ability to remarket the property for sale or use it as collateral for a loan. The audit generally involves two distinct phases: an information search and an analytic site evaluation.

As shown in Exhibit 4.22, three types of due diligence audits can be made to attain "innocent landowner/purchaser status." Federal regulations, especially CERCLA, regulate more than 700 pollutants and require owners and potential purchasers to perform environmental audits to satisfy CERCLA requirements or the courts should an environmental problem arise. Failure to perform the audit and act on the findings could result in a judgment against the facility professional's company regardless of when the hazardous condition was created. The owner or previous owner with the deepest pockets usually becomes the party charged to pay for the cleanup. To protect the facility professional's company, the environmental audit for a proposed site must be both accurate and defensible. The audit and any subsequent cleanup must be performed by competent professionals and must produce comprehensible information that will satisfy CERCLA or the courts.

Environmental issues have also been addressed at the state and local level by the enactment of legislation that in many areas is more restrictive or requires more corrective action than is required by federal regulations. New Jersey, for example, has stringent environmental auditing requirements; the state must issue an environmental permit and clear the site as clean before a site construction permit can be issued by a local New Jersey governmental authority. Also, states are requiring wetlands investigations as part of the permit process; this can limit the amount of building area or site work the facility professional's company can perform on a site with wetlands as defined by that state. The EPA estimated that as

WINDSHIELD AUDIT
(7 to 14 Days)
Visual site and area inspection and historical use review.

Visual inspection turned up no apparent environmental concerns; History of use is satisfactory.	**DEAL KILLER** Obvious visual detection of environmental problems; Substantial cost to remedy problems; Adjacent property problems; No further interest in the site.

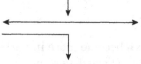

PHASE I
ENVIRONMENTAL AUDIT
(30 Days)
Records review, compliance evaluation, close visual inspection including sampling suspect asbestos, PCB's, RADON, operations review, adjacent site review and recommendations.

Records review revealed no problem compliance issues; Evaluation is good; Visual inspection acceptable; Sampling results are favorable; and operation review is acceptable. If there is concern with waste, UST, adjacent property activities or groundwater contamination, then recommend PHASE II ENVIRONMENTAL AUDIT.	**DEAL KILLER** Previous use is unacceptable; There are compliance problems; Analytical testing results are unsatisfactory, previous disposal practices are unacceptable, and current operations are unacceptable.

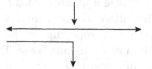

PHASE II
ENVIRONMENTAL AUDIT
(15 to 30 Days)
Sampling of additional buildings, materials or equipment, soil sampling, ground water sampling, waste disposal sampling and recommendation of action with cost estimate.

Sampling indicates no problems or sampling indicates property not source of the problem or result indicates a problem that can be solved at a cost that still makes the deal profitable or affordable.	**DEAL KILLER** Major problem in clean-up procedures and cost is revealed through sampling results. Potential liability is unacceptable.

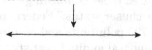

Due diligence completed.
Innocent landowner and/or purchaser provision established.

Exhibit 4.22   Environmental Audit Process

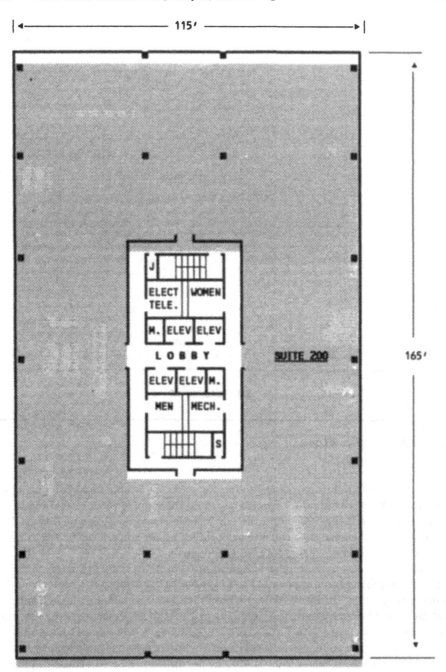

Exhibit 4.22A   Floor Plan

300.00'

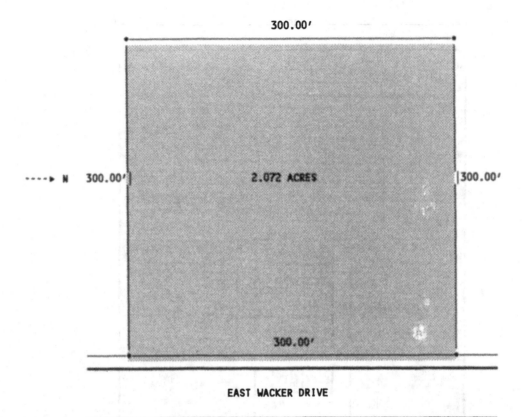

----▶ N   300.00'   2.072 ACRES   300.00'

300.00'

EAST WACKER DRIVE

Exhibit 4.22B   Site Plan

many as 750,000 buildings around the nation contain friable asbestos, and the
cleanup of this environmental hazard occupied the capital resources of many
owners throughout the 1990s and the early 2000s. Obviously, the facility professional wants assurance that the site or building under consideration contains
none of the hazardous waste material listed earlier.

With the increased awareness of health and safety in the workplace, many
cities are requiring building owners to upgrade their building life safety and fire
protection systems. Building owners whose facilities lack smoke alarms, sprinkler
systems, smoke doors, smoke corridors, or exit distances that meet current code
are being cited in many cities and given a specific period in which to upgrade
their structures. In some cases, local governments are providing property tax
relief or incentives to assist the building owner in taking care of these requirements. Corporate facilities must meet local code requirements; associated
expenses could influence the facility professional's company to move or expand
within newer facilities. Fire safety and owner liability are important considerations, and if the facility professional's company owns or leases a facility that is
severely out of date in terms of life safety requirements, the continued use of the
facility in as-is condition may be an unacceptable liability and may generate
undesirable public relations within and outside the corporation.

SAMPLE PROPERTY ENVIRONMENTAL EXECUTIVE SUMMARY

Property Owner: ABC Company

Property Location: 301 East Wacker Drive
Chicago, IL

Property Size: Approximately 6.0 Acres or 324,000 Square Feet

Property Building: Approximately 53,250 Square Feet
Warehouse: 94,000 Square Feet
Office: 6,000 Square Feet

Property Tax Info.:   Cook County
Unit Number: 54–6512 C
Parcel Number: 44–64-6–33-1.000-AR

Environmental Statement:

The property was acquired by ABC Company through an acquisition by XYZ Company, a wholly owned subsidiary of ABC Company, in the 1980s. The property had been in use for many years, with a resultant environmental impact to portions of the site.

In early 2001, ABC Company undertook a voluntary environmental assessment of the property and subsequently, under the guidance of the State of Illinois Department of Environmental Management and USEPA Region VI, a cleanup program was initiated at the property and completed in the summer of 2004.

The cleanup included the removal of PCB-contaminated soil from predetermined areas on the site and the removal of PCB-contaminated concrete from the interior of the building.

Clean soil replaced the removed soils, was compacted, and a 6-inch asphalt cap was placed on areas to serve as an engineering control. A top soil cap was placed on other areas of the property to serve as additional engineering controls. These areas were then appropriately landscaped. Portions of the concrete in the building interior were replaced. The entire concrete surface was then sealed with 2 applications of 2-part epoxy coating paint to provide appropriate control. These remedial steps were taken pursuant to 40 CFR 761, which regulates PCB material and remediation of it.

The upper one-third of the exterior of the building is composed of asbestos transit siding. The entire building, inside and out, was painted to contain and encapsulate this siding.

After site work was completed, four (4) groundwater wells were installed on the property, and periodic monitoring and test sample results have shown no detection of any groundwater contaminants.

Utility Requirements

The facility professional's annual and long-range planning for site evaluation requirements must include the ability to secure adequate and high-quality electrical service to meet the company's business needs. Some states and consumer groups have discouraged the building of additional power production facilities in their state, and these locations must be identified early in the site selection process. Adequate and reliable electrical power is essential for today's computer-driven manufacturing and financial requirements, and states or localities that favor growth usually encourage additional electrical capacity. The facility professional's review of existing buildings should ensure that electrical service is copper, properly grounded, quality/consistent voltage, and adequate for the facility professional's current and future load requirements. Also, the facility professional may determine that a site needs emergency backup electrical service by means of a backup generator. The fuel to run the generator may have to be chosen based on environmental or legislative considerations, and these may impose design, cost, or public relations constraints that the facility professional's company may or may not choose to accept. Because the monitoring of buried septic and fuel storage tanks may require extensive site modifications, a clean site without these liabilities may prove the best choice. The EPA has estimated that as many as 100,000 underground storage tanks may be leaking regulated substances into the soil and groundwater. This serious problem must be identified early in the site evaluation process.

LEGAL DOCUMENT REVIEW PROCESS

A site has been identified and management approval has been obtained. A proposal letter (often prepared by the landlord or seller) that includes all the main and important negotiated business and legal points and exhibits has been reviewed and signed by both parties, and your customer is ready to move forward with a lease or purchase agreement. The landlord or seller usually provides completed copies of the standard lease or purchase agreement, with the business and legal points and exhibits included for review and signature. This phase can be a time-consuming yet critical part of the real estate assignment. It is your responsibility to protect the legal and business interests of your customer and the corporation during this phase.

All contingency items must be satisfied before closing on the property. Once title changes hands and the deed is recorded, your corporation has little chance of returning the property to the seller. Purchasing property is a serious undertaking, and your corporate legal department must ensure that all legal issues, corporate property acquisition policies, and requirements are addressed before closing takes place. Your sale and purchase agreement should provide that either party can terminate the contract and all earnest money deposit and additional funds in escrow will be returned to you if you cannot obtain all licenses, permits, and other authorizations within a specified time.

A diligent and detailed review of the lease or purchase agreement should be made together with your customer, legal counsel, and real estate broker. The review comments are often transmitted to the landlord or the seller by your real estate broker or legal counsel, who should then follow up to ensure that the next draft includes these comments and requested revisions. If not, further business or legal negotiations must take place. Depending on the complexity of the requirement and the legal or business issues to be resolved, the review process could take a week to months. Sometimes, even though all parties felt they had a meeting of the minds, this review process brings out issues such as subleasing or assignment, asbestos, or major structural damage that one side cannot accept. If you reach an impasse, your customer should be prepared to walk away from the deal.

For purchased property and for certain leased property, you will use this time to work with either the seller or landlord on securing contingency items: zoning, permits, confirmation of utility services that meet your requirements, financing, total project costs, legal documentation, title binder and title insurance, closing time, date and location, due diligence inspection, audit of the site for hazardous materials, and so on. Only after these contingencies are met should you close on the sale and purchase of the property or proceed with the lease.

Deposit or Earnest Money

The size of your company and its net worth, sales, and reputation can influence the amount (if any) of deposit for a lease or earnest money for a sale and purchase that it is required to pay before the lease or sale and purchase agreement will be effective.

A deposit for leased property or space (usually equal to one or more month's rent) is a method landlords use to protect their investment. If your company can demonstrate sales volume, reputation, name presence, and history of business in the community, you may be able to require the landlord to waive the deposit requirement on the basis that the deposit represents risk and your company offers no payment risk to the landlord's investment. Wherever possible, try to negotiate with the landlord to waive the deposit, thereby reducing the cash outlay for your customer and corporation. Every dollar your customer does not have to pay up front could contribute to meeting the overall cash objectives for the year. If your customer must pay a deposit, ensure that it is placed in a separate, interest-bearing account and that your customer understands the requirements and time frame wherein to get the deposit back with the earned interest.

The purchaser's earnest money payment for a property is the seller's method of ensuring that the purchaser is serious, has financial resources, and will make a commitment that will take the property off of the market for a specified period. The amount of earnest money is negotiable and may be deposited with the seller, the seller's brokerage company, or, better yet, the title insurance company. Where the earnest money will reside (bank or savings and loan) can be negotiated. The sale and purchase agreement should detail who will receive the interest, how the earnest money will be applied to the purchase price, and how the earnest money will be refunded should the seller not be able to satisfy all the contingency items. You and your customer must be careful to ensure that *all* contingency items are met before agreeing to close on the sale. After closing, the property belongs to your customer; unless there is fraud, the purchaser must live with any problems that are discovered. You should consider involving your real estate broker in this process as a facilitator, especially when dealing with zoning, permits, and financing issues.

The lease approval process can take from a few weeks to many months. A number of critical phases are identified as follows:

Process Phases[4] include:

- Lease document prepared by the landlord or tenant
- Queue time with a focus on reducing iterations and changes to the signature process
- Business terms with a focus on a more detailed RFP
- Normal coordination with legal counsel
- Transfer of documents, automation, communication, and word processing
- Cycle of the lease document process including the number of iterations
- External and internal requirements the tenant and landlord must address
- Process time with a focus on the development and use of a lease document log to record and document process time

Lease Document Steps[5] include:

- Prenegotiated document or model lease, including a business term sheet. This could be developed between the tenant and the landlord or for the real estate industry in a format similar to standard contract documents used regularly in other business areas (engineering, design, architectural services, general construction, etc.). Model leases may pose a problem if corporate legal counsel insists that each document have their imprint. Corporate legal may want a say in the drafting of the document, no matter how minor, precluding the use of a model lease.
- Administration of the lease through word processing; communications via electronic mail, modem, or corporate network; the ability via software to redline changes to the lease; and a readability index of 40 where the lease can be read and understood by a person with a high school education before and after it is signed.
- Unique local legal requirements that could affect the rights and responsibilities of either or both parties to the lease.
- Landlord- or tenant-driven business, legal issues, and contingencies to complete the lease.
- Lender or financial partner whose financial interest may become a major obstacle or opportunity to completing the lease agreement. Ideally, the lender's legal and business requirements are understood before all business terms are agreed on.

[4]Source: "The Office Lease Approval Process" by Edmond P. Rondeau, Benchmarking Research Study for the Industrial Development Research Foundation (IDRF), June 1992.
[5]Ibid.

- Local market conditions, where the local real estate economy or business terms of the lease reflect local real estate values with respect to such items as concessions, rents, operating expenses, upfit, and free rent.

- Process time, including all the steps and time required to develop the lease document from the agreement of the business terms to the execution of the lease document. Process time is one of the key items to address and reduce where possible to improve productivity and obtain a signed lease.

- Format provides standardization of the business and lease terms, contents and wording, arrangement, and the ability to make and receive changes to the lease document manuscript electronically.

The Lease Agreement

The following items should be considered while negotiating a lease agreement to ensure that your customer, the tenant, is properly represented and protected. Other items unique to your business or location should be considered and may be required by your corporation's legal counsel. A sample lease is reproduced in the next section.

Lease agreement date

Landlord (lessor) name, a (state) corporation or limited partnership, etc.

Tenant (Lessee) name, a (state) corporation

Rental agreement: Total rentable square footage (RSF) per floor being leased, and how it is calculated by the landlord (as defined by BOMA or the commonly accepted/recognized local method). Total usable square footage (USF) per floor and how it is calculated by the landlord (as defined by BOMA or the commonly accepted/recognized local method). The common area factors (as defined by BOMA or the commonly accepted/recognized local method). The property area in square feet and acres if this is a ground lease. The property street address, suite number(s), county, city, ZIP code.

Location of premises: Where the premises are located (often the legal description of the property is included as Exhibit B).

Parking: Parking that is provided by the landlord is often expressed as (_____) per 1,000 square feet of usable office space. Parking for visitors, reserved parking (ideally at no cost), and the cost of parking (if not free for the term of the lease, try to lock in the rate for the term and option periods) should be included here.

Term: Effective or commencement date, occupancy date, termination date, and total initial term of lease in years/months/days.

Base rental: Rental rate per rentable square foot, total rent per year, and monthly amount _____ and_____ /100 dollars ($_____._____) due to the landlord, usually by the first day of the month, including the name the rent check is to be made payable to and the rent payment address.

Operating and common area maintenance expenses: Operating expenses per month are often expressed to an amount per square foot for a specific year as a peg or expense stop. This can be a complicated and expensive item that should be thoroughly detailed in the lease, especially with regard to the percentage of expense pass-through, the base amount and base year, etc. Common area mainte-nance expenses per month are often found at warehouse properties where the site maintenance is managed by the landlord and you pay utilities, janitorial costs, and so on for your space.

Rental adjustment: Sometimes called *rent escalation*, these stated increases establish future rents with specific information on what is being escalated. The increases usually occur yearly and may include increases to the base rent and/or to the operating expenses by:

- A specific percentage increase
- The CPI or a percentage of the CPI with a minimum and a maximum increase
- An additional $_____._____ cost per rentable square foot
- A set amount based on a specific $_____._____ cost per rentable square foot
- A combination of the above
- Whatever you negotiate

Use: What your customer will be legally doing in the space.

Landlord repairs and services included in the lease:

- None
- Janitorial
- Plumbing repair
- HVAC
- Grounds/CAM
- Lighting
- Electricity
- Roof
- Exterior/window repair
- Snow removal
- Window washing schedule
- Parking lot repair
- After-hours HVAC and cost
- Hours of normal HVAC service (Is Saturday morning included?)
- Holidays observed at the property
- Service elevator hours
- Porter service and costs

- Loading dock hours and trash disposal
- Security: guards, access card (cost), cameras, parking, after-hour access, fire stair access, keys, etc.
- Fire and life safety
- Basement or tenant storage
- Interior signage: suite, lobby directory, etc.

Repairs by the tenant: Such as repair of construction within the tenant's premises.

Possession: Lessor may or may not warrant that your customer can occupy the space on the commencement date of the lease.

Inspection: Usually, the requirement is that the landlord give the tenant 24-hour notice to enter the premises at reasonable hours to inspect the premises to see that the tenant is complying with all of the tenant's obligations.

ADA compliance: The lease property (site and building) meets the requirements of the federal Americans with Disabilities Act (ADA) and any other state and local rules and regulations.

Default: States what will happen if the tenant fails to pay the rent within a specific period, thereby defaulting on the terms of the lease.

Reletting by landlord and other remedies: Usually states that if tenant is in default, the landlord can rent the space to another tenant and that doing so does not mean the landlord has waived the right to seek further legal action against the original tenant.

Exterior signs: States whether or not the tenant can place an exterior sign on the building wall, roof, or grounds. If this is permitted, then a description of what can be installed and where, the approval process, and who will pay for the sign is included.

Removal of fixtures: Tenant is usually permitted at the end of the lease term to remove tenant-owned furnishings and removable items not included as part of the base building. This item should be carefully reviewed, especially if your customer will be spending capital funds to install a computer room and associated systems; ensure that the customer can take the raised floor, HVAC units, fire suppression, alarm system, etc., when moving out.

Assignment and subleasing: Ability to assign or sublease the lease, specific restrictions, and landlord approval, if any. Your customer should be able to sublease the space to any similar operation division without having to secure the landlord's approval.

Destruction or damage: Addresses what happens to the lease agreement if the building is destroyed or damaged by fire.

Condemnation by governmental authorities: Addresses what happens to the lease if the premises or the building is permanently taken or condemned by a governmental authority.

Alterations and improvements: Often stipulates that the tenant can make no alterations in or to the premises without first obtaining the landlord's prior written consent. This can also be less restrictive: The tenant may be able to redecorate, repaint, move a partition, recarpet, make nonstructural changes and changes that do not affect the mechanical, electrical, plumbing, and life safety systems of the space and building without first obtaining the landlord's prior written consent. Some landlords are using this section to try to require tenants to use the landlord's construction services and charge a management fee for alterations or improvements to the space.

Attorney's fee: Usually requires that the tenant agrees to pay all attorney's fees and expenses the landlord incurs in enforcing any of the tenant's obligations of the lease.

Waiver of subrogation: Briefly, the landlord and tenant waive all rights to recover against each other or against any other tenant or occupant of the building for any loss or damage arising from any cause covered by any insurance required to be carried by each of the parties or any other insurance actually carried by the landlord or the tenant.

Indemnification: Briefly, this usually provides that the tenant will indemnify the landlord, its agents, and employees against, and hold the landlord, its agents, and employees harmless from any and all demands, claims, causes, fines, damages, etc., arising at any time from the tenant's occupancy of the premises unless damage or injury results from the negligence of the landlord. If any action or proceeding is brought against the landlord, its agents, or employees by reason of any such claim, tenant, upon notice from the landlord, will defend the claim at tenant's expense with counsel reasonably satisfactory to the landlord.

Rules and regulations: Landlords adopt rules and regulations for the building operation and safety of their tenants, and these are usually attached as an exhibit to the lease. The rules can be fairly restrictive and should be carefully reviewed, and changes or modifications should be requested and approved by the landlord in writing before or when the lease is executed. For example, the rules and regulations may prohibit drink machines in tenant suites. If your customer plans to have a drink machine in the break room for the exclusive use of employees, an exception in writing should be requested for approval by the landlord during lease negotiation.

Holding over: Can the tenant stay on in the premises after the end of the lease on a month-to-month basis? If yes, will the monthly rental increase, and by how much? This can range from no increase to 200 percent of the monthly rental.

Surrender of the premises: At the termination of the lease, the tenant shall surrender the premises and keys to the landlord in the same condition as at the commencement of the term, natural wear and tear, fire, or other casualty only excepted. This item can be used by the landlord to withhold the return of a deposit where substantial abuse to the vacated premises is readily apparent and will need major repair.

Notice: Tenant and Landlord correspondence notification address refers to the legal addresses where each party must send their formal notices when informing the other party of an issue that is informational or legal in nature.

Parties: The "Landlord" or "Lessor" is usually used in the lease as the first party. The "Tenant" or "Lessee" is usually used in the lease as the second party.

Mortgages: The tenant's rights shall be subject to any bona fide mortgage or deed to secure debt that may be placed on the building by the landlord. The tenant has a right to remain at the premises under the terms of the lease regardless of default on the mortgage by the landlord.

Late charges: If the tenant is late in the payment of rent, a specific late charge is often required in the form of a greater of a minimum dollar amount or a maximum percentage of the amount due for every _____ (_____) days the rent payment is late.

Cancellation penalties: If your customer (the tenant) desires to cancel the lease at a specific time(s) during the term of the lease, an amount should be negotiated with the landlord and included in this section.

Tenant's insurance: Landlords require that their tenants provide a certificate of insurance for minimum amounts of coverage specified in the lease, with the landlord named as an insured in the tenant's public liability policies.

Options: If your customer wants to have a specific option to stay in the space, the lease should include a number of options with years for each option period and dates that the options will begin and end. The agreement should state the number of days required to notify the landlord to take an option; option for other space within the property with amount of space being optioned, the amount of rent for the option period(s)—fixed, consumer price index (CPI), percentage per year, or market; specific option information unique to the location; and the right of first refusal of specific floors or space.

Deposit: Is a deposit required? Your company may adopt or have a policy not to pay a deposit, as the deposit represents risk that your company may not pose to a landlord. If a deposit cannot be negotiated out of the deal, ideally it should be no more than one month's rent, with interest on the deposit to accrue to your company.

Rent abatement: In today's rental markets, a number of months of free rent is an appropriate way to gain financial benefit and reduce the effective rate to your company or your customer.

Improvements to the premises: The design and construction of the premises your customer will occupy often require work before the space can be used. The cost of this work is paid for by the landlord or the tenant, or prorated between them. As part of the negotiating process, who will pay and be responsible for what work, at what cost, and within what design and construction schedule must be identified in writing before the lease is executed. The cost, responsibility, design, and construction schedule often take one of the following forms in an exhibit attached to the lease:

- A landlord's work letter and construction schedule, which include design and construction completion dates, cost, and work the landlord will pay for before the premises is delivered to the tenant, the cost and work the landlord will do but the tenant will pay for, and the work the tenant will pay for and do during or after the landlord finishes its work.

- A dollar allowance per usable square foot provided by the landlord; the landlord schedules all design and construction work to provide the space as requested, pay all design and permit fees, and pay for all construction work; the tenant reimburses the landlord for costs over the total allowance amounts.

- A dollar allowance per usable square foot provided by the landlord; the tenant takes responsibility for all design work, obtains permits and fees, schedules the work, hires a general contractor, completes and pays for all work, and requests reimbursement from the landlord for all costs up to the total allowance amounts.

Contingencies or special stipulations: Items unique to your business or this lease may be included, such as:

- Purchase option; if yes, cost and date to notify landlord of date of purchase

- Density of employees restriction; for example, the landlord may require that your customer's premises can accommodate only one employee for every 200 rentable square feet. If additional employees assigned to the premises reduce that ratio, then the landlord could find your customer in default of the lease terms.

- Pro rata share of property taxes if these are not included in the operating expenses

- Occupancy or use tax established by local governments that you must pay either to the local government or to the landlord and is not included in the operating expenses

- Business noncompetitive tenants, where the landlord cannot lease space within the building to your customer's competition without prior approval

- The landlord and tenant to meet certain key dates to complete preliminary plans, develop design, and secure construction permits; obtain construction, permanent financing, or mortgage, etc.

- A bonus/penalty, which may be monetary, etc., if certain key dates or events are not met by either party

- Written confirmation from an independent testing firm that the site, building, and adjacent sites (subsurface, surface, and airborne) do not contain soil pollutants, hazardous waste, buried obstructions, etc.

- Continued warranties for major building mechanical and electrical systems

- Food service (type, location, hours of operation, etc.) that the landlord agrees to provide in the building or site

- Change and vending machines provided by the landlord, by type and location, to be serviced _____ times per week

- Statement of no-smoking areas or policies for the building, a floor, etc.

- A tenant conference room that will hold _____ people with projection, coat, and storage rooms that the landlord will provide within the building to the tenant at no initial cost or use fee for the term of the lease

- A health/fitness center that the landlord will provide within the building or on-site to include: (specify requirements).

- Retail services: bank, copy center, laundry, etc.
- Mail or postal facility in the building or on-site
- Access to the building: pedestrian, vehicular, and services
- Handicapped parking, access, rest rooms, etc.
- Shared telephone switch, telephone services, etc.

Commissions: Any and all commissions, compensations, or other broker or finder fee expenses as part of this lease shall be paid by the landlord.

Changes to the agreement: No term or condition of the agreement will be considered to have been waived or amended unless expressed in writing and agreed to by both parties, and shall be binding upon the parties, their heirs, succors, or assigns.

Execution of the lease agreement: Space should be provided for the:

- Signature(s) of the landlord and a witness, a notary public seal and signature, and the landlord's corporate seal, if appropriate
- Signature(s) of the landlord's agent, if required, and a witness; a notary public seal and signature; and the agent's corporate seal, where appropriate
- Signature(s) for the tenant's corporate officer(s), and a witness, a notary public seal and signature, and the tenant's corporate seal

Exhibits: Attached.

A table of contents at the beginning of your lease document enables you and those who manage and administer the lease terms to locate specific items quickly during the lease development process and after your customer has moved in. The contents may help you develop and manage your own real estate lease process. The Lease Agreement Sample for ABC Company follows the basic contents and includes additional items unique to the specific lease requirement.

LEASE AGREEMENT SAMPLE FOR ABC COMPANY

LEASE AGREEMENT

This Lease Agreement is made and entered into this 10th day of August 2004 by and between West Wacker Towers, L.P., an Illinois Limited Partnership ("Landlord"), and ABC Company, a Delaware Corporation ("Tenant").

In consideration of the agreements hereinafter set forth, the parties hereto mutually agree as follows:

1. DEMISED PREMISES. Landlord hereby leases to Tenant, and Tenant hereby leases from Landlord, certain space (the "demised premises ") on the second floor of the Building (the "Building") situated at 4425 West Wacker Drive, Chicago, Cook County, Illinois 60630, assigned Suite #200 (outlined on Exhibit A, attached hereto). The demised premises constitute approximately 16,535 square feet of net rentable area.

2. TERM. This lease agreement shall be for a term of five (5) years and no (0) months beginning of the Lease Commencement Date, which shall be October 1, 2004, and ending on September 30, 2009 (the "Expiration Date"), provided, however, that in the event the demised premises are not substantially completed in accordance with the provisions of Article 6 by said date, for any reason or cause, then the Lease Commencement Date shall be the earlier of (i) the date the demised premises are occupied by Tenant or (ii) the day which is fifteen (15) days after Landlord has certified in writing to Tenant that all work to be performed by Landlord pursuant to Article 6 has been substantially completed, in which event Landlord shall not be liable or responsible for any claims, damages, or liabilities by reason of such delay, nor shall the obligations of Tenant hereunder be affected. In the event the demised premises are occupied by Tenant prior to the Lease Commencement Date, such tenancy shall be deemed to be by the day, and Tenant shall be responsible for payment of monthly rental, for each day of such occupancy prior to the Lease Commencement Date. Within thirty (30) days after the Lease Commencement Date, Landlord and Tenant shall execute Exhibit E, attached hereto and made a part hereof by reference, confirming the dates of commencement and expiration of the term of this Lease Agreement in accordance with the provisions of Article 2.

3. USE. Tenant will use and occupy the demised premises solely for general purposes, such other purposes as Landlord consents to in writing in advance, and as a part of its present business operations and for uses incidental thereto in accordance with the use permitted under applicable zoning regulations, and for no other purpose. Tenant will not use or occupy the demised premises for any unlawful, disorderly, or hazardous purpose, and will not manufacture any commodity or prepare or dispense any food or beverage therein without Landlord's written consent. Tenant shall comply with all present and future laws, ordinances, regulations, and orders of all governmental authorities having jurisdiction over the demised premises.

4. RENTAL. Tenant shall pay to Landlord an annual rental, payable in monthly installments of Twenty-Eight Thousand Nine Hundred Thirty-Seven and 25/100 Dollars ($28,937.25), in advance, on the first day of each calendar month during the term of this Lease, equal to Three Hundred Forty-Seven Thousand Two Hundred Forty-Seven and 00/100 Dollars ($347,247.00) per year for the period beginning with the Lease Commencement Date through September 30, 1996. Beginning on the first anniversary date of the Lease Commencement Date and at each anniversary date thereafter, the annual rental due each year shall be increased by 4.5%. If the Lease Commencement Date occurs on a day other than the

first day of a month, rent from the Lease Commencement Date until the first day of the following month shall be prorated at the rate of one-thirtieth (1/30th) of the monthly rental for each such day, payable in advance on the Lease Commencement Date. Tenant will pay said rent without demand, deduction, set-off, or counterclaim by check to Landlord at 4425 West Wacker Drive, Suite 2100, Chicago, IL 60630, or to such other party or address as Landlord may designate by written notice to Tenant. If Landlord shall at any time or times accept said rent after it shall become due and payable, such acceptance shall not excuse delay upon subsequent occasions or constitute a waiver of any or all of Landlord's rights hereunder.

5. DEPOSITS. Upon execution of this Lease, Tenant shall deposit with Landlord the sum of Twenty-Eight Thousand Nine Hundred Thirty-Seven and 25/100 Dollars ($28,937.25) as a deposit to be applied against the first month's rent. In addition, Tenant shall pay to Landlord as a security deposit the sum of Twenty-Eight Thousand Nine Hundred Thirty-Seven and 25/100 Dollars ($28,937.25). Such security deposit (which shall bear interest at the then market rate) shall be considered as security for the performance by Tenant of all of Tenant's obligations under this Lease. Upon expiration of the term hereof, Landlord shall (provided that Tenant is not in default under the terms hereof) return and pay back such security deposit including interest to Tenant, less such portion thereof as Landlord shall have appropriated to cure any default by Tenant. In the event of any default by Tenant hereunder, Landlord shall have the right, but shall not be obligated, to apply all or any portion of the security deposit to cure such default, in which event Tenant shall be obligated to deposit with Landlord upon demand therefor the amount necessary to restore the security deposit to its original amount and such amount shall constitute additional rent hereunder. In the event of the sale or transfer of Landlord's interest in the Building, Landlord shall have the right to transfer the security deposit to such purchaser or transferee, Tenant shall look solely to the new Landlord for the return of the security deposit, and the transferor Landlord shall thereupon be released from all liability to Tenant for the return of such security deposit.

6. WORK LETTER AGREEMENT. Landlord will finish the demised premises in accordance with the provisions set forth in Exhibit B, attached hereto and made a part hereof. Landlord shall have no obligation to make any alterations or improvements to the demised premises except as set forth in Exhibit B.

7. REIMBURSABLE EXPENSES.

   a. Reimbursable Expenses Defined: Reimbursable Expenses are based on certain mutually agreed concepts as herein defined. There is established under this Lease a Base Year that is the first full calendar year of the Lease Term ("Base Year"). All subsequent calendar years shall constitute a comparison year ("Comparison Year") for Reimbursable Expense calculation purposes. The terms "Reimbursable Expenses" and "Operating Expenses" are interchangeable for purposes of this Article. Building Operating Expenses comprise two (2) cost categories for purposes of this Lease:

      1) Controllable Costs ("Controllable Costs") include all Reimbursable Expense items other than Noncontrollable Expenses, described below.

      2) Noncontrollable Costs ("Noncontrollable Costs") include taxes, insurance, and utility charges. Controllable and Noncontrollable Costs, when combined, constitute Operating Expenses ("Reimbursable Expenses"/"Operating Expenses"). Allowable Operating Expenses shall be limited to the line-item categories and amounts provided by Landlord as estimated Operating Expenses for the first calendar year of occupancy ("Commencement Year"), said estimate being attached hereto and

incorporated herein by reference as part of Exhibit F. Base Year Operating Expenses shall equal annualized actual expenses incurred for Building operation by the Landlord during the Commencement Year and shall serve thereafter as the basis for Comparison Year calculations per Exhibit F in accordance with the methodology set forth therein.

b. Controllable Costs: In the event that the Controllable Costs for each Comparison Year of this Lease shall be greater than Controllable Costs for the Base Year, Tenant shall pay to Landlord, as Reimbursable Expenses, adjusted amounts calculated in accordance with Article 7e—provided, however, that Tenant's pro rata share of the amount of the increase of the Controllable Costs for any Comparison Year shall be subject to the limitations and methodologies set forth herein.

c. Noncontrollable Costs: In the event that the Noncontrollable Costs for each Comparison Year of this Lease shall exceed the amount of the Noncontrollable Costs fixed for the Base Year, Tenant shall pay to Landlord as Reimbursable Expenses for Noncontrollable Cost categories the amounts as calculated in accordance with the methodologies stipulated below and the applicable prorations per Article 7e.

1) Real Property Taxes and Assessments. Taxes payable as Reimbursable Expenses, as used herein, shall mean any form of assessment imposed by any authority having the direct power to tax, including any city, county, state, or federal government, or any school, agricultural, lighting, drainage, or other improvement or special assessment district thereof, as against any legal or equitable interest of Landlord in the Premises ("Ad Valorem Taxes and Assessments"), to include the following:

a) Any assessment, tax, fee levy, partially or totally, of any assessment, and/or tax included within the definition of Ad Valorem Tax. It is the intention of Tenant and Landlord that new and/or increased assessments and taxes included within the definition of Ad Valorem taxes and Assessments be allowable as a Reimbursable Expense for the purposes of this Lease.

b) An assessment or tax allocable bases on area measurement of the Premises that increases Ad Valorem Taxation shall be allowable as a Reimbursable Expense for purposes of this Lease.

In addition to the above limitations, reimbursable tax expenses shall not include revenue taxation, Landlord's federal, state or local income, franchise, inheritance, estate taxes, nor sundry charges, fees, or levies in substitution thereof. Allowable Tax increases occurring between Comparison Years shall be included as Reimbursable Expenses under the provisions of this Article provided that a minimum occupancy of 80% has been achieved for the taxable parcel upon which the Premises are included.

2) Insurance amounts payable as Reimbursable Expenses shall be limited to the types and coverages insured as of the Commencement Date and applicable prorations of any cost increases for said insurance occurring between any Comparison Years shall be included as Reimbursable Expenses payable under the provisions of this Article.

3) Utility amounts payable as Reimbursable Expenses shall be limited to increases in rates and consumption between Comparison Years and applicable prorations

thereof shall be included as Reimbursable Expenses payable under the provisions of the Article.

d. Proration Calculation:

1) Tenant's pro rata share of Controllable Costs and Noncontrollable Costs is the percentage which the rentable area of the Demised Premises bears to the total Premises.

2) For Operating Expense calculation purposes, costs shall be computed based upon 95% occupancy with Landlord bearing all cost and expenses for vacant building space excluding the Demised Premises. Accordingly, allowable Reimbursable Expenses to which the pro rata share calculation from (1) above are applied shall not exceed actual allowable expenses incurred during any full or partial Lease Year times the appropriate pro rata share.

e. Calculation and Payment of Cost Increases:

1) Landlord shall provide to Tenant within thirty (30) days after the close of any Comparison Year an accounting of Landlord's actual Operating Expenses. Thereafter, Tenant shall have thirty (30) days to review Landlord's expense in order to verify Landlord's calculation and to assess the appropriateness of amounts claimed. For purposes of this review, Tenant shall have access to Landlord's cost records as provided in Article 7f.

2) Subject to the limitations of Sections 7b and 7c, and within thirty (30) days of Tenant's receipt of Landlord's annual Operating Expense statement for the first Comparison Year, Tenant shall pay to Landlord a lump sum amount for that portion of allowable annual operating expense increases, representing the period from the close of the first Comparison Year to the date respective (which shall be on or about the sixtieth (60th) day of the then current Lease Year).

3) With each monthly payment of Base Rent for the remainder of the current Lease Year, one twelfth (1/12) of the amount of the prior Lease Year's Operating Expenses as increased in accordance with the foregoing shall be remitted to Landlord as Reimbursable Expenses.

4) Operating Expense increases shall be calculated in accordance with Exhibit F and with the provisions of this Article throughout the Base Year and any extension years of this Lease.

f. Operating Expenses Inclusions:

Operating Expenses shall include all reasonable and necessary costs of operations and maintenance consistent with the definitions of this article and Exhibit F, as determined by a Certified Public Account ("Accountant") in accordance with Generally Accepted Accounting Practices (GAAP) to include the following costs:

1) Real property (ad valorem) taxes and assessments;

2) Utilities including water and sewer charges;

3) Insurance premium;

4) Janitorial services;

5) Labor;

6) Costs incurred by the direct management of the building;

7) Air conditioning and heating;

8) Elevator maintenance;

9) Supplies, materials, equipment and tools;

10) Maintenance, costs, and upkeep of all parking areas and common areas, including landscaping;

11) Costs incurred in compliance with applicable laws, regulations and ordinances.

The foregoing notwithstanding, Operating Expenses shall be limited to the amounts shown and increase methodologies stipulated as part of Exhibit F.

g. Operating Expense Exclusion's:

The following items shall be expressly excluded from Operating Expenses:

1) Cost incurred in connection with the construction of the project;

2) Cost of (including increased real estate taxes and other Operating Expenses related to) any additions to the Building after the original construction;

3) Cost (to the extent such cost constitutes capital costs under Generally Accepted Accounting Principles) of correcting defects in or inadequacy of the construction of the project, the building equipment, major systems, or the improvements in any rentable area of the project (including the Leased Premises);

4) To the extent such cost constitutes capital cost under Generally Accepted Accounting Principles, the cost of replacement of HVAC, mechanical, security, electrical, plumbing systems, or of any substantial component of subsystems beyond the scope of routine maintenance and repair, replacement or repair of the foundations, floor, walls, roofs, and structural elements of the building outside the scope of routine maintenance and repair; resurfacing of the parking area or of the driveways or roads on the project, or any other cost which is capital in nature;

5) Cost of Leasehold/Construction Improvements for Tenant or any other tenants, including alterations, painting, or decorating of the Leased Premises, and the Premises of other tenants or in preparation for a tenant's occupancy;

6) Salaries and benefits of Building Manager, officers, directors, executive personnel, and leasing agents of Landlord;

7) Legal fees (other than those relating to the general operation of the project) for specific Tenant matters, space planning fees, architectural fees, engineering fees (other than those relating to the general operation of the project), real estate commissions, marketing and advertising expenses incurred in connection with the development and leasing of the Building or any improvements on the project;

8) Any cost included in Operating Expenses, including management fees, representing an amount paid to a person, firm, corporation, or other entity related to Landlord unless it is demonstrated that an "arm's-length" transaction based on the lowest cost of at least three documented and competitively secured bids served as the basis for selection and it is concurred in writing by the Tenant that cost arising from said selection are no more than said costs would be in absence of such relationship;

9) Costs of selling, syndicating, financing, mortgaging, or hypothecating any of Landlord's interest in the project or the improvements located on the project;

10) Cost associated with the operation of the business of the legal entity which constitutes Landlord as the same is separate and apart from the cost and operation of the Building including legal entity formation, internal entity accounting, and legal matters;

11) Cost of disputes between Landlord and any third party regarding matters not related to the project;

12) The cost of any disputes between Landlord and any employee or agent of Landlord;

13) Cost of defending any lawsuits with mortgagees or ground lessors;

14) Cost for which Landlord is reimbursed whether by insurance, by its carriers, or otherwise to the extent to which Landlord is entitled to be reimbursed;

15) The cost of any work or service performed for any tenant (including Tenant) at such tenant's costs;

16) Charges (including applicable taxes) for electricity or any other utilities for which Landlord is entitled to reimbursement from any tenant;

17) The cost of any HVAC, janitorial, or any other service provided to other tenants during other than normal business hours;

18) Insurance premiums to the extent Landlord is entitled to reimbursement other than through the Operating Expenses;

19) Any late fees, penalties, interest charges, or similar fees incurred by Landlord;

20) Interest, principal payments, and other costs of any indebtedness encumbering the project;

21) Any bad debt losses, rent losses, or reserves for bad debt or rent losses;

22) The proceeds of all amounts received by Landlord as fees, rent, or other considerations for use of any public portions of the project (including but not limited to shows, promotions, kiosks, lockers, advertising, etc.) shall be deducted from and reduce the total Operating Expenses; and

23) Lease payments for rented equipment, the cost of which equipment would constitute a capital expenditure if the equipment were purchased.

24) New items of maintenance not included in Landlord's statement to respect of the Base Year Operating Expenses.

25) Any expense for repairs or maintenance covered by warranties and service contracts.

26) Building and equipment depreciation.

27) Taxes of any nature (excluding Ad Valorem Taxes) and interest and penalties for late payment of taxes.

28) Rent payable under any lease to which this Lease subject.

29) Managing agent's commissions in excess of rates customarily charged by managing agents for building in the area.

30) Expenses resulting from any violation by Landlord of the terms of any lease of space in the building or any ground or underlying lease or mortgage to which this lease is subordinate.

31) Costs associated with the replacement of HVAC and other building equipment due to the unavailability, excess cost, or statutory ban on the use of chlorofluoro-carbon in such equipment.

h. Right to Audit: Tenant reserves the right to inspect Landlord's books and records and Accountant's materials in order to verify the applicability and calculations of amounts claimed as Reimbursable Expenses. Tenant or Tenant's representative shall have full access to said materials at Landlord's and Accountant's place of business during normal business hours and be provided workspace, access to a telephone, and duplication equipment at no charge to Tenant for purposes of this audit.

8. ASSIGNMENT AND SUBLETTING. Tenant may not assign, transfer, mortgage, or encumber this Lease, nor shall any assignment or transfer of this Lease be effectuated by operation of law or otherwise, without the prior written consent of Landlord, which consent shall not be reasonably withheld. Tenant may not sublet (or permit occupancy or use of demised premises, or any party thereof) without the prior written consent of Landlord, which shall not be unreasonably withheld. If at any time during the term of the Lease the legal or beneficial ownership in Tenant of fifty percent (50%) or more of any of the stockholders, part-ners, or other beneficial owners of Tenant should change, or if the legal entity through which Tenant does business should change, by reason of sale, assignment, transfer, encumbrance, operation of law, reorganization, merger, consolidation, bankruptcy, other disposition, or other event, such change shall be deemed and shall constitute an assignment, transfer, mortgage, or encumbrance of the Lease, and shall require the prior written consent of the Landlord. If such change of ownership is done without the prior written consent of the Landlord, then Ten-ant expressly agrees that such change shall be deemed and shall constitute a default of Ten-ant under the Lease and Landlord may, at its sole option, elect to pursue any of the remedies set forth in Article 20 of this Lease. In the event that Tenant defaults hereunder, Tenant hereby assigns to Landlord the rent due from any subtenant of Tenant and hereby authorizes each such subtenant to pay said rent directly to Landlord. The consent by Landlord to any assignment, transfer, or subletting to any party shall not be construed as a waiver or release of Tenant from the terms of any covenant or obligation under this Lease, nor shall the collection or acceptance of rent from any such assignee, transferee, subtenant, or occupant constitute a waiver or release of any covenant or obligation contained in this Lease, nor shall any assign-ment or subletting be construed to relieve Tenant from obtaining the consent in writing of Landlord to any further assignment or subletting.

9. MAINTENANCE BY TENANT. Tenant shall keep the demised premises and the other fix-tures and equipment therein in clean, safe, and sanitary condition, will take good care thereof, will suffer no waste or injury thereto, and will, at the expiration or other termination of the term of this Lease, surrender the same, broom clean, in the same order and condition in which they are on the commencement of the term of this Lease, except for ordinary wear and tear and damage by the elements, fire, and other casualty not due to the negligence of the Tenant, its employees, invitees, agents, contractors, and licensees: and upon such termination of this Lease, Landlord shall have the right to reenter and resume possession of the demised premises. Tenant shall make all repairs to the demised premises caused by any negligent act or omission of Tenant or its employees, invitees, agents, contractors, and licensees.

10. ALTERATIONS. Tenant will not make or permit anyone to make any alterations, addi-tions, or improvements, structural or otherwise (hereinafter referred to as "Alterations"), in or to the demised premises or the Building, without the prior written consent of Landlord, which

consent shall not be unreasonably withheld. If any mechanic's lien is filed against the demised premises, or the Building for work or materials done for, or furnished to, Tenant (other than for work or materials supplied by Landlord), such mechanic's lien shall be discharged by Tenant within ten (10) days thereafter, at Tenant's sole cost and expense, by the payment thereof or by the filing of any bond required by law. If Tenant shall fail to discharge any such mechanic's lien, Landlord may, at its option, discharge the same and treat the cost thereof as additional rent hereunder, payable with the monthly installment of rent next becoming due and such discharge by Landlord shall not be deemed to waive the default of Tenant in not discharging the same.

Tenant will indemnify and hold Landlord harmless from and against any and all expenses, liens, claims, or damages to person or property which may or might arise by reason of the making by Tenant of any Alterations. If any Alteration is made without the prior written consent of Landlord, Landlord may correct or remove the same, and Tenant shall be liable for all expenses so incurred by Landlord. All Alterations in or to the demised premises or the Building made by either party shall immediately become the property of the Landlord and shall remain upon and be surrendered with the Demised Property as a part thereof at the end of the term hereof; provided, however, that if Tenant is not in default in the performance of any of its obligations under this Lease, Tenant shall have the right to remove, prior to the expiration of the term of this Lease, all movable furniture, furnishings, or equipment installed in the demised premises at the expense of Tenant, and if such property of Tenant is not removed by Tenant prior to the expiration or termination of this Lease, the same shall at Landlord's option, become the property of the Landlord and shall be surrendered with the demised premises as a part thereof. Should Landlord elect that Alterations installed by Tenant be removed upon the expiration or termination of this Lease, Tenant shall remove the same at Tenant's sole cost and expense, and if Tenant fails to remove the same, Landlord may remove the same at Tenant's expense and Tenant shall reimburse Landlord for the cost of such removal together with any and all damages which Landlord may sustain by reason of such default by Tenant, including cost of restoration of the premises to their original state, ordinary wear and tear excepted.

11. SIGNS, SAFES, AND FURNISHINGS. No sign, advertisement, or notice shall be inscribed, painted, affixed, or displayed by Tenant on any part of the outside or the inside of the Building except on the doors of offices, and then only in such place, number, size, color, and style as is approved by Landlord, and if any such sign, advertisement, or notice is exhibited without Landlord's approval, which approval shall not be unreasonably withheld, Landlord shall have the right to remove the same and Tenant shall be liable for any and all expenses incurred by Landlord by said removal. Any such permitted use, including directories and name plates, shall be at the sole expense of Tenant. Landlord shall have the right to prescribe the weight and position of safes and other heavy equipment or fixtures that Tenant desires to install in the demised premises. Any and all damage or injury to the demised premises or the Building caused by moving the property of Tenant into or out of the demised premises, or due to the same being on the demised premises, shall be repaired by and at the sole cost of Tenant. No furniture, equipment, or other bulky matter of any description will be received into the building or carried in the elevators except as approved by Landlord. All moving of furniture, equipment, and other material within the public areas shall be at such times and conducted in such manner as Landlord may reasonably require in the interests of all tenants in the Building. Tenant agrees to remove promptly from the loading docks and sidewalks adjacent to the Building any of Tenant's furniture, equipment, or other property.

12. ENTRY FOR REPAIRS AND INSPECTION. Unless due to an emergency, Landlord will provide reasonable notice for Tenant to permit Landlord, or its representatives, to enter the demised premises, without diminution of the rent payable by Tenant, to examine, inspect, and protect the same, and to make such alterations and/or repairs as in the judgment of Landlord may be deemed necessary, or to exhibit the same to prospective tenants during the last one hundred twenty (120) days of the term of this Lease.

13. INSURANCE RATING. Tenant will not conduct or permit to be conducted any activity or place any equipment in or about the demised premises, which will, in any way, increase the rate of insurance premiums on the Building; and if any increase in the rate of insurance premiums is stated by the insurance company or by the applicable Insurance Rating Bureau to be due to any activity or equipment in or about the demised premises, such statement shall be conclusive evidence that the increase in such rate is due to such activity or equipment and as a result thereof, Tenant shall be liable for such increase, as additional rent hereunder, and shall reimburse Landlord therefor.

14. TENANT'S EQUIPMENT. Tenant will not install or operate in the demised premises any electrically operated equipment or other machinery, other than electric typewriters, adding machines, radios, televisions, tape recorders, fax machines, refrigerators, calculators, monitors, computers, printers, paper shredders, coffee makers, vending machines, microwave ovens,, and clocks, without first obtaining the prior written consent of Landlord, which consent shall not be unreasonably withheld, who may condition such consent upon the payment by Tenant of additional rent in compensation for such excess consumption of utilities (including additional air conditioning costs) and for the cost of additional wiring, if any, as may be occasioned by the operation of said equipment or machinery. Tenant shall not install any other equipment of any kind or nature whatsoever which may necessitate any changes, replacements, or additions to, or in the use of, the water, heating, plumbing, air conditioning, or electrical systems of the Building without first obtaining the prior written consent of Landlord, which consent shall not be unreasonably withheld. Business machines and mechanical equipment belonging to Tenant which cause noise or vibrations that may be transmitted to any part of the Building to such a degree as to be objectionable to Landlord or to any tenant in the Building shall be installed and maintained by Tenant, at Tenant's expense, on vibration eliminators or other devices sufficient to eliminate such noise and vibration.

15. INDEMNITY AND PUBLIC LIABILITY INSURANCE. Tenant will indemnify and hold harmless Landlord from and against any loss, damage, or liability occasioned by or resulting from any default hereunder or any willful or negligent act on the part of Tenant, its agents, employees, contractors, licensees, or invitees. Tenant shall obtain and maintain in effect at all times during the term of this Lease a policy of comprehensive public liability insurance naming Landlord and any mortgagee of the Building as additional insureds, protecting Landlord, Tenant, and any such mortgagee against any liability for bodily injury, death, or property damage occurring upon, in, or about any part of the Building or the demised premises arising from any of the items set forth in this Article 15, against which Tenant is required to indemnify Landlord with such policies to afford protection to the limit of not less than Five Hundred Thousand Dollars ($500,000) with respect to bodily injury or death to any one person, to the limit of not less than One Million Dollars ($1,000,000) with respect to any one accident, and to the limit of not less than Five Hundred Thousand Dollars ($500,000) with respect to damage to the property of anyone owner. Such insurance policies shall be issued by responsible insurance companies licensed to do business in the State of Illinois. Neither the issuance of any insurance policy required under this Lease, nor the minimum limits specified herein with

respect to Tenant's insurance coverage, shall be deemed to limit or restrict in any way Tenant's liability arising under or out of this Lease. The term "Landlord" as used in this Article 15 shall be deemed to include in all instances not only West Wacker Towers, L.P., but also Universal Financial Life, Inc., and its assigns as the owner of the Building.

16. SERVICES AND UTILITIES. As long as Tenant is not in default under any of the provisions of this Lease, Landlord shall provide the following facilities and services to Tenant without additional charge to Tenant (except as otherwise provided herein):

1) Automatically operated elevator service.

2) Rest room facilities and necessary lavatory supplies, including hot and cold running water, at those points of supply provided for general use of other tenants in the Building, and routine maintenance, cleaning, painting, and electric lighting service for the Building in the manner and to the extent that is standard for first-class office buildings in the Chicago, Illinois, metropolitan area.

3) Heating, ventilating, air conditioning, and electricity as is customary in first-class office buildings in the Chicago, Illinois, metropolitan area, provided that it is understood that heating, air conditioning, and ventilation may be operated only during the hours from 7:30 AM to 6:00 PM (CT) Monday through Friday, exclusive of generally recognized holidays and on Saturdays from 7:30 AM to 12:30 PM (CT).

4) Access to the demised premises on a full-time, twenty-four-hour basis, subject to such reasonable regulations Landlord may impose for security purposes.

5) Provide janitorial services from 5:00 PM weekdays exclusive of generally recognized holidays.

Any failure by Landlord to furnish the foregoing services as a result of governmental restrictions, energy shortages, equipment breakdowns, maintenance, repairs, strikes, scarcity of labor or materials, or from any cause beyond the control of Landlord, shall not render Landlord liable in any respect for damages to either person or property, nor be construed as an eviction of Tenant nor work an abatement of rent, nor relieve Tenant from Tenant's obligations hereunder. If the Building equipment should cease to function properly, Landlord shall use reasonable diligence and make best efforts to repair the same promptly.

17. RESPONSIBILITY FOR DAMAGES TO DEMISED PREMISES. All injury or damage to the demised premises or the Building caused by Tenant or its agents, employees, contractors, licensees, and invitees shall be repaired by Tenant at Tenant's sole expense. If Tenant shall fail to do so upon reasonable demand, Landlord shall have the right to make such repairs or replacements, and any cost so incurred by Landlord shall be paid by the installment of rent next becoming due under the terms of this Lease. All injury or damage to the demised premises or the Building caused by the willful or negligent act of Landlord, or its agents or employees, shall be the responsibility of Landlord and shall be repaired with due diligence and as soon as practicable, at Landlord's sole expense, and in no event shall Tenant be liable for any such injury or damage caused by the willful or negligent act of Landlord.

18. LIABILITY FOR DAMAGE TO PERSONAL PROPERTY AND PERSON. All personal property of Tenant, its employees, agents, contractors, licensees, and invitees in the demised premises shall be and remain at their sole risk. Landlord shall not be liable for any damage to or loss of such personal property arising from any act or negligence of any person, or from any cause other than any damage or loss resulting directly from the negligence of Landlord. Landlord shall not be liable for any interruption of loss to tenant's business, and shall not be liable

for any personal injury to Tenant, its employees, agents, contractors, licensees, or invitees, arising from the use, occupancy, and condition of the demised premises other than from the negligence of Landlord. Notwithstanding the foregoing, Landlord shall not be liable to Tenant for any loss or damage to personal property, or injury to person, whether or not the result of Landlord's negligence to the extent that Tenant is compensated therefor by Tenant's insurance.

19. FIRE AND OTHER CASUALTY DAMAGE TO DEMISED PREMISES. If the demised premises shall be damaged by fire or other casualty, other than the willful fault or neglect of Tenant, Landlord shall as soon as practical after such damage occurs repair such damage (taking into account the time necessary to effectuate a satisfactory settlement with any insurance company) at the expense of Landlord, and the rent shall be reduced in proportion to the extent the demised premises are rendered untenantable until such repairs are completed. No compensation or reduction of rent will be allowed or paid by Landlord by reason of inconvenience, annoyance, or injury to business arising from the necessity of repairing the demised premises or any portion of the Building.

20. BANKRUPTCY OR INSOLVENCY. If a petition shall be filed, either by or against Tenant, in any court or pursuant to any federal, state or municipal statute, whether in bankruptcy, insolvency, for reorganization or arrangement, for the appointment of a receiver of Tenant's property, or because of any general assignment made by Tenant of Tenant's property for the benefit of Tenant's creditors, then after the happening of any such event or in the case of an involuntary petition, then (if such petition is not discharged within sixty (60) days from the filing thereof), Landlord shall have the right, at its option, to terminate this Lease by sending written notice to Tenant, in which event Landlord shall be entitled to immediate possession of the demised premises and to recover damages from Tenant in accordance with Article 21 thereof.

21. DEFAULT OF TENANT. If Tenant shall fail to pay any monthly installment of rent as aforesaid or shall violate or fail to perform any of the other conditions, covenants, or agreements herein made by Tenant, and if such violation or failure shall continue for a period of ten (10) days after written notice thereof to Tenant by Landlord, or if Tenant shall abandon or vacate the demised premises before the Expiration Date of this Lease, then and in any of said events Landlord shall have the right, at its election, then or at any time thereafter while such event of default shall continue, either:

(i) To give Tenant written notice that Landlord has elected to terminate this Lease on the date of such notice or on any later date specified therein, and on the date specified in such notice Tenant's right to possession of the demised premises shall cease and this Lease shall thereupon be terminated; or

(ii) Without demand or notice, to reenter and take possession of the demised premises, or any part thereof, and repossess the same as of Landlord's former estate and expel Tenant and those claiming through or under Tenant and remove the effects of both or either, by summary proceedings, or by action at law or in equity or by force (if necessary) or otherwise, without being deemed guilty of any manner of trespass and without prejudice to any remedies for arrears of rent or breach of covenant. If Landlord elects to reenter under this clause, Landlord may terminate this Lease, or from time to time, without terminating this Lease, may relet the demised premises, or any part thereof, as agent for Tenant for such term or terms and at such rental or rentals and upon such other terms and conditions as Landlord may deem advisable, with the right to make alterations and repairs to the demised premises. No such reentry or taking of possession of the demised premises by Landlord shall be construed as an election on Landlord's part to terminate this Lease unless a written notice of such intention is given to Tenant under clause (i), above, or unless the termination thereof be decreed by a court of competent jurisdiction at the instance of the Landlord. Tenant waives any right to the service of any notice of Landlord's intention to reenter provided for by any present or future law.

If Landlord terminates this Lease pursuant to this Article 21, Tenant shall remain liable (in addition to accrued liabilities) for (i) the (A) rent and all other sums provided for in this Lease until the date this Lease would have expired had such termination not occurred, and (B) any and all reasonable expenses incurred by Landlord in reentering the demised premises, repossessing the same, making good any default of Tenant, painting, altering, or dividing the demised premises, putting the same in proper repair, protection and preserving the same by placing therein watchmen and caretakers, reletting the same (including any and all attorney's fees and disbursements and brokerage fees incurred in so doing), and any and all expenses which Landlord may incur during the occupancy of any new Tenant, less (ii) the net proceeds of any reletting prior to the date when this Lease would have expired if it had not been terminated. Tenant agrees to pay to Landlord the difference between items (i) and (ii) of the foregoing sentence with respect to each month during the term of this Lease, at the end of such month. Any suit brought by Landlord to enforce collection of such difference for any one month shall not prejudice Landlord's right to enforce the collection of any difference for any subsequent month. In addition to the foregoing, and without regard to whether this Lease is terminated, Tenant shall pay to Landlord all costs incurred, including reasonable attorney's fees with respect to any successful lawsuit or action taken instituted by Landlord to enforce the provisions of this Lease. Landlord shall have the right, at its sole option, to relet the whole or any part of the demised premises for the whole of the unexpired term of this Lease, or longer, or from time to time for shorter periods, for any rental then obtainable, giving such concessions of rent and making such repairs, alterations, decorations, and paintings for any new tenant as Landlord, in its sole and absolute discretion, may deem advisable. Tenant's liability as foresaid shall survive the institution of summary proceeding and the issuance of any warrant thereunder. Landlord shall be under no obligation to relet the demised premises but agrees to use reasonable efforts to do so. If Landlord terminates this Lease pursuant to this Article 21, Landlord shall have the right, at any time, at its option, to require Tenant to pay Landlord, on demand, as liquidated and agreed final damages in lieu of Tenant's liability for damages hereunder, the rent and all other charges which would have been payable from the date of such demand to the date when this Lease would have expired the demised premises for the same period. If the demised premises shall have been relet for all or part of the remaining balance of the term by Landlord after a default but before presentation of proof of such liquidated damages, the amount of rent reserved upon such reletting, absent proof to the contrary, shall be deemed the fair rental value of the demised premises for purposes of the foregoing determination of liquidated damages. Upon payment of such liquidated and agreed final damages, Tenant shall be released from all further liability under this Lease with respect to the period after the date of such demand. For purposes of this Article 21, the term rent shall include monthly rental, additional rent, and all other charges to be paid by Tenant under this Lease. All rights and remedies of Landlord under this Lease shall be cumulative and shall not be exclusive of any other rights and remedies provided Landlord under applicable law.

22. WAIVER. If under the provisions hereof Landlord shall institute proceedings and a compromise or settlement thereof shall be made, the same shall not constitute a waiver of

any covenant herein contained nor of any of Landlord's rights hereunder. No waiver by Land-lord of any breach of any covenant, condition, or agreement herein contained shall operate as a waiver of such covenant, condition, or agreement itself, or of any subsequent breach thereof. No payment by Tenant or receipt by Landlord or a lesser amount than the monthly install-ments of rent stipulated shall be deemed to be other than on account of the earliest stipulated rent, nor shall any endorsement or statement on any check or letter accompanying a check for payment of rent or any other amounts owed to Landlord shall be deemed satisfactory. Land-lord may accept such check or payment without prejudice to Landlord's rights to recover the balance of such rent or other amount owed or to pursue any other remedy provided in this Lease. No reentry by Landlord, nor acceptance by Landlord of keys from Tenant, shall be con-sidered an acceptance of a surrender of this Lease.

23. ATTORNMENT. Tenant understands that Universal Financial Life, Inc., as Owner of the Building, has mortgaged the Building to the Fidelity National Bank, Limited (Mortgagor), San Francisco Branch. Tenant further understands that Owner and any future mortgagee will agree not to disturb Tenant's rights and possession so long as Tenant is not in default hereunder, and that any purchaser of said property under foreclosure or other suit or proceeding shall take said property subject to this Lease. Tenant further agrees to execute such subordination and attornment agreements or other similar instruments as may be required by Landlord or such mortgagee. It is further understood and agreed that in the event of default of Owner under its mortgage with Mortgagor, Mortgagor or any other party who becomes Landlord here-under by virtue of any such default may, at such party's sole option, require Tenant to pay as additional rent for each year of the lease commencing with the year of default its proportion-ate share (being the percentage that the square feet of net rentable space occupied by it bears to the entire rentable space in the Building) of any increase in operating expenses and real estate taxes for the base year. For this purpose, the base year is defined to be the calendar year 2004, and such base year costs and rental year costs shall be as determined by Owner's accountant. In the event the final lease year does not coincide with the base year, Tenant shall pay a percentage of such proportionate part equal to the number of days of occupancy divided by the number of days in the year.

24. CONDEMNATION. If the whole or a substantial part of the demised premises shall be taken or condemned by any governmental authority for a public or quasi-public use or pur-pose, then the term of this Lease shall cease and terminate as of the date when title vests in such governmental authority, or if earlier, the date of occupancy by such authority, and the rent shall be abated on such date. If less than a substantial part of the demised premises is taken or condemned by any governmental authority for any public or quasi-public use or pur-pose, the rent shall be equitably adjusted on the date when title vests in such governmental authority and this Lease shall otherwise continue in full force and effect. For purposes hereof, a substantial part of the demised premises shall be considered to have been taken if more than fifty percent (50%) of the demised premises are unusable by Tenant. In the case of any such taking or condemnation, whether or not involving the whole or a substantial part of the demised premises, Tenant shall have no claim against Landlord or the condemning authority for any portion of the amount that may be awarded as damages as a result of such taking or condemnation or for the value of any unexpired term of this Lease, and Tenant hereby assigns to Landlord all its rights, title, and interest in and to any such award; provided, however, that Tenant may assert any claim that it may have against the condemning authority for compen-sation for any fixtures owned by Tenant and for any relocation expenses compensable by stature, and receive such awards therefor as may be allowed in the condemnation proceeding

if such awards shall be made in addition and state separately from the award made for the land and the Building or the part thereof so taken.

25. RULES AND REGULATIONS. Tenant, its agents, employees, invitees, contractors, and licensees shall abide by and observe the rules and regulations attached hereto as Exhibit C. Tenant, its agents, employees, invitees, contractors, and licensees shall abide by and observe such other rules or regulations as may be promulgated from time to time by Landlord for the operation and maintenance of the Building provided that the same are in conformity with common practice and usage in similar buildings and are not inconsistent with the provisions of the Lease and copy thereof is sent to Tenant. Nothing contained in the Lease shall be construed to impose upon Landlord any duty or obligation to enforce such rules and regulations, or the terms, conditions, or covenants contained in any other lease, as against any other tenant, and Landlord shall not be liable to Tenant for violation of the same by any other tenant, its employees, agents, contractors, invitees, or licensees.

26. RIGHT OF LANDLORD TO CURE TENANT'S DEFAULT: LATE PAYMENTS. If Tenant defaults in the making of any payment or in the doing of any act herein required to be made or done by Tenant, then after ten (10) days' notice from Landlord, Landlord may, but shall not be required to, make such payment or do such act, and the amount of the expense thereof, if made or done by Landlord, with interest thereon at the rate of the prime interest rate charged by the Chicago National Bank during the period of such default plus two percent (2%) per annum (hereinafter referred to as the "Default Interest Rate"), from the date paid by Landlord, shall be paid by Tenant to Landlord and shall constitute additional rent hereunder due and payable with the next monthly installment of rent; but the making of such payment or the doing of such act by Landlord shall not operate to cure such default or to estop Landlord from the pursuit of any remedy to which Landlord would otherwise be entitled. If Tenant fails to pay any installment of rent on or before the first day of the calendar month when such installment is due and payable, such unpaid installment shall bear interest at the rate of the Default Interest Rate, from the date such installment became due and payable to the date of payment thereof by Tenant. Such interest shall constitute additional rent hereunder due and payable with the next monthly installment of rent. In addition, Tenant shall pay to Landlord, as a late charge, five percent (5%) of any payment herein required to be made by Tenant which is more than ten (10) days late or cover the costs of collecting amounts past due.

27. NO PARTNERSHIP. Nothing contained in this Lease shall be deemed or construed to create a partnership or joint venture of or between Landlord and Tenant or to create any other relationship between the parties hereto other than that of Landlord and Tenant.

28. NO REPRESENTATION BY LANDLORD. Neither Landlord nor any agent or employee of Landlord has made any representations or promises with respect to the demised premises or the building except as herein expressly set forth, and no rights, privileges, easements, or licenses are granted to Tenant except as herein set forth. Tenant, by taking possession of the demised premises, shall accept the same "as is," and such taking of possession shall be conclusive evidence that the demised premises are in good and satisfactory condition at the time of such taking or possession.

29. BROKERS. Tenant represents and warrants that it has not employed any broker other than Professional Brokerage Company in carrying on the negotiations relating to this Lease. Tenant shall indemnify and hold Landlord harmless from and against any claim for brokerage or other commission arising from or out of any breach of the foregoing representation and warranty. Any representation or statement by a leasing company or other third party (or

employee thereof) engaged by Landlord as an independent contractor which is made with regard to the demised premises or the Building shall not be binding upon Landlord or serve as a modification of this Lease and Landlord shall have no liability therefore, except to the extent such representation is also contained herein or is approved in writing by Landlord.

30. NOTICE. All notices or other communications hereunder shall be in writing and shall be deemed duly given if delivered in person or sent by certified or registered mail, return receipt requested, first class, postage prepaid,

(i) if to Landlord: West Wacker Towers, L.P.
4425 West Wacker Drive
Suite 2100
Chicago, IL 60630
Attention: Vice-President-Property Management

and (ii) if to Tenant: ABC Company
4425 West Wacker Drive Suite 200
Chicago, IL 60630
Attention: Facility Manager

unless notice of change of address is given pursuant to the provisions of this Article 30.

31. ESTOPPEL CERTIFICATE. Tenant agrees, at any time and from time to time, upon not less than five (5) days prior written notice by Landlord, to execute, acknowledge, and deliver to Landlord a statement in writing (i) certifying that this Lease has been unmodified since its execution and is in full force and effect (or if there have been modifications, that this Lease is in full force and effect, as modified, and stating the modifications), (ii) stating the dates, if any, to which the rent and sums hereunder have been paid by Tenant, (iii) stating whether or not to the knowledge of Tenant, there are then existing any defaults under this Lease (and, if so, specifying the same), and (iv) stating the address to which notices to Tenant should be sent. Any such statement delivered pursuant hereto may be relied upon Landlord or any prospective purchaser or mortgagee of the Building or any part thereof or estate therein. Tenant also agrees, at any time or times after Tenant has assumed possession of the demised premises, upon not less than five (5) days' prior written notice by Landlord, to execute, acknowledge and deliver to West Wacker Towers, L.P., an estoppel statement in the form attached hereto as Exhibit D, inserting the appropriate information in the blank spaces therein and making any changes thereto (if any) that are necessary to make the statements contained therein letter correct.

32. COVENANTS OF LANDLORD. Landlord covenants that it has the right to make this Lease and that if Tenant shall pay the rental and perform all of Tenant's obligations under this Lease, Tenant shall, during the term hereof, freely, peaceably and quietly occupy and enjoy the full possession of the demised premises without molestation or hindrance by Landlord or any party claiming through or under Landlord. In the event of any sale or transfer of Landlord's interest in the demised premises, the covenants and obligations of Landlord hereunder accruing after the date of such sale or transfer shall be imposed upon such successor-in-interest (subject to the provisions of Article 23 hereof) and any prior Landlord shall be freed and relieved of all covenants and obligations of Landlord hereunder accruing after the date of such sale or transfer.

33. LIEN FOR RENT. Tenant hereby grants to Landlord a lien on all property of Tenant now or hereafter placed in or on the demised premises (except such part of any property as may be exchanged, replaced, or sold from time to time in the ordinary course of business), and

such property shall be and remain subject to such lien of Landlord for payment of all rent and all other sums agreed to be paid by Tenant herein or for services or costs relating to the demised premises that Tenant may hereafter agree to pay to Landlord. Said lien shall be in addition to and cumulative of the Landlord's lien rights provided by law.

34. HOLDOVER. In the event that Tenant continues to occupy the demised premises after the expiration of the term of this Lease, with the written consent of Landlord, such tenancy shall be from month to month at 125% of the yearly rental at the end of the term of the Lease and shall not be a renewal of the term of this Lease or a tenancy from year to year.

35. PARKING. Landlord grants to Tenant the right to park fifty (50) automobiles for no additional monthly rental for the first year of the Lease term, and Landlord grants to Tenant the right to park five (5) automobiles for no additional rental for the balance of the Lease term on parking levels 1, 2, and 3 as set forth in Exhibit H. Starting October 1, 2004, through the balance of the term of the Lease, Landlord grants to Tenant the right to park forty-five (45) automobiles for additional rent which shall be the then market rate for comparable parking in a Class A office building in the Chicago, Illinois, metropolitan area. Nothing herein shall be construed to grant to tenant the exclusive right to a particular parking space, and at such appropriate time or times, Landlord may rearrange parking spaces or may provide assigned spaces, and may provide attendant parking or such other system of management of parking as it deems necessary. Landlord shall not be liable to Tenant, its invitees, employees, or guests because of failure to promptly remove snow, ice, or water from the parking area and/or structure or because of any injury or damage that may be sustained due to holes of defects that may develop or arise in the parking areas or due to any inconvenience that may arise due to temporary closure of parking areas for repair, maintenance or snow, ice, or water removal.

36. GENDER. Feminine or neuter pronouns shall be substituted for those of masculine form, and the plural shall be substituted for the singular number, in any place or places herein in which the context may require such substitution.

37. BENEFIT AND BURDEN. The provisions of this Lease shall be binding upon and inure to the benefit of the parties hereto and each of their permitted successors and assigns. Landlord may freely and fully assign its interest hereunder.

38. ENTIRE AGREEMENT. This Lease, together with the Exhibits and any Addenda attached hereto, contain and embody the entire agreement of the parties hereto, and no representations, inducements, or agreements, real or otherwise, between the parties not contained in this Lease, Addenda (if any) and Exhibits, shall be of any force or effect. This Lease may not be modified, changed, or terminated in whole or in part in any manner other than by an agreement in writing duly signed by both parties hereto.

39. SPECIAL STIPULATIONS. Landlord and Tenant agree to the following special stipulations to this Lease which shall take precedence over other Articles in this Lease:

1) Tenant shall pay to Landlord as additional monthly rent the direct cost of operating and providing above Building standard air conditioning and electrical services to the Tenant's Computer Room in Space 231. This additional rent shall be determined by multiplying the gallons of additional chilled water provided to Tenant's Computer Room air conditioning units times a cost of chilled water not to exceed $0.0.5 per gallon for the first year of the Lease, and electrical usage within the Computer Room for all items except general-purpose lighting and general-purpose electrical wall outlets shall be on a separate electrical meter and billed to Tenant at the Landlord's cost.

2) Landlord shall provide to the Tenant, at no additional rental for the term of the Lease, use of the Building's 250-square-foot Conference Room which Landlord shall construct at no additional cost to the Tenant. The Conference Room shall be located on the first floor of the Building adjacent to the public rest rooms, as shown and specified in Exhibit I, and shall be available for Tenant use on a first-come basis from 7:30 AM to 6:00 PM Monday through Friday and from 7:30 AM to 12:30 PM on Saturday.

3) Landlord shall provide to the Tenant, at no additional rental for the term of the Lease, use of the Building's unattended Fitness Facility, which shall be available for Tenant use on a first-come basis from 6:00 AM to 8:00 PM Monday through Friday and from 7:00 AM to 4:30 PM on Saturday and Sunday. The Fitness Facility is located on the ground floor of the Building as shown in Exhibit J.

4) Landlord shall provide the Tenant with one (1) Option to renew the Lease for an additional five (5) year term which shall commence on October 1, 2000, and terminate on September 30, 2005. Tenant shall notify the Landlord a minimum of 180 calendar days in advance of the beginning of the Option date should Tenant choose to exercise this Option to extend the Lease. Should Tenant choose to exercise this Option, Tenant shall pay a monthly rental equal to the then market rate for a Class A office building within a one-mile radius of the Building. Should Tenant choose to exercise this Option, Landlord shall provide to Tenant a painting and carpet allowance of $5.00 per usable square foot to be completed by Tenant within one year of the Option date.

5) Landlord shall provide the Tenant with nine (9) months of Rental Abatement commencing on October 1, 2004 and ending on June 30, 2005. Tenant shall pay as monthly rental during this Rent Abatement period Tenant's share of 2004 Operating Expenses which are $6.45 per rentable square feet which shall be Eight Thousand Eight Hundred Eighty-Seven and 56/100 Dollars ($8,887.56).

In WITNESS WHEREOF, Tenant and Landlord have each executed this Lease as of the day and year first above written.

TENANT:
ABC Company

Attest: By: _____

_____   Its: <u>Vice President</u>_____

(Corporate Seal)

LANDLORD:
WEST WACKER TOWERS, L.P.

Attest: By: _____

_____   Its: <u>General Partner</u>_____

EXHIBIT B

WORK LETTER AGREEMENT

In consideration of the terms and conditions of the Lease, the work shown in Exhibit A to this Lease Agreement and in the terms and conditions hereinafter contained, Landlord and Tenant agree as follows:

A. Landlord's Standard Work

1. Landlord has selected certain building standard materials and building standard designs for the Premises (hereinafter "Landlord's Standard Work"). Except as provided in Section B of this Work Letter Agreement, Landlord shall furnish and install Landlord's Standard Work in the Premises. Landlord's Standard Work shall include the following:

   a. Partitions—(number of) lineal feet of floor-to-finished-ceiling drywall partitions with 5/8" gypsum board and 4" vinyl cove base molding.

   b. Painting—Two (2) coats on partitions throughout the Public Areas, Core, and Premises, in colors selected by Tenant from Landlord's standard paint colors and not more than two (2) colors in any one (1) room or space.

   c. Ceilings—Suspended 2' × 2' regular acoustical ceiling installed in accordance with the building standard design. Ceiling height 9' 0".

   d. Lighting Fixtures—(number of) recessed 2' × 4' fluorescent lighting fixtures installed in accordance with the building standard lighting design with three (3) fluorescent tubes per fixture.

   e. Sprinkler System—A sprinkler system including recessed sprinkler heads in accordance with the building standard sprinkler design and with City of Chicago Bureau of Buildings requirements.

   f. Heating, Ventilating, and Air Conditioning (HVAC)—A heating, ventilating, and air conditioning system, including ducts, supply distribution, and return air plenum. The Building Standard mechanical and electrical system is designed to accommodate loads generated by lights and equipment up to a maximum of 3.5 watts per square foot in specific areas (e.g., word and data processing areas, copying rooms, mail rooms, kitchens, special equipment areas) in the Premises.

   g. Doors—(number of) 3' 0" wide × 8' 6" high × 13' 4" thick full-height, solid-core, oak veneer faced doors with frames, hinges, doorstops, and latch sets. The entrance door to the Premises and all public corridor doors shall each have a lock set and closer.

   h. Electrical and Telephone Outlets—(number of) 120 volt duplex electrical outlets and (number of) telephone outlets not including wiring, equipment, or fixtures customarily furnished by telephone suppliers. A single floor-mounted device may contain one duplex electrical outlet, one telephone outlet, two duplex electrical outlets, two telephone outlets, or one duplex electrical outlet and one telephone outlet. Although provided through a single device, each shall be counted separately for purposes of determining the number of outlets Landlord is obligated to provide. Telephone conduit provided by Landlord is minimum 3/4" and maximum r in diameter. Landlord has not included any work, outlets, or conduit in this Work Letter for Tenant's computer cabling. Should Tenant require additional outlets for computer cabling, Landlord shall charge Tenant a separate fee for such outlets. Tenant or Tenant's independent contractor shall provide and install computer cabling and where such cabling is in the return air plenum, Tenant shall ensure that such computer cable meets the City of Chicago's fire and smoke rating requirements.

   i. Carpeting—Carpeting throughout the Premises shall be of a type and color selected by the Tenant from Landlord's standard types and colors.

   j. Sun Control—Landlord shall provide 1" aluminum horizontal blinds on all exterior windows. All such blinds shall be manufacturer's standard design, style, and color as selected by the Landlord.

   k. Public and Core Areas—Landlord shall provide public and core areas within the Building as outlined in Exhibit A and finished in accordance with plans and specifications for the Building.

   l. Floor—Landlord shall provide finished concrete prepared to receive floor covering. Floor loading capacities: 50 pounds per square foot live load, 20 pounds per square foot partition load or per square foot in nonpartitioned areas.

B. Tenant's Nonstandard Work

  1. Tenant may request work in addition to or different from Landlord's Standard Work (hereafter "Tenant's Nonstandard Work").

  2. Landlord shall, upon Tenant's request in accordance with Sections C and D of this Work Letter Agreement, install the following Tenant's Nonstandard Work:

   a. Quantities and qualities of Landlord's Standard Work in excess of those provided by Landlord.

   b. Lighting fixtures, sprinklers, and/or any mechanical equipment in other than Building standard design locations due to the location of partitions.

   c. Additional mechanical and electrical equipment and controls required by Tenant's design or use of the Premises generating loads in excess of those described in subparagraph A.1.f. of this Work Letter Agreement.

   d. Tenant's computer and telecommunication equipment, cabinets, modems, switching units, consoles, and terminal boards.

   e. Tenant may request Landlord to install any other Tenant's Nonstandard Work in accordance with Sections C and D of this Work Letter Agreement including but not limited to substitution of materials or change in design from Landlord's Standard Work. Any such request shall be subject to the written approval of Landlord, which Landlord may reasonably withhold.

   f. Landlord shall, upon Tenant's request and at Tenant's expense, alter, remove, and/or replace acoustical ceiling tiles or exposed mechanical suspension system after initial installation due to installation of Tenant's computer, telephone or intercommunication system.

   g. All Tenant's Nonstandard Work shall be located within the Premises except where permitted by the Landlord in writing.

  3. Improvements Constructed by Tenant: If any Work is to be performed in connection with improvements to the Premises by Tenant or Tenant's contractor:

a. Such work shall proceed upon Landlord's written approval of (i) Tenant's contractor, (ii) public liability and property damage insurance carried by Tenant's contractor, and (iii) detailed plans and specifications for such work.

b. All work shall be done in conformity with a valid building permit when required, a copy of which shall be furnished to Landlord before such Tenant's work is commenced, and in any case, all such work shall be performed in accordance with all applicable governmental regulations. Notwithstanding any failure by Landlord to object to any such work, Landlord shall have no responsibility for Tenant's failure to meet all applicable regulations.

c. All work by Tenant or Tenant's contractor shall be done with Union labor in accordance with all Union Labor agreements applicable to the trades being employed.

d. All work by Tenant or Tenant's contractor shall be scheduled through Landlord.

e. Tenant or Tenant's contractor shall arrange for necessary utility, hoisting, and elevator service with Landlord's Contractor and shall pay such reasonable charges for such services as may be charged by Landlord's Contractor.

f. Tenant's entry to the Premises for any purpose, including without limitation, inspection, or performance of Tenant construction by Tenant's agents, prior to the Lease Commencement Date as specified in Paragraph 2 of the Lease shall be subject to all the terms and conditions of the Lease except the payment of Rent. Tenant's entry shall mean entry by Tenant, its officers, contractors, licensees, agents, employees, guests, invitees, or visitors.

g. Tenant shall promptly reimburse Landlord upon demand for any extra expense incurred by Landlord by reason of faulty work done by Tenant or its contractors, or by reason of any delays caused by such work, or by reason of inadequate cleanup.

C. Responsibilities of Landlord and Tenant

1. Time is of the essence with regard to the responsibilities of Landlord and Tenant under this Work Letter Agreement.

2. On or before (month, day, year) hereinafter known as the Preliminary Plan Delivery Date, Tenant shall provide Landlord with all necessary information, including all specifications and requirements for any Tenant's Nonstandard Work, to enable Landlord and/or Landlord's Architect to prepare a fully dimensioned floor plan and a reflected ceiling plan showing the location of the following:

a. Partitions, doors, electrical, telephone and computer outlets;

b. Equipment requiring electrical power, such as copiers, appliances, word processors, computers, printers, computer-related equipment, and clocks;

c. Furniture, fixtures, including trade fixtures, refrigerators, ice makers, coffee makers, microwave ovens, ovens, range hoods, can openers, water coolers, disposers, stoves, vending machines, cabinets, and counters;

d. Plumbing fixtures;

e. Lighting;

f. Special finishes to floors, walls, and ceilings; and

g. Special mechanical, electrical, or structural requirements, special features, facilities, or additions.

3. From the information provided by Tenant, Landlord and/or Landlord's Architect shall prepare a fully dimensioned preliminary floor plan and reflected ceiling plan which Landlord shall submit to Tenant.

4. Tenant shall have ten (10) calendar days to review and approve the preliminary plans. Tenant shall also, at or prior to the time of approval, select paint color(s) and carpet type(s) and color(s) from Landlord's standard types and colors, and provide Landlord with any additional information Landlord needs in order to prepare working drawings and specifications.

5. Following Tenant's approval of the above preliminary plans and selections, and Landlord's receipt of necessary information, Landlord and/or Landlord's Architect and Engineer shall prepare working drawings and specifications which Landlord shall submit to Landlord.

6. Tenant shall have five (5) calendar days to review and approve the working drawings and specifications. Tenant shall also, at or prior to the time of approval, select paint color(s) and carpet type(s) and color(s) from Landlord's standard types and colors, and provide Landlord with any additional information Landlord needs in order to prepare working drawings and specifications.

7. Following Tenant's approval of the above working drawings and specifications and if Tenant has not requested Tenant's Nonstandard Work, Landlord shall authorize Landlord's Contractor to commence construction.

8. If Tenant has requested and Landlord has granted necessary approvals for Tenant's Nonstandard Work, Landlord will have the requested work incorporated into the work drawings and specifications and Landlord shall obtain a firm price for the Tenant's Nonstandard Work from the Landlord's Contractor. Landlord will provide Tenant the firm price for the above Work and Tenant shall review and approve Landlord's Contractor's price within five (5) calendar days. Upon Tenant's written approval of Landlord's Contractor's price, Landlord shall authorize Landlord's Contractor to commence construction. In the absence of such written approval, Landlord shall not be required to authorize commencement of construction.

9. Tenant shall be responsible for delays in completion of the Premises and additional costs in Landlord's Standard Work and Tenant's Nonstandard Work caused by:

   a. Tenant's failure to provide information or approvals in a timely manner;

   b. Request for materials, finishes, or installations other than Landlord's Standard Work;

   c. Tenant's changes in any plans, drawings, or specifications; and

   d. Inaccuracies, omissions, or changes in any information provided by Tenant.

   Delay in completion of Landlord's Standard Work or Tenant's Nonstandard Work for any of the foregoing reasons shall be considered the fault of Tenant and shall not serve to extend the Commencement Date under Paragraph 2 of the Lease.

10. If Tenant shall request any change after construction commencement, Tenant shall request in writing to Landlord, and such request shall be accompanied by all plans and specifications necessary to show and explain changes from the approved working drawings and specifications. After receiving this information, Landlord shall give Tenant a written estimate of the maximum cost of engineering and design services to prepare working drawings and incorporate the changes in accordance with such request. If Ten-

ant approves such estimate in writing, Landlord shall have such working drawings prepared and Tenant shall reimburse Landlord for the cost thereof not in excess of such estimate. Promptly upon completion of such working drawings, Landlord shall obtain a cost, if any, for the change from Landlord's Contractor and Landlord shall notify Tenant in writing of the cost, if any, which will be chargeable or credited to Tenant for such change, addition, or deletion. Tenant shall within five (5) calendar days notify Landlord in writing to proceed with such change, addition, or deletion. In the absence of such notice, Landlord shall proceed in accordance with the working drawings and specifications prepared pursuant to the previously approved working drawings and specifications.

11. No Landlord's Standard Work or Tenant's Nonstandard Work shall be performed by Tenant or Tenant's contractor unless approved in writing by Landlord.

D. Financial

1. If Tenant does not request any Tenant's Nonstandard Work, Landlord shall install and furnish Landlord's Standard Work at Landlord's expense, including expense related to preparation of the fully dimensioned preliminary floor plan, reflected ceiling plan, and the working drawings and specifications.

2. If Tenant requests Tenant's Nonstandard Work, Tenant shall pay Landlord all costs related to Tenant's Nonstandard Work, including but not limited to:

a. The cost of professional services (including services of architects, interior designers, engineers, and consultants) required to incorporate Tenant's Nonstandard Work into the working drawings and specifications;

b. The cost of materials other than Landlord's Standard Work materials and the cost of installing such materials; and

c. The cost of structural changes in the Building.

Whether or not Tenant requests Tenant's Nonstandard Work, Tenant shall not be entitled to any credits whatsoever for Landlord's Standard Work not utilized by Tenant.

3. Following commencement of construction, Landlord shall bill Tenant monthly for the cost of Tenant's Nonstandard Work. Tenant shall pay Landlord the entire amount of each statement within ten (10) calendar days after receipt.

4. Notwithstanding Paragraphs 6 and 9 of the Lease, any sums payable by Tenant to Landlord under this Work Letter Agreement which shall not be paid upon the due date shall bear interest at a rate equal to the Prime Rate as determined by First Bank of Chicago plus one (1) percentage point, as the rate may vary from time to time.

TENANT: LANDLORD:
ABC COMPANY   WEST WACKER TOWERS, L.P.

By: _____   By: _____

Title: Vice President_____   Title: General Partner_____

Date: _____   Date: _____

EXHIBIT C

RULES AND REGULATIONS

1. Common Areas. The sidewalks, halls, passages, exits, entrances, elevators, and stairways of the Building shall not be obstructed by any of the tenants or used by them for any purpose other than for ingress to and egress from their respective premises. The halls, passages, exits, entrances, elevators, and stairways are not intended for use by the general public, and Landlord shall in all cases retain the right to control and prevent access thereto of all persons whose presence in the judgment of Landlord would be prejudicial to the safety, character, reputation, or interest of the Building, Landlord, or tenants, provided that nothing herein contained shall be construed to prevent access by persons with whom any tenant normally deals in the ordinary course of its business, unless such persons are engaged in illegal activities.

2. Use and Occupancy of Premises. For the safety, efficiency, and protection of the tenants and the Building, Tenant shall not nor permit any employee, agent, or invitee of Tenant to use its Premises for:

   a. Storage of merchandise held for sale to the general public;

   b. Lodging;

   c. Cooking except for private use by Tenant or its employees with Underwriters Laboratory approved equipment for brewing coffee, tea, or hot chocolate. Such limited quantities shall be only stored in containers approved by appropriate regulatory agencies;

   d. Use or keeping or storing any foul or noxious gas or substance, kerosene, gasoline, or inflammable or combustible fluid or material other than limited quantities thereof reasonably necessary for the operation or maintenance of office equipment is prohibited;

   e. The business of stenography, typewriting, printing, photocopying, or any similar business for the service or accommodation of occupants of any other portion of the Building, unless specifically authorized in the Lease;

   f. Any use which would be reasonably offensive to other tenants or Landlord or which would tend to create a nuisance or damage the reputation of the Premises or Building.

3. Prohibited Activities. Tenant shall not, nor permit any employee, agent, or invitee of Tenant to:

   a. Interfere in any way with other tenants or those having business in the Building;

   b. Use in its Premises of ice, drinking water, beverages, or catering service except at such reasonable hours and under such reasonable regulations as may be fixed by Landlord;

   c. Bring into the Building or keep within its Premises any birds or animals other than seeing-eye dogs and like animals;

   d. Load any floor beyond the point considered safe by a competent engineer or architect selected by the Landlord;

   e. Use any method of heating or air conditioning other than that provided by the Landlord;

    f. Attach or install curtains, draperies, blinds, shades, sun control devices, or screens on or adjacent to any window or glass situated within its Premises without Landlord's written consent, which shall not be unreasonably withheld;

    g. Use in the Building or its Premises any hand trucks except those equipped with rubber tires and side guards or such other material handling equipment without Landlord's prior written consent;

    h. Operate any television, radio, recorder, or sound system in such a manner as to cause a nuisance to any other tenant of the Building;

    i. Engage in any activity which would make it impossible to insure the Premises against casualty, would increase the insurance rate, or would prevent Landlord from taking advantage of any ruling of the State and local regulatory insurance agencies and Landlord's insurance company, unless Tenant pays the additional cost of insurance.

4. Tenant Requirements. Tenant shall, and shall require its employees and agents to:

    a. Keep window coverings in its Premises closed when the effect of sunlight or cold weather would impose unnecessary loads on the Building's heating or air conditioning system;

    b. Keep the doors to Building corridors closed at all times except for ingress and egress and ensure that the doors of its Premises are closed and locked and that all water faucets, water apparatus, and utilities are shut off before leaving the Premises each day; and

    c. Store all its trash and refuse within its Premises. No material shall be placed in trash boxes or receptacles if such material is of such nature that it may not be safely disposed of in the customary manner of removing and disposing of office building trash and refuse in the City of Chicago without being in violation of any law or ordinance governing such disposal. All trash and refuse disposal shall be made only through entrances and elevators provided for such purposes and at such times as Landlord shall designate.

5. Keys and Locks. Landlord will furnish each tenant two keys to each entry door lock to its Premises. Landlord may make a reasonable charge for any additional keys. Tenant shall not have any such keys duplicated. Tenant shall not alter any lock or install a new or additional lock or any bolt on any door of its Premises. Upon the Termination of the lease, Tenant shall deliver to Landlord all keys to doors in the Premises.

6. Janitorial Service. Tenant shall not employ, authorize, or permit any person, persons, or firm other than the janitor of the Landlord for the purpose of cleaning its Premises. Landlord shall not be responsible to any tenant for any loss of property on the premises, however occurring, or for any damage done to the effects of any tenant by the janitor or any other employee or any other person. Janitor service will not be furnished on nights when rooms are occupied after 6:00 PM unless, by prior agreement in writing, service is extended to a later hour for specifically designated rooms.

7. Use of Service Elevator. The Landlord shall designate appropriate entrances and a service elevator for deliveries or other movement to or from the Premises of equipment, materials, supplies, furniture, or other property, and Tenant shall not use any other entrances or elevators for such purposes. The service elevator shall be available for use by all tenants in the Building, subject to such reasonable scheduling as Landlord at its discretion shall deem appropriate.

8. Movement of Equipment. All persons employed by the Tenant who have the means or methods to move equipment, materials, supplies, furniture, or other property in or out of the Building must be approved by Landlord prior to any such movement. Landlord shall have the right to prescribe the method of protection to the Building, lobbies, corridors, elevator, and Premises to be provided by the Tenant before such movement and prescribe the maximum weight, size and positions of all equipment, materials, furniture, or other property brought into the Building. Heavy objects shall, if considered necessary by Landlord, stand on a platform of such thickness as is necessary to properly distribute the weight. Landlord will not be responsible for loss of or damage to any such property from any cause, and all damage done to the Building by moving or maintaining such property shall be repaired at the expense of the Tenant.

9. Building Services. Landlord establishes the hours 8:00 AM to 6:00 PM (CST) of each weekday and 8:00 AM to 1 :00 PM (CST) on Saturdays as reasonable and usual business hours for the purposes of this Lease. If Tenant requests heat or air conditioning during any hours other than the above and if Landlord is able to provide the same, Tenant shall pay Landlord such charges as Landlord shall establish from time to time for providing such services during such hours. Any such charges which Tenant is obligated to pay shall be deemed to be additional rent under this Lease, and should Tenant fail to pay the same within twenty (20) days after demand invoice, such failure shall be a default by Tenant under this Lease.

10. Access to Building after Hours. Landlord reserves the right to exclude from the Building all persons who do not present identification acceptable to Landlord between the hours of 6:00 PM and 7:00 AM (CST) and at all hours on Saturdays, Sundays, and legal holidays. Tenant shall provide Landlord with a list of all persons authorized by Tenant to enter its Premises and shall be liable to Landlord for all acts of such persons. Landlord shall in no case be liable for damages for any error with regard to the admission to or exclusion from the Building of any person. In the case of invasion, mob, riot, public excitement, or other circumstances rendering such action advisable in Landlord's opinion, Landlord reserves the right to prevent access to the Building during the continuance of the same by such action as Landlord may deem appropriate.

11. Building Directory. A building directory will be provided for the display of the name and location of tenants and a reasonable number of the principal officers and employees of tenants. Landlord reserves the right to restrict the amount of directory space utilized by any tenant.

12. Rest Room Use. Rest rooms and all fixtures and apparatus located therein shall not be used for any purpose other than that for which they were constructed.

13. Tenant's Requests. Special requests of tenants will be considered only upon receipt of a written and signed application on Tenant's letterhead stationery addressed to the Landlord. Landlord reserves the right to deny any such special requests. Employees of Landlord shall not perform any work or do anything outside of their regular duties unless under special instructions from Landlord.

14. Canvassing in the Building. Canvassing, soliciting, distribution of handbills or any other written material, and peddling in the Building are prohibited, and Tenant shall cooperate to prevent the same.

15. Signs. No sign, placard, picture, name, advertisement, or notice visible from the exterior of any tenant's premises shall be inscribed, painted, affixed, or otherwise displayed by

any tenant on any part of the Building without the prior written consent of Landlord. Landlord will adopt and furnish to tenants general guidelines relating to signs inside the Building. Tenant agrees to conform to such guidelines. All approved signs or lettering on doors shall be printed, painted, affixed, or inscribed at the expense of the Tenant by a person approved by Landlord. Material visible from outside the Building will not be permitted without the prior written consent of Landlord.

16. Building Name and Street Address. Landlord shall have the right, exercisable without notice and without liability to any tenant, to change the name or street address of the Building.

17. Landlord Access. Landlord shall, at reasonable hours, have the right to enter premises leased to tenants, to examine same or to make such alterations and repairs as may be deemed necessary, or to exhibit the same to prospective tenants.

18. Noise and Building Utilization. Tenants shall not make or permit any improper noises in the Building, or otherwise interfere in any way with other tenants or persons having business with them.

19. Rules and Regulations. Landlord may waive any one or more of these Rules and Regulations for the benefit of any particular tenant or tenants, but no such waiver by Landlord shall be construed as a waiver of such Rules and Regulations in favor of any other tenant or tenants, or prevent Landlord from thereafter enforcing any such Rules and Regulations against any or all of the tenants of the Building. These Rules and Regulations are in addition to, and shall not be construed to in any way modify or amend, in whole or in part, the agreements, covenants, conditions, and provisions of any lease of premises in the Building. Landlord reserves the right to make such other rules and regulations as in its judgment may from time to time be needed for the safety, care and cleanliness of the Building, for the preservation of good order therein, and to meet and require tenants to observe and comply with additional federal, state, and local regulations as they pertain to the tenant's occupancy of the Building and the tenant's Premises.

EXHIBIT D

ESTOPPEL CERTIFICATE

_____,
of _____, the Tenant, gives this
estoppel certificate to _____,
of _____, the Purchaser. The
Tenant has entered into a lease dated _____, with _____,
as Landlord, for the following space: _____

The Purchaser has requested the information and representations in this certificate
with regard to the Lease because it wishes to acquire an interest in the property known
as _____, which includes the property that is subject to the Lease. The
Tenant acknowledges that the Purchaser intends to rely on the information and representations the Tenant makes in this certificate in Purchaser's acquisition of the property.

The Tenant states as follows:

1. A copy of all documents that constitute its Lease are attached to this certificate, and
there are no understandings or verbal agreements that affect or amend the terms of the Lease.

2. The monthly Base Rate payments under the Lease are $_____, with addi-
tional rent due under the Lease as follows:

3. The Lease term ends on _____, with the following renewal options:
_____

4. To the best knowledge of Tenant, no notice has been received by Tenant of any default
which has not been cured.

5. The Lease is in full effect.

Dated: _____   Tenant: _____

EXHIBIT E

COMMENCEMENT DATE AGREEMENT

An Agreement made this _____ day of_____ , 20_____, by and between _____ (hereinafter called "Landlord") and _____ (hereinafter called "Tenant").

WITNESSETH:

WHEREAS on_____ , 20_____, Landlord and Tenant entered into a lease (the "Lease") relating to certain office premises located at _____;
and

WHEREAS the term of the Lease has commenced, pursuant to Section _____ of the Lease; and _____.

NOW, THEREFORE, in consideration of the mutual covenants contained, Landlord and Tenant agree as follows:

1. The Term Commencement Date of the Lease is

2. Tenant's obligation to pay Rent under the Lease commenced on

3. The Term Expiration Date of the Lease is

4. The execution of this Agreement shall not constitute the exercise by Tenant of any option it may have to extend the term of the Lease.

5. The Lease is in full force and effect and is hereby ratified and confirmed.

IN WHEREAS WHEREOF, Landlord and Tenant have caused this Agreement to be duly executed on the date first written above.

Landlord: _____   Tenant: _____

EXHIBIT F

OPERATING EXPENSES AND CALCULATIONS
(Applicable to Gross and Modified Gross Leases Only)

Operating Expenses for the base period are expressly limited to the items and amounts shown in the matrix (not included in this Exhibit) as guided by the following general principles to include the reasonable and necessary cost of building management, labor, superintendents, and their administrative fees not to exceed five percent (5%) of Controllable Costs and all reasonable and necessary costs for equipment, personnel, material, and supplies for maintenance, repair, and operation of the Project.

Expressly excluded from Operating Expenses are replacement of capital investment items, general expenses of Landlord's building office, executive salaries, rental and similar commissions, advertising and legal expenses except those arising from property tax litigation resulting in savings to the Tenant, building and equipment depreciation, specific costs billed to and paid by Tenant and other tenants, appraiser's fees and expenses, and accountant's fees and expenses which do not relate to the operation of the building and principal, interest, and other costs directly related to financing.

With regard to the foregoing, Tenant shall have the right to inspect Landlord's books, records, and other information for purposes of verifying the appropriateness of Operating Expense Charges.

EXHIBIT G

LANDLORD COVENANTS: BUILDING SERVICES

Landlord agrees to provide the following services to Tenant under the Base Rental amounts under Article 16 of the Lease:

1. Heating, ventilation, and air conditioning sufficient to meet the criteria set forth in the ASH RAE Applications Handbook, latest edition, "General Design Criteria for Office Buildings," for the city in which the Demised Premises are located in order to maintain temperature and humidity with a constant range of 70 d/f to 74 d/f and 45% to 60% humidity respectively. Outdoor design temperatures are to be as set forth in ASH RAE Fundamentals Handbook and should meet the 97.5% design dry-bulb winter and 2.5% design dry-bulb and mean coincident wet-bulb summer. Design considerations must take into account partitioning and special occupancy requirements as shown on approved floor plans in order to maintain uniform heating/air conditioning and lighting levels throughout. Special provisions for conference rooms shall include remote low-velocity exhaust fans for smoke removal providing a minimum of twelve (12) circulation air changes per hour.

2. Electrical energy to provide a minimum of 4 watts per square foot illumination and 5 watts per square foot service throughout the Demised Premises. Lighting plan shall provide a minimum of 70 foot-candles at all locations except corridors and rest rooms that shall be provided a minimum of 40 foot-candles illumination. Electrical design shall exceed these minimums if necessary to accommodate heat and power loads from the operation of all business machines and other equipment used by Tenant in the conduct of its business excepting operation of any computer room that may be separately metered.

3. Hot and cold domestic water and sewer capacity for office requirements to meet the design occupancy included in the attached Tenant improvement plans and specifications.

4. Removal of snow and ice from driveways, parking areas, and sidewalks. If snow and/or ice conditions develop during normal business hours, Landlord agrees to keep said areas as clear as weather conditions permit, to allow ingress and egress to and from public roads and to minimize hazards. If snow and/or ice conditions develop or prevail during other than normal business hours, Landlord agrees to have said areas cleared of snow and/or ice by 7:30 AM of the next business day.

5. Maintenance of any lawns, planters, or other plantings surrounding the Building in which Demised Premises are located, including prompt replacements as needed to maintain quality standards of a first-class office building.

6. Supply, install, and replace lighting lamps, tubes, starters, ballasts, and fixtures as required; service and clean all lighting fixtures at the end of each lease year.

7. Within 45 days prior to the commencement of the first Option Term, refurbish the Demised Premises as follows:

   - Repaint painted surfaces (two coats) in colors to be selected by Tenant;
   - Clean and refinish natural wood surfaces;

- Clean, repair or replace wall covering;
- Replace defaced, discolored, or broken floor or ceiling tiles; and
- Replace carpeting which has become worn or damaged through normal wear and tear.

Tenant shall have no repair and replacement obligation under this Lease. However, Tenant shall cooperate with Landlord in Landlord's performance of duties as established herein. Landlord's failure to perform or to comply with the foregoing shall constitute a material default under this Lease subject to the provisions of Article 16.

EXHIBIT H

PARKING PLAN FOR LEVELS 1, 2, AND 3
(not included)

EXHIBIT I

CONFERENCE ROOM PLAN
(not included)

EXHIBIT J

FITNESS FACILITY PLAN
(not included)

EXHIBIT K

BUILDING OWNERS AND MANAGERS ASSOCIATION
METHOD FOR SPACE MEASUREMENT
(not included)

EXHIBIT L

SCHEDULE OF RENTAL AND ALLOWABLE OPERATING EXPENSES
(not included)

EXHIBIT M

BUILDING HOLIDAY SCHEDULE
(not included)

EXHIBIT N

JANITORIAL SPECIFICATION AND CLEANING SCHEDULE
(not included)

EXHIBIT O

BUILDING SECURITY SPECIFICATIONS
(not included)

EXHIBIT P

ENVIRONMENTAL PROVISIONS
(not included)

EXHIBIT Q

SUBORDINATION AGREEMENT
(not included)

Conclusion

With the Lease Agreement, the legal and financial obligation begins for leased property, except for contingency items whose noncompliance may void the lease—not a usual circumstance. The due diligence phase for the sale and purchase agreement usually begins a process of resolving contingency issues and then moves into the detailed design development and construction document phases discussed in chapters 5 and 6. Closing can take place when the building permit has been issued and all other contingency issues have been resolved. These include zoning, financing, corporate board approval of the purchase and its funding, clear title and title insurance, property insurance, a general warranty deed and clear access to the property and/or building(s) on the site, a payoff of all indebtedness on the property/building(s) by the seller, a check or wire transfer of the funds required for the purchase less earnest money at closing, and, finally, the recording of the property deed—usually within a few days of closing.

Chapter Five

Architectural and Engineering Planning and Design

The real estate process reviewed in chapter 4 corresponds with completing step 1 as shown in Exhibit 5.1, a step-by-step chart of the building programming implementation process. In examining this process, we look at steps 2, 3, 4, and 5 in this chapter. As we concentrate on the development of the site and building, we keep in mind that interior building functions required by the corporate owner or tenants drive the exterior envelope of the building. As the project manager for your customer, it is your responsibility to ensure that planning and completion dates are met. We review the details of the interior design process in chapter 6.

DESIGN REQUIREMENTS AND LAYOUT

The design of a facility can have a substantial impact on productivity and profitability. Capacity planning, discussed earlier, is intimately involved in determining the physical size of a facility. The focus of this section is on the layout of a facility apart from its size. While the issue of layout certainly arises when a new facility is being constructed, it can also come up when there is a significant change in product or service volume, product, or product mix, as well as in technology or production or service methods. Optimization or productivity analysis might also lead to changes in a facility's design for the purpose of maximizing production or service volume and control; minimizing production equipment investments and operating costs (e.g., handling and work-in-process inventory); and even enhancing corporate image and worker productivity. In addition, as noted in the discussion on alternatives to building new space, facility layout may become an issue when space utilization is sub-optimal. These matters apply equally well to manufacturing, distribution, and service firms.

Corporate Functions and Design Requirements

Corporations engage in a wide variety of activities that require different kinds of space. The universe of operational functions includes those shown in Exhibit 5.2. Some of these functions are conducted in or on facilities that are solitary and single purpose with respect to design. Many more are likely to be juxtaposed in the same building shell, in proximity, as in a corporate campus, or even within

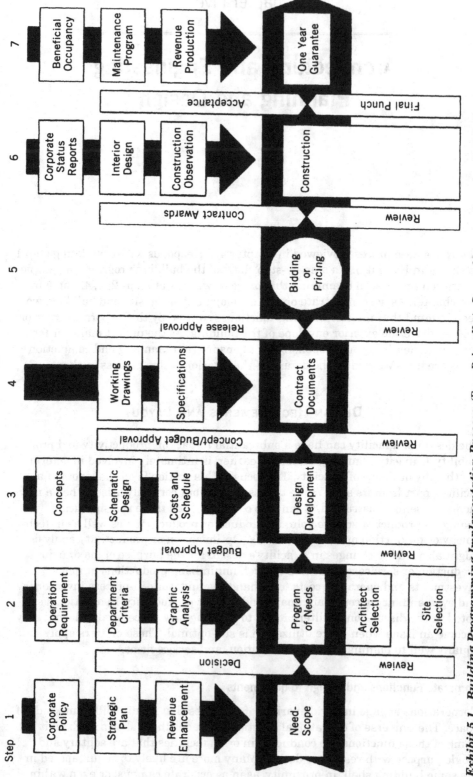

Exhibit 5.1 Building Programming Implementation Process *(From Robert Kevin Brown, Managing Corporate Real Estate, Copyright © 1993 by John Wiley & Sons, Inc. Reprinted by permission.)*

Functions	Building Space Required
Administrative	Executive offices, general office, supporting office
Manufacturing	Fabrication, assembly, processing, refining
Utilities	Electrical generation and transmission, telecommunications switching, cable lines, microwave stations
Extraction	Mines and wells
Agriculture	Farmland, timberlands
Distribution	Warehouses, ports, pipelines
Selling	Wholesale marts, retail, office (services, etc.)

Exhibit 5.2   Design Requirements for Corporate Functions

the same space. The latter alternative is being pursued by many companies that are now trying to return management (and their administrative office functions) to the shop floor in order to cultivate far better awareness, communication, and productivity.

The internal functions of a corporation must also be located in a manner that encourages overall operating efficiency. The degree of operating efficiency is, again, measured by the impact on overall corporate profitability. As the critical internal linkages must be identified and coordinated in the physical design and layout of a facility, so must the linkages between internal functions and external interfaces be coordinated. For example, showroom space is so located in a showroom/office/warehouse facility that customers have ready access to it; the facility's warehouse space is positioned to readily accommodate truck or rail deliveries.

Perhaps one of the most notable aspects of economic conditions since the 1960s has been the rate of change. The rate of change, also known as *churn*, has increased in two respects in particular: the length of furnishing product life cycles has gone from 8 years to 4 years and the rate of change in technology has gone from 4 years to 2 years. Consequently, manufacturing and service firms must provide for flexibility in their space design to accommodate changes in product types, design, volume, and the transformation processes applied thereto. Provisions for change in operations should include the manner in which facilities function as an input of production. This can be accomplished, in part, by incorporating wider spans between columns and walls, higher ceilings, floors with greater weight-bearing capacity, oversized chases, and less permanent methods of attaching personality.

Not only should buildings be designed with flexibility in mind but also the site itself should reflect this consideration. While each aspect of site selection should be considered for flexibility (transportation, energy, water supplies, etc.), the ability to expand at the site should be of principal importance. Incorporating flexibility is important not only for the corporation's operations but also for unrelated subsequent users (future purchasers) of the same facility. A facility that is adaptable to a large number of potential users is likely to have greater value in the marketplace and thus greater residual value. In real estate appraisal parlance, a facility so designed is said to have greater functional utility. Therefore, flexibility may increase the corporation's return on assets, depending on the incremental costs (initial and continuing) involved in providing the additional flexibility.

Before we examine facility scale and layout in detail, note that in addition to the general methods of space programming discussed later, special determinants pertain to manufacturing space layout. Much corporate space (e.g., office, warehouse, retail space) is capable of being reused (with relatively minor modifications) by subsequent users. However, manufacturing and processing facilities are a frequent exception with respect to uncomplicated reuse because they are constructed to house product-related production/transformation processes that are not generally standardized between products. Consequently, the product lines or product mix a corporation manufactures at a facility substantially determine its configuration. Taken a step further, production methods, technology, and so on, are selected or required on the basis of several factors: the stage of the product life cycle and its impact on the scale of the operation; the manufacturing processes used; the handling systems required; and materials storage requirements. With respect to the manufacturing processes, a corporation must use one of several types: nonrepetitive (fixed-position) processes (e.g., building airplanes), intermittent processes (sequential and differentiated batches, typical of job shops), assembly lines (as in most automobile production), or processing/refinement operations (as used in the oil refining, grain, and chemical industries). Each of these processes, technology types, production methods, and ancillary activities requires a different layout. Facility planners must carefully consider these permutations, which are responsible for the wide variation in facility configuration.

LEED: Leadership in Energy and Environmental Design[1]

In assessing site and building design requirements, many facility professionals include LEED requirements in their overall energy and environmental design specifications. The U.S. Green Building Council has developed the Leadership in Energy and Environmental Design (LEED) Green Building Rating System(R), which is a voluntary, consensus-based set of national standards for developing high-performance, sustainable buildings. Members of the U.S. Green Building Council representing all segments of the building industry developed LEED and continue to contribute to its evolution. LEED standards are currently available or under development for:

New commercial construction and major renovation projects (LEED-NC)

Existing building operations (LEED-EB)

Commercial interiors projects (LEED-CI)

Core and shell projects (LEED-CS)

Homes (LEED-H)

Neighborhood Development (LEED-ND)

[1]U.S. Green Building Council, *http://www.usgbc.org/DisplayPage.aspx?CategoryID=19*, Display page information on LEED (Leadership in Energy and Environmental Design).

LEED was created to:

Define *green building* by establishing a common standard of measurement.

Promote integrated, whole-building design practices.

Recognize environmental leadership in the building industry.

Stimulate green competition.

Raise consumer awareness of green building benefits.

Transform the building market.

LEED provides a complete framework for assessing building performance and meeting sustainability goals. Based on well-founded scientific standards, LEED emphasizes state-of-the-art strategies for sustainable site development, water savings, energy efficiency, materials selection, and indoor environmental quality. LEED recognizes achievements and promotes expertise in green building through a comprehensive system offering project certification, professional accreditation, training, and practical resources. Many corporations have adopted the LEED standards for the development of new and major renovation projects.

Determining Facility Scale and Layout

This section discusses the process used by the facilities planner to estimate space requirements. In the context of facilities planning, *space requirements* refer to the volume, type, and design of space needed to achieve the corporate goals and objectives. The term *space* includes both site and building considerations. (We focus on interior elements in chapter 6.) Most of the work of space programming, however, focuses on translating the elements of building requirements into site selection and facilities design criteria. Most often, an examination of the corporation's space requirements precedes a specific action the company intends to take—adding a new production or support activity, expanding into a new region, consolidating two or more existing operations, and so on. Space requirements are also examined and forecasted for the firm as a whole in the preparation of a strategic facilities plan. Even if the focus is on a single facility, planners should consider the impact of the facility on other corporate facilities. Establishing space requirements involves four basic steps, as follows:

1. Identifying the type and volume of activities to be accommodated.
2. Establishing the basis and criteria for space utilization.
3. Developing and applying space standards.
4. Calculating space requirements for the activity and for the firm.

Depending on the nature of the planning effort, these steps might be broken into several smaller steps to address specific project concerns. Each of these steps is discussed in order, followed by an example of their application, in a later subsection.

Identification and Analysis of Activities to Be Accommodated

This step requires identifying each activity to be performed in a facility, describing its role in production or service, and considering its relationship to other activities. The analysis starts with a charge to plan for space-consuming corporate activities and the facilities to house those activities. The space planner's first task in forecasting space requirements is to understand the kinds of activities to be housed in planned facilities over the next period (or within the planning horizon, if it extends over several periods). To begin, the space planner examines corporate documents (the strategic planning documents, if they are available) that establish the following key expectations of corporate production and growth:

1. Revenue forecasts for each productive activity—to ascertain the level of production expected and the relative importance of that activity to the financial health of the corporation.

2. Type and scale of activities required to support the revenue forecasts—to identify the productive and support activities to be accommodated and their interrelationships.

3. Forecasts of the number of employees by type of activity—to determine the type and quantity of workstations and support facilities and services.

4. Productivity forecasts, such as amount of revenue per employee or workstation—to help establish relative importance of activities and budget constraints.

5. Other statements or data that give direction to the space-planning effort—to use in setting design standards, budget allowances, and so on.

After identifying the basic activities and corporate criteria for the facility, the planner must break down the activities into subactivities and examine the interrelationships of each. One tool for accomplishing this task is the adjacency diagram (see Exhibits 5.10 and 6.6). These diagrams use bubbles and other geometric forms to illustrate schematically where activities and subactivities are conducted in space. The linkages between activities are shown as connecting lines between the geometric forms.

The Basis and Criteria for Space Utilization

Next, the space planner must specify the amount and type of space each activity needs. This process begins by examining each activity to isolate characteristics that require space or special design features.

Two procedures typically are required to carry out this task. First, a technical analysis is performed to list and describe spatial characteristics. Then, inputs from occupants or potential occupants of the space must be obtained to help ensure the space will function adequately.

Following is a list of items normally included in the technical analysis.

1. Number of employees by activity area and type of work activity to be performed. For each employee, find out:

   a. The individual workspace required

   b. Exclusive support required for the tasks performed in that workspace

   c. Shared support required for the tasks performed in that workspace

2. Equipment and furnishings required in the workspace

3. Work activity characteristics that require special design or spatial solutions (noise, temperature control, special security, limited accessibility, special utility connections, etc.).

4. Accessibility features. Type and frequency of access needed for:

   a. Other internal activities

   b. Visitor and core function areas

   c. External entrances and exits

   d. Loading and utility areas

5. Core functions required to support work areas. These include:

   a. Reception and visitor areas

   b. Rest rooms, lounges, and rest area

   c. Cafeterias, kitchens, and eating areas

   d. Passageways, vertical transportation devices, and emergency exits

   e. Utility and building support areas

   f. Other common areas or special features (recreation and exercise areas, day-care facilities, etc.)

After completing the technical analysis, the planner often finds it desirable to test the conclusions with people who will actually occupy the facility by eliciting input from corporate employees, potential occupants who might lease or purchase the facility, and occupants of comparable facilities elsewhere. The last two groups of respondents constitute samples from the market and can provide information about market expectations and norms. Either an interview or written question-naire format is suitable for gathering the information. The following concerns are usually surveyed:

1. Security features

2. Privacy requirements

3. Special accessibility requirements

4. Special support functions

5. Personal preferences, where applicable

6. Work environment characteristics

7. Other spatial design elements

The results of the technical analysis and the inputs from occupants are used in developing specifications for the quantity, quality, and special design features needed in the facility.

Development and Application of Space Standards

The two basic components of space standards are design standards and spatial standards. The design standards are, by far, the more technical and more complicated.

Design standards for particular types of space can be found in architectural and engineering manuals, and these usually serve at least as a point of beginning. Design standards may also be derived from previous facilities-planning experiences within the company or at other companies or consulting groups. These standards can be modified to reflect specific corporate requirements or other considerations derived from the technical analysis and inputs from occupants. Essentially, the design standards for a particular facilities plan reflect:

1. Minimum requirements according to architectural/engineering standards, local and state codes, and relevant federal requirements (OSHA requirements, handicapped design requirements, etc.)

2. Special corporate requirements imposed on the particular activity or facility or on all facilities of the company

3. Requirements derived from user/occupant input

4. Budget constraints

Spatial standards specify the quantity and/or dimensional requirements. These standards are often specified as the square feet of floor area per employee, workspace, or activity space. Sometimes the cubic volume of space is needed, and in other situations the floor area plus ceiling heights may be required to determine adequacy. Dimensional requirements may be more important than unit measures for some types of operations, such as some production line processes or the stage area of an auditorium. The most common measure used in spatial standards is the number of square feet of floor area by type of activity.

Calculation of Space Requirements

The last two tasks in estimating space requirements are performed simultaneously and flow from the prior tasks. The calculation of space requirements takes each activity and subactivity in the facilities plan and establishes the quantity of space required by applying the appropriate spatial standard. Space allocations are derived by assigning square footage requirements to the various activities. Identifying and classifying the activities and the space required is the allocation mechanism. Once space for the principal activities is allocated, space for support areas and core functions must be allocated.

Furnishing standards, discussed in chapter 6, and spatial standards, discussed here, are usually established on the basis of net floor area. Two conversions are necessary to translate space allocations to usable measures for cost estimation and other planning purposes. First, you must convert net floor area to gross floor area, which usually involves taking into consideration exterior and interior wall thicknesses. A detailed analysis may be necessary if the building has exterior elements such as attached loading docks, storage sheds, or utility rooms.

The second conversion is to establish minimum site requirements for the facility. Space must be allotted for all buildings and structures to be built on the site and the footprint of the buildings placed in exact locations. A site plan must then be developed that provides the most advantageous access for the buildings, all of the on-site circulation requirements, adequate parking, and other specified site elements. Ratios of site area to building area for various types of facilities are sometimes used to estimate site requirements. These ratios may suffice for rough estimates but should not be relied on for detailed planning purposes. A well-thought-out site plan addresses such factors as irregular site configuration, unusual access features, and special natural features (topography, vegetation, drainage).

In summary, a forecast for corporate space requirements involves the following actions:

1. Summation of activity space requirements
2. Addition of space requirements for core functions and accessibility features
3. Conversion of net floor area to gross floor area
4. Conversion of building area to minimum site requirements to accommodate:
   a. Buildings and other structures
   b. General access and circulation
   c. Loading, utility, and service access
   d. Specialized transportation features (rail, docking facilities, etc.)
   e. Parking
   f. Landscaping, recreational areas, and signage

Building Cost Estimates

Corporations require cost estimates for the construction, renovation, conversion, and reconfiguration of facilities because they are a necessary element of the capital budgeting process, the development of annual operating plans, and the calculation of corporate performance. Even if a corporation acquires existing buildings, making no changes to the building shell or structural components, the interior space probably must be modified to make it usable for the new occupant. Furthermore, if a facility provides no utility whatsoever to the corporation or others, it may need to be razed to make the underlying land reusable or marketable, and the facilities planner must secure a cost estimate for the razing (which could be substantial if, for example, the structure contained asbestos). These estimates might be preliminary or developed in some detail by architects, engineers, interior designers, or general contractors (perhaps with bids). Some corporations can justify maintaining this expertise in-house.

Different types of cost estimates are required for different purposes. Preliminary or detailed cost estimates can be developed or obtained for the following:

- Initial construction costs, including hard costs (e.g., materials, labor, construction management) and soft costs (e.g., professional fees, permits, construction period interest, taxes) to construct new space or to modify existing space (see Exhibit 5.3)

Project:	**ABC CORPORATION TECHNICAL CENTER**
Date:	**October 1, 2005**
File Number:	**0520 0115**
Phase:	**Program**

$ 50,000	Site clearing, removal and demolition
384,513	Site development—Estimated 10% of building cost
3,845,130	Building construction
	$1,667,400 Office 27,790 GSF @ $60/SF
	$1,999,530 Lab 22,217 GSF @ $90/SF
	$ 178,200 Plant 5,940 GSF @ $30/SF
	(Average) 55,947 GSF @ $68.73/SF
50,000	Elevator—2-stop hydraulic
25,000	Utility connections from off-site
384,513	Fixed equipment—Estimated 10% of building cost
461,416	Movable equipment/furnishings—Estimated 12% of building cost
(Not Included)	Additive options—Provisions for expansion, skywalk connections, additional site improvements, special appointments, or other amenities
$ 5,200,572	Subtotal
364,040	Contingency—Estimated 7% of subtotal
$ 5,564,612	Total Construction Cost
333,877	Architectural/Engineering, professional fees @ 6%
25,000	Miscellaneous Costs
	Property survey
	Soils testing
	Plans and specs
	Agency reviews
	Environment assessment
225,000	Land acquisition
$ 6,148,489	**Total Project Cost**

Exhibit 5.3 **Project Cost Summary** *(From Robert Kevin Brown, Managing Corporate Real Estate, Copyright © 1993 by John Wiley & Sons, Inc. Reprinted by permission.)*

- Operating costs, including utilities, maintenance and repairs, property taxes, property management, and property insurance (casualty and liability, if not covered under a corporate umbrella)
- Retirement or salvage costs (include all costs necessary to decommission and dispose of buildings and other improvements to land)

Some facilities can have fairly low initial costs yet experience elevated operating costs, and vice versa. Life cycle cost is determined by integrating the costs of constructing, operating, and retiring a facility into a single present-valued amount. Identifying this cost is useful for capital budgeting, for projecting corporate performance, and especially for comparing one facility alternative with another. However, initial cost and resulting value must be considered together in determining which alternative is or was more profitable for any accomplished or planned corporate activity. Identifying financial values (market value, value in use, residual value), is not part of the facility planning function. Value estimation is a responsibility of the larger real estate function, for which the facilities planning function develops cost estimates.

With this information, you can proceed with step 2 as shown in Exhibit 5.1, which we call the *design firm selection process*.

DESIGN FIRM SELECTION PROCESS

During lease negotiations, preliminary design work is completed by either your landlord's design firm or one you previously interviewed or selected. An activity at the bottom of step 2 is *architect selection*. In this discussion, the word *architect* is interchangeable with the words *engineering* and *interior design*, and the term *design firm* may refer to any of these disciplines.

The scope of your project, common sense, and the laws of the state where your project is located often dictate which discipline(s) you require, and in fact you may need all three. The process for selecting a design firm is similar for all types.

Because the design of a facility (see Exhibit 5.2) can have a substantial impact on productivity and profitability, the planner's selection of the appropriate design firm can strongly influence the success or failure of the facility. Therefore, selection of your customer's design firm is a critical step in the process.

Ideally, you should have a preferred design firm in place before a customer asks for your help on a real estate, design, or construction assignment. In many ways, the selection process is the same as that used to select a real estate broker or general contractor for ongoing facility management requirements. "Suggestions for Selecting a Design Firm" is included in the next section.

Each metropolitan area has a number of qualified, creative, and professional design firms that understand the local market and have contacts in other metropolitan areas if you have an out-of-town requirement. Check with your management, other facility professionals, corporate real estate managers, real estate brokers, bankers, and landlords to identify design firms with a superior reputation for design, project completion estimating, and customer service. If you are currently using a design firm you inherited or your customer wishes to use, determine whether or not the firm can provide the services you need and is identified as one of the best in your inquiries.

The object of this research is to identify a design firm that will increase your capabilities, effectiveness, and efficiency, and will save you and your customer time. Using the firm's services and developing an ongoing professional relationship before you have a specific design and planning requirement should help create value for your company. Develop a request for proposal (RFP) for design services presentation format and invite several of the recommended design firms to respond to the RFP in writing and to make presentations. (A sample RFP is included in the next section.) In your research, you will discover that design firms can differ in many ways. Some have considerable project-specific experience; others are more design-oriented. They may be larger or smaller firms, have one or multiple offices, or listen and respond better than others.

When reviewing responses to the RFP and presentations, evaluate these factors:

- Customer service orientation
- Available in-house services

  Construction document production

  Construction estimating and scheduling capability

  Creative design and problem-solving capability

  Construction management

  Specializations (office, retail, industrial, warehouse, etc.)

- Contacts with other design firms in other cities
- History and ownership of the design company
- Experience as architects, engineers, interior designers, etc.
- Financial capability
- Follow-up procedures
- Computer-aided drafting and design (CADD) and other software capability (word processing, spreadsheet, project cost tracking, project scheduling; see Exhibit 5.4)
- Methods of compensation for services

  Percentage fee

  Time and materials (T&M)

- Means of measuring the firm's performance and service
- Reputation and references

After this review, select the best two or three design firms to make a presentation. These will help you determine how well you and your customer feel each firm:

- Will be sensitive and flexible in quickly adapting to your and your customer's special needs.
- Will listen and act to provide creative alternatives if the requirement runs into major problems.
- Will work with you and your customers. Is this a good match?
- Are able to use the estimating, scheduling, and construction management expertise they profess to have.

You may find that using a design firm evaluation matrix similar to Exhibit 4.19 is helpful in objectively rating each presentation. It is usual for the design firm's fee for services to be paid by your organization unless the design firm is working for the landlord (leased property) or the seller (purchased property). Where appropriate, the lease agreement or sale and purchase agreement should

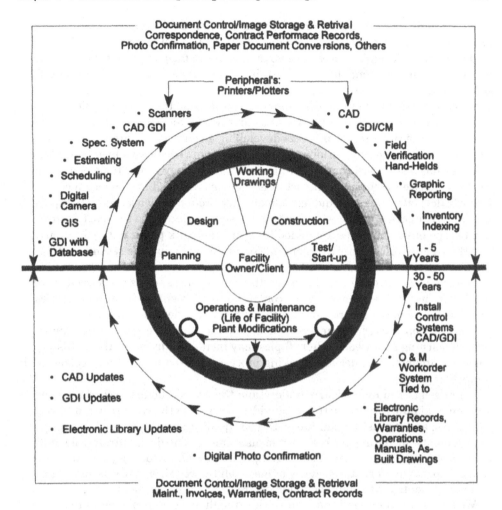

Exhibit 5.4   PC-Based Project Control Tools

spell out the design firm's work and fee responsibilities. The design firm's fee is negotiable, and you or your customer may feel that the best fee arrangement for the project could be:

- A percentage of the total construction cost
- A time and material agreement, which may include a guaranteed not-to-exceed fee
- A flat fee based on a specific scope of the work
- An amount per square foot of rentable area (often used for tenant work in office buildings)
- A fee based on specific tasks, with each task identified and priced separately. This arrangement is often used on complex projects.

We strongly recommend that neither you nor your customer select your design firm based solely on the lowest fee. The old adage "you get what you pay for" holds true with design services. Use your network of facility professionals to verify that the fee is reasonable and in keeping with comparable design firm fees for similar quality and type of work.

When you feel comfortable that one firm can provide the design services you and your customer desire, select it and begin the commitment and investment process. Part of this process involves developing a contract or agreement for services between your organization and the design firm. The design firm you select probably has a standard contract or agreement form they prefer to use, and your RFP should cite the form of contract or agreement required by your legal counsel. Many boilerplate contracts and agreements are produced by associations representing architects, engineers, and interior designers. Most are two-part documents: The business issues are added to fill-in-the-blank pages in the first part, and the legal requirements and general conditions make up the second part. These documents can be modified to meet your specific project requirements.

You and your customer should ensure that the business terms are agreed on with the design firm before developing the contract or agreement and that both parties complete and sign the contract or agreement before the design firm begins work.

With the contract or agreement signed, you and the chosen firm must invest time in learning about each other. Topics may include your corporation's history, business, organization, decision-making process, position in the marketplace, and competition.

Your design firm must clearly understand the project, budget, schedule, your mission, and how your department provides services to the corporation and your customers, and it must be familiar with your quality, excellence, and service requirements, including performance measurement. The design firm's role and the services you expect should be thoroughly reviewed, including your and their post-occupancy performance review of how well the requirement was satisfied and adjustments that should be made before the next assignment.

We strongly recommend that you work through *one* senior person in the design firm; this person will be your prime contact and responsible for coordinating all activities with you.

SUGGESTIONS FOR SELECTING A DESIGN FIRM

The suggestions for interviewing and selecting a design firm are similar to many of those for selecting a real estate broker:

- Be frank about what you or your customer needs and answer the design firm's questions during the interview and evaluation process.

- Respond as appropriate to a considered, well-thought-out phone call or letter requesting an appointment.

- Be willing to make decisions on behalf of your customer and company.

- Take responsibility for gathering project information and developing a complete program at the appropriate stage.

- Be straightforward with respect to the selection procedure—whether or not it is an opportunity for the design firm.

- Have a standard design RFP and a format for interviewing and evaluating design firms—a set of rules that all competing design firms must play by.

- Create a reference list of local, regional, and national design firms; give a new design firm a chance to sell itself as time permits.

- Understand the design firm's role with the team—to act as a bridge and facilitator between you, your customer, the landlord, the general contractor, and other associated service and product suppliers.

- Be an owner or tenant, not a design firm, landlord, or general contractor.

- Be a constructive, technically competent team member dedicated to solving your customer's design, engineering, and facility requirements.

- Be honest about the possibility of working together (or otherwise).

- Be honest about what services you expect, your time and budget constraints, and the fees charged.

- Where possible, stay with your decisions regardless of corporate pressure.

- Spend sufficient time checking references and the specific design or engineering work a firm has done that may relate to your customer's work at hand.

- Be accessible, open, and direct—treat everyone professionally.

- Conduct generic interviews involving several decision makers from your corporation.

- Continue conversations over an extended period to get to know the design firm better.

- Define what is unique about your organization's interests and your budgets, schedules, contract, design, construction, bidding, furnishings, and other service requirements.

- Be willing to share full information about needs and concerns with those you interview.

- Clarify—state as clearly as possible your needs, objectives, and constraints, including budget and schedule demands.

- Be consistent—establish and convey your priorities and job criteria consistently, thus ensuring more responsive and comparable responses to your RFP.

- Define in advance the design/engineering services you want, need, and expect. If you are unsure, your design firm should be willing to help you define the scope of work.

- Allow sufficient time for you and your prospective design firm to exchange information. The design firm will better understand your wants and needs and be in a position to clearly identify the most responsive areas of their expertise.

- Maintain continuity by having the same key staff in control/attendance on your behalf throughout the interview process and the design, construction, and occupancy phases of the project.

- Limit your interviews. Even if you have a great many firms under consideration, limit the number of interviews to approximately three to five.

- Even if a design firm has a substantial history of comparable design or engineering projects, check whether the people with that specific experience are still with the firm and available for your project.

- Check references with the firm's prior clients, with chief executives, heads of real estate, facilities, and users.

- If your customer is an owner or is going to be leasing office space, define the scope of work consistently to each design firm. Your objective is to select the design firm most likely to effectively respond to the unique needs of you and your customer.

- Focus your negotiations on design firms that fully meet your stated criteria. The selection will result in a relationship that can be rewarding to you, your customer, and company, or that will require change if expectations are not met.

- If you are not sure about what the prospective design firm has told you or if what was said gives you anxiety or concern, ask for clarification.

- Before making a selection, be sure your design or engineering requirement and assignment is ready to go. As appropriate, verify corporate support, program definition, site acquisition, and the allocation of corporate funds. A false start can damage your credibility as well as that of your organization and your project.

- If you are faced with a once-in-a-lifetime design or engineering requirement and are unsure how to proceed, following the preceding process can get you off to a good start.

SAMPLE: REQUEST FOR PROPOSAL FOR ARCHITECTURAL CONSULTING SERVICES

REQUEST FOR PROPOSAL
FOR
ARCHITECTURAL CONSULTING SERVICES

September 25, 2005

A. SCOPE OF WORK

1. ABC Company (Owner), a Chicago, Illinois–based division of XYZ Corporation International, is planning to open a number of Regional Distribution Centers around the United States to better serve its internal XYZ Corporation customers. These centers are to be designed based on a model Regional Distribution Center currently under construction in St. Louis, Missouri. The model shall be used as a guide to provide a consistent design for site adaptation at each location shown below.

2. Attachment A provides project requirements and an outline of the model concepts and design criteria to be considered in your response to this Request for Proposal. The occupancy dates shown below are based upon the Owner securing (lease or purchase) the appropriate zoned property in a timely manner.

3. The Owner plans to retain a Chicago, Illinois–based Architectural Consultant to provide professional architectural, engineering, and interior design consulting services for all planning and construction documents necessary to enable the Owner to bid or negotiate and construct the projects at any of the locations and states shown below. Design and construction documents shall meet federal, state, and local code requirements.

B. THE FOLLOWING WORK AND SCHEDULE IS PLANNED:

	Approx. Project Location	Approx. Site Acreage	Approx. Warehouse Sq. Ft.	Proposed Fenced Site Storage	Occupancy Date
Facility I	Jefferson, NY	11	35,000	200,000	Sep, 2006
Facility II	Williams, AL	10	40,000	200,000	Nov, 2006
Facility III	Washington, DC/ Northern, VA area	12	60,000	200,000	Jan, 2007
Facility IV	Dallas, TX area	10	35,000	200,000	Mar, 2007
Facility V	Ontario/ Victorville, CA area	10	45,000	200,000	May, 2007

C. <u>DESIGN FIRM EVALUATION CRITERIA</u>

Please address the following in your Proposal:

1. Contact Person Name and Title

2. Firm Name

3. Address

4. Telephone No.

5. Fax No.

6. Year Firm Was Established

7. Branch Offices:

<u>Location</u>	<u>Year Established</u>	<u>No. of Employees</u>

8. Design Specialization (based on fee volume)

Warehouse	_____%	Schools	_____%
Office	_____%	Banks	_____%
Retail	_____%	Hospitals	_____%
Hotel	_____%	Other	_____%

9. Financial Data (furnish one or more of the following for the two most recent years).

   A. Annual Report

   B. Balance Sheet

   C. Profit and Loss Statement

   D. Statement of Changes in Financial Position

10. Client References—Furnish client references for projects similar in size and scope. Provide names and telephone numbers of contacts familiar with your firm's expertise. The Owner may choose to visit and review relevant completed projects as part of the selection process.

11. Number of employees (do not include contract personnel):

<u>Discipline</u>	<u>No. of Employees</u>
Principals	
Project Directors	
Architects	
Designers	
Programmers	
Schedulers	
Engineers	
Draftsmen	
Construction	

Discipline	No. of Employees
Field Supervisors	
Secretarial	
Clerical	
Others (identify)	

12. Provide organization chart proposed for this project with names and titles.

13. Describe your firm's philosophy and approach to accomplishing the scope of work. Identify by name and title the responsibilities of your team members and percentage of time for each to be assigned to this project.

14. Provide a description of applicable experience and capabilities of team members who will work on this project.

15. List projects currently assigned to the proposed team members and expected completion dates.

16. List projects currently under contract or projected within next twelve months.

Name	Location	RSF/USF	Completion Date

17. Define your firm's method of project control. Address cost control, project documentation, and schedule control.

18. Provide samples of forms for budget preparation, programming records, field changes, conversation/meeting records, and change orders.

19. Identify the type(s) of outside consultant (if any) and identify by firm name (primary and secondary) consultants you will require for this project.

20. Provide a detailed schedule of the Architectural Consulting services you believe should be provided for this type of facility.

21. Provide amount of insurance coverage (Professional Liability—$10,000,000; Workers' Compensation—$1,000,000; Comprehensive General Liability—$1,000,000; Bodily Injury—$1,000,000; Property Damage—$1,000,000; Comprehensive Excess Indemnity (Umbrella)—$25,000,000; Other) for your firm and proposed consultants.

22. Fee Schedule—Describe the fee structure per square foot and estimated time for each of the following facilities, including site engineering by a local engineering consulting firm retained by the Architectural Consultant:

Facility I	Facility II	Facility III	Facility IV	Facility V
Fee/SF FT:	Fee/SF FT:	Fee/SF FT:	Fee/SF FT:	Fee/SF FT:

a. Programming

b. Schematic Design

     c. Design Development

     d. Construction Documents

     e. Contract Administration

23. Would you be opposed to a lump-sum fee arrangement?

24. Indicate all services that would be required but not billed on a square footage basis. Include method of billing for these additional services.

25. List your typical reimbursable items.

26. Anticipate reimbursable costs as a percentage of the total fee.

27. What is your markup for overhead and profit?

28. Indicate your normal multiplier for direct billing costs.

29. Include a statement that a named officer or principal in the firm has an NCARB certificate, is a registered architect in each project state, or can and will obtain registration in additional states as required by the Owner. Included is a current listing of architectural registration by states.

30. The Architectural Consultant and his/her consultants shall state, acknowledge, and recognize in the response to this proposal that the Owner shall have ownership of all designs, completed construction documents, and originals derived from the selection of their proposal for all facilities described herein.

D. ADDITIONAL INFORMATION

1. The Owner intends to provide a quality and safe work environment for the employees that will also provide a sound investment to the corporation and will be economical in *all* aspects of performance. Particular attention must be paid by the Architectural Consultant and especially his consultants to evaluate their designs and proposed engineering systems based on practical, hands-on knowledge. The construction document phase for each facility shall be based upon a specific budget agreed upon by the Owner and the Architect before work begins.

2. Selection by the Owner of the Architectural Consultant shall be based upon but not limited to a combination of the following criteria:

     a. The fee schedule and compensation requirements

     b. Proposal completed as required

     c. History and experience of project firm

     d. Project philosophy

     e. Project team members, education, training, and experience in similar warehouse distribution facilities and their systems

     f. NCARB certification and states where architectural registration has been obtained

     g. Professional attitude, reputation, and perceived relationship with Owner's staff to meet project time, schedule, and budget requirements

3. At the Owner's discretion, the architectural consultant may be selected and a Notice to Proceed may then be issued by the Owner for all or part of the work. The Owner expects to make a selection before the end of October 2005.

4. Upon notification of selection, the Architectural Consultant shall be prepared to begin preliminary planning and cost estimates for all facilities. The Owner requires that the preliminary plans, elevations, and cost estimates be completed by not later than November 27. The Owner will present the preliminary cost estimates and associated information for approval to XYZ Corporation International management in December. It is expected that XYZ Corporation International management will release the Owner to proceed in late December, and the Architectural Consultant should be prepared to begin construction documents for the first facility at the beginning of January, 2006. Should XYZ Corporation management not approve the project(s), the project may be stopped by the Owner as described below in paragraph D.7.

5. Upon notification of selection, the Architectural Consultant shall prepare and forward three (3) copies of the A 1 A Form "Contract Between the Owner and Architect for Designated Services," A 1 A form B 162, which upon execution by both parties shall serve as the contract between the Owner and the Architectural Consultant for each project.

6. The successful Architectural Consultant shall be prepared to meet as required with the Owner's representative, his staff, and the Owner's personnel to meet the objectives of this proposal. The Architectural Consultant shall take meeting minutes of all meetings and distribute typed minutes as requested.

7. The Owner reserves the right to stop the Architectural Consultant's Work and reimburse the Architectural Consultant and its consultants for time and expenses as of the date of the notice to stop the Work.

8. The Architectural Consultant shall keep separate time and expenses for each project facility and bill each project separately every 30 days. The Owner shall have 30 days from receipt to review and process invoices with expense receipts for services and make payment to the Architectural Consultant.

9. The Owner proposes to engage the services of a Fee Developer in early November 2005 for these projects. The Fee Developer shall be responsible for working with the Owner and the Architectural Consultant during preliminary design, cost estimating, and construction document review. The Fee Developer shall hire a local civil engineer to prepare the project civil engineering site plans, foundation plans, and foundation details, hire a local landscape architect to provide landscaping design and landscaping plans, permit, construct, and close out each project. The Architectural Consultant shall be prepared to work with and assist the Owner and the Fee Developer as requested during all phases of each project.

10. The Owner may choose to increase or decrease the Scope of the Work. Should the facility need to house other co-located requirements to support other XYZ Corporation divisions, the increase in the Scope may include additional site and building requirements to house a Part Center, a Service Center with associated office space, Conference Room, Break Room, etc., and parking for service center employees, service trucks, etc., as is the case with the model under construction in St. Louis,

Missouri. Should this occur, the Scope of the Work for the particular project will be amended and the Architectural Consultant's fee and expenses will be negotiated accordingly.

11. A topographic and boundary survey, soil borings, and a perk test are currently being performed for the Jefferson, New York, site. The Owner is in the process of requesting proposals for identified sites in the Washington, DC/Virginia area and is in the process of reviewing sites in the Williams, Alabama, area.

E. PROPOSAL REQUIREMENTS

1. Based on the above requirements, the Architectural Consultant shall deliver three (3) copies of a Letter of Proposal and other requirements listed in this Request for Proposal not later than 2:00 P.M. EST., Tuesday, October 12, 2005, to ABC Company, 324 Circle Center Parkway, Chicago, IL 60646, Attn: Martin K. Smith.

2. Questions regarding this Request for Proposal should be directed to Martin K. Smith at (312) 555–8351 or FAX (312) 555–1876.

3. The Proposal shall include the proposed Fee Structure by square feet and time required for each phase. Reimbursable Expenses such as travel via automobile or tourist class plane fare, reproduction charges, and other varied authorized expenses will be reimbursable by the Owner to the Architectural Consultant at cost and shall be shown separately on the Architectural Consultant's invoice with original copies of expenses attached. The proposal shall show a breakdown of the Architectural Consultant's fee, the fees of the Architectural Consultant's other consultants, and estimated reimbursable expenses totaled by project and location.

4. The Proposal shall state and list the additional Architectural Consultant services and their consultant's additional services not included in the proposal. Fees for additional services shall be listed by employee category and shall be billed on a time card basis with a (specified) Multiplier of Direct Personnel Expense (OPE). Fees and invoices for additional services and time from consultants retained by the Architectural Consultant will be billed at cost.

5. The Owner shall review the proposals, and those responding to this Request for Proposal will be provided with an opportunity to make a 1 1/2 hour presentation on Friday, October 27, at the Owner's office at a time to be scheduled. The Architectural Consultant should be prepared to discuss the proposal and the firm in detail, and the presentation should include no more than 3 representatives who are key members of the Architectural Consultant's team. The Owner may also choose to visit each respondent's office before making a final selection.

ATTACHMENT A

CONTENTS

SECTION

PROJECT REQUIREMENTS

SITE CONCEPTS

SITE PLAN DRAWING

CIVIL DESIGN CONCEPTS

FLOOR PLAN DRAWING

FLOOR PLAN CONCEPTS

ARCHITECTURAL/STRUCTURAL CONCEPTS

ARCHITECTURAL FINISHES

MECHANICAL DESIGN CONCEPTS

ELECTRICAL DESIGN CONCEPTS

PROJECT REQUIREMENTS

A. PROJECT DOCUMENTS:

1. Based upon the model design being built in St. Louis, Missouri, the program for each facility, including equipment, and security contained herein and as described in the Request for Proposal dated September 25, 2005, the Architectural Consultant shall develop and prepare all project documents for Owner review and approval for all related work to include but not be limited to:

   a. Preliminary plans, elevations (⅛ scale), specifications, and cost estimates

   b. Architectural Floor Plan—¼ scale

   c. Exterior Elevations—¼ scale

   d. Architectural Reflected Ceiling Plan—¼ scale

   e. Architectural Roof Plan, Toilet Elevations, and Details

   f. Architectural Wall Sections and Details

   g. Security Plans and Details

   h. Warehouse Equipment, Plans, and Elevations with Equipment Legend

   i. Interior Furnishing Plans and Elevations

   j. Canopy Plan—¼ scale; Sections and Details

k. HVAC Plans—¼ scale

l. HVAC Roof Plan—⅛ scale

m. Electrical Reflected Ceiling Plan—¼ scale and Panel Board Schedule and Details.

n. Plumbing Plan—¼ scale

o. Plumbing Riser Diagrams—Isometric and Elevation

p. The Project Manual, which shall include Owner-furnished requirements, specifications, and Cut Sheets for warehouse equipment

q. Structural, Energy, Seismic, and Wind Load Calculations as required by each state

2. Original drawings shall be 24" × 36", and all blue line prints for the Owner's projects shall be 24" × 36". Title blocks shall include the ABC Company logo and shall include this statement: "These designs and plans are the property of ABC Company."

3. The Project Manual shall be printed on both sides of each sheet where appropriate, shall be bound, and shall be printed on 8 ½" × 11" white paper with an appropriate front and back cover as approved by the Owner. The ABC Company logo shall be included on the front cover of the Project Manual with the name of the project, the Architectural Consultant, and other consultants as appropriate, Project No., and date.

4. Certain items will be provided by the Owner for installation by the General Contractor or by others. This information will be provided by the Owner to the Architectural Consultant to be included in the Construction Documents and the Project Manual.

5. Preliminary plans, site elevations, specifications, and cost estimates will be prepared by the Architectural Consultant and issued to the Owner on or before November 27, 2005.

6. The Architectural Consultant shall also provide the Owner review and approval plans and specifications to include but not limited to:

a. Interior Design

(1) Floor plan

(2) Carpet types and colors

(3) Plastic laminates and colors

(4) Wood species and stains

(5) Break room and rest room flooring and color

(6) Vinyl wall covering types and colors

(7) Window treatment types and colors

(8) XYZ Company Workplace open-plan furniture systems and office furniture

(9) Furnishings

(10) Accessories

(11) Interior Signage

SITE CONCEPTS

A. SITE CONSTRAINTS:

   1. Identify any site constraints such as rights-of-way, flood plains, easements, setbacks, zoning, etc.

B. SITE DESIGN CONCEPTS:

   1. Provide 150,000 square feet of secured, lighted site storage yard laydown area for cable reels, telephone poles, etc. (See the model Distribution Center Site Plan) [not shown in this sample].

   2. Provide adequate maneuverability for ingress and egress to the receiving and shipping dock areas and within the storage yard area.

   3. Provide a standalone concrete ramp in the storage yard for cable reel unloading.

   4. Provide adequate lighted, paved parking as a minimum for:

      a. Employee Parking 30 spaces

      b. Visitor Parking 5 spaces

      c. Truck Parking 2 spaces

   5. Provide future expansion for the warehouse, storage yard, and parking.

C. DISTRIBUTION CENTER SITE PLAN CONCEPTS:

   1. From the main ingress/egress road, visitors, employees, and truck and van drivers will access parking areas and roadways to the loading docks and storage yard.

   2. The Distribution Center shall be located on the site with designated warehouse expansion. A drive to the receiving and shipping docks shall be shown.

   3. The Distribution Center should permit a frontal image to the main access street with a lighted monument sign at the main access street/ingress-egress road.

   4. A curbside loading zone shall be provided for the use of vans.

   5. The storage yard will be secured by a 6' 0" high chain-link fence with manual sliding gates.

   6. There will be no requirement for on-site storage of truck fuel or motor oil.

   7. The site may require a designated area for the temporary storage of hazardous waste products.

CIVIL DESIGN CONCEPTS

A. SITE DRAINAGE:

   1. Address site drainage and water detention requirements.

B. SITE UTILITIES:

   1. Identify size, location, and service of existing water, sanitary sewer or septic tank system, electrical, natural gas, telephone, etc.

   2. All utilities shall be underground from the site boundary or main access street into the facility.

MODEL DISTRIBUTION CENTER SITE PLAN
[not provided in this sample]

MODEL DISTRIBUTION CENTER FLOOR PLAN
[not provided in this sample]

C. SITE IMPROVEMENTS:

1. The functional layout is similar to the model distribution center site plan drawing shown previously, and modifications/changes to the layout will be required as defined below.

2. Asphalt paving shall be provided in the automobile areas.

3. Pavement subject to heavy truck or tractor trailer loads shall have a base with a wearing surface of asphalt.

4. At turnaround areas and at the Receiving and Shipping Loading Dock areas, concrete paving shall be provided over a base designed for heavy truck and tractor trailer loads.

5. In the site storage yard, a granular base will be designed to meet local soil and code requirements for heavy truck or tractor trailers.

6. All curbs and sidewalks will be concrete with gravel base.

7. All exposed subgrade will be scarified to a 6" depth and recompacted.

FLOOR PLAN CONCEPTS

A. FUNCTIONAL LAYOUT:

1. The functional layout is similar to the model floor plan drawing as shown below, and modification/changes to the layout will be required as defined below:

		Area Sq. Ft.
a) Warehouse Area		33,600
b) Repair and Return		6,400
Subtotal		40,000
c) Office Area		
1) Office(s)		
2 × 200 sq. ft.	400	
2) Open Plan area	2,700	
3) Conference	500	
4) Break room	200	
5) Storage	400	
6) Clerical	200	
7) Rest Rooms	400	
Subtotal		4,800
Building Total		44,800 Sq. Ft.

2. Warehouse area shall include:

    a) Crossdock Warehouse design with linear flow

        1) Overhead Receiving Doors

            (a) Dock High Min. 4 each

            (b) Drive-in Min. 1 each

        2) Overhead Shipping Doors

            (a) Dock High Min. 4 each

            (b) Drive-in Min. 1 each

    b) Provide three-pallet-high stacking initially in the warehouse.

    c) Use racking in bulk storage to optimize cube.

    d) Utilize automation at Flow Racks for shipping.

    e) Mezzanine in intermediate storage (expansion).

    f) Re-locatable storage components to achieve flexibility.

    g) Battery charging area for electric forklift trucks.

3. Repair and Return shall require heating and cooling for the warehouse and mezzanine levels.

4. The Distribution Center Manager's office shall be designed adjacent to a door directly accessing the warehouse and. include appropriate windows looking into the warehouse from the Manager's office.

ARCHITECTURAL/STRUCTURAL CONCEPTS

A. BUILDING STRUCTURE:

1. The facility shall be based on 40' × 40' bays. The steel columns will support beams with bar joists which will have a minimum of 24' (high bay) clear to the concrete floor. The high bay area for the Dallas, Texas, location only will include the Warehouse and the Repair and Return and will be 200' × 200', which is 5 bays by 5 bays. The Office area should also be based on a 40' module and may be high or low bay. Skylights, where appropriate, with security bars will be installed to provide natural light in the warehouse area.

2. The building walls will be tilt-up concrete, precast concrete, or reinforced concrete block bearing walls with structural pilasters based upon cost and experience to determine the best exterior building wall material for each location.

3. An expansion wall will be included in the architectural and building structure design.

4. The warehouse floor will be clear epoxy—sealed concrete.

5. The loading docks will be equipped with overhead doors, dock seals, dock levelers, and canopies.

6. The Owner shall furnish and the contractor shall assist in the installation of a number of items which include but are not limited to: open-plan furniture, signage, conveyor system, pallet shelving, computer equipment and cabling, security, fire and telephone system, warehouse equipment, trash dumpster, etc.

ARCHITECTURAL FINISHES

A. EXTERIOR:

    1. Combinations of color and texture in concrete or concrete block will be the predominant finish.

    2. Aluminum storefront with insulating glass will be utilized at the public entry (reception/office areas).

    3. Roof will be designed to pitch rainwater to downspouts located as required within the facility at the inside face of the exterior wall, and shall be designed to meet code and provide insulation as required. An elastomeric or equal roof membrane system is desired.

    4. Hollow metal doors and frames will be painted and utilized for the Warehouse exterior entry doors.

B. INTERIOR:

    1. Offices, Conference Room, Clerical, and Open Plan Areas will have furring and painted drywall mounted on the exterior walls, metal studs and painted drywall on interior walls, painted metal door frames and stained wood solid core doors, lay-in ceilings, and carpet tile with 4" vinyl cove base.

    2. Break Room walls to have vinyl wall covering with a 4" cove base with carpet tile and a vinyl tile floor at the base cabinet area. Break Room to have plastic laminate countertop and plastic laminate base cabinets with a two-bowl stainless steel (5.5) sink, space for a 19.0 cu. ft. refrigerator, space for a drink machine, a coffee maker, and a microwave oven area with plastic laminate wall cabinets below a lay-in ceiling.

    3. Conference Room to have a movable, sound-attenuating partition which will enable the division of the Conference Room into two equal small conference rooms.

    4. Rest rooms will meet handicapped requirements and will have a lay-in ceiling. Rest room walls to have vinyl wall covering, a ceramic tile base with ceramic tile floor, and a mirror above a plastic laminate countertop over plastic laminate base cabinets. Toilet partitions shall be floor-supported plastic laminate.

    5. Open-plan office systems provided by the Owner will be used for workstations in open areas.

    6. Return and Repair and Storage will have furring and painted drywall mounted on the exterior walls, metal studs and painted drywall on interior walls, painted metal door frames and stained wood solid core doors, lay-in ceilings, and vinyl tile floor with 4" vinyl cove base.

    7. The interior finish in the Warehouse will be paint on concrete.

    8. Hollow metal doors and frames will be painted and utilized for the Warehouse interior doors.

MECHANICAL DESIGN CONCEPTS

A. HEATING, VENTILATING, AND AIR CONDITIONING:

1. The Warehouse areas will be heated and ventilated by multiple gas-fired or electric rooftop heating and ventilating units. Multiple relief fans will be provided for summer ventilation. The battery charging area will have a process exhaust.

2. The Repair and Return and the Office areas will each be served by a separate package rooftop air conditioner with gas or electric heat. Exhaust fans will be provided for toilet rooms.

B. PLUMBING:

1. A domestic water main and a sanitary sewer main will serve the building. Where public sewer is not available, a septic tank and system will be designed by the civil engineer to serve the facility. Building roof drains will be served by storm sewers. Domestic hot water will be provided to all lavatories by a gas fired or electric water heater.

2. Emergency eye wash/shower will be provided in the Warehouse at the battery charging area.

C. FIRE PROTECTION:

1. The entire building will be fully sprinklered. The office areas will be served by a light hazard wet pipe sprinkler.

2. The warehouse areas are to be served by an ordinary hazard wet pipe sprinkler system. If research and discussions with Factory Mutual reveal that an extra hazard wet pipe system would be required, an in-rack sprinkler system with multiple hose stations may be required.

3. A sprinkler main will be brought into the building from an existing water main. If the building is located at the end of the existing water main, there may not be sufficient water pressure without a fire pump. Therefore, if this case occurs, a fire pump may be required to boost the sprinkler system pressure.

ELECTRICAL DESIGN CONCEPTS

A. SERVICE:

1. Electricity will be from a pad-mounted transformer. Service capacity requirements will be designed for this specific location and are not expected to exceed 800 amperes at 277/480 volts, three-phase, four-wire. Entrance will be in an underground duct bank to the main switchboard located in the electrical closet.

2. Telephone service will be underground, encased in PVC conduits.

B. POWER DISTRIBUTION:

1. The main switchboard will include the metering current transformers and will distribute radially. Space will be provided in the switchboard for the future expansion.

2. Lighting and HVAC equipment will be fed at 277/480 volts, and receptacle panel boards will be fed through dry type transformers at 120/208 volts.

3. A separate feeder (120/208 volts) will be provided for the warehouse conveyor panel.

C. GROUNDING:

1. A ground grid will be provided in the green area adjacent to the electrical closet.

2. The main switchboard will be grounded to a ground grid and to the cold water service.

3. The metal conduit system will serve as the equipment grounding conductor. If PVC conduits are used, a separate green ground conductor will be installed with the circuit conductors.

4. A copper grounding strap will be provided at the telephone service and will be connected to the ground grid.

D. LIGHTING:

1. The office lighting will be 35 to 40 foot-candles with ½" × ½" × ½" chrome-plated, plastic louvers in a 2' × 4' lay-in fixture. This lighting will be supplemented with task lights located in open-office furniture.

2. Entry lighting will be recessed incandescent fixtures.

3. Toilet and break room lighting will be recessed fluorescent fixtures.

4. Repair and Return (50 foot-candles) and Warehouse office lighting (70–75 foot-candles) will be with strip fluorescent fixtures.

5. Pallet storage (30 vertical foot-candles) and conveyor lighting (20 foot-candles) will be with metal halide fixtures.

6. Wall-mounted telescoping dock lights will be provided for all dock doors.

7. Emergency lighting will be provided in the corridors and office area with inverter ballasts located in the fluorescent fixtures.

8. Exit lighting will be provided by battery-powered red-on-white exit lights.

E. EXTERIOR LIGHTING:

1. Parking lot lighting will be 0.150 foot-candle with pole-mounted metal halide fixtures.

2. Driveway and roadway (0.75 foot-candles) lighting will be with pole-mounted metal halide fixtures.

3. Entryway lighting will be with bollards.

4. Floodlighting will be provided for the sign.

5. Van and semi parking and storage yard lighting will be 1.0 foot-candle with pole-mounted floodlights.

F. RECEPTACLES:

1. Duplex convenience outlets will be provided as required to fit the space.

2. Ground fault receptacles will be provided in toilets.

3. Weatherproof duplex convenience outlets will be provided outdoors at the main entry, truck docks, exterior doors, and at the rooftop equipment.

G. MOVABLE OPEN-PLAN FURNITURE WIRING:

1. Branch circuits for the movable open-plan furniture will be provided in boxes located in the furred columns. The final connections will be provided with the open-plan furniture.

H. <u>TELEPHONE:</u>

1. Telephone outlets will be provided, which will include a box and empty conduit into the accessible ceiling. All telephone wiring will be provided and installed by the Owner, and where applicable will be plenum-rated cable.

I. <u>FIRE ALARM:</u>

1. The fire alarm system will be a low-voltage, zoned, noncoded supervised system with battery backup.

2. Ceiling-mounted smoke detectors will be provided for the room cavities. Duct-mounted smoke detectors will be provided for the air-handling equipment in accordance with NFPA codes.

3. Manual fire alarm pull stations will be provided at all exits or in the path of egress in accordance with NFPA codes.

4. Combination horn/flashers will be provided for audible/visual alerting.

5. The fire alarm system will be tied to the local fire department via leased telephone line.

J. <u>PAGING/SOUND SYSTEM:</u>

1. A voice paging system will be provided for the complete complex.

   a) Office area—ceiling speakers with wall-mounted volume control switches.

   b) Warehouse, conveyors, and storage areas—horn-type speakers.

   c) Truck parking and storage yard—pole-mounted weatherproof horn-type speakers.

2. AM/FM tuner will be provided for music source.

3. Provisions will be provided for a future tape deck.

4. Paging will be accessed by the telephone system.

K. <u>SECURITY SYSTEM:</u>

1. Door access into the building will be by card and card reader. The system shall be a Schlage microprocessor-controlled system, with the PC located in the office area.

2. The security system will be connected through a modem over leased telephone wire.

3. Door monitoring will also be included, with an annunciator located locally at the reception area.

L. <u>MOTOR CONTROL:</u>

1. Packaged mechanical equipment will be provided with built-in motor controls.

2. Individual motors will be controlled by combination magnetic motor starters or manual motor starters as required.

M. <u>GENERAL:</u>

1. The electrical system will be designed to allow an expansion of two tiers of (2) bays. This will add approximately 24,400 square feet of warehousing and storage space.

2. If the Owner elects to add 100,000 square feet of Warehouse space, the electrical system will be designed to allow for that expansion including the expansion stated in item M.1.

Programming and Design

As with a real estate or construction project, design and planning must be managed through strong lines of communication between all members of the team so that everyone understands the mission, what is to be accomplished, and who is responsible for specific actions based on an established schedule (see Exhibit 4.13, Gantt Chart—Relocation of XYZ Corporation International) and the building process functions shown in Exhibit 5.5. We now move through steps 3 and 4 as shown in Exhibit 5.1. These steps take you and your customer through the development of building plans and contract documents that physically describe your customer's physical requirements before bidding the project.

We find that holding a predesign meeting at the design firm office with your customer, major members of your in-house project team, and the design firm's staff who will work on the project is one of the best ways to get the project moving in a positive direction. Agenda items should include schedules for the design firm's work, owner-furnished items, budgets, cost estimates, a meeting schedule, document reviews and turnaround time, bid document requirements, bidding, bid review, bid award, managing construction, and so on.

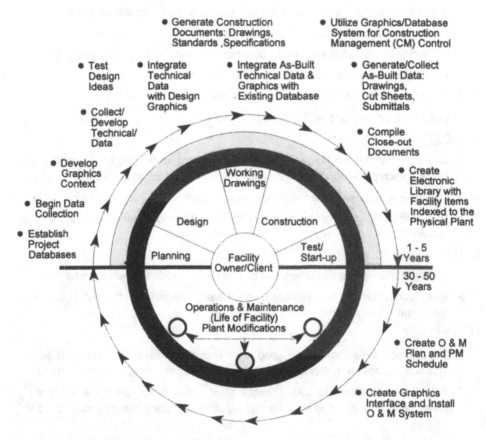

Exhibit 5.5   Building Process Functions

If your project is a fast-track, just-in-time, or hypertrack project, as discussed in chapter 6, some of these steps will be compressed or running concurrently with work being performed by the general contractor and others. It may be that to meet your customer's business schedule, certain longer-term acquisition items (e.g., HVAC equipment, furniture, electrical) must be decided on and purchased before detailed design is complete. These decisions definitely affect your approach to the project and determine many of the steps that must be taken to keep on schedule and on budget.

The actual programming and design phase for your customer's requirements by your design firm is often an intense and sometimes enlightening period for both parties. It is not unusual to discover that your customer and his or her staff have completely different ideas and views on how work gets done and why things are done in a particular way. At times, your customer may have to stop the project to ensure that he or she fully understands the impact of the information being discovered and reported.

A redefinition of your customer's, the organization's, or department's mission or its critical service path may be an outcome of the interviews and research being conducted by the design firm on current space utilization, growth plans, equipment, and furnishing inventories. A reengineering or business process improvement program, discussed in chapter 2, may be the next logical step before continuing with the project.

The programming phase reviews the previously collected information and verifies the material; from this, you can begin to review project concepts. With concepts in place (see the sample RFP, Attachment A) and adjacencies defined, it is possible to produce a first-pass schematic design—a rough layout—of the building, space, or engineering requirement.

At this phase, your customer must begin to address the plan's departmental, personnel, and locational issues. No plan is perfect, nor would you have the time or funds to develop such a plan. There are always trade-offs because the creative solution must exist within the constraints of the chosen site, schedule, or building.

As discussed in chapter 4, your real estate/project team members should review the schematic design to ensure that all components of the program are shown and will work. Often their comments identify problems, items that were forgotten or not considered, and suggestions to improve the design and overall project solution.

BUDGETING

Capital budgeting, discussed in chapter 3, should take into account not only construction costs but also all owner-furnished items that can be capitalized or expensed by your customer. These capital costs can include furnishings, telecommunication and computer cabling, security systems, and items provided by the customer to the contractor such as carpet, light fixtures, raised floor, signage, art and specialty millwork, and built case work. It is imperative that your customer understand and have the funds available to complete the project. Should the budget (see Exhibit 3.5) require revision during any stage of the design process, your customer must agree to any increase or decrease.

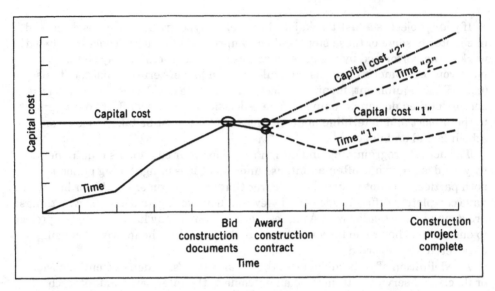

Exhibit 5.6   Project Control of Expenses—Time

Two components that must be considered in the planning and budgeting process are *time* and *cost*. Experience shows that adequate quality time is essential to develop a detailed project program and subsequent budget information that can serve as the foundation for a realistic schedule and capital budget and, ultimately, a project completed on time and on or under budget. Exhibit 5.6 shows that when a project's costs are well defined and budgeted, the corresponding time requirements should remain within schedule. Exhibit 5.7 shows that when appropriate time is devoted to programming and budgeting before construc-

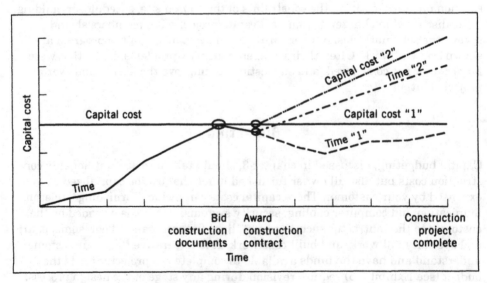

Exhibit 5.7   Project Control of Expenses—Cost

tion documents are bid, the project should remain within the approved capital budget (subject to last-minute changes requested by your customer).

Construction costs are subject to the same supply and demand and inflationary pressures that all businesses face. There are no guarantees in bidding a project. The prudent facility professional and his or her customer ensures that the capital budget includes contingency funds (between 5 and 10 percent, depending on your risk aversion and company policy) for unexpectedly high bids and for undetectable items discovered during construction (e.g., rock, springs, environmental hazards, unknown utilities and structural members in areas being demolished, changes in building code and/or occupancy requirements).

CONTRACT DOCUMENTS

After you and your customer approve and sign off on the design development documents (see Exhibit 5.1, step 3), revise the cost estimates, and review the project schedule developed by the design firm, you, your customer, and the design firm are ready to continue into the contract documents phase. Your lease or purchase agreement should include a schedule of completion and review of the design development and contract documents, budget, and necessary design revisions. You may find that the cost of the project is exceeding the up-fit allowances stated in the lease or the funds available from your customer; these costs may need to be reduced and brought back into budget. You should monitor this work to ensure that all conditions of the lease documents are being met. The continued involvement of your real estate broker may facilitate the schedule, the flow of meetings, and understanding of the terms of the lease agreement.

The design firm plays a key role in the preparation of the contract documents (working drawings and specifications) that translate your customer's business and design requirements into a set of legal documents defining what is to be constructed and occupied within the approved time frame and budget. You and the customer must remain actively involved to ensure the design development plans are accurately drawn as specified and converted into contract documents.

Progress meetings with the design firm are needed to exchange information and confirm details, colors, materials, finishes, and revisions to the design. If sufficient information was provided in the design development planning phase, the construction document phase should not require major time extensions or changes. Again, experience shows there is no perfect set of contract documents, but the more quality time you spend during this stage of the project finalizing details and making material and color selections, the better your bid results, the better the start to construction, and the fewer questions leading to change orders during construction.

BIDDING

Many corporate customers have the option to bid the project to a list of selected bidders (see Exhibit 5.1, step 5) for all items required for the project. Customers with this option may also choose to identify a general contractor or suppliers with whom they desire to negotiate a fee plus the cost for the work or a not-to-exceed cost. In requesting bids, the more common process, the customer seeks to obtain the lowest price from a qualified bidder who agrees to provide the desired quality at fixed cost and within a specific time frame. The low bidder may not be selected if your reference check of the bidder's past work, credit, or current workload does not provide your customer with the required security of completion. The bidding documents (see sample, chapter 7) should make specific requirements of the bidder and your customer.

With receipt and opening of the bids, you, your customer, and often your design firm should develop a bid comparison matrix to determine that all bids have addressed all cost issues and other items (see Exhibit 7.3). If bids come in at or below budget, your customer may choose to proceed with the project. If the bids or a bid comes in over budget, you, your customer, and the design firm should review the project for items to be deleted or revised. Rebidding or negotiating with the low bidder or bidder of choice may also be used (if permitted by company policy) to bring the project in or under budget. Also, a specific item or time constraints may be changed by your customer to obtain the required reduction(s) in cost. We describe in more detail the bidding and award of the construction and other contracts in chapter 7.

CLOSING AND COSTS

Property purchase agreements often require that you (representing the purchaser—your customer) and the seller proceed with certain contingency work such as obtaining rezoning; completing construction documents; obtaining utility, building, and use permits; and procuring dedication and acceptance by the local government of covenants and restrictions, streets, rights-of-way, and utilities installed by the seller. Many corporations have a strict policy that closings take place only when all contingency items are successfully resolved and acceptable to the purchaser (your customer) and when the purchaser has obtained all zoning and permits required for the work and occupancy. When all the contingency items are satisfied, then the closing can take place, the deed can be recorded, and possession of the property and construction or renovation can begin. After closing or after your customer moves into the leased space, you may consider sending out a customer satisfaction survey (see chapter 1) for feedback on your services and staff and the product supplier's services and performance.

BUILDING PROGRAMMING AND DESIGN ILLUSTRATED

The following examples[2] illustrate the preceding steps and the application of the principles involved in building programming and design. In these examples, a specific project—a combined office and R&D facility—is identified following

[2]Exhibits 5.1, 5.3, 5.8, 5.9, and 5.10 illustrate the building and space programming examples and are provided by Mr. Roger D. Roslansky, AIA, a registered architect residing in La Crosse, Wisconsin, from *Corporate Real Estate: Forms and Procedures,* John Wiley & Sons, New York, NY, 1994, pp. 295, 296, 301, 303, and 305.

the establishment and confirmation of overall corporate objectives and strategic planning documents. Subsequently, space requirements are determined by analyzing corporate intent for a specific physical facility. Corporate goals and objectives for this facility are then established, along with facilities design criteria, also termed *space programming*. In this case, seven sequential steps are pursued as follows:

1. The programming for building and site requirements is determined and presented (see Exhibit 5.1).
2. Project goals, a personnel listing, and site influences for this project are developed as follows:

Project Goals:

a. Develop a building organization with appropriate internal relationships to make efficient use of all spaces.

b. Provide comprehensive, state-of-the-art laboratory space.

c. Develop a creative high-technology image that relates to corporate headquarters.

d. Provide effective interior space that is sympathetic to human resources and promotes productivity.

e. Recognize the site influences while developing the site to its highest and best use.

f. Relate to adjacent properties, the community, and environmental concerns.

g. Employ energy conservation methodologies in all disciplines of architecture and engineering, including life-cycle costing.

h. Meet the construction budget target, set at $5,565,000.

i. Meet the schedule of phase completion points, reviews, and approvals, plus the required occupancy date.

j. Provide for a reasonable degree of flexibility, plus the ability to expand the space by 50 percent or more.

Personnel Listing (not including future growth or expansion):

Department	Personnel
Administration	2
Operations—North America	20
Operations—International	2
Product Marketing	29
Human Resources	7
Finance	41
Engineering	26
Technology and Plant	41
Total	166

Site Influences (key factors that will affect the design concept):

    a. Site area and configuration—amount and shape of the land available to support the site requirements, plus the building footprint

    b. Topography—the slope of the land and drainage aspects

    c. Existing vegetation—locations and areas of existing trees

    d. Freeway noise—traffic noise generated by nearby interstate highway

    e. Site access—vehicular routes of access to the site

    f. Adjacent land—use of parcels adjacent to the site

    g. Location—position of site in the area and community in terms of visibility and potential image

    h. Sun and wind—climatological conditions

    i. Views—vistas outward from the site

3. A summary list of spaces by departments or major components is compiled and supplemented or amplified by an expanded and detailed list of spaces for each department. The schedules included in Exhibit 5.8 illustrate this important compilation of items, presenting both the project summary and the details for each of the departments. To complete each department and, eventually, the grand total of required area, a circulation factor must be included for conversion from net assignable feet (NASF) to gross square feet (GSF). Often a relative sizes diagram (see Exhibit 6.5) is included as a comparative device for initial scope understanding and space perception.

4. A list of site requirements is developed, often accompanied by site use diagramming, as shown in Exhibit 5.9. Site design requirements are as follows:

    a. Provide parking for 10 visitors, 150 staff, and future space for 75 additional automobiles, using the essentially level areas in the center of the site relating to access points.

    b. Locate service access from the east, near the northeast corner, due to topography. Provide a service zone away from the main entry.

    c. Locate the main entry from the west on Oak Street.

    d. Consider the building location or footprint centralized on the site, with the potential for two levels utilizing the terrain and a northerly direction to gain a portion of the knoll.

    e. Take advantage of the existing trees for locational purposes and the near views, plus the long views to the northeast, east, and southeast.

    f. Use the existing vegetation and sufficient setback to achieve barriers for the interstate freeway noise.

5. Overall project organization, using the major departments or components, is described in an adjacency diagram similar to Exhibit 5.10. Often, it is advisable and helpful to show relationships in a matrix chart as well, as in Exhibit 6.6.

6. Each department or major component is broken down and described graphically, with significant relationships shown (see Exhibit 6.7). Occasionally,

Department	Area, SF	
Administration	736	
Operations—North America	2,515	
Operations—International	331	
Product marketing	4,047	
Human resources	4,658	
Finance	5,986	
Engineering	4,885	
Subtotal (office space)	23,158	SF
	× 1.20	Building Gross Factor
	27,790	GSF
Technology/Laboratory	18,514	SF
	× 1.20	Building Gross Factor
	22,217	GSF
Experimental plant	4,950	SF
	× 1.20	Building Gross Factor
	5,940	GSF
Total building	55,947	GSF

DEPARTMENT AREA SUMMARY

Administration

Space	Quantity	Planning Standard	Net Area	Net/ Gross	Dept. Gross	Comments
President	1	320	320	1.10	352	Closed office
Executive secretary	1	96	96	1.25	120	Includes file space
Conference room	1	240	240	1.10	264	Closed conference area
Total Area					736 SF	

OPERATIONS—NORTH AMERICA

Space	Quantity	Planning Standard	Net Area	Net/ Gross	Dept. Gross	Comments
Vice president	1	192	192	1.10	211	Closed office
Executive secretary	1	96	96	1.25	120	Includes file space
Managers	4	144	576	1.10	634	Closed office
Engineers	5	96	480	1.20	528	
Safety supervisor	1	96	96	1.20	115	
Clerks	6	64	384	1.20	154	
Director	1	192	192	1.10	211	Closed office
Purchasing agent	1	64	64	1.20	77	
Vendor interview	1	144	144	1.10	158	Closed conference Area—adjacent lobby
Total Area					2,515 SF	

Exhibit 5.8 Project Summary and Detailed Schedules (From Robert Kevin Brown, *Managing Corporate Real Estate.* Copyright © 1993 by John Wiley & Sons, Inc. Reprinted with permission.)

OPERATIONS—INTERNATIONAL

Space	Quantity	Planning Standard	Net Area	Net/ Gross	Dept. Gross	Comments
Vice president	1	192	192	1.10	211	Closed office
Executive secretary	1	96	96	1.25	120	Includes file space
Total Area					331 SF	

PRODUCT MARKETING

Space	Quantity	Planning Standard	Net Area	Net/ Gross	Dept. Gross	Comments
Vice president	1	192	192	1.10	211	Closed office
Executive secretary	1	96	96	1.25	120	Includes file space
Managers	6	144	864	1.1	950	Closed office
Product managers	4	144	576	1.1	634	Closed office
Marketing specialist	1	128	128	1.2	154	
Pricing representative	1	64	64	1.2	77	
Engineers	7	96	672	1.2	806	
Customer service reps	6	64	384	1.2	461	
Planners	2	64	128	1.2	154	
Conference room	1	400	400	1.2	480	Closed conference area
Total Area					4,047 SF	

HUMAN RESOURCES

Space	Quantity	Planning Standard	Net Area	Net/ Gross	Dept. Gross	Comments
Director	1	192	192	1.10	211	Closed office
Executive secretary	1	96	96	1.25	120	Includes file space
Manager	1	144	144	1.10	158	Closed office
Loading dock/ Staging area	1	1,000	1,000	1.10	1,100	Two loading areas
Clerks	2	64	128	1.20	154	
Mailroom	1	440	440	1.10	484	
Lunchroom	1	1,000	1,000	1.10	1,100	Include vending machines, micro-wave, refrigerator
Interview room	1	100	100	1.10	110	
Reception/waiting	1	320	320	1.25	400	
Copy room	1	92	92	1.1	101	
Men's lockers/ showers	1	300	300	1.2	360	Adjacent exterior access
Women's lockers/ showers	1	300	300	1.2	360	Adjacent exterior access
Total Area					4,658 SF	

Exhibit 5.8   Project Summary and Detailed Schedules (Continued)

FINANCE

Space	Quantity	Planning Standard	Net Area	Net/ Gross	Dept. Gross	Comments
Vice president	1	92	192	1.10	211	Closed office
Executive secretary	1	96	96	1.25	120	Includes file space
Managers	7	144	1,008	1.10	1,109	Closed office
Controller	2	144	288	1.10	317	Closed office
Director information systems	1	192	192	1.10	211	Closed office
Asst. Controller/ Specialists	2	64	128	1.20	154	
Accounting	13	64	832	1.20	988	
Credit representatives	4	64	256	1.20	307	
Coordinators	4	64	256	1.20	307	
Computer operators	2	64	128	1.20	154	
Data center	1	1,480	1,480	1.10	1,628	Raised flooring
Personal computer stations	4	64	256	1.20	307	
Conference	1	144	144	1.20	173	Open conference area

| Total Area | | | | | 5,986 SF | |

ENGINEERING

Space	Quantity	Planning Standard	Net Area	Net/ Gross	Dept. Gross	Comments
Director	1	192	192	1.10	211	Closed office
Executive secretary	1	96	96	1.25	120	Includes file space
Managers	5	144	720	1.10	792	Closed office
Engineers	14	96	1,344	1.20	1,613	
Designer/Draftsman		396	288	1.20	346	
Secretary	2	64	128	1.20	154	
Conference room shared with technology group	1	216	216	1.10	238	Closed room
Personal computer stations	3	64	192	1.20	230	
Engineering storage	1	300	300	1.20	360	
Blueprint & copy machine	1	240	240	1.20	288	
Library	1	300	300	1.20	360	
Conference	1	144	144	1.20	173	Open conference area

| Total Area | | | | | 4,885 SF | |

Exhibit 5.8 **Project Summary and Detailed Schedules** *(Continued)*

TECHNOLOGY/LABORATORY

Space	Quantity	Planning Standard	Net Area	Net/ Gross	Dept. Gross	Comments
Director	2	192	384	1.10	422	Closed office
Executive secretary	2	96	192	1.25	240	Includes file space
Manager offices	5	144	720	1.10	792	Closed office
R&D chemist or engineer	12	96	1,152	1.20	1,382	
Analytical lab chemist or technician	12	96	1,152	1.20	1,382	
International technologies chemist or technician	7	96	672	1.20	806	
Personal computer stations	3	64	192	1.20	230	
Conference	1	144	144	1.20	173	Open conference area
Secretary	1	64	64	1.20	77	
Library	1	300	300	1.20	360	
Laboratory space	1	11,000	11,000	1.10	12,100	Area for R&D and analytical lab space included for manager office 144 SF
Lab support	1	500	500	1.10	550	Storage area for labs
Total Area					18,514	SF

EXPERIMENTAL PLANT

Space	Quantity	Planning Standard	Net Area	Net/ Gross	Dept. Gross	Comments
Experimental plant	1	4,500	4,501	1.10	4,950	
Total Area					4,950	SF

Exhibit 5.8   Project Summary and Detailed Schedules (Continued)

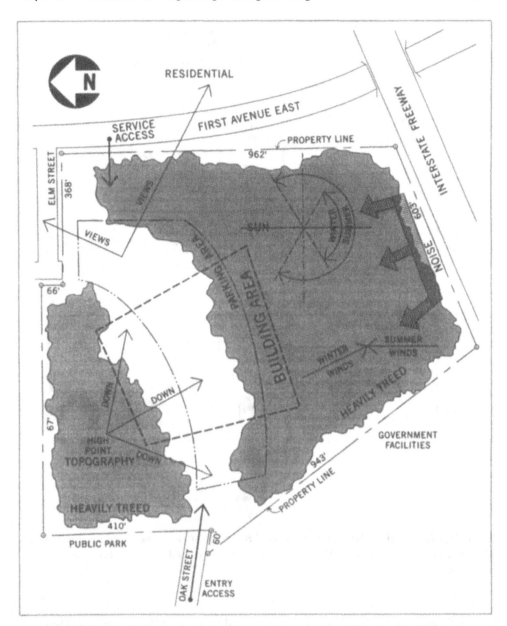

Exhibit 5.9   Site Conditions and Analysis *(From Robert Kevin Brown, Managing Corporate Real Estate. Copyright © 1993 by John Wiley & Sons, Inc. Reprinted with permission.)*

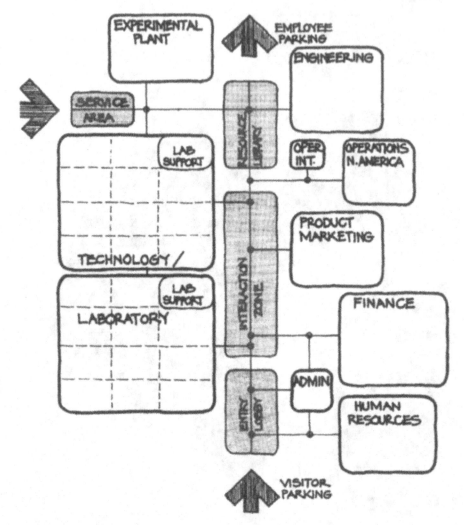

Exhibit 5.10   Project Organization and Relationships *(From Robert Kevin Brown, Managing Corporate Real Estate. Copyright © 1993 by John Wiley & Sons, Inc. Reprinted with permission.)*

supplemental analysis diagrams are used to visually depict certain other planning aspects, such as movement of people and services, flow of materials handling, manufacturing process, communications, robotic configuration, and security barriers.

7. Finally, the space programming or building and site programming of needs presents the first opportunity to develop sufficient information for a preliminary estimate of probable construction costs. The cost estimate analysis must account for all items in order to establish the economic parameters, or the project budget. Depending on the time frame for implementation, escalation factors to the midpoint of construction should be included. The schedule

in Exhibit 5.8 presents a summary of the pertinent cost factors for the project, exclusive of soft costs such as financing and legal costs and fees.

Space Utilization Measures

The facilities planning function is often concerned with space utilization measures. Such measures—typically ratios—are intended to gauge the performance of facilities design and operations. The standards of performance are generally set forth as objectives relating to the decision to acquire, reconfigure, or operate a facility. Standards may be calibrated either by using data internal to the corporation or through industry benchmarking. Therefore, evaluation of performance is against either project or operational goals, most of which can be based on competitive concerns. The evaluation of performance against the standard developed can serve to identify immediate remedial requirements or to determine appropriate objectives for future facilities (and the planning thereof). To the extent that individual responsibility can be assigned to facility performance measures, those measures may also serve as the basis for employee performance evaluation.

There are two classes of space utilization measures: (1) those that measure physical performance, and (2) those that measure financial performance. The principal difference between the two classes is the management level at which each is used to convey performance data. Physical performance measures originate within the facilities planning function and are rarely conveyed beyond reports to those involved in real estate asset management, except in cases in which management of operating divisions is concerned with production quotients. Financial performance measures may originate within the facilities planning function, though it is more likely that the asset management personnel participate in developing these measures, some of which are included in reports to senior management. Financial measures are generally concerned with the impact of facilities on revenue and expenses and specifically concerned with two issues: corporate productivity and the consumption of resources (e.g., operating funds). Physical measures are generally concerned with functional efficiency, which is typically equated with profitability, though this can be a presumption worth examining when the effect of the trade-offs made to achieve efficiency is uncertain.

Examples of physical performance measures include items such as (1) the number of square feet per employee, and (2) the ratio of net to gross building area. These two examples might look somewhat familiar, and they should, as they were used to plan the building project discussed in the previous section. These measurements describe different types of functional efficiency. Recall, however, the caveat regarding functional efficiency: Trade-offs are nearly inevitable. Minimizing the number of square feet per employee is likely to affect adversely worker morale and productivity. Therefore, maximizing such measures of functional efficiency should not be the only goal. Rather, these measures should be regarded as diagnostic tools for identifying potential problems that may require greater definition. Still, as prevention is better than cure, facility planners use such measures in planning new facilities. There are often guidelines, rules of thumb (e.g., 200 sq. ft. per employee), or industry standards that may, if incorporated into a facility design, work to the corporation's overall benefit and profitability. However, after a new facility is up and operating, the operations it houses continue to evolve. Therefore, it is advisable to measure its physical performance periodically to determine whether any changes might enhance corporate profitability.

Financial performance measures focus on two aspects of corporate facilities: how facilities consume resources, and how they contribute to the creation of value. With this perspective on both input and output, these measures can form the basis for a cost-benefit analysis of corporate facilities. With respect to resource consumption, the most common measures include facility operating costs per square foot and facility operating costs as a percentage of incremental value attributable to the use of a facility (as in revenues or sales). The degree of incremental value just noted is also the ordinary measure of value contribution, the other financial measure. However, except for retail (or some service) facilities, it is often difficult to determine an amount of value contribution for facilities such as office space, warehouses, or factories, although a value-added factor might be established in some cases. The usual denomination for all of these financial measures is dollars per square foot, which allows facilities to be compared with one another.

Using the facilities of a corporation's competitors as a basis for comparison and evaluation of the corporation's own performance is termed *benchmarking* (see also chapter 1). Benchmarking usually involves the participation of several companies, each of which is interested in obtaining similar performance data. This practice is possible within an industry or across industries, provided the facilities themselves are reasonably comparable. Benchmarking is becoming an increasingly popular approach to determining performance measurement results. The special benefit that accounts for this popularity is due to the ability of benchmarking group participants to identify the management and design practices associated with the facilities that appear to perform better than their own. Consequently, a corporation may be able to improve its performance by adopting established and tested practices. The information exchange is accomplished on a confidential basis and may be facilitated and coordinated by an outside consultant.

CAMPUS AND HIGH-RISE OFFICE CONCEPTS

Campus and High-rise Issues

During your initial discussion and interviews with your customer and senior management, you may find that a number of design-related terms such as *campus* and *high-rise* may engender a number of meanings and concepts. To ensure that the campus environments and concepts discussed during your interview process are consistent, you may choose to review and compare the traditional suburban campus office site concept (Exhibit 5.11), today's urban campus office concept (Exhibit 5.12), and today's high-rise office concept (Exhibit 5.13).

Campus

Corporate campus development is usually found where the senior officers of a corporation and the corporate style and culture have generated a suburban or urban approach to customer business and public relationships. The campus has a low- to mid-rise profile with multiple buildings and a landscaped setting, and it tends to be found outside of the downtown business area and adjacent to major highways, large areas of single-family and multifamily housing, and shopping areas.

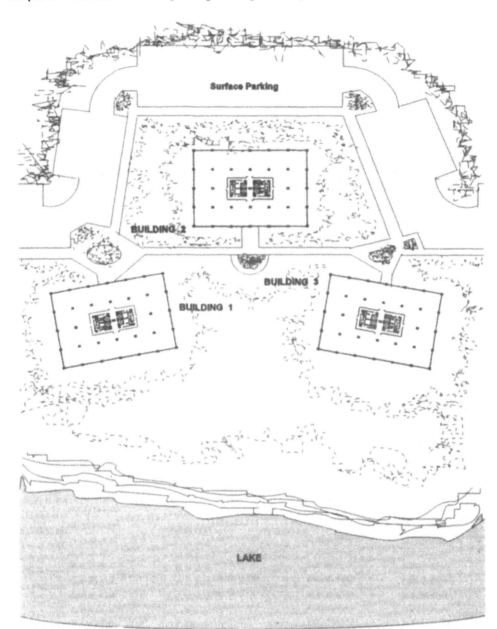

Exhibit 5.11 Suburban Campus Office Site Concept

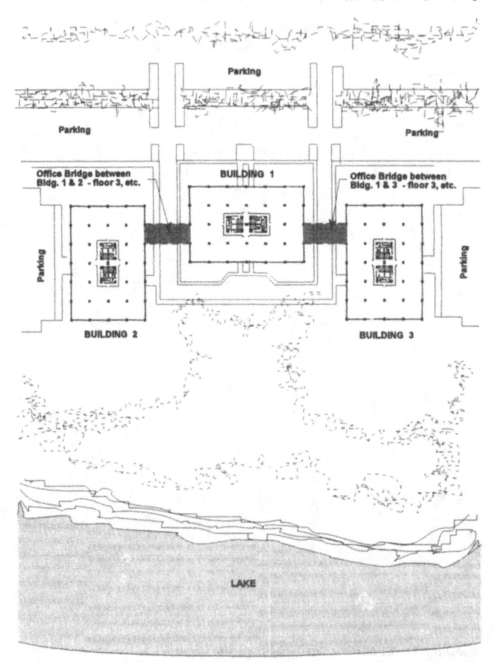

Exhibit 5.12   Urban Campus Office Site Concept

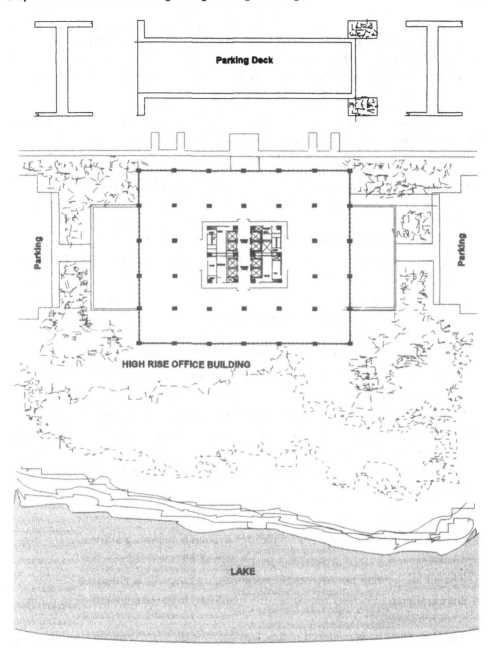

Exhibit 5.13   High-Rise Office Site Concept

Lower land prices and zoning use, size, and height restrictions encourage or require multiple buildings with surface and at times two levels of structured parking. Corporations often select the campus as an opportunity to develop a more cost-effective headquarters, especially if they were previously located in a downtown high-rise building.

Campus buildings generally require less costly foundation and structural systems and less complicated mechanical, plumbing, electrical, and elevator systems. Maintaining and modifying campus buildings are often less difficult tasks because the lower height and smaller volume of the buildings allows for simpler and more locally available materials as well as easier construction. Campus settings have the following additional advantages and disadvantages:

Advantages

They can allow easier and faster expansion opportunities.

They can have larger floor plate square footage and bridges to connect buildings.

Building image can be less formal and less imposing.

Large departments can often be located on one or two floors; building vacant space is more horizontal, which often permits easier departmental expansion or reorganization.

Parking can be closer to the building for more employees.

There is less concrete and more open area for outside activities.

Setup fosters ad hoc relationships between teams.

Various levels of floor plan flexibility can be designed into separate buildings.

Elevators are less of a bottleneck; employees do not have to change elevator banks; shorter vertical travel distance and travel time can be realized.

Campuses may be more environmentally acceptable to local community and neighborhood groups.

Disadvantages

Travel back and forth between buildings is time-consuming and causes delays.

Use of several buildings causes a perception of physical separation.

The buildings may not project the corporate business image desired.

Informal meetings may not be readily available with team members in different buildings.

Weather must be considered before leaving to walk to an adjacent building.

More horizontal walking is required.

It is harder to obtain building visibility and meaningful building signage.

All employees cannot be housed in one building.

Amenities such as cafeteria, reprographics, human resources, and employee health facility are not in all buildings.

Security between buildings, access to, and control of the buildings can be difficult to achieve.

High-Rise

Corporate high-rise development is usually found where the senior officers of a corporation and the corporate style and culture have generated a downtown or business district approach to customer business and public relationships. The high-rise makes an immediate statement as a highly visible symbol of the corporation's presence in the marketplace.

High land prices, zoning use, and size with no height restrictions enables the corporation to make economical use of the site and provide structured parking on or adjacent to the site. Corporations often select the high-rise office building to be in the vicinity of their customers or as a more central location for doing business versus the less costly but more distant urban or suburban space.

High-rise buildings generally require more costly foundation and structural systems and more complicated mechanical, plumbing, electrical, and elevator systems. Maintaining and modifying high-rises are often difficult tasks because of the height and volume of the buildings. High-rises have the following additional advantages and disadvantages:

Advantages

There is no need to travel back and forth between buildings.

There is no perception of physical separation.

The building can project a world-class corporate business image.

Informal meetings can take place readily with team members in the same building.

Weather is not a consideration, as employees do not need to leave the building.

There is less horizontal walking.

It is easier to obtain building visibility and meaningful building signage.

All employees can be housed in one building.

Amenities such as cafeteria, reprographics, human resources, and employee health facility can be in one building.

Building, site, and parking security, access, and control can be easier to achieve and monitor.

Disadvantages

High-rise expansion opportunities are often more time-consuming to fund, construct, and bring on line.

The building usually has smaller floor plates.

Building image can be too formal and too imposing.

Large departments may be located on two or more floors; building vacant space is more vertical, which often makes it harder to accommodate departmental expansion or reorganization.

Parking lots or decks may be farther from the building and require employees to walk considerable distances.

There is more concrete and less open area for outside activities.

Vertical separation may not foster ad hoc relationships between teams.

A high-rise facility may not accommodate various levels of floor plan loading and design flexibility.

Elevators may be bottlenecks; employees may have to change elevator banks; longer vertical travel distance and travel time may be required.

Local community and neighborhood groups may find the high-rise more environmentally objectionable.

CONCLUSION

In this chapter, we reviewed the planning and design processes that generally apply to architectural and engineering projects related to the site and the building shell, core, and utility requirements. As you have seen, however, and as is discussed more fully in chapter 6, the inside of the facility—the customer's work process and space requirement—almost always drives the design of a building. The building and site must provide a venue that serves the interior work environment. Some of the major interior requirement drivers of building and configuration and site design are floor plate size, efficient core design, passenger and service elevators, bay/column spacing, open plan and office layouts, floor circulation requirements, computer, network and telecommunications requirements, heating and cooling loads, building orientation, security and life safety issues, ceiling height, and building amenities.

The site and the building must provide an aesthetic, efficient, effective, safe, and secure working environment. When these goals are met, employees and management do not have physical obstacles to distract them and so can focus more effectively on the business of the organization.

Chapter Six

Interior Programming and Space Planning

In chapter 5, we reviewed architectural and engineering planning and design (step 5 in Exhibit 6.1); this chapter focuses on the interior programming and space planning process (step 6). While this chapter concentrates on the development of the interior requirements, we keep in mind that the site and building required by the owner or customer drives the interior and exterior envelope design of the building (see Exhibit 6.2). We review the details of the construction process in chapter 7.

Interior design is evolutionary in nature, a process of expanding, modifying, and refining, each step building on the preceding one. In this process, a design first takes shape as a written document, an analysis of needs. That analysis evolves into a two-dimensional approach and finally unfolds into a three-dimensional concept.[1]

SPACE AND FURNISHING STANDARDS

Space and furnishings are expensive and important items that call for management involvement. Previously, little or no advance planning meant that each project was an isolated and independent decision, not tied to an overall strategy. The use of space and furnishing standards now allows management to organize and provide consistent, high-quality, and cost-effective space and furnishings for all employees. These standards ensure that what others provided under previous organizational administrations would work for those who inherited these standards. A sample furnishing standards document is shown in the next section.

Standards are designed to ensure that employees have adequate space and furnishings to accomplish the tasks assigned and are not usually subject to the whim of a supervisor. The reuse and relocation of furnishings in space designed to accommodate change gives management the ability to reorganize and relocate groups and departments in a short span of time, often with little or no physical construction. While standards have reduced overall furnishings and space requirements and associated costs, they can be a bottleneck for groups or departments that do not fit into the traditional organizational space and furniture groupings. You must take care to allow for some flexibility with standards, as the

---

[1]Julie K. Rayfield, *The Office Interior Design Guide, An Introduction for Facilities Managers & Designers* (New York: John Wiley & Sons, 1994), p. 53.

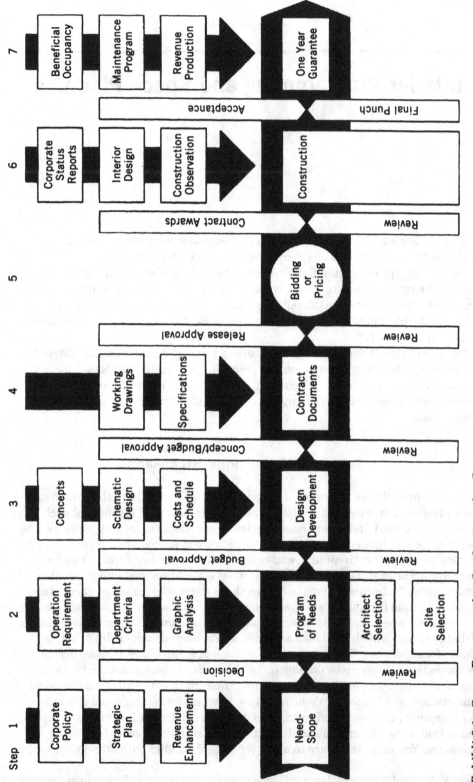

Exhibit 6.1 Space Programming Implementation Process

Functions	Building Space Required
Administrative	Executive offices, general office, supporting office
Manufacturing	Fabrication, assembly, processing, refining
Utilities	Electrical generation and transmission, telecommunications switching, cable lines, microwave stations
Extraction	Mines and wells
Agriculture	Farmland, timberlands
Distribution	Warehouses, ports, pipelines
Selling	Wholesale marts, retail, office (services, etc.)

Exhibit 6.2   Design Requirements for Corporate Functions

purpose of the facility management function is to provide service, not to let standards make your life easier.

Space and furnishing standards are generated based on:

- Functional requirements of each position
- Tasks performed
- Surface area requirements
- Technology/equipment requirements

   Size

   Built-in, freestanding, or work surface

   Power, telecommunications, and/or computer requirements

   Heat release

   Acoustic constraints

   Cabling requirements

   Special requirements such as special HVAC (heating, ventilation, or air conditioning) or plumbing

- Storage requirements
- Configuration requirements
- Lighting
- Wire management
- Accessories
- Conference/meeting requirements
- Organizational culture
- Organizational status—job classification
- Industry or professional standards

Space and furnishing standards form the basic planning units in the development of a space program. During the data analysis portion of programming, these space standards are multiplied by the number of personnel required for each standard in a current period and forecasted for future incremental periods of growth.

Exhibit 6.3 shows an example of a closed-plan approach, which is appropriate for organizations with strong privacy requirements and for which planning flexibility is not a priority. Exhibit 6.4 provides an example of an open-plan approach, which is appropriate where significant planning flexibility is required. The following items should be considered when using space and furnishing standards to design open-plan and office areas:

- Whenever possible, orient high splines of systems furniture perpendicular to a window wall to maximize visibility to the natural light sources.

- Design corridors along window walls whenever possible.

- Place ceiling-high enclosures strategically together; these may include conference rooms, fully enclosed offices, and common areas. Try hard to keep these enclosures off window walls, where they obscure natural light sources.

- Intersperse common conference, file, and copier areas throughout the layout to service the groups.

- Lay out workstations so that individual stations can be converted to cluster stations with a minimum amount of rework.

- When setting up computer graphics, create a drawing layer so the systems furniture panels may be plotted separately. This drawing may be used to locate and plan dimension heights of accent panels.

- Panel thickness is measured in inches. This dimension must be calculated when planning layout.

- When laying out runs of systems furniture, design equal perpendicular spines so as to keep the clusters of equal length. Avoid unequal spines. However, if there is no alternative, keep the main aisle panel locations even and locate uneven ends in a less prominent area.

- Main systems furniture spines should be designed with perpendicular intersections not more than 18 feet apart.

- During the analysis phase, the design firm's analyst should arrange to show users a mock-up station to determine the correct height for work surfaces. This will expedite the ordering process and lead to the most cost-effective installation process.

- Right- or left-handed drafting area stations may be designed to meet individual needs.

- Provide adequate coat storage in all office areas. Please do not use coat trees.

- Design enclosed storage areas for recycling bins in all office areas.

- Do not design systems furniture panels to run flush parallel to hard walls. Utilize wall electrical, telephone, and computer outlets and mount binder bins directly to hard walls, if possible.

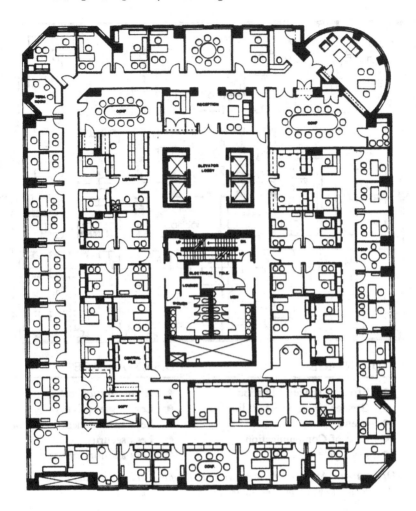

ADVANTAGES

- Controlled environment
- Security
- Visual privacy
- Physical separation
- Traditional and systems furniture applications

DISADVANTAGES

- Less efficient than open plan
- Lack of flexibility
- Cost of relocation
- Restricted individual and group interaction
- Views
- More extensive mechanical systems required

Exhibit 6.3 Closed-Plan Approach (From Julie K. Rayfield, The Office Interior Design Guide. Copyright © 1994 by John Wiley & Sons, Inc. Reprinted by permission.)

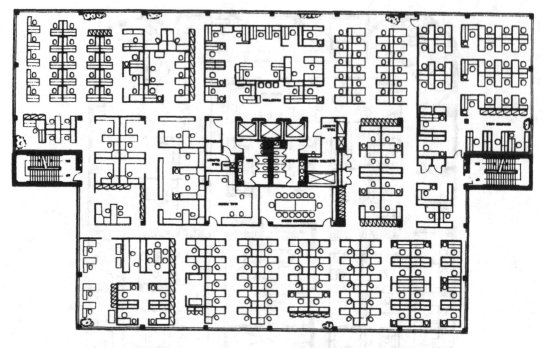

ADVANTAGES	DISADVANTAGES
• Efficient space utilization	• Higher *initial* cost
• Greater planning flexibility	• Less visual privacy
• Views	• Less environmental control
• Ease of Communication	• Less security
• Life cycle cost lower	• Less auditory privacy

Exhibit 6.4   Open-Plan Approach *(From Julie K. Rayfield, The Office Interior Design Guide. Copyright © 1994 by John Wiley & Sons, Inc. Reprinted by permission.)*

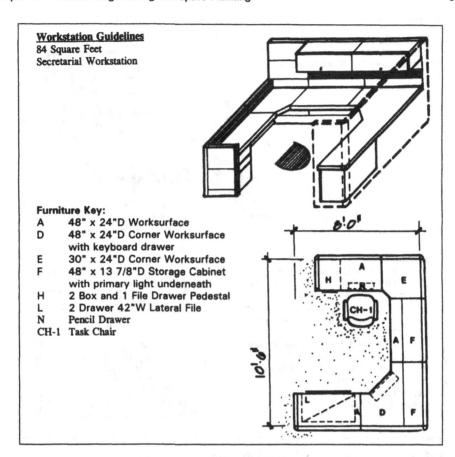

Workstation Guidelines
84 Square Feet
Secretarial Workstation

Furniture Key:
A   48" x 24"D Worksurface
D   48" x 24"D Corner Worksurface
       with keyboard drawer
E   30" x 24"D Corner Worksurface
F   48" x 13 7/8"D Storage Cabinet
       with primary light underneath
H   2 Box and 1 File Drawer Pedestal
L   2 Drawer 42"W Lateral File
N   Pencil Drawer
CH-1   Task Chair

Exhibit 6.4   Open-Plan Approach (Continued)

Workstation Guidelines
110 Square Feet
Exempt Supervisor Workstation

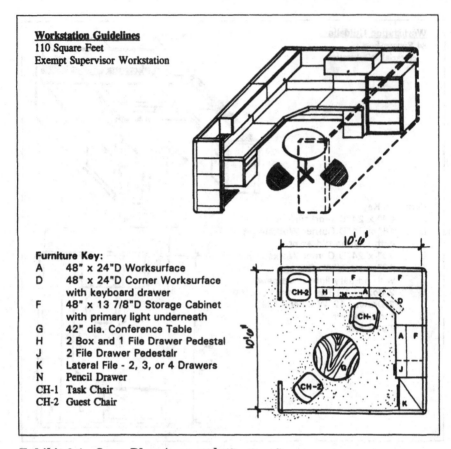

Furniture Key:

A	48" x 24"D Worksurface
D	48" x 24"D Corner Worksurface with keyboard drawer
F	48" x 13 7/8"D Storage Cabinet with primary light underneath
G	42" dia. Conference Table
H	2 Box and 1 File Drawer Pedestal
J	2 File Drawer Pedestalr
K	Lateral File - 2, 3, or 4 Drawers
N	Pencil Drawer
CH-1	Task Chair
CH-2	Guest Chair

Exhibit 6.4 Open-Plan Approach (Continued)

Workstation Guidelines
108 Square Feet
Senior Staff Workstation

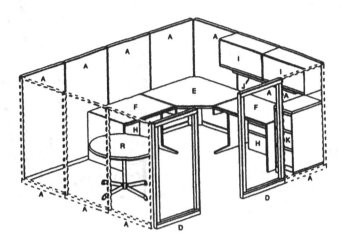

Furniture Key:

A.   65"H x 36"W tackable acoustical panel
      with power.

D.   65"H x 36"W glass panels.

E.   30"D x 45"W corner worksurface with
      back panels and clear access end
      panels.

F.   30"D x 42 3/4"W right or left
      worksurface with back panel, clear
      access end panel, right or left end panel
      and lock.

H.   30"D x 15"W box over letter file
      pedestal.

1.   36"W binder bin with lock.

J.   53" task light to be installed under
      binder bins. 40 watt fluorescent tube
      ordered separately.

K.   41 1/4"H x 28 9/16"D x 14 7/8"W 3
      drawer vertical letter file with lock.

R.   42" round laminate table with vinyl
      edge.

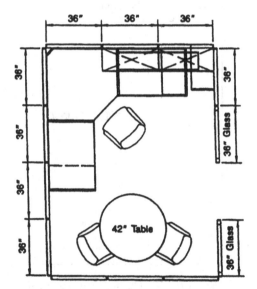

Exhibit 6.4   Open-Plan Approach (Continued)

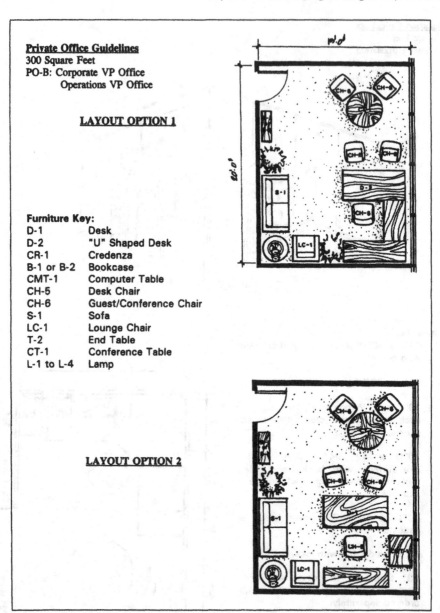

Private Office Guidelines
300 Square Feet
PO-B: Corporate VP Office
        Operations VP Office

LAYOUT OPTION 1

Furniture Key:

D-1	Desk
D-2	"U" Shaped Desk
CR-1	Credenza
B-1 or B-2	Bookcase
CMT-1	Computer Table
CH-5	Desk Chair
CH-6	Guest/Conference Chair
S-1	Sofa
LC-1	Lounge Chair
T-2	End Table
CT-1	Conference Table
L-1 to L-4	Lamp

LAYOUT OPTION 2

Exhibit 6.4 Open-Plan Approach (Continued)

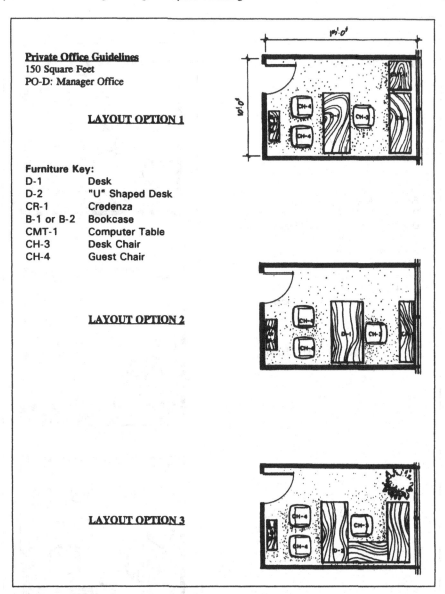

Private Office Guidelines
150 Square Feet
PO-D: Manager Office

LAYOUT OPTION 1

Furniture Key:

D-1	Desk
D-2	"U" Shaped Desk
CR-1	Credenza
B-1 or B-2	Bookcase
CMT-1	Computer Table
CH-3	Desk Chair
CH-4	Guest Chair

LAYOUT OPTION 2

LAYOUT OPTION 3

Exhibit 6.4   Open-Plan Approach (Continued)

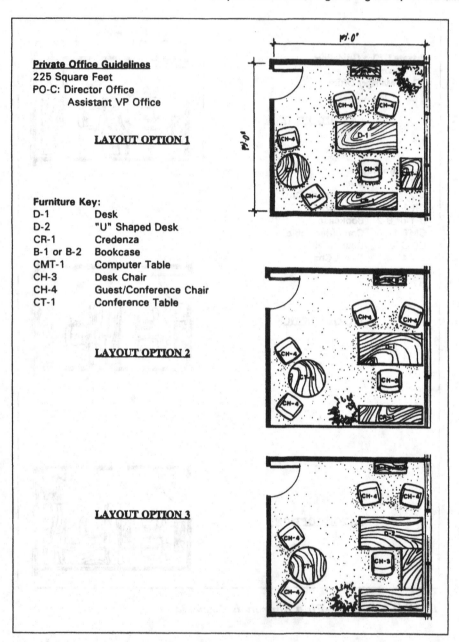

Private Office Guidelines
225 Square Feet
PO-C: Director Office
        Assistant VP Office

LAYOUT OPTION 1

Furniture Key:

D-1	Desk
D-2	"U" Shaped Desk
CR-1	Credenza
B-1 or B-2	Bookcase
CMT-1	Computer Table
CH-3	Desk Chair
CH-4	Guest/Conference Chair
CT-1	Conference Table

LAYOUT OPTION 2

LAYOUT OPTION 3

Exhibit 6.4   Open-Plan Approach (Continued)

Workstation Guidelines
81 Square Feet Each
Staff Workstation Configuration

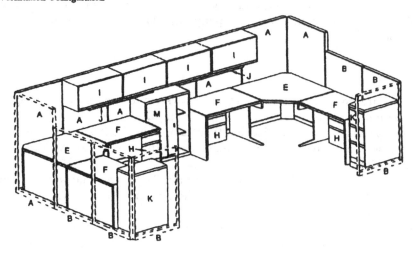

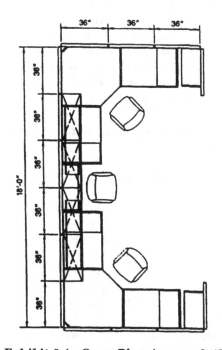

Furniture Key:

A.   65"H x 36"W tackable acoustical panel with power.

B.   53"H x 36"W tackable acoustical panel.

E.   30"D x 45"W corner worksurface with back panels and clear access end panels.

F.   30"D x 42 3/4"W right or left worksurface with back panel, clear access end panel, right or left end panel and lock.

H.   30"D x 15"W box over letter file pedestal.

I.   36"W binder bin with lock.

J.   53"W task light to be installed under binder bins. 40 watt fluorescent tubes ordered separately.

K.   41 1/4"H x 28 9/16"D x 14 7/8"W 3 drawer vertical letter file with lock.

M.   42"H x 36"W x 15"D adjustable 3 shelf bookcase with sliding steel doors.

Exhibit 6.4   Open-Plan Approach (Continued)

SAMPLE: ABC COMPANY FURNISHING STANDARDS

To serve our employees with high-quality and ergonomically sound furnishings for their work environments, ABC Company has adopted the following Furnishing Standards:

Workstations

PQR Furniture Co. WorkPlus is the standard system for workstations in open areas. Evaluation of job function and employee needs, including privacy, storage requirements, and equipment size and type, as well as the flexibility, maintenance, and maximum use of square footage led to the selection of WorkPlus for standardization.

Workstation types are dictated by job function. The secretarial workstation is presented with a scaled coded plan, a three-dimensional view drawing, and a listing of each component.

The flexibility of the finishes allows for the establishment of identities for the Corporate Headquarters and the Operations Division. In the Corporate Headquarters, the basic gray values are accented with blue and burgundy tweed fabrics and a mahogany wood veneer. In the Operations Division, the basic gray values are accented with blue and burgundy solid fabrics. Accent colors are located on the upholstery fabric of the guest seating, the face of the storage cabinets within each workstation, and the exterior panel finishes of each workstation. All work surfaces have a laminate top with a wood edge. Each workstation has 8 feet of rail tiles to hold accessory items, as well as rail tiles in overhead storage units. Secretarial stations have an additional 6' 6" of half-height rail tiles along the front of the workstation.

Below is a comparison of the existing (Exist. Furn.) workstation standards and the new PQR Furniture Co. WorkPlus standard.

Workstation Type	Exist. Furn.	PQR Furniture Co. WorkPlus
Secretarial		
Overall size	30 sq. ft.*	84 sq. ft.
Work surface	18.75 sq. ft.*	43.03 sq. ft.
Open shelving	0	0
Closed shelving	0	8 lin. ft.
6" box drawer	2 @ 18"D	2 @ 24"D
Total filing storage	4' 6" letter*	10' 3" letter

*The above figures for the Exist. Furn. secretarial workstation are based on the workstation as defined in the current ABC Company Furnishings Standards Manual. They do not reflect additional tables or built-in filing storage that may actually be in a secretarial station. An executive secretary is currently in 180 square feet.

NOTE: All above filing storage totals are based on letter-size filing. If the same units are used for a combination of letter and legal filing or all legal filing, the total quantity per workstation will vary. Total filing storage includes pedestal file drawers and two-drawer units located below a work surface.

Secretarial Workstation

Below is a comparison of the existing Exist. Furn. work surfaces and the new PQR Furniture Co. WorkPlus work surfaces.

Workstation Type	Exist. Furn.		PQR Furn. Co. WorkPlus	
	Qty	Size	Qty	Size
Secretarial	1	20" × 42"	3	24" × 48"
		(type ht.)	3	30" × 30"
	1	30" × 60"	1	48" × 48" corner

Below is a list of organizing tools available for use on the rail tiles or within the overhead storage unit. Each employee will have the opportunity to select the organizing tools he or she will require.

Shelf Divider	Paper Tray
Armature	Vertical Tray
Document Stand	Diagonal Tray
Machine Support Tray	Organizer Tray
Mini-Shelf	

Exempt Supervisor Workstation

PQR Furniture Co. WorkPlus is the standard system for workstations in open areas. Evaluation of job function and employee needs, including privacy, storage requirements, and equipment size and type, as well as the flexibility, maintenance, and maximum use of square footage led to the selection of WorkPlus for standardization.

Workstation types were dictated by job function. The supervisor workstation is presented with a scaled coded plan, a three-dimensional view drawing, and a listing of each component and freestanding furniture item used.

The flexibility of the finishes allows for the establishment of identities for the Corporate Headquarters and the Operations Division. In the Corporate Headquarters, the basic gray values are accented with blue and burgundy tweed fabrics and a mahogany wood veneer. In the Operations Division, the basic gray values are accented with blue and burgundy solid fabrics. Accent colors are located on the upholstery fabric of the guest seating, the face of the storage cabinets within each workstation, and the exterior panel finishes of each workstation. All work surfaces have a laminate top with a wood edge. Each workstation has 8 feet of rail tiles to hold accessory items, as well as rail tiles in overhead storage units.

Below is a comparison of the Exist. Furn. workstation standards and the new PQR Furniture Co. WorkPlus standard.

Workstation Type	Exist. Furn.	PQR Furniture Co. WorkPlus
Exempt Supervisor		
Overall size	Does not exist	110 sq. ft.
Work surface	Currently	38.39 sq. ft.
Opening shelving		0
Closed shelving		8 lin. ft.
6" box drawer		2 @ 24"D
Total filing storage		16' 6" letter
Guest chair		2

NOTE: All above filing storage totals are based on letter-size filing. If the same units are used for a combination of letter and legal filing or all legal filing, the total quantity per workstation will vary. Total filing storage includes pedestal file drawers and two- or four-drawer freestanding units.

Below is a comparison of the Exist. Furn. Work surfaces and the new PQR Furniture Co. WorkPlus work surfaces.

Workstation Type	Exist. Furn.		PQR Furn. Co. WorkPlus	
	Qty	Size	Qty	Size
Exempt Supervisor	Does not exist		2	24" × 48"
	Currently		1	48" × 48" corner
			1	42" diam. table.

Below is a list of organizing tools available for use on the rail tiles or within the overhead storage unit. Each employee will have the opportunity to select the organizing tools he or she will require.

Shelf Divider	Paper Tray
Armature	Vertical Tray
Document Stand	Diagonal Tray
Machine Support Tray	

Private Offices B, C, and D

PQR Furniture Co. Executive is the standard casegood furniture series for private offices. Standard furnishings for private offices varies due to job function. Two furniture layout options for each office type B and three furniture layout options for each office type C and D are presented for each employee's selection in relation to his or her tasks. Each furniture layout option is presented with a scaled coded plan and a listing of each freestanding furniture item.

Private Office B (PO-B) is for Corporate Vice Presidents and Divisional Vice Presidents. They will receive the option of a desk/credenza with an optional VDT table or U-shaped desk arrangement. Casegoods and upholstered seating styles have been standardized for this office size. Furnishings for a PO-B office include a desk/credenza arrangement, guest seating, a small lounge seating area, and a conference table and chairs.

Private Office C (PO-C) is for Directors and Assistant Vice Presidents. They will receive the option of a desk/credenza with an optional VDT table or U-shaped desk arrangement. Casegoods and upholstered seating styles have been standardized for this office size. Furnishings for a PO-C office include a desk/credenza arrangement, guest seating, and a conference table and chairs.

Private Office D (PO-D) is for Managers. They will receive the option of a desk/credenza with an optional VDT table or U-shaped desk arrangement. Casegoods and upholstered seating styles have been standardized for this office size. Furnishings for a PO-D office include a desk/credenza arrangement and guest seating.

The PQR Furniture Co. Executive Collection is of a transitional style featuring mahogany veneers with a catalyzed lacquer finish. All desk configurations, desk and credenza or U-shaped, come with Centra locking. This enables the user to lock all pedestals within the desk or credenza with one key. The center drawer bottom is lined in polysuede. Black chrome hardware is standard on all drawers. Credenzas and modified credenzas in the U-shaped unit offer a combination of storage and filing. File drawers accommodate legal, letter, and/or 8½" × 14⅛" EDP filing. Conference tables and bookcases are also from the Executive Collection.

National Purchasing Contracts

In the 1980s, with the widespread adoption of space and furnishing standards, the next logical extension of the standards program was for facility professionals to develop long-term and ongoing national purchasing contracts with major suppliers and manufacturers. This policy ensures favorable, below-retail costs for one or more years for specific products and services, is designed to yield a specific and consistent level of quality, and allows for special requirements such as special finishes, short-time delivery (2 to 4 weeks rather than the usual 6 to 10 weeks), and so on.

National purchasing contract programs have been a blessing and a curse for some facility professionals. With these contracts in place, you are usually locked in to a specific price for specific items. Should your needs change and your customer require furnishing items not part of the program, the costs can be more than expected, as your customer may be able to purchase the required furnishing items through normal dealer channels for a lower price than you can obtain from the manufacturer. These contracts are good for budgeting and planning purposes, but you must stay aware of the marketplace. Last year's sweet deal may be this year's expensive project.

Ideally, national purchasing contracts for furnishings are for one year with options to extend the contract for specific periods and with product, delivery, freight, tax, storage, installation, and parts costs identified for your unique standards program. Many furnishings, carpet, and specialty dealers specialize in working with national purchasing contract accounts either as the originator of the contract or as a third party assigned by the manufacturer and approved by the facility customer to provide day-to-day services for the manufacturer.

Space Programming Illustrated[2]

Chapter 5 provided a number of building programming and design examples. The following illustrates the application of space programming for the office and R&D facility project described in that chapter.

1. Often, a relative sizes diagram is included as a comparative device for initial scope understanding and space perception. Exhibit 6.5 provides a comparative department size/scope for the office and R&D facility project.

2. Overall project organization, using the major departments or components, is described in a diagram similar to Exhibit 5.10. Often, it is advisable and helpful to show relationships in a matrix chart as well, as in Exhibit 6.6.

3. Each department or major component is broken down and described graphically and with significant relationships shown, as Exhibit 6.7. Occasionally, a series of supplemental analysis diagrams are used to depict other aspects of planning such as movement of people and services, flow of materials handling, manufacturing process, communications, robotic configurations, and security barriers.

ALTERNATIVE PROJECT DELIVERY SYSTEMS

Many facility professionals do not realize there are alternatives to the traditional design project delivery system under either the design-bid-build model or the fast-track method for building and interior construction and renovation.

Traditional Project Delivery Procedure

As discussed in chapter 5, the traditional project delivery procedure is to hire an appropriate design firm to handle the proposed project size; complete all the design planning and programming months in advance of the construction, move, or consolidation; bid the work; and implement the design plans.

Some facility professionals feel that much of the design and planning for new facilities is wasted effort because of subsequent reorganization. It seems that facility professionals have always had to deal with the costs of reorganization using the traditional design approach. The old rallying cry of "Given enough time and money, we can do anything" is no longer valid. Today's question is, "How do we hit a moving target?" in terms of organizational analysis and planning. The business environment is rapidly changing, and the time has come to consider alternatives to project delivery that offer quicker results, greater flexibility, and greater value to the customer and the corporation. Two of these alternatives are *just-in-time* and *hyper-track*, which are discussed in the following sections.

[2]Space planning Exhibits 6.1, 6.5, 6.6, and 6.7 used in this subsection to illustrate space programming are provided by Mr. Roger D. Roslansky, AIA, a registered architect residing in La Crosse, Wisconsin, from *Corporate Real Estate: Forms and Procedures,* (New York: John Wiley & Sons, Inc., 1994) pp. 295, 300, 302, and 304.

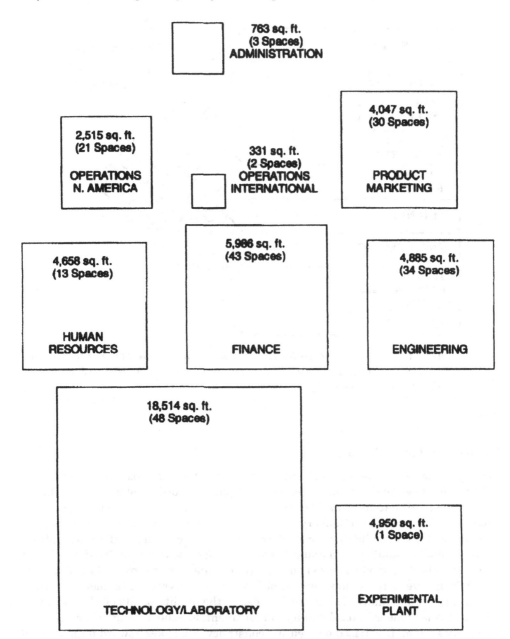

763 sq. ft.
(3 Spaces)
ADMINISTRATION

4,047 sq. ft.
(30 Spaces)

2,515 sq. ft.
(21 Spaces)

OPERATIONS
N. AMERICA

331 sq. ft.
(2 Spaces)
OPERATIONS
INTERNATIONAL

PRODUCT
MARKETING

4,658 sq. ft.
(13 Spaces)

5,986 sq. ft.
(43 Spaces)

4,885 sq. ft.
(34 Spaces)

HUMAN
RESOURCES

FINANCE

ENGINEERING

18,514 sq. ft.
(48 Spaces)

4,950 sq. ft.
(1 Space)

TECHNOLOGY/LABORATORY

EXPERIMENTAL
PLANT

Exhibit 6.5   Comparative Department Size/Scope (From Robert Kevin Brown, Managing Corporate Real Estate. *Copyright © 1993 by John Wiley & Sons, Inc. Reprinted by permission.)*

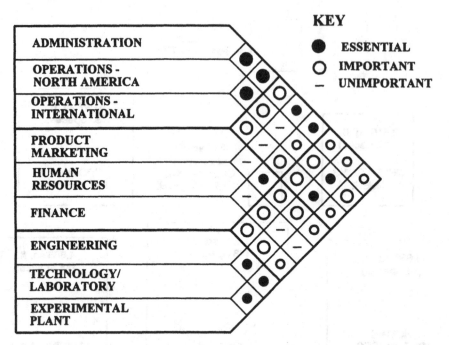

Exhibit 6.6   Relationships Matrix—Major Components *(From Robert Kevin Brown,* Managing Corporate Real Estate. *Copyright © 1993 by John Wiley & Sons, Inc. Reprinted by permission.)*

Just-in-Time Project Delivery[3]

Just-in-time-project delivery (JIT/PD) is based on the manufacturing process of the same name. As the name indicates, each phase of design, planning, building, and move coordination is implemented *only* just before it is needed (see Exhibit 6.8). Just-in-time project delivery assumes that, for whatever reason (a corporate reorganization, consolidation, or modernization of an existing facility), a significant number of small design and construction work packages can be accomplished sequentially. This mode is based on high quality and service from all team members. It involves a total management philosophy, empowered team members, communications, and many details. All fourteen of the quality points of W. Edwards Deming, the pioneer in total quality management, are the driving factors in the delivery system. It is based on creating constancy of purpose toward improvement of service and building quality into the product rather than checking it after completion. The most important point is that in traditional methods, the individual is often powerless to influence quality. It is only by changing the process (i.e., just-in-time project delivery) that quality can be improved.

[3]The information in this section, including Exhibits 6.7 and 6.8, is taken from "Just-in-Time Project Delivery," by Sheri Raiford, Corporate Interiors, Inc., Atlanta, GA, and Barry Lynch, R.J. Reynolds Tobacco Company, Winston-Salem, NC, IFMA Atlanta. IFMA Chapter program presentation and handout, April 1992.

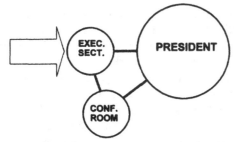

ADMINISTRATION - 736 SF - 2 STAFF

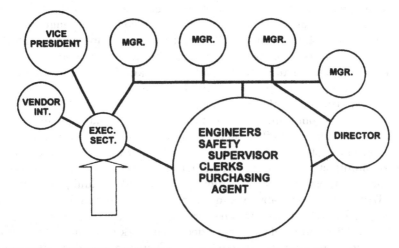

OPERATIONS - NORTH AMERICA - 2,515 SF - 20 STAFF

OPERATIONS - INTERNATIONAL - 331 SF - 2 STAFF

Exhibit 6.7   Departmental Graphic Analysis (From Robert Kevin Brown, Managing Corporate Real Estate. Copyright © 1993 by John Wiley & Sons, Inc. Reprinted by permission.)

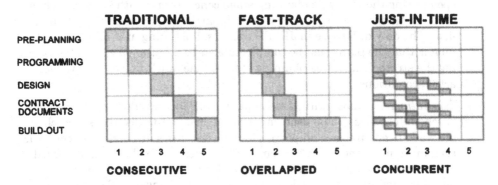

Exhibit 6.8   Project Delivery Methods

Another difference between JIT/PD and the traditional method of project delivery is that it assumes multiple small work packages can be accomplished sequentially to completely renovate or consolidate a fully occupied building while allowing unimpeded use of the facility. Similar to fast-track, work is accomplished sequentially through the building. Unlike fast-track, spaces are occupied as they are completed, allowing a 50 percent improvement in median personnel relocation time. Unlike fast-track projects in unfinished raw spaces, the renovation of an owner-occupied building requires extensive coordination with and from a great number of operational support groups, the contractor, and the existing departmental customer group. A goal of JIT/PD is to minimize the impact of construction activities on existing building departmental groups. Because construction is completed on the day shift, the construction coordinator must go to great lengths to check with departmental customers on adjacent floors before starting noisy activities.

JIT/PD requires a comprehensive team that includes, in addition to the facility professional, your customer representative(s), and the design firm planner, the building maintenance and operations staff (including the dock crew), the furniture movers (including the warehouse dock team, the installers and move coordinators), the telecommunications and computer/MIS (management information system) staff, mail and office services, signage and art coordinator, as well as other corporate staff, the contractor and all his or her subcontractors, and the furniture manufacturer. The crucial element in getting members to make decisions is to provide them with enough information to make sound judgments.

JIT/PD puts accountability and control on the individual and can exist only in an organizational culture that encourages change and does not punish risk.

With JIT/PD, all levels of project documents take on a new form. Program documents, space plans, interior construction documents, and specifications are used by design professionals to communicate the project intent. Examples of JIT/PD documents and methods include:

- *Programming.* The standard questionnaire and interview procedure is replaced with top-down executive-level interviews, on-site observation, documentation by planners, and quick-fit space-planning studies. The traditional program report is replaced by quick-fit space plans that verify exactly how many people will fit in the existing space.

- *Universal planning.* JIT/PD requires that a universal space plan be developed during the strategic planning stage concurrently with space plan standards in order to be sure the customer department population will fit on a floor. The only difference in JIT/PD universal planning and traditional planning is that the plan must be completed as a part of the program effort during the strategic facilities planning stage so the quick-fit sketches reflect actual conditions.

- *Scheduling.* The most critical element of JIT/PD is scheduling. Many types of scheduling aids can be used on a project. The most effective is the schedule wall. To ensure that all parties know what floors are in design, construction, move-in, or move-out for demolition stages, a schedule wall designed by the project team can depict all floors of the project facility and other buildings undergoing consolidation. Color-coded plans on a floor-by-floor basis can illustrate weekly progress of the schedule over the project period. Current occupancy plans showing existing or new approved layouts can be updated daily by the design team or the move coordinators.

- *Personalized schedule.* To ensure that each responsible party understands his or her commitments, an individual schedule is also developed for the many nonconstruction activities—hanging artwork, installing plants, cleaning the floor, pulling furniture from the warehouse, installing furniture, and so on—that must be accomplished for each move.

  The personalized schedule is a critical tool for empowerment of team members because information is crucial to empowerment. Using both the schedule wall and the personalized schedule as communication tools, everyone should understand his or her workload and be able to plan time so no project delays are incurred.

- *Design concepts, presentations, and pricing documents.* The schedule allows a minimum amount of time to develop base building and select finishes and furniture design concepts for the project. Design concepts should be presented in a schematic form using sketch paper, loose finishes, and a detailed listing of pricing items for the contractor. Construction should start within a few weeks after the design concept presentation. You may choose to use a renovated area as an on-site mock-up for all team members.

- *Interior construction / specification items.* Carpet tiles are often selected for a project because of the ease of installation in working with a high density of existing partitions. Carpet tiles usually have a higher first cost than roll goods, but they allow faster installation with less installation labor. Carpet is commonly the largest budget line item in modernization projects. To minimize total costs, it is important to look at the overall cost of a product, including first cost of the item, cost of installation, costs of storage if you are required to accept delivery prior to installation, and the costs of overhead involved in the installation time.

- *Interior construction drawings.* Interior construction drawings are provided as they are needed, demolition plans are supplied when demolition begins, and construction drawings and details are developed in a universal format and released as they are needed. If the contractor requires information prior to the release of drawings, the schedule wall can show current plans for his or her use in preliminary takeoffs. Design details become standards for the project as new conditions appear.

- *Furniture / move coordination documents.* Your design firm must work with you and your staff to ensure that existing furniture is used. Several design standards may be developed that maximize the use of existing furniture with different colors and fabrics coming from several locations. The design firm staff and the furniture installer may make substitutions on the floor or prior to installation to meet the schedule. Workstation drawings (8 1/2" × 11") may be used to build out a particular workstation module. These elements may later become part of the furniture standards manual (see Sample: ABC Company Furniture Standards) that will allow you to change and update the floors as needed with minimum furniture drawings.

- *Facilities operations manual.* Meeting and exceeding customer expectations is a key to quality. Construction documents and specifications are legal documents intended to ensure that work is completed in a satisfactory manner. By taking critical information and formatting it in an easy-to-use reference manual, considerable product research time can be saved by maintenance and operations departments when they must repair, replace, or maintain renovated space.

You may wish to use Exhibit 6.9 to determine if this nontraditional project delivery process is appropriate for your organization.

Hyper-Track[4]

A second alternative project delivery procedure meant to accelerate the design and construction process is called *hyper-track*. At issue is how facility professionals can respond to ever-increasing demands to deliver construction projects more quickly without sacrificing acceptable levels of quality, objectivity, or cost.

The options available to design and implement facility projects are many. Typically, though, two scenarios are considered. The traditional approach involves hiring a professional architectural, engineering, interior design (A/E/I) firm to provide design services for a complete package, which is then bid and built (see chapter 5). This obviously requires the most time. The second scenario is hyper-track, whereby a few phases of design and bidding occur simultaneously with construction. This approach requires the use of the A/E/I and a construction manager or a design/build firm. Where traditional approaches involve one major issue of a design package delivered to the contractor, fast-track can have from four to seven phases of Project Documents. There is a similarity between the two—all issues of Project Documents are complete packages.

Hyper-track is similar to just-in-time, essentially taking it one step further. Hyper-track can have up to 50 issues that are incomplete, small packages, sometimes not much more than one fax ahead of the contractor. As you can imagine, hyper-track is not for the faint of heart!

A few examples may help illustrate this point. Meeting schedule demands meant site work had to start almost immediately after authorization due to the upcoming winter season. Programming of divisions moving from New York and other regions had just begun, and a full evaluation and payback analysis of alternate centralized HVAC systems (including ice storage) was being conducted while construction documents were being prepared for parking lot, detention, lake, and site utilities. Schedules also required that a key lobby entry and kitchen/cafeteria location be set right away, before programming was complete. During finalization of programming and start of space planning, construction documents were being prepared for utility cores. While the interior designers were in the process of space planning and working side by side with the office systems furniture dealership, demolition and construction began.

[4]The information in this section is taken from "Hyper-Track: A New Reality in Construction Projects," by Bruce F. Mirrielees, AIA, Hixson Architecture Engineering Interiors, Cincinnati, Ohio, *IFMA '93 Presentation Proceedings,* October 1993, pp. 206–212.

Fill out the table below. Assign a rating for your organization for each of the issues listed in the right-hand column. If your score totals over 70 you might consider using a non-traditional project delivery approach. Reference scoring analysis below.

Issue	Range	Your score
Importance of speed in plan implementation.	Not Important Important 0---------5---------`10---------15-------20	
Importance of speed in marketplace.	Not Important Important 0---------5---------10----------15--------20	
Organizational growth.	Significant Growth No Growth 0---------0----------3-------------6----------12	
USF / Person (density) in existing facilities.	175 sf/person 225 275+ 0---------3----------6------------9----------12	
Percentage of owned vs. leased space.	100% Owned 100% Leased 12--------9----------6------------3--------0	
Total sf of facilities involved in plan.	150,000 sf over 750,000 sf 1----------2----------3------------4----------5	
Prior experience with phased planning /const.	None Once Several Times (-30)----(-25)----(-20)---------0--------12	
Expected churn rate during planning period.	0% 15% 25% or more 0---------4----------8----------12----------16	
Current occupancy plans continuously updated.	10% Complete 75% 100% 0---------4----------8----------12----------16	
Availability of detailed historical project costs.	10% Complete 75% 100% 0---------4----------8----------12----------16	
Your corporate problem-solving methodology.	Fix-as-fail Anticipation (-30)----(-25)----(-20)---------0----------16	
Organization supports employee empowerment.	No Support Support 0---------1----------2------------4---------5	
Organization supports risk taking.	No Support Support (-30)----(-25)----(-20)---------0---------12	
TOTAL SCORE		

	SCORING ANALYSIS	
Total score	**Below 70:** Risks outweigh benefits.	
Total score	**70–85:** Some gains to organization related to reduced cost and increased project speed.	
Total score	**Above 85:** Significant benefits to organization related to reduced cost and increased project speed.	

Exhibit 6.9 Just-in-Time Project Delivery (From "Just-in-Time Project Delivery," by Sheri Raiford, Corporate Interiors, Inc., Atlanta, GA, and Barry Lynch, R.J. Reynolds Tobacco Company, Winston-Salem, NC, IFMA Atlanta. IFMA Chapter program presentation and handout, April 1992.)

Use just-in-time project delivery for:

- **Large or complex reorganizations**
- **Office space consolidations**
- **Reconfiguring existing fully occupied space**
- **Moving out of leased space**
- **Department restacking in high "churn" organizations**

Definitions

USF Person	Usable square feet per person: The total building area less nonusable spaces such as toilets, building lobbies, elevator lobbies, stairs, etc.
Density	The total facilities square footage divided by the total population. In this case use usable area.
Churn rate	The total number of people moved per year divided by the total customer population. Includes "briefcase" moves and project moves.
Problem-solving methodologies	Fix-as-Fail: Normal operating procedure — fix problems as they arise (Crisis Management).
	Prevention: Allocating resources to identifying defects on a real time basis.
	Root Causes: Fewer problems create time to find underlying causes.
	Anticipation: Changes to the system generate time to improve the process.

Exhibit 6.9   Just-in-Time Project Delivery *(Continued)*

Another example involves a company that supplied products to the U.S. Armed Forces as part of Operation Desert Storm. A total conversion of an abandoned facility was designed, engineered, and constructed within 6 months into a 180,000-square-foot processing operation. This project involved the issuance of over 35 hyper-track design packages. The purpose of the move was to expand the company's production capability twelvefold to meet increased demand.

Without a doubt, the essential ingredient of the process is coordination—making sure what is on one package coordinates with the whole job as it develops. Repeated checking is an ongoing task. All design disciplines must bend over backward to make sure they are integrated. Also, during construction, detailed field data are shared regularly with the design team for their immediate feedback.

Two important points to note:

1. Hyper-track does not involve completed design—it is the integrated design of a moving target.
2. This approach is not design/build in any way. The A/E/I and general contractor are independently contracted to the owner. This maintains the positive checks and balances between design and construction.

Criteria

While the need for speed is an obvious criterion when considering whether or not to utilize hyper-track, it is hardly the only one. Many projects must come on line as soon as possible for a variety of reasons: production capacity, seasonal relationships (agriculture/holidays), needed selling capacity, special occurrences (Desert Storm), or allowing major capital investment to more quickly show a return. "As soon as possible" is the operative phase. The degree of risk associated with cost, quality, and potential business disruption based on decisions stemming from schedule commitments is significantly higher with hyper-track. Therefore, it is critical that a company take a long, serious look at several issues.

The foundation of this approach is that it is a *team effort*. The project team includes the owner, internal supporting departments, A/E/I, and the contractor, all of whom must be able to work together, with each player having a defined responsibility. Team selection must be based on qualifications and the cultural compatibility of each partner—not price alone. The following is a suggested guide for considering your team as well as your approach to regulatory agencies.

Criteria for the Owner

1. The owner should set the stage by having upper management's total commitment—a clear understanding of the company's vision and mission.
2. The owner should develop realistic expectations and objectives.
3. The owner should be willing to make quick decisions. Management does not have the luxury of studying plans for long periods—they either comment quickly or abdicate.
4. The owner should make any staff member available whom the team needs to get program and criteria established.
5. Top decision makers should either be accessible themselves or delegate the authority.

Criteria for Selection of a Design Firm (A/E/I)

1. The A/E/I should have as many design disciplines in-house as possible.
2. First choice would be an A/E/I your company has worked with successfully.
3. The A/E/I should have specific knowledge and experience with the project type and schedule demands.
4. The A/E/I should have demonstrated ability to produce partial plans without large coordination errors developing as the total design progresses.

5. The A/E/I should be open-minded so the project can benefit from owner and contractor's design input. A/E/I must put the interests of the project first.

6. The A/E/I should be large enough to handle the project but not so large that your project has little significance for it. The preferred company has design firm principals directly involved in the project; not removed by several layers of management.

7. The firm's individuals, not just the company's past projects, should be compatible with the job.

Criteria for Selection of a Contractor

1. First choice would be a contractor your company and/or the A/E/I has worked with successfully.

2. The contractor should have specific knowledge of and experience with the project type and schedule demands.

3. The contractor should be able to perform general carpentry and cleanup. A pure construction management organization only adds another layer of bureaucracy.

4. The contractor must emphasize quality—there is little time to do things twice.

5. The contractor should be large enough to handle the project but not so large that your project is insignificant for it. The preferred company has corporation officers directly involved in the project, not removed by several layers of management.

6. The firm's individuals, not just the company's past projects, should be compatible with the job.

7. The contractor should have a strong following of qualified subcontractors and product suppliers.

8. The contractor should have demonstrated success in performing and completing negotiated contracts.

Strategy for Regulatory Involvement

In addition to the issues of senior management commitment, partnering, and trust among the qualified team members, relationships with city, county, state, and federal regulatory agencies must be carefully evaluated. Uncooperative building departments can easily kill a hyper-track project even if all other elements are in place. Therefore, it is crucial to discuss expectations early with any involved agencies on issues such as the need for ongoing partial permits like foundations only or site only. All agencies must be treated as valuable partners in the process.

Construction Contracts

As with any construction project, developing the appropriate contractual arrangements with your contractor is important. Generally speaking, work that is not on the critical path schedule should be bid, and therefore a lump-sum contract is advantageous. Due to the nature of items on the critical path, time does not allow for large design packages. These smaller packages are usually incomplete and feature overlapping responsibilities, making time and materials (T&M) contracts appropriate. A mix of both can be used also. As an example, modifications to a lump-sum contract can be on T&M to avoid bidding or pricing delays. Due to the aggressive schedules, the owner may preorder equipment and assign installation to the contractor. Both overtime and shift work must be defined before either lump-sum or T&M contracts are signed.

Because the hyper-track project will have significant portions of the work going T&M or fixed subprices being administered by a T&M general contractor, a contract format designed for the specific situation is prudent.

Selecting the appropriate American Institute of Architects (AIA) owner-contractor A Series forms is a good starting point, but it does not go far enough. Define and differentiate the contractor's home office expenses versus field expenses. Understand and agree on what kind and how many supervisors/managers will be provided and which ones are to be covered by the fee and which will be reimbursable. The same logic applies to job site general conditions (e.g., office trailers, dumpsters, computers, vehicles, chemical toilets).

Small tools are always a point of contention. Unless you want to be in the tool business during and after the project, a small tool fee should be established either as a percentage of direct labor costs or, preferably, as a lump-sum fee for the project. All labor burden percentages should be agreed on so there are no surprises. All components of the contractor's progress billing should be supported by backup invoices and certified payroll registers.

Similar logic holds for a contract with the A/E/I, but there are fewer components. If possible, the A/E/I and contractor contracts should be based on a guaranteed maximum price to be established as the scope of the work becomes more defined. With the right controls and systems, the costs can be monitored, but nobody gets a blank check; for instance, all overtime must have prior owner approval and all subs and material suppliers are selected by the team, not unilaterally. It is critical that a change order system be established at the earliest stages of the project. In any case, if a level of trust between all team members cannot be established, this arrangement will not work.

Financial Management

As is always the mandate, cost must be controlled. Under the constraints of a rapidly moving project, however, this takes on added importance. Moving at the speed of light can expend dollars at twice the speed of light! The only way to control costs effectively is through constant monitoring relating back to the construction cost estimates. Any bookkeeper can tell you where you are today; the real value of financial management is the ability to determine where you will be at the end of a project. Several tools can be used from the standpoint of both soft costs such as design fees and, more importantly, construction cost.

A logical question at this point is who should perform this task? Any of the three primary team members—the owner, A/E/I, or contractor—can do it, but it is essential that some singular entity take responsibility for the project's financial management.

Our experience is that the A/E/I is best suited because of knowing the most about the project from the owner's and the construction side. (An important assumption here is that the A/E/I has the technological systems in place and experienced *construction* professionals on staff who have hands-on experience in the field.) This arrangement may work well since the contractor is busy trying to meet a demanding schedule and the owner is concerned with the logistics of start-up, move-in, and/or maintaining business during construction. This setup also establishes necessary objectivity.

In managing construction costs, developing an estimate is the obvious starting point. This estimate takes on added significance in hyper-track because it quickly becomes a living, breathing document and is used for negotiation of contracts with selected subcontractors to verify price competitiveness. It is during the actual construction process though that financial management plays its greatest role. In conjunction with site representation, financial management consists of:

- Establishing a project cost accounting system to monitor and control the total project cost (see chapter 3, Capital Project Tracking). The system tracks costs associated with various packages such as steel, furniture, and electrical work, as well as major components within those areas.

- Determining amounts owed to the contractor, based on quality of work, work accomplished, and materials stored on site.

- Evaluating changes to determine if they were part of the project scope and recommending a course of action including determining financial responsibility for the changes.

- Preparing regular reports summarizing the status of the budget compared with project progress and schedule.

Is Hyper-Track For You?

Speed has in fact become the great differentiator for many in our rapidly changing world. Finding ways to deliver quality service, products, and information quicker than the competition is the challenge before many of our companies if we hope to flourish in the global marketplace. This new reality trickles down and affects how facility projects come together. For this reason, we see hyper-track will only increase in frequency.

It is something though that has to be approached with eyes wide open. Definite risks are involved.

Disadvantages

Essentially, you are not dealing with lines on paper. Constructing parking lots while programming and space planning can be scary. What if a major item is uncovered during programming that would dictate relocation of a major element? If a better solution presents itself through the design process, it may be too late to change if the lesser solution has already been constructed. Changes mean tearing out or demolishing something built as opposed to just erasing the wall or equipment on a drawing.

The cost of change can be significantly higher than with a more moderately paced project. Preliminary construction cost estimate overruns when bid could limit the ability to value-engineer other aspects of the project if they are already constructed. The importance of excellent construction cost estimating cannot be overemphasized.

Without proper and constant monitoring, quality could certainly suffer. This is why a trustworthy team that provides the needed checks and balances throughout the process is a must.

It does not take much imagination to see how a project that can have up to 50 design packages issued can run into trouble. As long as all parties understand clearly the potential pitfalls involved and have made the necessary commitments to minimize risk, it can and has worked.

Advantages

The advantages to successfully completing a hyper-track project can be numerous depending on your situation. Avoiding paying interest on unproductive land or facilities, improving corporate operation or moving people sooner, gaining efficiency of a new facility more quickly after a decision to relocate, expanding or remodeling as well as reducing the time it takes to get a product to the market all can have a profound impact on a company's bottom line and overall competitiveness. In instances where there may be no alternative, the outline we have provided can prevent major problems.

And facility professionals who can successfully navigate through projects requiring "hyper-speeds" will no doubt be seen as an extremely valuable asset to any company.

ERGONOMIC AND LIFE SAFETY ISSUES

Ergonomics

Ergonomics is a very important design criterion, stemming from concern for maximizing human resource efficiency through a high-quality environment. The term *ergonomic* describes a design created specifically to fit human dimensions and respond to functional requirements. Crucial to the success of any ergonomic plan is the adjustability of equipment and furniture in the workplace. Adjustable ergonomic chairs are essential, as are adjustable ergonomic computer accessories such as keyboards, document holders, and computer mouse pads.

The argument in favor of ergonomic furnishings and accessories is supported by numerous statistics. An estimated 280,000 U.S. workers between the ages of 18 and 69 report inability to use their upper extremities because of paralysis, severe incoordination, or complete absence of feeling in the arms. To accommodate these workers, one ergonomic solution is to provide adjustable seating and a worksurface that is height and angle adjustable. Adjustable keyboards, document holders, and computer mouse pads can further enhance a fully accessible work space. Use of these products can help not only impaired workers, but also all workers at keyboards. They can help prevent disabling ailments such as carpal tunnel syndrome (CTS) and upper limb disorders (ULD). At present, CTS is the leading cause of occupational illness in the United States, with combined absenteeism and medical expenses costing the industry some $27 billion a year.

Studies show that the position of the user's wrist-bent with the palm higher than the wrist joint (positive slope) constitutes a major health problem for computer key operators. In this position, arms and wrists become tense, placing considerable stress on nerves and tissues, possibly causing cumulative damage to the carpal tunnel, resulting in CTS. The health problem can be more severe for keyboard operators working at speeds of up to 13,000 keystrokes per hour. Research has shown that an ergonomically safe keyboard system must have an integral palm rest and must be optimally preset to slope downward to match the natural angle of forearms and hands. This supports the wrist in a healthier, "vertically neutral" position.[5]

Handicap Requirements

In addition to the requirements of the Americans with Disabilities Act (ADA), most states have added to their handicap site, building access legislation. Most corporations meet these regulations as a norm in their new facilities and now face retrofitting older facilities to achieve compliance. The need for more accessible parking, building entrances, stairs, elevators, rest rooms, and workstations could reduce the usable site and building size. And as each state has its own handicapped code, which may or may not be more restrictive than federal codes, ADA, or adjacent state requirements, it is an ongoing process to stay abreast of changes and how these impact the facility professional's properties. A local design firm should be consulted whenever possible for a detailed local interpretation of each legislated requirement.

Life Safety

As a facility professional, you must be thoroughly versed in the life safety requirements mandated by local, state, and federal codes and regulations. At times, good old common sense must step in when a building may be in conformance with the code but the health and welfare of your fellow employees are at stake. For example, the code may not require a second means of exit from a space, but because you know in detail the activities and possible use of the spaces concerned, a second means of exit makes common sense to design in and install now regardless of the code requirements.

Fire evacuation plans, fire extinguishers, sprinkler systems, panic hardware, unlocked exits, emergency lighting, lighted and unlighted exit signage, emergency speaker system, emergency power, smoke detectors, fire alarms, adequate passage width and unobstructed exitways are some of the basic life safety concerns and issues that must be addressed by the design firm and the facility professional during the interior design process. Neither you nor your design firm

---

[5]Leonard Kruk, Peoformix, Inc., "Complying with the ADA Can Save You Money," *Facility Management Journal,* November/December 1993, p. 30. Copyright 1993.

ever want to be second-guessed should a life safety issue be directly linked to a loss of life event.

In reviewing life safety issues, remember that the building systems and furnishings within a facility are subject to building and life safety codes. Building fire annunciator systems and noncombustible, flame-resistant, and smoke-inhibiting materials must be specified for building systems and furnishings including carpet, wall coverings, paint, ceilings, furniture, and drapes. Also, the interior design must encourage and assist in the maintenance, repair, and cleaning of all spaces.

ADDITIONAL PLANNING AND DESIGN REQUIREMENTS— CURRENT TRENDS

The information revolution will continue to drive changes in how our companies do business. Computer-aided management tools such as decision, knowledge-based, expert systems, computer-aided design (CAD), computer-aided facility management (CAFM), and facility management information systems (FMIS), both server based and Internet based, will continue to develop and assist all levels of management and staff in forecasting, processing, and accessing more *pertinent* information faster. Computer technology has become more sophisticated with greater networking and integration of differing systems. Hardware, communications systems, fiber optics versus cable, laser technology, laptop PCs, bubble memory, and other information advancements still in development (including security issues) has changed, grown, and expanded into the home, office, and at any workplace around the world.

The use of file servers, proxy servers, networks, e-mail, wireless communications, special telecommunications systems (fax, satellites, cellular), video conferencing, web casts, net meeting technology, and other new technologies to speed communication and the flow of information to more and remote locations will become a common part of doing business at work and at home. The rapid growth and implementation of business information systems has continued to challenge facility management. You must become aware and comfortable with computer hardware and software technology. Your challenge includes integrating new more sophisticated technology into your planning with an emphasis on a long-term flexible approach that will reduce obsolescence in your increasingly more complex facility environments. Workplace systems and facilities must be able to accommodate the rapid growth of business technology. Laser, fax, VSAT, optical fiber, and other emerging technologies will require rapid transitions from obsolete systems to new facility and utility requirements that were not initially incorporated or even considered.

FACILITY MANAGEMENT INFORMATION SYSTEM

Diversified, divisionalized corporations, particularly those that combine all the line and staff functions on national and international market levels, have a significant logistical problem in creating and maintaining accurate, adequate, and responsive data systems relating to real property and facility management.

There are two primary reasons for computerizing the facility management information system: First, to save time and thus the cost of information, and second to deal efficiently with complex and diverse data. For example, if management requires a quarterly facilities report, two to three employee-weeks of time may be required for data collection, compilation, and review. Thus, it may be four or five weeks into a new quarter before the report on the previous quarter is available. In addition, the report may lack important information on facilities simply because the sheer burden of collecting and modifying that information prohibits its inclusion. Additionally, the report may lack uniformity, particularly if the base data are prepared at a variety of sources, such as different operating divisions of the corporation.

A computer-based system (see Exhibit 6.10 and Exhibit 6.11) can alleviate these problems while providing a broad base of current and comprehensive facility information for other corporate departments such as executive management, corporate accounting, industrial engineering, risk management (insurance), security, tax, transportation, legal, and distribution.

The potential benefits would include the following:

- A broad base of logically associated information concerning all facility-related activities, which could be made available to any authorized users throughout the corporation.

- Consistent facility management information since all users would draw their information from one source.

- The elimination of quarterly and monthly peak/valley data collection periods in the corporate, group, and operating locations. Data could be distributed continuously, and the users would always have the most current data available.

The improvement to reports are as follows:

- Faster turnaround time in the generation of reports.

- Uniformity of the data reported.

- The availability of data not currently compiled.

- The acquisition and use of information across corporate operations lines with a single request or inquiry.

- Easily compiled and consolidated corporate reports through a shared data file if a corporation maintains two or more divisional headquarters, for example, one on the East Coast and one on the West Coast; and the immediate availability of information at both headquarters, without regard to East Coast/West Coast time differentials.

- Ability to interface with other corporate information systems, such as a financial data system, if the system is designed and implemented under the database concept.

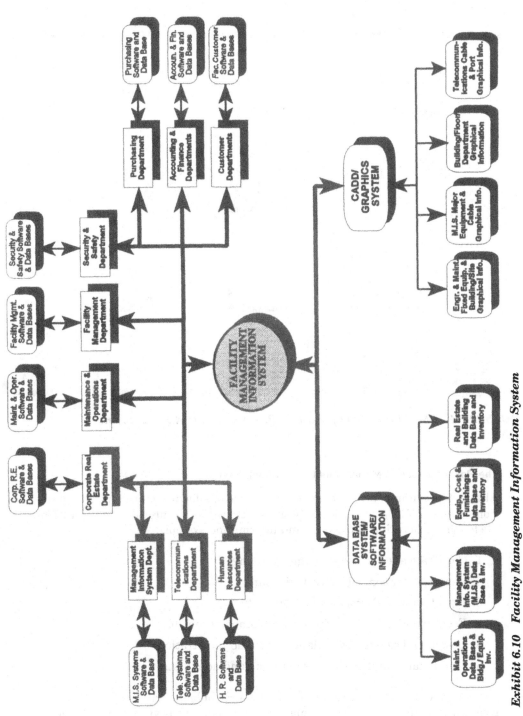

Exhibit 6.10 Facility Management Information System

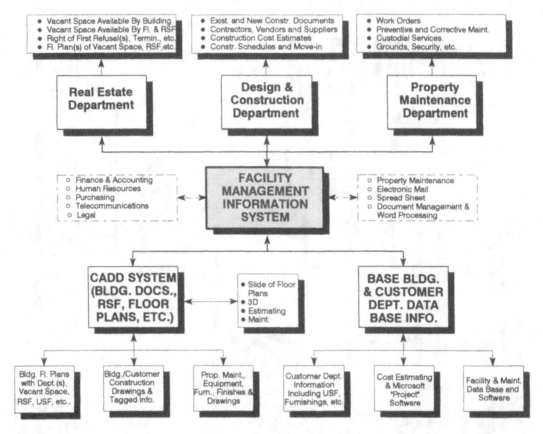

Exhibit 6.11   FMIS Flowchart for a Facility Management Department

The Role of a Facility Management Information System

Although providing data is the generic purpose of a facility management information system (FMIS), we can identify six critical roles that provide the key rationale for the structuring of the data and information systems:

1. Corporate and facility strategic planning

2. Reporting for control of strategic plans

3. Facility and real property administration

4. Facility budgeting, scheduling, and financial controls

5. Design and construction planning and administration

6. Maintenance and operations planning and administration

Understanding the source, nature, and degree of long-term legal and financial
commitments involved in facility management decisions is vital, or implementing
and realizing corporate and facility strategic plans becomes an exercise in futility.
The effectiveness of strategy will be a function of the quality of information with

respect to assumptions and constraining conditions. With this in mind, an effective facility management information system becomes imperative. For example, a leased facility will be governed primarily by a leasehold agreement and an owned facility will be governed primarily by the sale and purchase agreement. The real estate and facility departments will need to know what matters covered in these documents affect corporate decision making for leased property, such as the term, manner, and amount of rental payment; the facilities leased; and special conditions. The real estate and facility department will need to know when a lease expires or is to be renewed so that the affected division can be notified sufficiently in advance of termination. Many times, leases contain a 6- to 12-month advance notice provision with respect to exercising a renewal option. Not fulfilling this requirement could, for example, sideline a corporate strategy of retaining a facility to capitalize on the value that has been created by virtue of the location.

Reporting and control enable performance evaluation as well as provide information for corrective action where appropriate. These reports may be restricted to real property per se or to facilities alone, or to a combination of the two. In any event, the timing of report preparation will be known in advance by the real estate and facility department. The FMIS provides speed of report assemblage that is usually lacking in manually performed functions and, assuming the accuracy of the raw data input, it will often provide a level of accuracy that may be lacking in manual real estate reporting operations. A periodic formalized report might include, for example, a quarterly status report on surplus property that the corporation wishes to dispose of or to swap around among its various divisions. Extending the example, management might wish to know about the current status of a particular parcel of surplus property at some time between two quarterly reports. If the FMIS is properly updated, it could furnish such information on what effectively becomes a real-time basis (see Exhibit 6.12).

The administrative requirements of the FMIS are utilized primarily to support day-to-day activities. The FMIS should be designed for a series of response capabilities ranging from annual summary reports to the answering of everyday queries about facility management issues such as strategic planning, real estate leases, and maintenance work orders. Additionally, the primary mission of FMIS administration is to update data files and maintain their integrity with respect to accuracy. The previously discussed roles of the FMIS underscore the necessity of treating data as an asset in this regard. This responsibility is not restricted to electronic data files and graphic files, but extends to hard copy files as well. For example, the complete file on a particular property can be maintained within the real estate department, with the summary sheet denoting the location within the file of relevant documents that communicate obligations and rights of the respective parties. This is particularly critical if real property is leased. If property is owned, the file summary would indicate the location of every legal document affecting ownership, from the sales contract, closing statement, and the deed to boundary surveys, plot plans, building plans and specifications, and photographs. Because this data administration is so important, proper stewardship of both hard copy documents and electronic data files is an imperative.

Another benefit of the FMIS program is that facility professionals can proactively manage their space, construction, and expenditure requirements with accurate and timely data supplied from other departments and from their design firm.

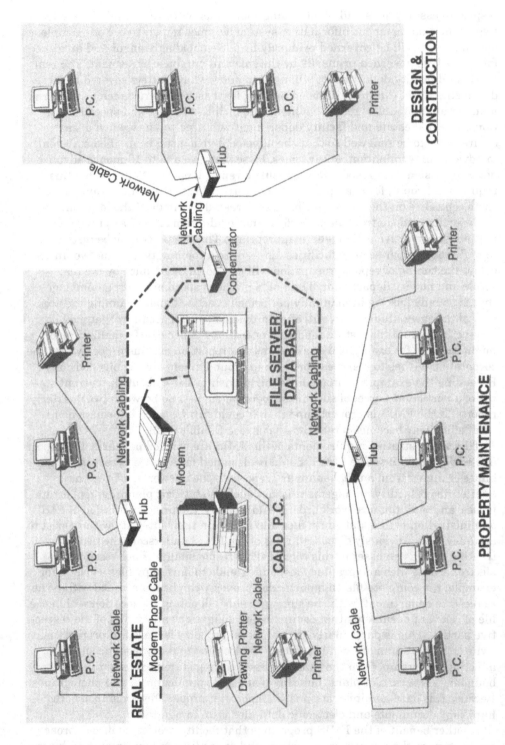

Exhibit 6.12   FMIS Flowchart for a Facility Management Department

Many design firms are managing their clients' graphics in computer-aided design and drafting (CADD) formats. When their facility client makes a change to the interior floor plan, the design firm can make that adjustment and keep the floor plan up to date with graphics and database information on furnishings, cost, and scheduled relocations. This capability can provide you with accurate information for strategic planning requirements and the quick and efficient performance of "what if" scenarios. Relocation planning of personnel and furnishings is less time consuming if your data can provide current inventories of furnishings for comparison with the requirements of the new configuration.

Disaster Prevention and Recovery[6]

With the growing awareness of facility management's significant impact on the corporate bottom line, the use of facility management information systems has also increased. Once in place, the FMIS (see Exhibit 6.10) becomes an integral and critical tool to the management of facilities. Therefore, it's integrity must be ensured. An FMIS disaster prevention and recovery plan is one component of the answer.

An effective disaster prevention and recovery plan consists of the following three steps:

1. Identify the disaster.

2. Develop prevention and preparation strategies.

3. Implement recovery procedures if disasters occur.

These three steps must be applied to the following five categories of FMIS infrastructure:

1. Personnel

2. Data

3. Equipment

4. Software

5. Vendors

The written plan should be contained in a three-ring binder and it should be reviewed annually and appropriate areas tested. Some areas of the plan may take time to develop and/or carry a cost. To justify either the time or cost, develop a list of risks that are exposed and estimate the impact to various business units and to various business functions. When these impacts include financial or service-level losses, it may be prudent to develop a level of protection. Exhibit 6.13 shows a breakdown of the three steps and five categories.

[6]The information in this section is taken from "CIFM Disaster Prevention & Recovery," by Susan J. Mosby, CFM, IBD, CDFM, Kansas City, MO, presentation and handout, IFMA Best Practices Forum, August 11, 1994, Danbury, CT. Copyright 1994.

Disaster	Prevention and Preparation	Recovery
Personnel		
Absences	• Training more than one operator. • Good working environment. • Documentation of system. • Responsibility and authority. • Scheduling of vacations.	• Reschedule backup's time. • Implement training for new.
Productivity	• Training new users. • Time allocation. • Allow time to develop productivity.	• Implement training as soon as possible. • Schedule "uninterrupted" time. • Bring vendor in.
Errors	• Training program. • System "lock-out." • Data auditing. • Work records.	• Locate errors or locate latest valid data. • Correct errors.
Malicious Actions	• Backup data and store separately. • Password security and change. • Physically isolate data. • Data auditing and system log.	• Restore data. • Change password. • Locate valid data. • Identify cause of problem.
Data		
Data Loss	• Power backup and conditioners. • Daily backup stored off-site. • Weekly backup stored out of area. • Check backups and restore monthly.	• Determine extent of loss. • Restore only lost data. • Test data to verify. • Check for computer virus and remove virus from the system.
Data Corruption	• Data auditing process. • Backup incrementally. • Work-order log of changes.	• Identify corrupt data. • Check for computer virus and remove virus from the system. • Restore noncorrupt data. • Destroy any corrupt backup.
Noncurrent Data	• Data maintenance process. • Record of facility changes. • Update and maintenance program.	• Identify extent of update required. • Determine in-house or service. • Update data.
Equipment		
Lost or Stolen	• Physical security. • Insurance coverage. • Store data separately. • Encrypt data. • Backup systems.	• Replacement policy. • Loaner equipment.
Breakdown	• Regular maintenance. • Power perfection. • Maintenance contracts. • Backup systems.	• Response time. • Loaner equipment. • Lead time for replacement.
Obsolescence	• Open architecture hardware. • Standard parts. • Upgradable.	• Determine upgrade required. • Upgrade or replace? • Other uses for system.

Exhibit 6.13   Disaster Prevention and Recovery

Software		
Faulty Software	• Research. • Test. • Standard data format. • Ease of use.	• Purchase compatible software. • Develop an in-house program.
Lost or Stolen or Damaged	• Store original disks separately. • Register software. • Insure any "lock." • Make backup disks.	• Request new disks from the manufacturer. • Re-install from backup. • File police report. • File insurance claim.
Obsolescence	• Buy from reputable maker. • Data in standard format. • Excess capacity.	• Purchase new software with same data format. • Convert formulas and programs. • Input data from old system.
Incompatibility	• "Standard data." • "Industry standard." • Hardware requirements.	• Change software. • Upgrade hardware. • Translation programs.
Vendors		
Poor Performance	• Selection of dependable and reliable vendors. • Multiple vendors.	• Select new vendor. • Change software. • Develop support in-house.
High Cost	• Ensure competition. • Negotiate.	• Alternate vendor. • In-house support.
Out of Business	• Multiple sources. • Manufacturer support.	• Alternate vendor. • In-house support.

Exhibit 6.13   Disaster Prevention and Recovery (*Continued*)

WORK ENVIRONMENT TRENDS

Facility management literature provides information that can be used to identify and document current and future facility design concepts and trends.

The traditional workplace in today's office environments consists of a private or semiprivate space separated by enclosed walls and supported by systems furniture. Larger offices, larger staff, and an office with a window are examples of traditional perks. Studies show that these traditional methods of space utilization, which require increasingly expensive lease space and human resources, represent ineffective space management for today's business environment. As a result, several concepts have been designed to achieve better results.

The term "hoteling" refers to a space-sharing concept in which work space is made available on advance notice from the employee. The hoteling system operates like a hotel, where a room is provided on request. This arrangement can be useful for companies with a group of employees who spend a great deal of their time outside their traditional offices.

"Nonterritorial" offices have been designed for projects involving short- or moderate-term teamwork. In a nonterritorial environment, no one person has an assigned workstation but shares space, resources, files, and quiet areas with other members of their team. The sharing of resources encourages interaction between team members. The nonterritorial concept works well for creative and development activities and for special teams of interdisciplinary personnel.

The "caves and commons" concept also emphasizes group work with shared resources. It is similar to the nonterritorial concept, except that employees are assigned a very small private work space. The caves and commons concept works well for organizations who aren't ready for the nonterritorial concept, or as a starting point for its implementation.

"Free addresses" is a term for a concept in office planning based on groups of people who need to be together to perform a specific type of task. These activity-specific work spaces include specially designed computer, telephone, and meeting rooms. In the free address system, reservations are not made very far in advance, and the work spaces can be used by any group in the company. In this environment, employees must request space based on the needs of their particular task.

"Telecommuting" is a concept encompassing a work environment rather than a workplace. Today, many types of work can be performed in any location that has access to information. In many cases, a computer, modem, fax, and telephone are all that an employee needs to successfully perform his or her job. As long as the information link is maintained, the employee can be located anywhere. Telecommuting initially evolved as a result of environmental concerns.

Each of these concepts has been used successfully to resolve some of the problems associated with traditional workplaces and environments. Each has unique advantages as well as drawbacks. Part of the challenge that the organization faces in improving its performance is to become more involved in studying and directing the workplace and work environment.

CONCLUSION

Interior programming and space planning are critical for the successful use and operation of a facility as well as for optimal work performance by the employees. The facility professional, customer, design firm, and members of the project team all make creative contributions to this effort. Within this process, the stages of document development discussed in chapter 5 also take place for interior projects. The success of the project rests with a good interior design solution, detailed contract documents, and a successful bidding of the project. All work must be thoroughly managed and coordinated by the facility professional and his or her staff to ensure that the customer can move into and occupy a work environment that meets current needs and is flexible enough to accommodate future needs.

Chapter Seven

Construction and Renovation Work

In chapter 6, we reviewed interior programming and design; now we consider construction and renovation work, which completes step 6 in Exhibit 6.1. We then initiate step 7 with issues of move-in and occupancy. Chapter 8 covers the details of maintenance and operations processes.

CAPITAL AND CHURN PROJECTS

Capital and churn construction and renovation projects are generally defined within organizations by the funding mechanism (capital or expense funds), by the number and cost to move employees, or by the complexity of the project.

Capital projects usually require the approval of the organization's finance committee, president, or chairperson depending on the size of the dollar/resource request. These projects are strategic in nature and call for substantial amounts of organizational time and financial resources.

Churn projects usually cost less and may involve varying amounts of preparation time, from little or none to many weeks of planning and internal coordination. Most churn projects deal with the relocation of employees, their personal belongings, furniture, equipment, and records. Construction or renovation within the occupied space is often a small matter compared with the overall relocation. Churn projects are either funded by the requesting department from their own funds or from the facility department's churn fund. In organizations that charge back the cost of churn projects to the requesting department, the facility management department may define churn as chargeable to the department, not to a capital project.

Capital Construction Projects

Once you and your customer select a location (chapter 4), your customer will require, in addition to legal documentation and design and construction documents (chapters 5 and 6), a managed process to ensure that the operations facility is constructed and relocation is completed on time and on budget. The in-house facility project manager must address the associated internal project management and coordination in a timely manner.

Exhibit 7.1 shows a capital project flowchart that documents the step-by-step process most capital projects must follow to satisfy senior management and operational requirements and to keep the project on schedule and on or under budget. At the top of the flowchart, a decision block asks the question "Funding Approved." Without capital funding, the project is not approved, and your customer must either resubmit the project or find an alternative solution. If capital funding is approved, the project can continue through the steps shown in the flowchart. To the left of Capital Project Manager is a dotted block that says "Real Estate." With capital fund approval, you need the assistance of your real estate department should your customer require a new facility; alternatively, real estate may be able to identify surplus corporate property or facilities for your customer.

The process shown in the flowchart is simplified for the sake of illustration. Larger projects have a more complex process in which numerous approvals are required and governmental regulation plays a prominent role in the approval, start, completion, and move into the facility.

Churn Projects

After moving into the new facility, the customer may find immediately or during occupancy that it is necessary to relocate staff, functions, walls, doors, equipment, and so on. This relocation during occupancy is known as *churn* (see Exhibit 7.2) and usually pertains to smaller moves or projects that rarely require separate capital funds. Your customer(s) will again require a facility project manager to ensure that their operations are addressed in a businesslike and timely manner. In leased facilities, the facility project manager often coordinates the work for the customer through the building landlord and with the approval of the landlord.

The churn project flowchart shown in Exhibit 7.2 documents the step-by-step process that most churn projects must follow to satisfy customer and operational requirements and to keep the project on schedule. The process shown in the flowchart illustrates a simplified review; the process for larger projects is more complex, as numerous approvals are required and governmental regulation plays a prominent role in the approval, start, completion, and move into the project.

PERMITS

During the documentation process, the design firm often issues a preliminary set of contract documents for review by local officials responsible for issuing construction permits. These review sessions, at times, can reduce the permitting process from many months to weeks and can uncover code issues before they become problems. Although the general contractor usually is responsible for obtaining the building permit, it is advantageous for the design firm and the facility professional to be involved in the process before the contractor applies for the building permit.

Once a site is ready to support a use, and construction documents are completed for the site improvements, the general contractor must obtain a building

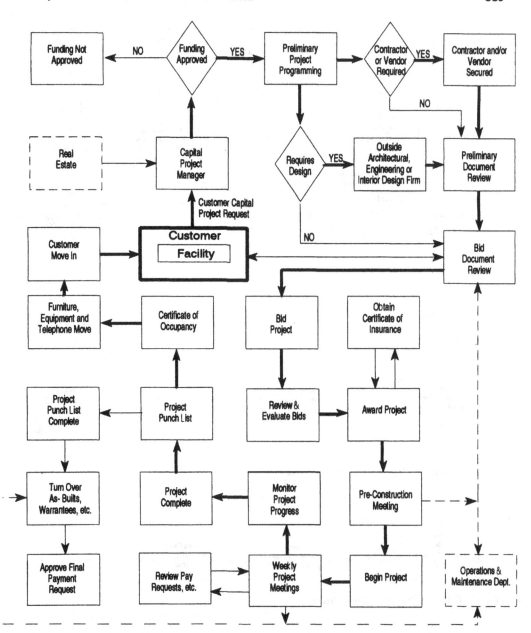

Exhibit 7.1   Capital Project Flowchart

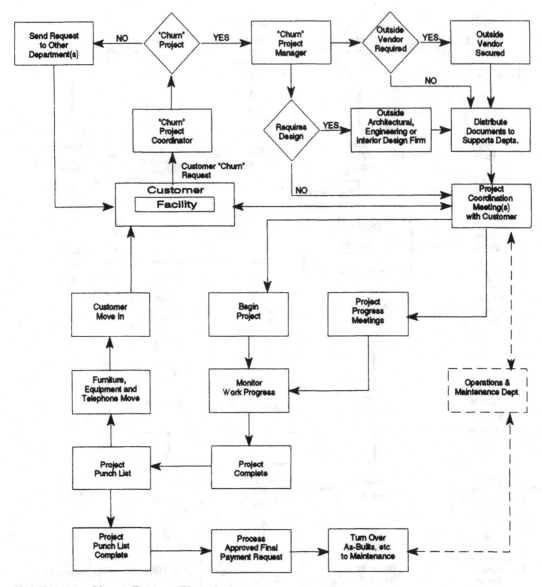

Exhibit 7.2   Churn Project Flowchart

permit before starting construction. The permit is required by the local governmental authority and cannot be issued until compliance with zoning and subdivision regulations is achieved.

The building permit and the local building code usually reference other construction codes: the HVAC code, the electrical code, the plumbing code, the gas code, and the life safety code. To obtain a building permit, the contractor's agent or the facility professional representing the corporation (property owner) must submit a complete set of construction documents for approval by the local governmental authority's building inspector. When construction starts, the work is inspected and approved on a regular basis by governmental field inspectors who work for the building inspector. If the construction work does not comply with all relevant requirements, the building inspector will not issue a certificate of occupancy, which is required before your customer can occupy and use the facility.

The key controls in the construction codes are the specification of materials and workmanship and requirements for essential components and design to meet health and life safety standards. Because the local government is not involved directly in any part of the construction, the only major points of coordination and negotiation, besides the building permit, are for hookup of essential services to the building, both during construction and for permanent occupancy.

When sites are already subdivided but have inadequate infrastructure improvements (storm drainage, sewer, power, water, stormwater retention area, roads, curbs, sidewalks, street lighting), the property owner must complete these improvements before building construction is complete and the certificate of occupancy issued. Several uses, such as individual office buildings or commercial buildings on freestanding sites, commonly call for infrastructure improvements, including dedications or payment of development or impact fees, as a condition of fulfilling obligations under the building permit.

REVIEWING AND AWARDING THE CONSTRUCTION CONTRACT

Reviewing the Contract

Bidding was discussed in chapter 5; we briefly review the subject here, as it leads to award of the construction contract. The next section contains the front-end portion of a sample bid document. The bid document usually contains the following items:

- Bid announcement
- Bid proposal form
- Detailed bid form
- List for subcontractors
- Unit prices
- Schedule of drawings
- Special conditions
- Owner-furnished items
- Project schedule
- Construction contract form
- General conditions to the construction contract
- Insurance requirements
- Project specifications
- Bid document addendum

The bid document sets the tone for the construction of the project. A good set of bid documents provides your customer with a tight spread of bids, generally all within 10 percent from the high to low bidder. A poor set of bid documents generally yields bids with a wide spread of 10 percent or more from the high to low bidder. This result indicates the information to bidders was unclear. A poor bid package leaves specifications and construction drawing interpretation open to debate and requires much clarification and probably a number of change orders.

It is incumbent upon you and your customer to review the bid package in great detail with your design firm by going over each page of the construction drawings and each page of the project specifications. When a good bid package is assembled, the construction phase of the project begins with solid information and a common understanding of the requirements. A project that starts out on a strong basis generally continues with that tone.

One document in the following sample bid announcement that is crucial to the cost and the quality of workmanship on the project is the list for subcontractors. It is your responsibility to learn the reputation of, obtain references for, and review the work of the major subcontractors on your customer's project. Your general contractor bid should provide full information on these subcontractors. Also, this list assures you of quality and prevents the general contractor from shopping the job with other subcontractors after you have awarded the contract. Just as you and your customer may choose to permit prequalified general contractor bidders to bid on your project, you may also choose to identify and prequalify selected subcontractors that the general contractor bidders must use.

The sample bid announcement includes a detailed bid form (Attachment No.1). This document is crucial to a good project bid and cost review. The detailed bid form requires bidders to provide to you and your customer specific line item costs in the format you have chosen. When bids are presented in a common format, you and your customer can compare each line item in your bid analysis, as shown in Exhibit 7.3. You can look for similar amounts for each line item and for large differences that may be cause for concern. If the spread is too large, you may need to discuss this with bidders to determine if a mistake has been made.

If the bids come in over your customer's budget, the bid evaluation form will help you identify candidates for cost reduction. You can go back to all bidders with your cost reduction requirements or choose to negotiate with your selected contractor before contract award. It is always best for both parties to agree on cost changes based on major revisions to the scope of project work *before* awarding the contract.

Please remember that it is not in the best interest of your customer or organization to award any contract if you feel or know the bidder has made a serious mistake or has misbid a large item, even if the firm has provided a bid bond. It is inevitable that even though you can require performance, the bidder will always try to make up for the loss by using shortcuts, choosing less than specified materials, or finding fault with the contract documents through many change orders.

Project Name: Relocation of ABC Company   Page 1 of 1
Project Number: 95.0023.00
Date: May 18, 1995

BID ITEM	BIDDER NO. 1	BIDDER NO. 2	BIDDER NO. 3
1. Demolition & Rubbish Removal	$8,324.00	$26,165.00	5,050.00
2. Metal Fabrication	16,525.00	16,524.00	17,210.00
3. Handrails and Railings	53,590.00	57,290.00	72,014.00
4. Carpentry (Rough)	28,180.00	18,758.00	41,950.00
5. Architectural Woodwork	1,263,207.00	1,145,204.00	1,290,880.00
6. Hollow Metal Doors & Frames	6,432.00	8,285.00	6,537.00
7. Wood Doors	81,902.00	197,135.00	200,553.00
8. Finish Hardware	73,246.00	73,246.00	85,878.00
9. Glass and Glazing	8,082.00	5,042.00	2,393.00
10. Partitions	209,781.00	212,200.00	209,781.00
11. Tile Work	in #14	1,750.00	2,900.00
12. Acoustical Ceilings	26,423.00	26,423.00	23,441.00
13. Wood Flooring	12,500.00	9,500.00	7,733.00
14. Interior Stonework	46,232.00	39,936.00	40,492.00
15. Resilient Flooring & Base	46,456.00	49,456.00	10,609.00
16. Paint and Wallcovering	183,615.00	184,571.00	184,571.00
17. Access Flooring	7,150.00	7,869.00	7869.00
Subtotal	2,071,659.00	2,079,354.00	2,209,861.00
18. Fire Protection	29,256.00	29,900.00	29,256.00
19. Plumbing	32,053.00	32,600.00	32,000.00
20. HVAC	173,855.00	169,305.00	153,400.00
21. Electrical	375,000.00	397,716.00	386,770.00
22. Appliances	12,638.00	11,900.00	12,453.00
24. Miscellaneous	32,459.00	22,753.00	51,159.00
Subtotal	655,261.00	664,174.00	665,038.00
Supervision, Cleaning, & Protection	46,582.00	42,400.00	1,920.00
Overhead & Profit	105,000.00	113,857.00	126,386.00
Subtotal	151,582.00	156,257.00	128,306.00
TOTAL BASE BID PROPOSAL	2,878,502.00	2,899,785.00	3,003,205.00
ALTERNATES			
1. Deduct for Carpet Type in Conf. Rooms	-680.00	-3,548.00	-787.00
2. Deduct for Carpet Type in Offices	-1,590.00	-634.00	-4,195.00
3. Deduct for Glue-Down Carpet	-4,891.00	-5,095.00	-6,189.00
4. Add for Concealed Sprinkler Heads	4,703.00	4,453.00	5,000.00
5. Deduct Office Shelving	-375.00	-2,957.00	-375.00
6. Add Paneling in President's Office	12,448.00	20,115.00	9,355.00
ALTERNATE TOTALS	9,615.00	12,334.00	2,809.00
TOTAL ADJUSTED BASE BID PROPOSAL	2,888,117.00	2,912,119.00	3,006,014.00

Exhibit 7.3   Bid Evaluation Form

SAMPLE: BID ANNOUNCEMENT

Sealed proposals in duplicate will be received by Mr. Bill Roberts, Project Manager for ABC Company, for furnishing all labor, materials, equipment, and services required for the construction of:

ABC Company's Corporate Headquarters
Demolition and Construction
XYZ Building
2538 North Michigan Avenue
Suite 3100
Chicago, IL 60632

until 2:00 PM CST on Tuesday, May 18, 2005, in the Office of the Director of Purchasing, ABC Company, 2107 East Wacker Drive, Suite 2150, Chicago, IL 60621, at which time and place they will be privately opened and evaluated. All bidders will be notified in writing on the outcome of the project award.

A certified check or bid bond payable to ABC Company in an amount not less than five percent (5%) of the amount of the bid but in no event more than $10,000.00 must accompany the bidder's proposal. Performance and statutory labor and material payment bonds will be required at the signing of the Contract.

Plans and Specifications dated May 2, 2005, may be obtained by the prequalified bidders from the office of Design Architects Limited, Suite 310, 2167 East Wacker Drive, Chicago, IL 60623 upon the deposit of thirty dollars ($30.00) per set. Deposits, *less five dollars ($5.00) to be retained as a proposal and plan fee per set,* will be refunded to all depositors upon return of all bid documents in good condition within ten (10) days after the date of opening of bids. Plans and specifications will be available for distribution on or about May 3, 2005.

The general nature of the project includes: Interior demolition and construction on the 30th, 31st, and 32nd floors of the XYZ Building for the relocation of ABC Company's Corporate headquarters.

All bidders bidding in amounts exceeding $20,000.00 must be licensed under the Provision of Title 34, Chapter 8, Code of Illinois, 1991.

No bid may be withdrawn after the scheduled closing time for receipt of bids for a period of thirty (30) days. ABC Company reserves the right to reject any or all bids and to waive informalities.

Mr. Harry M. Phillips
Vice President
Facility and Administrative Services
ABC Company
Chicago, IL 60621

SAMPLE PROPOSAL FORM

To: Office of the Director of Purchasing   Proposal No. _____
     ABC Company
     2107 East Wacker Drive
     Suite 2150
     Chicago, IL 60621
     Attn: Mr. Bill Roberts

                                        Date _____, 2005

The Undersigned, as Bidder, hereby declares that the only person or persons interested in the Proposal as Principal or Principals is or are as herein named and that no other person than herein named has any interest in this Proposal or in the Contract to be entered into; that this Proposal is made without connection with any other person, company, or parties making a bid or proposal; and that it is in all respects fair and in good faith, without collusion or fraud.

The Bidder further declares that he has examined the site of the Work and informed himself fully in regard to all conditions pertaining to the place where the Work is to be done, and that he has examined the Drawings and Specifications, including Addenda Nos. _____, for the Work and the other Contract Documents relative thereto, and that he has satisfied himself relative to the Work to be performed.

In compliance with your Bid Announcement and subject to all the conditions thereof, the undersigned _____ Illinois Registration No. _____ Classification _____, a corporation organized and existing under the laws of the State of _____ or a Partnership consisting of _____or an Individual trading as of the City of _____ hereby proposes to furnish all labor and materials and perform all work required for the construction of a _____
_____
_____
_____

in accordance with Drawings and Specifications dated _____, 2005 prepared by _____Architects and approved by the ABC Company, Facility Management Department.

BASE BID: For construction complete as shown and specified, the sum of _____ Dollars ($_____ . _____)

DEDUCTIVE ALTERNATES   ADDITIVE ALTERNATES

For No.1 Alternate (deduct) _____   Alternate (add) _____ No.1

For No.2 Alternate (deduct) _____   Alternate (add) _____ No.2

For No.3 Alternate (deduct) _____   Alternate (add) _____ No.3

DEDUCTIVE ALTERNATES   ADDITIVE ALTERNATES

For No.4 Alternate (deduct) _____   Alternate (add) _____ No.4

For No.5 Alternate (deduct) _____   Alternate (add) _____ No.5

For No.6 Alternate (deduct) _____   Alternate (add) _____ No.6

The Bidder agrees to complete the Work within _____ consecutive calendar days from date of Notice to Proceed.

DETAILED BID FORM (See Attachment No.1)
LIST OF SUBCONTRACTORS (See Attachment No.2)
UNIT PRICES (See Attachment No.3)

(To be filled out if certified check accompanies bid)
The undersigned further agrees that in case of failure on his part to execute the Contract Agreement and required Contract Bonds within ten (10) consecutive calendar days after being given written notice of the Award of the Contract, the check accompanying this Bid and the monies thereon shall be paid into the funds of the ABC Company as liquidated damages for such failure; otherwise the check accompanying this Proposal shall be returned to the undersigned.

Attached hereto is a certified check on the _____Bank of _____ for the sum of _____Dollars ($_____ . _____).

(To be filled out if bidder's bond accompanies bid)
The undersigned further agrees that in case of failure on his part to execute the Contract and required Contract Bonds within ten (10) consecutive calendar days after being given written notice of the award of the Contract, the Bidder's Bond accompanying this Bid is callable and the surety will be called upon by the ABC Company for the liquidation; otherwise said Bidder's Bond shall be returned to the undersigned.

Attached hereto is a bidder's bond of _____for the sum of Dollars ($ _____ . _____) made payable to _____

WITNESSES:

_____ (L.S.)

                                               (Bidder or Bidders)

_____ (L.S.)

The full names and addresses of persons and firms interested in the foregoing Bid as Principals are as follows:

_____   _____

ATTACHMENT NO.1

ABC COMPANY
DETAILED BID FORM
Relocation of ABC Company

BID ITEM   BID AMOUNT

1. Demolition and Rubbish Removal
2. Metal Fabrication
3. Handrails and Railings
4. Carpentry (Rough)
5. Architectural Woodwork
6. Hollow Metal Doors and Frames
7. Wood Doors
8. Finish Hardware
9. Glass and Glazing
10. Partitions
11. Tile Work
12. Acoustical Ceilings
13. Wood Flooring
14. Interior Stonework
15. Resilient Flooring and Base
16. Paint and Wallcovering
17. Access Flooring

Subtotal

18. Fire Protection
19. Plumbing
20. HVAC
21. Electrical
22. Appliances
23. Miscellaneous

Subtotal

Supervision, Cleaning, and Protection
Overhead and Profit

Subtotal
TOTAL BASE BID PROPOSAL

ALTERNATES

1. Deduct for Carpet Type in Conf. Rooms
2. Deduct for Carpet Type in Offices
3. Deduct for Glue-down Carpet
4. Add for Concealed Sprinkler Heads
5. Deduct Office Shelving
6. Add Paneling in President's Office

ALTERNATE TOTALS

TOTAL ADJUSTED BASE BID PROPOSAL

ATTACHMENT NO. 2
ABC COMPANY BID FORM
LIST FOR SUBCONTRACTORS

The undersigned affirms that their Base Bid as described in the Proposal Form is based upon quotes from the following subcontractors and suppliers and furthermore that if awarded the contract and upon approval of the subcontractors by ABC Company, the undersigned will retain the following subcontractors and suppliers to accomplish the work indicated.

TRADE   SUBCONTRACTOR

1. Flooring   _____

2. Partitions   _____

3. Ceiling   _____

4. Painting, etc.   _____

5. Casework   _____

6. Computer Flooring   _____

7. Plumbing   _____

8. HVAC   _____

9. Electrical   _____

10. Computer and Telecommunications Cabling   _____

                        FIRM   _____

                        BY   _____

Illinois General Contractor's LICENSE NO.   _____

ATTACHMENT NO. 3

ABC COMPANY BID FORM
UNIT PRICES

The Undersigned agrees that additions and deletions which may be called for in this work shall be done for cost in accord with GENERAL CONDITIONS Article 19 and shall not in any event exceed the following unit prices. Unit prices govern items which cannot be predicted by examination of exposed surfaces or may be requested as an extra or deleted as a credit by the ABC Company.

                        FIRM   _____

                        BY   _____

Illinois General Contractor's LICENSE NO.   _____

WORK	EXTRA	CREDIT	UNIT
1. Concrete Cutting & Patching	$_____	$_____	Square Feet
2. Partition	$_____	$_____	Linear Feet
3. Office Door	$_____	$_____	Each
4. Office Door Hardware	$_____	$_____	Hardware Set
5. Lay-in Acoustical Tile Ceiling	$_____	$_____	Square Feet
6. Painting Partitions	$_____	$_____	Square Feet
7. Wallcovering	$_____	$_____	Square Feet
8. Plastic Laminate Casework	$_____	$_____	Lin. Ft./Counter Top
9. Carpet (Corridor and Open Plan)	$_____	$_____	Square Yard
10. Carpet w/Pad (Office)	$_____	$_____	Square Yard
11. Computer Flooring	$_____	$_____	Square Feet
12. Duplex Electrical Receptacle	$_____	$_____	Each
13. Lighting Fixture Wall Switch	$_____	$_____	Each
14. 34" x 3" x 48" Lay-in Lighting Fixture	$_____	$_____	Square Feet
15. Concealed Sprinkler Head	$_____	$_____	Each

SCHEDULE OF DRAWINGS

Demolition and Construction
for ABC Company
30th, 31st, and 32nd Floors
2538 North Michigan Avenue
Suite 3100
Chicago, IL 60632

Sheets	Nos.	
1	X-1	Title Sheet, Project Location Map, and Abbreviations
2	AS-1	Demolition of Existing Structure Plans and Details
3	S-I	Interior Steel Stair Framing Plan, Sections and Schedule
4	A-1	Demolition Floor Plans
5	A-2	30th and 32nd Floor Plans
6	A-3	31st Floor Plans and Notes
7	A-4	30th and 32nd Floor Reflected Ceiling Plans
8	A-5	31st Floor Reflected Ceiling Plan and Details
9	A-6	Door and Interior Window Sections and Details
10	A-8	Door and Hardware Schedule
11	A-9	Interior Stair/Entrance Sections and Details
12	A-11	Interior Sections and Details
13	A-12	Interior Sections and Details

14	A-13	Room Finish Schedule
15	A-14	Partition Sections and Details
16	A-15	Computer Room Plan, Reflected Ceiling Plan, and Elevations
17	A-16	Library and Records Storage Plans and Details
18	M-1	Schedules and Notes
19	M-2	30th and 32nd Floor Demolition Plans
20	M-3	31st Floor Demolition Plan
21	M-4	30th and 32nd Floor HVAC Plans
22	M-5	31st Floor HVAC Plan
23	M-6	30th and 32nd Piping Plans
24	M-7	32nd Floor Piping Plan
25	M-8	Base Building Plans and Diagrams
26	M-9	XYZ Building Mechanical Room Plans and Details
27	P-1	Schedules and Notes
28	P-2	Water and Sewer Riser, Supply, and Sprinkler Piping Diagrams
29	P-3	Demolition Plans—30th and 32nd Floor Plans
30	P-4	Demolition Plan—32nd Floor Plans
31	P-5	Plumbing Plan—Crawlspace and Basement Areas
32	P-6	New Plumbing—30th and 32nd Floors
33	P-7	New Plumbing—32nd Floor
34	E-1	Schedules and Notes
35	E-2	30th and 32nd Floor Demolition Plans
36	E-3	32nd Floor Demolition Plans
37	E-4	30th and 32nd Floor Lighting and Power Plans
38	E-5	31st Lighting and Power Plan
39	E-6	Power Riser and Distribution Plans

SPECIAL CONDITIONS

1. Time of Completion:

The Contractor shall complete all work in connection with this contract within 120 consecutive calendar days of the date of Notice to Proceed.

2. Options:

Wherever the phrase "or and approved equal!" is referred to in the specifications, it shall mean that written approval of such substitute product or method must be obtained from the Architect.

Where special brand names or trademarks are included in the specifications, it is intended to be descriptive of a type, style, and quality required. Other brands of equal quality, utility, and design will be given full consideration subject to the Architect's approval.

In the event that the Contractor desires to submit a bid based on a type not included in the specifications, he must submit full data such as comprehensive literature cuts, complete specifications and/or major samples covering the product, to the Architect in ample time to be intelligently evaluated and an Addendum issued no later than four (4) days prior to the date for the opening of bids.

Items other than those covered in the specifications or included in an Addendum as approved will not be acceptable for this Project.

3. **Demolition:**

Demolition consists of the removal of any and all existing components required for the installation of new work. The Contractor shall be responsible for the protection of adjacent existing conditions that are to remain and shall be required as part of this contract to replace or repair damaged areas as required by the Landlord of XYZ Building to restore them to their present state.

4. **Fire Exits:**

All corridors on all floors of the XYZ Building serve the building as required fire exits. The Contractor shall not store materials or equipment in these corridors. The Contractor shall not place any debris from required demolition in the corridors. All debris shall be moved directly from the building immediately after it is displaced, and the corridors shall be kept broom clean at all times.

5. **Preconstruction Conference:**

Before the contractor begins any of the work on site and not later than five (5) days after the Notice to Proceed is issued to the contractor, the ABC Company Project Manager will set the agenda and chair a preconstruction meeting for the Project. This meeting shall be attended by selected members of the ABC Company Project Team, the general contractor, major subcontractors, the architect and engineer, the landlord's representative, and others invited by the Project Manager. The meeting will cover issues such as:

- Building permits and start-up
- Project schedule
- Construction contract
- Requests for payment
- Project progress inspections
- Payments
- Change order procedures
- Utilities

- Insurance
- Security and safety
- Trash removal
- Keys and locks
- ABC Company—furnished items
- Project punchlist and completion
- Certificate of occupancy
- Move-in phases and date(s)

INSTRUCTIONS TO BIDDERS

1. **INTENT OF INSTRUCTIONS**

Instructions to Bidders are included in the Contract Documents to amplify the Bid Announcement, which is abbreviated because of cost and space limitations, and to give other details which interested parties must or should know in order to prepare bids properly. Modifications hereof for this contract, if any are deemed necessary or advisable by the Architect and/or ABC Company, will be added hereto.

2. PREQUALIFICATION OF BIDDERS:

Bidders for work costing in excess of $20,000.00 must be licensed under terms of existing State laws. Any exceptions are noted in the Modifications to Instructions to Bidders. In case of a joint venture of two or more contractors the amount of the bid shall be within the maximum bid limitation as set by the State Licensing Board for General Contractors of the combined limitations of the partners to the joint venture.

Copies of the Contract Documents may be obtained from the Architect only upon payment of the deposit, and proposal and plan fee, as stated in the Bid Announcement, plus postage if delivered by mail or other courier service. Deposits will be returned to all depositors upon return of all documents in good condition within ten (10) days after date of opening of bids. The proposal and plan fee is nonrefundable and will be retained by the Architect.

3. EXAMINATION OF CONTRACT DOCUMENTS AND OF THE SITE OF THE WORK:

Before submitting a proposal for the Work, the bidders shall carefully examine the Contract Documents, visit the site, and satisfy themselves as to the nature and location of the Work, and the general and local conditions, including weather, the general character of the site or building, the character and extent of existing work within or adjacent to the site, any other work being performed thereon at the time of submission of their bids. They shall obtain full knowledge as to transportation, disposal, handling, and storage of materials, availability of water, electric power, and all other facilities in the area which will have a bearing on the performance of the Work for which they submit their proposal. The submission of a proposal shall be prima facie evidence that the bidder has made such examination and visit and has judged for and satisfied himself as to conditions to be encountered regarding the character, difficulties, quality, and qualities of work to be performed and the material and equipment to be furnished, and as to the contract requirements and contingencies involved.

If, in the performance of the Contract, subsurface or latent conditions are found to be materially different from those indicated by the Drawings and Specifications, or unknown conditions of an unusual or impractical nature are disclosed differing materially from conditions usually inherent in work of the character shown and specified, the attention of the Architect and ABC Company Project Manager shall be called immediately to such conditions before they are disturbed. Upon such notice, or upon such observation of conditions, the Architect will promptly make such changes in the Drawings and/or Specifications as he finds necessary to conform to the different conditions, and any increase or decrease in the cost of the Work resulting from such changes will be adjusted as provided under CHANGES IN THE WORK or EXTRA WORK as set forth in the GENERAL CONDITIONS as he and the ABC Company Project Manager decide.

4. EXPLANATIONS AND INTERPRETATIONS:

Should any bidder observe any ambiguity, discrepancy, omission, or error in the Drawings and Specifications, or in any other Contract Document, or be in doubt as to the intention and meaning thereof, he should at once report such to the Architect and request clarification, in writing, with copy of his request to the ABC Company Project Manager.

Clarification will be made only by written Addenda sent to all prospective bidders. Neither the Architect, ABC Company Project Manager, or ABC Company will be responsible in any manner for verbal answers regarding intent or meaning of the Contract Documents, or for any verbal instructions, by whomsoever made, prior to the award of the Contract.

Should conflict occur in or between Drawings and Specifications, a bidder will be deemed to have estimated on the more expensive way of doing the work involved unless he shall have asked for and obtained the written decision of the Architect before submission of his proposal, as to method, materials, or equipment which will be required.

5. CONTENTS OF PROPOSAL FORM:

The Architect or the ABC Company Project Manager, as stated in the Bid Announcement, will furnish bidders blank Proposal Forms for the Work contemplated, indicating the lump-sum bid items, alternate bid items, and unit price bid items. Blank proposal quantity forms will also be furnished.

Where bids are requested on a unit price basis, final payment to the Contractor will be made for only the actual quantities of the respective unit price pay items of the Work performed, at the contract unit prices bid in the Proposal, as finally determined during the progress or after completion of the Work.

6. COMBINATION BIDS OR PROPOSALS:

If the ABC Company so elects, Proposal Forms may be issued for projects or parts of projects in combination or separately. In any case, the Bid Procedures as set forth in the Bid Documents must be adhered to. Award or awards will be made to the qualified bidder or bidders strictly in accordance with the bidding procedures.

7. LIQUIDATED DAMAGES:

Time is of the essence of the Contract, and the bidder's attention is called to that clause of the GENERAL CONDITIONS which requires the deduction of a stipulated time charge equal to six percent (6%) interest per annum on the total Contract Price for the Work for the entire period that any part of the Work remains uncompleted after the time specified in the Contract Documents for completion of the Work which will be deducted by the ABC Company Project Manager from the final estimate and retained by the ABC Company out of the moneys otherwise due the Contractor in the Final Payment, not as a penalty but liquidated damages sustained by the ABC Company.

8. PREPARATION OF PROPOSAL:

The Bidder's Proposal must be submitted on the Proposal Form furnished him by the Architect or the ABC Company Project Manager as stated in the Bid Announcement.

The Bidder must specify, both in words and figures, without interlineations, alterations, or erasures a lump-sum price for each lump-sum item including alternate prices—a unit price for each of the separate items, as well as the gross sum for which he will perform all of the estimated Work as required by the Contract

Documents. In case of discrepancy between the prices shown in figures and in words, the words will govern.

The Proposal shall be properly signed by the Bidder. If the Bidder is an individual, his name and post office address must be shown; if a firm or partnership, the name and post office address of each member of the firm or partnership must be shown; if a corporation, the president, vice president, or secretary shall sign and affix the corporate seal, or if the person signing the Proposal is an agent, the said agent must attach written authorization from the president, vice president or secretary of the corporation, and the Proposal must show the name of the corporation, the name of the state under the laws of which the corporation is chartered and the names, titles, and business address of the officers.

9. PROPOSAL GUARANTY:

No Proposal submitted will be considered unless accompanied by a certified check or Bid Bond made payable to the ABC Company in an amount not less than five percent (5%) of the Contractor's bid, but in no event more than twenty thousand dollars ($20,000.00), as a guaranty that the Bidder will enter into a contract with the ABC Company for the performance of the Work and furnish Contract Bonds for the Work if it is awarded to him.

10. DELIVERY OF PROPOSALS:

Each Proposal shall be placed, together with the Proposal Guaranty, in a sealed envelope on the outside of which is written in large letters "Proposal" and so marked as to identify the Work bid on and the name of the Bidder. Proposals may be delivered in person, or by mail if ample time is allowed for delivery. When sent by mail, preferably special delivery or registered, the sealed Proposal, marked as indicated above, shall be enclosed in another envelope for mailing. Proposals will be received at the place stated and until the hour of the date set in Bid Announcement for their opening unless notice is given of postponement. No proposal will be accepted or considered which has not been received prior to the hour of the opening date.

11. WITHDRAWAL OR REVISION OF PROPOSALS:

A Proposal may be withdrawn at any time prior to the hour fixed for opening of Proposals, provided a request in writing executed by the Bidder or his duly authorized representative is filed with the Architect or ABC Company Project Manager prior to that time, in which case such Proposal when received will be returned to the Bidder unopened. Telegrams, facsimiles or written communications to correct Proposals will be accepted and the Proposal corrected in accordance therewith if received by the Architect or ABC Company Project Manager prior to the hour set in the Bid Announcement. No Proposal shall be withdrawn, modified, or corrected after the hour set for opening such Proposals.

12. OPENING OF PROPOSALS:

Proposals will be opened and read privately by ABC Company management. Bidders or their authorized agents are not invited to be present.

13. IRREGULAR PROPOSALS:

Proposals may be rejected if they contain any omissions, alterations of forms, additions not called for, conditional bids, alternate bids unless called for, incomplete bids, erasures, or irregularities of any kind. Proposals in which the unit or lump-sum prices bid are obviously unbalanced may be rejected.

14. ERRORS IN BID:

In case of error in the extension of prices, the unit price will govern. In case of discrepancy between the prices shown in the figures and in words, the words will govern.

15. DISQUALIFICATION OF BIDDERS:

Any Bidder using the name or different names for submitting more than one Proposal upon any unit, portion, part, or section of work will be disqualified from further consideration on that part of the Work. Evidence that any bidder is interested, as a principal, in more than one Proposal for the Work (for example, bidding in a partnership; as a joint partnership or association and as a partnership, association, or individual) will cause the rejection of any such Proposal. A bidder may, however, submit a Proposal as a principal and as a subcontractor to some other principal, or may submit a Proposal as a subcontractor to any other principals as he desires, and by so doing will not be liable to disqualification.

If there is reason for believing that collusion exists among the bidders any or all Proposals may be rejected, and participants in such collusion may not be considered in future Proposals for the same work. Proposals in which prices are obviously unbalanced or unresponsive to the Bid Announcement may be rejected.

The right is reserved to reject a Proposal from a Bidder who has not paid, or satisfactorily settled, all bills due for labor and material on former contracts in force at the time of letting.

16. CONSIDERATION OF BIDS:

After the Proposals are opened and read, the Contract Bid Prices will be compared and the results of such comparison and recommendations will be delivered by the ABC Project Manager to ABC Company management for review and consideration. Until the final award of the Contract, however, the ABC Company reserves the right to reject any and all Proposals, and to waive technical error if, in his judgment, the best interests of the ABC Company will thereby be promoted.

17. DETERMINATION OF LOW BIDDER BY USE OF ALTERNATES:

Where deductive alternate bids are deemed necessary in order to reduce the base bid to an amount within the funds available for the project, any alternatives from the base bid shall constitute cumulative deductions from the base bid, and in determining lowest bidder the ABC Company management will proceed to consider the bids upon the basis of the base bids of all bidders minus the respective reductions sited for the first alternate. If the lowest bid so determined is not then within the funds available, ABC Company management will proceed to consider the base bids minus the first and second alternates together to determine the lowest bidder, and in like manner throughout all alternates, if necessary, so that in no event will there be any discretion as to which alternate or alternates will be used in determining the lowest bidder.

Where additive alternate bids are deemed necessary in order to obtain prices for the addition of necessary items not included in the base bid because of possible bid variations from the estimated cost, and the lowest base bid is less than the amount of funds available for the project, any additive alternates included shall constitute cumulative additions to the base bid and in determining the lowest bidder ABC Company management will proceed to consider the bids upon the basis of the base bids of all bidders plus the respective additions stated for the first alternate. If the lowest bid so determined is not then within the funds available, ABC Company management will proceed to consider the base bids plus the first and second alternates together to determine the lowest bidder, and in like manner throughout all alternates, if necessary, so that in no event will there be any discretion as to which alternate or alternates will be used in determining the lowest bidder.

When the lowest responsible bidder has been determined as set forth above, ABC Company management may accept or reject any alternates, deductive or additive.

18. AWARD OF CONTRACT:

The Contract will be awarded to the lowest responsible bidder complying with all established requirements of the Contract Documents unless ABC Company management finds that his bid is unreasonable or that it is not to the interest of the ABC Company to accept it.

A bidder to whom award is made will be notified by telegram, facsimile, or letter to the address shown on his Proposal at the earliest possible date.

19. RETURN OF PROPOSAL GUARANTIES:

All Proposal Guaranties, except those of the three lowest bona fide bidders, will be returned immediately after Proposals have been checked, tabulated, and the relation of the Proposals established. The Proposal Guaranty of the three lowest bidders will be returned as soon as the Contract Bonds and the Contract of the successful Bidder have been properly executed and approved. When the Award is deferred for a period of time longer than fifteen days after the opening of the Proposals, all Proposal Guaranties except that of the successful Bidder will be returned. Should no award be made within thirty (30) days, all Proposals will be rejected and all guaranties returned, unless the successful Bidder agrees in writing to a stipulated extension in time for his/her bid, in which case the ABC Company may, at their discretion, permit the successful Bidder to substitute a satisfactory bidders bond for the certified check submitted with his/her Proposal as a Proposal Guaranty.

20. EXECUTION OF CONTRACT:

The Contract shall be signed by the successful Bidder, in the number of counterparts provided in the Contract Agreement, and returned to the ABC Company Project Manager through the Architect with satisfactory Contract Bonds within ten (10) days after the date of Notice of Award.

21. REQUIREMENTS OF CONTRACT BONDS:

In order to insure faithful performance of each and every condition, stipulation, and requirement of the Contract and to indemnify and save harmless ABC Company from any and all damages, either directly or indirectly (arising out of any failure to perform same), the successful Bidder to whom the Contract is awarded shall, within ten (10) days from the date of award, furnish at his expense and file with the ABC Company Project Manager an acceptable Surety Bond in an amount equal to one hundred (100) percent of the Contract Price of the Contract as awarded. Said Bond shall be made on the approved Bond form, shall be furnished by a surety duly authorized and qualified to make such bonds in the State of Illinois, shall be cosigned by an authorized agent resident in the State who is qualified for the execution of such instruments, and shall have attached thereto power of attorney of the signing official. Should extenuating circumstances prevail, the ABC Company may grant an extension of time not exceeding five (5) days for the return of the Contract and Contract Bond. In case of default on the part of the Contractor, all expenses incident to ascertaining and collecting losses suffered by the ABC Company under the Bond, the direct costs of administration, architectural, engineering, and legal services, shall lie against the Contract Bond for Performance of the Work.

In addition thereto the successful Bidder to whom the Contract is awarded shall, within ten (10) days, furnish at his expense and file with the ABC Company Project Manager another Bond with good and sufficient surety payable to the ABC Company in an amount not less than fifty percent (50%) of the Contract Period, with the obligation that the Contractor shall promptly make payment to all persons furnishing him or them with labor, material, or supplies for or in prosecution of the Work provided for in the Contract and for the payment of reasonable attorney's fees, incurred by successful claimants or plaintiffs in suits on said Bond.

22. APPROVAL OF CONTRACT:

No Contract is binding upon the ABC Company until it has been approved by ABC Company management and executed by the Vice President, Real Estate and Facility Services. The date of the final execution of the Contract shall be the date on which it is signed by the Vice President, Real Estate and Facility Services.

23. FAILURE TO EXECUTE CONTRACT:

Should the successful Bidder or Bidders to whom a Contract is awarded fail to execute a Contract and furnish acceptable Contract Bonds within ten days following the date of Award, ABC Company shall retain from the Proposal Guaranty if it be a certified check or recover from the Principal or the Sureties if the guaranty be a bid bond the difference between the amount of the Contract as awarded and the amount of the proposal of the next lowest bidder. If no other bids are received, the full amount of the Proposal Guaranty shall be so retained or recovered as liquidated damages for such default. Any sums so retained or recovered shall be the property of the ABC Company. In the event of the death of the low bidder (if an individual and not a partnership or corporation) between the date of the opening of the bids and the ten (10) days following the date of award of Contract, allowed for furnishing the Contract Bonds, the ABC Company shall return the Proposal Guaranty intact to the estate of the deceased low bidder.

Failure by the Owner to compete the execution of a Contract and to issue a Notice to
Proceed within ten days after its presentation by the Contractor shall be just cause,
unless both parties agree in writing to a stipulated extension in time for issuance of a
Notice to Proceed, for withdrawal of the Contractor's bid and Contract Agreement
without forfeiture of certified check or bond.

Awarding the Contract

When you and your customer are ready to award the construction contract, you
may wish to notify the general contractor with a letter to proceed, which basically
awards the contract to their firm under the conditions of the bid and any agreed-
on changes, requests their detailed project schedule, insurance, and bond documents, and sets up preconstruction meeting with the major parties in the project.
In the next section is a sample contract agreement for construction. Some organizations require that both parties sign this kind of contract before any work
begins; they do not permit the use of the letter to proceed without a signed construction contract. The American Institute of Architects (AIA, A Series), the Association of General Contractors, and other associations have standard boilerplate
construction contracts that you may choose to use.

SAMPLE: CONTRACT AGREEMENT FOR CONSTRUCTION

THIS AGREEMENT, entered into this _____ day of _____, 20____, by and between the ABC Company, a subsidiary of XYZ Corporation and party of the first part (hereinafter called the Owner), and _____ party of the second part (hereinafter called the Contractor).

WITNESSETH that the Owner and the Contractor, in consideration of premises of the mutual covenants, considerations, and agreements herein contained, agree as follows:

STATEMENT OF WORK: The Contractor shall furnish all labor and materials and perform all work for the_____

_____

_____

_____

in strict and entire conformity with the Contract Documents dated _____, 20___, prepared by Architect(s), and approved by the ABC Company Real Estate and Facility Services Department, including Addenda thereto dated _____ all of which are hereby made a part of this Agreement as fully and to the same effect as if the same had been set forth at length in the body of this Agreement.

TIME OF COMPLETION: The Work shall be commenced on a date to be specified in a written proceed order of the ABC Company Vice President of Real Estate and Facility Services, and shall be completed within _____ (_____) calendar days from and after said date as provided in the Contract Documents.

COMPENSATION TO BE PAID: The Owner will pay and the Contractor will accept in full consideration for the performance of the Work, subject to additions and deductions (including liquidated damages) as provided in the Contract Documents, the sum of _____ Dollars ($_____._____), being the amount of the Contractor's Base Bid for the aforesaid work, including the following Alternate Prices:

_____

_____

_____

_____

_____

_____

_____

_____

_____

_____

PARTIAL PAYMENTS: In making partial payments, there shall be retained 10 percent on the estimated amounts until completion of 50 percent of the contract, after which 5 percent shall be withheld and paid to the Contractor at the completion of the Work with the final payment.

OTHER CONDITIONS OR PROVISIONS: _____

_____

_____

_____

_____

_____

    The Contractor and the ABC Company for themselves, their successors, executors, administrators, and assigns, hereby agree to the full performance of the covenants herein contained.

    IN WITNESS WHEREOF, The Parties hereto on the day and year first above written have executed this Agreement in four counterparts, each of which shall, without proof or accounting for the other counterparts, be deemed an original.

    In compliance with the approval of the Board of Directors of ABC Company, the ABC Company hereby certifies that this contract was let in accordance with the provisions of the ABC Company Construction Policy No. 04–01 and as amended on February 12, 2005.

ABC COMPANY   **CONTRACTOR**

_____   _____

PRECONSTRUCTION MEETING

All successful projects start off with a definite plan so that all parties understand their responsibilities and performance requirements. To help kick off your customer's project, we strongly recommend that you hold a preconstruction meeting as soon as possible after project award and before any work begins on site.

A preconstruction meeting agenda similar to that shown in Exhibit 7.4 should be developed and sent to attendees before the meeting to ensure that they are prepared to address their part in the project. Attendees should include the facility project manager, your customer, selected in-house project team members (MIS, telecommunications, maintenance, and operations), the design firm representative and special consultants, the general contractor, major subcontractors, and others as required.

In real estate, the buzzword is location, location, location. In construction, the buzzword is time, time, time. There are situations were no amount of money can make up for lost time. (Time is not really lost, but it has not been managed.) It is your responsibility at the preconstruction meeting to stress the management of time and information. Review communication requirements and your role as the project manager for your customer. Each project has its own problems, but they can be resolved with no loss of overall project time or additional cost if addressed promptly. It is when members of the project team, the contractor, or his or her suppliers or subcontractors wait until there is no time to implement the easier alternate solution that projects run into time and cost troubles. Being honest and candid during this meeting and during the entire construction process are major recommendations for project success. You and your customer don't want any major surprises during the project, and ongoing communication among all concerned should avoid them.

During this meeting, review in detail the project schedule (see Exhibit 4.13). It must address critical path items for construction and other items your customer must provide. Verify with the contractor that he or she will be providing all specified name-brand items that your customer has requested and agreed to pay for. Some contractors try to reduce their costs by providing alternate products for approval late in the construction process, claiming that the specified items could not be obtained in time. Should the design require a specified material that may not be available when needed, the general contractor must make certain to identify, order, and secure these items in a timely manner. You or your customer must also ensure that delivery and installation of owner-furnished items (e.g., carpet, security systems, millwork) and items such as furnishings, telecommunications, and computer requirements are coordinated with the project schedule.

The meeting should cover progress payments, the format required, who they should be sent to, who will review them, how they will be reviewed, when they will be sent to accounting, the check-processing time, and other payment documentation requirements such as lien waivers and schedule updates. Also, you should review change order procedures. We strongly recommend that all requests for change orders be made in a timely manner and managed through the facility project manager. Neither the customer, design firm, nor the general contractor should have unilateral permission to proceed with a change order without prior approval by the facility project manager. We have seen an otherwise good project

Date: Monday, June 26, 2005
Place: XYZ Building, Suite 2510
Purpose: ABC Company Construction and Relocation Preconstruction Meeting
Attendees: ABC Company: John Smith
                                       Susan Martin
                                       Bob Philips
                                       Russ Abbott
               Interior Designers & Assoc.:   Richard DeVane
               Consulting Engineers, Inc.:   Jerry Murphry
               Specialty Construction Co.:   Terry Dodd
               XYZ Building: James Zoss
                                         Sarah Pitman

<u>Discussion Items:</u>

1. XYZ Building requirements
   a. Building access
   b. Preconstruction review of the condition of finished core areas
   c. Freight and passenger elevator usage
2. Construction contract
3. Certificate of insurance
4. Bonds
5. Construction schedule
6. Permits and construction documents
7. Long lead items
8. Communication requirements
9. Change orders
10. Progress payments
11. Construction progress meetings
12. Carpet and plastic laminate provided by ABC Company
13. Keying and test and balance
14. Alternates:
    a. Customer furniture
    b. Wood parquet flooring
15. Voice and data cabling
16. Telephone switch
17. Security system
18. Paging system and sound system for the multipurpose room
19. High-density library and file room shelving

Exhibit 7.4   Preconstruction Meeting Agenda

20. Dumbwaiter
21. Specialty items:
    a. Systems furnishing
    b. Chandeliers
    c. Custom rugs
    d. Secretarial desks
    e. Library circulation desk
    f. Reception desks
    g. Board room conference table
21. Miscellaneous items:
    a. Safety
    b. Smoking, etc.
    c. Visitors
22. Other items

Exhibit 7.4 Preconstruction Meeting Agenda (Continued)

come to a sad ending at completion because the general contractor provided a number of change orders that the customer orally approved without understanding the magnitude of costs or the legal implications of that approval. Make sure everyone at the preconstruction meeting understands who controls the project purse strings.

Be sure to clarify items unique to your customer's business requirements. Finally, discuss safety and security at the project site, progress meetings, coordination with the landlord and his or her staff, the certificate of occupancy, the punchlist process, and the final payment process.

By the end of the preconstruction meeting, all attendees should have a better understanding of the project as well as its unresolved issues and items requiring further research. Within three days of the preconstruction meeting, issue a contact listing sheet (see Exhibit 7.5) and meeting minutes to all attendees and project team members with assignments for follow-up reports at the first construction progress meeting.

CONSTRUCTION

Your role during construction is to ensure that your customer's plans and requirements are constructed, installed, and completed on time and within budget. Your customer, your staff and in-house project team members, design firm, project consultants and vendors, general contractor, and the subcontractors are key players in making the project a success.

Before work starts at the project site, the general contractor must provide to you the required certificate of insurance and any bonds (i.e., performance and payment) and must acquire the permits for the project as required by the local permitting authority.

Progress Meetings

Weekly or biweekly project meetings on major projects are necessary. These meetings should be onsite whenever possible to enable a candid review of progress, problems, and proposed solutions; cost to date; change order items and their costs; schedule adjustments and delivery requirements; shop drawing submittals; and sample and color approvals. Items requiring action at the previous progress meeting should be reviewed to ensure that the matters were resolved and approved by you and your customer.

Payment and Change Order Review

Monthly progress payments must be made based on actual costs of the work and material in place and stored on the site. Change order work must be carefully reviewed, approved, and managed in a timely manner (see Exhibit 3.6).

As the work progresses, you must continue to ensure that all construction and nonconstruction items are being installed and completed as required. During this time and throughout the project, it is vital that your customer remain involved in project review, decisions, payment, and changes, if required, to the schedule.

SERVICE OR PRODUCT	CONTRACTOR/VENDOR	CONTACT	PH. #(312)/FAX#
ABC Company	ABC Co. Facility Management Department	Susan Martin	FAX #
Interior Design/Construction Administration	Design Firm		FAX #
HVAC/Plumbing/Electrical Engineer	Engineering Firm		FAX #
General Construction	Construction Company		FAX #
Voice and Data Cabling	Voice & Data Cabling Vendor		FAX #
Security System	Security System Vendor		Fax #
Paging and Sound System	Paging and Sound System Vendor		Fax #
H. D. Mobile and Library Shelving	H.D. Mobile Shelving Vendor		Fax #
General, Office, and Systems Furniture.	Furniture Dealer/Installer		FAX #
Custom Public Area and Secretarial Furniture	Custom Furniture Manufacturer		FAX #
Window Treatment (Drapery and Blinds)	Window Treatment Vendor		
Telephone Switch and Voice Mail	Telephone Switch Vendor		FAX #
Furniture Reupholstery and Refinishing	Reupholstery Vendor		
Copy Tracking System	Tracking System Vendor		
Copy Center Service	Copy Center Vendor		
Coffee, Soft Drinks and Vending	Refreshment Vendor		
Interior Room Signage	Signage Vendor		FAX #
Elevator Lobby Signage	Elev. Lobby Signage Vendor		
Special Custom Rugs	Special Custom Rug Vendor		FAX #
Computer Equipment Relocation	Computer Relocation Vendor		
Furniture and Equipment Relocation	Moving Vendor		FAX #
Plants and Planters	Plant Vendor		FAX #
Artwork	Rematting and Reframing Vendor		FAX #
Landlord Construction Representative	Landlord Constr. Rep.		FAX #
Landlord Building Manager	Landlord Prop. Mgmt.		FAX #

Exhibit 7.5   ABC Company–XYZ Building, Chicago, IL Contact List

PROJECT COSTS

During the project, the facility project manager is responsible for managing all costs associated with the project, including the general contract and owner-furnished items. Your original approved budget (see Exhibit 3.5) is the basis for all project costs. As the project progresses, commitments are made, contracts are awarded, and purchase and change orders are issued, you must track the project costs versus project commitments versus project payments and the balance of funds remaining (see Exhibit 3.7). Without this information, neither you nor your customer can truly know what all phases and items in the project are costing.

If you are managing the project, it is your responsibility to ensure and protect your customer's time and financial resources. Your proactive management of all project costs is essential to bringing the project in on time and within or below budget in every segment, not just general construction.

Chapter 3 describes a corporate capital tracking system whose integrated, consistent methodology creates and manages a computerized database in conjunction with the capital budget approval process, preliminary budgets and approved funding, purchase and change orders, invoices, payments, and project closeout. Whether you have an automated or manual process, your responsibility for project funds and time is critical and essential to success.

Allowances

Many lease agreements provide allowances (funds) that can be used by your customer to cover all or a portion of the costs for the design, construction of the premises, relocation, and so on. Your customer often requires construction work to get the space ready before it can be occupied. The cost of this work is paid for either by the landlord or your customer, or it is prorated between the landlord and your customer. As part of the negotiating process, the lease identifies who pays and is responsible for what work, at what cost, and within what design and construction schedule before the lease is executed. The construction allowance can take one of the following forms and is often attached as an exhibit to the lease:

- A landlord's work letter and construction schedule, including design and construction completion dates, cost, and work the landlord will pay for before the premises is delivered to the tenant, the cost and work that the landlord will do but the tenant will pay for, and the work that the tenant will pay for and do during or after the landlord finishes its work.

- A dollar allowance per usable square foot provided by the landlord; the landlord will schedule all design and construction work for the space as requested, pay all design and permit fees, and pay for all construction work; the tenant will reimburse the landlord for costs over the total allowance amounts.

- A dollar allowance per usable square foot provided by the landlord; the tenant will be responsible for all design work, permits and fees, scheduling the work, hiring a general contractor, and completing and paying for all work;

the tenant will request reimbursement from the landlord for all costs up to the total allowance amounts.

The cost, responsibility, design and construction schedule should specify in detail:

- Landlord coordination or management fees (if any)
- Design and/or engineering firm/fees/services
- Design and construction documents/changes
- Work to be completed by the landlord
- Work to be completed by the tenant (your customer)
- Access to the premises
- The definition of substantial completion tied to receipt of the certificate of occupancy
- Improvement schedule/milestone dates
- Change order procedures
- Insurance
- Lien waivers
- Permitting and certificate of occupancy
- Bonus/penalty or late penalty clause

Other allowances can include a dollar amount per rentable (preferable) or usable square foot for design and/or engineering fees, moving, telecommunications, carpet, furnishings, and so on. These nonconstruction allowances can be paid to your customer in cash, usually as a reimbursable expense. Should the allowance not be totally expended, your negotiation should include your customer's option to take the balance due in cash or apply it to operating expenses or rent abatement.

As the facility project manager, you should be aware of these clauses in the lease agreement and manage these funds to ensure that your customer obtains the maximum benefit from them.

CERTIFICATE OF OCCUPANCY AND PUNCHLIST

The certificate of occupancy is a key document issued by the local permitting authority. When construction is complete and final building inspections are passed, you should obtain the original of this certificate or a copy from the general contractor before move-in. Your customer's lease should be tied to that certificate of occupancy date as being the lease commencement date as of which your customer can operate his or her business from this new address. You may also wish to tie the lease commencement date to the acquisition of all or certain utilities needed for the customer's business. If, for example, the customer must have two feeders of main electrical power to the facility and only one has been installed, the customer may not want to begin operation without the second feeder.

Punchlist

Before the customer physically moves into the leased or owned facility, a punchlist of incomplete construction, business items, and building services should be made by you with your customer, the design firm, other in-house support department representatives (maintenance, MIS, security), and the general contractor with his or her subcontractors. As a minimum, before the punchlist inspection, these conditions should pertain in the project space:

- The site should be clean of debris, construction material, and all tools belonging to the general contractor or subcontractors.

- Ceiling tiles should be in place, sprinkler heads on, light fixtures on with all lamps burning.

- Rest room toilet partitions should be up and fixtures in place and working.

- All mechanical and electrical systems should be up, running, and tested and balanced.

- Wallcovering or finished paint coat on walls and touch-up painting should be complete.

- Doors and door frames should be in place, operable, and painted or stained.

- Door and window hardware should be installed and operable, including keys and cylinders.

- Floors should be vacuumed in carpeted areas and cleaned and finished in wood and other hard-surface areas.

- Electrical, telephone, and computer receptacles, switches, and cover plates of the right color and design should be in place.

- Major mechanical and electrical rooms should be broom clean; equipment should be tested, balanced, and operational. Pumps and piping should be coded, painted as required, and labeled. Electrical panel boards and circuits should be labeled.

- Exhaust fans should be tested and the HVAC system balanced on each floor and in each zone on each floor. Thermostats should be tested and set for each zone.

- Fire protection system equipment should be in place, tested, and adjusted.

- Boxes and cutouts for owner-furnished security system should be in place and ready for system installation.

- Owner-furnished items that the general contractor was responsible for installing, such as carpet, wallcovering, and special light fixtures, should be installed, cleaned, and adjusted.

- Exterior site work should be complete: Road and parking paving complete; parking striped; sidewalks installed; electrical and natural gas service installed and operational; storm drainage installed and operating; fire hydrants (if required) in place, tested, and operational; site rough grading complete; landscaping complete, with all grass, plants, and trees installed; parking lot lighting installed and operational.

When the punchlist inspection is complete, copies of the punchlist should be distributed to all concerned parties, including the landlord, for review and correction as necessary and where required.

The punchlist should *not* be used as a means by which the general contractor can abdicate management or responsibility to complete all parts of the project. We have seen projects where a contractor who has obviously not kept up with the work of the subcontractors tries to use the punchlist as a management tool at the end of the project. Before you agree to schedule a punchlist meeting, walk the project and inspect the work. If numerous incorrect or incomplete items are plainly visible in most spaces during your walk-through, then the contractor is not ready for the punchlist meeting. You are not helping your customer or yourself by doing an early punchlist for the general contractor.

When the general contractor completes the punchlist satisfactorily, project closeout can be completed. Before the general contractor and other major suppliers and contractors receive final payment, all tests should be completed successfully, training on specific equipment should be completed, and all as-built drawings, service manuals, warranties, guarantees, and lien waivers must be executed and turned over to you, your customer, or maintenance and operations.

Also, if your project was produced by your design firm on a CADD system and if your design agreement requires that you receive a copy of the CADD information at the end of the project, you should now obtain that copy on a CD.

OWNER-FURNISHED ITEMS

As discussed in chapter 6, your customer will be occupying the facility and space to provide a service or product. Furniture, telephone system and equipment, computers and printers, raised floor, emergency power supply monitoring equipment, computer networks, fax machines, sound systems, mail and copy room equipment, file room shelving, carpet, window shades, blinds or drapes, refreshment center equipment, special light fixtures and hardware, security system, electronic door locks, keys and cylinders, signage, artwork, and other items not included in the construction contract must be identified, inventoried, designed, specified, bid, ordered, received and inspected, installed, adjusted, and cleaned before your customer can begin to work in the space or facility. Exhibit 7.5 lists a number of owner-furnished items and suppliers for these services and products.

It is important to manage these contracts as well as you manage the construction contract. Working successfully with service and product suppliers means that information and scheduling must be coordinated with your contractor, customer, in-house project team members, and landlord.

Your major owner-furnished-item suppliers and installers should be included at appropriate progress meetings to obtain their input and to review with the general contractor their requirements, especially for getting into the space and into areas, walls, and ceilings before they are closed off. Protection of contractor work in progress and completed work should be discussed in detail to reduce finger-pointing should damage occur.

Delivery notice, receipt, inspection, storage (if required), installation, adjustment, cleaning, and cleanup of trash and shipping debris must be fully coordinated to ensure a smooth transition from one owner-furnished item to another. With literally dozens of owner-furnished item contracts, the facility project manager must be fully aware of the staging and delivery requirements of all suppliers and product suppliers to ensure that they can get into the space and complete their work without running into each other.

Your goal as the facility project manager for capital and churn projects should be to have your customer move in with all items in place and all equipment fully tested and operational, including signage and artwork. This goal can be achieved and, with the right team, it becomes the rule, not the exception (which your customer expected anyway).

RELOCATION

As the facility project manager, you spend considerable time planning and coordinating the relocation of the customer's employees, production equipment, signage, furnishings, artwork, valuables, records, computer, and telecommunications equipment, both the overall project and the details. As the construction phase of the project draws to a close, the actual move becomes paramount to your customer. Relocation can be traumatic to some employees, and you should help the customer keep employees informed about their situation before, during, and after the relocation. Maps, keys, building rules and regulations, transportation, food service, telephone numbers, signage, street and mailing addresses, new business cards, and parking should be discussed in detail with the employees to ensure their comfort with the new space.

For large or multiple relocations, you may recommend your customer hire a relocation company that specializes in coordinating large and complex moves, especially from one city to another. Detailed announcements about the move must be made in a timely manner to all employees, vendors, and suppliers, and to the public where necessary.

The cost, timing, and services of a number of suppliers and vendors must be coordinated to ensure that the previous building, the new location, and the new work are protected during the move by qualified and insured suppliers and vendors. Major moves, which often occur after work hours, may require security (provided by either in-house or an outside company), a furniture refinisher, furniture installer, general furniture mover or a system furniture mover and installer, computer transport vendor, food service vendor, telecommunications vendor, computer vendor, signage vendor, art installer, and so on.

The furniture installers should be onsite the day the employees start work for miscellaneous furniture relocation requirements, the removal of boxes, and so on. A furniture touch-up vendor should be contracted to be onsite after the move to take care of scratches and minor furniture damage.

Cleanup from the move must be completed as soon as possible so employees can be productive the day they start to work in their new space. All services including security, parking, telephone, computer, mail, reprographics, food service, and building services including heating and air conditioning must be tested and operational *before* employees begin work. The facility professional must be the catalyst and coordinator to ensure that all loose ends are tied and that the move is a success.

SAMPLE: RELOCATION AND MOVING PROPOSAL

PROPOSAL INVITATION

Project Name:	ABC Company
Project Location:	XYZ Building, 20th, 21st, and 22nd Floors
Date:	October 14, 2005

RELOCATION AND MOVING

You are invited to submit a proposal to contract and provide all labor, materials, services, vehicles, permits, licenses, and equipment necessary for the relocation and moving of furnishings and associated items for ABC Company (Customer) from 2 West Wacker Drive, Suites 1400, 1500, and 1600, Chicago, IL 60621–2501, and from 343 West Wacker Drive, Suite 800, Chicago, IL 60615–1010, to the XYZ Building (Building) at 1230 North Michigan Street, Suites 2000, 2100, and 2200, Chicago, IL 60615.

The work shall be as described in the General Conditions and Requirements; in the attached Project Furnishings Report dated October 14, 2005; and in the enclosed existing floor plans and the enclosed Furniture Plans dated October 10, 2005: Sheet F-1 X, Furniture Plan—20th Floor East; Sheet F-2X, Furniture Plan—20th Floor West; Sheet F-3X, Furniture Plan—21st Floor East; Sheet F-4X, Furniture Plan—21st Floor West; Sheet F-5, Furniture Plan—22nd Floor East; and Sheet F-6X, Furniture Plan—22nd Floor West.

Please return your Lump Sum written proposal not later than 10:00 A.M., Tuesday, October 28, 2005. Three (3) copies of the proposal shall be delivered to Russ Abbott; ABC Company, 2 West Wacker Drive, Suite 1400, Chicago, IL 60621. Any exceptions to the General Conditions and Requirements must be identified with specific qualifications.

RELOCATION AND MOVING

Project Name:	ABC Company
Project Location:	XYZ Building, 20th, 21st, and 22nd Floors
Date:	October 14, 2005

GENERAL CONDITIONS AND REQUIREMENTS

1. The Relocation and Moving Contractor (Contractor) shall provide evidence that the work shall be performed by skilled, properly attired personnel and that the number of personnel assigned to the job will be adequate to complete the Work as scheduled.

2. The Contractor shall not subcontract any portion of this Work without the knowledge and written approval of the Customer.

3. The Contractor shall supply new materials as specified and suitable to achieve the intended results.

4. The Contractor shall be responsible for coordinating all schedules, vehicles, loading docks, deliveries, and installation activities with the Customer and respective building Property Management agencies and shall provide the work in accordance with the enclosed Moving Policy for the 2 West Wacker Drive Building, the XYZ Building Tenant Move-in Rules and Regulations, the XYZ Building Contractor Rules and Regulations, and the move requirements of the building management agency.

5. The Contractor shall provide the Customer with a schedule to complete the Work as follows:

Move Phase	Day and Date	From Building	Requirements
Phase I	Friday, 5:30 P.M. November 10, 2005	2 W. Wacker Dr.	Accounting/Data Processing and Central Files
Phase II	Monday, 7:30 AM November 13, 2005	2 W. Wacker Dr.	Library
Phase III	Friday, 7:30 AM November 25, 2005	2 W. Wacker Dr. 3343 W. Wacker Dr.	Balance remaining

The Contractor shall also provide in the Proposal an alternate price should the Customer choose to schedule Phase III to occur on Friday, November 17, 2005.

6. The Customer has contracted with:

   a. Specialty Contractors as general contractor for general construction work on the project, which is scheduled for completion on or before December 1, 2005.

   b. Howard Post Company to pack, move, deliver and install all computer-related equipment to be coordinated with the above move schedule.

   c. T&S, Inc., to refurbish and refinish selected furniture items. This vendor is responsible for removing these items from 2 West Wacker Drive in November 2005 and for delivering and installing these items at the XYZ Building in coordination with the above schedule.

   d. Corporate Furnishings to provide and install new furnishings in coordination with the above schedule. The Customer is planning to contract with this vendor for the disassembly, move, and reassembly of the existing Knoll Zapf workstations located in the 14th floor Word Processing Room to the 20th floor Central File Room. The Contractor *may* also provide an alternate price for this work and, if an alternate price is provided, must provide the Customer with satisfactory evidence of experience with this Systems furniture.

   e. Mid-West Business Systems, Inc., to provide and install new high-density mobile storage system in the 20th floor Central File Room, shelving in File and Case Rooms, and high-density mobile shelving and fixed and stationary shelving in the 22nd floor Library. This vendor will be responsible for disassembling existing Library shelving on the 14th floor of the 2 West Wacker Drive Building and removing it from the building the morning of November 10, 2005. In coordination with this work, the Contractor shall pack the Library books on the Contractor's mobile shelving carts beginning the morning of November 10, 2005, and the mobile shelving carts will remain within the 14th floor Library for Customer use of Library books until November 18, 2005. On Monday morning, November 21, 2005, Mid-West Business Systems will deliver and reinstall the existing but newly painted Library shelving within the 22nd floor Library high-density mobile shelving. The Contractor shall move the books on the mobile shelving carts from the Library, from corridor shelving on the 14th and 15th floors and all other tagged boxes and contents from the 14th floor Library to the XYZ Building on November 21, 2005.

7. The Contractor shall ensure that the work of others is not damaged. The Contractor shall promptly correct any damages and any defect or deficiencies found in his work as a result of the Customer's inspection. Upon final approval by the Customer, the work shall be declared complete. The Contractor shall be responsible for obtaining all necessary permits, licenses, and inspections from appropriate permitting and licensing authorities.

8. The Contractor shall as part of the proposal provide sufficient equipment, labor, and material to assist the Customer at the XYZ Building with minor furnishing relocations on, within, and between any of the three floors and to remove all empty packing boxes and material on the Saturday, Sunday, Monday, and Tuesday of the Phase III move.

9. The Contractor shall:

   a. Provide instructions, guidelines, assistance, and requirements to the Customer for the move and relocation. Unless noted otherwise, the Customer will be responsible for packing, tagging, and labeling all items including but not limited to paper, supplies, and personal items in file cabinets, desks, credenzas, cabinets, etc.

   b. Provide sufficient packing boxes, labels for tagging in different colors for each Phase, tape for boxes for files, miscellaneous, and personal items for the Customer to pack which the Contractor will move and relocate. Contractor shall break down and remove all empty packing boxes and material from the Building during and after each Phase of the move.

   c. Protect, move, deliver, and install all tagged items including but not limited to desks, credenzas, desk chairs, guest chairs, sofas, chairs, tables, folding tables, side tables, end tables, table lamps, floor lamps, lampshades, secretarial desks with returns, typing tables, stools, file cabinets, safes, mirrors, paper shredders, trash containers, larger common area accessories, tagged equipment such as typewriters, mail room equipment, hand trucks, etc., excluding computer-related equipment, metal shelving, artwork, portraits, pictures, decorative screens, area rugs, boxes, containers, statues, vases, plant stands, plants in containers, etc.

   d. Provide sufficient mobile shelving carts and labor to pack, move, relocate, and reinstall the Central File Room records in Phase I and the books in the Library and in corridor shelving on the 14th and 25th floors in Phase II.

10. The Contractor shall provide evidence of required insurance to the Customer before beginning the Work. Contractor shall hold the Customer harmless and shall be responsi-

ble for any damages, paying for any damages, and coordinating and settling any damages made by Contractor's forces to the 2 Michigan Street Building, 3343 Michigan Road Building and 1230 North Michigan Street Building (XYZ Building). Contractor shall be responsible for notifying the Customer as soon as possible of any damages made during the Work to the facilities and to any of the items being moved and relocated. Contractor shall be responsible for paying, repair, coordination, and settlement of any damages to the Customer's furnishings, equipment, and property within the limits of the Contractor's insurance requirements. The Customer reserves the option and right to contract separately for the repair or replacement of any item damaged in the move.

11. Payment for the Work by the Customer shall be made within thirty (30) days after the Contractor's invoice has been submitted to the Customer, provided the Work has been completed to date and in full to the satisfaction of the Customer.

12. The following will be required as consideration for final payment:

    a. Completed punchlist, signed by the Customer.

    b. Satisfactory evidence that all claims for items damaged in the Work are being addressed. The Customer reserves the right to retain up to ten percent (10%) of the contract price but not more than the estimated damage claim amount.

SAMPLE: RELOCATION INSTRUCTIONS MEMORANDUM

MEMORANDUM

TO: _____   FROM: (Name, Director of Administration)

DATE: _____, 2005   RE: Instructions for the (Company Name)
                                            Move to (Building Name), (Building
                                            Address, City, State, and ZIP)

In order to make your move as smooth as possible to (Building Name) and keep downtime to a minimum, we have prepared the following for your review and action:

1. *All items (moving boxes, furnishings, and pictures) must be labeled* with a *black* Magic Marker on the appropriate color coded labels to identify your new location by floor and location number. Officer and firm furnishings will also be identified by piece letter. If a moving box, item, or furniture does not have a moving label, it *will not* be moved. Please ensure that you are using the right color label for your move in one of the following phases:

PHASE	LABEL COLOR	FL.	CHECK OUT DAY	CHECK OUT DATE	MOVE DAY	MOVE DATE
I	GREEN	30	Thursday	Nov. 9, 2005	Friday	Nov. 10, 2005
II	YELLOW	32	Monday	Nov. 13, 2005	Tuesday	Nov. 14, 2005
III	BLUE	30	Wednesday	Nov. 22, 2005	Friday	Nov. 24, 2005
III	ORANGE	31	Wednesday	Nov. 22, 2005	Friday	Nov. 24, 2005
III	RED	32	Wednesday	Nov. 22, 2005	Friday	Nov. 24, 2005

2. *Each office, work area, storage area, etc. at (Building name) will have a location number* posted at each door jamb or area location just before the move by a member of the Move Team.

   Your Move Team Coordinator is: _____ at Ext. _____. Please contact your Move Team Coordinator if you have any questions before, during, or after the move.

   You are moving in   Phase _____ to
                       the _____ floor.
                       Your location number is _____.

   Please write your floor and location number on all moving labels to identify your boxes and items to be moved; turn back the upper right-hand corner of the location label to allow for easier removal.

(PLACE SAMPLE OF MOVING LABEL HERE)

3. *Each office, work area, storage area, etc. at (Building Name) will have a floor plan posted* by a member of the Move Team just before the move showing the locations of all existing furnishings being relocated to your office or work area. The movers from *(Moving Co. Name)* will use this floor plan to place all furniture.

Officers:	Only Officer office furnishings with location labels will be moved. You are responsible for packing items from your desk and from other furnishings in your office into moving boxes and placing a completed location label on your moving boxes, furnishings, chair mat, trash can, and pictures. (Facility Coordinator Name) will be checking with you to verify the furnishings you wish moved to (Building Name). Your Move Team Coordinator will complete the furnishings location label by writing the appropriate piece letter on each furnishings label to correspond with the piece letter on your office floor plan.
Dept. Managers:	No existing Dept. Manager furniture will be moved, as Dept. Manager offices will contain new office furniture, including new desk pads, which will be in place before your move. You are responsible for packing items from your desk and from other furnishings in your office and placing a completed location label on your moving boxes, chair mat, trash can, and pictures.
Staff:	No existing Staff furniture will be moved, as Staff offices will contain a new desk chair, an existing secretarial unit, and one or more lateral file cabinets. You are responsible for packing items from your desk and file cabinet contents and placing a completed location label on your moving boxes, chair mat, and trash can.
Secretaries:	No existing secretarial furniture will be moved, as Secretarial areas will contain new furniture, including a new chair mat. You are responsible for packing items from your desk and file cabinet contents and placing a completed location label on your moving boxes and trash can.
Administrative:	Existing secretarial units, credenzas, desk chairs, guest chairs, bookcases, chair mats, etc., will be moved and reused. You are responsible for packing items from your desk and file cabinet contents and placing a location label on your moving boxes, chair mat, and trash can.

4. *All packing and labeling must be completed prior to your check-out date.* In addition, your personal items, including personal plants, valuables, and fragile items should be packed and taken with you *after* you have completed the Check-out Process.

IMPORTANT FOR ALL OFFICERS

Please inspect all furnishings moving from your current office *PRIOR* to the move. We ask that you do this to familiarize yourself with *ALL PREEXISTING DAMAGE*. This is very important, as people usually inspect their furniture only after it has been moved by the moving company. Once moved, they see damage and assume the mover did it when in many cases the damage was already there. Please help yourself and your Move Team Coordinator by inspecting your furniture before and after the move. We suggest making notes to refresh your memory. This will improve your overall satisfaction with the move, which will be provided by the moving company (Moving Co. Name).

GENERAL INFORMATION

1. Phase I employees: Please plan to come to (Building Name) on Saturday, November 11, or Sunday, November 12, from 2:30 P.M. to 6:00 P.M. to unpack your boxes to be ready for work on Monday morning, November 13.

2. Phase III employees: Please plan to come to (Building Name) on Saturday, November 25, or Sunday, November 26, from 2:30 P.M to 6:00 P.M to unpack your boxes to be ready for work on Monday morning, November 27.

3. As you unpack from your move on Saturday or Sunday, please break down your moving boxes and place them on the floor outside of your office or work area. The movers will be picking up these boxes throughout both days.

4. The movers will be available on Monday, November 27, to assist with minor furniture relocations. Please contact your Move Team Coordinator on Saturday or Sunday after-noon to request and schedule this assistance.

5. On whichever day you plan to unpack at (Building Name), please remember to bring your security access card with you to get you into the building and past the elevator entry doors on your floor. Also, we ask that, if you feel you need to bring *family* members with you, you limit your family help to not more than two to help you unpack, etc. If you drive to (Building Name) to unpack and you park your car in the building parking garage, you can take your parking ticket to be validated by your Move Coordinator on the 30th floor.

6. Please remember to be *SECURITY CONSCIOUS* during and after the move. Should you see someone who does not seem to work for the firm, our movers, or another vendor, or who does not belong in your existing area or at (Building Name), please contact (Name of Person responsible for move security). Please remember to protect your valuables, including money, credit cards, keys, wallets, purses, and access cards, at all times by keeping them out of sight or, better yet, by locking them up as appropriate.

   During a move of this size, items have been known to disappear. It is important that you take your personal items, plants, and valuables home with you on your Check-out day. If you want to bring them back to your office or work area, consider doing so two or three days after you start work in your new location.

7. We realize that you may wish to hang your photographs, pictures, etc., while you are unpacking. Please resist this temptation, as the firm will provide this service to you starting on Monday, November 27.

8. All personal liquid containers should be packed and moved with the personal items you will be taking home.

9. In the event keys are not available for file cabinets, the cylinder lock should be wrapped in tape to prevent the lock from being pushed in.

10. Please use only the moving boxes and location labels provided by (Moving Company Name) through your Move Team Coordinator. Moving boxes must be packed full or packed to prevent items from shifting about loose inside the box.

    Do not use the *Business Records* storage boxes when packing your desk or file cabinet contents.

11. Please read the attached information on what to pack and how to pack and label the items you will be taking with you. If we've omitted something or if you have any questions, please call your Move Team Coordinator.

12. Items for which no specific location for the location label has been given or shown in this information should be placed on any flat, easily visible surface.

13. Information on your Move Team is attached that you may wish to review.

14. Part of the Check-out Process will include a formal sign-out of your responsibilities to take place on your check-out date. A copy is attached for your review.

15. Information on phone numbers, phone, and voice mail training, CRT backing up, etc., will be provided in a follow-up memo.

16. Please remember there will be no smoking other than in designated areas on each floor or otherwise in accordance with the firm's Smoking Policy.

PACKING AND LABELING INSTRUCTIONS

ITEM	INSTRUCTIONS
Packing box	These will be provided through your Move Team Coordinator. Place a location label on the small end of box.
Desk	Contents must be packed in moving boxes.
Credenza	Check with your Move Team Coordinator for packing sensitive materials.
Secretarial unit	All staff office and secretarial unit furniture should be unlocked, with keys taped to the bottom of lowest drawer.
	Officer furniture should be locked; officers should take all keys with them.
	Place location labels on top of desks, credenzas and secretarial units.
Glass top on desk	Leave as is. However, papers under glass should be removed.
	Place a location label on top of the glass (don't forget to label the desk).

Bookcase	Contents must be packed in moving boxes.
	Place location label on the front upper corner or top of the Bookcase.
Desk chair	If chair has casters which are loose, remove and pack in.
Guest chair	Moving box
Side chair	Place a location label on the rear of the back rest, leg, or base.
Sofa	Place a location label on front right leg or on manufacturer's label under center cushion.
Pictures	Small pictures may be packed in moving boxes or left on the wall.
	Large pictures should be left on the wall.
	Place a location label on the front, lower-right corner.
Lamp	Unplug lamp and wrap cord around base securely.
	Removable lampshades should be left on the lamp. Place a location label near the base of the lamp and place a location label on the wire frame at the top of the removable lamp shade.
Personal belongings	These are your responsibility. Personal desk items may be placed in moving boxes at your own risk.
Card files	Place in moving boxes.
Desk organizers	If these are too large for moving boxes, they may be kept loose.
Other desk accessories	Place a location label on the top if too large for a moving box.
	These will remain loose.
Chair mat	Do not place a location label on these, as the best of the existing chair mats will be reused.
	New chair mats will be installed only in Secretarial areas.
Desk pad	These will remain loose.
	Dept. Managers only should not place a label on their existing desk pads as new desk pads will be installed in all Dept. Manager offices.
File tray	Place single trays in bottom of moving boxes. Secure post to tray with tape. If trays are too large for moving boxes, they may be kept loose.
	Place a location label on the top if too large for a moving box.
Portable calculator	Pack in moving boxes.
Dictation equipment	
Waste basket	Please provide empty and clean.
	Place a location label on the side.
Lateral filing cabinet	Contents must be packed in moving boxes.
	Unlock all drawers with keys taped to the bottom of the lowest drawer.

	Place a location label on the front of the cabinet.
Side table	Pack material on top or in drawers in moving boxes.
Table	Unlock all drawers with keys taped to the bottom of the lowest drawer.
Work table	Place a location label on the tabletop.
Storage cabinet	Contents must be packed in moving boxes.
	Unlock all doors with keys taped to the bottom shelf. Place a location label on the front of the cabinet.
Metal shelving	Contents must be packed in moving boxes.
	Place a location label on front upper right of the shelf.
Filing cabinet safe	Leave material in place in the cabinet.
	Lock all drawers and keep keys with you.
	Place a location label on the front of cabinet.
Typewriter	Leave dust cover and power cord in place. Wrap cord around the machine and secure with tape. Secure typewriter carriage by setting both margins at center. Do not place a location label on your typewriter. A separate location label will be placed on it by the Move Team.
	Please note that you may or may not have the same typewriter at your new location, especially at secretarial areas, where the work area layout includes the sharing of one typewriter by two secretaries.
Calculator	Remove dust cover and cord if removable, then pack in a moving box. If cord is not removable, wrap around machine and secure with tape.
Telephone	*Do not* pack your telephone(s) in your moving boxes.
	Do not place a location label on your telephone.
	Unplug your telephone(s) from the wall and bring your telephone and phone cable with you when you Check Out.
	A new telephone will be provided at your new location and operational before you arrive to unpack.
Monitor CPU Printer	Back up all directories and files on properly labeled floppy or CD disks from your CPU hard drive on your Check-out morning.
Modem	Take backup floppy disks with you when you go home—*do not* pack them in your moving boxes.
	Do not place a location label on your CRT, CPU, printer, or modem. A separate location label will be placed by MIS, which will also unplug all cables and prepare your CRT, etc., for moving on your Check-out or Move-out day. Your CRT, etc., will be packed and moved by (Computer Moving Company Name).

Your CRT, etc., will be at your work area and will have been tested before you begin work at your new location. *Please note that you may or may not have the same Printer at your new location, especially at secretarial areas, where the work area layout includes the sharing of one Printer by two secretaries.*

Copy machine   All copiers will be packed and moved by (Equipment Moving Company Name).

WHAT ARE THE RESPONSIBILITIES AND JOB DESCRIPTION OF THE MEMBERS OF YOUR MOVE TEAM?

One of the key elements of a smooth relocation is good coordination and management by the (Company Name) Move Team. Don't ignore the move and hope it will go away. Specific people have been assigned to the Move Team, and their responsibilities have been defined below.

Move Team:

1. *Move Team Supervisor—_____:*
   a. Readily available to firm and (Moving Company) supervisor prior to, during, and after the relocation.
   b. Knowledgeable about the items to be moved and placement of items in the new location.
   c. Distributes information and forms from firm and (Moving Company) planning sessions to the members of the Move Team and to firm personnel.
   d. Coordinates with the (Moving Company) supervisor to ensure that the existing and new location is properly protected from damage to the floor and walls and ensures that new location space numbers and room and area plans have been installed prior to arrival of the first shipment.
   e. Coordinates with members of the Move Team for arrangements for all third-party vendors for the following:
      • Servicing copiers, postage machine, etc.
      • Disconnecting and reconnecting computer equipment
      • Moving plants owned by the firm
      • Coffee service connections
      • Connection of phone, database, network, and modem service
      • Disconnection and connection of Library Database Services (i.e., Lexis, West Law and Information America)
      • Installing drapery, signage, new furnishings, and artwork
      • Special packing
      • Elevators (reserved for exclusive use)

    f. If there is any damage, receives reports from Move Team Coordinators and reports it to (Moving Company).

    g. Signs all necessary paperwork after completion of the move.

2. *Move Team Coordinators—*

Jack Williams	22nd Floor—Legal Section (Rose)
Jill Stone	21st Floor—Marketing Section (Hahn)
Natalie Cohen	20th Floor—Accounting (Smith)
Sherri Koll	21st Floor—H. R. Section (Brown)
Martha Rae Adams	26th Floor—Executives (Stevens)
Stephen Fields	22nd Floor—Finance Section (Tyson)
Wilma Miller	20th Floor—MIS, Facilities, etc.

    a. Readily available to specific section personnel and (Moving Company) personnel prior to, during, and after the move.

    b. Have complete knowledge about the items to be moved and placement of items in the responsibility areas at the existing space and at (Building Name).

    c. Distribute information and forms developed from the firm and (Moving Company) planning sessions.

    d. Arrange for the distribution of moving boxes, tape, labels, furniture placement plans, Instructions for the (Company Name) Move to (Building Name), and related material to firm personnel.

    e. (Move Team Coordinator Name) checks with Officers to verify the furnishings they wish moved to (Building Name). The Move Team Coordinator completes the furnishings location label by writing the appropriate piece letter on each furnishings label to correspond with the piece letter on the Officer's office floor plan.

    f. Answer questions from firm personnel regarding labeling and packing.

    g. Prior to Check-out and the arrival of (Moving Company), check to see that each office or work area is properly packed and labeled, phone and keys have been turned in, and that each person has been issued the appropriate security access card and signed their Check-out Process sheet.

    h. Coordinate with (Moving Company) supervisor to ensure all labeled items are moved from old location. Check proper placement of items at new location.

    i. Arrange for removal of cartons after unpacking.

    j. If there is any damage, report it to the Move Team Coordinator, who will see that it is reported to (Moving Company). The Move Team Coordinator serves as your contact for the repairperson.

CHECK-OUT PROCESS

Name: _____   (Previous Building Name) Floor: _____

(Building Name) Floor: _____   (Building Name) Location Number: _____

Check off each item when completed:

☐ Location labels have been placed on all moving boxes, furnishings, pictures, etc.

☐ Desk, tables, file cabinets, and storage cabinets have been unlocked and keys taped to the bottom of the last drawer or shelf.

☐ Officer has inspected his/her furniture for damage, noted damage in writing before the move, has locked his/her furniture, and has the keys.

☐ Personal items have been packed to be taken home.

☐ CRT has been backed up and floppy disks have been packed to be taken home.

☐ Phone set(s) have been turned over to the Move Team Coordinator.

☐ Floor entry door key(s) at (Previous Building Name) has (have) been turned over to your Move Team Coordinator (if applicable).

☐ Office door key at (Previous Building Name) has been turned over to your Move Team Coordinator (if applicable).

☐ Telephone Calling Card at (Previous Building Name) has been turned over to your Move Team Coordinator (if applicable). Card Number: _____.

☐ Security access card for building and floor entry doors at (Building Name) has been signed out and provided to you. Card Number: _____.

☐ Security access card for parking at the (New Building Name) Parking Garage has been signed out and provided to you (if applicable). Card Number: _____.

☐ Telephone Calling Card for use at (New Building Name) has been signed out and provided to you (if applicable). Card Number: _____.

Signature: _____   Date: _____ _____, 2005

Move Team
Coordinator
Signature: _____   Date: _____ _____, 2005

BUILD-TO-SUIT CONCERNS (TURNKEY ACQUISITION)

Sometimes corporate management desires to develop a facility but lacks the expertise or the initial capital. With a build-to-suit turnkey arrangement, a corporation provides performance specifications and, in time, obtains a completed facility without having to manage the details of real estate acquisition, design, construction, and inspection. Instead, a developer or developer/general contractor with major expertise and purchasing resources undertakes to provide all services for the project and, when it is completed, turns over the keys to the corporation.

Regardless of the procedure, someone must represent the corporate customer. As the facility management professional, you must ensure that your customer receives the agreed-on value and premises. As seen earlier in the chapter, your role also entails the relocation and management of owner-furnished items that must be delivered, installed, tested, adjusted, and cleaned. Finally, you must arrange to have rubbish removed before your customer's employees occupy the build-to-suit facility.

The concept, in many ways, is similar to contracting for the construction of a home where you have agreed on a site, floor plan(s), specifications, and purchase price with the developer or general contractor, who then hires the necessary workers and provides all services. The developer of a build-to-suit facility generally takes responsibility for the following:

- Property—properly zoned and subdivided
- Architectural, interior, and landscape design and engineering services
- Construction schedules and documents
- Construction financing, bonds, and payments to subcontractors
- Project utilities, permits, and insurance
- Site and building construction, finishes, supervision, and coordination for corporate-furnished items
- Interim construction payments, inspections, and the certificate of occupancy
- As-built drawings, completed punchlist work, lien waivers, warranty, and final construction payments
- Training for corporation operations and maintenance staff on building systems and presentation of the building keys at closing

But why should the corporation choose the build-to-suit option? The following are the most common reasons:

- *Lack of capital funds.* The corporation may have insufficient funds to finance the property acquisition and construction of the project. The developer purchases the property and obtains construction financing. The corporation and developer agree on a price and delivery date, which removes development risk from the corporation while it works to obtain the best financing for the permanent mortgage or the cash required at closing.

- *Timing issue.* The corporation does not have the total amount of funds available to begin the project at a specific time, needs the facility in a timely manner for business requirements, and will have the necessary funds at closing.

- *Business implications.* Cash is needed for business operations, or the delay of a major expenditure or financing will help the balance sheet in the short term.

- *Tax implication(s).* The arrangement allows the corporation to defer taxes or depreciation to a more favorable tax period, especially where closing takes place just after the start of the new tax year such that the corporation will have a full year of depreciation.

- *Lack of available sites.* Appropriate locations may not have utilities, zoning, or completed infrastructure (roads, stoplights, utilities, etc.). The build-to-suit developer can, controls, or has the political know-how to promptly secure the necessary site requirements, permits, and approvals. In some areas, local developers control the more desirable sites and often have the connections to move the project through the state or local bureaucratic maze.

- *Difficulties doing business in the location.* In acquiring and developing the property, there may be considerable delay while the corporation tries to understand local ways and the timing of doing business. The developer may be able to acquire an option on additional adjacent property for an attractive price, whereas the corporation's deep pockets may inflate the adjacent property owner's expectations.

- *Lack of expertise within the corporation.* This type of development is not an ongoing requirement, or the corporation does not wish to deal with development details. Many corporations may build a major facility once in ten years and do not have skilled or experienced staff readily available to manage the project on a day-to-day basis. The developer has the expertise and is hired to provide an acceptable solution with a minimal expenditure of corporate staff and management time.

- *Need to remain flexible.* Corporate resources that were scheduled to finance the project have been transferred to other requirements, and this solution allows the project to continue while deferring fund requirements to a later date. Other business issues may also be pending, and until they are resolved, flexibility remains an immediate corporate requirement.

- *Requirement not to own the project.* Certain other events or timing must take place prior to ownership. Again, balance sheet expenditures and asset disclosures may be more advantageously deferred to a later time and, in some cases, other corporate leadership.

Advantages to the corporation may include:

- Corporation is not the owner until the project is complete.

- Corporation can walk (within reason) if the developer cannot deliver the project as specified.

- Corporation leverages its resources by using other people's money (capital).
- The developer is responsible for zoning, utilities, and so on.
- Corporation retains its capital for interim purposes.
- Options to purchase additional property later at a specific price can be included.
- Turnkey concept provides a fixed cost for the corporation to finance at closing.
- Corporation obtains a site and a facility built to its specifications.
- Developer can provide the project to the corporation on a fast-track basis.
- Corporation does not have to staff up for the project.

Disadvantages to the corporation may include:

- Corporation is not the owner until closing.
- Time frame may be critical, but corporation has no direct control over schedule.
- Paying for the use of other people's money could prove costly.
- Corporation must rely on the financial ability and stability to the build-to-suit developer.
- Quality of construction may be more difficult to control with lack of available and qualified staff.
- Corporation must develop a detailed RFP.

SAMPLE: REQUEST FOR PROPOSAL FOR A BUILD-TO-SUIT

FOR
ABC COMPANY
June 18, 2005

ABC Company (Tenant), a Chicago, IL–based division of XYZ Corporation, is soliciting formal responses to this Request for Proposal for the leasing of a build-to-suit facility from a Landlord with the Tenant having the option to purchase the property and facility as specified below.

Tenant proposes to lease property and a 44,800-square-foot Regional Distribution Center with 150,000 square feet of adjacent outside storage in the Chicago, IL, area to better serve its customers.

Attachment A (see chapter 5, "Sample Request for Proposal for Architectural Consulting Services") provides the Tenant's specific site and project requirements and an outline of the model concepts and design criteria to be incorporated at this facility which the Tenant desires that the Landlord construct and lease to the Tenant.

Tenant has identified a Chicago, IL–based Architectural Consultant to provide professional architectural, engineering, and interior design consulting services for all planning and construction documents necessary to enable the Tenant's Landlord to construct this project. Design and construction documents shall meet federal, state, and local code requirements. Tenant has also identified a Fee Developer to provide value engineering, planning, estimating, and project closeout services for this project and other similar projects around the United States.

A. PREMISES:

1. Approximately 12 acres zoned for the construction and operation of a warehouse with outside storage as required below and as described in Attachment A.

2. Provide a plot plan of the proposed property showing the major access roads to the property, the proposed property's street address, legal description, covenants and restrictions, size in acres and square feet, and current owner's name, address, and telephone number.

B. PROPERTY ZONING:

1. State the governmental agency which has zoning jurisdiction for the property, current zoning of the proposed property, and that this zoning permits the Tenant's intended use of the property.

C. TERM:

1. Twenty (20) years.

D. TERM COMMENCEMENT DATE:

1. Approximately July 1, 2006, to June 30, 2026.

E. OPTION FOR ADDITIONAL PROPERTY:

1. Tenant requires a lease option for approximately two (2) adjacent acres for the construction of approximately 100,000 square feet of additional warehouse space. The Tenant shall have a period of six (6) months after the initial Term Commencement Date to elect to take the lease option.

2. State the proposed per square foot lease cost per month, the proposed number of square feet of property, and the lease cost per year exclusive of common area maintenance, taxes, commissions, or other fees.

3. Provide a plot plan of the proposed optional lease property, the proposed property's street address, legal description, size in acres and square feet, and current owner's name, address, and telephone number.

F. BUILD-TO-SUIT LEASE CONTINGENCIES:

1. Tenant's obligation to lease the property and the facility is contingent upon but not limited to Landlord obtaining for the Tenant:

   a. Written confirmation from governmental authorities of zoning, utilities available to the site, acceptance of covenants and restrictions, acceptance of the rights of way and streets, etc.;

   b. Written plan approval from development and construction permitting authorities and a copy of the Landlord's construction permit;

   c. Written confirmation from an independent testing laboratory that the site does not contain soil pollutants or contaminants, etc.;

   d. Property owner's clear title and title insurance for the property; and

   e. Initial and final approval by the Purchaser's parent company.

G. RENTAL ABATEMENT:

1. Specify the rental abatement offered for the initial term and option terms.

H. RENTAL RATE:

1. Specify the lease rental rate per month, per year, per square foot per month, and per square foot per year for the initial term and option periods.

2. Specify the method by which the Landlord proposes the Tenant pay for services to the property and facility through a Net or a Net Net Net (see definitions on page 569) for Operating Expenses, Common Area Maintenance, Taxes, etc.

I. ESCALATION AND OTHER RENTAL ADJUSTMENT:

1. Specify and illustrate method(s). Provide your definition of Operating Expenses, Common Area Maintenance, or any expenses/costs that are reimbursable by Tenant to the Landlord.

J. TENANT IMPROVEMENTS:

1. Tenant requires the Landlord provide an estimate cost of the project to understand and approve the expenditures which will become part of the Landlord's basis for

determining rent for the Tenant's capital lease and for the Tenant's purchase option price.

2. Furnish to the Tenant the Landlord's estimated site development and construction costs for the improvements to the property based upon the proposed site and the improvements specified herein. Cost estimate items shall include but are not limited to site investigation, site and foundation engineering and design, general conditions, overhead and profit, permits, site work, foundations, structural, exterior skin, carpentry, finishes, dock equipment and specialties, sprinkler, HVAC, plumbing, electrical, landscaping, cleanup, etc.

K. RENEWAL OPTIONS:

   1. Two (2) consecutive renewal options:

      a. One (1) for Ten (10) years; and

      b. One (1) for Five (5) years.

L. PURCHASE OPTION:

   1. Tenant desires the option of purchasing the property and the facility from the Landlord, including the initial and expansion option, if taken, as a package at a future date.

   2. Specify a proposed future date the Tenant would have to notify the Landlord to execute the option and the proposed time requirements in working days for the Landlord and Tenant to close the sale and purchase.

   3. Specify a separate and total purchase price of the improved property and the facility exclusive of closing costs, taxes, commissions, or other fees.

M. PROPERTY MANAGEMENT AND TENANTS:

   1. Specify who provides property management services.

   2. Provide a list of other Tenants in the development with your proposal.

N. TENANT'S BUILD-TO-SUIT EVALUATION CRITERIA: Address the following in your response to this RFP.

   1. Contact Person Name and Title

   2. Firm Name

   3. Address

   4. Telephone No.

   5. Fax No.

   6. Year Firm Was Established

   7. Branch Offices:

Location	Year Established	No. of Employees

8. Development Specialization (based on # of sq. ft. constructed)

Warehouse	_____%	Schools	_____%
Office	_____%	Banks	_____%
Retail	_____%	Hospitals	_____%
Hotel	_____%	Other	_____%

9. Financial Data (furnish one or more of the following for the two most recent years).

   a. Annual Report   c. Balance Sheet

   b. Profit and Loss Statement   d. Statement of Changes in Financial Position

10. Client References—Furnish tenant references for projects similar in size and scope. Provide names and telephone numbers of contacts who will be familiar with your firm's expertise. The Tenant may choose to visit and review relevant completed projects as part of the selection process.

11. Number of employees (do not include contract personnel).

Discipline	No. of Employees
Principals	
Project Directors	
Project Managers	
Schedulers	
Construction	
Field Supervisors	
Accounting	
Secretarial	
Clerical	
Others (identify)	

12. Describe your firm's philosophy and approach to accomplishing the scope of work.

13. Identify the one contact person the Landlord will assign to the Tenant's Project Team, provide an organization chart proposed for this Project, and provide a description of applicable experience and capabilities of Landlord's team members with names, titles, and percentage of time for each person who will work on each project.

14. Provide a description of applicable development and construction experience and the value of construction completed since 2000.

15. Specify the Landlord's team which will accomplish permitting and coordination meetings with all local authorities and building trades.

16. Current projects—List projects currently assigned to the proposed team members and expected completion dates.

17. List projects currently under contract or projected within next twelve months.

Name	Location	Sq. Ft.	Completion Date

18. Define your firm's plan that will demonstrate savings to this build-to-suit project and your firm's method of project control, project documentation, and schedule control.

19. Provide samples of forms for budget preparation, programming records, field changes, conversation/meeting records, and change orders.

20. Identify the type(s) of outside consultant and, by firm name (primary and secondary), consultants which you will require for this project.

21. Provide a detailed listing of the build-to-suit services you believe should be provided for this type of facility.

22. Schedule—Describe the scheduled time required for each phase of the project:

    a. Preliminary design, value engineering, and preliminary estimates

    b. Code review, site investigation, and construction documents

    c. Permitting

    d. Construction

    e. Punchlist and occupancy permitting

    f. Project closeout

23. The Landlord and his/her consultants shall state, acknowledge, and recognize in the response to this proposal that the Tenant shall have ownership of all designs, completed project construction documents, and originals derived from the selection of their proposal for the Work described herein.

O. TENANT'S ADDITIONAL BUILD-TO-SUIT CRITERIA:

Address the following in your response to this RFP where Landlord shall:

1. Retain a local registered survey firm to prepare a legal description and boundary and topographic survey drawings including but not limited to the following information: main access street to the site, site street or highway address, benchmarks, floodplain, surface rock, setbacks, easements, encroachments, rights of way, overhead and underground utilities (electricity, natural gas, water, fire main, fire hydrants, telephone, etc.), major trees and types over 6" in diameter, water retention, groundwater, storm sewer, culverts, pipes, existing structures, telephone/power poles, curb and curb cuts, and paved and unpaved roads. Also, provide the Tenant with a copy of all Work and provide an as-built survey of the completed project;

2. Retain a local soils testing engineering firm to perform soil testing, testing for toxic waste, and provide recommendations for soils and foundation design. If the site is not served by gravity sanitary sewer and will require a septic tank and drain field system, provide the required perk tests and tank and system design. Provide the Tenant with a copy of all Work and testing results;

3. Retain a local civil engineer to review all code requirements, and provide civil engineering design and site plans and site details, foundation design, plans and details, and specifications. The Landlord shall ensure coordination between the civil engineer and the Tenant's Architectural Consultant for the site design, foundation design, plans and details, and specifications. Provide the Tenant with a copy of all Work and testing results;

4. Retain a local material testing firm to provide testing of material placed on the site during construction, including but not limited to: fill soil, concrete, and asphalt. Provide the Tenant with a copy of all Work and testing results;

5. Retain a local landscape architect to provide landscaping design and plans. Provide the Tenant with a copy of all plans and specifications;

6. All site, foundation, and landscape design and construction document plans provided through the Landlord's Consultants shall be drawn and be capable of being printed on 24" × 36" blue line printer paper. Title blocks shall include the ABC Co. logo and shall include this statement: "These designs and plans are the property of ABC Company."

7. The Landlord's Consultants shall prepare their specification documents in accordance with the Tenant's Project Manual requirements, which shall be prepared by the Tenant's Architectural Consultant, be printed on both sides of each sheet where appropriate, shall be bound, and shall be printed on 8½" × 11" white paper with an appropriate front and back cover as approved by the Tenant.

8. Obtain all governmental permits including but not limited to:

   a) plan review

   b) excavation

   c) construction

   d) utilities

   e) occupancy

9. Hold monthly progress meetings (or more often, if needed) to provide the Tenant with a detailed and itemized monthly review and progress schedule that monitors construction schedule against the approved schedule;

10. Provide a construction safety and security program acceptable to the Tenant. Tenant may request a periodic safety and/or a security audit from ABC Co. divisional safety/security personnel.

11. Provide and manage a quality assurance program which meets the Tenant's approval;

12. Assist the Tenant as requested in the installation of Tenant-furnished items, which include but are not limited to: furniture, open-plan furniture, signage, conveyor system, pallet shelving, security, computer, fire and telephone systems, warehouse equipment, and trash dumpster.

13. Closeout of project to include but is not limited to:

   a) General site and facility cleanup;

   b) Removal of all debris, temporary utilities, and construction material and equipment from the site;

   c) Requesting and passing of all necessary governmental and Tenant inspections;

   d) Testing of all systems and utilities to the Tenant's satisfaction;

   e) Acquiring and turning over to the Tenant three sets of keys;

   f) Completion of all punchlist items before final payment is made by the Landlord;

g) Provision to the Tenant of a set of as-built blueprints;

h) Obtaining and turning over the Certificate of Occupancy to the Tenant;

i) Reconciling all accounts with approved budgets and payments made, including providing the Tenant with a listing of work and costs by the Tenant's Asset Code; and

j) Reviewing the final request for payment and ensuring that all lien waivers have been received and that all general contractor and subcontractor obligations have been met.

14. The Landlord shall be prepared to work with and assist the Tenant and the Tenant's Architectural Consultant as requested during all phases of the project.

15. The Tenant intends to provide a quality and safe work environment for its employees while obtaining a sound investment that is economical in all aspects of performance. Particular attention must be paid by the Landlord and especially his General Contractor, Subcontractors, and consultants to evaluate their designs and proposed site development construction and engineering systems based on practical, hands-on knowledge.

16. Selection by the Tenant of the Landlord shall be based upon but not limited to a combination of the following criteria:

a) The Rental Rate, Rent Abatement, Upfit Allowance, Project Cost, Option(s), and Option to Purchase

b) Proposal completed as required

c) History and experience of Build-to-Suit Landlord

d) Project philosophy and perceived quality of the Landlord's Development and of the Build-to-Suit Project

e) Project team members, education, training, and experience in similar warehouse distribution facilities and their systems

f) Professional attitude, reputation, and perceived ability of Tenant's staff and Tenant's Architectural Consultant to meet project time, schedule, and budget requirements

P. INSURANCE COVERAGE:

1. Provide amount of insurance coverage for the Landlord and general contractor, and proposed consultants as follows on page 445.

Q. SECURITY:

1. Describe the proposed security services for the park (if any).

R. OTHER LANDLORD SERVICES:

1. Specify all Landlord Services that *are* and *are not* provided to the Tenant by the Landlord under the proposed build-to-suit lease (e.g., grounds maintenance, property taxes.).

	Workers' Compensation (Employers' Liability)	Workers' Comprehensive General Liability	Automobile Liability	Umbrella	Professional Liability**
Landlord and General Contractor	$500,000	$1,000,000/Occ.—B.I. $500,000/Occ.—P.D. or $1,000,000—CSL* Commercial General Liability policy form* $1,000,000/Occ. $3,000,000 general Annual aggregate and $3,000,000 products Completed operations Aggregate	$1,000,000/Occ.—B.I. $500,000/Occ.—P. D.	Not less than $10,000,000	-0-
Landlord Consultants	$500,000	$500,000/Occ.—B.I. $250,000/Occ.—P.D. or $500,000—CSL * Commercial General Liability policy form* $1,000,000 general Annual aggregate and $1,000,000 products Completed operations Aggregate—excluding Professional E&O	$500,000/Occ.—B.I. $250,000/Occ.—P.D.	$5,000,000	$10,000,000

*CSL—Combined Single Limit; B. I.—Bodily Injury; P. D.—Property Damage.
Either general liability form must contain coverage for products/completed operations, contractual liability, broad form property damage, independent contractors, and explosion, underground, and collapse hazards.
ABC Company should be included as an additional insured.
**Professional liability insurance shall be active for the project and expire at the end of five (5) years from the date of owner's occupancy of the facility.

S. AGENCY DISCLOSURE:

   1. Professional Brokerage Company is acting as Agent for the Tenant/Purchaser in this transaction and will be paid a commission by the Owner of the property should a transaction between the parties be consummated.

T. PROPOSAL DUE DATE:

   1. The response to this Request for Proposal is due not later than 10:00 A.M. (CST), July 15, 2005.

   2. Please submit six (6) copies of your Proposal to:

   Ms. Sandra K. Broker
   Vice President
   Professional Brokerage Company
   304 East Wacker Drive Chicago, IL 60631
   Telephone No. (312) 555-8067
   Fax No. (312) 555-0449 [end CG]

NEW PARADIGMS[1]

A successful project manager today must be clairvoyant, have the skills of a psychologist, know the principles of running a day-care program for children, and be able to direct the complex demands of completing a project, be it a relatively simple remodel to a multimillion-dollar facility expansion. Many more skills than those in standard project management are juggled to bring a project to successful fruition.

Experience and research show that successful project managers apply a multitude of skills to the overall direction of a project. Two important tools that project management should have are the concepts and application of partnering and team building. These are paradigms because they are not among the normal rules and boundaries utilized in corporate project management.

Managing a corporate project is basically organizing yourself and materials into a process that will deliver a product within a set amount of time for a given amount of cost. "On time and within budget" is the bottom line for upper management.

What some facility professionals in the quest of successful project management may have a hard time doing, or at least doing well, is managing people. That is where team building and partnering come into play. Some in this field may feel left in the cold when they try to manage and direct people in diverse and often competing relationships. A basic understanding of the principal tenets of partnering and team building will give you additional power in your project management endeavors. In fact, you may be surprised to learn that partnering and team-building principles are found in the concepts of total quality management (TQM). Total quality management is different things to different people, but in many ways it is doing more with less and doing a better job of it. This certainly fits project management as well.

Our resources of people, time, and money are always in short supply. The trick is how to make the greatest impact with the human resources that are at hand from top management down to the bottommost tier. You must recognize and deal with the liabilities and assets of all the players involved in a project. If you can accomplish that goal, then you've probably solved 90 percent of your problems from the outset, or at least you will have a process in hand to deal with people problems.

What is partnering? Partnering is not a new way of doing business. It is the way people used to do business when a person's word was his or her bond and everyone accepted responsibility. Partnering is not a contract but rather the recognition that every contract includes an implied covenant of good faith.

The partnering process attempts to establish working relationships among the parties (we can call them *stakeholders*) through a mutual commitment for communication. Trust and teamwork are the primary elements, and disputes are resolved in a recognized and agreed-on process.

---

[1]The information in this section is taken from "Applying New Paradigms to Project Management," by M. Boone Hellman, IFMA '93 Presentation Papers, University of California, San Diego, San Diego, CA, October 1993, pp. 164–167.

The key elements of partnering are as follows:

- *Commitment.* Everyone involved is committed to the overall success of a project.

- *Equity.* Everyone's perspective and interests are considered in the creation of mutual goals for a successful project by utilizing a win-win philosophy.

- *Trust.* Open communication about motives, risks, and individual goals creates a better understanding among the involved entities. With an understanding of your associates' problems and risks, and their reciprocal understanding of your motives, risks, and goals, you can develop and nurture mutual trust.

- *Development of mutual goals and objectives.* Jointly developed goals and objectives allow unclouded thinking about mutual project decision making. In essence, all parties possess a joint investment in the project.

- *Implementation.* All parties jointly participate in the implementation of their mutual goals and objectives.

- *Continuous evaluation.* Like everything else, partnering needs attention and work for it to be successful. Difficulties must be addressed. Successes must be analyzed and repeated.

- *Timely responsiveness.* Mechanisms for quick communication are delineated and utilized. Issue resolution is handled effectively and expeditiously.

Partnering has tremendous benefits for all concerned. It definitely can save money and time when correctly and effectively applied.

Team building is the other project management tool that can contribute to attaining a successful project. Everyone on a project wants to be a part of the team, a recognized and utilized team member. Team building is a part of the partnering process as well, but it is easier to use in everyday circumstances than the more formal partnering process.

Understanding your colleagues, both internal and external, is the primary ingredient of successful team building. This is where the recognition of others' assets and utilities comes into play. If you can deal with people's personalities and behaviors to the point of influencing them in the outcome of decisions, then you can, to a large degree, influence the decision-making process. In other words, you must determine how to appeal to their desires. This results in effective decision making, or getting the decision you want.

The key to effective lateral relationships is the ability of managers to negotiate (see chapter 1). You must recognize the limitations of a counterpart's negotiating capabilities. Work toward win-win negotiations, and the other person also feels a sense of accomplishment.

What do people want on a team?

- To be informed.
- To be respected.
- To be listened to.

- To have their needs met.
- To feel safe.
- To have a sense of control.
- To belong.
- To be recognized and rewarded.
- To feel competent.
- To have a sense of power.
- To feel job satisfaction.

What are the characteristics of a well-functioning team? Team members have a strong commitment to do the following:

- Communicate openly and frankly.
- Actively listen.
- Recognize the personal style of others and stretch to meet their needs.
- Participate in the problem-solving process.
- Confront each other's assumptions without interrupting further contributions; regard conflict as a healthy and necessary part of the problem-solving process.
- Recognize that there is room for new ideas and that team members can use both competing and cooperating behaviors.
- Realize that a cohesive bond exists among individual team members. This strong unity is the basis for the energetic support of organizational objectives.
- Recognize task (content) and maintenance (process) roles.
- Feel responsible and committed to the successful implementation of the team's decisions and objectives.
- Assure that team leadership is appropriate and clear by shifting the leadership role to whoever has the expertise and by making sure that much of the decision making is by consensus. However, be alert for the wrong-decision-for-the-wrong-reason syndrome.

If you can apply and utilize some of these people-oriented attitudes, you will have a fully complemented project management toolbox. You still have to be a jack-of-all-trades, but knowing when and how to use the right tool is as important as anything else in the project management process.

Private Funding Initiatives

We see the increasing use of private funding initiatives (PFIs), where an organization contracts with a legal entity (developer, mortgage lender, general contractor, or facility management company) to design, build, and manage all aspects of a facility development project. The organization, in effect, borrows funds on a 15- to 30-year basis and makes a monthly lease payment. This frees the organization's capital for other business uses and provides the entity with a cash flow stream to pay off the debt and provide ongoing facility management services to their tenant.

This advanced turnkey approach not only provides for a completed site and facility but also includes the day-to-day facility management maintenance and operations of the facility long before it is ready for occupancy. This also provides the outsourcing facility management company with an opportunity to make recommendations to the design team and to review construction and building commissioning processes before they take over management of the site and facilities.

Conclusion

The construction and remodeling process is an ongoing and often daily activity at most organizations. When technology and office furnishing systems permit management to reorganize with moderate cost and time loss, then management will make that reorganization decision. As facility professionals improve their project management skills, harder projects become old hat, and customers expect to be able to meet even tighter construction, renovation, and relocation schedules. No one admits an upper limit has been reached although some may feel they have already given their best.

As the facility project manager, you may have just completed your assigned project and your customer has satisfactorily moved in. Now maintenance and operations personnel must ensure that all building mechanical and electrical systems perform year round and that all spaces are maintained so as to keep the facility and site operational. Their job is never done, but you will have made it easier if you included them on your project team, kept them informed and involved during construction as well as through relocation, and made sure that they underwent training on new building systems and received operations manuals, equipment warranties, and as-built drawings. In turn, they will be able to help you when you need their information for your next construction, renovation, or relocation project.

Chapter Eight

Maintenance and Operations

A facility's physical appearance often gives corporate clients, customers, investors, lenders, visitors, and employees their first impression of an organization. Accordingly, the ongoing management, maintenance, and operations of these owned or leased facilities are critical considerations. Many organizations, unfortunately, do not recognize the significance of the contribution the facility maintenance and operations function makes to the success or failure of the business.

Exhibit 8.1 shows a facility maintenance and operations process flowchart documenting the steps most corporate maintenance and operations departments must address to satisfy their customers' operational, regulatory, and code requirements and to keep the owned facility operating every day as designed. The process in the flowchart shows the most common maintenance and operations functions:

1. Customer service/help desk

2. Engineering and energy management

3. Supply

4. Preventive and corrective maintenance

5. Custodial (janitorial) services

6. Site and exterior building maintenance are also included in the preceding functions.

The dotted Landlord block in Exhibit 8.1 indicates where the facility maintenance and operations personnel may coordinate customer requirements in leased facilities with the landlord and review and inspect (where allowed in the lease) the landlord's ongoing and preventive maintenance and operations program.

Exhibit 8.1 illustrates the coordination of the corporate real estate, design, and construction management functions. It is vitally important that maintenance and operations personnel take part in new site and facility reviews and acquisitions as well as planning, budgeting, and executing churn and capital projects. Participation should include design review, construction document review, specifications review, and construction review; a maintenance and operations representative should be on the punchlist team.

For example, it is not unusual, in many organizations, for maintenance to paint an area as part of their ongoing maintenance plan, only to have the area

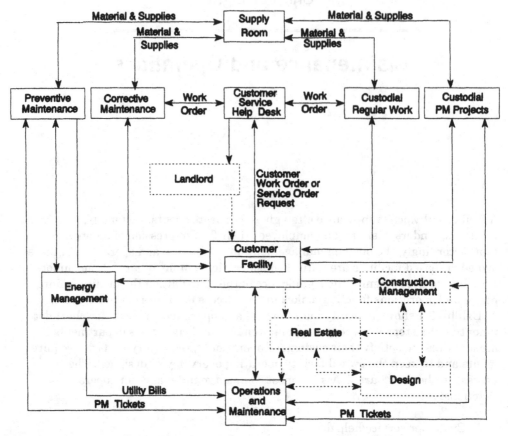

Exhibit 8.1   Facility Maintenance and Operations Process Flowchart

demolished the next day as part of a churn or capital project (see chapters 5, 6, and 7) of which they were unaware. The obvious conclusion (but often overlooked) is to ensure that maintenance and operations personnel are active members of the project team so they know about scheduled changes well in advance. This enables them to exchange feedback and suggestions about how these projects may affect the operation, maintenance, safety, and security of the facility and site.

Just as any business needs a plan to succeed, the maintenance and operations of a company facility requires a maintenance and operations plan and yearly budget.

THE IMPORTANCE OF MAINTENANCE AND OPERATIONS

Current Trends

For almost 30 years now, the positive effects of good maintenance and operations have received increased attention, largely because corporations appreciate the strategic importance of real estate and facilities to a company's financial structure. The vast numbers of leveraged buyouts have focused attention on the mar-

ket value (versus book value) of sites and facilities owned by acquired companies
and the ability to finance acquisitions with those assets.

In addition, with sale-leaseback transactions becoming a common source of
capital for the selling company, the relationship of the value of corporate property
and the impact of good management on that value has received a lot of recognition. Corporate facility professionals and trade and professional associations have
been reasonably successful in demonstrating the significant relationship of maintenance and operations and investment performance.

These trends—combined with aggressive and, at times, inept and unscrupu-
lous real estate lending practices in the late 1980s by savings and loan concerns,
commercial banks, and the demise of Internet boom companies in the 1990s and
early 2000s—highlight the importance of effective maintenance and operations.
Organizations and individuals that recognize their problem real estate and troubled real estate loan portfolios early are often able to overcome many threats.
Without exception, decisive, high-quality maintenance and operations are credited with making a significant contribution to the workout and restructuring
process. Accordingly, organizations are trying to improve the quality of their
maintenance and operations and facility management services.

Today, corporate property owners are focusing on management operations as
they look for ways to reduce operating costs, dispose of excess properties, or hold
on to troubled properties by improving their operating income (and reducing their
operating losses). The proliferation of published commercial real estate operating
data makes it easier to evaluate commercial property performance, but not corporate property performance. This need for corporate property data has helped
establish the importance of maintenance and operations capabilities and performance, which are becoming recognized as a cornerstone of every successful corporation's strategy and operations.

PREDICTIVE MAINTENANCE

Facility maintenance and operations costs for facilities in North America often
represent 50 to 70 percent of total annual facility operating costs. Many facility
professionals are now seeking leading-edge and best practices, processes, and procedures to manage, plan, and complete work. While the majority of the work continues to be preventive maintenance (60 percent) rather than reactive
maintenance (35 percent), many are now including predictive maintenance programs in their work activities.

Predictive maintenance uses a number of non-invasive techniques such as oil
analysis, infrared scanning, and vibration analysis to test a piece of equipment's
state of repair. If these tests show the piece of equipment has no problems, expensive annual teardown can be postponed or delayed. Equipment downtime is
reduced, maintenance staff are reassigned to other equipment and work, and the
facility management customer experiences a longer time between the stopping of
services for preventive maintenance work. Predictive maintenance, especially for
facility management customers who have large, mission-critical facilities, provides the opportunity to increase equipment life and to reduce equipment failure
to a very rare event.

The Multiplier Effect

Senior management and corporate facility executives are learning to take into consideration the multiplier effect as it relates to all recurring property expense (and income) items. All too often, undue attention is given to negotiating one-time high-cost items like property and casualty insurance, while small recurring cost items are ignored.

While a $3,000 reduction on an insurance premium results in a one-time saving of $3,000, a seemingly small decrease in expenses (e.g., lowering cleaning costs) for each square foot of office or support space can have a much more significant effect on cash flow and, ultimately, property and business value. For example, a decrease in maintenance costs of $0.03 per month for each square foot of a 300,000-square-foot office building decreases monthly and annual maintenance costs by $9,000 and $106,000, respectively. All these savings fall to the bottom line, making the business more profitable and, very likely, the corporate property more valuable.

The property value becomes significant in terms of its use as collateral for obtaining financing, engineering a sale-leaseback, and leveraged buyouts (LBOs). In fact, in the preceding example, the $106,000 annual reduction in costs might increase the value of the property by over $1,200,000. In contrast, the $3,000 savings on casualty insurance would increase the building's value by $36,000.

The multiplier effect must also be considered in its application to increases in costs and their related reduction in income and in its power to turn a marginally profitable business into a sizable cash drain. For example, a seemingly small increase in cleaning costs for a 150,000-square-foot office park, where such costs have typically totaled 10 percent of the building's expenses, would significantly decrease the cash flow and adversely affect the property's value by hundreds of thousands of dollars.

The greater the size of the property (in square footage or acres), the greater the impact of the multiplier effect. Its importance is enhanced even further as the organization's property and facility holdings grow.

GOALS OF MAINTENANCE OPERATIONS

Maintenance and operations must conform to overall corporate strategy and two goals. The first goal, which is both strategic and operational, is to ensure that clients, customers, employees, and other constituencies are able to visit or work in a certain type of location and, along with that, a specific type of environment. At minimum, this goal is likely to include a safe and clean environment and prompt attention paid to real estate—and facility-related problems (e.g., maintenance and repair). If this goal is ignored, the business may have difficulty attracting and retaining employees, clients, and customers, thereby decreasing revenues and increasing costs.

The second important goal includes target financial performance for property in terms of costs per square foot, costs per employee, costs as a percentage of revenues, costs as a percentage of total expenses, and costs in relation to prior period and budgeted costs. In addition, companies managing excess property or property leased to noncorporate entities, offers financial targets that should be addressed.

These should include target revenue and net income numbers, estimates of real estate values, and even disposition values.

These goals are accomplished through the implementation of appropriate strategies. These strategies should be defined and stated in a business or management plan developed by the corporate facility executive and senior management.

MAINTENANCE AND OPERATIONS ALTERNATIVES

Maintenance and operations issues should be considered and addressed early in the development of the company's corporate and facility management strategy (see chapter 2). At that time, strategy decisions and the related implementation plans should dictate or, at minimum, indicate which of three basic maintenance and operations alternatives is preferred or mandated:

1. Property that requires no management
2. Internal management of corporate property
3. Outsourcing maintenance and operations functions

In addition, companies that choose to sublease property to other (nonaffiliate) companies, either by strategic decision making or because of economic necessity, can accomplish this in conjunction with the preceding alternatives.

Deciding which alternative will best serve the company's overall strategy depends on the types of corporate property involved, and the choice may change many times throughout a company's life. Each management alternative has its advantages and disadvantages. Regardless of the maintenance and operations strategy, the goal should be to maximize corporate and real estate objectives by using the highest-quality and most cost-effective maintenance and operations resources available.

No Management Requirements

Companies that lease facilities under a standard lease agreement should have no maintenance and operations responsibilities; the burden of those responsibilities should be shifted to the building owner and, if applicable, the owner's maintenance and operations agent. The lease should address in detail all the rights and responsibilities of both the tenant and the landlord.

The track record, experience, and financial stability of the building owner and agent should be examined carefully. This review should include visiting the properties being managed by the owner/manager and speaking with clients, vendors, and others in the real estate community for references.

Managing Corporate Properties

Traditionally, corporations have managed the properties they own and those they lease under a net lease. While the organization of the facility management department varies (see chapter 1), its functions include, at minimum, managing the physical asset. This preeminently significant function includes developing and administering a maintenance plan; selecting, training, and supervising departmental and property-level employees; hiring and monitoring independent contractors; and making capital improvements.

Additional facility management department responsibilities may include preparation of related operating budgets and detailed recordkeeping; purchase of maintenance and repair supply items; risk management; and compliance with federal, state, and local laws. In many organizations, these functions are performed by other departments, including accounting, insurance, and legal.

Outsourcing—Selecting a Maintenance and Operations Firm

The past decade has seen significant interest in outsourcing the maintenance and operations functions related to corporate-owned and net-leased properties to independent maintenance and operations companies. This interest is increasing and includes joint ventures formed by corporations with facility management organizations. Historically, corporations outsourced only specific management functions, such as general cleaning and the maintenance and repair of elevators and other major equipment. Exhibit 8.2 shows a typical process flowchart for outsourced tasks.

There are many advantages to hiring an experienced maintenance and operations organization. Because professional management firms handle all the routine and time-consuming facility-level management maintenance and operations activities such as related purchasing, maintenance, employee/tenant communications, and staffing and other human resource management issues, corporate management is free to focus on strategic management issues, not to mention other opportunities. Seasoned professional facility management firms have the management proficiency (experienced management and staff) to manage a facility well while decreasing its operating costs and increasing its long-term value. Local outside management organizations are privy to market trends and legislative proposals that could affect the value of the facility. In addition, the purchasing skills and buying power of a large management organization often result in significant savings for the corporation.

If outsourcing is chosen as the method of managing corporate facilities, corporate management still must have an adequate understanding of the maintenance and operations function. This may include at least one knowledgeable in-house person to negotiate and manage the contract—a detailed specification describing the level of service(s) required and benchmarks to measure daily and long-term vendor performance and contractor(s).

Additionally, if a company chooses to outsource, consideration should be given to the impact of that choice on the company's employees. For example, which employees should be reassigned within the company or hired by the vendor as part of maintenance and operations contract?

Selection of an organization to manage a corporation's facilities may be accomplished in conjunction with outsourcing all the facility management functions or just the management of the maintenance and operations function (see chapter 1).

A vendor's past performance and depth of experience are important considerations when selecting a maintenance and operations organization. Interviewing a

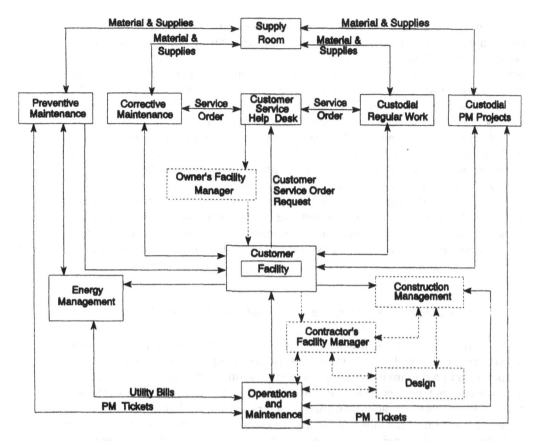

Exhibit 8.2   Outsourced Facility Maintenance and Operations Process Flowchart

management company's clients, tenants, vendors, and others in the real estate and facility management community, and inspecting the facilities being managed by the organization can give a good indication of the organization's management experience, level of service, effectiveness, methods, and style.

After reviewing the preceding information for each firm under consideration, the corporation should schedule a personal visit to each management firm to compare services, costs, firm size, structure, and operation. Such comparisons help ensure that the chosen organization is capable of performing facility services using an appropriate level of resources for successful management of the facilities.

Traditional Maintenance and Operations

Companies that choose to lease or sublease property to other (nonaffiliated) companies, either by strategic design or because of economic necessity, may need to perform all the tasks required by a traditional maintenance and operations company. These tasks include marketing and leasing property, determining rental rates and collecting rents, and dealing with the associated financial accounting and reporting.

Traditional maintenance and operations places the company in the owner/manager role, and with it the company assumes all the accompanying responsibilities. This is the reverse of leasing space from an owner/manager, where the corporation has minimal or no maintenance and operations responsibilities. Accordingly, the corporation should give careful consideration to the traditional management function prior to entering the market. Real estate and facility management consultants and maintenance and operations experts can provide valuable information about traditional management responsibilities. If a decision is made to enter the traditional real estate property marketplace, outsourcing the maintenance and operations function may still be the best decision and, accordingly, should be carefully considered.

The anticipated revenues, additional related costs, and level of service to be provided should be carefully estimated and documented prior to embarking on a strategy that requires traditional maintenance and operations. Nevertheless, in recent years, many corporations have found themselves with additional space and forced to enter the competitive marketplace of traditional real estate operators.

THE FACILITY MAINTENANCE MANAGEMENT FUNCTION

To many newcomers to the facility management industry, maintenance and operations appears to involve little more than property supervision—maintaining the property and paying invoices. Surprisingly, this limited perspective of building management is found, occasionally, within the facility maintenance and operations industry itself. In actuality, the importance of the facility maintenance management function in the site and facility investment process cannot be overstated.

Corporate facility maintenance and operations is a service industry requiring frequent interactions with in-house customers, onsite service personnel, contractors, governmental officials, and other professionals; therefore, it is useful for the corporation to develop a plan for its own operation—ideally, a maintenance manual (see Exhibit 8.3) that can be updated as needed and an organizational chart depicting management roles and responsibilities. A carefully developed plan and the selection of well-qualified employees to carry it out can maximize both company efficiency and income, giving corporate owners, managers, and customers a sense of security about the management of their property.

Successful maintenance and operations must begin with a carefully constructed plan, prepared with or approved by corporate management. The plan must strive to ensure that policies on costs and expenses, staffing, maintenance, and operational services enhance the value of the property to the corporation. Even undeveloped parcels of land adjacent to an industrial park or shopping center call for attention to such management-related issues as site hazards, local development trends, taxes, zoning, and legal codes.

If management functions are allowed to follow an uncharted course, as they are in many corporate facilities, it is difficult to make necessary modifications in direction when problems arise. The result is a lack of control that can quickly develop, by crisis, into reactive and ineffective management. It should be noted that adherence to a management plan does not preclude flexibility. Meeting the management demands of retail, office, and industrial real estate requires an

1. Custodial maintenance
   - Task descriptions
   - Memorandums
   - Articles
2. Corrective maintenance
   - Common maintenance problems
   - Performance standards
   - Memorandums
   - Articles
3. Preventive maintenance
   - Policy
   - Inspection reports
   - Property detail records and service detail
   - Preventive maintenance checklist
   - Winterization checklist
   - Operating instructions
   - Memorandums
   - Articles
4. Emergency maintenance
   - Emergency call list
   - Emergency procedures
   - Memorandums
   - Articles
5. Service contracts
   - Service contract summary
   - Service contract analysis
   - Contractor's references
   - Memorandums and correspondence
   - Articles
6. Security
   - Policy
   - Procedures
   - Memorandums
   - Articles
7. Safety
   - Procedures
   - Memorandums
   - Articles

Exhibit 8.3   Maintenance Manual: Sample Table of Contents ongoing reevaluation of decisions on staffing, repairs and maintenance, insurance, and other aspects of maintenance and operations.

Management Activities

While maintenance and operations has always been an essential component of achieving corporate goals, only fairly recently have senior managers started to recognize its full importance.

To simplify understanding of the broad range of management activities it encompasses, we break down maintenance and operations into six basic areas of responsibility:

1. *Management of the physical asset.* Administration of the maintenance plan, hiring and monitoring independent contractors, tenant construction, and capital improvements.

2. *Intracompany and customer management.* Interdepartmental and customer relations, rent collections, and evictions.

3. *Financial reporting and controls.* Preparation of the operating budget, detailed recordkeeping, and purchasing/inventory control.

4. *Administration.* Employee selection, training, and supervision; development of appropriate insurance programs; operation of the management office; compliance with federal, state, and local laws.

5. *Communicating performance.* Development of communication systems between senior management, customers, and vendors with the facility management department.

6. *Marketing and leasing.* Market research, marketing strategy, broker selection, lease preparation, leasing techniques, and tenant selection.

The services required by the corporate facility management department vary depending on corporate strategy, type and size of real estate and facility holdings, remaining term(s) on leased and subleased properties, organization of company, and stage of corporate development. In many corporations, the facility management or real estate department may primarily have responsibility for managing the physical asset; in others, it may have responsibility for all six of the functions listed.

Facility Maintenance Management Organization

The purpose of defining a corporation's structure is to demonstrate how the constituent positions and functions are related. Some corporations may choose to operate with an informal structure—one without titles or specified lines of responsibility and reporting. With few exceptions (e.g., small companies), an informal structure is not recommended for the corporate facility management or maintenance and operations function (see chapter 1).

An organization chart should be prepared to visually depict the company's maintenance and operations structure; this facilitates company maintenance and operations by defining what is to be done, and by whom. The chart's detail and narrative should be determined, in part, by the size of the company's facility holdings, its stage of development, and its management preference.

Human Resources

Well-qualified employees supported by a strong training program, compensated competitively, and supervised properly help increase the probability of a facility meeting corporate objectives. Employees should be given clear, specific definitions of duties and responsibilities to reduce misunderstandings and to promote good personnel relations. One of management's responsibilities is letting employees know what is expected of them. Without a clear understanding of what is expected, employees are not able to perform effectively or efficiently. Accordingly, job descriptions should be prepared for all maintenance and operations employees.

A job description should specify in writing the areas of responsibility and authority and the duties of a particular position within the company. It should also define the significant relationships of the individual performing the job with others in the organization, the level of service to be provided, how performance is evaluated, and how often and in what manner this is accomplished.

Maintenance Manual

Preparing a maintenance manual (see Exhibit 8.3), which standardizes a company's policies and procedures, forces management to address, in detail, every aspect of the management process. A maintenance manual increases the likelihood that management and employees will make consistent decisions and act in accordance with federal, state, and local laws.

An up-to-date maintenance manual is an important permanent resource for maintenance and operations managers, supervisors, and employees and an integral part of the training process. It should reflect the company's basic maintenance and operating policies and procedures. A maintenance manual should be a primary source of information, providing consistent answers to questions that arise and solutions to most problems that occur. A maintenance manual enables decisions to be made quickly and empowers employees at lower levels in the company, thereby freeing management to attend to responsibilities such as planning and control.

Because a maintenance manual covers a large portion of the maintenance and operations program, it must be amended and updated on a regular basis to keep pace with changing company, property, and industry conditions. One source of recommendations that often goes unrecognized is feedback from onsite staff responsible for implementing the policies and procedures of the company.

MANAGEMENT PLANNING PROCESS

A formal, written plan stating the financial and non-financial goals for a facility or group of facilities is essential for a successful maintenance and operations program. The planning process for managing facilities is similar to that for any other aspect of business planning.

Planning requires the development of a course of action based on an understanding of the responsibilities and capabilities of the company and of the expectations and goals of management. The planning process should result in a comprehensive plan that covers all areas of concern. Developing a good plan requires the commitment of everyone involved in the maintenance and operations process, including senior management, corporate facility management, maintenance and operations management, and onsite employees. The plan must reflect an understanding of the current situation, the company's objectives, and the method of measuring performance.

The Management Plan

To ensure delivery of the exact services agreed on, the maintenance and operations manager, the facility executive, and senior management together should prepare a business or management plan for each site and facility. The purposes of the management plan are to (1) direct the operation toward realization of corporate objectives for that property, (2) provide a standard by which the manager's progress can be measured, and (3) allow for the implementation of programs to improve the facility's performance and value.

A good management plan is the foundation of a well-managed site and facility. After stating the agreed-on objectives for the facility, the management plan should outline and analyze current and expected demographic and economic conditions of the facility and surrounding area. The plan should then state a strategy for achieving management goals based on this analysis. Because it documents what is expected and from whom, the plan is an invaluable communication and performance measurement tool for management, onsite employees, senior management and, in many cases, lending institutions.

The type and amount of information required to prepare an effective management plan varies with requirements dictated by the type and size of the site and facility. It is often useful to prepare a preliminary plan that identifies the areas to be addressed and the information to be gathered. This preliminary plan should undergo revision and fine-tuning until the facility executive and senior management approve a final version. Even the final plan is subject to revision as time passes in order to accommodate changes in circumstances, objectives, and goals. Although the initial preparation of a management plan is time-consuming and tedious, the revision process is easier with each successive plan.

Generally, the management plan should address the following issues:

1. Objectives: Profile of company.

   Degree of senior management participation in management (e.g., monthly written reports)

   Expected duration of ownership

2. Neighborhood and regional description:

   Population growth and area characteristics (economic, social and political)

   Occupancy and rental-rate trends

   Significant opportunities and risks (e.g., major competitor moving in or out of the area, number of new commercial properties, etc.)

3. Description of the facility and maintenance requirements:

   Detailed physical description

   Technical equipment considerations (e.g., security system, energy management, HVAC)

   Maintenance and repairs (routine and extraordinary)

   Optimal improvement of the maintenance program

   Recommendations for capital improvements—rehabilitation, modernization, or conversion

   Manual or computerized maintenance management system

4. Financial management:

   Structure and details of real estate financing

   Accounting and bookkeeping systems

   Type and frequency of reporting

   Preparation of operating budget and pro formas

   Breakeven analysis

   Purchasing procedures and limitations

   Insurance requirements

   Tax management

5. Administrative responsibilities:

   Management company organizational structure

   General personnel requirements and policy

   Management office hours, staffing, procedures

6. Communication and decision making:

   Summary of type and frequency of reports

   Schedule of meetings

   Situations requiring notice

   Decisions critical to the facility

   Decision-making authority and relevant factors

Systems for Control

For management to accurately and effectively control the management function, the management plan should provide for reporting, communicating, and decision-making systems. This control should be one of the overall objectives of the management plan.

Control is impossible without a plan—and without control, it is difficult to be aware of the need for changes in policies and procedures or modification to the current strategy. There are too many variables—expense items, staffing, turnover, and competing properties—to expect the desired outcome to emerge without planning and the accompanying controls. The basics of successful maintenance and operations practices, while specialized, are basically no different from successful business management practices, of which planning and control are integral parts.

By regularly and frequently documenting operating results, the reporting system provides the information necessary for evaluation and subsequent appropriate modification. If, for example, a plan is developed that projects a 4 percent increase in maintenance and operations costs over the next year, it is crucial for both the maintenance and operations manager and accounting to be aware that two months into the period, maintenance and operations costs have already increased 3 percent. Without timely reporting, it is difficult to give accurate credit for a property's success or to identify and rectify the problems causing a property's failure.

Operating Budget

The operating budget, as shown in Exhibit 8.4, is a critical part of the management plan and the control system. Accordingly, its preparation should take into consideration the impact of both financial and non-financial factors. The operating budget portion of a typical management plan should provide the means for comparing the actual operations with budgeted projections for the current month, year to date, and the corresponding month from the previous year, if available. This budget should be reviewed monthly by the property manager and, if desired, by accounting and other members of senior management. Depending on discrepancies between actual and projected numbers and changes in relevant economic conditions, the budget and operating procedures should be revised as necessary.

To assist in determining rental income and operating expenses, the manager should compare the current operating data with those of similar corporate properties by contacting their corporate maintenance and operations managers. Additional sources of current operating data could be a knowledgeable local real estate or property management firm, building maintenance trade associations, or the yearly operating expense reviews sold by national real estate and property management trade associations. Definitions of operating costs may vary among companies, organizations, and associations; accordingly, exercise care when using such information.

Published operating data is available from the Building Owners and Managers Association (BOMA), Washington, DC; Institute of Real Estate Management (IREM) and the Society of Industrial and Office Realtors (SIOR), Chicago, IL; International Facility Management Association (IFMA), Houston, TX; National Association of Industrial and Office Parks (NAIOP), Merrifield, VA; and the Urban Land Institute (ULI), Washington, DC.

The management plan and the operating budget should be viewed as guidelines or points of reference for asking questions about performance and for improving operations. Questions such as "Why are maintenance and operations costs over or under the plan?" and "Why is a particular expense over or under budget?" may lead to additional questions about related items. Both the questions and answers improve the planning process and operating results. Comparing actual with projected performance keeps management aware of changes in the operations and improves the skills required to develop future plans. In this respect, planning is more of a process than an end in itself—as skills improve, so do the plans.

ABC BUILDING (ACCOUNT NO. 1456)
2005 INCOME AND OPERATING PLAN

SEPTEMBER 5, 2004
PREPARED BY: STEVEN ADAMS

CODE ACCOUNT	JAN	FEB	MAR	APR	MAY	JUN	JUL	AUG	SEP	OCT	NOV	DEC	TOTAL
42260 RENTAL INCOME	163,014.00	163,269.00	171,112.00	169,972.00	170,026.00	170,472.00	171,220.00	172,248.00	172,362.00	172,362.00	173,480.00	173,608.00	2,043,145.00
EXPENSES													
42264 Utilities													
Electric	9,559.00	8,869.00	9,089.00	10,078.00	10,622.00	15,359.00	14,323.00	15,215.00	15,878.00	14,744.00	10,207.00	7,978.00	141,921.00
Gas/Fuel Oil	4,042.00	4,417.00	4,716.00	2,795.00	1,152.00	679.00	35.00	35.00	35.00	150.00	2,079.00	4,725.00	24,860.00
Water	0.00	0.00	2,576.00	0.00	2,767.00	0.00	0.00	0.00	3,360.00	0.00	2,887.00	0.00	11,590.00
Total Utilities	13,601.00	13,286.00	16,381.00	12,873.00	14,541.00	16,038.00	14,358.00	15,250.00	19,273.00	14,894.00	15,173.00	12,703.00	178,371.00
42269 Mechanical	13,421.00	30,971.00	18,821.00	14,621.00	15,571.00	13,421.00	13,421.00	14,971.00	15,030.00	13,430.00	13,780.00	13,430.00	190,888.00
42270 Electrical	2,676.00	2,325.00	450.00	450.00	825.00	3,887.00	450.00	2,425.00	450.00	450.00	825.00	450.00	15,663.00
42274 Fire Protection	3,126.00	573.00	62.00	244.00	231.00	62.00	244.00	4,063.00	62.00	254.00	241.00	62.00	9,224.00
42267 Cleaning	9,154.00	9,154.00	9,154.00	9,154.00	11,920.00	9,154.00	9,154.00	9,154.00	9,154.00	9,154.00	9,154.00	9,154.00	112,614.00
42268 Landscaping	955.00	955.00	985.00	985.00	4,185.00	985.00	985.00	985.00	985.00	2,185.00	985.00	985.00	16,160.00
42273 Security	808.00	808.00	808.00	808.00	808.00	1,372.00	872.00	872.00	872.00	872.00	872.00	872.00	10,644.00
42271 Elevators	872.00	872.00	872.00	898.00	898.00	898.00	898.00	898.00	898.00	898.00	898.00	898.00	10,698.00
42269 Snow Removal	1,400.00	1,200.00	0.00	0.00	0.00	0.00	0.00	0.00	0.00	0.00	750.00	500.00	3,850.00
42269 Miscellaneous	485.00	799.00	785.00	1,335.00	1,045.00	1,206.00	1,292.00	806.00	542.00	492.00	806.00	492.00	10,085.00
42924 Management Fee	6,655.00	6,655.00	6,655.00	6,655.00	6,655.00	6,655.00	6,655.00	6,655.00	6,655.00	6,655.00	6,655.00	6,655.00	79,860.00
42280 Taxes/Insurance	0.00	0.00	0.00	0.00	0.00	0.00	0.00	0.00	198,535.00	0.00	0.00	0.00	198,535.00
42265 EWO Work	0.00	0.00	0.00	0.00	0.00	0.00	0.00	0.00	0.00	0.00	0.00	0.00	0.00
10504 Leasehold Improv	0.00	0.00	0.00	0.00	5,000.00	0.00	0.00	0.00	0.00	0.00	0.00	0.00	5,000.00
Total Expenses	53,153.00	67,598.00	54,973.00	48,023.00	61,679.00	53,678.00	48,329.00	56,079.00	252,456.00	49,284.00	50,139.00	46,201.00	841,592.00
OPERATING INCOME	109,861.00	95,671.00	116,139.00	121,949.00	108,347.00	116,794.00	122,891.00	116,169.00	(80,094.00)	123,078.00	123,341.00	127,407.00	1,201,553.00
42265 SWITCH EXPENSES													
Maintenance	0.00	6,678.00	0.00	0.00	6,678.00	0.00	0.00	6,678.00	0.00	0.00	6,678.00	0.00	26,712.00
XYZ CORP. Payments	(4,913.00)	(4,913.00)	(4,913.00)	(4,913.00)	(4,913.00)	(4,913.00)	(4,913.00)	(4,913.00)	(4,913.00)	(4,913.00)	(4,913.00)	(4,913.00)	(58,956.00)
Total Switch	(4,913.00)	1,765.00	(4,913.00)	(4,913.00)	1,765.00	(4,913.00)	(4,913.00)	1,765.00	(4,913.00)	(4,913.00)	1,765.00	(4,913.00)	(32,244.00)
NET OPERATING INCOME	114,774.00	93,906.00	121,052.00	126,862.00	106,582.00	121,707.00	127,804.00	114,404.00	(75,181.00)	127,991.00	121,576.00	132,320.00	1,233,797.00
CHECKBOOK BALANCE													
Account Minimum	5,000.00	5,000.00	5,000.00	5,000.00	5,000.00	5,000.00	5,000.00	5,000.00	5,000.00	5,000.00	5,000.00	5,000.00	
Net Oper Income	114,774.00	93,906.00	121,052.00	126,862.00	106,582.00	121,707.00	127,804.00	114,404.00	(75,181.00)	127,991.00	121,576.00	132,320.00	
ABC COMPANY A/C	0.00	0.00	0.00	0.00	0.00	0.00	0.00	0.00	0.00	0.00	0.00	0.00	
Transfer to ABC CO.	(114,774.00)	(93,906.00)	(121,052.00)	(126,862.00)	(106,582.00)	(121,707.00)	(127,804.00)	(114,404.00)	75,181.00	(127,991.00)	(121,576.00)	(132,320.00)	
Balance Sheet Items	20,027.21	20,027.21	20,027.21	20,027.21	20,027.21	20,027.21	20,027.21	20,027.21	20,027.21	20,027.21	20,027.21	20,027.21	
MONTH END BALANCE	25,027.21	25,027.21	25,027.21	25,027.21	25,027.21	25,027.21	25,027.21	25,027.21	25,027.21	25,027.21	25,027.21	25,027.21	

Exhibit 8.4   ABC Building Income and Operating Budget—2005

A sample operating budget for a 250,000-square-foot build-to-suit building is included as Exhibit 8.4. The building, located in a suburban mid-Atlantic city, is managed by the facility services division of a corporation and is 50 percent leased to a nonaffiliated tenant. The rental income reflects income from both the affiliated and nonaffiliated tenants.

Management Contract

If a corporation outsources the management of its site and facilities, a maintenance and operations contract should be prepared and executed. (A management contract is also commonly called a *management agreement* or *service level agreement*.) In addition, corporate facility management or a facility maintenance or real estate department that manages corporate property should consider using a management contract. This is a legal contract that establishes an agency relationship between the corporate facility owner (the "owner") and the maintenance and operations entity (the "contractor"). It should state specifically the rights and responsibilities of both the contractor and the corporate facility owner and should itemize in detail the duties of the contractor as well as the method and frequency of their performance. A sample table of contents, confidentiality agreement, and contract agreement for a request for proposal for outsourced maintenance and operations services appears in the next section. The detailed specifications are not included.

Like the management plan, the management contract should be executed between the contractor's organization and the corporate facility owner. In some cases, the management contract provides for the preparation of the management plan. In other cases, the management plan is prepared prior to hiring a contract management company.

The management contract should include desired limitations or restrictions (e.g., minimum contract length of six months, corporate facility owner approval of all vended service contracts after three competitive bids are obtained) and a statement that all management duties are to be performed in compliance with federal, state, and local laws (e.g., ADA, OSHA, wage and hour laws).

Every management contract should be reviewed and approved by corporate legal counsel to ensure compliance with current federal, state, and local laws and with corporate policies, standards, and requirements. In addition, counsel should review the facts and circumstances influencing management of a particular site and facility and discuss and clarify sections that might lead to misunderstandings or litigation. The following items appear in most management contracts:

- Identification of the site(s) and facility(ies) to be managed
- Identification of the parties—the corporate property owner and contractor and the form of organization of each
- Duration of contract
- Commencement and expiration dates
- Renewal and termination clauses—how, by whom, when, and what type of notice must be given

- Type and frequency of reports to be issued to owner
- Authority to enter into vended service contracts, leases, and other agreements, including any restrictions or limitations
- Specific management duties of agent
- Authority to employ, train, supervise, set salary for, and terminate onsite employees
- Clarification of whether onsite employees are employees of the corporate property owner or the contract manager
- Banking instructions
- Specific purchasing authority, including setting limits, authority to pay bills for property expenses, and specification of party responsible for paying the taxes, insurance, and mortgages
- A detailed list of insurance coverage on the property
- An indemnity clause holding the agent harmless for liability arising out of management of the property
- Confidentiality agreement
- Amount of fees, or formula(s) for their calculation, to be paid to the agent for management, leasing, and other duties (e.g., remodeling, major repairs), as well as frequency and timing of payments
- If appropriate, specific authority to collect rents, security deposits, and other income; to deposit monies; and to institute legal actions to collect rents and other income
- Signature of both parties

If a management plan is not prepared, certain information that would otherwise be covered in the plan should be added to the management contract, including a statement of the corporate property owner's objectives and first-year operating budget. A well-drafted management contract addresses all areas of primary concern to the contract manager and the owner to reduce the possibility of conflict from misunderstanding, to increase the probability that each party will act in accordance with the other's expectations, and to provide a basis for settling disputes that may arise.

Charge-Backs

There are several ways to allocate the cost of facility management, maintenance, and operation services among corporate business segments (e.g., subsidiaries, divisions, departments, and products). This allocation is commonly known as a *charge-back*, *corporate allocation*, or *transfer pricing*—artificial prices used when goods or services are transferred from one segment to another within the same company. The charge-back or transfer price is recorded as either revenue or expense recovery to the facility management department and as a cost, or expense, of the business segment occupying the facility and using the services of the facility management department.

The charge-back price for facilities should be the amount that would be charged to a business segment if the same facility or space and related services were purchased from a nonaffiliated party. Without this market price, charge-back prices can be determined (a) on a cost basis, (b) on a cost-plus-profit basis, or (c) by estimating market price. The application of each of these methods has its complications; accordingly, internal conflict is likely regardless of the method chosen.

The method used for charge-back prices should be consistent with the company's organizational structure and policy for determining whether the facility management service departments are cost centers or profit centers.

SAMPLE: OUTSOURCING MAINTENANCE SERVICES REQUEST FOR PROPOSAL GUIDELINES AND STATEMENT OF WORK

TABLE OF CONTENTS

4.0 FACILITY MAINTENANCE

    1. Service Desk

    2. Parking Lot Services and Maintenance

    3. Painting and Wallcovering

    4. HVAC Equipment Preventive Maintenance

    5. Minor Construction

    6. Fire Pump/Sprinkler

    7. Pantry/Food Service Equipment Maintenance

    8. Water Treatment

    9. Furniture Keys

    10. Electrical Work

    11. Plumbing Maintenance

    12. Switch Gear

    13. Telephone and Equipment Cabling

    14. Standby Power—UPS and Emergency Power Generator

    15. Elevators

    16. Building and Energy Management System and Building Fire Alarm System

    17. Computer-aided Maintenance Management

    18. Light Bulb Replacement

    19. Ceiling Tile Replacement

5.0 ADMINISTRATION

    1. Mail Room Services

    2. Office Services

    3. Convenience Copiers

    4. Additional Services

    5. Audiovisual Equipment Services

    6. Typewriter Maintenance

    7. Conference Room Scheduling

    8. Reprographics Vending

    9. Switchboard/Receptionist

6.0 ATTACHMENTS

    1. General Offices/Public Spaces Cleaning Schedule

    2. Rest Room Cleaning Schedule

    3. Kitchen and Pantry Areas Cleaning Schedule

    4. Stairs, Vinyl and Terminal Floors Cleaning Schedule

    5. Cafeteria Cleaning Schedule

    6. Carpet Care Cleaning Schedule

    7. Special Projects Cleaning Schedule

8. Day Porter Duties Schedule

9. Special Projects Matrix Cleaning Schedule

10. Window Cleaning Schedule

11. Unit Pricing for Minor Construction

12. Unit Pricing for Painting

13. Pricing Schedule for System Furniture, Inventory, Reconfiguration, and Removal

14. Pricing Schedule for Electrical Work

15. Pricing Schedule—Plants

16. Schedule of Unit Prices for Housekeeping Services

17. Pricing Schedule for Moving Services

18. Service Request Form

19. HVAC Maintenance Schedule

20. Equipment Schedule

21. Detailed Facility Description

22. Site Plan

23. Floor Plans

24. Confidentiality Agreement

25. Contract Terms and Agreement

ATTACHMENT 24

CONFIDENTIALITY AGREEMENT

CONFIDENTIALITY AGREEMENT, dated_____, _____, 20_____, between ABC Company ("Owner"), a Delaware corporation with an office at 2124 South Wacker Drive, Chicago, IL 60606, and _____("Contractor"), with an office at _____;

WHEREAS, the parties to this Confidentiality Agreement have determined to establish terms governing the confidentiality of certain information, one party ("Owner") may disclose to the other party ("Offeror or Recipient");

NOW THEREFORE, the parties agree as follows:

1. For the purposes of this Confidentiality Agreement, *Confidential Information* means all information regarding RFP-0500 7 ABC, in whatever form transmitted. relating to the past, present, or future business affairs, including without limitation research, development, or business plans, operations, or systems of Owner or another party whose information Owner has in its possession under obligations of confidentiality, which (a) is disclosed by Owner or its affiliates to Recipient or its affiliates, bearing an appropriate legend indicating its confidential or proprietary nature or otherwise disclosed in a manner consistent with its confidential or

proprietary nature, or (b) is produced or developed during the working relationship between the parties and that would, if disclosed to competitors of Owner, give or increase such competitors' advantage over Owner or diminish that Owner's advantage over its competitors. Confidential Information shall not include any information of Owner that: (a) is already known to Recipient at time of its disclosure; (b) is or becomes publicly known through no wrongful act of Recipient; (c) is received from a third party free to disclose it to Recipient; (d) is independently developed by Recipient; (e) is communicated to a third party with express written consent of the Owner or is lawfully required to be disclosed to any governmental agency or is otherwise required to be disclosed by law, but only to the extent of such requirement, provided that before making such disclosure the Recipient shall give the Owner an adequate opportunity to interpose an objection or take action to assure confidential handling of such information.

2. For a period of five (5) years from the date of disclosure to Recipient, Recipient shall not disclose any Confidential Information it receives from Owner to any person or entity except employees of Recipient and its affiliates who have a need to know and who have been informed of Recipient's obligations under this Confidentiality Agreement. Recipient shall use not less than the same degree of care to avoid disclosure of such Confidential Information as Recipient uses for its own confidential information of like importance.

3. All Confidential Information disclosed by Owner to Recipient under this Confidentiality Agreement in tangible form (including, without limitation, information incorporated in computer software or held in electronic storage media) shall be and remain facility of Owner. All such Confidential Information shall be returned to Owner promptly upon written request and shall not thereafter be retained in any form by Recipient. The rights and obligations of the parties under this Confidentiality Agreement shall survive any such return of Confidential Information.

4. Owner shall not have any liability or responsibility for errors or omissions in or any business decisions made by Recipient in reliance on any Confidential Information disclosed under this Confidentiality Agreement.

5. The parties agree that, in the event of a breach or threatened breach of the terms of this Confidentiality Agreement, Owner shall be entitled to an injunction prohibiting any such breach. Any such relief shall be in addition to and not in lieu of any appropriate relief in the way of money damages. The parties acknowledge that Confidential Information is valuable and unique and that disclosure in breach of this Confidentiality Agreement will result in irreparable injury to Owner.

6. Either party may terminate this Confidentiality Agreement by written notice to the other. Notwithstanding any such termination, all rights and obligations hereunder shall survive with respect to Confidential Information disclosed prior to such termination.

7. Neither party hereto shall in any way or in any form disclose, publicize, or advertise in any manner the discussions that give rise to this Confidentiality Agreement or the discussions or negotiations covered by this Confidentiality Agreement without the prior written consent of the other party.

8. The term *affiliate* shall mean any person or entity controlling, controlled by, or under common control with a party.

9. This Confidentiality Agreement: (a) is the complete agreement of the parties concerning the subject matter hereof and supersedes any prior such agreements; (b) may not be amended or in any manner modified except in writing signed by the parties; and (c) shall be governed by and construed in accordance with the laws of the District of Columbia without regard to its choice of law provisions. If any provision of this Confidentiality Agreement is found to be unenforceable, the remainder shall be enforced as fully as possible and the unenforceable provision shall be deemed modified to the limited extent required to permit its enforcement in a manner most closely approximating the intention of the parties as expressed herein.

IN WITNESS WHEREOF, the parties have executed this Confidentiality Agreement as of the date first above written.

	ABC Company
_____	_____
	Kathy K. Smith
Name	Name
_____	_____
Signature	Signature
	Sr. Contract Administrator
_____	_____
Title	Title
_____	_____
Date	Date

ATTACHMENT 25

ABC COMPANY
CONTRACT TERMS AND CONDITIONS

Title Page

CONTRACT AGREEMENT

THIS AGREEMENT is made by and between ABC Company ("Owner"), a Delaware corporation with offices located at 2124 South Wacker Drive, Chicago, IL 60606 and _____ ("Contractor"), a _____ corporation with offices located at _____. In consideration of the mutual promises and agreements set forth herein, the Parties agree that to the extent goods and services are ordered by Owner, Contractor agrees to provide the goods and services specified herein in accordance with the terms below.

1. DEFINITIONS

   A. *Agreement* and *Contract* mean the TERMS AND CONDITIONS, including the STATE-MENT OF WORK and any other exhibit or document made a part of this Agreement, or incorporated therein by reference, which have been signed by duly authorized representatives of the Parties.

   B. *Owner* and *Buyer* mean Owner Telecommunications Corporation, its divisions, affiliates, subsidiaries, and assignees.

   C. *Contractor* means _____.

   D. *Purchase Order* means Owner's standard purchase order or change order form.

   E. *Work* means _____.

   F. *Services* means _____.

   G. *Goods* means any needed material, part or piece of equipment for the repair, inspection, or replacement of HVAC equipment.

   H. *Owner Representative* means the site manager, building engineer, site supervisor, or manager's staff assistant.

   I. *Acceptance* means the Owner Representative has verified the work was completed as stated and the Systems Maintenance Management Engineer has verified the work was within the contract scope (rate and description).

2. TERM

The term of this Agreement shall be three years, from July 1, 2005, to June 30, 2008, unless terminated pursuant to the Article of this Agreement entitled "Termination." Continuance of the Agreement will be contingent on the performance of the Contractor as evaluated by the Buyer. Buyer may extend the original Agreement in one-year increments, under the same terms and conditions of the original Agreement if in his evaluation the performance level has been maintained as herein specified.

3. SCOPE OF WORK

Contractor shall provide the services as requested by Owner in accordance with Exhibit A, entitled "Statement of Work," which is attached hereto and hereby incorporated into and made a part of this Agreement.

4. PRICE AND PAYMENT

   A. For the full, satisfactory, and timely performance of any Work performed by Contractor as requested by the issuance of an Owner Purchase Order and accepted by Owner, Owner shall pay Contractor in accordance with the fees set forth in the Bid Schedule. In no event shall Owner be obligated to take or pay for Work by Contractor under the Agreement unless a Purchase Order has been signed and issued to Contractor by Owner for said work.

   B. Contractor shall submit original invoices to the Owner Accounts Payable department stating the amounts due as set forth herein. The applicable amounts due Contractor shall be paid within thirty (30) days net in United States dollars after receipt of a correct and properly executed invoice in which Contractor has certified that the Work that is the subject of the invoice has been completed in accordance with the requirements of this Agreement.

C. Contractor shall submit all original invoices to:

ABC Company
701 South 12th Street
Chicago, IL 60606
Attn: Accounts Payable Department (0206/943)

Contractor shall also submit duplicate invoices to the location specified on the individual purchase order(s).

5. INDEPENDENT CONTRACTOR

Contractor's relationship to Owner in the performance of this Contract is that of an independent contractor. Personnel furnished by Contractor (hereinafter "Contractor's Employee(s)") to perform services hereunder shall at all times remain under Contractor's exclusive control and direction and shall be employees of Contractor and not employees of Owner. Contractor shall pay all wages, salaries, and other amount due Contractor's Employee(s) relative to this Contract and shall be responsible for all obligations respecting them relating to FICA, income tax with holdings, unemployment compensation, and other similar responsibilities and as such Contractor is filing all required forms and necessary payments appropriate to the Contractor's tax status. In the event the Contractor Employee(s)' independent status is denied or changed and the Contractor or Contractor's Employee(s) are declared to have common law status with respect to Work performed for Owner, Contractor agrees to hold Owner, its paren, and its affiliates and subsidiaries harmless from all costs, including legal fees, which may incur as a result of such changes in status.

Nothing contained in this Agreement shall be deemed or construed as creating a joint venture or partnership between Contractor and Owner. Neither Party is by virtue of this Agreement authorized as an agent, employee, or legal representative of the other. Except as specifically set forth herein, neither Party shall have power to control the activities and operations of the other and their status is, and at all times will continue to be, that of independent contractors. Neither Party shall have any power or authority to bind or commit the other.

6. INSURANCE AND INDEMNITY

During the term of this Contract, Contractor shall maintain insurance, the kinds and in the amounts specified with insurers of recognized responsibility, licensed to do business in the State(s) where the work is being performed, and having an A. M. Best's rating of AS. If any work provided for or to be performed under this Agreement is subcontracted, Contractor shall require the subcontractor(s) to maintain and furnish him with insurance equivalent to that which is required of Contractor.

In accordance with the above, Contractor and any subcontractor shall maintain the following insurance coverages:

A. COMPREHENSIVE OR COMMERCIAL GENERAL LIABILITY INSURANCE as follows:

$1,000,000 per occurrence with combined single limit of $2,000,000 general aggregate coverage, will include coverage for contractual liability, and coverage for the use of independent contractors, products, and completed operations. This will not contain an exclusion for explosion, collapse, and underground coverage.

B. BUSINESS AUTOMOBILE LIABILITY, including coverage for owned, hired, leased, rented, and non-owned vehicles as follows:

$1,000,000 combined single limit per accident

C. WORKER'S COMPENSATION AND EMPLOYERS' LIABILITY as follows:

Workers' Compensation—Statutory Limits

Employers' Liability:

Bodily Injury by Accident $1,000,000 each accident

Bodily Injury by Disease $1,000,000 policy limit

Bodily Injury by Disease $1,000,000 each employee

A combination of primary and excess/umbrella liability policies will be acceptable as a means to meet the limits specifically required hereunder. THE REQUIRED MINIMUM LIMIT OF COVERAGE SHOWN ABOVE, HOWEVER, WILL NOT IN ANY WAY RESTRICT OR DIMINISH CONTRACTOR'S LIABILITY UNDER THIS CONTRACT.

D. EXCESS OR UMBRELLA LIABILITY at a limit of no less than $5,000,000 per occurrence and aggregate in excess of the underlying coverages required above.

E. ALL-RISK PROPERTY insurance in a minimum amount equal to the replacement cost of any and all equipment owned, leased, or borrowed while in Contractor's or subcontractor's care, custody, or control, including while in transport at the direction of Contractor or subcontractor.

F. PROFESSIONAL LIABILITY INSURANCE covering the effects of errors and omissions in the performance of professional duties, with a minimum limit of $5,000,000 each occurrence and aggregate (if applicable), associated with work performed under this Agreement.

G. FIDELITY insurance providing coverage for any losses resulting from dishonesty or fraudulent acts of Contractor's employees.

GENERAL PROVISIONS:

1. Contractor will submit to Owner a standard Accord insurance certificate (or comparable form acceptable to Owner), signed by an authorized representative of such insurance company(ies), certifying that the insurance coverage(s) required hereunder are in effect for the purposes of this Agreement. Said insurance certificate shall certify that no material alteration, modification, or termination of such coverage(s) shall be effective without at least 30 days advance written notice to Owner.

2. All policies (excluding Workers' Compensation) shall name Owner, its subsidiaries, and affiliates, as Additional Insureds with respect to work performed under this Agreement.

3. Contractor's insurers shall waive all rights of recovery against Owner for any injuries to persons or damage to property in the execution of work performed under this Agreement.

4. Contractor shall permit any authorized representative of Owner to examine Contractor's original insurance policies, should Owner so reasonably request. Should Contractor at any time neglect or refuse to provide the insurance required herein, or should such insurance be canceled or nonrenewed, Owner shall have the right to terminate this Agreement, or costs of securing substitute coverages shall be deducted from payments owed the Contractor.

5. Contractor's insurance shall be considered primary and not excess or contributing with any other applicable insurance.

6. Contractor and all subcontractors shall ensure full compliance with the terms of the Occupational Safety and Health Administration (OSHA) and all locations' and jurisdictions' safety and health regulations during full term of this Agreement.

7. Contractor shall defend, hold harmless, and indemnify Owner against any and all claims, expense (including attorney's fees), loss, or liability for injury to or death of any persons (including property owned, leased, or borrowed by Owner) incurred during the performance of work associated with and under this Agreement, unless by reason of any and all acts or omissions or negligence by Owner, its agents, or employees.

8. Contractor assumes entire responsibility and liability for losses, expenses, demands, and claims in connection with or arising out of an injury or alleged injury (including death) to any person, or damage or alleged damage to property of Owner or others sustained or alleged to have been sustained in connection with, or have arisen out of, or resulting from the performance of the work by the Contractor, his subcontractors, agents, and employees, including losses, expenses, and damages sustained by Owner. Contractor shall also agree to indemnify and hold harmless Owner, its agents, and employees from any and all suits or actions brought against them, or any of them, based on any such alleged injury or damage, and pay all damages, costs, and expenses in connection therewith or resulting therefrom.

9. Contractor shall comply with the safety provisions of the National Fire Codes and Factory Mutual Engineering's cutting and welding procedures whenever such Work is performed.

10. Contractor agrees to assume all responsibility, risk of loss, and liability for and shall defend, hold harmless, and indemnify Owner, its parent, and its subsidiaries and affiliates, from and against any and all liabilities, losses, demands, claims, suits, damages, causes of action, fines or judgments, expenses (including attorney's fees and allotted in-house legal expenses) for injuries to persons (including death) and for loss of, damage to, or destruction of property (including property of Owner) arising out of or in connection with this Agreement unless caused by the gross negligence or willful misconduct of Owner, its officers, agents, or employees. In the event any demand or claim is made or suit is commenced against Owner, Owner shall give prompt notice thereof to Contractor, and Contractor shall have the right to settle or defend the same to the extent of its own interest.

7. PROTECTION OF INFORMATION AND PROPERTY RIGHTS:

Trade secrets and proprietary information of Owner (hereinafter collectively referred to as "information") shall mean information disclosed to Contractor or an employee hereunder as being proprietary to Owner in connection with this Agreement which is either identified as being proprietary to Owner or which is information that a reasonable person would understand to be such information. Examples of information include, but are not limited to, customer lists, pricing policies, market analyses, business plans or programs, software, specifications, manuals, print-outs, notes and annotations, performance data, drawings, photographs, and engineering, manufacturing or technical information related to Owner's products and services, as well as duplicates or copies thereof. Information furnished to Contractor and that to which employees hereunder are exposed shall remain Owner's proprietary property. Neither Contractor or any of its employees shall disclose information to any third party, and each shall take all reasonable precautions to prevent the disclosure of information to third parties.

Any invention, discovery, proprietary information, maskwork, software, system, data, or report resulting from the Work performed under this Agreement shall be the sole property of Owner. All patents, copyrights, trade secrets, trademarks, maskworks, or other intellectual property resulting from Work under this Agreement shall be the sole property of Owner. Owner shall have the full right to use such property in any manner without any duty to account to the Contractor for such use. The Parties agree that, to the extent allowed by law, any original work of authorship created under this Agreement is a work made for hire for purposes of copyright ownership, and to the extent any such work does not qualify as a work made for hire, to whatever extent the Contractor has any interest in any original work of authorship created under this Agreement, Contractor agrees to assign and hereby assigns its entire interest in such work to Owner, including all rights to derivative works.

Contractor agrees that each person employed by it for work under this Agreement will be bound by written agreement with Contractor to the extent necessary to give effect to the provisions of the foregoing two (2) paragraphs, and Contractor further agrees that Owner may enforce any such agreement as a third-party beneficiary thereof. In addition, at Owner's option in each case, it may require that each person assigned by Contractor for work hereunder shall enter into a separate agreement with Owner to more fully provide for any of the matters of said foregoing two (2) paragraphs. In such event, the separate agreement in accordance with the immediately proceeding paragraph shall take precedence over any agreement between Contractor and the assigned person, to the extent of any conflict there between.

8. RESPONSIBILITY FOR MATERIALS

Unless otherwise specifically provided in this Contract, all equipment, material, and articles incorporated in the work covered by this Contract are to be new and free from defects and of the most suitable grade for the purpose intended. Owner may, in writing, require the Contractor to remove from the work any employee Owner deems incompetent, careless, or otherwise objectionable. Unless otherwise specifically provided in this Contract, reference to any equipment, material, article, or patented process by trade name, make, or catalog number shall not be construed as limiting competition, and the Contractor may, at his option, use any equipment, material, article, or process which, in the judgment of Owner, is equal to that named. The Contractor shall furnish to Owner for its approval the name of the manufacturer, the model number, and other identifying data and information respecting the performance, capacity, nature, and rating of the machinery and mechanical and other equipment which the Contractor contemplates incorporating in the work. When required by this Contract or when called for by Owner, the Contractor shall furnish to Owner for approval full information concerning the material or articles which he contemplates incorporating in the work. When so directed, samples shall be submitted for approval at the Contractor's expense, with all shipping charges prepaid. Machinery, equipment, material, and articles installed or used without required approval shall be at the risk of subsequent rejection.

All work under this Contract shall be performed in a skillful and workmanlike manner and shall be consistent with the best practices of the industry. If at any time Owner notifies Contractor that any Work fails to meet the foregoing standards, Contractor shall promptly take all remedial steps required to meet those standards. Except as specifically otherwise provided in this Contract, Contractor shall be responsible for supplies meeting the requirements of this Contract until final inspection and acceptance thereof by Owner and shall bear all risks as to rejected goods or goods requiring correction after notice of rejection notwithstanding any prior acceptance.

9. DEFECTIVE WORK

Owner, notwithstanding any prior acceptance, at its option, may reject or require prompt correction (in place or elsewhere), of any goods which are defective in material or workmanship or otherwise fail to meet the requirements of this Contract. All goods furnished under this Contract shall be subject to inspection at destination notwithstanding any previous source inspection, and Contractor shall be given notice of defects, other than latent defects, within a reasonable time after receipt of the goods and all records (such as affidavits, test reports, drawings, etc.) required to be furnished herewith. Owner may, in addition to any rights it may have by law, prepare for shipment and ship the goods to Contractor, require Contractor to remove them, direct their correction in place, or, with authorization by Contractor, correct them, and the expenses of any such action, including transportation both ways, if any, shall be borne by Contractor. If Contractor fails promptly to remove such supplies and to proceed promptly to replace or correct them, Owner may replace or correct such goods at the expense of Contractor, including any excess costs, or may terminate the Contractor's right to proceed in accordance with the Article of this Contract entitled "Termination." Contractor shall not again tender rejected or corrected supplies unless Contractor discloses the former tender and rejection or requirement of correction.

10. LIENS

Contractor warrants that it has title to the goods to be delivered to be incorporated in the Work under this Contract and shall deliver same free of all liens, claims, and encumbrances.

11. CLEANUP

Contractor shall at all times keep his work area in a neat, clean, and/or safe condition and remove from the right of way owners' premises and the vicinity thereof and properly dispose of all debris and rubbish caused by Contractor's operations. Upon completion of the Work, Contractor shall promptly return unused materials furnished by Owner and remove from the premises all of Contractor's equipment, material, and like items, leaving such premises and the vicinity clean, safe, and ready for use. All work areas shall be restored by Contractor and his subcontractors to their original conditions or to their original state of cleanliness prior to completion of Work.

In the event Contractor or any of his subcontractors shall fail to maintain the work area as described above in a manner satisfactory to Owner or other authorities with jurisdiction, or fail to effect such cleanup or removal in compliance with the applicable regulations, codes, or Owner's requirements within forty-eight (48) hours after notice by Owner, Owner shall have the right, without further notice to Contractor, to perform such cleanup and remove such items on behalf of, at the risk of, and at the expense of Contractor. Any and all costs and expenses so incurred by Owner will be deducted from any monies due Contractor.

12. INSPECTION, TESTING, AND QUALITY CONTROL

All Work shall be subject to inspection and test by Owner at all reasonable times and at all places prior to acceptance. Any such inspection and test is for the sole benefit of Owner and shall not relieve the Contractor of the responsibility of providing quality control measures to assure that the work strictly complies with the Contract requirements. Contractor shall prepare and submit a Quality Control Plan to Owner. The Quality Control Plan shall be revised and submitted to Owner for joint review on a monthly basis. Owner's failure to inspect materials, equipment, or the Work, or to object to defects therein at the time Owner inspects the same, shall not relieve Contractor or any of his subcontractors and suppliers of their responsibilities for defective material, equipment, or Work, nor be deemed to be a waiver of Owner's rights to subsequently reject defective Work. Inspection or test shall not relieve the Contractor of responsibility for damage to or loss of the material prior to acceptance nor in any way affect the continuing rights of Owner after acceptance of the completed Work under the terms of paragraph 6 of this clause, except as herein above provided.

Contractor shall, during the course of performance of the Work hereunder, make or cause to be made all tests required by this Contract. Owner may require additional inspections and tests. Contractor shall furnish Owner with documentation satisfactory to Owner of the results of all inspections and tests. Owner shall be given not less than five (5) working days' notice of any tests to be made by Contractor in order that Owner may witness any such tests.

Owner and others as may be required by applicable laws, ordinances, and regulations shall have the right at all reasonable times to inspect the Work and all material, supplies, and equipment or the Work at the job site and at Contractor's and its suppliers' or subcontractors' shops. Contractor shall provide or cause to be provided access and sufficient, safe, and proper facilities for such inspections.

All Work performed by Contractor shall be subject to coordination and inspection by Owner representatives, the representatives of permitting agencies, railroads and other right-of-way owners, and the city, county, or state inspectors. Work rejected by any such inspectors and representatives shall be corrected by Contractor and his subcontractors at their sole cost, as expeditiously as possible, until it passes the inspection.

The Contractor shall furnish promptly, without additional charge, all facilities, labor, and material reasonably needed for performing such safe and convenient inspection and tests as may be required by Owner. All inspection and tests by Owner shall be performed in such manner as not to unnecessarily delay the work. Special, full-size, and performance tests shall be performed as described in this Contract. Owner reserves the right to charge to the Contractor any additional cost of inspection or test when material or workmanship is not ready at the time specified by the Contractor for inspection or test or when reinspection or retest is necessitated by prior rejection.

Unless otherwise provided in this Contract, acceptance by Owner shall be made as promptly as practicable after completion and inspection of all work required by this

Contract or that portion of the work that Owner determines can be accepted separately. Acceptance shall be final and conclusive except as regards latent defects, fraud, or gross mistakes as may amount to fraud, or as regards Owner's rights under any warranty or guarantee.

13. SAFETY

Contractor shall develop an appropriate safety management plan and take all necessary safety and other precautions to protect property and persons from damage, injury, or illness arising out of the performance of the Work. The safety management plan shall be submitted to Owner for review prior to the commencement of Work. Contractor agrees and warrants that it will comply strictly with local, municipal, provincial, state, and federal laws, orders, and regulations pertaining to health or safety which are applicable to Contractor or to the Work, including, without limitation, the Occupational Safety and Health Act of 1970 (84 USC 1590), as amended, and any state plans approved thereunder and regulations thereunder to the extent applicable, and Contractor warrants the materials, equipment, and facilities, whether temporary or permanent, furnished by Contractor in connection with the performance of the Work shall comply therewith.

Contractor shall be responsible for complying with all federal Environmental Protection Agency (EPA) regulations and state and local laws regarding water chemicals, CFC, HCFC, and HFC usage. In addition, Contractor shall indemnify and hold Owner, its parent, and its affiliates and subsidiaries harmless from and against any and all liabilities, claims, losses, costs, damages (including without limitation, punitive, or special damages) and expenses (including attorney's fees and allotted in-house legal expenses) arising out of any chemical, CFC, HCFC, or HFC accident as well as any breach of the foregoing warranties.

The Contractor shall warrant that the chemicals used in the treatment of water for use in all heat transfer equipment and associated systems, such as, but not limited to, steam and condensate systems (including water systems, chilled water systems, and condenser water systems) will not endanger the health or safety or persons coming in contact with the chemicals, will not endanger the health and safety of the general public, and will not harm personal or real property. The Contractor shall warrant that the chemicals used in the water treatment program shall have no effect on any surfaces of the systems being treated and that the Contractor shall bear any and all costs associated with any repairs made necessary by their use.

14. TERMINATION

A. Without limiting Owner's right to terminate this Agreement for default of Contractor as provided below, Owner, by written notice to Contractor, may immediately terminate this Agreement, in whole or in part, at any time prior to the Agreement's expiration date for the following reasons:

   (i) Owner's convenience; or

   (ii) Contractor applies for or consents to the appointment of or taking of possession by a receiver, custodian, trustee, or liquidator of itself or of all or a substantial part of its property; makes a general assignment for the benefit of creditors; commences a voluntary case under the Federal Bankruptcy Code (as now or hereinafter in effect); or fails to contest in a timely or appropriate manner or acquiesces in writing to any petition filed against it in an involuntary case under such Bankruptcy Code or any application for the appointment of a receiver, custodian, trustee, or liquidation of itself or of all or a substantial part of its property, or its liquidation, reorganization, or dissolution.

B. In the event of termination under paragraph A alone, in accordance with Article 4, PRICE AND PAYMENT herein, Owner shall be liable only for payment to Contractor for Work performed prior to the effective date of the termination notice plus any reasonable costs incurred by Contractor in complying with the termination notice. In no event shall Owner be liable for anticipated profit or fee on Work not performed.

C. Contractor shall continue to perform all portions of the Agreement not terminated. Owner shall have no obligation to Contractor with respect to any terminated portions of this Agreement except as provided in this Agreement.

D. Owner may, by written notice of default to Contractor, terminate this Agreement in whole or in part if the Contractor fails to:

(i)   perform the Work within the time specified in the Agreement;

(ii) make progress so as to endanger performance of this Agreement; or

(iii) perform any of the other provisions of this Agreement.

E. If Owner terminates this Agreement for Contractor's default, in whole or in part, Owner may acquire, under the terms and in the manner Owner considers appropriate, goods and services similar to those terminated, and Contractor will be liable to Owner for any excess costs for those goods and services.

F. In the event of termination, and regard less of any dispute between the Parties, all Owner property, materials, equipment, and Work in the Contractor's possession, including any and all documents in the possession of Contractor, its employees, or subcontractors, in any way pertaining to this Contract, shall be delivered to Owner within thirty (30) days of the notice of termination.

15. INDEMNIFICATION

Contractor agrees and warrants that Contractor and all Work shall comply with all applicable permits and licenses and all requirements of applicable federal, state, and local laws, orders, regulations, and standards ("Provisions") including, without limitation, Provisions relating to equal employment opportunity, nondiscrimination based on race, color, creed, religion, sex, age, disability, or ethnic origin, wages and hours, occupational safety and health, and immigration. In addition, Contractor agrees to indemnify and hold Owner, its parent, and its affiliates and subsidiaries harmless from and against any and all loss, cost (including attorney's fees and allocated in-house legal expenses), liability, or damage (including without limitation punitive or special damages) by reason of Contractor's violation of any applicable law, permit, license, executive order, or regulation.

Contractor agrees and warrants that it will:

A. Comply with all applicable provisions and requirements of Title VII of the Civil Rights Act of 1964, as amended, the Age Discrimination in Employment Act of 1967, as amended, the Americans with Disabilities Act of 1990, and all other applicable federal, state, and local employment laws and regulations; and

B. Indemnify and hold Owner, its parent, and its affiliates and subsidiaries harmless from and against all liabilities, claims, costs, losses, damages (including without limitation punitive or special damages), and expenses (including attorney's fees and allocated in-house legal expenses) arising out of the breach of the foregoing warranty.

Use of the defined term "Contractor" presumes that the defined term either includes subcontractors or that the terms of the Agreement specifically precludes subcontracting or assignment with Owner's prior written approval, at which time such subcontractor shall be required to meet the same provisions.

16. AUDIT

Contractor shall maintain such books and records as will adequately substantiate charges and hours worked hereunder and shall produce such books and records for Owner's inspection upon Owner's request for a period of three (3) years after final payment hereunder. Owner shall give timely notice of its intent to inspect such records. Contractor shall refund to Owner any overpayment indicated by such audit.

17. ASSIGNMENT AND SUBCONTRACTING

Contractor may not assign or delegate its obligations, rights, or duties under this Contract, in whole or in part, without Owner's prior written approval. Owner may assign this Contract in whole or in part without the consent of Contractor. In such event, Owner shall notify Contractor in writing of such assignment. Owner shall be entitled to the right of set-off against any amounts payable under this Contract.

Contractor shall not subcontract all or substantially all Work to be performed under this Contract without the prior written consent of Owner. Contractor further agrees to select subcontractors, including suppliers, on a competitive basis to the maximum practical extent consistent with the objectives and requirements of this Contract.

18. ORAL MODIFICATIONS

No oral statement shall in any manner modify or otherwise affect the terms of this Contract.

19. NOTICES

All notices, requests, reports, demands, and other communications under this Contract or in connection therewith shall be in writing and sent to Owner or Contractor by registered mail or Federal Express Standard Overnight Delivery at the following address:

Owner: ABC Company
2124 West Wacker Drive
Chicago, IL 60606

ATTN.: Procurement Officer

Reference Contract No.: 05–0001 ABC

CONTRACTOR: _____

_____

_____

ATTN.: _____

20. GOVERNING LAW

This contract shall be interpreted, construed, and governed by the laws of the State of Delaware without regard to its conflict of laws provisions.

21. RELEASE OF NEWS OR ADVERTISING INFORMATION

Contractor shall obtain the prior written approval of Owner's Procurement Officer concerning the acceptability, including the content and timing, of news releases, articles, brochures, advertisements, prepared speeches, and other information releases concerning the Work performed hereunder by Contractor, within a reasonable advance time prior to the scheduled release of such information to permit review and approval by Owner. Contractor shall send a copy of all such information release requests to the Owner Public Relations Department, located at 2124 West Wacker Drive, Chicago, IL 60606, as well as to the Procurement Officer.

22. COMPLIANCE WITH IMMIGRATION LAWS

The Contractor warrants, represents, and agrees that it will not assign any individual to perform work under this Contract who is an unauthorized alien under the Immigration Reform and Control Act of 1986 or its implementing regulations. In the event any employee of the Contractor working under this Contract is discovered to be an unauthorized alien, the Contractor will immediately remove this individual from the contract and replace that individual with one who is not an unauthorized alien.

Contractor shall indemnify and hold harmless Owner, its parent, subsidiary, and affiliated companies from and against any and all liabilities, claims, costs, damages (including without limitation punitive or special damages), losse,s or expenses (including attorney's fees and allocated in-house legal expenses) arising out of any breach by Contractor of this Article.

23. SUSPENSION

Without affecting any right of cancellation or termination set forth in this Agreement, either party may suspend this Agreement at any time because of strike of its personnel, war, declaration of a state of national emergency, acts of God, including fires, floods, and unusually severe weather, by giving the other party written notice of such suspension and the reason for the same.

Payments to be made and services rendered hereunder shall be made and rendered to the date of such suspension and shall thenceforth cease until the period of such suspension has ended. Nothing herein contained shall prevent Owner, in the event Contractor suspends the operation of this Contract, from securing the services herein contemplated from such other source as it so desires during the period of such suspension.

24. WARRANTIES

Contractor warrants that all Work furnished under this Contract shall be free from defects in materials, design, and workmanship and shall conform to the design, specifications, drawings, samples, or other descriptions and requirements of this Contract, and, to the extent that the Contractor knows or has reason to know of the purpose for which the Work is intended, will be fit and sufficient for such purpose. Owner's approval of designs furnished by Contractor shall not relieve Contractor of its obligations under this warranty.

Notice of defect or nonconformity under this Contract shall be given to Contractor within one (1) year from the date of final acceptance; provided, however, that notice of a defect that is latent or was caused or concealed by fraud or such gross mistakes as amount to fraud may be given at any time.

Owner shall have the right at any time during the period of this warranty, and irrespective of prior inspections or acceptances, to reject Work not conforming to the above warranty, and to require that Contractor, at its own expense, correct or replace such Work with conforming Work. If Contractor fails to correct or replace such nonconforming Work promptly after notification, Owner may, by contract or otherwise, correct or replace such nonconforming Work, and Contractor shall be liable for and shall pay to Owner all costs associated with such correction or replacement. After notification to Contractor of a defect, Owner may elect not to require correction or replacement of such nonconforming Work, and, in such event, Contractor shall repay to Owner such portion of the price as is equitable under the circumstances.

In addition to the foregoing, Contractor agrees to assign, and hereby does assign, to Owner any other warranties as Contractor or its subcontractor(s) customarily offer in connection with the sale of similar goods, including sales to Contractor's or the pertinent subcontractor's most favored purchaser. Any such assignment shall not relieve Contractor of any of its responsibilities under this Contract. Contractor shall notify Owner of each warranty and, upon receipt of such warranty, shall deliver to Owner any documents issued by the warrantor evidencing such warranty.

25. CHANGES

The Owner's Procurement Officer may, by written change order, without notice to any surety, make any changes within the general scope of work, including additions to and deletions from the number/type of Work originally ordered; or in the specifications or Statement of Work; or in the time and place of performance. If any change affects the amount due or the time of performance hereunder, an equitable adjustment shall be made by Owner. Any claim for adjustment hereunder must be asserted in writing within thirty (30) days from the date when the change is ordered or claim will not be considered. Nothing hereunder shall relieve the Contractor from proceeding with the Work as changed.

26. CONTRACTOR RELIEF

In the event of damage to HVAC equipment, whose maintenance and repair are provided for hereunder, due entirely from acts of God, including fires, floods, and unusually severe weather, the Parties agree that the repair and check of such HVAC equipment shall be provided for in accordance with Article 25, entitled "Changes," and shall not be considered Time and Material Work.

27. ORDER OF PRECEDENCE

In the event of possible conflict between the body of this Agreement and any Exhibit attached hereto or Purchase Order issued hereunder, the provisions shall be read to the extent possible as if they were reconcilable; in the event such a reading is not possible, the terms of this Agreement shall control.

28. ALTERNATE DISPUTE RESOLUTION

Any dispute or disagreement arising between the Parties in connection with this Agreement which is not settled to the mutual satisfaction of the Parties within thirty (30) days (or such longer period as may be mutually agreed upon) from the date that either Party informs the other in writing that such dispute or disagreement exists shall be settled by arbitration in the District of Columbia in accordance with the Commercial Arbitration Rules of the American Arbitration Association then in effect on the date that such notice is given.

Decision of the arbitrator(s) shall be final and binding upon the Parties, except that errors of law are subject to appeal to a court of competent jurisdiction. Each Party shall bear the cost of preparing and presenting its respective case. The cost of the arbitration, including fees and expenses of the arbitrator(s), will be shared equally by the Parties unless award otherwise provides.

29. SWBE UTILIZATION

A. Owner recognizes the need for and the benefits of aiding and stimulating the growth of small disadvantaged and small women-owned business enterprises (SWBE), and, consequently, has adopted a policy of seeking such businesses as sources of supply. Contractor agrees to aggressively and competitively increase the participation of SWBEs in the performance of its obligations under this Contract. Contractor's SWBE support under this Contract may be satisfied through any one of the following associations with SWBEs: partnerships, joint ventures, subcontracts, purchase orders, and/or other contractual arrangements.

B. Contractor understands that if Contractor has proposed to Owner that it will use SWBEs in the performance of this Contract, such representation by Contractor is a material factor, among others, for its selection by Owner for this contract award. Therefore, for Owner to determine Contractor's compliance with its representation regarding its SWBE utilization under this Contract, Contractor agrees to comply with all reporting requirements requested by Owner with respect thereto.

C. Contractor grants to Owner, during Contractor's business hours and upon reasonable notice, a right to audit Contractor's records from time to time for compliance with Contractor's SWBE utilization plan and further agrees to make all such records available for Owner's inspection.

D. Owner assumes no liability in connection with Contractor's selection and use of any subcontractors to perform its obligations under this Contract, and the relationship of Contractor and Owner shall at all times remain that of independent contractors; however, Contractor agrees that Owner shall have the right, reasonably exercised, to reject in connection with Contractor's undertakings under this Article, any subcontractor deemed by Owner to be unacceptable to satisfy Contractor's SWBE utilization plan requirements.

E. Notwithstanding the foregoing, Owner and Contractor do not intend to create any interest in any third party by this Contract except to the extent as may be expressly provided herein.

30. CONFLICT OF INTEREST

Contractor agrees to inform Owner immediately if an employee of Owner requests any form of payment, gift, gratuity, or other consideration of any amount, to be paid or delivered by Contractor or on Contractor's behalf, to or for the benefit of the Owner employee. Contractor also agrees that it will not provide any type of gift, load, gratuity, or consideration of any value to any Owner employee without first informing Owner's Office of the General Counsel, located at 2124 West Wacker Drive, Chicago, IL 60606, in writing of such action. Contractor also represents that it has in place a system or process for determining if the foregoing transactions occur.

31. DELIVERY

Time is of the essence. Deliveries are to be made in quantities and at the times specified herein, F.O.B. Destination. If Contractor fails to make scheduled deliveries, Owner may, without limiting its other rights or remedies, either: (a) direct expedited routing, and any excess costs incurred thereby shall be paid by Contractor and subject to offset by Owner; or (b) in accordance with Article 14, "Termination," terminate all or part of this Contract. Owner shall not be liable for Contractor's commitments or production arrangements in excess of the amount or in advance of the time necessary to meet this Contract's delivery schedule. Goods which are delivered in advance of schedule may, at Owner's option, either: (1) be returned at Contractor's expense for scheduled delivery; (2) have payment therefore withheld by Owner until the date that goods are actually scheduled for delivery; or (3) place goods in storage for Contractor's account and at Contractor's expense until the scheduled delivery date(s). Delivery in accordance with this Contract does not constitute acceptance by Owner under this Contract. Risk of loss of goods shall remain with the Contractor until final acceptance.

32. TAXES

The price specified herein, unless otherwise expressly stated, includes (a) all taxes and duties of any kind which Contractor is required to pay with respect to the Work covered by this Contract; and (b) all charges for packing, packaging, and loading. Contractor's prices are exclusive of any federal, state, or local sales, use or excise taxes levied upon, or measured by the sale, the sales price or use of goods supplied hereunder. Contractor shall separately list on its original invoice any such tax collectible by Contractor at the time of the sale which is lawfully applicable to any such goods otherwise payable by Owner and not subject to exemption or resale certificate.

33. WAIVER

The failure of Owner at any time to insist on the strict observance of any of the provisions of this Contract, or to exercise any rights in respect thereto, or to exercise any election herein provided, shall not be construed as a waiver of such provision, right, or election, or in any way affect the validity of this Contract. The exercise by Owner of any of its rights of election herein shall not preclude or prejudice Owner from exercising any other right it may have under this Contract. No waiver under this Contract shall be valid unless it is given in writing and signed by Owner's Procurement Officer.

34. PATENT INDEMNITY

A. Contractor, at its own expense, shall indemnify and hold Owner, its parents, and its affiliates and subsidiaries, directors, officers, employees, agents, customers, designees, or assignees harmless from any loss, damage, liability, or expense on account of any claim(s) or other proceedings, based on an allegation that the manufacture of any item in the performance of this Contract, or the use, lease, or sale of any item delivered or scheduled to be delivered under this Contract, infringes any United States or foreign Patent(s) or other proprietary right(s). Contractor shall pay any royalties and other costs or expenses, including attorney's fees, related to the defense, settlement, or dispositions of such infringement claim(s). Owner shall promptly notify Contractor in writing of any such infringement claim or action and give Contractor authority and any assistance or information reasonably available to Owner for the defense of such claim(s). Any such assistance or information which is furnished by Owner at the request of Contractor is to be at Contractor's expense.

B. If the manufacture of any item in the performance of this Contract, or the use, lease, or sale of any item delivered or scheduled to be delivered under this Contract, is enjoined as a result of a suit based on any such claim(s) of infringement, Contractor agrees to utilize its best efforts (a) to negotiate a license or other agreement with the claimant so that the item is no longer subject to such injunction, or (b) to modify such item suitably or substitute a suitable item therefore (subject to the technical approval of Owner), which modified or substituted item is not subject to such injunction, and to extend the provisions of this Article thereto. In the event that neither of the foregoing alternatives is suitably accomplished by Contractor, Contractor shall be liable to Owner for Owner's additional costs and damages arising as a result of such injunction.

C. Contractor agrees to use its best efforts to design, develop, and manufacture the items to be delivered under this Contract so that the manufacture, use, lease, or sale of any such items shall not infringe any United States or foreign Patent(s) or other proprietary right(s). Contractor further agrees to use its best efforts to identify and promptly report to Owner any unexpired Patents or other proprietary rights of third parties which may be infringed by the manufacture, use, lease, or sale of any item delivered under this Contract.

D. Owner neither represents nor warrants that the performance of any Work or the manufacture, use, lease, or sale of any deliverable item will be free from any third-party claim(s) of infringement of any United States or foreign Patent(s) or other proprietary right(s).

E. The foregoing indemnity shall not apply to any infringement resulting from a modification or addition by other than Contractor to an item after delivery thereof.

F. Contractor shall not be bound by any settlement of any charge of infringement made by Owner without Contractor's written consent.

35. SEVERABILITY

If any provision of this Contract is or becomes void or unenforceable by force or operation of law, the other provisions of this Contract will remain valid and enforceable.

36. SMOKE-FREE ENVIRONMENT

As part of Owner's efforts to provide a safe and healthy working environment for all personnel, Owner has adopted a Smoke-Free Workplace policy. Contractor understands this policy and agrees to observe and enforce its prohibitions against smoking in all Owner locations and vehicles, including offices, hallways, rest rooms, elevators, meeting rooms, and common areas such as cafeterias and employee lounges. Contractor understands that this policy applies to all Owner employees, Contractor's employees, subcontractors, clients, vendors, and visitors.

37. DRUG-FREE WORKPLACE

Prior to assignment to the Owner facility, Contractor shall provide written certification that Contractor's employees, including temporaries, assigned to perform Work at the Owner facility have passed a drug test for cocaine, marijuana, opiates, phencyclidine, and amphetamines. This requirement shall not apply to administrative/secretarial temporaries whose time of assignment at the Owner facility is less than thirty (30) days, nor shall it apply where such drug testing is prohibited by law.

38. HEADINGS

Article headings contained in this Contract are included for convenience only and will have no substantive effect or form any part of the agreement and understanding between the Parties.

39. GENERAL

A. Owner reserves the right to accept, reject, or request the replacement of any Contractor personnel furnished hereunder which it considers to be unsuitable for the tasks to be performed.

B. Owner reserves the right to contract with other firms or individuals during the term of this Agreement to provide services similar to those being performed by Contractor.

C. Contractor shall provide written certification to Owner that police background checks have been performed on all Contractor's employees, including temporaries, prior to their assignment to perform Work at the Owner facility.

D. Contractor shall be responsible for ensuring that its employees are fully trained in all safety procedures relevant to their work.

E. Owner may, at any time, at its discretion, suspend all or a portion of Contractor's Work for safety-related reasons. In such case, Contractor shall take immediate corrective action. Notwithstanding any other provision herein, neither the suspension of Contractor's Work nor any corrective action taken will result in any increase in Contract price or the price of any applicable Purchase Order.

F. In the event Owner requires that furniture be stored for a period up to forty-eight (48) hours, such service shall be provided by Contractor at no charge to Owner.

40. ENTIRE AGREEMENT

This Agreement contains the entire agreement and understanding between Owner and Contractor as to the subject matter of this Agreement; and merges and supersedes all prior agreements, commitments, representations, writings, and discussions between them. This Agreement may not be modified or amended in any way except by an instrument in writing executed by both Parties.

IN WITNESS WHEREOF, the Parties hereto have caused this Agreement to be executed by their duly authorized representatives as of this _____ day of _____, 2005.

_____   ABC Company

_____   Kathy K. Smith_____
Name   Name

_____   _____
Signature   Signature

_____   Sr. Contract Administrator_____
Title   Title

_____   _____
Date   Date

Managing The Physical Asset

Management of the physical asset is a crucial part of the overall management process, as it significantly affects the value of the site and facility. The appearance and condition of the building and grounds help determine the type of clients and employees attracted, the occupancy cost structure, customer satisfaction, and quality-of-life factors for management and employees.

Maintenance Activities

Maintenance of the physical asset is an ongoing process, as you saw in Exhibit 8.1. It can be broken into four main categories:

1. *Custodial maintenance.* Routine, day-to-day housekeeping activities, including policing the grounds; vacuuming and cleaning the offices, lobby, and other common areas; trash sorting where required; and trash removal.

2. *Corrective maintenance.* Repair and restoration of items after problems are identified but before major breakdowns occur.

3. *Preventive maintenance.* Scheduled inspections, service, and repair to maximize the level of services at the property, prolong equipment life, and reduce equipment breakdowns and service interruptions.

4. *Emergency maintenance.* Corrective action that must be taken immediately to protect life, health, or property.

A fifth type of maintenance, called *deferred maintenance*, occurs when needed maintenance is not or cannot be performed until some later date. The reasons for delay include cash limitations, management plan or budget restrictions, or negligence. Deferred maintenance is the antithesis of preventive maintenance. In fact, it is often non-maintenance. There are times, however, when work is necessarily delayed, as when parts are not available or timing is not appropriate for repair. Deferred maintenance should be listed in the maintenance reporting system, as both management and the owner must be aware of items that have not been serviced. It is important to ensure that deferred maintenance does not result in environmental, health, security, or safety hazards.

The type of maintenance program, staffing, and monies allocated to the maintenance and operations function should be established in the management plan, which should reflect the condition of the facility and the company's overall and specific site and facility objectives. Some facilities are best suited to a minimal maintenance program (e.g., back office or startup manufacturing facilities), while others require an extensive maintenance program (e.g., corporate headquarters, showroom space, Class A office buildings).

A good maintenance program requires support and cooperation from everyone involved in the management process, from the maintenance staff to the building's corporate owner. It must be developed with care and continually reexamined to achieve the desired objectives, which include satisfying in-house customers and maintaining the integrity of the physical assets. A good program seeks a balance among planned maintenance (custodial and preventive), responsive maintenance (corrective and emergency), and deferred maintenance.

The facility maintenance manager is responsible for the satisfactory performance of all preventive maintenance functions and should be aware of all maintenance work on the property, as well as the overall conditions, property operations, and work being performed on surrounding properties. The manager's effectiveness depends on the quality of the preventive maintenance program, which, in turn, largely depends on the performance of the maintenance staff and maintenance contractors. Therefore, it is important that the facility maintenance manager follow up on maintenance system reports and information and personally inspect the building and equipment on a regular basis.

Custodial Maintenance

Custodial maintenance encompasses all day-to-day routine maintenance activities. Generally, these tasks are performed at least once a day, although some may be performed more often. Because of its routine nature, custodial maintenance can easily be scheduled, assigned, and controlled. This activity is one of the more visible areas of facility maintenance and often the one that receives the most complaints and work orders. Maintaining quality requires daily ongoing supervision.

While custodial maintenance may be performed by full-time onsite employees, some maintenance (custodial, corrective, and preventive) tasks may be contracted out to independent contractors (e.g., cleaning, elevator, and HVAC maintenance and repair).

Corrective Maintenance

Corrective maintenance is performed to repair and restore items after problems are identified but before major breakdowns or emergencies occur. Even the best-maintained equipment develops operating problems and, occasionally, breaks down. In fact, all building components are susceptible to breakdown and may need corrective maintenance regardless of the quality of the preventive maintenance program. While the onsite staff identifies much of the corrective maintenance required, customer requests for service probably are the most common source for corrective maintenance. Room temperature that is too hot or cold, leaky or noisy plumbing, and electrical malfunctions are common problems reported by in-house customers. Also, adverse weather conditions, such as extreme cold or heavy rain, can cause broken water pipes, leaky roofs, and other problems.

All requests for service should be monitored by management to determine the effectiveness of the corrective and preventive maintenance program and revise services as required. Also, it is important to identify the source of the problem (e.g., customer negligence, inadequate maintenance, faulty equipment) and take action to eliminate it.

Work Order Procedures

To control the corrective maintenance function (and the deferred and emergency maintenance functions), work order forms, service request forms, and a work order log should be used to document, schedule, and control the maintenance function. For larger facilities, an automated maintenance system should be considered. Without a reliable system to record and analyze information, there will inevitably be additional problems amounting to far more than the administrative time and cost of developing and maintaining such a system.

For proper control and scheduling of maintenance functions, a work order form (see Exhibit 8.5) should be completed by an authorized maintenance employee in response to each request for service. The work order form should include the name of customer requesting work, location of problem, time and date of service request, phone number where individual requesting service can be reached, nature of problem and its priority, time when maintenance or repairs can be performed, amount of time spent on repairs and materials used, cost of labor and materials, billing codes, and initials of staff member taking request and of individual performing work.

The maintenance staff member should also outline on the work order the nature of the problem and its priority and arrange for a time for the maintenance person to enter if the area is secure or information-sensitive. In addition, the form should be used to record the amount of time spent on repairs and the materials used, the cost of labor and materials, and applicable billing codes.

Typically a five-part, prenumbered form, the work order consists of one office copy and four copies for use by the maintenance staff. One copy should be left with the requester or requesting department. One copy should be filed in the building/floor/department unit file and another in the maintenance file. If the requesting department is to be charged for the work, the final copy is sent to accounting and should subsequently be filed in the accounting department's maintenance file. If the requesting department and/or accounting copies are not needed, they may be discarded. After the office copy is matched to the completed work order, the office copy may also be discarded.

Service Request

A service request form (Exhibit 8.6) may be used in conjunction with a work order form. Requests for service typically are recorded by a maintenance staff member directly onto a work order form (Exhibit 8.5), but if a request is made by a customer or other non-employee, a service request form can be filled out by that individual. This documents the individual's exact request (in his or her handwriting). From the information provided on the service request form, the maintenance staff should prepare a work order form. Some maintenance managers prefer to skip the service request and have a maintenance staff member directly prepare the work order form.

Management should establish specific service request, control, and filing procedures for each location. For instance, prenumbered, multipart forms should be used. The first copy is for use in preparing the work order and may be attached to it, the second copy should be given to the individual requesting service, and a third copy should be filed numerically for control purposes. For control and scheduling purposes, all service requests must be scheduled from the maintenance office.

Proper procedures for requesting service should be discussed with corporate customers when they move in and be included in printed information given to them at that time.

                                    Time   Work Order Number: _____
Date: ___/___/___   Received: ___:___ AM/PM Initials: _____   Priority Code (1): _____

Location Name: _____
Address: _____   Floor: _____
         _____   Space No.: _____

Service Requested by: _____   Date Requested: ___/___/___

Telephone Number: _____   Time Requested: ___:___ AM/PM

Permission to Enter: □ Anytime □ By Appointment only, with _____
                Date: ___/___/___ Time: ___:___ AM/PM Telephone: _____

Maintenance Service Requested: _____ Type of Service (2): _____
_____
_____ Requestor's Initials: _____

FOR OFFICE USE ONLY

Maintenance Service Performed: _____
_____
_____

Materials Used: _____
_____
_____
_____ P.O. No (s): _____

□ Completed work: Date: ___/___/___ Time: ___:___ AM/PM New Work Order No. _____
□ Unable to complete work, explain: _____

Notes: _____
_____

Total hours:	Accounting:

Cost of labor: $_____   Bill to: _____
Cost of materials: $_____   Accounting _____ Amounts $_____
         Total: $_____   Codes   _____ $_____
                                                   _____ $_____

(1)Priority Code: 1 = Emergency, Immediate service required;
                   2 = Corrective, Rush;
                   3 = Routine;
                   4 = Custodial;
                   5 = Preventive.
(2)Type Service - Optional.

	By	Date
Prepared	_____	_____
Authorized	_____	_____
Performed	_____	_____
Approved	_____	_____
Reviewed	_____	_____

Exhibit 8.5   Work Order Form

```
                          Time                    Service
Date: ___/___/___    Received: ___:___ AM/PM     Initials: _____    Request Number: _____

┌──────────────────────────────────────────────────────────────────────────────────────────┐
│ Location Name: _____                                      │
│ Address:       _____        Floor: _____               │
│                _____        Space No.: _____           │
├──────────────────────────────────────────────────────────────────────────────────────────┤
│ Service Requested by: _____           Date Requested: ___/___/___        │
│                                                                                            │
│ Telephone Number: _____      Time Requested: ___:___ AM/PM      │
└──────────────────────────────────────────────────────────────────────────────────────────┘

┌──────────────────────────────────────────────────────────────────────────────────────────┐
│ Permission to Enter:  □ Anytime   □ By Appointment only, with _____         │
│               Date: ___/___/___  Time: ___:___ AM/PM  Telephone: _____           │
└──────────────────────────────────────────────────────────────────────────────────────────┘

┌──────────────────────────────────────────────────────────────────────────────────────────┐
│ Service Requested: _____               │
│ _____                  │
│ _____                  │
│ _____                  │
│ _____                  │
│ _____                  │
│ _____                  │
│ _____        Requestor's Initials: _____    │
└──────────────────────────────────────────────────────────────────────────────────────────┘

┌──────────────────────────────────┐               ┌──────────────────────────────┐
│ Work Order Number Assigned:      │               │               By      Date   │
│                                  │               │ Prepared  _____  _____     │
│                                  │               │ Reviewed  _____  _____     │
│                                  │               │                              │
└──────────────────────────────────┘               └──────────────────────────────┘
```

Exhibit 8.6   Service Request

Service Priority

A system of assigning work orders according to priority should be established using a service priority list (Exhibit 8.7). Descriptions of work required on a service priority list help the maintenance staff categorize and code work into emergency, immediate service, corrective, rush, routine, custodial, and preventive work. All emergency requests should be handled as they are received; other service requests should be scheduled to maximize maintenance staff efficiency.

Common Maintenance Problems

Preparation of a common maintenance problems form increases the efficiency of the preventive and corrective maintenance function. Preventive and corrective maintenance are performed to repair and restore items during regular maintenance or after problems are identified but before major breakdown or emergencies occur. Even the best-maintained equipment develops operating problems and occasionally breaks down; therefore, it is helpful to develop problem/solution worksheets for common maintenance problems as they occur.

Also, it is important that common maintenance problems be addressed in the maintenance manual. Example 8.3 shows a sample table of contents for such a manual.

Location Name:_____   Manager:_____

All requests for service should be assigned a priority code number, and all service calls should be attended to in accordance with the assigned priority code.

Priority Code	Type	Description
1	Emergency Immediate service	Any breakdown or malfunction in which life, health, or property is threatened if corrective action is not taken immediately. Examples: fire, flood, no heat in winter, no air conditioning in the summer, broken elevators in a high-rise, accident, no water, no electricity, open gas line, burglary, vandalism, security system malfunction.
2	Corrective Rush	Repair or restoration of an item before a major breakdown or emergency occurs. Non-emergency service request that is important to corporate user, tenant or property. Examples: broken or stopped up plumbing fixtures, make-ready work orders still outstanding after corporate user or tenant has moved in, keys or security system pass cards.
3	Routine	All other corrective maintenance calls that can be scheduled for same day or within a reasonable time period.
4	Custodial	All of the day-to-day routine maintenance activities. Example: cleaning common areas.
5	Preventive	All work that is part of the formal preventive maintenance program. Preventive maintenance is performed on a regular basis to maximize the level of services at the location and reduce equipment breakdowns and service interruptions.

	By	Date
Reviewed	___	___
Reviewed	___	___

Exhibit 8.7   Service Priority List

Detailed records should be kept for all maintenance and repairs on all office and support space, the building, grounds, and equipment. These records should enable the quick review of work performed for each space and user (e.g., department or tenant).

Work Order Log

A work order log should be used to monitor and control work orders. A work order log (Exhibit 8.8) is a place to record the work order number, a description of the work required, the location of work, and completion information. It also enables maintenance management to prioritize the work orders, to make applicable notes, and to monitor the work orders for such items as location, type, and volume of services required. The level of detail of the log can be increased to include such information as time spent and total cost of service. A computer-based system provides the greatest degree of detail with the least amount of work.

Location Name:					Month:		Day:		Year:

Work Order No.	Floor/ Space No.	Work Requested	Priority(1)	Type(2)	Work Assigned To	In/Completed Date/ Time	Date/ Time	Remarks

(1)Priority Code: 1 = Emergency, Immediate service required; 2 = Corrective, Rush; 3 = Routine; 4 = Custodial; 5 = Preventive.
(2)Type Service - Optional.

	By	Date
Reviewed	_____	_____
Reviewed	_____	_____

Exhibit 8.8   Work Order Log Form

Location/Floor/Space Service

Records of maintenance service should be kept for each location, floor, and space number. This detailed recordkeeping provides a quick reference overview of the work that has been performed and when. Copies of all location/floor/space service record forms (Exhibit 8.9) should be kept in the facilities maintenance office. These can be updated monthly or weekly (or as the work is completed, for computerized systems) from the work order and service detail. Work orders can be

Location Name:						Floor/Space No.:	
Work Order No.	Date	Maintenance Performed	Type(1)	By	Estimated Cost	Remarks	

(1) Type of maintenance: P - preventive; C - corrective; D - deferred; E - emergency.

	By	Date
Reviewed	_____	_____
Reviewed	_____	_____

Exhibit 8.9   Location/Floor/Space Service Record

used as substitutes for the location/floor/space service records, but the lower level of detail will make the review and planning processes more difficult.

Property Service

Property service records should be kept for maintenance performed on the building, grounds, and equipment. Similar to location/floor/space service records, the property service records (Exhibit 8.10) serve as a quick reference to work per-

Location Name:						Item:	

Work Order No.	Date	Maintenance Performed	Type(1)	By	Estimated Cost	Remarks

(1) Type of maintenance: P - preventive; C - corrective; D - deferred; E - emergency.

	By	Date
Reviewed	___	___
Reviewed	___	___

Exhibit 8.10   Property Service Record

formed on the property. Copies of these records should be kept in the facilities maintenance office.

To service the majority of corrective maintenance requests on a timely basis, each property should maintain an inventory of maintenance supplies, replaceable parts, appliances, tools, and equipment. These maintenance, repair, and operating supplies are often referred to as *MRO supplies*.

Inventory is also necessary for custodial, preventive, and emergency maintenance. The size of the inventory is determined by the size and condition of the facility and the types of problems encountered. In addition, an inventory control system is essential for a smooth maintenance program. For large facilities, you may consider implementing a formal supply room function, as shown in Exhibit 8.1.

Preventive Maintenance

Preventive maintenance is performed on a regular basis to keep the level of services at the facility high and to reduce equipment breakdowns and service interruptions. Maintenance staff and the onsite maintenance manager must make regular inspections in order to repair and replace items before problems occur. Preventive maintenance reduces emergencies by anticipating wear and tear on the property, buildings, and equipment.

Preventive maintenance is one of the most important components of successful maintenance and operations, and it requires the commitment of everyone from the maintenance and operations staff to the site and corporate facility owner. Accordingly, an appropriate preventive maintenance program should be developed for both large and small facilities, regardless of whether building staff consists of a part-time maintenance worker or a large number of employees supported by a computerized maintenance program.

Careful preventive maintenance eliminates corrective and emergency repairs later. While some managers consider preventive maintenance a poor use of cash and some companies claim to have no time for it, the truth is that preventive maintenance, by identifying problems in early stages, saves both money and time.

The following four steps are required to develop a good preventive maintenance program:

1. Preparing an inventory of all items that require servicing during the year.
2. Determining the type of service, frequency, and cost efficiency of performing the work required by each item, and who should do the work (in-house staff or contractor).
3. Scheduling the work throughout the year.
4. Controlling and revising the preventive maintenance program as needed.

The building, major equipment, and grounds should be inspected regularly by the maintenance supervisor to note both the unusual and normal wear and tear. This inspection is, by and large, a quick visual one, and the details of this inspection need not be entered on any form. For work that must be performed, a work order should be prepared.

Detailed inspection reports can be used as a reference for the daily inspections. These forms should be completed on a regular basis in accordance with the maintenance plan. In general, inspection reports should be completed at least once each month. The maintenance manager should inspect the exterior and interior of the property.

Evidence of building settlement, structural damage, leaks, and corrosion should be among the items noted during site and facility inspections. In addition to regular daytime inspections, night inspections should be held to test and examine lighting, signage, safety, and security features. Night inspections should also include an evaluation of the facility's appearance to clients, visitors, customers, and, if applicable, prospective tenants.

Emergency Maintenance

Emergency maintenance is a form of corrective maintenance. Immediate action must be initiated to correct emergency situations that threaten the life and health of customers and other occupants as well as the integrity of the facility. Situations requiring emergency maintenance can be created by fires, floods, burglaries, or the malfunctioning of major equipment (e.g., broken elevator, gas or water main leaks).

Preparation for emergency should begin well in advance of occupancy, during the site selection, development and property negotiation, planning, design, and construction stages. Response plans for mechanical, electrical, plumbing, roofing, elevator, security, and snow and other weather-related emergencies should be developed. For services contracted with outside vendors, the contract should include detailed specifications for emergency response procedures and response times.

Customers, risk management, safety, security, facility, and building personnel should be versed in emergency procedures such as evacuation, and they should receive a list of telephone numbers for the local police, fire department, and utility repairpersons as well as the building's 24-hour emergency number. Because of the dangerous conditions surrounding an emergency situation and the swift response its correction requires, emergency maintenance is the most costly of all maintenance types.

Maintenance and Operations Staff

While overstaffing a site and facility can be expensive, so can understaffing. Poor facility maintenance shows in the appearance of the building and grounds, which may interfere with the achievement of corporate objectives—which, in turn, will affect net income and property value.

Personnel requirements should ensure that onsite staff can effectively perform routine maintenance and operations responsibilities. The maintenance supervisor is responsible for the operation and maintenance of the physical and mechanical aspects of the facility. The maintenance supervisor's duties should be spelled out in detail in a job description. Typical duties are:

- Training and supervising the maintenance crew.
- Establishing and controlling a preventive maintenance program, including costs.

- Conducting regular inspections of maintenance-related items.
- Identifying maintenance problems.
- Assigning and supervising the execution of work orders.
- Maintaining a clean, orderly, well-stocked, and safe maintenance shop.
- Maintaining the parts and supplies inventory.
- Maintaining the tools and equipment inventory.
- Maintaining records and operating manuals for equipment, machinery, and fixtures.
- Completing special assignments for the facility maintenance manager.

The maintenance supervisor should report directly to the onsite facility maintenance manager, if there is one, or to the overall facility management manager. If a facility is not large enough to support a maintenance supervisor, the maintenance manager is responsible for these duties, or one supervisor may be hired to cover two or more sites and facilities.

Contract Services

Contract services, also known as *vended services*, are those services performed regularly by an independent contractor for an agreed-on fee. These contracts may cover cleaning services, trash and snow removal, roof inspection and maintenance, pest and rodent extermination, security, plumbing, electrical, elevator and other mechanical maintenance, and amenities maintenance. The facility and maintenance manager should approve all service contracts after securing and reviewing several service contract bids. A contractor's references should be checked for quality of service, reliability, and consistency.

Service Contract

All service contracts should be in writing and address the following items:

1. Identification of parties
2. Service to be performed, where, and how often
3. Performance standards and measurements
4. Hourly, weekly, monthly, and yearly costs
5. Start and expiration dates of contract
6. Special provisions (e.g., insurance coverage, emergencies, overtime, etc.)
7. Termination provisions
8. Signatures of both parties

Contracts that involve a substantial amount of labor are likely to contain clauses for escalations to offset increases in labor costs or material costs. Be certain to analyze the method of escalation and base rates. A limit should be put on the amount of increase acceptable during the life of any contract, and the contract should include the right to audit the contractor's books regarding labor and material costs for the job. A copy of each contractor's appropriate licenses, liability insurance, fidelity bonds, and workers' compensation insurance should be obtained and retained by the company.

The facility maintenance manager is responsible for all work done on the site, whether it is performed by onsite staff or outside contractors, and to see that service contracts are fulfilled to standard and on time.

Maintenance Contractor References

One of the best lines of defense against inferior contractors is a policy of obtaining customer references before selecting a contractor for a major job. A contractor's references, including current and former clients, should be checked for the quality, reliability, and consistency of the service. Usually, a contractor can supply a list of references (6 to 20 companies) for whom the contractor has recently done satisfactory work.

The facility maintenance manager should randomly select two or three references from the list and ask them about their experiences with the contractor. If there is any doubt or if the reference simply does not seem definite or well informed about the job, calling one or two more references should provide more information. If the contractor later asks the company to serve as a customer reference, the manager should not hesitate to agree. A contractor who does satisfactory work has earned a good reference. If problems crop up while the contractor is using the company as a reference, the contractor has an extra incentive to keep doing a good job.

Safety and Security

Safety and security are primary concerns of management. Crime and accidents cannot always be prevented, but risks can be reduced by taking certain precautions.

Correcting and preventing safety hazards should be primary maintenance concerns. The safety of clients, visitors, and customers is an extremely high priority.

Safety programs should comply with the Occupational Safety and Health Act (OSHA), which imposes comprehensive, detailed safety and health standards and recordkeeping requirements for employers. The act states that each employer "shall furnish to each of his employees employment and a place of employment which are free from recognized hazards that are causing or are likely to cause death or serious physical harm to his employees." Employees are also required to comply with OSHA standards and "all rules, regulations, and orders issued pursuant to this Act which are applicable to his own actions and conduct." A copy of the act can be obtained from the U.S. Department of Labor.

Security systems may include changes to the physical site (e.g., lighting and fencing), human resources (e.g., security guards), and electronics (e.g., closed-circuit television and access control systems). A good security system significantly reduces the risk of crime, but even the best system cannot guarantee that crime will not occur.

Maintenance Reporting and Control

Regular reporting and control programs should be set up for each site and facility. The type and frequency of each depends on the size of the site and facility, the structure of the organization, and the company philosophy. Specific reporting requirements should be included in each employee's job description and indicated on each report, either on the face or back of the form.

In general, monthly reviews and reporting serve as an adequate control, but in many situations, weekly reporting is warranted. The frequency of review should be indicated on the appropriate forms (site and facility inspections, work orders, and work order log). The monthly report should include work order statistics, maintenance deferred, and notes on unusual events at the property. For the unusual items or occurrences, an interoffice memo can be prepared or a standard report developed to assure that all significant topics are addressed.

Maintenance Goal Setting

The maintenance program should include a set of goals developed by management in conjunction with the maintenance staff. These written goals might address such items as:

1. The amount of money spent per month on a square-foot basis. This amount should probably be set for variable expenses, such as supplies and equipment repairs, and should not include employee salaries.

2. The desired percentage of compliance with the custodial maintenance program. This might be set at 90 percent (no more than 10 percent of missed custodial routine procedure tolerated by management without investigation).

3. The desired percentage of compliance with the preventive maintenance program. This should be higher than the custodial compliance percentage because, unlike a missed office cleaning that can never be made up, neglected preventive maintenance tasks can be performed on another day. Consequently, this percentage might be as high as 98 to 99 percent.

4. The desired percentage of responses within 24 hours to service or work order requests. This might vary depending on the site and facility, the type of request, and the company's facility management strategy, from as low as 70 percent to a more reasonable 90 to 95 percent satisfaction rate.

5. Emergency on-call coverage and response to emergencies. This category of response should demand a 100 percent success rate.

Technology and Computerization

The effects of technology and computerization have been demonstrated in the areas of energy management, security systems, and the entire maintenance management process. Many computerized maintenance management systems (CMMS) are available in the market today, and their application is becoming more widespread throughout the industry. An appreciation for the efficiency of a computer-based maintenance program is still developing in the industry. While the tedious and time-consuming recordkeeping tasks of accounting, including cost management and financial reporting, have been computerized for some time, computerized maintenance systems are beginning to proliferate.

A good computer-based system generates and updates most of the records discussed here from one source, typically the work order. The entire work order can be prepared at a terminal and should be automatically posted to the work order log. On completion of the work, the information added to the work order by the maintenance staff is entered into the system. A good system then updates the work order log, the unit service record, the inventory of supplies, and the billing system. This process eliminates the need to enter the same information on several forms and eliminates duplicate entry.

Another application of a computer-based maintenance system is the initiation and monitoring of the preventive maintenance system. A properly developed system lists daily, weekly, and monthly tasks, initiates the work orders, and assigns the work. As the work is performed and subsequently entered into the system, the system updates the related records, as described previously, along with the property service record. All items not attended to appear as items outstanding that require attention.

Reports for items not attended to, work order statistics, and other reports can be generated by the system, thereby minimizing tedious work by the staff. In addition, a computerized system enables management staff to spend more time planning and maintaining the site and facility and supplies more accurate information more promptly.

Maintenance Manual

The maintenance manual data gathering described here is likely to expand to the point at which it is advisable to use separate binders and sets of files for some of the maintenance information. In particular, the volume of forms and operating instructions may become so large that multiple binders and files will provide for easier handling.

With a separate maintenance manual, a more detailed format can be used for referencing and filing materials. Dividers can separate the information in the manual by maintenance type and form.

INTRACOMPANY AND CUSTOMER RELATIONS

One of the primary goals of maintenance and operations is to ensure that clients, visitors, customers, tenants, and other constituents are able to visit or work in a safe and clean environment and have their facility maintenance-related problems attended to promptly. If this goal is ignored, the business may have difficulty attracting and retaining employees and clients. Accordingly, it is essential for the maintenance and operations staff to cultivate and preserve good relations with all constituencies.

Management and staff should remember that an individual's initial impression is often a lasting one; therefore, consideration should be given to these impressions and to improving relations with current customers, employees, tenants, and other constituencies as discussed in chapter 1 under Total Quality Management (TQM). In addition, these people are the best source of referrals for new clients, customers, and tenants.

Communications

Good communication among senior managers, facility management staff and the facility maintenance managers and staff, other supporting departments, and facility users (e.g., clients, visitors, and customers) is an important aspect of successful maintenance and operations. The communication process should be ongoing, from the moment management creates a management plan based on the established objectives through the dissemination of daily, weekly, monthly, and annual financial reports.

The communication system includes both formal and informal components. Formal components can be specified and quantified in organizational charts, financial reports, and maintenance statistics. The primary vehicle of communication is established with the reporting system and its associated financial and narrative reports. All reports to be included in the reporting system, as well as their frequency, should be agreed on and specified in the management contract.

The informal system emerges regardless of the formal system. It can include such interactions as those between a customer and a maintenance employee or a supervisor and a subordinate. It includes discussions a visitor may have with maintenance workers or employees.

Meetings between the facility maintenance manager and other members of management should be scheduled at regular intervals to discuss management-related issues such as maintenance, special programs, schedules, ongoing programs, safety, security, major repairs, disaster recovery, and problems with personnel. The facility maintenance manager should communicate serious problems immediately to his or her superior so they can be addressed in a timely and cost-effective manner.

The importance of open communication cannot be overemphasized. Without mechanisms for formal communication and encouragement of informal communication, the company's maintenance organizational structure may become too unyielding to field the host of people-related problems inherent in the maintenance and operations business. This leads quickly to employee and client dissatisfaction and jeopardizes management's goals of protecting the real estate and facility investment, maximizing returns, and achieving corporate objectives.

Traditional Maintenance and Operations Requirements

Companies that set up their maintenance and operations departments as separate profit centers and those that lease or sublease property to nonaffiliated companies must perform additional intracompany and tenant relations tasks. These additional requirements are the same as those required of traditional maintenance and operations companies.

Because traditional maintenance and operations places the company in the owner/manager role with responsibilities to nonaffiliated tenants, the following sections describe owner/manager responsibilities relating to occupancy and rules and regulations.

Occupancy Procedures

The seeds of the manager-tenant relationship are planted when the tenant first takes occupancy. Everything possible must be done to ensure that the tenant moves into a clean, well-maintained space. A tenant who is not satisfied at move-in will be difficult to turn around later.

Move-in procedures should include an inspection by the manager followed by a walk-through inspection with the new tenant and the preparation of a move-in inspection report. At this time, the manager should explain the operation of equipment, answer questions, and provide the tenant with an information package detailing building hours, parking policies, security, and emergency procedures. Building keys, office keys, and ID and parking stickers should also be given to the new tenant at this time.

Property Rules and Regulations Violations

Violations of building rules and regulations should be addressed promptly. In many cases, it is sufficient to advise the tenant or send a notice outlining the offense and possible penalties should the violation be repeated. For habitual violations and serious offenses, the manager should seek legal counsel. In cases where the tenant refuses to cooperate, legal action and eviction should be considered.

FINANCIAL REPORTING AND CONTROLS

Good financial reporting and strong controls are essential to successful maintenance and operations. Financial reporting is a product of the accounting and bookkeeping systems. To enable management to analyze the performance of the site, facilities, and employees, reporting should provide for the comparison of anticipated income and costs with actual income or back charges (if any) and expense items.

Computer technology has simplified recordkeeping and improved reporting accuracy while permitting comparative analyses on a more timely basis. Whether computerized or manual, a good reporting system requires the use of certain reports, the type and format of which may be partially dictated by the company's current systems or by the particular system the facility maintenance manager uses.

Components of Reporting and Control System

The basic components of an effective reporting and control system include the following items, each discussed in the following sections:

- Operating budget
- Statement of operations
- Comparative statements
- Narrative reports

- Management summary information
- Other reports

Operating Budget

The operating budget is a projected summary of all income (if any) and expenses for a given period. It is developed considering management's objectives for the site and facility, recognized trends (as indicated by surveys, demographic studies, or reports), anticipated changes in economic factors, and detailed information on the site and facility's physical and fiscal condition. The facility manager's ability to recognize market and financial patterns and to correct problems is greatly enhanced by a well-planned budget. Reports should be designed to allow individuals to monitor and control those items for which they are responsible (see Exhibit 8.4).

The operating budget estimates income and expense items on a monthly basis and usually includes projections for a one-year period. In preparing this budget, management must determine future maintenance expenses, charge-backs, and revenues (if any). Management must also forecast increases and changes in expense categories such as payroll, maintenance and repairs, taxes and insurance, marketing and leasing, and general and administrative costs. Seasonal variances in income and expense items (e.g., utilities, snow removal) and expenses that are not paid on a monthly basis (e.g., real estate taxes, insurance) should be anticipated and accounted for.

Statement of Operations

The statement of operations—also called *income statement, profit and loss statement, statement of earnings,* and *summary of operations*—is an accounting of all site and facility revenues and expenses during a given reporting period. It enables management to determine the result of the period's operating activities.

Supporting documentation for the statement of operations includes the rent roll, schedule of miscellaneous receipts, and a schedule of cash disbursements.

Comparative Statements

Comparative statements for financial analysis should be prepared monthly and address every revenue and expense item. The statements should allow management to review income and expense for both the year to date and the current reporting period. Comparisons of current income and expenses with prior periods and with the same period for the previous year should also be prepared. In addition, revenue and expenses should be reported as percentages of possible gross revenue by square foot and by employee.

Financial guidelines presented by the operating budget should be continually reassessed and compared with actual operating results so as to monitor budget compliance and control operations. Operating results should be compared with similar buildings for which industry statistics are available. In addition, cost figures should be discussed with vendors for comparison purposes (e.g., utility bills, cleaning costs, and services).

Narrative Reports

Narrative reports should accompany numerical reports to senior management to explain activities for the period. They should provide information about transactions and events found in the financial reports such as employee turnover, back charges, and unusual site or facility charges. The reports should explain variances in the comparative statement, major repairs, or deferred maintenance. Suggested improvements should also be included.

Management Summary

Information contained in a management summary report is useful for comparing management effectiveness by the month. It can include monthly results of income and miscellaneous receipts, disbursement totals, and net cash flows and balances.

Other Reports

Depending on the scope of management requirements, the facility manager may have additional reporting responsibility. These reports might include:

- *Balance Sheet (or Statement of Financial Position).* A report of all assets, liabilities, and net worth or equity (the difference between total assets and total liabilities) as of a specific reporting date.

- *Statement of Changes in Owner's Equity.* A report of the additional investments by owner, retirement of owner's interests, and similar events to the owner's capital account(s).

- *Statement of Cash Flows.* A report of the cash effects of an organization's operations, investing transactions, and financing transactions.

Purchasing

The development of a strong purchasing and control system enables management to purchase maintenance-related items at the best prices and maintain inventory and operations supplies at costs and quantities that are efficient to operations. The purchasing function of the maintenance and operations process depends on the company's normal purchasing procedures, the size of the corporation's real estate portfolio, and the specific facility types.

The facility manager or the facility maintenance manager is usually responsible for controlling, reviewing, and approving all purchase orders. Orders should be placed with approved supply sources and service firms. If no supply source is established, the purchasing manager should obtain price quotations from several firms before choosing the best source.

Authorized purchase orders should be obtained for every purchase, except in emergency situations where life or property is in danger (e.g., flood, fire, electrical outages). The purchase order is a contract between the corporation and vendor regarding the purchase of supplies, equipment, or services. Prices, specifications, delivery dates, and special payment arrangements should be agreed on before any purchase is made and should be noted on the order. Some corporations provide their facility maintenance manager with a corporate charge card for the purchase of common and needed supplies and equipment under $100 per purchase.

Service contracts for items such as custodial support, elevator service, mechanical equipment maintenance and repair, extermination, and landscaping should be handled in accordance with standard purchasing procedures.

Taxes

The facility manager or a member of senior management must be familiar with real estate and personal property taxes. These taxes are based on the assessed value of the property, and the determination of that value can be both complicated and subjective. In most cases, a tax specialist should be employed to determine if the value and rates are correct and to identify avenues that might reduce the tax assessment.

Because taxes must be paid whether or not a bill is received, management must be aware of the payment dates and keep a good tax information file. Estimated tax amounts and the timing of their payment should be included in the budget and cash flow statements.

Safeguarding Assets

Assets under management should be protected against three types of losses:

1. Losses from casualty
2. Losses from theft
3. Losses from conversion of an asset to another form (receivables to cash, inventory to cash)

Casualty losses can be protected by a good internal control system combined with adequate insurance and an ongoing risk management program. Theft and conversion can be protected by a strong system of internal control combined with periodic internal auditing to check for compliance with the system's policies and procedures.

Controlling conversion (by implementing an efficient inventory procedure and an effective preventive maintenance program) reduces the time that assets are at risk from casualty or theft. It also lowers expenditures for interest, inventory, insurance, handling, storage, obsolescence, and bad debts. Money saved from reduced spending can be invested elsewhere.

Internal Control

Good internal control maximizes the probability that the corporate facility management and maintenance and operations objectives are met and that operations are in compliance with corporate policies and all applicable laws. It is management's responsibility to develop policies and procedures that achieve this control.

Systems of internal control vary by company because of unique policies and procedures, management philosophy, and organizational size and structure. A system of internal controls encompasses numerous safeguards to provide reasonable assurances that (1) assets are used properly and protected from misappropriation, (2) transactions are accurately recorded and reported, and (3) operations are in compliance with management policies.

Insurance

Corporate sites and facilities should be insured against risks of loss if such insurance coverage is cost-effective. While the facility manager is not expected to be an insurance expert, he or she should be knowledgeable about the types of insurance available.

The manager should be familiar with workers' compensation, fidelity, fire, rent loss, and liability insurance as well as other coverages. Insurance companies often can eliminate the need for separate policies by combining such coverages into a single, cost-effective package.

Being overinsured serves no purpose, and being underinsured can ruin the company. Insurance coverage should be reviewed and approved by senior management prior to purchase.

The purpose of a risk management program is to identify the risks of potential liability presented by each facility leased, owned, or managed. A risk management program can reduce potential losses that insurance cannot efficiently cover (e.g., insurance coverage may not be available for certain risks, or the cost of the coverage may be prohibitive). In addition, it can reduce the cost of insurance coverage (e.g., accurate loss exposure data generated by the risk identification program may persuade underwriters to renew insurance coverage at lower prices).

Management should appoint someone to be in charge of creating the risk management program, such as (a) a full-time risk manager, (b) one person to both manage risk and deal with the insurance brokers, or (c) a risk management consultant (either to conduct periodic audits or provide continuous support). This individual, along with other members of senior management, should be familiar with local property owner liability laws, estimate accurately the stakes involved in an uninsured loss, and purchase sufficient liability insurance when it is available.

ADMINISTRATIVE RESPONSIBILITIES

The facility maintenance manager performs administrative duties related to human resources, from hiring, training, and supervising onsite employees to managing the employee payroll, risk control, and insurance programs. The manager must abide by antidiscrimination and wage and hour laws, establish working standards acceptable to OSHA guidelines, and see that license and notice requirements, such as OSHA and workers' compensation, are met. Because more than one hundred different forms and reports may be required to manage larger facilities effectively, the manager must maintain a good forms control, review process, and filing system.

Operations Manual

The facility maintenance manager should develop a formalized standard for maintenance and operations by creating an operations manual that specifies the policies and procedures under which the company operates.

An operations manual is a useful resource for maintenance and operations employees and should be an integral part of training. The manual should reflect the policies and methods under which the company operates and be a primary source of answers to questions that arise in the process of managing properties, thereby enabling employees to make consistent decisions.

A good operations manual consists of three main elements—policies, procedures, and forms—defined as follows:

1. A *policy* is a guiding principle adopted to influence or determine decisions and actions.
2. A *procedure* is a step-by-step course of action for implementing a particular policy.
3. A *form* is a procedural byproduct, a document that is a mechanism for following a procedure.

The greatest value of an operations manual is the operational continuity it allows given the effects of personnel turnover and/or management changes. In addition, an operations manual enables employees to perform at their best, clearly understanding their functions and roles.

The manual should offer specific directives to save time and effort in making minor decisions at all levels. Because an operations manual should cover the complete maintenance and operations program, it must be updated regularly to keep pace with rapidly changing industry conditions.

MARKETING AND LEASING

Corporate-owned and occupied properties have minimal marketing and leasing requirements, while for properties leased to nonaffiliated tenants these requirements may be quite extensive. For the latter, the amount of revenues generated from a property is directly related to the success of the marketing, leasing, management, and control functions.

For example, one manager may have 100 percent of the company's excess space leased with rents 20 percent below the market rate, while another may be skilled at obtaining higher rents and attracting qualified prospective tenants but poor at securing signed leases. The professional facility manager must be able to balance both marketing and leasing efforts.

The prime purpose of the marketing and leasing effort is to attract qualified prospective tenants who will sign leases at market rent—and then pay the rent! Factors affecting this goal include the property's:

- Location
- Overall appearance, including building style and size
- Condition, as well as that of adjacent grounds
- Amenities
- Rental structure
- Reputation of the property, the company, and staff
- Competition

These factors, along with occupancy trends, employment changes, competition, and other market influences, must be considered in determining accurate tenant profiles and appropriate rental rates for the property.

A carefully planned marketing program is necessary to attract new tenants. If not constrained by law, rent and rent increases should be established on the basis of periodic market surveys, which are designed to define maximum income possible while maintaining the property's competitiveness in the marketplace. It should be kept in mind that every marketing decision has an impact on building services and amenities and on the number and compensation package of property employees.

Chapters 2 and 3 discuss the disposition of assets, including a detailed listing of disposition strategies you may wish to review before beginning a marketing and leasing program.

CONCLUSION

Maintenance and operation services should be designed by the facility manager to support the business operations with services to protect the real estate investment and facility operations and the value of the owned or leased capital improvements. As part of these services, the facility manager and staff must remember that the built environment must be maintained on a regular and ongoing basis based on a series of quality decisions that reflect the physical image of the organization. The quality of maintenance and operations services expresses your organization's success and image to the public and to staff who will want or not want to work in that environment.

The management of day-to-day work orders and customer service requirements by facility management staff and service vendors is the basis for high customer satisfaction. Over time, that experience by customers provides the facility manager and staff with a reputation that can support a career at the company or that must be changed and improved. The physical environment is the stage where we work. Maintenance and operations can support and improve the quality of our work environment.

Chapter Nine

General Administrative Services and Technology

Chapters 4, 5, 6, and 7 dealt with ongoing project activities. Chapter 8 reviewed the day-to-day maintenance and operations of the facility, and in this chapter we review general administrative services and technology that supports the employees' performance of their required administrative and technology tasks in a safe and secure environment. These services can include providing or relocating a phone, fax, modem, computer, printer, furnishings, files and records, copies, mail and courier services, office supplies, safety and security, food and beverage services, transportation, purchasing, switchboard, pest control, artwork, signage, energy management, stockholder services, library, archives, and transportation pool.

These daily functional services, which many employees take for granted, must be managed and provided in a timely and cost-effective manner.

GENERAL ADMINISTRATIVE SERVICES

Security and Safety

The horror of September 11, 2001, affected corporate business strategies, including facility management, primarily because the event put planning and activities on hold and prolonged the economic downturn for a number of years. Business leaders have sought to continue businesses in these economic and security challenging times. Security and safety are primary concerns of management. Crime and accidents cannot always be prevented, but the risks can be reduced by taking precautions. Security and safety departments of larger organizations are charged with these responsibilities. In smaller organizations, it often falls within the realm of the facility management department to hire security providers and to serve as the organization's safety representative.

Security

Security systems may include changes to the physical site (e.g., lighting, fencing, parking spaces for employees and visitors), human resources (e.g., security guards), and electronics (e.g., closed-circuit television and access control systems). A good security system significantly reduces the risk of crime, but even the best system cannot guarantee that a crime will not occur.

Crime, including blue-collar crime and domestic and foreign terrorism, can happen anywhere; therefore, as the facility professional, you, your corporate security counterpart (if available), and your management must take the necessary steps to reduce the risks of crime to the facility and to employees while at the facility. While it may not take a thief to catch a thief, it can be helpful to look over the facility as if one were a criminal. You should, therefore, walk the property and look for ways to enter the facility. List facility features that might make it attractive to criminals; efforts to improve security at the facility should address these weaknesses first. You may also want to enlist the help of trained professionals such as corporate security, police, insurance experts, and other security specialists who are familiar with the ways in which criminals operate and may spot opportunities you or your staff might have missed.

Crime prevention efforts fall into two major categories: efforts that prevent a criminal from gaining access to property (e.g., locks, bars, gates, fences, and other access control devices) and efforts that increase the criminal's risk of being detected and caught (lighting and alarm systems).

Safety

Safety, especially in light of workplace violence, 9/11, and other terrorist activity around the world, is an important area of concern with an increasing amount of attention, time, and resources being spent by the facility professional and his or her staff to alert and train employees in safety and related workplace issues such as violence in the workplace, drug and alcohol abuse, and employee nondiscrimination awareness. Most organizations have established a zero tolerance program for drug and alcohol abuse by employees and contractors or their employees who come to the organization's site or facilities. The facility professional and his or her staff have become monitors for these issues and often work closely with their organization's security, human resources, and legal departments on organizational awareness and crisis response programs.

Facility professionals must be aware of and understand local, state, and federal safety and environmental requirements. They must ensure that their employees and contractors obtain the proper permits and comply with appropriate laws and regulations. Regulatory officials are monitoring construction and renovation projects more closely for safety and environmental compliance. Neighborhood, local, regional, and national nonprofit groups are tracking and reporting safety and environmental problems and violations to local or state and federal government regulatory agencies and officials.

Correcting and preventing safety hazards should be primary concerns in managing, constructing, and performing maintenance work at the facility. The safety of customers, visitors, and employees is an extremely high priority.

Safety programs should be designed to comply with the Occupational Safety and Health Act (OSHA), which imposes comprehensive and detailed safety and health standards and recordkeeping requirements on employers. OSHA states that each employer "shall furnish to each of his employees employment and a place of employment which are free from recognized hazards that are causing or are likely to cause death or serious physical harm to his employees." Employees are also required to comply with OSHA standards and "all rules, regulations, and orders issued pursuant to this Act which are applicable to his own actions and conduct." A copy of the act can be obtained from the U.S. Department of Labor.

Work areas may involve dangerous tools, slippery surfaces, electrical cords or ropes stretched across walkways, and other conditions that pose hazards to the unwary customer, visitor, or employee who enters the work area. To protect these people, workers should consider each of the following every time a job is begun, completed, or left unattended.

1. *Limit Access to Work Areas.* Employees should take reasonable steps to keep people out of dangerous areas. Roof doors, for example, should be locked, unless fire regulations require otherwise; work sheds, where tools and dangerous chemicals are stored, should be locked at all times. Elevators that are not running properly should be turned off, and HVAC, electrical, and telephone room entrances should be locked.

2. *Post Warnings of Danger.* Examples of warnings that can be used to alert customers, visitors, employees, and others to danger are signs announcing "Wet floor," "High voltage," and "Danger" where applicable. Yellow is the standard color for drawing attention to a hazard. Yellow tape or paint can be used along with appropriate signs to alert potential accident victims to the dangers of tripping over a wire, stepping in a hole, or touching a hot surface.

3. *Do Not Create Unnecessary Hazards.* Avoid leaving wires, ropes, and hoses stretched across walkways where people are likely to trip. Tripping is a common cause of injuries to passersby. Employees should look for a way to run the cord or rope along the wall or to attach it at another location to avoid running it across a walkway. If this is not possible, the area should be well lit and a "Danger" sign placed on top of the extended cord. The hazard should be removed as soon as the work is finished.

4. *Cleaning Up Work Areas Promptly.* Areas should be straightened and tools and supplies returned to locked storage as soon as work is completed. This also helps prevent theft of tools and supplies.

Suggestions for On-the-Job Safety

Employees and contract workers can help reduce the chance of work-related accidents by heeding the following suggestions:

1. *Be Cautious in the Use of Unfamiliar Products or Equipment.* Read the manufacturer's directions for safe use and follow them with care. Read all cautions closely. If the manufacturer has sent a product to market with a warning on the label, there is a good reason for it.

2. *Be Cautious When Dealing with Electricity.*
   - Be sure hands and work surfaces are dry when handling electrical tools or appliances.
   - Unplug electrical tools and appliances before performing even simple repairs.

- Never perform repairs on a live circuit. Use switches and circuit breakers to run off current before starting work.

- If unable to avoid working near a live circuit, workers should put as much insulation as possible between themselves and the circuit in the form of heavy rubber gloves, tools with well-insulated handles, and the like.

3. *Dress for the Job.*

- Long hair worn loose can catch in motorized equipment, obscure vision at crucial moments, or be set ablaze by a carelessly handled torch.

- Work shoes with a nonslip sole are a plus when handling heavy loads, crossing wet floors, or scaling a ladder.

- Clothing that can fall forward or get in the way, such as full sleeves or long ties, can be dangerous on the job.

4. *Be Aware of Fatigue.* Difficult or dangerous work is best scheduled for early in the day when most workers are alert. Accident statistics show the late afternoon is prime time for accidents.

5. *Work Neatly.* Take steps to minimize the chances that employees or others will trip or slip in the work area. Wipe up spills as they occur. Do not leave materials where someone may trip over them. Wires, hoses, and string should not be placed where they will cross pedestrian paths. If there is no alternative, draw attention to the hazard with a "Please watch your step" sign and remove the hazard as quickly as possible.

6. *Be Careful about Leaving Equipment Unattended.* Anything that is sharp, motorized, flammable, or poisonous should be kept out of the way of passersby.

7. *Use Personal Protective Equipment.* Goggles protect the eyes from flying particles. In some cases, a heavy apron should be used to protect the rest of the body, along with work gloves to protect the hands.

8. *Be Careful When Lifting or Carrying Equipment.*

- When handling brooms, mops, or long tools or pipes, take care that the free end does not hit a passerby or knock into ceiling sprinklers or smoke detectors.

- Make sure the way is clear before moving heavy equipment.

- Use hand trucks and dollies whenever possible to spare both the worker's back and the building's floors.

- Lift loads properly to prevent back problems. Keep the spine as straight as possible while lifting, and keep the load as close as possible to the upright spine. Bending and straightening should come from the knees.

9. *Be Careful When Working with Chemicals.*

- Poisonous and caustic materials should be carefully marked and controlled, and should be handled only by people familiar with the hazards and the rules for safe handling.

- Do not work with solvents in small, closed rooms. Follow the warnings on the label and find a well-ventilated work area.

- Keep solvents capped tightly to avoid leakage through evaporation.

- Protect the skin from exposure to strong chemicals.

- If a chemical gets on your hands or skin, wash and dry the affected area right away.

- In diluting chemicals, pour the strong chemical into the water or neutral chemical. Pouring water into a chemical may cause dangerous splashes.

- Never mix bleach and ammonia, as this releases chlorine gas.

- Where a battery backup exists, provide emergency eye wash and emergency shower facilities.

Corporate facilities, security, safety, and maintenance services should use a safety evaluation checklist similar to the one shown in Exhibit 9.1 to ensure that all necessary safety precautions are taken for each property and that no step is overlooked.

The safety and health of each employee of your company is of primary importance. Company policy should be to maintain a safe and healthy working environment at all times and to comply with OSHA regulations and state and local safety requirements. The prevention of occupationally induced injuries and illnesses should be a priority of management and employees and should be given precedence in all operational matters. The company should not knowingly allow unsafe conditions to exist (see Exhibit 9.2) or permit employees to participate in unsafe activities (see Exhibit 9.3).

Occupancy Codes

After your customer moves in, your organization has a responsibility to maintain the facility to protect the health and welfare of employees, visitors, clients, and service and product suppliers. Occupancy codes include fire codes, life safety codes, sanitary codes, health codes, and other regulations that apply after a building is occupied and in operation. Code officials have the authority and in many cases are required to inspect certain types of facilities periodically or upon complaint. If noncompliance is found and not corrected, your customer's certificate of occupancy may be revoked, whereupon the facility can no longer be legally operated. Some occupancy codes require a minimum level of structural soundness and repairs. If your facility does not meet these standards, the local government may pursue a condemnation action against your company to have the building demolished.

During your periodic inspection visits to your organization's owned or leased space, you should ensure that a secure, safe, and healthy environment exists for those who occupy it. This may require a meeting with the landlord to review specific items and to insist that problems be corrected in accordance with the lease and local occupancy codes.

PROPERTY: _____ COMPLETED BY: _____

DATE COMPLETED: _____ Page 1 of 2

ITEM	ITEMS TO BE EVALUATED	YES	NO	N/A	COMMENTS
1.	**Fire Protection and Security**				
	a. Floor Fire Extinguishers in place as required by code and the Fire Marshall?				
	b. Fire Extinguisher inspected and serviced in past 12 months?				
	c. Smoke alarms in common areas and in tenant areas?				
	d. Smoke alarms tested and serviced in past 12 months?				
	f. Pull stations and sound/light alarms in common areas and in tenant areas tested in past 12 months?				
	g. Sprinklers, piping, risers and fire department connection tested in past 12 months?				
	h. Fire alarm panel(s), security camera, monitors and card access system serviced and tested in past 12 months?				
2.	**Public Areas**				
	a. Exits properly marked and lighted?				
	b. Illuminated exit lighting tested?				
	b. Exit ways, and exits free of obstructions?				
	c. Floor surfaces free of slipping and tripping conditions?				
	d. Safety/tempered glass in full length glass doors and sidelights?				
	f. Elevators inspected and Certificate of Inspection on file?				
3.	**Stairs, and Exit Doors**				
	a. Handrails securely fastened?				
	b. Treads and risers in good condition?				
	c. Stairways free of obstructions				
	d. Stairways well lighted and lights working?				
	e. Stairway emergency lighting tested?				
	f. Stair and exit doors operating properly and unlocked in path of travel to the outside?				
	g. Door locks and security system operating properly?				
4.	**Custodial Services**				
	a. Combustible trash stored in covered metal containers?				

Exhibit 9.1   Safety Evaluation Checklist

DISASTER AVOIDANCE AND RECOVERY

Today's business and facility environment requires that we work to avoid business disasters and, when disasters do happen, that we quickly recover. The events of 9/11 dramatically showed that there were businesses that were not ready for this disaster while other organizations were up and running the next day at their backup data facility. The facility professional must understand and

ITEM	ITEMS TO BE EVALUATED	YES	NO	N/A	COMMENTS
	b. Trash disposed frequently and in accordance with local ordinances?				
	c. Flammable paints and liquids kept in fire resistant metal lockers?				
	d. Flooring in good repair with no tripping hazard(s)?				
	e. Recycling containers properly labeled, placed and emptied regularly?				
5.	Maintenance and Repair Operations				
	a. Ladders in good condition?				
	b. Safety glasses worn during hazardous operations?				
	c. Fire extinguisher and protective blanket on hand during cutting/welding operations?				
	d. Emergency generator and back-up batteries tested and inspected each month?				
	f. Natural gas supply, diesel fuel storage tank, and electrical service inspected each month?				
	g. Drinking water and air quality tested and inspected quarterly?				
6.	Sidewalks, Steps, and Parking Areas				
	a. All areas free of slipping and falling conditions?				
	b. Adequate exterior night lighting?				
	c. Steps and ramps equipped with securely fastened handrails?				
	d. Speed bumpers clearly marked?				
	e. Pedestrian crossing areas clearly marked?				
	f. Storm drains free of obstructions?				
Notes:	1. On all "No" answers, show anticipated correction date and make appropriate comments.				
	2. Forward completed form to:				

Exhibit 9.1   Safety Evaluation Checklist (Continued)

maintain a plan in conjunction with other company departments to respond should any disaster, whether caused by people or nature, come to the organization. Here are issues to consider:

What does *quickly recover* mean to senior management, to the information technology group, to the human resources department, to the security department, to the facility professional, and to his or her staff at their home office headquarters and division/branch office locations around the world? Each department should be included and coordinated in the response plan.

Does *quickly recover* have different meanings in different countries or regions? This question is important because technology and database maturity can differ with respect to what is available, what employees are trained to

---

Safety Suggestion Sheet

Prepared by:_____   Date:_____

Department:_____

Describe the potential safety hazard and what areas it could effect:_____

_____

_____

_____

Recommendations or suggestions for eliminating or minimizing hazard:_____

_____

_____

_____

Department Manager:_____

Disposition or Action Taken:_____

_____

_____

_____

_____

_____   _____
Safety Manager   Date

Exhibit 9.2   Safety Suggestion Sheet

handle, and what physical resources are available to respond to the emergency. The facility professional must be aware of and plan for these differences so as to support emergency efforts wherever the company operation is located.

How can we better help operational business units quickly recover from a natural disaster or personnel or terrorist event? What are the critical issues that the facility professional and his or her staff must address to support the business unit(s) should an emergency event happen? The answer should

Department(s) Inspected: _____   Inspection Date(s): _____

Safety Coordinator: _____

Scope: This checklist is by no means all-inclusive. You should add to them or delete items that do not apply. The General Industry Safety and Health Standards and DSAA's self-inspection checklists should be reviewed for additional items that may be needed to update this checklist. The scope of the self-inspection should consider and include the following:

☐ Processing, Receiving, Shipping and Storage—equipment, job planning, layout, heights, floor loads, projection of materials, materials-handling and storage methods.

☐ Building and Grounds Conditions—floors, walls, ceilings, exits, stairs, walkways, ramps, platforms, driveways, aisles.

☐ Housekeeping Program—waste disposal, tools, objects, materials, leakage and spillage, cleaning methods, schedules, work areas, remote areas, storage areas.

☐ Electricity—equipment, switches, breakers, fuses, switch-boxes, junctions, special fixtures, circuits, insulation, extensions, tools, motors, grounding, NEC compliance.

☐ Lighting—type, intensity, controls, conditions, diffusion, location, glare and shadow control.

☐ Heating and Ventilation—type, effectiveness, temperature, humidity, controls, natural and artificial ventilation and exhausting.

☐ Machinery—points of operation, flywheels, gears, shafts, pulleys, key ways, belts, couplings, sprockets, chains, frames, controls, lighting for tools and equipment, brakes, exhausting, feeding, oiling, adjusting, maintenance, lock out, grounding, work space, location, purchasing standards.

☐ Personnel—training, experience, methods of checking machines before use, type clothing, personal protective equipment, use of guards, tool storage, work practices, method of cleaning, oiling, or adjusting machinery.

☐ Hand and Power Tools—purchasing standards, inspection, storage, repair, types, maintenance, grounding, use and handling.

☐ Chemicals—storage, handling, transportation, spills, disposals, amounts used, toxicity or other harmful effects, warning signs, supervision, training, protective clothing and equipment.

☐ Fire Prevention—extinguishers, alarms, sprinklers, smoking rules, exits, personnel assigned, separation of flammable materials and dangerous operations, explosive-proof fixtures in hazardous locations, waste disposal.

☐ Maintenance—regularity, effectiveness, training of personnel, materials and equipment used, records maintained, method of locking out machinery, general methods.

☐ Personal Protective Equipment—type, size, maintenance, repair, storage, assignment of responsibility, purchasing methods, standards observed, training in care and use, rules of use, method of assignment.

Completing the Self-Inspection: Each item should be reviewed and checked if it can be answered in the affirmative or is not applicable. For No responses, a brief description of the problem or concern should be forwarded to the Workplace Safety Action Plan. If during the inspection, additional items or concerns are discussed, they should also be forwarded to the Workplace Safety Action Plan for follow-up.

Exhibit 9.3   Workplace Safety Self-Inspection Checklist

be fully documented and realistically rehearsed where possible by all related departments and business units in all countries where business units must quickly recover.

What are our internal and external plans and funds? The facility professional must know what he or she must do internally and externally and what funds are available to accomplish the work.

Where is the offsite recovery facility? Is one in place for each region of the world, or does one serve all locations? Are they or is it adequate? When was the last time the company ran disaster simulations with service and operational units?

Is the company prepared? If no, what else should the facility professional and staff do and recommend for customer(s) and senior management?

Are the other service departments with which facility management interacts—for example, security, human resources, information technology—prepared? This is a vital question to which any answer other than yes is not good for the organization and must be addressed.

Be prepared to manage and promote facility professional change as business trends and technology continues to change:

Be attuned to your corporate business situation. What is senior management planning, in what time frame, and with what expected results? The facility professional must be privy to and aware of the strategic and tactical realities of business within the organization.

What is the economy doing in the company's headquarters country, regionally and globally? Where are sales strong, stable, or weak, and how does this information affect the need for real estate and facilities?

What is the economic situation where the facility professional is located if not at the corporate headquarters? Depending on the economy in a particular location or region, the facility professional and his or staff will have unique location or region issues to manage.

What is senior management doing? What information is being shared with the facility professional?

What are your internal customers doing? Are they aggressively planning to move their business unit product or service forward, to enter a no-growth mode, or want the facility professional to help them reduce their portfolio of real estate assets rapidly?

What are your peers doing? The facility professional must be aware of peer activity, as it could prove to be a best practice that the facility professional could adapt to fit his or her situation. Being involved in a professional association is a good way to support your profession, obtain education and research information, network with peers, and remain aware of what is happening in your city, region, country, and planet.

What should the facility professional do in support of proactive change? It is important that the facility professional be aware of the business, political, and personnel issues that are important to the company, customers, fellow employees, profession, peers, and acquaintances.

The result should be a better service or product, greater customer satisfaction, and a higher return on investment that will support management and company regardless of changes in global business trends.

Depending on the organization and what is important to its survival, disasters can take different forms, including fire, tornado, hurricane, flood, earthquake, electrical failure, strikes, and terrorism.

The National Fire Protection Agency has determined that out of one hundred businesses that experience a disaster, 43 percent never reopen and 29 percent close after three years, which equates to 72 percent of the companies never recovering from the disaster.[1]

Businesses, for their own survival, must be prepared for all emergencies that may affect their ability to continue to do business. Plans must be developed and implemented to assure that all critical business functions continue in the event of disaster.

An emergency plan must be prepared and implemented prior to a disaster occurring. Several scenarios must be developed that address all types of disasters and degrees of severity. To have an effective emergency preparedness and response program, you must consider all priorities and include all applicable local, state, and federal codes concerning emergencies and emergency preparedness/response.

Any worthwhile emergency plan must address the organization's critical needs for survival and the best ways to protect these needs. All organizations must identify their most important assets and devise means to safeguard them. Some organizations may feel their most important assets are their staff, financial, and accounting records. Other organizations may classify equipment as more important than financial records, while some may decide buildings are most important.

For some emergencies, especially earthquakes, city and emergency task forces have advised building and business owners that they should not plan on help arriving for at least 72 hours. They recommend that each floor have an emergency cabinet placed near the core of the building. Each cabinet should contain medical supplies, stretcher, emergency blankets, flashlights, radios, climbing rope, grounded axe, crowbar, jack, utility gloves, large plastic bags, toilet paper, and extra batteries. Cabinets containing water and emergency food should be placed in central areas of the facility.

Emergency floor coordinators should be assigned within each floor, area, and department. Each floor coordinator should be certified in first aid and cardiopulmonary resuscitation (CPR). Floor coordinator training should take place annually to review emergency evacuation procedures, the responsibilities of the floor and emergency response procedures.

New employees should be issued an emergency preparedness packet with information defining *disaster*, what to do during one, who the floor emergency

---

[1]*Source:* "What Is an Emergency Plan? Why Do We Need One?" by Phylis Meng, *Facility Management Journal,* January/February 1993, pp. 5–6.

coordinators are, and the locations and content of emergency cabinets. Emergency evacuation and preparedness training should be provided monthly for all staff. During training, staff should be briefed as to stairwell locations, fire extinguishers, fire alarms, and floor coordinators. The floor coordinators should understand their responsibilities in case of fire, bomb threat, earthquake, or medical emergency. All participants should receive a listing of floor coordinators plus a "What to do in an emergency" cover page/instruction sheet.

To protect irreplaceable assets (financial, accounting, and other valuable papers), you may choose to develop and implement a vital records emergency plan. Under this plan, vital records should be stored at two locations, one out of state and the other within a 50-mile radius of your facility. The following items are usually stored offsite:

- Backups of your organization's current financial and accounting files
- Backups for your local area network (LAN)
- Backup magnetic tape for your master document index
- Copies of all organizational archival microfilm rolls or archival scanned backup tapes
- Microfilmed or scanned corporate meeting agendas and meeting minutes
- Organizational correspondence
- Original legal documents and real estate records where state law does not prohibit their storage out of state

The records management department may be assigned the responsibility for developing and implementing the procedures to capture, index, and store all vital information and records pertaining to the organization.

Several staff emergency response team members should be issued instructions and the locations of stored data and codes so they can access the offsite data. They should also receive instructions on retrieving the stored information and necessary equipment.

After the Disaster

Each organization must decide what important issues it will address after an emergency. The most critical are to retrieve vital records and to obtain and provide office space for staff to work.

A business resumption plan should be developed and implemented describing the actions to be taken, the resources to be used, and the procedures to be followed after an unlikely event occurs that renders your organization operational capacity partially or fully inactive. As part of your business resumption plan, you may consider obtaining a mailbox from your telephone company that originates and terminates in a different location than your office phone lines. After a major disaster, all staff can call this number to find out when and where to report to work.

You might also consider making arrangements with your leasing agent, furniture supplier, equipment suppliers, stationery suppliers, mechanical and electrical maintenance contractors, and vendors with four-wheel-drive vehicles to work with your emergency response team. Working together, they could arrange for alternate office space, procurement and delivery of furniture and equipment, and delivery of additional supplies as required. This plan should assist the emergency response team in setting up temporary office space in three to seven days after a disaster.

After the disaster, the previously assigned engineering team should evaluate the damage and determine whether the offices can be utilized or contingency plans should be implemented.

Developing an Emergency Plan

Every organization should have an emergency preparedness/contingency/recovery plan in place. During planning, consider the following items:

- Identify the assets needed to survive the disaster, including emergency cash funds and insurance coverage where available and affordable.
- Identify how to protect those assets. If you are building a new facility, this protection should be part of the planning and construction program.
- Plan what to do during an emergency.
- Plan what to do after the disaster to ensure the organization survives.
- Inform and train staff in emergency preparedness/recovery requirements. Ensure that local fire and police authorities are included in your planning and training process.
- Monitor and test your plans regularly to ascertain that all contingencies are addressed.
- Make adjustments in your plan(s) as required.

Emergency plans are vital for business and personnel survival. Facility staff members, their support departments, and product and service suppliers should be constantly testing, monitoring, and reviewing the plans to see how the organization can be better prepared to respond to an emergency and better able to make an easy transition after a disaster occurs.

RECORDS MANAGEMENT

Space in a working facility is a valuable and costly commodity. Many organizations have spent untold dollars, built out considerable office quality space, and purchased numerous file cabinets to keep heavy and costly paper files and records not only onsite but in the immediate department area. With the advent of microfilm, microfiche, and document management through document scanning, imaging, and retrieval, having the original document at hand is seldom necessary except for certain legal purposes.

In addition to the high cost of maintaining old documents onsite is the question of whether they should be kept, stored, or (dare we say it?) destroyed.

Records management has evolved as a profession (represented by the American Records Management Association) and has developed an organized process for handling and managing the thousands—often millions—of files and pieces of paper that organizations and their employees accumulate.

Records management provides an organized mechanism to store and retrieve valuable documents, a process to examine, retain, and destroy documents no longer important to the organization or required for legal purposes, and a method to ensure that workers periodically purge their files by throwing away specific documents and sending others to an on- or offsite records storage facility.

Your company should have a records management plan to retain and dispose of records in an orderly fashion for periods that comply with legal and governmental requirements and as needed for general business requirements.

The records management procedure applies to all business documentation generated by your organization. However, this does not necessarily cover internal or certain day-to-day business correspondence.

Current Filing System

To ensure efficient access, filing centers should be established in each department. To reduce duplicate and unnecessary record retention, individual desk files should be avoided unless they are used in daily operations. All other departmental or company records should be filed in the departmental central filing areas.

Unless necessary, records should be retained by the originator or sender and not by the receiver. This practice avoids duplicate filing systems. Adhering to the following filing guidelines optimizes filing efficiency and records access:

1. All file cabinets and files should follow recognized rules of order, such as left to right, top to bottom, front to back, and, in the case of chronological records, new to old.

2. File markers or label headings should be placed at the front of a file or group of files.

3. Alphabetical files should be filed under broad topical categories. Files should never be filed under individual employee names (except personnel files) to avoid confusion and refiling in the event of turnover. Files should be always filed under the proper or company name whenever appropriate. In the case of individuals, files should be maintained according to the person's last name, then first name and middle initial.

Record Retention and Long-term Storage

Archived records should be maintained in locked storage areas at the facility or offsite in long-term storage. Access to these areas should be limited to organizational individuals, the records manager, and his or her staff. In some organizations, the facility customer must receive approval from the records manager before the facility project manager can order, purchase, and install additional file cabinets. We recommend you adopt this policy, as it ensures that your customer must comply with the records retention policy and positively influences conservation of valuable floor space. A sample proposal for high-density mobile shelving follows this section.

Nonpermanent files should be stored in cardboard file boxes. Each file box should be labeled on the front with the contents, dates covered, and destruction date, if applicable. Permanent records should be maintained in metal fire-resistant file cabinets.

Files should be stored only in boxes with similar items, dates, and retention periods. This allows easier access and purging of records. As a general rule, it is better to half-fill a file box than to store dissimilar files in the same box. The records manager should be responsible for categorizing and maintaining a listing of records maintained and the location (by wall unit and shelf or row number).

The following list suggests the holding periods for various documents. Questions regarding documents not listed should be directed to the records manager.

Document	Holding Period in Years
Accident reports after settlement	8
Accounts payable (vouchers and invoices)	6
Bank statements and reconciliations	6
Canceled checks	6
Cash receipts books	Permanent
Claim files (against us)	6
Claim files (by us)	3
Contracts, agreements, and leases after expiration	8
Credit files	6
Employee records (terminated)	6
Engineering and scientific records	Permanent
Financial statements (internal)	5
Financial statements (external)	Permanent
General ledgers and journals	Permanent
Income and other tax returns	6
Insurance claims after settlement	10
Patents and licenses	17
Payroll registers and time sheets	6
Payments and reports to governmental agencies	6
Physical inventory records	6
Purchasing correspondence	6
Sales correspondence	2
Sales invoices	6
Stock certificates (canceled)	Permanent
Travel and expense reports	6

Record Destruction

Three to six months after each year end, the records manager should proceed with destruction of all files that have exceeded their recognized holding period. A listing of file categories to be destroyed should be circulated to all managers 30 days prior to destruction for review and comment. The listing of records destroyed should be maintained permanently.

Destruction of the files should be performed by an independent shredding and disposal service. Disposal of records via the company's general trash service should not be permitted.

Furnishings and Equipment Inventory

Ten years ago, if you asked about an organization's furniture and equipment inventory, you might have found that at best it was out of date, incomplete, and did not match the fixed asset register managed by the finance department. Manual recordkeeping for systems furnishings and equipment within a facility was especially difficult in high-churn companies because what was in the warehouse one day might be gone the next, and probably no one knew where it had gone. Archaic at best, the system was cumbersome just to maintain, which no one did.

What furniture and equipment do we own or lease, and what is the strategy for keeping our records up to date? These and other questions can, in large part, be answered by providing, installing, and maintaining an asset-based bar code database system.

Today's workplace is a complex combination of systems furniture, personal computers, and equipment that can be moved and recombined with other components daily. To cope with this ever-changing environment, facility professionals are now turning to database inventory systems, often networked with computer-aided design systems (CADD), for furniture and equipment inventory information.

Some are using PC-based bar code asset management systems that provide information for inquiry or reporting purposes. These furniture and equipment inventory systems use bar code labels that are placed on the item, room, and building. Almost anyone can scan the bar codes with an appropriate reader, and after the information is downloaded into the computer system, an inventory of items in a particular room, on a floor, by department, and in a particular building can be generated in a standard report in minutes.

Bar code labels are a series of lines that represent numbers, and these lines can be scanned accurately by a handheld bar code reader. The number is cross-referenced in the computer database, and the system can then provide up-to-date information with accuracy far superior to that of any manual system. On a daily basis, inventory personnel can send the data collected to the host computer or file server by cable or over telephone lines.

The bar code system can also work in a warehouse setting where furniture and equipment are stored in an organized and bar-coded bin location system. It allows you to inquire how much you have on hand of a particular item in the warehouse, where it is located, and in what physical shape it is. The system reports current inventory, its value, replacement orders, and expected delivery dates.

The more complex the facility in its combination of open-plan furnishings, the more an automated bar code scanning system makes financial and business sense.

As a part of the furnishings and equipment inventory requirement, the facility professional should ensure that surplus furnishings are disposed of in accordance with corporate policies and procedures (see Sample Request for Proposal for Disposal of Surplus Furnishings). Furnishings and equipment, like any asset, must be maintained and reused where possible. Metal furnishings and equipment may require cleaning and painting to extend their useful life and to ensure that their color blends in with other facility furnishings and equipment (see Sample Request for Proposal for Electrostatic Spray Painting).

MAIL AND COPY CENTER SERVICES

The administrative services department often resides and is a support group within the facility management department. The mail and copy center services usually are part of the administrative services department and provide daily or round-the-clock service to meet the mail and copy center needs of its customers.

Mail Room Services

The mail services department provides mail room services. The volume of mail depends on the organization it is supporting for outgoing mail and the type of product or service the organization provides to its clients. The types of inbound and outbound mail handled are usually:

- Post Office services, including registered, certified, and overnight mail
- Internal mail
- Freight
- Courier service, including overnight deliveries

The mail services department processes incoming mail by picking it up daily from the Post Office or having it delivered to the facility. In larger organizations, one or two mail runs per day are made to mail stops on each floor. Certified and registered mail is accepted by mail services and the ultimate recipient notified immediately that it is available for pickup with an authorized signature.

Mail services often provides a fax and customer center where it receives faxes, local courier packages, and special handling mail. It also receives incoming overnight mail, courier deliveries (UPS, RPS, Federal Express, DHL, etc.), and other freight carrier shipments; logs in packages, delivers them to the recipients; and obtains their signature indicating receipt.

Another service, at some organizations, is the receipt of company payroll in envelopes; each envelope is logged in, and an authorized signature is required to pick up the envelopes.

Outgoing mail is processed, and mail services must maintain sufficient funding in the postage machine. All outgoing mail, including certified and registered mail, is metered and processed the same day it is received. Overnight mail and deferred freight shipments are made utilizing the carriers contracted by the organization. Local courier service is usually provided, and the correct charge to department or location for every shipment is logged and forwarded to accounting.

Copy Centers

Copy centers are generally provided one and sometimes two per floor, depending on the volume and type of copies to be made. For high-volume copying projects, a central print center is often found in the service area of a facility. This center may be staffed with in-house employees or an outsourced local service company that specializes in managing high-volume copy centers.

The center generally provides high-volume copying, specialty copying, color copying, offset copying, bindery services, covers, tabs, and so on. Print projects are completed based on time of delivery to the copy center with a priority for completion on a job ticket that lists the specifications of the job, point of contact, due date of job, and charge to department or location. As the copy center provides a valuable service to the organization, the copy center manager must provide the administrative services manager or facility manager with a monthly report detailing the number of jobs vended, types of jobs, and total costs.

The copy center generally provides and maintains convenience copiers throughout the facility. The center manager keeps records of copier performance and maintenance and reports these records monthly. The copy center manager takes monthly meter readings and reports the monthly impressions per machine. He or she also purchases and tracks monthly usage of paper, toner, and staples per machine and provides monthly totals. Copy staff check copiers daily and add paper, staples, and toner, and clean the glass shelf as needed. Copy staff provide minor copier maintenance and coordinate copier service issues and preventive maintenance with the appropriate service company.

AUDIOVISUAL EQUIPMENT SERVICES

The audiovisual (A/V) equipment services department is responsible for A/V equipment and for tracking and maintaining it for the use of the employees throughout the facility. This support department has become more visible with the detailed and timely communication service equipment it provides to general staff and to management. This department works closely with information technology (IT) and telecommunications, maintains the A/V equipment in conference rooms, and keeps extra units available for temporary use. Generally, reservations to borrow equipment specify that it cannot be checked out longer than one week. The department must ensure that all A/V equipment, including teleconferencing equipment, is in working order, repair malfunctioning equipment, and provide supplies such as bulbs for overhead and slide projectors.

The A/V department manager should provide a monthly report detailing the number of times each type of equipment was checked out and the amount and types of supplies used; the inventory of equipment should include make, model, serial number, date of purchase, and storage location. For corporations where numerous marketing presentations are made each week, the A/V department fills a key service role.

CONFERENCE ROOM SCHEDULING

Another service provided by most administrative services departments is conference room scheduling. This service may be accessed through the work order system or a separate system connected through the intranet or organizational e-mail system. The service schedules conference room usage throughout the facility, usually on a first-come, first-served basis.

The conference room scheduler should take the following information from the person calling to reserve a conference room:

- Name of person making reservation
- Department/location of person responsible for meeting
- Conference room location preference
- Start and ending time for use of conference room
- Number of people in meeting
- Topic of meeting
- Number of chairs and table configuration required
- A/V equipment requirements

This information is then provided to the appropriate departments—A/V, catering, security, maintenance—for their scheduling of required staff.

FOOD AND BEVERAGE SERVICE

Most buildings, whether owned or leased by the corporation, contain some form of food and beverage service. Where the number of employees does not support a full-service cafeteria or sandwich shop, the service may consist of vending machines.

If your customer is housed in a leased facility, the landlord may provide space for a food service vendor within the building as an amenity feature. If your customer has leased a large portion of the building or owns the building, management may choose to provide food service to its employees on a subsidized or nonsubsidized basis.

Organizations that provide food service to their employees almost always retain a contract food service vendor in lieu of staffing the facility with its own food service employees. The organization usually purchases all food service equipment, builds out the space, and hires a food service vendor to manage the operation. This management contract may include:

1. Preparing monthly menus for the employee cafeteria.
2. Providing food service for senior management and catering special events.

3. Catering food service requirements in conference rooms.

4. Coordination and maintenance of all furnished pantry and food service equipment.

5. Purchasing all food, beverages, and replacement items.

6. Visually inspecting all kitchen equipment, including electrical and mechanical components, quarterly.

7. Cleaning the coils and checking the refrigerant charge on all condensing coils quarterly.

8. Recording the amperage readings on all electrical equipment quarterly.

9. Replacing filters on city water supply lines where applicable quarterly.

10. Testing pressure relief valves on water heaters and hot water boosters quarterly.

11. Checking belts, bearings, pulleys, air filters, and duct conditions on dish-washer exhaust systems quarterly.

12. Supervising the testing of fire-suppressing hood systems by a certified fire protection company annually.

13. Performing quarterly preventive maintenance routines on and repairs as needed to the following equipment:

Food warmers

Refrigerators

Freezers

Ice makers

Freezer cabinets

Coffee and tea urns

Convection ovens

Microwave ovens

Food steamers

Food mixers

Sinks

Dishwashers

Hot water booster heaters

Toasters

Dishwasher exhaust systems

Fire-suppressing hood system

Exhaust systems and fans

Other services may include maintaining and repairing coffee stations and vending machines located throughout the facility. For some organizations, collecting and reporting monies obtained from the vending machines is required.

RECYCLING AND CONFIDENTIAL DESTRUCTION SERVICES

As organizations become more environmentally aware of paper, plastics, and other products that are choking landfills, a strong movement has developed among corporate organizations to recycle these products as many times as possible, especially in response to local regulations requiring recycling programs.

Many facility management departments now contract with waste management companies to provide receptacles for recycling paper, glass, and aluminum cans. These containers are usually placed at strategic locations on each floor throughout the facility.

A related service is confidential shredding. Again, a local vendor is retained to provide lockable containers that serve as the holding and transporting containers for the confidential materials. The vendor must be able to document that all the confidential materials, including microfiche, were shredded promptly and disposed of in an environmentally safe and legal manner.

TECHNOLOGY

In the past 30 years, the business world has gone from mainframe computers in a specialized room to computer stations to personal computer workstations to laptop computers and now to handheld information devices and beyond. Information, communications, and e-mail is at your fingertips 24 hours per day, 7 days a week. Computers have become smaller and lighter; they hold more information and are faster each year. Color monitors that once were bulky are now available in flat monitor displays with large screens in high-definition color. Phone systems are more sophisticated and have more features. With some technologies, local and long-distance phone service is available through the high-speed digital communication system and even over the Internet. Cell phones are available at lower costs, with greater memories and features, are available as picture phones, can send and receive text messages, and, with the right technology, can be used in most parts of the world.

Technology at the corporate office is being used by the corporate customer who has kept pace with the rapid development, use, and implementation of new software, the Internet, e-business, online purchasing, and online communications. Web telecasts, net meeting technologies, and the use of CDs and personal/removable drives are changing the way business communicates and stores information. And we have seen the business concerns that spam, computer viruses, identity theft, and computer hackers have brought to our use of technology. Computer and communication security as it relates to the transfer of money and information is a big business, and a secure corporate intranet is important to the information and business health of today's organizations, governments, and individuals.

Surprisingly, while security is perceived as important, many corporate and corporate facility professional decision makers have invested more funds in technology. They seem to be more focused on how to continue business in the face of the 9/11 disaster and its aftermath.

Incorporating technology into operations is one way the facility professional is working to review and improve the cost-effectiveness and efficiency of services. For example:

Consider the initial and maintenance costs and benefits of technology in the workplace and the on-going operational requirements (database, CIFM, etc.) which must be maintained on a regular basis.

Assess the current role of facility technology.

Decide whether or not facility technology is appropriate for your information requirements.

Explore whether or not current manual processes can be easily translated to facility professional technology and, if yes, how long it will take and how much it will cost.

Consider incorporating facility technology if not currently being used.

Increase facility technology if and where appropriate.

Assess the current role of technology in the information technology, human resources, security, finance, and accounting departments as well as the compatibility of the systems.

Seek the most current data available.

Seek relevant technology and data and consider how to integrate the data.

As the facility professional for your organization, you must be able to plan, direct, use, and manage facility management and related business and operational technologies. Also, you must be aware of the technologies your customers use and require for their business operations. Today's technologies utilize space, volume, weight, electrical, HVAC, raw material, and environmental requirements to provide specific services or products for your customers. It is important that the facility professional and his or her staff:

Monitor information and trends related to facility management technologies.

Identify and interface with internal and external accountable resources—for example, external vendors, internal or external information technology systems.

Identify evaluation criteria, evaluate, and recommend facility management technologies solutions.

Assess how changes to facility management technologies will affect current infrastructure, processes, and building systems.

Oversee the acquisition, training, installation, operation, maintenance, and disposition of components supporting facility management technologies.

Recommend and communicate facility management technology policies.

Establish facility management technology practices and procedures.

Develop and implement training programs for facilities staff and ancillary resources.

Monitor facility management technology performance and make appropriate recommendations if modifications are needed.

Manage corrective, preventative, and predictive maintenance.

Develop, test, and implement, when necessary, emergency procedures and disaster recovery plans.

TELECOMMUNICATIONS AND COMPUTER INTEGRATION

Over the past 30 years, office, service, and manufacturing technology has rapidly improved the ability of the employee to access vast amounts of information. At times, the process of electronic information storage and retrieval has grown too fast for employees to master the associated technology. The computer has moved from the large encased, raised-floor room to a smaller space that requires little or no special ventilation or cooling. Power consumption is down per piece of equipment but up per workstation; the size of equipment is smaller; printers are printing faster and with higher quality on standard copy paper.

During this time frame, telephone service has moved from the large, solely owned electromechanical telephone switch to a number of refrigerator- or smaller-sized fully computerized boxes that digitally send and receive pulse information. Now the two technologies, the telephone and the computer, once far apart, are moving closer and closer together in the technology used and the services provided.

State of the art today may be obsolete in six months or less. In 1986, the IBM AT personal computer was the state of the art, and today laptops, cell phones, and the handheld personal digital assistant (PDA) are available for use by office and industry workers in most parts of the world. Telephone switch service has moved from the long distance or local phone carrier's central office to the organization's phone room through deregulation of the telephone industry. The on-site computerized telephone switches provide more services, in less space, with more reliability for the organization; often it is onsite, in the basement, where changes and expanded service can be made as and when needed.

Telephone and Computer Services Today

Today, in many smaller organizations, the director of administration often has the overall responsibility for technology, including telephone and computer services. These two services now are often housed in the same room using the same or similar technology. The management information system (MIS) manager often supervises the maintenance and operation of computer and telecommunication requirements, including the telephone switch and associated equipment.

The ability to digitize information and send it over telephone lines has rapidly expanded into a common feature allowing employees to use telephone lines and modems to access, use, and retrieve information from computers almost anywhere in the world. Fax machines are tied into the office computer network via a fax server, and employees can send faxes straight from their computer terminal.

Telephone and computer integration has made the facility professional's job easier and harder at the same time. Where moving a telephone or a computer terminal used to be a two- to four-week process, it can now be done while the employee is walking to the new office or workstation if the facility is wired appropriately.

Today, offices, conference rooms, break areas, touchdown areas, and workstations are wired in more than one location for telephone and computer use via separate twisted pair cable or fiber-optic cable rated to accommodate higher speeds; thus, information can now be transmitted to any location in the office, service, or manufacturing facility. We may soon see the use of a single cable to receive and send telephone and computer information, including real-time video of the person we have contacted. The flat computer screen and keyboard may become, in time, fully integrated with the telephone, with one piece of equipment providing computer and telephone features.

Electronic mail, voice mail, and the cell phone are essential to managers who are often out of their offices. In most organizations, managers leave messages for and receive replies from their employees and customers at all times of the day and night, especially from international locations.

The ability to send information via voice, e-mail, or fax poses problems for the receiver of the mountain of information—some important and some time-robbing. Organizations with these problems have developed guidelines and etiquette procedures for when to call, when to use e-mail, and when to send a fax. These services have a cost, and some organizations have experienced information block: their telephone voice mail, computer electronic mail, and fax file servers lock up because they are full.

As a facility professional, it is your responsibility to provide the environment in which this equipment and service resides. The computer/telephone room must be able to accommodate growth; be designed and installed in an organized layout with backup power as required; include smoke and fire detection equipment, shelves for reference manuals, and desks and ergonomic chairs for operators; and have appropriate HVAC, power, and cabling that is convenient, labeled, and organized for rapid change via plug-in blocks. Cabling overhead and under-floor must meet fire code requirements and be neatly installed, bundled, and secured from the structure—not lying on top of the ceiling.

Keeping the computer and telephone room clean and tidy (with no extension cords on the floor or cabling snaking from one machine through a walking path) helps ensure that equipment is properly ventilated and that operators and repair technicians can find the equipment, cables, and power they need for their work.

These requirements will continue to be a major part of the organization's business requirements. It is essential for the facility management department to be fully aware of the requirements of telecommunications, e-mail, and MIS departments. Discussion about services required by customers and how these will be physically and safely provided must be ongoing.

CONCLUSION

This chapter concludes our review of the facility management responsibilities described in Exhibit 1.2 and presented graphically in Exhibit 1.4. Our goal has been to demonstrate the interplay of facility management–related services and the information relationships you must develop to meet the requirements of your customers. In your efforts to fulfill these responsibilities, the general administrative and technology services that provide day-to-day support for management and employees are vital to your success.

Chapter Ten

Successful Facility Management

Throughout this second edition, we have reviewed the concepts, methods, and processes used by successful facility professionals. Some of the information may have been familiar to you; other concepts will have been new. The test of the usefulness of all the material we have provided is its successful application. To grow and move forward with your facility management career, you must risk trying new or slightly different ways of doing things. Before you jump in, however, check for obstacles and issues that may lie just below the surface of your work environment.

This chapter reviews applying what you have read, heard, and know through hands-on experience, discusses further education and information support you may require, and looks at the future of the profession.

Hands-on Experience

"Nothing beats experience" is a saying many corporate officers feel is appropriate to facility management. But the saying really requires an additional phrase: ". . . , but you had better not fail while getting that experience." Leasing space or purchasing property, designing, planning, bidding, constructing, managing, maintaining, subleasing, or selling property provides you with detailed, hands-on experience beyond the scope of this book, but the goal of this experience is not merely to survive but to excel at the services you and your staff provide.

To excel, you will find it helpful to become familiar with terminology, negotiation strategies, financial models and analysis techniques, and the major legal issues associated with facility management as discussed throughout this book. Based on the size of community where your company is located, you may find a number of other corporate real estate, facility, or asset management professionals who have experience in your markets. These are people you should get to know.

Your project team should be able to help with additional information and publications, and you may want or need to obtain detailed training in financial, legal, real estate, project management, maintenance and operations, and business areas.

Ideally, you begin with what you know and move into areas of the process where you require more detailed information or outside help. As with all tasks, you must apply your business skills to organize and manage the process you are responsible for completing. Many people lose their way in new responsibility areas by focusing on the details first instead of trying to understand the big picture—that is, the mission and corporate goals.

Where possible, tackle and complete small projects. Small successes help build confidence and provide hands-on experience you can build on. For example, if you have never built out an entire building, it is more prudent to tackle the build-out of a floor than to tackle the build-out of an entire building. Using what you know as a foundation from which to develop experience with new situations is a successful approach to the problem solving that is an everyday occurrence for the facility professional.

We briefly discussed networking with others and through professional associations, and we cannot overstress the need for all facility professionals to be aware of what is going on in their profession outside their unique sphere of influence and understanding. Networking helps you benchmark your knowledge and problem-solving capabilities. It also can help you avoid making small and large mistakes due to ignorance of the marketplace. By knowing peers, vendors, and service providers throughout your business and in your geographic area, you ensure that you and your customer do not make the simple but expensive errors that can sometimes stop a major project. You would never knowingly hire a general contractor or buy from a supplier who is about to go bankrupt. But how can you gain this information except by networking and seeking information from others in the industry?

Facility professionals are developing increasingly large peer networks in order to track current practices, identify vendors or consultants in their area, and ascertain the rule-of-thumb requirements and normal costs for others in similar circumstances. This trend is spreading into international markets with the establishment of international association programs, chapters, and written information on international facility management practices.

Networking is especially useful for those who find themselves out of a job. The informal network can be a source of information about career opportunities that are seldom advertised in the newspaper. People do not like to hire strangers and instead seek applicants who trusted peers can recommend. Without networking (which also helps the hiring manager) to extend your slim resources, you may find your job search a lonely experience.

EDUCATION

Traditionally, on-the-job training is the major component in facility management education and training. In the context of this chapter, *education* means increased awareness and formal training in several areas: understanding the corporation's internal and external politics and business, learning facility and related business requirements, analyzing customers' needs for service, and keeping abreast of complex technical issues and products.

An increasing number of high-quality facility management training programs are available to you, your staff, consultants, vendors, and corporate senior management. These educational services are offered in-house by corporate training departments, facility departments, professional associations, vendors and consultants, and colleges and universities.

Many colleges and universities (e.g., Brigham Young University, Cornell University, Eastern Michigan University, Ferris State University, George Washington University, Georgia State University, Georgia Institute of Technology, Indiana State University, Iona College, Michigan State University, North Dakota State University, Oklahoma State University, State University of New York, University of Southern Colorado) offer continuing education programs addressing facility management and related issues, and a growing number are establishing undergraduate and master's degree programs in facility management. Many vendors and design consultants are supporting these programs with their time and financial resources as they realize that successful management of their corporate clients' problems and requirements increasingly depends on knowledgeable facility professionals.

You may wish to take courses offered by a local college, the state real estate commission, or a professional association. Numerous self-help books deal with negotiation, strategic planning, real estate, design, construction, project management, maintenance and operations, and administrative management. These sources of basic and advanced facility management information can form the foundation for further learning. The International Facility Management Association (IFMA), CoreNet Global, the Industrial Asset Management Council (IAMC), the Institute for Real Estate Management (IREM), and the Building Owners and Managers Institute (BOMI) are just a few of the associations that offer educational programs for facility professionals.

IFMA Recognized Programs are formal college/university FM-related education programs that are available at the locations shown below. The steps to achieving recognition are explained in the IFMA document "Standards for Recognized Programs, First Professional Facility Management Degree Programs." The process involves completing a detailed self-study that is reviewed by a committee of peers who decide whether or not to grant recognition.

Brigham Young University, Provo, Utah, offers a B.S. degree in Facilities Management with a Business Management minor from the nationally recognized Marriott School of Management, part of the College of Engineering and Technology in the School of Technology Facilities Management.

Colorado State University—Pueblo offers a B.S. degree in Facilities Management and Technology Studies through the College of Education, Engineering, and Professional Studies.

Cornell University, Ithaca, New York, offers B.S. and M.S. degrees in Facilities Management. The programs are offered through the New York State College of Human Ecology. The school also offers periodic continuing education units (CEUs) in major cities such as New Orleans, New York, and San Francisco.

Ferris State University, Big Rapids, Michigan, offers a B.S. program in Facilities Management through the College of Technology.

FHS Kufstein BildungsGmbH, Kufstein, Austria, offers a Magister (FH) in Facility Management.

Georgia Institute of Technology, Atlanta, Georgia, offers an M.S. in Integrated Facility and Property Management through the College of Architecture, Building Construction Program.

The Hong Kong Polytechnic University, Hung Hom, Kowloon, Hong Kong, offers a graduate program in Facility Management.

Wentworth Institute of Technology, Boston, Massachusetts, offers a B.S. in Facilities Planning and Management through the Department of Design and Facilities.

Obviously this book does not cover in detail all the information you may need. Your challenge is to apply business and corporate skills and abilities to your opportunities as you master your current facility management challenges and opportunities.

Integrated Asset Management

In a business environment featuring mega-mergers, corporate takeovers, and buyouts, the surviving organization gives the highest priority to ensuring long-term financial viability. This requires a redirection away from traditional capital investment and a strengthening of infrastructure management regimes—that is, integrated asset management (IAM).

The adoption and implementation of IAM throughout the organization is monitored as part of the overall process of capital asset planning and implementation. The IAM planning process also integrates with the corporate strategic planning cycle.

Integrated asset management is defined as the sum of all those activities leading to infrastructure that is appropriate to the cost-efficient delivery of service, those activities having the following strands:

Identification of the need for an asset

Provision of the asset, including its renovation

Operation of the asset, including its maintenance

Disposal and thus the effective removal of the asset from the organization's portfolio

In this context, asset requirements are driven by business/service needs and not viewed as a need in themselves. This ensures that scarce capital resources are properly allocated and managed to maximize the return on investment.

Concept and Application

IAM is a concept that organizations use to optimize and integrate the number, type, size, location, initial capital costs, and ongoing maintenance expenses of unique owned or leased requirements. The concept identifies the quality of facilities an organization chooses to provide for the people whom it employs; the cultural values the organization seeks to promote, including quality of life within a community; and the environment that supports and sustains all facets of the organization, now and in the foreseeable future.

IAM is a tool to match corporate infrastructure resource planning and investment with corporate service delivery objectives with the following criteria:

An asset has an enduring value.

Assets should exist only to support service delivery strategy.

Assets are only one input in the corporate planning process.

All assets must have a value.

All assets must have a service potential.

Assets can be financial, physical, or intangible.

Assets can be current or non-current.

Assets must, by their individual physical definition, distinguish between physical and useful life.

International Trends

The impact of trends on the management of infrastructure supporting service delivery to the community is forcing organizations to adopt innovative and integrated approaches to planning and decision making. The concept and use of IAM has both national and international applications and is a logical process for looking at:

The globalization of markets

Pressure on cost of service and competition

Acquisitions, mega-mergers, and takeovers

Common products and profit margins

The public and private sectors in a number of countries have embraced and are using the concept, while in other countries, more research must be done and local benefits identified through case studies before IAM can be used on a regular basis.

Private-sector Industry Trends

A number of organizations in North America have embraced IAM. To do so, senior management at the highest levels must have the vision and determination to understand and apply the concept in a proactive course of action that requires a multi-year commitment to achieve success. The facility professional must not only deal with the realities of day-to-day work, costs, and the politics of IAM but be willing and able to address IAM requirements to:

Be customer and business focused.

Be an ongoing internal program to reduce assets, costs, and head count.

Look at business infrastructure, services, and costs from an integrated/ portfolio perspective.

Outsource non-core services as an integral part of the IAM program.

Establish and use financial and performance measurement/benchmarking programs.

Team with internal and external service providers.

Develop partnering, alliances, etc., as strategic methods of conducting FM business.

Take a business case analysis (BCA) approach to identify current business methods, identifying risks to the organization, and developing risk assessments that lead to recommendations for changing the way facility and organizational business is conducted.

Identify risk sharing and the realities of fee-at-risk contracts with service providers.

Develop and use service level agreements with facility customers.

Use a balanced scorecard with customers to assess and quantify performance.

Use off–balance sheet financing when and where appropriate, especially in a sale-lease-back environment.

Use quality and performance measurements to establish a baseline of service and to establish progress over time toward improvements in facility quality and performance.

IAM Principles and Processes

Integrated asset management is a tool to better match infrastructure planning and investment with community and industry service needs with the following considerations:

Review of the organization's broader economic strategy

Coordinating divisional and/or business unit budgetary process

Organizationwide, whole-of-life asset management

Context of one single coordinated program delivery framework

Best practice management, including the development of a detailed service management process. Develop a centralized coordination and management process for real estate and facility strategy development and implementation to ensure that:

Real savings are provided to the organization regardless of the strategy implemented/

The IAM approach maximizes organizations purchasing power.

There is a realistic and verifiable return on investment.

The strategy provides improved performance standards for facility accommodation, management, and disposal.

Sustainable development must be incorporated into the IAM policy and program. Leadership and services supports an organization's (public and private sector) commitment to maintaining its stewardship role in regard to:

Long-term economic development

Social responsibility

Environmental sustainability

History and evolution

IAM has been practiced to some degree by centralized organizations for many years. Few have embraced it fully because the strong centralized research and decision concepts must be delivered over a long period—often three to ten years. The concept requires that organizations follow through with quality research; an objective, not subjective, process; and a full program of option development before decisions are made.

From a historical viewpoint, the process requires that within the organization there:

Is a demand for efficiency and effectiveness.

Is a perceived piecemeal approach that is not working well and must be changed.

Is a threat to the organization's perceived and actual wealth.

Is a robust management framework that can allow the financial, cultural, and political commitment to IAM.

Are viable internal processes that are compared to current and proposed outcomes.

Is a current lack of an overall coordinating body at the senior management leadership level for asset management.

Is a high cost of asset creation.

Are identified and validated costs for maintaining and staffing the organization.

Are aging assets with strategic maintenance program requirements.

Are changing expectations from employees, especially with respect to technologies.

Are financial risks to the organization.

Are fixed assets, capital fund requirements, and service delivery needs.

Are better infrastructure investments with community and industry service needs.

Are alternative ways of delivering services that do not require creation of infrastructure.

Are planning tools.

Are decision tools.

Is a performance monitoring program.

Is a best practice program for:

Energy/environmental management

Real estate and facility management

Human resources and personnel services

Information technology

Financial management

Asset management

Heritage assets

Total cost planning

Community infrastructure development

IAM Objectives

An organization that chooses to use IAM does so for competitive business and sustainable growth reasons and as a process or solution to address those competitive pressures. IAM objectives are strategic and are designed to:

Achieve the best possible match of assets and service delivery strategies.

Reduce demand for new assets by adopting non-asset solutions.

Maximize the service potential of existing assets.

Lower the overall cost of owning assets through life cycle costing techniques.

Ensure bottom-line focus by establishing clear accountability and responsibility.

Master Plan

Within IAM is a master planning process (see Figures 10.1 and 10.2) that includes:

Identifying the problem

Describing the implications of not fixing the problem

Research and benchmarks

Influences

Desired outcomes and objectives

Individual strategies

Integration of selected strategies

The net cost of implementation, including capital, operational, personnel, and associated program costs

The net savings to the organization both in actual and intangible dollars, time, and competitive advantage

Selling the concept

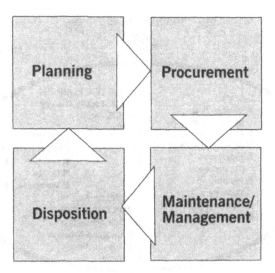

Figure 10.1   Integrated Asset Strategies

Identifying the Problem

The first step in developing the IAM master plan requires identifying IAM problems. These may include:

Higher-than-industry-average occupancy costs

Average maintenance expenditure on owned assets outstripping organizational funding

Divisions or business units having sole control of property acquisition and disposition

Multiple individually negotiated leases for multiple divisions or business units housing thousands of people

Diminished organizational purchasing power

Aging facility/property stock with limited flexibility

High ownership ratio of facilities and real estate

Increasing churn costs as a result of organizational change costing millions of dollars per year

The Strategic Plan

The IAM strategic plan is designed to integrate strategies at the corporate level of the organization, as shown in Figures 10.1 and 10.2. To be effective, the strategic plan must:

Assess asset functions against and be matched to specific service delivery strategies.

Include the planning time frame against the corporate planning horizon as shown in Figure 10.2, the integrated site/asset cycle.

Figure 10.2   Integrated Site/Asset Cycle

Strategically incorporate capital, personnel, one-time expenses, and recurrent costs linked to the financial management strategy.

Result in an integration of strategies into business plans to optimize the service potential of new and existing assets.

The Acquisition Plan

This plan requires a thorough research program with alternatives and options identified, including:

Plans and details for the rationale acquisition and replacement of sites and facilities

Facts establishing that existing assets are fully utilized and meet service delivery requirements

Consideration of non-asset solutions

All express and implied costs in life cycle analysis

A review of all infrastructure management, client relationship issues, and the issues identified in the case study

The result should be an efficient and effective acquisition framework that reduces the demand for new assets and funds and enhances the organization's business programs.

The Management Plan

The management plan provides reliable, relevant, and timely data with which to make informed asset management decisions. It should include:

Policies and procedures

Asset registers

Accommodation databases

Internal/actual rent charge-back systems

Infrastructure management, including integrating all corporate facility and asset services such as

Portfolio management

Corporate real estate

Facility management services

Human resources

Information technology

Telecommunications

Purchasing, etc.

The result should be an effective internal control system within whose framework improvements to assets are effected.

The Disposition Plan

Embarking on an IAM program will identify assets to consider for disposal. Legal, financial, personnel, community, technology, and cultural issues must be considered in the decision-making process to determine:

Which assets are utilized, are underperforming, and have been identified as part of a systematic review

Reasons for underperformance and corrective action to take

Appropriate disposal methods with regard to potential market, timing, and ability to maintain service delivery

The result should be an effective disposal management process that minimizes surplus holdings and underperforming assets and maximizes the ROI on portfolio.

Functional Service Silos and Vertical Processes

IAM includes a functional review of all asset-related services with special emphasis on:

Vertical processes (within functional areas). These provide a detailed analysis of each functional area with the intent of identifying best practices in facility management and strategies that can be applied to improve performance and reduce cost (see Figure 10.3).

Vertical Processes (*within functional areas*) **Detailed analysis of each functional area, with the intent of identifying best practices in facility management and strategies that can be applied to improve performance and reduce cost**

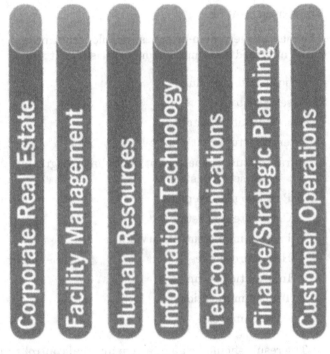

Figure 10.3   Functional Service Silos and Vertical Processes

Integrating corporate services. While a review of vertical processes is important, the integration of work among these processes is a key requirement of a successful IAM program (see Figure 10.4).

Horizontal processes (between functional areas). These involve the identification of opportunities for consolidation or integration of personnel, processes materials, etc., between functional areas.

Integrating functions (combining support functions). These involve evaluation of management systems and other processes that apply to all functional areas.

Client Relationship Management

For the IAM process to work, there must be a client relationship management program that incorporates the senior management of divisional or business unit leaders. This requires an understanding of each business and:

An interface with senior management from all businesses to develop major strategies for business, real estate, and asset initiatives

A consolidation of like business functions to reduce redundancies, foster synergies, and promote reengineering

The elimination of phantom planning and design work

Horizontal Processes (*between functional areas*) Identification of opportunities for consolidation and/or integration of personnel, processes, materials, etc. between functional areas

Integrating Functions (*combining support functions*) Evaluation of management systems and other processes that apply to all functional areas

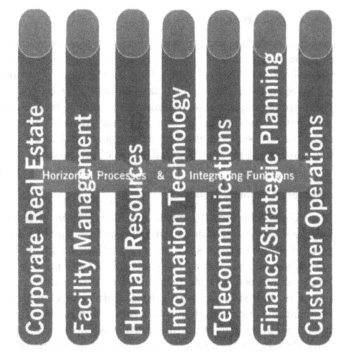

Figure 10.4   Integrated Corporate Services

The confirmation of occupancy—direct staff, full-time equivalents (FTEs), consultants, and vendors

A focal point for organizational space engagement processes with senior management regarding significant changes planned by the businesses

The above information (see Figure 10.4) can be subject to criticism as an abstract process without practical application or examples.

Governmental Legislative and Worker Trends

Businesses are becoming more active in addressing political, environmental, and human resources issues. Political forces are changing at the local, national, and international level, which affects the way we do business. Businesses are addressing and at times lobbying for and against issues such as no-growth and environmental policies, tariffs, property and income taxes, stock and bond prices, and other personal and business regulatory codes, laws, and administrative policies.

Worker benefits such as elective and selective health, dental, and life insurance plans, elderly care plans, health and fitness programs, maternity leave, day care and child care, retirement and profit-sharing plans, food service, and special training programs are becoming more important in attracting and retaining the skilled workforce the business of the future must.

Technological Changes

As businesses face widespread changes in their markets and global competition becomes more intense, we will see shifts in business philosophy, organizations, operations, information, technology, and political, environmental, and human resources issues. These shifts have already started and will continue. Business philosophies require that management and the workforce be ever more responsive, flexible, and efficient. Managing for growth, value creation, and the long term are key issues that many businesses must be able and willing to address and implement to meet the challenges of the future.

Information Industry Trends

The information revolution will continue to drive changes in how companies do business. Computer-aided management tools such as decision, knowledge-based, intelligent, and expert systems will continue to develop and provide all levels of management and staff with additional ways to forecast, process, and access larger amounts of pertinent information faster. Information systems are becoming more sophisticated, with greater networking and integration. Hardware, communications systems, fiber optics versus cable, laser technology, laptop PCs, bubble memory, and other information advancements still in development (including storage and security issues) will continue to change, grow, and proliferate in the home, office, and workplaces around the world.

Other technological trends such as the use of special telecommunications systems (fax, VSAT, cellular telephones, videoconferencing) to speed communication and the flow of information to more and remote locations will become a common way of doing business at work and at home. The rapid growth and implementation of business information systems will continue to challenge management, the facility professional, and the facility professional's facilities. The facility professional must be aware of and comfortable with computer hardware and software technology. The challenge includes integrating this sophisticated technology into planning, with an emphasis on a long-term flexible approach to reduce obsolescence in increasingly complex facility environments. Workplace systems and facilities must be able to accommodate the rapid growth of business technology and be ready for rapid transitions from obsolete systems to previously inconceivable facility and utility requirements.

Possibly the most challenging test to your professional skills in the next ten years will be participation in finding the solutions to political, environmental, and human resource issues that affect you and your company. Your approach must continue to shift from being a technician to being a businessperson.

No-growth policies, local, state, and federal legislation, codes and regulation changes, sewer and water moratoriums, permit procedures, rapid transit, taxes and insurance, health and safety requirements, union issues, purchasing policies, environmental impact studies, brownouts, asbestos, soil contamination, radon, sick building syndrome, VDT issues, child and health care, wellness programs, flex time, and physical and information system security issues are just a sample of what you must be ready to respond to, directly or indirectly, by staying informed and aware of what is going on in the world around you.

The future of facility management is evolving, and as we see by the application of the process in countries around the world, the scope of the profession is gaining strength. The specific applications may be different, but the ongoing development of literature and understanding of the benefits to an organized and creative process have financial and organizational implications that cannot be ignored. As the profession has grown in following and understanding, its relationship to strategic business development and business success has become more apparent. The future of the successful facility professional is bright with the promise of creative challenges and opportunities to help the corporation in its evolving work environment.

COMMUNICATIONS AND LEADERSHIP

The FM has many ways to share and communicate information, reports, and events, whether in person on a one-to-one basis, via written material or a formal presentation, through staff, or through the intranet or website. The financial, business, and leadership aspects of that communication must be delivered in the language the audience and users of the information understand. With increasing competition inside and outside of the organization for scarce resources, it is the FM's responsibility to communicate all aspects of an issue to senior management and related department leaders, to seek their support, and to help them make the best decision possible. How, when, where, what kind, and how much information is provided remains the FM's leadership responsibility, challenge, and opportunity.

Good to Great

At times, the FM must review his or her communication and leadership responsibilities, deciding what to look at and understand and what he or she can do to improve financial and operational performance to help the organization meet stated goals. This requires that the FM look at what is expected of him or her.

To this end, we believe the FM must review not only FM literature but also review recent business, financial, communications, and leadership information and literature. A recent book, *Good to Great*, by Jim Collins (Random House, 2001), is one we recommend the FM obtain, read, and share with staff. The FM should know and understand if the corporation is a good or a great organization and understand how, in his or her business, financial, communication, and leadership role, he or she fits into the current organizational program. The FM should also know if the FM department is good or great.

Certification and Testing

The Certified Facility Manager (CFM) program, implemented in 1994 through the International Facility Management Association (IFMA), based in Houston, Texas, has matured, and there are now thousands of facility professionals who have passed the exams and received CFM designation. The CFM recertification program requires that facility professionals continue to participate in FM-related educational programs to ensure continued awareness.

Another international association, CoreNet Global, offers a certificate program known as the Master of Corporate Real Estate (MCR). This is part of the CoreNet Global Professional Development Series. The MCR is a professional designation focused on the strategic management of corporate real estate, on urgent and critical business issues, and in the management of one or more real estate functions. Another certification program sponsored by CoreNet Global is the Senior Leader of Corporate Real Estate (SLCR) series. This certificate program is focused on developing the essential leadership skills needed to drive strategies that create value in corporate real estate. It is designed for those positioning themselves for a greater role in their organization.

An educational organization, the Building Owners and Managers Institute (BOMI), has a certificate program known as the Facilities Management Administrator® (FMA) designation program. This is designed to enhance the FM's career by increasing his or her effectiveness and knowledge and positioning him or her as a key strategic professional in the organization. This program teaches the FM to manage facilities in a way that best supports staff, fits into the organization's overall objectives, and maximizes productivity.

To earn the FMA designation, the FM must complete these seven mandatory courses plus the one-day Ethics Is Good Business® Short Course™:

Fundamentals of Facilities Management

Technologies for Facilities Management

Facilities Planning and Project Management

Environmental Health and Safety Issues

The Design, Operation, and Maintenance of Building Systems, Part I

The Design, Operation, and Maintenance of Building Systems, Part II

Real Estate Investment and Finance

These courses provide information on the evolutionary changes, both minor and major, that the facility management profession and the facility professionals have faced in the last ten years. Obviously, these courses provide only a brief insight into these educational changes. The continued growth and rapid pace of economic activity expected in North America in the twenty-first century indicates an optimistic outlook for corporate real estate and facility management professionals.

MOVING TOWARD THE FUTURE

In a number of organizations, facility management has moved from the boiler room to the board room. The facility professional, who was stuck with whatever design, building, furniture, or system he or she was handed, now leads the team that solves complex corporate facility problems.

Facility management has learned to resolve many old and new issues. "Service, Service, Service" is a facility professional's motto because in-house customers expect the same service and quality their paying clients expect of them.

Some organizations and facility departments are committed to injunctions such as these:

- Bring issues to the person you are charged to serve; refer people to the people they have issues with.
- If you come with a problem, come with at least one nonlethal solution.
- Be 100 percent accountable for your results—no blaming, no justifying.

Today's corporate facility professionals face numerous daily and long-term challenges. These highly qualified technological professionals often find that these challenges mean resolving management and leadership issues, including problems related to corporate politics. Professional facility managers have had to develop and use known but often neglected concepts such as leadership, excellence, service, unifying principles, tradition, and positioning to help them cope, survive, and excel in today's ever-changing corporate environment.

So how has the facility professional learned to excel? The following program has led to success.

Leadership, Excellence, and "Service, Service, Service"

In implementing an ongoing leadership versus management role within the corporation, facility professionals must:

1. *Arrange* the things necessary to get the job done.
2. *Establish* standards of service.
3. Set an *example* of service and excellence.
4. *Handle* challenges and opportunities.
5. Do what it takes to get the job done.

This leadership role provides the facility professional with five key responsibilities:

1. *Educate* self, staff, and customers.
2. *Sponsor* staff by delegating responsibility and authority.
3. *Coach* staff to obtain their best performance.
4. *Counsel* staff about what and how they are performing.
5. *Confront* issues in a timely, tactful, and responsible manner before they become significant.

Facility professionals continue to develop, adopt, and use *vision* statements like this one:

Success is built on:

- Understanding and satisfying current and future customer needs
- Integrity and trust in dealings among ourselves and with others

- A fun, challenging, and entrepreneurial environment in which people grow and prosper

- Excellence as a standard, prosperity and personal satisfaction as rewards

Service, Service, Service has become the way corporate professional managers must do business. They must achieve:

- Customer *satisfaction* with the services performed

- *Efficient* service provided in a timely manner

- *Reliable* service the customer can count on

- *Value* in the services performed

- *Integrity* in their work and relationships with others (see chapter 1, "Ethics")

- *Commitment* to their customers, with professional services and results

- *Excellence* as the only standard of doing business (see chapter 1, "Total Quality Management")

Facility professionals should consider management by walking around (MBWA) as one means of becoming more visible—to speak, listen, learn, share, and seek customer, vendor, and consultant feedback on how they are doing as a professional and how they and their staff, as service providers, are perceived by their boss, customers, and the public.

In addition to observing the preceding guidelines, facility professionals should give back to their community and profession through personal programs:

- *Volunteer.* Step forward and raise your hand to serve—to be a leader in your community and profession. *Volunteer* and, as a volunteer, ask others to volunteer to serve their community and profession. The profession's continued success will remain a function of the health and commitment of leaders to provide *quality* to the profession and *quality* services to their customers.

- *Lead.* Seek opportunities to speak, listen, and write for the profession. Encourage others within the company to participate and spread the message of service and excellence through leadership.

Unifying Principles

The book *Time Power*,[1] by Charles R. Hobbs, discusses how to take charge of time and how to manage it at work and at home. In particular, Hobbs lists four critical unifying principles that apply to everyone in an organization from top to bottom:

1. Have *personal integrity.*

2. Build *trust* in others.

3. Have *concern for others.*

4. Commit to *excellence.*

[1]Selected excerpts from pages 98–99 of *Time Power* by Charles R. Hobbs. Copyright © 1987 by Charles R. Hobbs. Reprinted by permission of Harper Collins Publishers, Inc.

The success of facility professionals often is determined by how well they manage and live the preceding principles and how effective they are as leaders.

As the facility management profession continues to evolve, we must concentrate on the development of leadership and management skills while strengthening technical skills. Hobbs reminds us that professionals and leaders must know, promote, and live by unifying principles that help them perform. The company or organization also must have a set of established unifying principles to ensure success.

Facility professionals must define and address leadership and excellence issues that provide challenges and opportunities for personal and professional development and growth.

The preceding principles should be reviewed and adopted. Within the organization, commitment to think and live these issues will extend the facility professional beyond a managerial role to a leadership role. This role of leadership and excellence must be sought, and striving to achieve it is central to success.

TRADITIONS

In a staff meeting in a Midwestern facility department, the issue of corporate departmental traditions at work was discussed. What does and should *tradition* mean to facility professionals?

Many older professions have developed traditions (unwritten and written) that reflect how members of their profession think about their work, how they do their work, how they celebrate their work and each other's successes, how they network, and how they look at their future. You, as a member of your profession, are setting traditions.

Traditions provide consistent and comfortable ideas and issues that repeatedly meet our needs and requirements. As the facility management profession continues to evolve, traditions such as celebration and networking become more important. Celebration serves as a focus to informally and formally enjoy doing what we do for a living and what we do after we leave work. It is not unusual to informally celebrate success by bringing in doughnuts, going out for lunch, or writing a thank-you card to someone who helped you.

Celebrating more formally is a way professionals who do not meet in informal settings can get to know each other. It may also serve to recognize those who have excelled and to communicate their accomplishments within the organization.

A tradition of celebrating both informally and formally by facility management departments is becoming a way of life. These celebrations help equalize the pressures you may be under and allow you to look at your projects from a different perspective. Hearing someone say "thank you" encourages the celebrant to continue providing high-quality service. Without something to look forward to—an event or objective—people tend to lose the sharp edge of their talents and interest in doing their job. Celebrations are a key method of improving repetitive contact and networking for professional and personal interests.

To improve your work life and that of your staff, establish and maintain traditions and foster celebrations. You have the opportunity to be part of an evolving and changing profession within your organization, and it is in your interest to develop programs and traditions that will help you and others cope and excel.

Facility management is growing and developing as a profession. When we look back at where we were and where we are going, our tradition of celebration should be an important part of remembering our success.

Leaders versus Managers

In the book *Leaders: The Strategies for Taking Charge,*[2] authors Warren Bennis and Burt Nanus focus on leading others and managing yourself. They state, "The problem with many organizations, and especially the ones that are failing, are that they tend to be over managed and under-lead." They continue with a crucial distinction: "Managers are people who do things right, and leaders are people who do the right thing." The ability to lead, to do the right thing, to be vision-oriented is crucial to all managers—especially to the facility professional, who is often in the middle of organizational politics.

Leadership in work life is but one area that facility professionals must strive to develop and achieve. Providing excellence and service is a quality you should also consider in your work and personal life. Adopting excellence means seeking to do everything to the best of one's ability or resources based on measurable excellence standards—and then to measure performance against these standards on a periodic or ongoing basis.

Excellence for a facility professional requires looking at what you do, how you perform, and what can be done to improve your performance in both small and big ways. When we complete a task, the result should be reviewed and improvements put in place to enhance the next opportunity to achieve excellence.

"Service, Service, Service" requires remembering that customers look to you as you look to vendors, contractors, and consultants to provide timely, quality, and cost-effective service—with a smile.

Positioning

Positioning: The Battle for Your Mind[3] discusses a new approach to communication called *positioning*. The authors state, "Positioning starts with a product," and it ". . . is not what you do with the product but is defined as what you do to the mind of the prospect."

The authors further state:

Many people misunderstand the role of communication in business and politics today. In our over-communicated society, very little communication actually takes place. Rather, a company must create a "position" in the prospect's mind. A position that takes into consideration not only a com-

---

[2]Selected excerpts from pages 21–22 of *Leaders: The Strategies for Taking Charge,* by Warren Bennis and Burt Nanus. Copyright 1985 by Warren Bennis and Burt Nanus. Reprinted by permission of HarperCollins Publishers, Inc.

[3]Al Ries and Jack Trout, *Positioning: The Battle for Your Mind.* Copyright 1986 by McGraw-Hill, Inc. Reprinted by permission.

pany's own strength and weaknesses, but those of its competitors as well. . . . The easy way to get into a person's mind is to be first. If you can't be first, then you must find a way to position yourself against the product, the politician, the person who did get there first.

The authors also include a chapter on positioning yourself and your career, where they discuss this advice:

- *Define yourself:* What are you? People suffer from the same disease as products. They try to be all things to all people.

- *Find a horse to ride:* Some ambitious, intelligent people find themselves trapped in situations where their future looks bleak. So what do they generally do? They try harder. . . . Trying harder is rarely the pathway to success. . . . Trying smarter is the better way.

What does all this have to do with being a corporate professional manager? You should review and evaluate the preceding concepts of leadership, excellence, and service as they apply to your position and what you want to do with your career and life.

As companies and markets change, so do your customers' expectations. The more aware you become in managing the nontechnical aspects of your life and work, the greater the possibility you are prepared to share in the management of your future.

Those who do not prepare for the future will in time be left behind. The management of your future will not be easy, but you can prepare, you can try smarter—not harder—and be ready for management challenges and opportunities as they appear.

FROM NOW TOWARD THE FUTURE

The development of user-friendly, economical mainframe computer and personal computer-aided facility management (CAFM) software integrated with associated low-cost computer-aided design and drafting (CADD) systems has opened many management opportunities for facility professionals, vendors, and consultants to provide corporate management with timely information not available by manual methods.

Many corporate facility professionals use these automated tools to manage strategic requirements and the details of their space inventories, furnishings, fixed assets, properties, capital expenditures, and ongoing financial obligations. The use of computers and automating information has had mixed success, but the trend is gaining support and shows value.

There is an ongoing evaluation of corporate staff and resources in almost all companies today. The facility professional is not exempt from proving that the services he or she provides add value and are more cost-effective than those provided by an outside firm. The middle manager role in facility management is disappearing. Staff sizes are being reduced, but the workload generally remains the same or is growing. Facility professionals are increasingly turning to outside consultants or vendors to help them meet their goals.

Real estate and facility management advisory services based in real estate bro-
kerages, accounting firms, and independent third-party companies have appeared
as consultants to help the facility professional with myriad services: long-range
planning; development; real estate acquisition; consolidation and disposal policies; inventories of corporate leased and owned properties; the auditing and management of leases, taxes, and operations; design and project management;
furnishing and equipment inventory; mail room; copy center; food service; word
processing; library; records management; security; payroll; and maintenance and
operations requirements and expenses. These consulting services are catching on
and filling a void for the facility professional.

A number of architectural, property management, and property maintenance
consulting firms are actively marketing facility management services to the facility professional. Many of these consulting firms have only limited expertise in
managing day-to-day corporate politics, service requirements, or corporate budgets and facilities. As a result, these consulting services have not caught on well
because few firms have personnel with corporate facility management experience,
and services and fees for these services are still being developed. However, some
of these firms have hired experienced facility professionals and are developing the
expertise, services, and fees necessary to fill this void.

The facility professional of the future will be a knowledgeable management
executive with minimal in-house staff. He or she will report to the president or
chief financial officer of the company and rely on facility management consultants
and outsourcing firms to get the job done.

THE FUTURE OF FACILITY MANAGEMENT

In chapter 1, we discussed the facility management overview. The future holds
many challenges and opportunities. Some facility professionals will not survive
because of their lack of managerial and leadership skills and abilities; because of
their senior management's shortsightedness, lack of education, or misunderstanding of facility issues; or because through mergers, acquisitions, or restructuring
their positions are abolished, downgraded, or combined with others.

The future for facility professionals and facility management will not be easy,
but it will offer tremendous opportunities for those who do their homework, prepare, keep current, and consistently perform.

We believe the evolution of facility management will result in the facility professional having:

- More authority with responsibility
- More workable and appropriate policies and procedures, but, ideally, less
  bureaucracy
- A greater management and strategic leadership role within the corporation
  providing additional promotions and career opportunities
- Increased requirements for quality service with excellence as the ongoing
  goal
- Less in-house staff and more outsourcing vendors and consultants

- Increased awareness and expertise in strategic business planning, asset management, safety, security, acoustics, air quality, ergonomics, ADA, and productivity issues and solutions
- More automation tools for reviewing alternatives and making quicker informed decisions or recommendations
- A greater likelihood of selling their services as a consultant to in-house customers and of effectively dealing with business and people issues by moving to a profit center operation
- More exposure and access to senior management and a voice in strategic business and facility planning and policy

The facility professional of the future will frequently work for an international firm with headquarters in another country. States and cities will compete for foreign investment and subsequent employment opportunities. The rise in the number of internationally owned facilities will create increasing management opportunities for facility professionals.

International investment has affected the economies of many markets, and facility management practices will be influenced by what internationally owned companies expect in the way of services and end product. Many architectural, engineering, interior design, and construction companies have identified these firms and are actively marketing their services to them.

Your customer's business will be changing, and its space and furnishings requirements will too. Each business unit must look at its financial capabilities and match future requirements within its investment plan for space costs, equipment costs, facility costs, labor costs, and land costs. Companies may choose to expand via acquisition or direct expansion; these requirements must be incorporated into the customer's annual, long-range, and strategic business facility plans.

Each facility acquired by your customer may provide the opportunity to improve the corporation's profitability, reduce annual expense and capital costs, and manage or reduce its legal asset commitments.

Facility management professionals will be challenged to do more with less, to manage more closely, to plan more carefully, to become more aware of the business community and economy, and to participate with senior management in setting goals and objectives that will ensure the profitability, health, and success of the company.

Many service and supplier groups to the facility profession are looking at the facility professional and the profession. Some wonder how the facility management profession will change. Others do not understand what facility management is. To survive, facility professionals must be:

- Leaders who as *businesspeople* understand and are supportive participants in the goals and objectives of their companies and customers
- Educated risk takers who are prepared to educate, train, nudge, and sell their management and their customers on the value-added benefits their services can provide to their company and customers

The problems and issues will not diminish but rather increase as the global information and service economy evolves.

Beleaguered executives are beginning to realize that the key to their organization's long-term survival may well not lie in faster and more powerful PCs, sophisticated telecommunications networks, or advanced furniture concepts but in the most wondrous of all things: the incredible ability of the individual human mind to acquire and apply knowledge to the corporation's short- and long-term advantage.

Ikujiro Nonaka, professor of management at the Institute for Business Research of Hitotsubashi University in Tokyo, Japan, sums up the situation: "In an economy where the only certainty is uncertainty, the one sure source of lasting competitive advantage is knowledge." Successful enterprises, he argues, are those capable of continuously creating new knowledge, disseminating this knowledge throughout the organization, and quickly embodying it in new products and services.

However, Nonaka warns that creating new knowledge is simply not a matter of processing objective information. Rather, he suggests, it depends on tapping the tacit and often highly subjective insights, intuitions, and hunches of individual employees and making those insights available for testing and use by the company as a whole.[4]

The theme of the knowledge-creating or learning organization has been quickly picked up by numerous pundits of the modern business organization. It would be easy to write off the hoopla as yet another management fad. What have knowledge-creating enterprises or learning organizations to do with the future of the corporate office workplace in general and the future of those who plan, design, build, and manage office workplaces in particular? Quite a lot, it turns out.

Before knowledge can be shared, it must acquired. Organizations don't learn; people do. If our goal is to create learning organizations, which it certainly should be, then we must provide tools and a social system that support the moment-by-moment learning behavior of individuals. This is true whether people work alone or in teams.

Common sense suggests that facilities, broadly construed, are often inextricably intertwined with individual learning. The goal is not to attempt to design workspaces for people but to create a sociotechnical infrastructure that allows individuals and teams to craft their own work spaces in response to the demands of the particular intellectual task at hand.

The bottom line is that organizations are not machines; they are not information factories. They are, in the most literal sense, extensions of the human mind. At the end of the day, it will be individuals doing their minds' best work—supported by the kinds of sociotechnical infrastructure being discovered—that will make the difference between competitive success and failure.[5]

Organizations have changed, and we see fewer management layers with less staff but more authority and responsibilities, greater integration of functions and

[4]Excerpts from Ikujiro Nonaka, "The Knowledge-Creating Company," *Harvard Business Review* (November–December 1991). Copyright © 1991 by the President and Fellows of Harvard College, Reprinted by permission of *Harvard Business Review*. All rights reserved.

[5]Reprinted by permission from Duncan B. Sutherland, Jr., "The Knowledge-Creating Enterprise," *The Construction Specifier* (January 1993) pp. 30–35. Copyright © 1993 by Duncan B. Sutherland, Jr.

cross training, and increased spans of control and communications at the business unit level. The workforce will be older and grow more slowly. Skilled workers will be more scarce and consultants used more frequently to address specific issues.

The way businesses operate is changing. Globalization is providing the opportunity and is requiring competitors to seek markets and customers around the world.

Customers are becoming increasingly well informed and are requiring and demanding quality, efficiency, and cost-effective products and services. Increased completion in the United States and internationally and changes in the European Common Market in 1992; the North American Free Trade Agreement (NAFTA) of the United States, Canada, and Mexico in 1994; a smaller increase in the skilled workforce; new efficient and cost-competitive products; and an increased awareness of environmental concerns and the need to conserve raw materials are requiring product and service suppliers to reassess all aspects of doing business. Businesses are also finding that to operate in this competitive world environment, decentralized decision making at lower levels in the organization, speed, flexibility, training, cross training, job integration, and productivity increases are required.

There's a lot of gum-flapping about the new breed of team-building visionaries occupying executive suites these days. To succeed in your management career, it seems you must embrace, as *Fortune* magazine dubs it, "post-heroic leadership" or "distributed leadership" or "servant leadership" or "virtual leadership" or . . . . Translation: Yesterday's table-pounding, my-way-or-the-highway organization man has given way to a more democratic coordinator and consensus-builder.

The way facility professionals operate must change just as the way business operations are changing. Your understanding of your company's business, political, and corporate culture requires you to maintain an ongoing program of developing work environments that remain flexible into the future. Because decision making is being decentralized, you must improve your listening, speaking, and writing skills, and your management and customers must be educated in effective facility management. You must improve the quality of the services you provide and make excellence a way of life for yourself and for the vendors and consultants who work with you.

CONCLUSION

Throughout this chapter and this book we focus on issues and concerns that make up the facility management practice. Our intent is to share what we and others have learned and experienced. Some material is theoretical and some (especially that used for the exhibits and samples) is based on real-world experiences. Regardless of the stage of your facility management career and interest, we hope we have provided helpful insights or shed new light on topics that interest you.

There is always more to say on every topic, and as we noted in the beginning of this chapter, you can expand your knowledge by reading excellent books and articles. Or perhaps you wish to share your wisdom and experience on facility management by writing a book yourself. We trust our volume will lead you to ask the next question and then find the answer, for that is the nature of our profession.

   We have been fairly serious in our presentation but feel it is appropriate to leave you with a little humor from an unknown facility customer who wrote the following poem:

Ode to a Move[6]

It's time again for trepidation
We're moving to a new workstation.
What's that you say?
You moved last month?
What made you think you'd pack just once?
At [*Fill in the Blank*] it's part of the fun
To keep employees on the run.
We're hidden, switched, and moved around—
It takes some work before we're found.
And once we are, it's just in time!
Despite the planning, reason, and rhyme
They've—understandably—changed their minds
About the space to which we've been assigned.
Empty your desk, unload your shelf—
You need some boxes? Find them yourself!
What's that again? You've *work* due when?
You don't have time to pack again?
Forget that notion—it's just folly!
Get those boxes on the dolly!
The mission is to move TODAY,
It's first and foremost—get out of the way!
So travel again through a sea of gray stalls
Up many stairs and down many halls
Until there like a beacon is your new spot—alas!
With boxes stacked high atop one that's marked "Glass."
Throw out the pieces, hook up the phone,
Unpack the boxes in your new home—on loan.
Organize the files, water your plants,
Hang up your calendar and poster of France.
You think you're now settled?
Don't be deluded.
They've drawn up NEW plans, and your names included!
It's the never-ending saga of musical cubes.

---

[6]Author unknown, "Ode to a Move" (submitted by Mary Klenieski, Shared Medical Systems, Malvern, PA), *IFMA Real Estate Council News*, November 1994, p. 4.

Glossary of Facility Management Definitions and Buzzwords

ABOVE-BUILDING STANDARD Materials not included in the work letter that are subject to negotiation between the landlord and tenant.

AMENITY AREA* Any area in a facility used by employees for nonwork activity, such as employee dining rooms, vending areas, lounges, day-care centers, and fitness or health centers.

AMORTIZATION OF TENANT ALLOWANCES The return to the landlord over the term of the lease of those costs included in the landlord's building standard work letter and any other costs that landlord has agreed to assume or amortize.

AMORTIZATION OF TENANT IMPROVEMENTS An agreement on the part of the landlord to pay for above-building standard improvements and amortize those improvements at a defined interest rate over a fixed term as additional rent.

AREA OF PENETRATION The sum of the area of those physical objects that vertically penetrate the space serving more than one floor (e.g., elevator or HVAC shafts, stairwells, flues, and their enclosing walls).

ASBESTOS/HAZARDOUS MATERIALS Materials in facility office structures that may pose a detriment to tenant's safe occupancy.

BASE RENTAL The initial rental rate, normally identified as the annual rent in a gross lease.

*Source: International Facility Management Association, *Benchmark Report,* 1991.

BASE YEAR The year of building operation, normally a calendar year, in which the landlord fixes or identifies the operating costs included in a gross or seminet lease. Any increase in operating expenses over the base year is "passed through" to the tenant on a pro rata share of rentable area.

BOMA STANDARD MEASUREMENT A defined way of measuring space by the Building Owners and Managers Association (BOMA). Landlords may choose their own method to measure space, normally by increasing the amount of common areas added to the usable area.

BUILDING CORE The "guts" of a building, which normally includes building elevators, rest rooms, smoke towers, fire stairs, mechanical shafts, janitorial, electrical, and phone closets.

BUILDING EFFICIENCY RATE The usable area divided by the rentable area, multiplied by 100.

BUILDING MAINTENANCE The preventive and remedial upkeep of building components (HVAC, electrical, plumbing, elevators, carpentry, painting, etc.), excluding janitorial and grounds maintenance.

BUILDING MODULE Standard dimensions within leased areas dictated by spacing of window mullions or columns (e.g., a 5-foot module dictates offices in multiples of 5-feet dimensions).

BUILDING STANDARD WORK LETTER A document that delineates the type and quality of materials and quantities to be furnished by the landlord as building standard.

CATEGORIES OF MOVES* *Employees moved to existing work spaces* means that no furniture is moved, no wiring or new telecommunications systems required. Files and supplies are moved. *Workstations/furniture moves* means that existing furniture is reconfigured and/or furniture is moved or purchased; no new wiring or telecommunication installation required. *Moves that require construction* means that new walls, new or additional wiring, or telecommunication systems are required, or other construction is needed to complete the move.

CHURN RATE* The total number of employee work space moves made in the last year divided by the total number of office employees in the facility multiplied by 100.

CODE COMPLIANCE TRIGGER Certain costs, structural changes, or other defined events that necessitate the compliance of a building to current codes.

CODE REQUIREMENTS Building code requirements that must be satisfied by either the tenant or the landlord in preparing space or building for tenant occupancy. Included are seismic (earthquake), life safety, energy, hazardous/toxic materials, and handicapped code requirements.

COMMON AREA That area with common access to all users within a gross space (e.g., public corridors, rest rooms, mechanical or utility rooms, vestibules). Equation:

$$\text{Common area} = \text{Rentable area} - \text{Usable area}$$

Source: International Facility Management Association, *Benchmark Report,* 1991.

COMMON AREA FACTOR (RENTABLE/USABLE RATIO)   The factor used to determine a tenant's pro rata share of the common area.

Equation:

$$\text{CAF (R/U Ratio)} = \frac{\text{Rentable area}}{\text{Usable area}}$$

COMPARTMENTALIZATION   A code requirement to divide large floor plates into smaller units to meet fire code requirements.

CONCESSIONS   Those inducements offered by a landlord to a tenant to sign a lease. Common concessions are free rent, extra tenant improvement allowances, payment of moving costs and lease pickups.

COST OF OPERATION*   The total costs associated with the day-to-day operation of a facility. It includes all maintenance and repair (both fixed and variable), administrative costs, labor costs, janitorial, housekeeping and other cleaning costs, all utility costs, and all costs associated with roadways and grounds.

COSTS OF PROVIDING THE FIXED ASSET*   Refers to capital costs, mortgage costs, capital improvements, taxes, insurance and depreciation charges. It does not include the lease costs, the security costs, or the relocation/rearrangement costs.

CROSS-OVER FLOOR   A floor in which one bank of elevators connects to another bank of elevators, allowing tenants to have access to floors in other elevator banks without returning to the lobby of the building.

DEMISING WALLS   Those walls between one tenant's area and another as well as walls between tenant areas and public corridors.

DIRECT CHARGE OF OPERATING EXPENSES   On a gross or seminet lease where the tenant does not pay costs directly, the pro rata share of occupancy costs that the landlord directly bills tenants. In most instances, this will be done on a "good faith," "best estimate" advanced payment basis, wherein the landlord bills the tenant for estimated operating expense costs during the lease term.

EFFICIENCY   The percent of rentable area that is usable area (i.e., a 90 percent efficient building offers 900 usable square feet for every 1,000 rentable square feet). *Note:* Efficiency and load factor are not the same.

EFFICIENT RENT   The dollar amount per square foot per year figure that the tenant pays on an average over the term of the lease. This would be the average of specified rents in a stair-stepped lease as well as the average of a lease with substantial free rent period. Example: A 5-year lease with 6 months' free rent offers a 10 percent discount from the face rate.

ENCLOSED SPACE   The floor area inside the enclosed space, measured to the inside surface of walls, major protrusions or other surfaces that define the limit of functionally usable floor surface. This does not include the area of freestanding columns that inhibit functional use of the space and does not include circulation area outside the space.

*Source: International Facility Management Association, *Benchmark Report,* 1991.

EXPENSE ALLOCATION   The allocation of all expenses (gross or seminet lease) or a proportionate share of increased expenses to a tenant based on tenant's pro rata share.

EXPENSE STOP   An identified dollar amount, either on a dollar per square foot per year basis or a pro rata share basis of the total operating expense cost, that the landlord is responsible to pay. Any increase over the expense stop will be allocated to the tenant.

FACE RATE (Contract Rate)   The identified rental rate in a lease that is subsequently discounted by concessions offered by the landlord, also known as contract rate.

FAIR MARKET VALUE   The rental value of space similar to the leased premises for comparison purposes in rental adjustments.

FIRE CORRIDORS   Special corridors with partitioning designed to create escape routes in time of fire.

"FIRE RATED"   Special building materials, such as partitioning and doors that have been constructed and have been tested to provide greater fire resistance than normal building standard materials.

FLOOR PLATE   A broker's buzzword for rentable floor size.

FREE RENT   Period of time in which the tenant occupies the premises under the lease but does not pay rent.

GROSS AREA   Building or floor footprint; the total area of the building or floor within the outline of the building extremities. This area is computed by measuring the inside finished perimeter of the dominant portion of the permanent outer building walls. The *dominant portion* shall mean that portion of the inside, finished surface of the permanent outside building wall which is 50 percent or more of the vertical floor-to-ceiling dimension measured at the outer building walls. If the dominant portion is not vertical, the measurement for area shall be to the inside, finished surface of the permanent outside building wall at the point of intersection of the vertical wall and the finished floor.

GROSS RENTAL (Gross Lease)   A rental rate that includes normal building standard services as provided by the landlord within the base year rental.

HANDICAPPED REQUIREMENTS   Code-required features designed to accommodate handicapped persons. Included are entry ramps, rest rooms, rest room fixtures, hardware, and special doors.

IMPROVEMENT ALLOWANCE   The estimated or dollar value of the building standard work letter being offered by the landlord.

INTRAOFFICE   The common area *between* departments, sections, etc. used for corridors, aisles, or walkways. These would generally be determined between users defined on the same *tier* as compared with the previous tier.

LAYOUT (Space Plan)   A plan created by a space planner/interior designer/architect showing locations of tenant improvements and the utilization of the space by the tenant.

LAYOUT EFFICIENCY   Efficiency of the usable area to meet tenant's workflow requirements, office design, personnel, etc. Efficiency of usable area is dictated by building shape, core location, floor size, leasing depth, corridors, etc.

LEASE BUYOUT A cash inducement offered by a landlord to a tenant's previous landlord or by the tenant to the current landlord to cancel the remaining term of tenant's lease.

LEASE PICKUP Landlord's commitment to assume that the costs associated with paying a tenant's rent in premises to be vacated that are still under lease.

LEASED RENTABLE AREA That area to which the base lease rate applies. This is defined as the tenant's usable area times the CAF. This area may then be multiplied by the lease rate to determine the lease amount.

Equation:

$$\text{Tenant usable area} \times \text{CAF}$$

LEASES* *Net lease-base* rent plus tenant pays directly a share of real estate taxes; *triple net lease-base* rent plus tenant pays directly a share of real estate taxes, insurance, maintenance, repair and operating costs; *gross lease-one* payment in which owner has included estimated cost of operations.

LEASING DEPTH The distance from the building window line to the building corridor.

LIFE SAFETY Government regulations and building code requirements for buildings relative to seismic, fire, handicapped, and existing requirements.

LOAD FACTOR/COMMON AREA ALLOCATION That percentage of the building in which common area is allocated to the tenants to increase their usable area to rentable area. A load factor of 10 percent means that 900 usable square feet (USF) would be 990 rentable square feet (RSF).

MOVING ALLOWANCE An offer by a landlord to pay all or part of a tenant's moving costs.

NET NET NET RENT (Triple Net Lease) A lease in which the tenant is responsible for every and all expenses associated with its proportionate share of occupancy of the building.

NET OR SEMIGROSS RENT (Net Lease) A rental rate that includes some services to be provided by the landlord; normally the tenant is responsible for cost of janitorial and utilities services.

OCCUPANCY COST* The total cost incurred by a company or organization to provide space for operations. It includes all the costs of operation plus the costs of providing the fixed asset.

OFFICE PLANS* *Private offices-enclosed* by floor-to-ceiling walls; *open-plan offices* spaces divided by movable partitions; *bullpen style offices-open* areas with no partitions.

OFFICE SPACE UTILIZATION RATE* The number of office workers divided by the facility's total number of work spaces (offices or workstations) and multiplied by 100.

OPEN SPACE The floor area available inside a workstation for furniture, equipment, and internal circulation. This area is measured from the inside face of furniture screens or panels, to the outside edge of furniture, equipment, or carpet

*Source: International Facility Management Association, *Benchmark Report,* 1991.

that bounds the intended work area. It does not include area of circulation out-side the immediate work area.

OPERATING EXPENSES   Those normal expenses associated with the operation of a standard office building included, but not limited to: management fees, utilities, janitorial service, consumable supplies, taxes, insurance, refurbishing of building common areas, maintenance and repair, etc.

OWNERSHIP COSTS   The cost to the owner to own the building, service existing debt, or receive a return on equity. Also included would be costs of capital improvements, repair, and upkeep, which would not be considered standard operating costs.

PANELS   Generally defined as modular furniture sections used to define the limits of a workstation. Panels do not extend from floor to ceiling.

PARTITIONS   Generally defined as inside floor-to-ceiling structures not other-wise meeting the criteria of walls. Partitions are movable or removable.

PARTITIONING   The divisions between offices, separate office suites, tenant areas, and corridors.

PRELEASE   Leasing of premises in a building under construction, which is not yet ready for occupancy.

PREVENTIVE MAINTENANCE*   A program in which wear, tear, and change are anticipated and continuous corrective actions are taken to ensure peak efficiency and minimum deterioration.

PRIMARY CIRCULATION*   The portion of the building that is public corridor, lobby, atrium, or hallway required for access to stairs, elevators, rest rooms, or building exits.

PROJECTED OPERATING EXPENSE INCREASE   A "good faith" estimate by the landlord as to the current operating expense increase over a base year, which is billed to the tenant as additional rent.

PRO RATA SHARE   The ratio between the tenant's percentage of occupancy of the rentable square footage of the building and the entire building rentable area.

RECAPTURE   The billing to tenants of their pro rata share of increased operating expenses after those expenses have been incurred and paid for by the landlord.

RENTABLE AREA   The area, in square feet, of a floor available for rental. It is computed by measuring to the inside finished surface of the dominant portion of the permanent outer building walls, excluding any major vertical penetrations of the floor. No deductions are made for columns and projections necessary to the building. Vertical penetrations include stairs, elevator shafts, flues, pipe shafts, vertical ducts, and their enclosing walls that serve more than one floor of the building.

RENTABLE AREA (RSF)   The area of a given space defined as the gross area less the areas of penetration. *Note:* This area is fixed to the life of the building unless major modifications such as the addition of elevators, etc. occur.

Source: International Facility Management Association, *Benchmark Report,* 1991.

Equation:

$$\text{Rentable area} = \text{Gross area} - \text{Area of penetration}$$

and

$$\text{Rentable area} = \frac{\text{Usable area}}{\text{Common area factor}}$$

Example: Rentable area of floor = 20,000 SF.

ABC Company usable = 17,500 SF.

$$\frac{R = 20,000}{U = 17,500} = 1.144 \text{ Common area factor (CAF)}$$

$$1,500 \text{ USF} \times 1.144 = 1,716 \text{ RSF}$$

$$\frac{1,716 \text{ SF}}{1.144 \text{ CAF}} \text{ Rentable} = 1500 \text{ SF}$$

RENTAL The cost charged per rentable square foot (RSF) on a monthly or annual basis for a leased area.

RENTAL INCREASE/RENTAL REVIEW Changes in the base rent during the term of the lease; not to be confused with operating expense recapture increase or expense billings, usually tied to "fair market" or CPI reviews.

SHARED TENANT SERVICES Services provided by a building to allow tenants to share the costs and benefits of sophisticated telecommunications and other technical services.

SMART BUILDING A building that has additional technical capabilities to provide enhanced building management and operating efficiency.

SPACE The generic definition of a particular enclosed area. A space may be a building, floor, or any defined area. As a practical matter, a space is defined as that area defined by the drawing.

SPACE LIMITS The area of a given space generally determined by some physical limit, most often walls, partitions, or panels.

SPRINKLERS A fire suppression system, usually water, designed into many buildings to reduce compartmentalization and to provide additional fire protection.

STAIR-STEPPED RENT A rental rate that increases by fixed amounts during the period of the lease term.

SUBLEASE Leasing of premises by the current tenant to another party for the remaining balance of an existing lease term.

SUBSTITUTION AND CREDITS The ability to substitute nonstandard materials for landlord-supplied materials as specified in the work letter, or to receive dollar amount credits for those materials if not utilized.

SUPPORT AREA Includes computer centers, mail rooms, reprographics/copy center, library space, training rooms, communications centers, auditoriums, conference rooms, security areas, and shipping and receiving area.

TENANT IMPROVEMENTS BUILDING STANDARDS   Standard building materials and quantities as identified by the landlord that are to be provided at no cost to the tenant to improve tenant premises. Normally included are partitioning, doors, walls, hardware, ceiling, lighting, window and floor coverings, telephone and electrical outlets, and HVAC (heating, ventilation, and air conditioning systems).

TIER 1   The overall working area of the space being considered. This may be the gross area of a floor or the rentable area of a floor. Tier 1 should describe the space as the *User of Tier 1* (e.g., "Globe Building, 8th Floor"). Tier 1 may have only *one* user.

TIER 2   A spatial area definition under the Tier 1 definition. This may be a tenant, section, department, etc. Tier 2 may have multiple users of similar definition (e.g., "XYZ and Associates," "Acme Computers"; or "Accounting Department," "Marketing Department").

TIER 3   A spatial area definition under the Tier 2 definition. This may be a department, unit, etc. Tier 3 may have multiple users of similar definition.

TIER 4   A spatial area definition under the Tier 3 definition. This may be a department, unit, etc. Tier 4 may have multiple users of similar definition.

TIER 5   The lowest level of spatial definition. This is generally used to define a workstation, room, or individual space.

A typical tier structure might be depicted as follows:

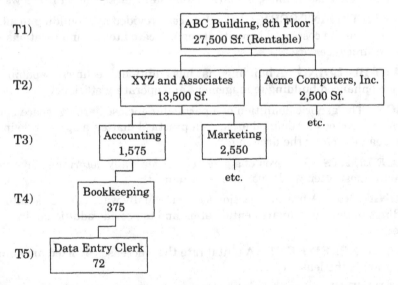

TURNKEY   A complete build-out of tenant's premises to the tenant's specifications.

UNDER-FLOOR DUCT SYSTEM   A system of ducts permanently located in floors to assist in the installation of telephone, computer, and electrical wiring.

USABLE AREA*   That area of a space that may actually be occupied by a user.

*Source: International Facility Management Association, *Benchmark Report,* 1991.

Equation:

Usable area = Rentable area – Common area

USABLE AREA (USF)   Office area actually occupied by a tenant for its sole and exclusive use. The usable area on a single floor of a building may vary depending on corridor configurations, whether the floor is a single-tenant or multiple-tenant occupancy, etc.

USER   The generic definition of the occupant of a space. This may be a tenant, a company, a department etc. A given space may have more than one user for each tier of definition except Tier 1.

VACANCY RATE*   The current vacant square footage/meters in a facility divided by the total usable area and multiplied by 100. For example, if the facility currently has 12,000 square feet vacant and the usable area is 200,000 then the vacancy rate is 6 percent.

WALLS   Generally defined as outside walls, load-bearing walls, fire walls, or those walls that are not considered to be movable or removable.

WORK LETTER   A document that includes building standards plus any additional items to be paid for by the landlord or by the tenant; the letter specifies who is responsible for each item.

WORKSTATION   Any space for which a function is accomplished. This may be an enclosed space or a space in an open area (e.g., a conference room, an executive office, a coffee station, a reception area, a data input station). A workstation does *not* necessarily require that a person or persons be assigned to that particular space.

WORKING DRAWINGS   Drawings necessary to fully price the work, to obtain a building permit and to construct the tenant improvements.

ZONES   The identified portions of an office area served by the HVAC system that have separate thermostatic and temperature controls.

Source: International Facility Management Association, *Benchmark Report,* 1991.

Index

Printed in the United States
By Bookmasters